THE  T

Good
University
Guide 2006

in association with

Edited by
John O'Leary

with
Andrew Hindmarsh
Bernard Kingston

TIMES BOOKS

Published in 2005 by Times Books
HarperCollins Publishers
77–85 Fulham Palace Road, Hammersmith, London W6 8JB
www.collins.co.uk

First published in 1993 by Times Books. Thirteenth edition 2005

Compilation © HarperCollins Publishers 2005
Chapters 1, 2, 3 (tables), 4–9, 12, 13, internet resources © Mayfield University Consultants 2005
All other material © Times Newspapers Ltd 2005

The Times is a registered trademark of Times Newspapers Ltd

ISBN 0–00–720303–9

ACKNOWLEDGMENTS

This edition has been produced in association with PricewaterhouseCoopers LLP (PwC).
To find out more about undergraduate opportunities with PwC, please visit their website:
www.pwc.com/uk/careers/

The tables and their underlying methodology have been created by Mayfield University
Consultants under the guidance of its partners, Bernard Kingston and Andrew Hindmarsh.
We wish to offer our best personal thanks to the many individuals who have helped with
this edition of The Times Good University Guide. We are indebted to Peter Elias and Kate
Pursell for permission to draw on their extensive research into graduate occupations; to
Nicola Bright who, once again, has lent her very considerable statistical expertise to the
rigour of the tables; to Hannah Brady and Alison Patterson for their assiduous research; to
Tabitha Birchall, Carole Finnigan, Andy Foster, Allan Johnson, Ana Kingston, Jon Simmons,
Richard Tyler and Zena Wooldridge for sharing professional insights; to Jonathan Waller for
his technical advice; to Christopher Riches for his editorial and publishing expertise, and to
Sarah Churchman and Elaine Marron of PricewaterhouseCoopers, our sponsors, for their
generous interest and support.
The publishers wish to thank BUSA for giving permission to reproduce their
championship tables and UNITE for access to the results of their Student Experience Report
2005. This was conducted by MORI through face-to-face interviews with full-time university
students in Autumn 2004. UNITE is the UKs largest provider of student accommodation.
To find out more visit www.unite-students.com.
Please see chapter 2 for a full explanation of the sources of data used in the ranking
tables. The data providers do not necessarily agree with the data aggregations or
manipulations appearing in this book and are also not responsible for any inference or
conclusions thereby derived.

Printed and bound in Great Britain by Clays Ltd, St Ives plc

Contents

About the Authors

John O'Leary is the Editor of *The Times Higher Education Supplement*. Until 2002 he was the Education Editor of *The Times*, having joined the paper in 1990 as Higher Education Correspondent and assumed responsibility for the whole range of education coverage in 1992. He has been writing on higher education for nearly 20 years. He has a degree in politics from the University of Sheffield.

Andrew Hindmarsh is Planning Officer at the University of Nottingham, where his responsibilities include providing management information and statistical returns to official bodies. Until 1998 he was head of the Undergraduate Admission Office at the University of Sheffield, where for ten years he worked closely with admissions tutors and UCAS. He has degrees in zoology and animal behaviour from the University of Oxford.

Bernard Kingston is now a university consultant, having been Director of the Careers Advisory Service and latterly Director of International Affairs at the University of Sheffield. He is a past president of the Association of Graduate Careers Advisory Services and has advised governments and universities in Asia, Africa, Australia and the UK. He has degrees in chemistry from the Universities of Leicester and Sussex.

Andrew Hindmarsh and Bernard Kingston are Partners in Mayfield University Consultants, who have compiled the main University League Table and the individual subject tables, as well as contributing ten chapters and the internet resources.

How to Use This Book

The Times Good University Guide 2006 provides a wealth of information to help you select the courses and universities of your choice and to guide you through the whole process of applying to study at university.

Which are the Best Universities?

The place to start is the main *Times* League Table on pages 39–43. This ranks the universities by assessing their performance not just in their teaching and research but also through another seven factors, including the student–staff ratio and the spending on student facilities. This table gives an indication of the overall performance of each university. Each measure used in making the assessment is described in the pages that precede the table.

It is also important to read chapter 1, which provides an invaluable introduction to the many aspects of selecting an appropriate university for you.

Which are the Best Universities for Particular Subjects?

Chapter 1 also provides guidance on how to start selecting courses that you are interested in. It is a good introduction to chapter 3, which gives detailed information on 61 different subject areas, where universities appear in ranked tables, with our assessment of the top universities for each subject. Background information is given about the subject, along with the latest data on what graduates did on completion of the courses. The notes on pages 44–5 explain the data that is included within these tables.

By using both the subject tables and the main university League Table, you can begin to narrow down your search for appropriate universities.

What is Each University Like?

Chapter 11 devotes two pages to each university, giving a general overview of the institution as well as data on student numbers, how to contact the university, the accommodation provided by the university, and the quality of teaching. There are also profiles of the main university towns in chapter 12, complete with travel information and websites for further information.

As an International Student, How Do I Choose?

In addition to using all the data on universities and subjects, chapter 9 is devoted to the needs of international students. As well as providing practical advice for students coming to the United Kingdom, this chapter gives details of the most popular subjects and the most popular universities attended by international students, so helping further in the selection of a university.

How Do I Apply?

Chapter 4 outlines the application procedure for university entry. It starts by advising you on how to complete the UCAS application, and then takes you step-by-step through the process that we hope will lead to your university place for autumn 2006.

How Much Will It Cost?

Chapter 5 provides advice on where to live during the course of your studies, while chapter 7 outlines the costs of studying at university (including the payment of fees) as well as sources of funds (including student loans). For English universities details of bursary and scholarship schemes that will operate from 2006 are given in chapter 13. Additionally, the range of charges for accommodation are given in each university profile in chapter 11.

What Parents Need To Know
Chapter 8 outlines some of the help parents can provide during the process of applying to and preparing for university.

How Do I Find Out More?
In each university profile (chapter 11) contact details are given (including e-mail addresses and websites), so you can obtain more information on any university you are interested in. More help is provided in the Internet Resources section (pages 504–7) which lists many appropriate websites for students, while a further listing (pages 501–4) provides contact details for Higher Education Colleges which are not covered elsewhere within the book.

We hope you find the information presented in the book useful in planning for your university career. If you have any suggestions for further information you would like to see, please send them to:
The Times Good University Guide
Reference Department
HarperCollins Publishers
Westerhill Road
Bishopbriggs
Glasgow G64 2QT
or contact us through our website, www.collins.co.uk

Introduction

This is the year that English universities have been waiting for – and students have been dreading – the start of the top-up fees era. At almost all universities in England and Northern Ireland, full-time students starting courses in 2006 will have to repay fees of £3,000 a year after they graduate. Those heading for Wales will at least have a year's grace, while in Scotland the cost of study will remain limited to a 'graduate endowment' of around £2,000 – although the cost of an extra year in higher education will usually outweigh the saving on fees.

In fact, the news is not all bad for applicants in 2006: it may be easier to win a place on previously oversubscribed courses, there is no requirement to pay fees of £1,200-plus upfront and grants, bursaries and scholarships will be available to bring down the cost for many students. This year's *Guide* includes a section detailing the (sometimes complex) arrangements at each university. Only time will tell if the prospect of bigger debts after graduation has a lasting effect on the demand for higher education places, but it is inevitable that there will be some impact in the first year of the new system. Applications for courses beginning in 2005 increased by 8 per cent, due partly to mature students bringing forward their study plans. This year, the pressure on places should be eased accordingly.

That does not mean, however, that it will be plain sailing for the class of 2006. The number of 18-year-olds is still rising, A-level pass rates are improving and the range of qualifications accepted by universities has expanded. In addition, the number of applicants from the accession countries of the European Union is growing and universities have stepped up their efforts to recruit students from other parts of the world, who pay even higher fees. It will still be difficult to win a place on a popular course at a prestigious university.

That is where this *Guide* comes in. A league table will not identify the most suitable course for any prospective student: that is a matter of personal preference, involving the location and character of a university, and above all the syllabus. But the rankings in this *Guide* will help place those choices in context. They take account of academics' own ratings of the standards of teaching and research in each of the 61 subject areas in British higher education, building in measures of other aspects of campus life and the all-important employment prospects after graduation.

When *The Times Good University Guide* first appeared more than a dozen years ago, it helped to explode the myth that any British degree was as good as any other. Although ranking universities proved predictably controversial, the statistics behind the tables confirmed sharp variations in performance within British higher education. Charles Clarke, Labour's former Education Secretary, was prepared to cite this *Guide* as evidence to demolish what he termed the 'emperor's clothes idea that all universities are broadly the same'.

The changes that Mr Clarke was advocating – chiefly the introduction of variable tuition fees, but also the encouragement of greater specialisation – will create a stark new pecking order in higher education. Employers already distinguish between universities as well as individuals. The need to know the standing of a university, both as an institution and in the various subjects it offers, can only become more important as time goes on.

Unlike most of the rankings that have sprung up in recent years, *The Times Guide* has maintained as much consistency as possible in the methods used to compare universities. Dated assessments of teaching quality were removed two years ago, but the only significant change in this year's tables is the introduction of new classifications of graduate jobs. The guide had already pioneered distinctions between different types of graduate employment. The new system – devised by Peter Elias, of Warwick University, and Kate Purcell, of the University of the West of England – adds to the sophistication in an area that will assume growing importance in the era of top-up fees.

There is also one change in the institutions covered by the rankings. Following last year's introduction of the University of the Arts, London, the latest new arrival is the University of Bolton. Approved as a university after a decade of campaigning, Bolton will be the first of a number of colleges and institutes of higher education to be promoted. However, while other colleges will become 'teaching-only' universities, Bolton secured enhanced status under the previous definition of a university, with full research powers. The total would have increased by two if London Metropolitan University had not again blocked the release of data from the Higher Education Statistics Agency. It took this action last year because it regarded statistics relating to its two predecessor institutions (London Guildhall and North London) as misleading. Although this objection no longer holds good, the university has maintained its stance and, regrettably for those seeking information on one of the capital's largest universities, it cannot be included in the new table, or in the many subject rankings for which it is eligible. London Met was 98th out of 100 universities in its one appearance in the ranking.

The first *Times* League Table effectively produced a dead heat between Oxford and Cambridge, with the light blues a fraction ahead. After several years of Cambridge domination, changes in methodology saw the roles reversed in the 2003 edition and Oxford subsequently extended its lead. The current table sees the ancient rivals take closer order once more. Cambridge has the better record in teaching and research assessments, which are the most heavily weighted elements in our rankings, but extra spending on computing and student facilities makes the difference. Accurate comparisons of the two are difficult because of the mix of college and central university responsibilities, but Oxford appears to include more college spending in its submission. Cambridge has widened the gap on Imperial College and the London School of Economics, but the most dramatic progress has been made by Edinburgh, which moves up eight places to fifth, overtaking St Andrews in the process to become the top university in Scotland.

For most readers, the scramble over a handful of points at the top of the overall ranking of universities will be literally academic. The key information is contained in the subject tables, which now cover every area of higher education. Ironically, however, the belated completion of official teaching quality assessments in England also marked the end of the process for universities. Although revamped quality audits will pass judgment on universities' procedures for ensuring that standards are maintained, only those departments that registered poor scores previously will be inspected in future. Only further education colleges will continue to undergo teaching quality assessments of the type that has been the norm over the past decade. And even they will switch to a lighter touch eventually if their grades are consistently good.

University Vice-Chancellors succeeded in persuading ministers that the assessment arrangements were wastefully bureaucratic and expensive without pointing up significant differences in quality. Grades had drifted inexorably upwards as academics learnt what was required to satisfy the system. Instead of devising a better method of external assessment of individual courses, the Vice-Chancellors and the national bodies responsible for quality and funding in higher education decided that universities should be responsible for their own quality assurance.

To compensate for the absence of detailed reports, universities are now required to publish particular statistics – some of which were already available nationally – as well as summaries of external examiners' reports. The Teaching Quality Information website (www.tqi.ac.uk) now provides a range of data and will eventually include results from a national student satisfaction survey. The switch has been overwhelmingly popular among academics, who resented the previous system, but its replacement is unlikely to be as effective at pointing up the gems (or duds) in unexpected places.

One of the strengths of this *Guide,* and others like it, has been to highlight the quality of hitherto underestimated universities such as York, and to celebrate the achievements of centres of excellence such as the social sciences at Essex. But, far from seeing the end of league tables as the critics of subject assessments intended, the likely impact will be to make them more influential. Universities' own research suggests that well over half of all applicants use newspaper guides and, as the one round of teaching quality reports becomes increasingly dated, more students will look for alternative sources of comparison. University rankings existed before teaching assessments were published and they will continue under the new system.

Any doubt that students would become more selective about the courses they chose has evaporated in recent years. Just as tuition fees and the withdrawal of maintenance grants have added to the financial pressures on students and their families, the winds of change have turned into a gale for some universities. Amid the Government's expansion plans, academics by the score have been made redundant in some institutions, and we have seen the first campus closures. Top-up fees, while promising a financial lifeline for many universities, may bring further institutional casualties if students become even more selective.

The most recent concerns, however, have been in particular subjects where students are in short supply and research costs can only be met with generous funding. Most attention has focused on chemistry, where there have been a number of closures, but other sciences and modern languages have proved vulnerable. The lure of a degree remains strong in some subjects and some universities, but by no means all. The demand for places on new universities' vocational degrees is often buoyant, for example, while applicants are looking elsewhere for traditional academic subjects.

Higher education had already seen important changes with the introduction of incentives to extend access to a wider share of the population, and much more selective allocation of research funds. The Government wants half of all young people to experience higher education by the time they are 30, many of them taking two-year foundation degrees rather than the traditional honours. The result is a gradual return to the hierarchical system that seemed to have been abandoned when the polytechnics acquired university status; only this time there are more than two tiers.

At the top, in terms of funding and prestige, is a group of fewer than 20 universities, which attract 90 per cent of the resources available for research and also take the lion's share of money for teaching, partly because they offer expensive subjects such as medicine and engineering. A middle group, composed mainly of traditional universities, has been recruiting more undergraduates – especially overseas – while trying to compete on research. The remainder are having to survive mainly by expanding, or at least maintaining, student numbers and interacting with local firms.

Universities in the last group have been feeling the squeeze, as several of the most popular institutions have taken advantage of a relaxation in recruitment controls to expand their numbers. But fears have also been expressed for some of those in the middle, which miss out not only on the Government's boost for leading research but also on the rewards for widening access to higher education. Applicants with the necessary qualifications will no doubt continue to migrate towards the more prestigious institutions.

Continuing confusion over sixth–form qualifications is complicating matters further for those hoping to begin a course in 2006. Although the Government has rejected proposals for an overarching diploma, teenagers and mature applicants would do well to examine the small print in universities' prospectuses and on their websites to gauge their approach to different qualifications. The demand for more than the conventional three A levels and attitudes towards Key Skills, AS levels and vocational qualifications still vary enormously from university to university. Most of the top universities continue to frame their offers in terms of A-level grades, but the majority of others now use the UCAS tariff to set a points requirement.

Whichever system is used, every grade may help in the race for selection. And the right choice of course remains vital. This book should help in the process of choice for, unlike other guides, its emphasis is on the quality of education. As well as the original university rankings, the book contains advice for both home and overseas students on how to choose a suitable course, and there are extended profiles of all the universities in our tables.

Mindful of the competition for graduate jobs, applicants are looking as never before for quality and are also gravitating towards the more vocational subjects. The pattern established in Australia, which began charging for higher education more than a decade ago, is being repeated in Britain. Courses that are perceived to offer a clear career path are seeing a significant rise in applications, while some traditional academic subjects are struggling. There will be a place somewhere in higher education for most of those hoping to start a course in 2006, but such are the uncertainties this year that candidates would be wise to consider a wide range of options. Some may choose to be more ambitious than they would have been in previous years, while including at least one 'insurance' course, for example, where entrance requirements are significantly lower than at the first-choice university.

The University Explosion

At first sight, choosing a university appears to have become simpler over the past decade. The distinction between universities and polytechnics was swept away in 1992 and the number of places expanded to the point where far more young (and not so young) people could benefit from higher education. Although the parties differed in the 2005 election about the scale of expansion, consensus has grown among politicians and business leaders that, quite apart from the benefits to the individual, a modern economy needs mass higher education. Countries such as the United States and Japan reached the same conclusion long ago but a combination of factors – not all of them planned – has seen Britain making up for lost time at a rate that has prompted concerns about the quality of some courses.

More than a third of 18-year-olds are now going on to higher education, compared with one in seven in 1980, while a much higher proportion will take a higher education course at some point in their life. Yet, paradoxically, by ridding Britain of its elite university system, the last Conservative Government sowed the seeds of a different form of elitism. The very process of opening up higher education ensured the creation of a new hierarchy of institutions. The old certainties could not survive in a nation of 100 diverse universities and a growing number of degree-providing colleges.

The New Hierarchy

There always was a pecking order of sorts. Oxford and Cambridge were world leaders long before most British universities were established, and parts of London University have always enjoyed a high status in particular fields. But few outside the higher-education world could discriminate between Aberdeen and Exeter, for example. Employers, careers advisers, even academics, had their own ideas of which were the leading universities, but there was little hard evidence to back their conclusions. Often they were based on outdated, inaccurate impressions of distant institutions.

The expanded higher education system has made such judgements more scientific as well as more necessary. Employers of graduates and those who commit their money to student sponsorship or funding research are comparing institutions department by department. This has become possible because of a new transparency in what a former higher-education minister described as the 'secret garden of academe'. Official demands for more and more published information may have taxed the patience of university administrators, but they have also given outsiders the opportunity to make more meaningful comparisons.

Many see the beginnings of a British Ivy League in the competitive culture that has ensued. Even before the recent upheavals, the lion's share of research cash went to a small group of traditional universities, enabling them to upgrade their facilities and attract many of the top academics. As student numbers have gone through the roof, however, general higher education budgets have been squeezed and the funding gap has widened. Beneath the veneer of a unified higher education system, it was inevitable that greater specialisation would arrive eventually. There is no need for formalised divisions because the market – and now Government policy – are already taking the university system in that direction.

Why University?

Doubtless some will be tempted, once the cost of living has been added to the new fees burden and the attractions of university life balanced against loss of potential earnings, to write off higher education. There are plenty of self-made millionaires who still swear by the University of Life as the only training ground for success. Yet even by narrow financial criteria it would be rash to dismiss higher education. With so many more competing for jobs, a degree will never again be an automatic passport to a fast-track career. But graduates' financial prospects still compare favourably with school leavers'. Indeed, the salary premium enjoyed by UK graduates is among the highest in the world, according to the Organisation of Economic Cooperation and Development. Even for those who cannot or do not wish to afford three or more years of full-time education after leaving school, university remains a possibility. The modular courses adopted by most universities enable students to work through a degree at their own pace, dropping out for a time if necessary, or switching to part-time attendance. Distance learning is another option, and advances in information technology now mean that some nominally full-time courses are delivered mainly via computers.

For many – perhaps most – students, therefore, the university experience is not what it was in their parents' day. There is more assessment, more crowding, more pressure to get the best possible degree while also finding gainful employment for at least part of the year. The proportion of students achieving first-class degrees has risen significantly, while an upper second (rather than the previously ubiquitous 2:2) has become the norm. Research shows that degree classification has a real impact on success in the labour market.

Toward the Future

The 2004 Higher Education Bill and the White Paper that preceded it have ensured that the pace of change will accelerate. In the future it is likely that more students will begin their degrees at further education colleges, more will opt initially for two-year courses and the range both of subjects and teaching methods will grow still further. Some predict the rise of the 'virtual university' or the demise of the conventional higher-education institution, as companies customise their own courses. However, universities have demonstrated enduring popularity and show every sign of weathering the current turbulence.

Overall competition for places may ease slightly this year, but demand will follow a familiar pattern. Especially in traditional universities, many arts and social science courses will remain oversubscribed and some science degrees, too, will have high entrance requirements. Places will again be plentiful, however, in all but the most prestigious engineering programmes, as well as in technology and the 'hard' sciences, such as physics, for those with the right qualifications.

Top-up fees in England may cause a rush for places in Wales particularly and, to a lesser extent, in Scotland. Those who opt for an English university may blanch at the thought of future debts, but the new system should reduce the immediate financial problems that students have experienced in recent years. Undergraduates from less-affluent homes will have their pick of bursaries, as well as the possibility of a grant, while middle-class families may be able to offer more financial support when they no longer have to help out with upfront tuition fees. The new system will take time to bed in, but there will be advantages to being in at the start.

Choosing a Course and a University

1

Choosing a course and a university are big decisions which will have an enormous impact on your future life. They will affect the place you live, the friends you make, and quite possibly your future career. They are also very difficult decisions: with tens of thousands of courses and over a hundred universities to choose from (nearer 150 if you include higher education colleges). It can be difficult to know where to start, let alone which to choose. And the problem is likely to get worse as the Government has expressed its desire for more, not less, diversity among universities.

So how do you go about it? There are no easy answers, but it is possible to list a range of factors which need to be looked

UNITE Student Experience Report 2005
87% of students have a favourable impression of their university.

at. Different people will attach different levels of importance to each one, but most will need at least to think about them all. HERO (www.hero.ac.uk), the national website for higher education in the UK, may help you to do this. In 2004 it commenced publication of much more information about the quality of universities, including summaries of external examiners' reports and detailed employment statistics. The full data should be available sometime in 2005. Some guidance on English-speaking alternatives to British universities is given at the end of this chapter. We will start by looking at the choice of course and then the place where you might study.

The Subject

For a few people, choosing a course is simple: they have always wanted to be a brain surgeon or have always had a passion for Tudor England. For most, however, there is a bewildering variety of courses, many of which involve subjects that are not taught in schools or colleges. Somehow you have to narrow down the thousands of courses to just a few.

When it comes to choosing a subject there are several things you need to take into account. First, you must make sure you understand the nature of the subject you are considering, especially if it is one you have not studied before. A course in ecology, for example, sounds as if it might deal with conservation and 'green' issues. However, many ecology courses are about the scientific study of the interaction between living organisms and may only deal peripherally with conservation issues. Language courses

UNITE Student Experience Report 2005
85% of students think their course meets or exceeds their expectations.

can vary considerably, from those concerned largely with literature to those which concentrate on translation and contemporary area studies. Psychology is another subject which may not be what is expected. It, too, can vary depending on whether the course focuses on the social or the scientific end of the subject.

Having made sure you understand the nature of the subject, you must be interested in it. You will spend a large proportion of three to six years immersed in the subject and that will be pretty dull if you find it boring. More important, you will probably perform better if you are excited by what you are studying. You are also likely to perform better if you have an aptitude for the subject. A course may be really interesting and lead to a guaranteed high-flying career, but if you are no good at it, you may end up performing badly or even failing altogether.

What Do Graduates Do?

Times Subject	Employed in Graduate Job	Employed in Graduate Job and Studying	Employed in Non-Graduate Job	Employed in Non-Graduate Job and Studying	Studying and Not Employed	Unemployed
Medicine	89%	2%	0%	0%	8%	1%
Dentistry	81%	17%	1%	0%	1%	0%
Nursing	86%	10%	2%	0%	1%	1%
Veterinary medicine	70%	3%	7%	1%	16%	2%
Pharmacology and pharmacy	55%	21%	8%	1%	12%	3%
Architecture	57%	16%	8%	1%	14%	4%
Civil engineering	67%	9%	10%	1%	8%	3%
Other subjects allied to medicine	68%	9%	11%	2%	8%	3%
Building	73%	10%	9%	0%	2%	5%
Education	70%	3%	14%	2%	9%	3%
Anatomy and physiology	56%	5%	15%	1%	19%	4%
Food science	61%	5%	15%	2%	12%	4%
Social work	63%	7%	17%	2%	7%	4%
Town and country planning and landscape	52%	6%	18%	3%	16%	6%
Chemical engineering	48%	7%	15%	2%	20%	9%
Chemistry	32%	4%	19%	2%	36%	7%
Law	18%	5%	21%	6%	46%	5%
Land and property management	55%	12%	21%	2%	3%	7%
Celtic studies	24%	4%	24%	3%	41%	5%
East and South Asian studies	50%	7%	24%	2%	11%	6%
Theology and religious studies	28%	6%	25%	3%	32%	6%
General engineering	48%	7%	21%	1%	14%	10%
Mechanical engineering	50%	5%	22%	2%	11%	10%
Mathematics	29%	10%	26%	3%	25%	8%
Middle Eastern and African studies	32%	2%	23%	5%	27%	10%
Russian	41%	6%	27%	3%	17%	7%
Physics and astronomy	21%	6%	24%	2%	36%	11%
Music	31%	4%	29%	4%	26%	6%
German	36%	6%	30%	4%	20%	5%
Aeronautical and manufacturing engineering	45%	6%	24%	2%	12%	11%
Economics	34%	10%	27%	4%	16%	8%
French	34%	5%	32%	4%	21%	5%
Biological sciences	28%	4%	29%	3%	28%	8%
Electrical and electronic engineering	42%	5%	24%	2%	13%	14%
Computer science	44%	4%	26%	3%	10%	13%
Classics and ancient history	27%	4%	32%	4%	26%	8%

Times Subject	Employed in Graduate Job	Employed in Graduate Job and Studying	Employed in Non-Graduate Job	Employed in Non-Graduate Job and Studying	Studying and Not Employed	Unemployed
Geology	29%	2%	31%	2%	27%	8%
Accountancy	25%	17%	33%	9%	8%	7%
Archaeology	27%	2%	30%	5%	24%	11%
Geography	32%	4%	35%	3%	20%	7%
Materials technology	37%	4%	33%	2%	15%	9%
English	28%	3%	35%	5%	22%	7%
Linguistics	26%	5%	36%	4%	23%	6%
Social policy	36%	4%	35%	5%	12%	7%
Politics	30%	4%	34%	4%	20%	8%
Philosophy	25%	4%	34%	5%	23%	8%
Iberian languages	33%	5%	37%	4%	16%	6%
History	24%	3%	36%	5%	25%	7%
Agriculture and forestry	40%	6%	38%	2%	9%	5%
History of art, architecture and design	29%	3%	35%	4%	20%	8%
Italian	35%	4%	38%	3%	15%	5%
Psychology	27%	6%	39%	5%	17%	6%
Business studies	40%	5%	38%	3%	7%	7%
Librarianship and information management	33%	5%	33%	5%	11%	12%
Anthropology	31%	4%	35%	3%	16%	11%
Hospitality, leisure, recreation, sport and tourism	33%	3%	43%	4%	12%	6%
Sociology	28%	5%	42%	5%	13%	6%
Drama, dance and cinematics	31%	3%	42%	4%	12%	8%
Art and design	36%	2%	38%	4%	8%	13%
American studies	25%	3%	43%	6%	16%	7%
Communication and media studies	36%	3%	43%	2%	6%	10%
All Subjects	39%	5%	29%	3%	16%	7%

The table is ranked by the sum of 'positive' destinations – Employed in Graduate Jobs, Employed in Graduate Jobs and Studying, and Studying and Not Employed.

Source: HESA 2002-03

Career opportunities are another important factor. If you know what you want to do after university, your subject must provide a suitable basis for that career. The choice may be wider than you think, as just under half of graduate jobs do not specify any particular subject at all. Conversely, a narrowly vocational course could restrict your career options if you subsequently change your mind about the direction you want to go in.

For many professional subjects, such as engineering, psychology or architecture, the course may be accredited by a professional body (such as the Institution of Civil Engineers). You will usually need to have followed an accredited course if you want to continue with the subject as your chosen career.

Students often refer to employment prospects when they are asked about why they chose their course. However, it is worth looking at the figures. The table on pages 14–15 gives the percentages of graduates in 2003 who, six months after graduation, obtained a graduate job (ie, one which normally recruits graduates), went on to further study, obtained a job but one that does not normally recruit graduates, or who were unemployed. The unemployment rate varies from 0 per cent (dentistry) to 14 per cent (electrical and electronic engineering) but for most subjects is within the range 5–10 per cent. In other words, for most subjects the chances of getting a job are about the same. Interestingly, business studies, a subject that is often considered to be highly employable, comes out in the middle at 7 per cent.

> **UNITE Student Experience Report 2005**
>
> 83% of students are optimistic about getting a job after university. Science and engineering students are rather more optimistic than those studying arts subjects.

The picture becomes more varied when you look at the proportions who obtain a graduate-level job. Some subjects, such as dentistry and nursing, do more or less guarantee a graduate-level job with over 95 per cent obtaining one. However, there are a number of subjects where over one third of graduates are in non-graduate jobs after six months. The proportion entering further study also varies considerably, usually because of the normal career paths followed by graduates. Forty six per cent of lawyers go on to further study because that is necessary to qualify as a solicitor or barrister and 36 per cent of chemists do the same because a higher degree is necessary for many chemistry careers.

Of course there will be some variability within these broad subject groups. Some courses may be tailored towards specific careers and so achieve a very high level of employability, but conversely may be seen as too specialised if you try for an alternative career. Also, the longer-term career prospects may be better than the figures for six months after graduation.

Ten Courses You Didn't Know You Could Do		Top Ten Most Popular Subjects		
BA	Adventure recreation	1	Design studies	19,772
BA	Animation	2	Law	19,395
BA	Hausa and Arabic	3	Medicine	17,826
BA	Byzantine studies	4	Psychology	14,957
BSc	Equine science	5	Management studies	13,982
BA	Packaging design	6	Computer science	13,715
BA	Playwork	7	Nursing	12,038
BSc	Law and property valuation	8	Teacher training	11,766
BSc	Science and football	9	Business studies	10,668
BA	War studies	10	English	10,056

AVAILABLE FOR ENTRY IN 2005, UCAS WEBSITE   APPLICATIONS, ENTRY 2004, UCAS

One study showed that the proportion of graduates in a non-graduate job after five years was less than half of that after just six months. Design studies graduates, for example, often take longer to establish their careers than those in some other disciplines.

One reason for some similarity in employment prospects is the point mentioned above, that a significant proportion of job vacancies do not specify any subject at all. You can take the most obscure subject in the UCAS Directory and still have nearly 50 per cent of jobs open to you. Another reason is that class of degree is important: students with first-class honours are very rarely unemployed whatever subject they studied.

Getting a job is one thing, but will it be a well-paid job? Graduate starting salaries also vary between subjects as the table on pages 18–19 shows. The tables are quite highly correlated so that subjects where graduates are likely to find a job are also those which are well paid (at least initially). However, there are some exceptions such as architecture, where graduate jobs seem to be easy to come by but starting salaries are very much in the middle. Do remember that these figures do not reflect your earning prospects as your career develops. For example, nursing graduates receive quite good starting salaries but the longer term earning potential may well be less than that of some other subjects lower down the table.

You also need to consider entry requirements. Some universities have a General Entrance Requirement, a basic minimum set of qualifications that all students have to have. For most students this is not a problem as they will meet the Requirement easily, but it is worth checking to make sure. It may include an English language requirement and a minimum age. Most universities will also have various escape clauses to enable them to admit good students with unusual backgrounds even if they don't meet the General Entrance Requirement.

Each course will also have its entry requirements, both in terms of subjects you must already have studied and the examination grades required for entry. Most mathematics courses, for example, will require previous study of mathematics. The UCAS website or the *Official UCAS Guide* are the easiest ways to check this. If you have the right subjects, the grades required will vary between universities and also between subjects. There is little point in applying for medicine unless you are confident of getting As and Bs at A level (or their equivalent in other qualifications) while Ds and Es will get you into a course such as engineering at many less popular universities.

Many universities now also provide entry profiles on the UCAS website, a much more detailed guide to entry requirements and what the university is looking for than can be

Top Ten for Average Tariff Score			Bottom Ten for Average Tariff Score		
1	Medicine	456	1	Social work	206.6
2	Veterinary medicine	454	2	Tourism, transport and travel	210.8
3	Dentistry	420	3	Building	244.1
4	Mathematics	410	4	Design studies	250.2
5	Physics	405	5	Education	250.6
6	Classical studies	377	6	Human resource management	252.3
7	Aerospace engineering	371	7	Information systems	253.3
8	Philosophy	368	8	Publishing	253.9
9	Statistics	365	9	Medical technology	254.2
10	Law	365	10	Dance	255.5

What do Graduates Earn?

	Subject	Average Starting Salary
1	Medicine	£31,353
2	Dentistry	£26,236
3	Chemical engineering	£21,049
4	Veterinary medicine	£20,765
5	Civil engineering	£19,388
6	Nursing	£19,333
7	General engineering	£19,327
8	Building	£19,217
9	Social work	£19,177
10	Mechanical engineering	£18,831
11	Aeronautical and manufacturing engineering	£18,589
12	Electrical and electronic engineering	£18,085
13	Economics	£17,859
14	Education	£17,548
15	Computer science	£17,424
16	Food science	£17,272
17	East and South Asian studies	£17,227
18	Anatomy and physiology	£17,060
19	Librarianship and information management	£17,034
20	Mathematics	£16,887
21	Materials technology	£16,861
22	Other subjects allied to medicine	£16,806
23	Land and property management	£16,745
24	Chemistry	£16,670
25	Town and country planning and landscape	£16,530
26	Russian	£16,503
27	Middle Eastern and African studies	£16,297
28	Business studies	£16,199
29	Physics and astronomy	£16,104
30	Accountancy	£15,902
31	Social policy	£15,850
32	Classics and ancient history	£15,628
33	Politics	£15,525
34	Celtic studies	£15,522
35	German	£15,352
36	Law	£15,219
37	History of art, architecture and design	£15,216
38	Geology	£15,172
39	Anthropology	£15,090
40	Architecture	£15,075
41	French	£15,054
42	Iberian languages	£15,004
43	Pharmacology and pharmacy	£14,977
44	Philosophy	£14,850

What do Graduates Earn?

	Subject	Average Starting Salary
45	Theology and religious studies	£14,765
46	Geography	£14,722
47	History	£14,712
48	Sociology	£14,601
49	Hospitality, leisure, recreation, sport and tourism	£14,469
50	Agriculture and forestry	£14,302
51	Biological sciences	£14,279
52	Psychology	£14,215
53	Italian	£14,212
54	English	£14,177
55	American studies	£14,042
56	Communication and media studies	£13,930
57	Music	£13,895
58	Art and design	£13,760
59	Linguistics	£13,760
60	Drama, dance and cinematics	£13,387
61	Archaeology	£13,308

SOURCE: *HESA 2002–03*

summarised in a prospectus. This information will also be in course or departmental booklets.

The Qualifications Jungle

The current post-16 curriculum allows universities to express their entry requirements in a wide variety of ways. They have to make choices about the number of units that should be taken, how many A2s or Advanced Highers will be required, whether Key Skills will be compulsory and so on. Inevitably different universities have made different decisions and so you will have to read their websites and prospectuses much more carefully to ensure that you can find your way through the new qualifications jungle.

On some things most universities are in agreement:
- at least two subjects should be taken at A2
- applicants who do not take AS levels in Year 12 will not be disadvantaged
- applicants with four or five AS levels will not be at an advantage
- neither Key Skills nor the Advanced Extension Tests will be compulsory

On others, however, there are differences:
- some universities require a total of 21 units, others require 18 units
- some include Key Skills in offers, others do not
- some use the new UCAS tariff (see *The UCAS Tariff* box, page 20), others do not
- some accept General Studies A2, others do not.

Generally speaking, universities that come higher up the ranking in our league table are more likely to require 21 units rather than 18, not to include Key Skills in offers, and not to use the tariff. However, there is a lot of variation so it is important to ensure you read the small print carefully.

In general, the new universities are more likely to accept the more vocationally-oriented A levels for particular courses, and are more likely to use the new UCAS tariff and allow points for Key Skills. However, in all cases you will need to check the university's prospectus and/or the *Official UCAS Guide* carefully.

Older students, or those with a non-traditional educational background, will generally be treated more flexibly by universities. While you will still be expected to demonstrate your ability and suitability for the course, you will be able to do this through a wide variety of qualifications or an access course or, in some cases, relevant work experience. The GCSEs you flunked as an unhappy adolescent before diving into the first job that became available will be ignored and the emphasis will be on what you can do now.

Bear in mind that entry standards are essentially market-related. Popular courses at popular universities can afford to be very choosy about whom they admit and so have the highest entry standards. That may not mean the courses are any tougher at those universities (though they could be for other reasons) but it does mean that most of the students on the courses will be very able.

Also, remember that published entry grades are usually the normal levels of offer. A very popular course might make offers of ABB or AAB but in practice only make those offers to applicants expected to get AAA. This is not wilful perversity on the part of universities but an aspect of the market. If they usually made AAA offers and published that, then application rates would plummet as applicants would have to be very confident of getting AAA before they would consider applying. But dropping the offer level means more

---

The UCAS Tariff

The UCAS tariff allocates a numerical score to a range of qualifications and attainments, establishing an equivalence between them and allowing the aggregation of scores from many different qualifications. It became available in 2002 for universities to use in making their offers of places, but not all universities are using it. Some do not agree with the equivalences and weights determined by UCAS while others simply prefer to make offers based on specific grades in specific subjects. In general, universities that appear higher up *The Times* League Table are less likely to use the UCAS tariff in making their offers. Even those using it are likely to require specific grades in certain key subjects as well as an overall tariff score.

Full details are on the UCAS website (www.ucas.com) but some of the main scores in the new tariff are as follows:

| Score | English Qualifications | | Scottish Qualifications | | Key Skills |
	GCE AS	GCE A Level	Advanced Higher	Higher	
120		A	A		
100		B	B		
80		C	C		
72				A	
60	A	D		B	
50	B				
48				C	
40	C	E			
30	D				Level 4
20	E				Level 3

applicants apply and so, if the actual selection criteria matched the offer level, too many students would be accepted.

In some cases conventional school examinations may not be enough. Many years ago, Oxford and Cambridge ran their own entrance examinations and the idea is being looked at again. A group of prestigious law schools (Birmingham, Bristol, Cambridge, Durham, East Anglia, Nottingham, Oxford and University College London) introduced an admissions test (LNAT) for entry in 2005. Similarly, Bristol, Cambridge, Oxford, the Royal Veterinary College and University College London use the BMAT test (www.bmat.org.uk) for entry to some courses in biomedical sciences, medicine and veterinary science. Cambridge has a Sixth Term Examination Paper (STEP) in mathematics and may require interviewees in other subjects to take a Thinking Skills Assessment (TSA).

There are also growing calls for the introduction of a general university entrance test, similar to the Scholastic Aptitude Test used in the United States, to enable universities to identify talent among large numbers of applicants.

Type of Course

Having decided what you want to study, you will be faced with a variety of ways of studying it. The most basic difference is between the levels of the courses. While most higher education courses lead to a degree, some lead to sub-degree qualifications such as a Higher National Diploma (HND) or a Foundation Degree. Foundation Degrees are becoming more common as the Government has decided that future expansion of higher education should largely be through the expansion of this type of course. In general sub-degree courses will be shorter, more vocationally orientated, and have lower entry requirements. Some will be linked to degree courses, giving you the option of progressing to a degree if you perform well enough on the early parts of the course.

Courses can differ markedly in length, varying from two years for most sub-degree courses to six years for a professional course in architecture, and possibly more for some

---

Eleven Things You Didn't Know About Universities

- The oldest university in the country, Oxford, was probably founded in 1096, but no one knows precisely. It was there in 1187, but must have been founded before that.
- There are over 50,000 courses to choose from.
- Fancy a degree in Brewing and Distilling? Go to Heriot-Watt.
- The total income of universities in 2002–03 was £15.6 billion, which is more than that of some countries.
- Women outnumbered men among first-year students in 1996–97 for the first time.
- In his will, the philosopher Jeremy Bentham instructed that his skeleton and head be preserved, clothed and mounted in a seated position. He has sat like that in University College London since 1850.
- There are 300,000 overseas students from 180 countries in the UK.
- At some Scottish universities the Rector is elected by the staff and students. This has sometimes resulted in the election of celebrities rather than distinguished academics.
- The student population in the UK has increased to over 2 million from just 200,000 in the 1960s.
- 'University' is a legally controlled title in the UK – only institutions with a Royal Charter or some other legal authority can call themselves a university.
- The total floor area of UK higher education buildings is 24 million square metres.

part-time courses. The majority of full-time courses are three years, but some add a 'sandwich' year (usually spent in work experience), most language courses last four years and many science and engineering courses lead to a Master's degree (such as MChem or MEng) after four years. In some cases it is possible to add a foundation year to the beginning of a course, making it a further year in length. These foundation courses vary somewhat in nature and entry requirements. Some are essentially a conversion course for students who have the 'wrong' subjects in their examinations and will expect the same or a similar standard for entry as the courses they lead on to (though key subjects for direct entry will not be required). Others are designed to take students who have performed below the normal entry requirements for a course to bring them up to speed. These courses will often have lower entry requirements.

In some cases the length of a course can be misleading if you intend to go on to a profession in the same subject. Five years of medicine or six of architecture will qualify you to start work as a doctor or an architect (though in both cases there are further hurdles before full qualification). However, three years of law does not qualify you to be a lawyer. You must undertake further training (often at your own expense) before you can work as a barrister or a solicitor. In the case of engineering, a four-year MEng course will give you maximum credit towards the status of Chartered Engineer, but if you take a BEng course you will have to undertake further study after you have finished.

The start of courses may vary, too. While the great majority still start in September or October there are a few that start in the spring. Many of these are nursing courses but some universities are offering a spring start in other subjects, too.

Some differences between courses relate to aspects of the subject itself. Only the very largest academic departments have expertise in all aspects of a subject and so, especially in the later years, the course will focus on the particular expertise of the department. You will need to decide whether a particular course offers the areas of the subject you want to study. Of course you may not know, or may change your mind as you go through the course. If you think this is likely, then a course in a large department with a wide range of options might be best.

Even for courses with a similar content, there may nonetheless be significant differences. Some of the opportunities you may want to consider are:

- spending a year or part of a year in Europe under an ERASMUS programme
- taking time out on a work placement
- extending the course to four years to obtain a Master's degree (common for engineering and some science courses)

Top Ten for Teaching Quality			Bottom Ten for Teaching Quality	
1	Dundee	23.5	1 Surrey Institute of Art and Design	19.0
2	York	23.2	2 East London	19.3
3	St Andrews	23.1	3 Bournemouth	19.5
4	Edinburgh	23.0	4 Thames Valley	19.6
5	Harper Adams	23.0	5 Derby	19.8
6	Cambridge	22.0	6 Central England	19.9
7	Loughborough	22.8	7 Buckinghamshire Chilterns	20.0
8	Glasgow	22.7	8 London South Bank	20.0
9	Strathclyde	22.7	9 Anglia	20.3
10	Warwick	22.7	10 University of Wales, Newport	20.3

- being taught part of your course by a media personality or a Nobel prize-winner who is a member of staff in the department.

Courses also differ in their structure. Some will concentrate on a single subject, some will allow you to combine two subjects in a single course (often called Dual or Joint Honours courses), and others will involve several subjects. Some will have a large proportion of the course fixed in advance, while others will allow you to choose options to make up a substantial part of the course. There are even 'pick and mix' courses where you can choose from a wide range of very diverse options.

Some courses are organised on a modular basis, usually with two semesters rather than three terms a year. Each module will require the same amount of study and will usually be assessed separately. This tends to increase the number of examinations and assessments you will have to do. In some cases the courses are organised in this way simply to assist a university with its administration, timetabling and so on. The courses themselves continue to be traditional single or joint honours courses. In some cases the modular courses are advertised as being very flexible, allowing you to choose your options from a very wide range of available modules. However, they may not be as flexible as they appear, as timetable clashes will restrict the real choice available to you. Also, in making your choices you should think about how they will appear to an employer, as they may well prefer to see a coherently structured programme of study rather than an eclectic mix of unrelated modules.

Across the varying course structures, there will be differences in teaching methods and assessment. Some courses will make more use than others of particular teaching methods, such as tutorials (though watch out for groups of 15-20 that are still called tutorials), computer-assisted learning or dissertations. If you seize up in formal examinations, you may want a course with a lot of continuous assessment. Alternatively, if you don't like the continuous pressure that this involves, you may prefer one with an emphasis on final examinations. If that isn't enough variety for you, there are differences between universities in the weight given to second and third-year modules in the final degree classification and there may be different rules about how often you are allowed to re-sit examinations.

Which Subject is Hardest to Get Into?

There is no simple answer to this question. Some courses are very popular – they get a lot of applications – but the standard of those applications may on average be low. For example, teacher training makes the top ten most popular subjects but the average UCAS tariff score of new entrants is one of the lowest for any subject. Similarly, veterinary science only gets 1,400 applications but has the top tariff score. Generally, the hardest subjects to get into will

Top Ten for Average Tariff Score			Bottom Ten for Average Tariff Score		
1	Cambridge	510.6	1	Bolton	147.8
2	Oxford	499.1	2	London South Bank	179.6
3	Imperial College	467.8	3	Thames Valley	180.2
4	London School of Economics	447.1	4	East London	181.1
5	Warwick	429.7	5	Buckinghamshire Chilterns	182.8
6	Durham	426.1	6	Teesside	187.3
7	Bristol	423.7	7	Luton	194.3
8	Nottingham	419.9	8	University of Wales, Newport	195.5
9	St Andrews	414.8	9	Greenwich	198.9
10	York	414.8	10	Middlesex	199.0

be those which both attract large numbers of applications and attract lots of good applicants and so have high average tariff scores. Having said that, an applicant with AAA (or AAAAA in Highers in Scotland) in the right subjects will find it easy to get into almost any course he or she wants.

For some, the choice of subject and type of course will narrow down the number of possible universities to just a few. If you want to study veterinary science, there are currently only six places you can go. If you want to study paper science, only one. For many though, particularly if you are interested in one of the major subjects such as English, chemistry, law or mechanical engineering, there may be 30 or more similar courses. Research into the reasons why students leave universities early in the course often finds that choosing the wrong course is important, so it is crucial to do good research and make a careful decision.

Now we will look at the choice of university, breaking the decision down into several components: location, type of university, quality and reputation, facilities and cost.

Location

Where do you want to go? Do you really like your parents or do you want to get as far away as possible? Do you want to visit your boyfriend or girlfriend every weekend (or, perhaps, want an excuse not to)? Do you want to find the cheapest way of going to university? One way or another, location is likely to be an important factor. If you want to live at home, the decision might be straightforward, though if you live in London there could easily be half a dozen local universities. If you want to go away from home, then distance or travel time will probably be a factor.

Going away to university and living at home will give you rather different experiences. Going away will be more of an adventure, taking you away from your parents and the town where you live, and any restrictions that implies, to a whole new city or region of the country. You will be free to study and socialise as and when you like, joining in with other students, without having to worry about getting the last bus to your parents' part of town. On the other hand, it will almost certainly be more expensive. You will also have to be much more self-reliant, possibly shopping and cooking for yourself, and generally not having any of the security and comfort of home. Your parents and their central heating can seem very appealing when you are trying to get to sleep in a cold bed-sit.

Incidentally, if you can go away from home it may be to your longer-term advantage to do so. Some recent research has shown that students who move away from home have better job prospects. This is probably because those who stay at home tend to end up with narrower horizons and have less self-confidence in new situations.

Top Ten for Library/Computing Spend			**Bottom Ten for Library/Computing Spend**	
1	Oxford	1,559	1	Worcester	329
2	Abertay Dundee	1,278	2	Liverpool Hope	335
3	SOAS	1,230	3	Canterbury	338
4	Cambridge	1,161	4	Teesside	345
5	Imperial College	1,138	5	Bucks Chilterns	351
6	University College London	1,131	6	Northampton	352
7	London School of Economics	1,091	7	Bournemouth	360
8	Edinburgh	901	8	Bath Spa	367
9	King's College London	870	9	Sunderland	367
10	Manchester	838	10	London South Bank	378

If a particular town or city is acceptable, you will need to look at the location of the university itself in relation to that town or city. Is it in the city-centre or several miles outside? The former will be handy for shops and transport but may be noisy and less than picturesque. The latter may be a beautiful setting, but if you have to live off-campus there could be high travel costs. Another factor might be security: is the university in a well-lit suburban area or in a less desirable and possibly less safe part of town?

The facilities of the town or city may be important for you, too. Your sojourn at university will be a time when you can pursue your interests in a way you may never be able to again. Access to many things, such as sports facilities, will be very cheap and you will have the time to take them seriously. Whether you like to dance the night away, follow the Premier League or take the theatre seriously, you will want to ensure you can do it.

Prospectuses frequently boast about the attractive surrounding countryside, so much so that it seems that every university is situated in the most picturesque region of the country. However, unless you have a particular interest that takes you there, such as climbing or fell walking, it is doubtful if you will spend much time taking in the sights.

Then, of course, there is cost. Generally, the south of England and London are more expensive places to live than the rest of the country, so if cost is significant for you, you will want to take this into account.

Type of University

Universities are not all the same, and nor is it easy to put them into simple categories. At one extreme is an ancient collegiate university, a world leader in terms of research, offering traditional academic courses, having most students with AAA at A level, and with large numbers of postgraduates, many from overseas. At the other extreme is a very locally orientated university which does little research, but offers more vocational courses to largely local students, many of whom are mature and do not have A levels. Both universities may be very good at what they do, but what they do is very different and they will feel very different to attend as a student.

Generally, older universities (pre-1970) will do more research, recruit a higher proportion of school leavers and offer more traditional academic courses, while newer universities will be more locally and vocationally orientated and recruit more mature and part-time students.

Universities also vary greatly in size, from fewer than 2,000 students to well over 20,000. A small university will be more personal and cosier but will have fewer facilities and non-academic activities; a big university will be busier and more impersonal (lectures may be to

Top Ten for Student Facilities Spend			Bottom Ten for Student Facilities Spend		
1	Harper Adams	650	1	Thames Valley	27
2	Surrey Institute of Art & Design	553	2	Glasgow Caledonian	72
3	Queen Margaret	479	3	Bournemouth	80
4	Imperial College	473	4	Liverpool Hope	88
5	Chichester	451	5	London South Bank	101
6	UWIC, Cardiff	408	6	Abertay Dundee	111
7	Bath	407	7	Exeter	120
8	Leicester	394	8	Leeds Metropolitan	122
9	University of Wales, Newport	392	9	Teesside	122
10	University of the Arts London	378	10	Robert Gordon	122

hundreds at a time) but there will be a lot more going on. Student numbers are a guide to where a university lies on this spectrum, but are not the whole story. Some large universities are divided into colleges, which helps to create a small university feel within a big university context, while others are on several sites, each of which may be relatively small.

Quality and Reputation

Most people want to go to a good university if they can, and this is where the rankings in this book are helpful. By bringing together a variety of measures they try to give a reasonable basis for deciding how good a university or a subject within a university really is. Differences of a few places in the table are insignificant, but a university in the top ten is doing a lot better than one in the bottom ten or even in the middle.

The subject tables rank universities on the basis of their teaching quality (where a reasonably recent assessment is available), research quality, the actual entry standards of their new students and how successful their graduates are. The teaching assessment (technically known as a Subject Review), when it is available, is given the highest weight in these subject tables.

The results of each Subject Review are available via the websites of the QAA or the higher education funding councils (HEFCE for England and Northern Ireland, SHEFC for Scotland and HEFCW for Wales). The full reports for England, Northern Ireland and Scotland are also available on the websites, so you can easily find out about the subjects and universities you are interested in (if you haven't got access to the internet you can buy copies). The older reports in England and Wales, which led to an Excellent or Satisfactory rating, were an attempt to judge the absolute level of teaching quality in each university for the subjects covered. This was very helpful but the reports are now so old that they are no longer used in the rankings in this book. The more recent reports, which lead to a score of 1 to 4 on six aspects of teaching (giving a total out of 24), and all reports in Scotland, are an assessment against the universities' own objectives in teaching. This is an important distinction. On the old English system you could be reasonably confident that a department with an Excellent rating was better at teaching than one with a Satisfactory rating (or at least it was back in 1994 or 1995 when the assessment was carried out – a lot could have changed since then). However, on the new English system, all you can say is that a department with a higher score was better at

> **UNITE Student Experience Report 2005**
> 39% of students have a very favourable impression of their university. However, more of those attending an old university report a favourable impression then those attending a new university.

Things to Look Out For
- Most degree courses in Scotland last four years, though many students with good A levels can be exempt from the first year.
- Where a university has a split site, check where your course will be based.
- Large adverts in the press usually mean a university is having difficulty filling its places
- Engineering courses are either MEng or BEng; only the MEng will give maximum credit towards Chartered Engineer status.
- Some courses offer the chance of spending a year or part of a year in Europe.
- Accommodation might be guaranteed, but check whether it is five miles down the road.
- Courses based in two or more departments can feel as if they are based nowhere – check for a 'home' department where you will belong.

meeting its own objectives than one with a lower score. A department with very high aspirations, trying to offer the best course in the country but not quite succeeding, could end up with a lower score than a much more modest department which aimed to achieve far less but did so completely. So if you read any Subject Reviews, remember to read the section on the department's objectives very carefully.

More recently still, some departments have been re-assessed using yet another methodology called 'academic review'. In Scotland quite a large number of departments have been assessed, but in England it is only those that did particularly badly first time around. This makes it difficult to use these new scores fairly in the league tables, particularly the subject tables, as not all universities have had an opportunity to

improve their scores. As a result, we have only used them in the main League Table and not in the subject tables. However, the review reports are available on the website of the Quality Assurance Agency.

A new departure is a series of Centres for Excellence in Teaching and Learning, which will be provided with substantial extra funding. There are 74 of them across the country, based in 54 universities and colleges. Some are focused on particular subjects while others cover broader aspects of teaching, such as enterprise or employability. If the course you are interested in is linked to a Centre, it is likely that at least some aspect of the teaching is a bit special.

The main university League Table uses a wider range of measures of quality (not all are available at subject level) and ranks the quality of the entire university. However, it is clear from the subject tables that even the best universities vary in quality across subjects. Some

---

Tricks of the Prospectus Trade

The claims made by universities are rarely untrue, but they do need to be read carefully and critically. Here are a few cases where *The Times* league tables can help you to interpret what the prospectuses and websites are saying. All the quotations were taken from university websites in January 2005.

"Statistics prove that the quality of our teaching and research is amongst the best in UK higher education." No, they don't. According to *The Times* League Table this university was not in the top 30 for either teaching or research.

"We consistently rate within the top ten of all UK universities for graduate employment." Well, that depends on how you measure it. On our measure of graduate employment this university didn't make the top 20.

"The University ... is one of the UK's leading universities. We are renowned for our teaching and research excellence. Our departments and schools are world-class and we have an outstanding reputation for student support." The research record is impressive, but in *The Times* League Table over 30 other universities were more impressive. And while the quality of teaching may have an international reputation, over 40 universities scored higher.

"The University ... is at the cutting edge of teaching and learning, as well as being one of the foremost research-led universities in the UK." The use of the phrase 'cutting edge' is presumably designed to suggest a university among the best. In fact this university did not make the top 50 for teaching or the top 20 for research.

universities perform consistently well and appear in the top 20 of many subject tables, while others come low down in the main table but have one or two very good departments that do well in the subject tables. So it is important to look at the main league table alongside the subject tables.

As ever, quality has to be paid for. A Mercedes costs more than a Ford, and Cambridge 'costs' more than other universities, though in this case the currency is examination results rather than cash (though see also the cost section below). Look at the entry standards column in the ranking and you will see that it follows the overall ranking fairly closely. In other words, universities high up the table will, in general, ask for higher grades in whatever qualification you are offering than those lower down the table. You will need to make a judgement about how well you are going to do in your school or college examinations and choose universities where you have a realistic chance of meeting the entry requirements. If you are taking A levels and are going to get AAA, there is no problem, but in many subjects CCC will exclude most of the universities near the top of the table.

Facilities

The facilities offered by universities are fairly similar in general terms. All will have a library, a sports hall, a health service, a careers service and so on. But there will be differences and if something is particularly important for you it is worth checking out. Sometimes this will be hard to do – all universities will claim to have a really good careers service, but it is difficult to find out how true those claims are. In other cases, however, it is more straightforward.

UNITE Student Experience Report 2005

50% of students think the availability of IT facilities at their university is very good. 27% of students think the availability of course books in the library is very good. 34% of students think the availability of journals in the library is very good.

Accommodation will be important if you are going away from home. Is there an accommodation guarantee for first-year students? What about later years? If you are a computer geek who spends the early hours on the internet, you will want to know if the rooms are wired up. If you are often out late (and how many students are not?) you may want to know where the accommodation is, how you can get back to it late at night and whether you will feel safe doing so. If you can't live in university accommodation for the whole of your course, where is the private accommodation? Is it all in a city five miles down the road (which could be good for access to shops, night-clubs and maybe the beach, but will probably be bad for travel costs), or in the grotty end of town, or in a leafy suburb by the university? For more detail on the accommodation options, see chapter 5, *Where to Live*.

If you have a particular minority interest you want to follow while at university, then this could be a factor. Most universities will have football pitches and a Liberal Democrats Society, but a climbing wall and a deep-sea fishing group may be harder to find. The students' union will be able to tell you.

Students' unions are an increasingly important aspect of student life and have come a long way from the traditional image of providers of cheap beer and student protests. The modern entrepreneurial union will have a wide range of services from food and stationery outlets through to comprehensive advice services. Increasingly they are providers of part-time employment for students and are becoming involved in personal skills development. Inevitably, some are more active and innovative than others, so they are worth looking at.

As the financial position of students has worsened, universities have responded by setting up employment agencies. These are generally based in careers services or students' unions and use their contacts with employers to identify employment opportunities and their contacts with students to identify suitable employees. The agency will also ensure that rates of pay and hours of work are reasonable. If you think you may be short of cash, a good agency of this type could be vital.

Finally, if you have any particular needs, you will want to know that they can be catered for. Support for students with disabilities has improved greatly in recent years but some universities are particularly good at supporting some kinds of disability, while others have old buildings that make wheelchair access difficult.

Cost

From 2006, cost is set to become another factor in the decision-making process as English universities will be allowed to charge up to £3,000 in fees for home students instead of the current maximum of about £1,175. Most will charge the full £3,000 with only three (at the time of writing) charging less. If that proves to be correct, then the difference in price may be a factor you will wish to, or need to, take into account. However, to complicate matters, most universities will also introduce bursary schemes to assist students who are from low-income backgrounds and, in some cases, students who want to study shortage subjects. So, in order to find out how much it will cost to study at a particular university you will have to

---

English–Speaking Alternatives to British Universities

While UK universities have a worldwide reputation, the UK is not the only country with good universities. You may dream of doing your first degree in the USA or a Commonwealth country and every year such dreams become a reality for some students. For example, over 8,000 UK undergraduates are enrolled at US universities. Many more go overseas for further study or employment once they have graduated.

The most common destinations are other English-speaking countries, including Australia, Canada, Ireland and the USA, and plenty of advice and information is available. For example, every October there is a 'College Day' in London and another in Edinburgh, organised by the Fulbright Commission, when around 100 US universities come to extol the virtues of an American university education. Interest in these events, and for possible study in other countries, has grown since the introduction of higher fees in the UK from 2006.

The web is the easiest source of information and the following sites are among the more useful:

Association of Commonwealth Universities	www.acu.ac.uk
College Board (USA)	www.collegeboard.com
Education Ireland	www.educationireland.ie
Finaid (USA)	www.finaid.org
Fulbright Commission (USA)	www.fulbright.co.uk
Study in Australia	studyinaustralia.gov.au
Study in Canada	www.studyincanada.com

There are also university ranking tables, similar to those found in *The Times Good University Guide*, for each of the major English-speaking countries. Among the more respected are:

Australia	*The Good Universities Guide* (www.thegoodguides.com.au)
Canada	*The Maclean's Guide to Canadian Universities* (www.macleans.ca)
USA	*US News & World Report* (www.usnews.com)

check their fees and your eligibility for any of their bursary schemes. For further details on bursary and scholarship schemes, see chapter 13.

Even then, this may not give you the full picture as there will often be a range of costs that you will have to bear but which you are usually not told about in advance. If you want to put an admissions officer on the defensive, try asking about how much it will cost for you to join the sports centre, connect your laptop to the university network, make a photocopy in the library or bring your parents to your graduation ceremony.

Making the Decision

For some, location will be critical and this will immediately narrow down the choice. Others may be keen to go to as prestigious or high quality a university as possible and then the key question will be whether they can meet the entry requirements. Others may be particularly keen to carry on with an obscure martial art and so will want to go to one of the two or three places where they can do this. But for most, a combination of factors such as these will result in the elimination of most universities so that a manageable list of perhaps five or ten emerges. Then the detailed work begins.

The first source of information will probably be the undergraduate prospectus. This is the main recruiting document that universities produce and should include most of what you will need to know, including details of courses, facilities and entry requirements. However, you need to bear in mind that it is not an impartial document; it is a form of advertising designed to make the university seem attractive. Strangely, the sun is always shining in prospectus photographs. They are rarely factually incorrect, though there have been a few legal cases where disappointed students have successfully argued that the course they experienced was not the same as the one advertised in the prospectus and received compensation. However, prospectuses can be incomplete and frequently make generalised claims of quality without any supporting evidence (see above, *Tricks of the Prospectus Trade*, page 27). In addition to the prospectus, many universities will produce a series of departmental booklets, which will give more detail about individual subject areas.

One easy way of obtaining a pile of prospectuses and departmental booklets is to visit a higher education fair where most universities will have a stand to give out information. You may also get an opportunity to talk to someone from the university if you have particular questions you want to ask.

Alternatively, universities usually have prospectuses available on their websites (addresses given in University Profiles, chapter 11). This will generally have the most up-to-date module choice and financial details. You can also often take a virtual tour of the university. Departments will usually have their own sites, too, and you can often access student handbooks aimed at current students for all the detail you will ever need about courses, options, teaching methods and assessment.

If you are still unclear about entry requirements, check them out in *University & College Entrance: the Official UCAS Guide* or the entry profiles on the UCAS website. If you want more information about employment or about what external examiners have had to say, you can go to the HERO website.

A personal visit can also be very helpful. You can get a feel for the atmosphere of a university and find out just how far you will have to walk between the lecture theatres and the students' union when it is raining. Don't forget that open days are designed to make you want to apply and so you should be critical of what you see and hear, just like when you read a prospectus. If you can't make the date of the open day, many will make arrangements for you to visit more informally during the summer. A few will offer residential visits, which allow a more extended and comprehensive look at the university.

While trawling through all these sources of information, you will no doubt talk to friends, parents, teachers, careers advisers and anyone else who comes within range. While it is good to talk, be critical of what you hear. A parent or teacher may know what they are talking about, but they may be telling you things based on their experiences of 20 or 30 years ago. Universities have changed a lot since then. Alternatively, your next-door neighbour, whom you rarely see, may just happen to work in a university admissions office and be a real source of good advice.

Finally, do a double-check to make sure your chosen university still exists. There are a number of actual and possible mergers around, such as the recent merger of Manchester with UMIST to form, with startling originality, the new University of Manchester. Alternatively, some new universities may have come along, such as Bolton University or the University of the Arts, London (formerly the London Institute).

Every course and every university is different, but every student wants different things, so the chances of finding a perfect match is not that high, despite the huge range of courses that are available. You will almost certainly end up having to decide what is most important to you. Do you want the best course or one which is quite good but offers the options you really want? Do you want the ideal work placement or the course with least continuous assessment?

In the end only you can decide. It won't be easy, but after all the reading, visiting, surfing and talking, you have got to do it. You have to decide which six will go on your UCAS application. Good luck!

Checklist

Choosing a course
❑ What do you enjoy?
❑ What are you good at?
❑ Will it lead to the career you want? If you are not sure, will it keep your options open?
❑ Are you studying the right subjects?
❑ What grades do you expect to get?
❑ Will there be an additional university entrance test to take?
❑ Do you want to study one subject, two subjects or several subjects?
❑ Do you want lots of options?
❑ What kinds of assessment do you perform best in?

Choosing a university
❑ Which universities offer your chosen subject?
❑ Where are they ranked in *The Times* league table and subject tables?
❑ How far away from home do you want to go?
❑ Which facilities are important to you?
❑ Have you got a copy of the prospectus(es)?
❑ Is there an open day you can attend?
❑ What are the costs likely to be?

2

The Top Universities

The Times first published a University League Table in October 1992 as a distinctive way of measuring the quality of British universities. Every year since then the Tables have been the subject of vigorous debate among academics. Subsequently, too, a number of other broadsheet newspapers have got in on the act with not dissimilar university tables and this has inevitably led to a certain amount of confusion. Nonetheless, *The Times* League Table retains its position as the most respected and authoritative guide to the quality of UK universities and is frequently used and quoted overseas. Indeed, it has been incorporated into recent attempts by some to produce global comparisons among universities across the English-speaking world.

Given that analyses of this type within higher education and elsewhere – in schools, health, etc – have come to be seen as legitimate aids, it is perhaps surprising that many universities remain opposed to the very notion of comparing one with another, and yet that is what applicants have to do all the time. They claim in defence that each is unique, has a distinct mission and serves a different student community. Be that as it may, universities have been known to quote favourable League Table rankings when these assist their cause. Nor will you find tables of the type reproduced in this book in any material published by UCAS or The British Council and yet we remain convinced that comparisons are valid and helpful to students and their mentors when it comes to choosing a university.

Interestingly, the Higher Education Funding Council for England (HEFCE) has itself published sets of performance indicators for each UK university. We have chosen to use one of them, a measure of completion, in *The Times* League Table. This set of 'official' performance indicators covers access, completion rates, teaching and learning outcomes, research output and employment. It is in many ways a commentary on how well each university is doing at delivering government policy and, as such, has a different purpose to the measures of quality used in *The Times* League Table.

The raw data for the League Table and other tables in later chapters all come from sources in the public domain. The Higher Education Statistics Agency (HESA) provided data for entry standards, student–staff ratios, library and computer spending, facilities spending, firsts and upper seconds, graduate prospects and overseas student enrolments. HESA is the official agency for the collection, analysis and dissemination of quantitative information about the universities.

The HEFCE, along with the Scottish Higher Education Funding Council (SHEFC) and the Higher Education Funding Council for Wales (HEFCW), are the funding councils whose remit it is to develop policy and allocate public funds to the universities. The 2001 Research Assessment Exercise, conducted by the funding councils, provides the data for the research measure used in the Tables. The funding councils also have a statutory responsibility to assess the quality of learning and teaching in the UK universities they fund. In England, Wales, Northern Ireland and, latterly, in Scotland, too, this duty is discharged through the Quality Assurance Agency for Higher Education (QAA) and we use their programme of Subject Reviews as a measure of teaching quality.

In a few cases the source data were not available and were obtained directly from the individual universities.

All universities were provided with complete sets of their own HESA data well in advance of publication. In addition, where anomalous figures were identified in the 2002–03 HESA data, institutions were given a further opportunity to check for and notify any errors.

Similarly, we consulted the universities on methodology. Once a year, a Review Group with university representatives meets to discuss the methodology and how it can be improved. Thus, every effort has been made to ensure accuracy, but no responsibility can be taken for errors or omissions. The data providers do not necessarily agree with data aggregations or manipulations appearing in this book and are also not responsible for any inferences or conclusions thereby derived.

A particular feature of *The Times* Tables is the way the various measures are combined to create a total score. In many other tables each institution's score, for each measure, is expressed as a percentage of the maximum score. Where there is little variation in the scores these percentages are often scaled to spread the variation out and so ensure that the measure contributes something to the overall score in the table. The percentages are then summed to form an overall score.

This approach has the advantage that it is possible to see how a particular institution is performing relative to the best performing institution for a particular measure. The main disadvantage is that year-on-year comparisons are not possible. For example, an institution which scored 86 one year (ie, had a score that was 86 per cent of the top score) might perform better the next year but still have a lower score if the top institution happened to perform even better still.

In *The Times* Tables the scores have undergone a Z-transformation. This is a statistical way of ensuring that each measure contributes the same amount to the overall score and so avoids the need for any scaling. (For the statistically minded, it involves subtracting the mean score from each individual score and then dividing by the standard deviation of the scores.)

Another feature of *The Times* League Table is that three of the measures have been adjusted to take account of the subject mix at a university. A university with a medical school, for example, will tend to admit students with a higher tariff score than one without simply because it has a medical school. The adjustment removes this subject effect. A side-effect of this is that it is impossible to recalculate the total score in the table using the published data, as you need full access to all the raw data to be able to do this.

Given the various changes and the continuing refinement of the process over the years, you have to be careful when making comparisons between positions in the League Table from year to year. The Open University and the privately funded Buckingham University, and universities like Cranfield with mainly postgraduate students, are not included.

Apart from noting the overall position of any one university of interest, you can home in on a particular measure of importance to you like entry standards or graduate destinations. But bear in mind that this composite table says nothing about specific subjects at a university and so should be scrutinised in conjunction with the Subject Tables and University Profiles in later chapters.

How the League Table Works

The League Table measures nine key aspects of university activity using the most recent data available at the time of going to press. A statistical technique called the Z-transformation was applied to each measure to create a score for that measure. The Z-scores on each measure were then weighted by 2.5 for teaching, 1.5 for research and 1.0 for the rest and summed to give a total score for the university. Finally, these total scores were transformed to a scale where the top score was set at 1000 with the remainder being a proportion of the top score. This scaling does not affect the overall ranking but it avoids giving any university a negative overall score. In addition some measures (Entry Standard, Good Honours, and Graduate Prospects) have been adjusted to take account of the subject mix at the institution. The details of how the measures were compiled, together with some advice about their interpretation, is given below.

Teaching Assessment

What is it? A measure of the average teaching quality of the university.

Where does it come from? The QAA sends teams of assessors to university departments and publishes the outcomes.

How does it work? The results of assessments of teaching quality are averaged for each university. The earliest results in England (those with outcomes of Excellent or Satisfactory) are now ten or more years old and have been excluded along with the corresponding subjects from Scotland and Wales. The Scottish (Excellent, Highly Satisfactory and Satisfactory) and Welsh (Excellent and Satisfactory) outcomes, along with the more recent Academic Review outcomes, have been converted to numerical scores on this scale in order to calculate an average.

What should you look out for? The earliest results included (1995–96) are now also quite old and a lot may have happened in a department since then. In England universities learned how to achieve good results and so subjects assessed later tended to have higher scores. This was taken into account when Scottish and Welsh outcomes were converted to numerical scores.

Research Assessment

What is it? A measure of the average quality of the research undertaken in the university.

Where does it come from? The 2001 Research Assessment Exercise undertaken by the funding councils.

How does it work? Each university department entered in the assessment exercise was given a rating of 5* (top), 5, 4, 3a, 3b, 2 or 1 (bottom). These grades were converted to a numerical scale and an average was calculated, weighted according to the number of staff in the department getting each rating. Staff not selected for the exercise were assumed to be conducting research at a level two grades below that of the outcome.

What should you look out for? The rating of 5*, 5, etc., is accompanied by a letter which indicates the proportion of staff included in the assessment. Thus a 5A indicates that most staff were of 5 standard but a 5F indicates that most staff were not included in the return (and so unlikely to be active at that level).

In Scotland, the SHEFC announced in advance that it would not distinguish between 5 and 5*-rated departments for funding purposes. This may have affected the strategies adopted by some Scottish universities with the result that they obtained fewer 5* ratings then they might otherwise have done.

Entry Standards

What is it? The average UCAS tariff score of new students with A/AS levels and Scottish Highers under the age of 21.

Where does it come from? HESA data for 2002–03.

How does it work? Each student's A level, AS, or Scottish Higher grades are converted to a numerical score (A level A=120, B=100 ... E=40, etc.) and added up to give a score total. HESA then calculates an average for all students at the university. The results were then adjusted to take account of the subject mix at the university.

What should you look out for? At present quality of data for the UCAS tariff is not good enough to include other qualifications such as BTEC awards, GNVQ, International Baccalaureate or Access courses, and so these are not included. This will not matter for some universities, where the majority of the intake has A levels or Highers, but for others the score will represent a smaller proportion of the intake. Universities which have a specific policy of accepting students with low grades as part of an access policy will tend to have their average score depressed.

Student–Staff Ratio

What is it? A measure of the average staffing level in the university.

Where does it come from? HESA data for 2002–03.

How does it work? HESA has calculated a student–staff ratio, ie, the number of students divided by the number of staff, in a way designed to take account of different patterns of staff employment in different universities.

What should you look out for? A low SSR, ie, a small number of students for each member of staff, does not guarantee good quality of teaching or good access to staff. Universities with a medical school, where SSRs are usually low, will tend to score better.

Library and Computer Spending

What is it? The expenditure per student on library and computing facilities.

Where does it come from? HESA data for 2000–01, 2001–02 and 2002–03.

How does it work? A university's expenditure on library and computing facilities (books, journals, staff, computer hardware and software, but not buildings) is divided by the number of full-time-equivalent students. Expenditure over three years is averaged to allow for uneven expenditure. (For example, a major upgrade of a computer network might cause expenditure to rise sharply in one year but fall back the next.) Libraries and information technology are becoming increasingly integrated (many universities have a single Department of Information Services encompassing both) and so the two areas of expenditure have been taken together.

What should you look out for? Some universities are the location for major national facilities, such as the Bodleian Library in Oxford and national computing facilities in Bath and Manchester. The local and national expenditure is very difficult to separate and so these universities will tend to score more highly on this measure.

Facilities Spending

What is it? The expenditure per student on staff and student facilities.

Where does it come from? HESA data for 2000–01, 2001–02 and 2002–03.

How does it work? A university's expenditure on student facilities (sports, recreation, health, counselling, etc.) is divided by the number of full-time-equivalent students. Expenditure over three years is averaged to allow for uneven expenditure.

What should you look out for? This measure tends to disadvantage some collegiate universities as it mostly includes central university expenditure. In Oxford and Cambridge, for example, a significant amount of facilities expenditure is by the colleges but it has not yet been possible to extract comparable data from the college accounts.

Good Honours

What is it? The percentage of graduates achieving a first or upper second class degree.

Where does it come from? HESA data for 2002–03.

How does it work? The number of graduates with first or upper second class degrees is divided by the total number of graduates with classified degrees. Enhanced first degrees, such as an MEng awarded after a four-year engineering course, are treated as equivalent to a first or upper second for this purpose, while Scottish Ordinary degrees (awarded after three years rather than the usual four in Scotland) are excluded altogether. The results were then adjusted to take account of the subject mix at the university.

What should you look out for? Degree classifications are controlled by the universities themselves, though with some moderation by the external examiner system. It can be argued, therefore, that they are not a very objective measure of quality. However, degree class is the primary measure of individual success in British higher education and will have an impact elsewhere, such as employment prospects.

Graduate Prospects

What is it? A measure of the employability of a university's graduates.

Where does it come from? HESA data for 2002–03.

How does it work? The number of graduates who take up employment or further study divided by the total number of graduates with a known destination expressed as a percentage. Only employment in an area that normally recruits graduates was included. The results were then adjusted to take account of the subject mix at the university.

What should you look out for? A relatively low score on this measure does not mean that many graduates were unemployed. It may be that some had low-level jobs, such as shop assistants, which do not normally recruit graduates. Some universities recruit a high proportion of local students. If they are located in an area where graduate jobs are hard to come by, this can depress the outcome. A measure of the employability of graduates has been included in the HEFCE performance indicators but this is only available at institution level. The HESA data was used so that a subject-mix adjustment could be made.

Completion

What is it? A measure of the completion rate of those studying at the university.

Where does it come from? HESA performance indicators, based on data for 2002–03 and earlier years.

How does it work? HESA calculated the expected outcomes for a cohort of students based on what happened to students in the current year. The figures in the League Table show the percentage of students who were expected to complete their course or transfer to another institution.

What should you look out for? This measure of completion is a projection based upon a snapshot of data. It is therefore vulnerable to statistical fluctuations.

Conclusions

Universities' positions in *The Times* League Table inevitably reflect more than their performance over a single year. Many of those at the top have built their reputations and developed their expertise over many decades or even centuries, while some of those at the bottom are still carving out a niche in the unified higher education system. Perhaps the least surprising conclusions to be drawn from the League Table are that Oxbridge and the University of London remain the dominant forces in British higher education and that, on the measures adopted here, the new universities still have ground to make up on the old. The former polytechnics have different priorities from those of any of their more established counterparts, however, and many can demonstrate strengths in other areas.

Even on the traditional measures adopted here, the table belies the system's reputation for rigidity. For example, a former polytechnic (Northumbria) continues to outperform a number of long-established universities. No doubt others will follow before long. The remarkable rise of universities such as Warwick and York, both founded around 40 years ago, shows what can be achieved in a relatively short space of time.

In an exercise such as this, some distortions are inevitable and the main ones have been identified in the *What should you look out for?* sections, above. The use of a variety of indicators is intended to diminish such effects, but they should be borne in mind when making comparisons.

Last year			Teaching assessment	Research assessment	Entry standards	Student–staff ratio	Library/computing spend	Facilities spend	Good honours	Graduate prospects	Completion	Total
		Max score	24.0	7.0	N/A	N/A	N/A	N/A	100.0	100.0	100.0	1000
1	(1)	Oxford	22.4	6.5	499.1	13.1	1559	376	86.4	77.5	97.9	1000
2	(2)	Cambridge	22.9	6.6	510.6	11.5	1161*	281	90.4	85.4	98.5	983
3	(3)	Imperial College	22.3	6.4	467.8	9.3	1138	473	72.7	78.9	96.4	958
4	(4)	London School of Economics	22.0	6.4	447.1*	13.0*	1091*	155*	74.5*	78.0*	96.8	891
5	(13)	Edinburgh	23.0	5.6	403.6	14.0	901	231	77.2	66.9	92.4	867
6	(6)	University College London	22.1	6.0	386.5	7.6	1131	172	74.4	76.0	93.5	864
7	(9)	St Andrews	23.1	5.7	414.8	10.1	609	207	78.0	68.6	86.0	860
8	(5)	Warwick	22.7	6.0	429.7	16.4	727	221	78.6	68.5	95.3	859
9	(7)	York	23.2	5.8	414.8	14.0	610	181	68.3	66.3	94.7	851
=10	(12)	Bristol	22.0	5.7	423.7	14.5	726	263	81.3	76.8	96.5	841
=10	(8)	Durham	22.2	5.7	426.1	15.6	724	313	72.3	68.6	97.7	841
12	(14)	Nottingham	22.4	5.3	419.9	15.7	715	298	76.7	69.3	97.3	838
13	(11)	Bath	21.6	5.7	375.1	15.2	568	407	74.8	76.7	96.7	828
14	(10)	Loughborough	22.8	5.1	345.6	20.3	644	303	67.5	68.0	93.4	818
15	(19)	SOAS	22.0	5.5	322.9	10.9	1230	147	71.8	73.5	83.5	810
=16	(16)	King's College London	22.2	5.5	368.5	11.4	870	183	70.6	79.9	93.0	806
=16	(17)	Manchester	22.1	5.7	372.0	12.7	838	249	68.6	67.2	92.3	806
=16	(15)	Royal Holloway	21.8	5.7	344.7	12.3	638	376	65.0	59.6	95.4	806

Last year		Max score	Teaching assessment 24.0	Research assessment 7.0	Entry standards N/A	Student–staff ratio N/A	Library/computing spend N/A	Facilities spend N/A	Good honours 100.0	Graduate prospects 100.0	Completion 100.0	Total 1000
19	(18)	Newcastle	22.2	5.2	366.8	16.7	777	282	67.0	75.0	93.0	803
20	(=22)	Glasgow	22.7	5.2	373.9	13.5	682	211	70.2	65.0	85.0	788
21	(26)	Sheffield	22.2	5.5	398.5	14.7	583	190	72.0	66.9	91.8	776
22	(21)	Cardiff	22.0	5.4	361.1	14.7	667	216	69.5	69.7	90.7	766
23	(20)	Birmingham	22.2	5.3	382.7	16.6	622	208	67.4	67.3	92.1	764
24	(29)	Leicester	22.3	5.0	330.2	16.9	545	394	66.8	62.5	91.7	762
25	(28)	Dundee	23.5	5.1	324.1	13.5	478	162	63.3	68.7	76.2	761
=26	(=22)	Aston	21.7	5.0	313.4	15.9	691	308	65.3	71.9	89.3	758
=26	(25)	Southampton	21.8	5.8	359.2	15.1	691	212	68.7	63.6	94.0	758
28	(=34)	Aberdeen	22.4	4.7	339.8	15.5	720	201	67.5	72.3	82.6	754
29	(27)	Essex	22.5	5.6	296.5	15.5	649	294	53.5	59.7	85.3	753
30	(24)	Lancaster	22.1	5.8	345.7	19.7	654	262	65.2	53.2	94.1	743
31	(33)	Queen's, Belfast	21.9	4.9	350.4	17.7	457	301	59.6	74.5	91.0	732
32	(37)	Strathclyde	22.7	4.7	361.0	17.3	535	159	66.9	63.4	84.7	731
33	(36)	East Anglia	21.5	5.4	349.8	15.9	594	352	65.6	54.2	92.2	725
34	(=31)	Exeter	22.0	5.2	359.0	16.5	576	120	68.5	59.5	95.1	724
35	(=31)	Keele	22.0	4.6	306.8	15.6	451	154	55.2	72.3*	95.8	715
36	(46)	Heriot-Watt	22.5	4.7	362.7	14.4	526	232	50.9	56.6	81.5	712

37	(39)	Sussex	21.3	5.5	333.3	17.2	601	263	69.7	61.6	85.6	711
38	(=34)	Leeds	21.5	5.3	364.0	17.8	563	148	67.3	66.6	93.4	709
39	(30)	Reading	21.8	5.3	315.2	15.4	591	175	64.8	59.4	89.2	707
40	(38)	Stirling	22.5	4.8	317.1	18.2	573	214	66.9	45.3	86.2	703
41	(41)	Liverpool	21.9	5.2	332.7	15.2	500	160	61.8	65.6	91.4	701
42	(50)	Swansea	22.1	4.6	275.1	15.5	495	209	57.1	65.8	89.1	699
43	(43)	Brunel	21.9	4.3	286.6	18.6	555	285	65.8	60.5	87.5	697
44	(42)	Queen Mary	21.8	5.0	289.8	12.5	561	165	59.3	69.4	90.6	694
45	(40)	Surrey	20.6	5.4	311.5	15.5	517	272	58.6	74.1	90.2	693
46	(44)	Kent	21.2	4.8	305.8	18.3	575	150	58.8	66.8	87.8	662
=47	(47)	Bradford	21.1	4.4	260.9	16.6	516	274	53.8	81.5	84.5	655
=47	(52)	Hull	22.2	4.3	283.8	19.1	422*	165	56.3	61.9	85.3	655
49	(48)	Northumbria	22.1	2.3	260.6	18.3	636	259	49.2	66.1	84.1	649
50	(49)	Aberystwyth	21.4	4.5	290.6	21.8	536	249	62.6	56.1	90.4	646
51	(45)	UWIC, Cardiff	21.6	2.7	232.9	18.6	408*	445*	48.5	65.1*	83.3	646
52	(=61)	Lampeter	22.5	4.7	231.0	23.8	427	151	60.1	60.8	89.8	644
53	(51)	Oxford Brookes	21.9	2.8	258.8	16.3	378	262*	57.1	68.1	82.6	642
54	(=59)	Goldsmiths College	20.3	5.3	288.3	16.2	509	163	63.6	60.8	85.6	626
55	(54)	Ulster	21.1	3.8	260.4	17.3	558	184	62.5	64.4	83.4	625
56	(55)	City	20.7	4.4	301.4	17.0	415	157	59.3	79.7	86.9	624
57	(53)	Plymouth	21.4	3.2	252.1	13.2	499	221	52.8	56.1	85.3	621
=58	(56)	Bangor	21.4	4.7	272.7*	16.9*	723*	201*	55.9*	43.0*	86.2	603
=58	(58)	Robert Gordon	21.5	1.9	294.6	18.1	496	122	58.0	69.9	81.4	603
60	(=59)	Hertfordshire	22.2	2.5	221.9	17.4	530	154	50.8	61.2	79.7	593
61	(65)	Kingston	22.3	2.7	214.3	21.9	498	144	54.9	62.4	80.7	591
=62	(57)	Nottingham Trent	20.7	2.8	268.4	18.3	641	157	57.3	59.8	89.0	589
=62	(=76)	Sunderland	22.1	2.8	225.9	17.0	367	186	53.2	58.4	72.6	589

Last year		Max score	Teaching assessment 24.0	Research assessment 7.0	Entry standards N/A	Student–staff ratio N/A	Library/computing spend N/A	Facilities spend N/A	Good honours 100.0	Graduate prospects 100.0	Completion 100.0	Total 1000
64	(67)	West of England	21.9	2.8	263.0	19.2	465	190	56.3	54.4	78.7	587
65	(72)	University of the Arts, London	21.1	4.7	248.6	20.8	378	119	52.8	48.7	86.7	583
66	(63)	Brighton	21.1	2.9	251.5	19.3	465	179	54.4	60.6	83.6	579
67	(68)	Sheffield Hallam	21.6	3.0	254.5	21.5	420	222	46.7	59.4	85.8	576
68	(69)	Salford	20.7	4.3	260.1	18.1	387	214	51.5	62.1	79.3	567
69	(=76)	Westminster	21.0	2.8	240.5	15.0	407	163	57.2	55.2	78.1	561
70	(64)	Roehampton	20.5	3.2	226.6	20.5	549*	356*	50.7	61.9	79.4	556
71	(=61)	Glamorgan	21.9	2.4	209.9	20.2	426	194	48.1	58.2	73.7	546
72	(80)	Huddersfield	22.2	2.4	210.9	18.2	384	132	45.3	53.4	77.5	544
73	(66)	Abertay Dundee	20.8	2.0	218.4	17.1	1278	111*	49.6	57.6	66.9	540
74	(=76)	Glasgow Caledonian	21.4	2.5	278.0	20.5	388	72	59.2	54.0	81.6	535
75	(73)	Manchester Metropolitan	21.3	2.9	252.7	21.4	458	128	49.1	54.4	81.6	532
76	(88)	Paisley	21.2	1.6	236.4	16.2	695	194	51.7	48.9	72.2	529
77	(71)	Portsmouth	21.2	3.2	229.0	19.8	433	136	46.1	56.5	83.6	527
78	(87)	Central England	19.9	2.2	235.6	16.3	481	281	58.2	60.1	78.9	522
79	(84)	Middlesex	21.1	2.7	199.0	17.8	489*	174	52.4	53.6	71.7	520
=80	(70)	Lincoln	21.3	1.7	241.4	23.3	493	159*	49.2	54.6	76.8	516
=80	(=85)	Staffordshire	21.2	2.2	223.6	17.9	627	189	45.5	46.9	80.3	516

Rank	(Prev)	University										Total
82	(=90)	Napier	21.2	2.3	222.3	16.6	505	150	61.0	57.4	62.0	515
83	(=85)	Liverpool John Moores	20.6	2.6	236.1	19.0	396	134	51.3	63.5	77.0	508
84	(89)	Wolverhampton	20.8	2.0	200.2	18.6	451	305	52.5	54.0	73.3	507
85	(83)	Bournemouth	19.5	1.9	281.2	15.5	360	80	57.3	62.4	84.7	504
86	(79)	Central Lancashire	20.9	2.2	249.0	22.8	406	217	52.8	56.5*	73.3	503
87	(=90)	Gloucestershire	20.7	3.0	241.9	17.5	385	173	41.1	54.3	77.6	499
88	(82)	Coventry	20.7	2.1	226.6	20.3	503	219	42.9	60.3	81.7	496
89	(81)	De Montfort	20.9	3.1	225.0	18.8	501	126*	39.7	57.7	77.0**	494
90	(75)	Leeds Metropolitan	20.7	2.2	251.6	25.2	453	122	52.7	56.0	83.0	486
=91	(74)	Luton	21.6	1.8	194.3	23.8	593	127	52.3	48.2	72.5	475
=91	(96)	Teesside	21.3	1.9	187.3	21.0*	345	122	40.3	71.1	76.2**	475
93	(92)	UWCN, Newport	20.3	3.0	195.5	21.9	392	239	48.1	58.9	77.0	474
94	(93)	Anglia	20.3	1.5	228.7	20.7	394	140	54.9	63.4	80.4	467
95	(97)	London South Bank	20.0	2.9	179.6	18.7	378	101	51.7	62.1	78.2	445
96	(95)	Derby	19.8	1.5	207.8	20.1	576	140	50.4	60.0	79.2	444
97	(94)	Greenwich	20.5	2.5	198.9	24.5	463	138	47.5	58.9	75.8	440
98	—	Bolton	21.2	1.5	147.8	20.0	498	329	47.5	47.1	63.9	438
99	(98)	East London	19.3	2.5	181.1	20.6	570	337	42.2	53.4	65.1	392
100	(99)	Thames Valley	19.6	0.5	180.2	25.4	388	27	47.3	57.3	72.4	326
		median	21.6	4.4	281.2	17.2	535	194	58.0	61.9	85.1	646
		min	19.3	0.5	147.8	25.4	345	27	39.7	43.0	62.0	326
		max	23.5	6.6	510.6	7.6	1559	473	90.4	85.4	98.5	1000

Note: data marked * have been supplied directly by the university concerned.
Note: data marked ** are from the previous year as the latest figures were unavailable.

For the second year running, London Metropolitan University refused to allow the release of data. Last year, the reason given was that the figures related to the two universities which merged to form it and not to LMU itself. This objection no longer applies. It was ranked 98th in the 2004 edition.

3

The Top Universities by Subject

Knowing where a university stands in the pecking order of higher education is a vital piece of information for any prospective student, but the quality of the course is what matters most. The most modest institution may have a centre of specialist excellence and even famous universities have mediocre departments. This section offers some pointers to the leading universities in a wide range of subjects. Expert assessors have produced official ratings for research and teaching. HESA data is used to provide information about students' entry qualifications, as a guide to the demand for places and the calibre of undergraduates on different courses, and the destinations of graduates. The destination information draws a distinction between different types of employment: graduate employment, where a degree is normally required, and non-graduate employment. The tables give the percentage of 'positive destinations' by adding those undertaking further study to the total in graduate employment.

The tables cover all the areas in which teaching has been assessed in England, although teaching quality grades from the initial rounds of assessment have been removed. Whether judged on four indicators or three, the tables give individual scores for each university included.

Where all four indicators are available, they are weighted as in the main university League Table: 2.5 for teaching; 1.5 for research; 1 each for average UCAS tariff and graduate prospects. Where only three indicators are used, they all have the same weighting. To qualify for inclusion in a table, a university had to have data for at least two of the measures. Differences in the outcomes used by the Scottish and Welsh funding councils have been accommodated by calculating an equivalent on the English scale.

The tables confirm the dominance of the traditional universities in most areas of higher education. This is to be expected in research, where decades of differential funding have left the former polytechnics struggling to compete. Less predictably, the ratings for teaching have usually told the same story. This is partly because the academics who inspect departments take into account facilities such as library stock, while the traditional universities' generally smaller teaching groups also give them an advantage.

Cambridge is again by far the most successful university, with 25 top places including 42 top-10 placings. Oxford has the next highest number of top places with ten, followed by Bristol and Nottingham with three each. The subject rankings demonstrate that there are 'horses for courses' in higher education. Thus the London School of Economics is more than a match for its rivals in social science, while Imperial College confirms its reputation in engineering. In their own fields, table-toppers such as Liverpool John Moores (hospitality) and Southampton (electrical and electronic engineering) are equally well-known.

In all the tables, the following information is provided when it is available.

Teaching Quality

The assessment is recorded either with a score (with a maximum of 24) or by a letter – E for Excellent, S for Satisfactory and, in Scotland, an additional category, HS for Highly Satisfactory. In the foot of each table, the dates of the teaching quality assessments in England are given. When the assessments were very old, and no longer relevant, they have been omitted altogether. This applies to 15 of the tables. The dates of assessments in

Who's in the Top Ten for Their Subjects?

		Appearances in Subject Tables	Top Places	Times in Top Ten	Percentage in Top Ten
1	Cambridge	43	25	42	97.7
2	Oxford	35	10	34	97.1
3	Warwick	26	1	20	76.9
4	Imperial College	16	1	12	75.0
5	York	22	0	15	68.2
6	Bristol	40	3	27	67.5
7	University College London	37	0	24	64.9
8	Bath	26	0	16	61.5
9	London School of Economics	13	2	8	61.5
10	Nottingham	44	3	25	56.8
11	Durham	32	0	18	56.3
12	St Andrews	25	0	14	56.0
13	Loughborough	28	2	15	53.6
14	Harper Adams	2	0	1	50.0
15	St George's Hospital	2	0	1	50.0
16	Edinburgh	43	0	20	46.5
17	Newcastle	38	0	17	44.7
18	Manchester	50	1	22	44.0
19	Sheffield	44	1	18	40.9
20	Queen's, Belfast	41	0	16	39.0

Scotland and Wales were usually different but in the majority of subjects took place before those in England. Recently, a new cycle of assessments has started in Scotland and a summary of these is given on page 245.

Research Quality

This provides a measure of the average quality of research undertaken in the subject area. The first figure gives a quality rating of 5* (top), 5, 4, 3a, 3b, 2 or 1 (bottom). The letter refers to the proportion of staff included in the numerical assessment, with A including virtually everyone and F hardly anyone. These data are from 2001.

Entry Standards

This is the average UCAS tariff score for new students with A levels and/or Scottish Highers under the age of 21, taken from HESA data for 2002–2003. Each student's A level, AS and Higher grades were converted to a numerical score (A level A=120, B=100, etc) and added up to give a total score. HESA then calculated an average score for the university.

Graduate Prospects

This is the percentage of graduates undertaking further study or in graduate job in the annual survey by HESA six months after graduation. Scores are withheld where the number of students is too small to calculate a reliable percentage. A low number on the measure does not necessarily mean that many graduates were unemployed – some could have obtained jobs that are not usually considered graduate jobs. The averages for each subject are given at the bottom of each subject table and in a table in chapter 1 (see pages 14–15).

The subjects listed below are covered in the tables in this chapter:

Accounting and Finance
Aeronautical and manufacturing
engineering
Agriculture and forestry
American studies
Anatomy and physiology
Anthropology
Archaeology
Architecture
Art and design
Biological sciences
Building
Business studies
Celtic studies
Chemical engineering
Chemistry
Civil engineering
Classics and ancient history
Communication and media studies
Computer science
Dentistry
Drama, dance and cinematics
East and South Asian studies
Economics
Education
Electrical and electronic engineering
English
Food science
French
General engineering
Geography
Geology

German
History
History of art, architecture and design
Hospitality, leisure, sport, recreation and
tourism
Iberian languages
Italian
Land and property management
Law
Librarianship and information management
Linguistics
Materials technology
Mathematics
Mechanical engineering
Medicine
Middle Eastern and African studies
Music
Nursing
Other subjects allied to medicine (see page
    134 for included subjects)
Pharmacology and pharmacy
Philosophy
Physics and astronomy
Politics
Psychology
Russian and East European languages
Social policy
Social work
Sociology
Theology and religious studies
Town and country planning and landscape
Veterinary medicine

Accounting and Finance

This is a new table, compiled from data extracted from the Business Studies ranking to reflect the growth of accountancy and finance degrees. Accounting alone was among the 20 most popular subjects at the start of 2005, with almost 28,000 applications. The LSE heads the first ranking, with a clear lead over Warwick, having entered a bigger proportion of academics in the last Research Assessment Exercise and doing slightly better on entrance qualifications and graduate prospects.

Old universities fill 29 of the top 30 places, although almost half of the institutions in the ranking are former polytechnics. Portsmouth is the one new university in the top 30, although Liverpool John Moores has one of the best employment scores. Only Queen's, Belfast, and Loughborough, where 95 per cent of the leavers were in graduate jobs or further training within six months, were more successful in the jobs market.

Teaching scores for business and management (which included accountancy and finance) are now too old to be included in the new ranking. Four universities were considered internationally outstanding for research: the LSE, Warwick, Lancaster and Manchester. Glasgow is just ahead of Edinburgh as the top university in Scotland, while Cardiff is the clear leader in Wales.

Entry scores are quite widely spread among the 67 universities in the table. Ten average more than 400 points, but eight are below 200 points. Employment prospects are better than in many areas of higher education, but in 2003 more than 40 per cent of graduates started their careers in low-level jobs. The unemployment rate of 7 per cent was on the average for all subjects.

- **The Chartered Institute of Public Finance and Accountancy:** www.cipfa.org.uk
- **The Institute of Chartered Accountants:** www.icaew.co.uk/students
- **The Association of Chartered Certified Accountants:** www.accaglobal.com

	Accounting and Finance	Research Quality/5	Entry Standards	Graduate Prospects %	Overall Rating
1	London School of Economics	5*A	443	80	100.0
2	Warwick	5*B	439	75	96.8
3	Loughborough	4C	391	95	94.7
4	Bristol	5B	404	80	94.6
5	Glasgow	5C	427	80	93.6
6	Queen's, Belfast	4B	382	85	93.2
7	Nottingham	5B	429	70	92.9
8	Edinburgh	5A	416	65	92.2
=9	Leeds	5C	410	75	91.2
=9	Durham	5A	336	75	91.2
=11	City	5C	373	80	90.9
=11	Southampton	4B	365	80	90.9
13	Lancaster	5*B	372	65	90.5
14	Aberdeen	4B	409	70	90.1
15	Manchester	5*A	384	50	88.3
16	Sheffield	4B	386	60	86.0

		Research Quality/5	Entry Standards	Graduate Prospects %	Overall Rating
17	Newcastle	5D	401	65	85.3
18	Birmingham	4D	382	70	84.7
19	Essex	5C	290	70	83.8
20	Exeter	5D	393	60	83.4
21	Cardiff	5B	349	50	83.1
22	Dundee	4A	302	60	83.0
23	Heriot-Watt	4D	425	55	82.5
24	Stirling	5B	333	50	82.3
25	Strathclyde	5C		60	81.8
26	Hull	4C	271	70	81.4
27	Salford	3aB	268	70	81.3
28	Kent	3aC	291	70	80.9
29	Portsmouth	4C	221	75	80.4
30	Liverpool	3aA	291	55	78.9
31	East Anglia	3aC	312	55	77.6
32	Ulster	3aD	283	65	77.3
33	London South Bank	3aE		70	76.6
34	Liverpool John Moores	3bE	223	80	76.4
35	Bangor	5B	268	40	76.2
=36	Reading		309	70	76.0
=36	Nottingham Trent	3bD	278	65	76.0
38	Bradford	4C	216		74.1
39	Robert Gordon		325	60	73.9
40	Glasgow Caledonian	4F	302	60	73.6
41	Aberystwyth	3bC	260	55	73.5
=42	Brighton	3aE	269	60	73.4
=42	Northumbria		254	70	73.4
44	Kingston		252	65	71.8
45	Napier	3bE	207	65	71.2
46	Manchester Metropolitan		258	60	70.6
47	Bournemouth		253	60	70.4
48	De Montfort	3aC	226	45	70.3
49	West of England	5E	260	45	69.9
50	Central Lancashire	3bE	234	55	69.6
51	Plymouth	3bE	251	50	69.0
=52	Northampton UC		196	60	67.5
=52	Glamorgan	3bD	224	45	67.5
54	Huddersfield	3bE	187	55	67.3
55	Paisley	5F	218	50	66.7
56	Brunel		292	40	66.4
57	Middlesex	3aE	185	50	66.3
58	Sheffield Hallam	3aF	237	45	65.8
=59	Hertfordshire		199	50	64.7

=59	Staffordshire		228	45	64.7
61	Abertay Dundee		168	50	63.2
62	Leeds Metropolitan		251	35	62.9
63	Teesside		189	45	62.8
64	Central England		209	40	62.3
65	Greenwich	3bF	186	40	61.6
66	Lincoln		191	40	61.4
67	Wolverhampton		202	35	60.5

Employed in graduate job: 25%
Employed in non-graduate job: 33%
Studying, not employed: 8%
Average starting salary: £15,902

Employed in graduate job and studying: 17%
Employed in non-graduate job and studying: 9%
Unemployed: 7%

THE LETTERS THAT APPEAR IN THE RESEARCH QUALITY COLUMN INDICATE THE PROPORTION OF STAFF INCLUDED IN THE ASSESSMENT, A SHOWING THAT ALMOST ALL STAFF WERE INCLUDED AND F SHOWING THAT HARDLY ANY WERE.

Aeronautical and Manufacturing Engineering

The courses under this heading focus mainly on aeronautical or manufacturing engineering, but include some with a mechanical title. To add to the confusion, manufacturing degrees often go under the rubric of production engineering (*see* General Engineering and Mechanical Engineering). In any case, it is a declining area, with 40 institutions in this year's ranking, compared with 52 a year ago.

Cambridge holds onto top place with maximum points for research and the best employment record. Bath stays in second place, with one of the other top research grades, but Nottingham's graduate employment rate and maximum points for teaching quality take it above Imperial College London into third. Cambridge does not separate its A-level scores for the different branches of engineering, so Imperial registered the highest entry standards, with seventh-placed Bristol next.

Aeronautical and Manufacturing Engineering	Teaching Quality/24	Research Quality/5	Entry Standards	Graduate Prospects %	Overall Rating
1 Cambridge	23	5*A		90	100.0
2 Bath		5*A	422	85	98.8
3 Nottingham	24	5B	356	85	95.9
4 Imperial College	22	5*B	507	80	93.9
5 Sheffield		5A	422	80	92.0
6 Loughborough	23	5B	391	75	90.1
7 Bristol	22	4B	474	75	86.4
8 Southampton	21	5*A	430	70	85.4
9 Liverpool	20	5*A	370	80	80.6
10 Heriot-Watt		4A	360		79.9
11 Kingston	24	3aC	265	60	79.1
12 Queen's, Belfast	21	5*B	385	55	77.8

		Teaching Quality/24	Research Quality/5	Entry Standards	Graduate Prospects %	Overall Rating
13	Leeds		5*B	245		76.4
14	Manchester	20	5A	361	55	71.4
15	Surrey		4B	293		69.7
16	Brunel	20	5C	309	65	67.0
17	Aston		5C	277		66.8
18	Glasgow		4A	369	40	66.6
19	Hertfordshire	22	3aD	233	55	64.8
=20	Salford		3aA	244	65	63.5
=20	Strathclyde		4D	367	60	63.5
22	Birmingham	20	4C			63.3
23	Queen Mary		5B	268	45	63.1
24	Portsmouth		4D	232	65	55.9
25	City	19	4D	242	65	54.7
26	Sheffield Hallam	21		216		54.2
27	University of Wales, Newport	S	3aD			53.6
28	West of England		3bD	230	70	53.2
29	Coventry	18	3aC	251	70	52.4
30	Derby		3aD	171	70	51.3
31	Northumbria		3bD	275		48.7
32	Anglia	19	2C			47.4
33	UWIC, Cardiff	S		216		45.8
34	Liverpool John Moores		3aE	239		43.1
35	Paisley		2C	208		41.4
36	Robert Gordon			320	40	40.3
37	London South Bank	17	3aD	218	45	37.8
38	Plymouth		4E		40	36.8
39	Northampton UC			208	50	36.5
40	Buckinghamshire Chilterns UC		2E	205		35.7

Employed in graduate job: 45%
Employed in non-graduate job: 24%
Studying, not employed: 12%
Average starting salary: £18,589

Employed in graduate job and studying: 6%
Employed in non-graduate job and studying: 2%
Unemployed: 11%
Teaching quality assessed 1996–98

THE LETTERS THAT APPEAR IN THE RESEARCH QUALITY COLUMN INDICATE THE PROPORTION OF STAFF INCLUDED IN THE ASSESSMENT, A SHOWING THAT ALMOST ALL STAFF WERE INCLUDED AND F SHOWING THAT HARDLY ANY WERE.

Like a number of universities in the ranking, Bath had its teaching assessed under a different category, so its other scores are averaged to produce an overall result. Liverpool, Southampton and Queen's, Belfast were the other top scorers for research, but none managed more than 22 points out of 24 for teaching.

Apart from Nottingham, only Kingston, the sole new university close to the top ten, was awarded maximum points for teaching. Loughborough and Cambridge were next best in an assessment that produced an unusually wide spread of points.

Failure rates in first-year exams are high – between 32 and 45 per cent when departments in England were assessed – but most students pass resits. Many graduates go on to further study or training to meet professional requirements and, particularly for aeronautical engineering graduates, employment prospects are bright. Three Cs at A level (and another at AS level) will secure a place on almost any course outside the top ten. The decline in the number of courses is not reflected in the latest application figures, which show a second successive rise in demand for aeronautical engineering and a small drop in the smaller production and manufacturing area.

- **The Engineering Learning Information Portal:** www.elip.info

Agriculture and Forestry

Nottingham tops the agriculture table with a teaching score matched only by fourth-placed Harper Adams University College and a research grade matched only by Reading in third place. Harper Adams, a specialist agricultural college in Shropshire, also has a high employment score, but has the lowest research grade in the table. Leeds and Bangor also reached grade 5 for research, but did not enter a full complement of academics for assessment.

Queen's, Belfast continues to boast the best employment record, with nine out of ten leavers finding graduate-level work within six months of graduating. Only sixth-placed Bristol comes near to challenging on this measure. In the absence of entry data for Nottingham, Bristol also has by far the highest average A levels.

Agriculture and Forestry	Teaching Quality/24	Research Quality/5	Entry Standards	Graduate Prospects %	Overall Rating
1 Nottingham	23	5A			100.0
2 Newcastle	22	4B	283	70	84.2
3 Reading	21	5A	266	70	81.7
4 Harper Adams UC	23	3bE	274	70	79.1
5 Queen's, Belfast	21	4C	264	90	78.3
6 Bristol			384	85	77.5
7 Leeds	20	5B			72.0
8 Plymouth	22	3aE	238	65	70.9
9 Imperial College	22			45	65.0
10 Aberystwyth		3aC	260	45	63.4
11 Aberdeen		3aC	253	35	59.5
12 Greenwich	20	3aD		50	59.2
13 Bangor	S	5C	213	35	58.4
14 Buckinghamshire Chilterns UC	20			55	53.7
15 Central Lancashire	18		214	35	38.2

Employed in graduate job: 40%
Employed in non-graduate job: 38%
Studying, not employed: 9%
Average starting salary: £14,302

Employed in graduate job and studying: 6%
Employed in non-graduate job and studying: 2%
Unemployed: 5%
Teaching quality assessed 1996–98

THE LETTERS THAT APPEAR IN THE RESEARCH QUALITY COLUMN INDICATE THE PROPORTION OF STAFF INCLUDED IN THE ASSESSMENT, A SHOWING THAT ALMOST ALL STAFF WERE INCLUDED AND F SHOWING THAT HARDLY ANY WERE.

Agriculture and Forestry CONT.

Plymouth is the only former polytechnic in the top ten, boasting one of the best teaching assessments. However, since the closure of its rural campus, courses in the subject are confined to two partner colleges. This is one of the few subject areas in which no university achieved full marks for teaching or research. Scores in both sets of assessments are tightly bunched, covering only three grades in the case of research.

A quarter of those enrolling for degrees in agriculture and more than a third in forestry do so without A levels, often coming with relevant work experience. Applications for degree places in agriculture were up by 11 per cent at the start of 2005 and the demand for foundation degrees had almost doubled. As befits a firmly vocational area, employment rates are high, although more than a quarter of graduates start in lower-level jobs.

- **The Sector Skills Council for the Environmental and Land-Based Sector (LANTRA):** www.lantra.co.uk
- **The Institute of Chartered Foresters:** www.charteredforesters.org

American Studies

A consistent performance again gives Warwick top place even though it outscores its nearest rivals only on entry scores, which are still lower than tenth-placed Birmingham's. Nottingham is only a whisker behind in second place, with the only 5* research grade, a better graduate employment record and virtually identical A levels. Warwick is the only English university to have had its teaching quality assessed under the original system.

Although the top ten places are filled by traditional universities, Central Lancashire shares with East Anglia and Keele the distinction of a maximum 24 points for teaching in the main assessment of the subject. Keele was one of six universities to reach grade 5 in the last research assessments, while Reading graduates have by far the best employment record.

Students' entry qualifications show wide variation, from more than 400 points at Birmingham, Nottingham and Warwick to less than 200 at Derby and Northampton University College. Nine out of ten students taking American Studies have A levels or equivalent qualifications.

There is an impressive level of firsts and 2:1s, but the subject has one of the highest proportion of graduates in low-level jobs or still unemployed six months after graduation. Only Reading, Warwick, Nottingham, Sussex, Leicester and Lancaster saw more than half of leavers go straight into graduate-level jobs or further courses, while the proportion was down to a quarter at two of the institutions in the table.

The number of places in American studies has been falling gradually – the 718 new recruits through UCAS in 2004 represented a drop of almost 9 per cent. Applications were down by 13 per cent that year, but there was a healthy increase of almost 8 per cent at the start of 2005, bringing the total close to 4,000.

- **The British Association for American Studies:** www.baas.ac.uk

American Studies

		Teaching Quality/24	Research Quality/5	Entry Standards	Graduate Prospects %	Overall Rating
1	Warwick	E	5A	410	60	100.0
2	Nottingham	22	5*B	408	65	99.6
3	Sussex	23	5B	321	65	97.0
4	Sheffield		5B	398	45	95.3
5	Manchester		5B	367	50	94.9
6	Keele	24	5B	312	35	94.8
7	Lancaster		4A	337	55	92.6
8	Liverpool		5A	285	45	91.9
9	East Anglia	24	4C	384	35	91.6
10	Birmingham	22	4B	415	50	91.4
11	Central Lancashire	24	3bA			90.9
12	Kent	21	4B	303		83.0
13	Ulster	22	4C	221		80.1
14	Leicester	23		331	60	79.5
15	Wolverhampton	21	4C			78.2
16	Aberystwyth	S	4B	253	50	77.0
17	Hull	23		301	50	76.6
18	Brunel	21	3aB	235	35	75.9
19	Swansea	S	3aA	261	50	75.8
20	Derby	21	3aB	195	35	74.5
21	Reading	21		302	75	74.2
22	Canterbury Christ Church UC	21		262	40	66.5
23	Winchester UC	18	3aD	237	35	60.7
24	Dundee			259	25	51.6
25	Northampton UC	18		199	20	50.4

Employed in graduate job: 25%
Employed in non-graduate job: 43%
Studying, not employed: 16%
Average starting salary: £14,042

Employed in graduate job and studying: 3%
Employed in non-graduate job and studying: 6%
Unemployed: 7%
Teaching quality assessed 1996–98

THE LETTERS THAT APPEAR IN THE RESEARCH QUALITY COLUMN INDICATE THE PROPORTION OF STAFF INCLUDED IN THE ASSESSMENT, A SHOWING THAT ALMOST ALL STAFF WERE INCLUDED AND F SHOWING THAT HARDLY ANY WERE.

Anatomy and Physiology

Bristol retains top position in the table with a 5* research grade in anatomy and one of the four maximum scores for teaching in England. Loughborough, the leader two years ago, is down to sixth place with one of the lowest employment scores in the table, while Newcastle, Cambridge and Liverpool all move up.

Surprisingly, the seven universities with full employment scores all appear in the bottom half of the table. None was assessed under this category for teaching or research. King's College London was the other research star in anatomy, while Manchester and Liverpool reached the top grade in physiology.

Anatomy and Physiology CONT.

In a high-scoring teaching quality assessment completed in 2000, Newcastle and Sheffield joined Bristol and Loughborough on maximum points. The absence of entries in the relevant categories of the Research Assessment Exercise keeps Sheffield out of the top ten. Oxford is restricted to tenth because it has one of the lowest teaching scores, despite having by far the highest entry grades and a good employment record.

Fifth-placed Cardiff, St Andrews, Dundee and Glasgow all achieved Excellent ratings for teaching in the Welsh and Scottish systems. A dozen new universities and one university college offer the subjects, but only Oxford Brookes and Robert Gordon appear in the top 20. The spread of entrance qualifications is wide, with students at Nottingham averaging more than 400 points while those at Westminster average less than 200.

In spite of the generally high marks for teaching, assessors in England found wide variations in some areas. The proportion of students awarded 2:1s, for example, ranged from 30 per cent in one unnamed university to 90 per cent in another. Some equipment was found to be outdated, but students acquired good knowledge of the subjects and skills that are in demand from employers.

There were more than 32,000 applications for anatomy, physiology or pathology by the start of 2005, an increase of more than 10 per cent. In 2004, just over 3,600 were successful. Employment prospects are bright, with only 4 per cent out of a job six months after graduation in the latest figures.

- **The Anatomical Society of Great Britain and Ireland:** www.anatsoc.org.uk
- **The Physiological Society:** www.physoc.org

	Anatomy and Physiology	Teaching Quality/24	Research Quality/5 Anaotomy	Research Quality/5 Physiology	Entry Standards	Graduate Prospects %	Overall Rating
1	Bristol	24	5*A	4A	423	95	100.0
2	Newcastle	24		5A	338	70	91.4
3	Cambridge	23	5A	4B			86.1
4	Liverpool	23	4A	5*A	361	75	85.8
5	Cardiff	E	5A		335	60	85.5
6	Loughborough	24		4A	343	50	84.9
7	Nottingham	22		5A	413	85	82.6
8	Aberdeen			5B	349		82.3
9	Manchester	23		5*B	349	55	81.7
10	Oxford	21	5B	5A	493	90	79.8
11	King's College London	22	5*B		350	75	77.6
12	University College London	22	5A	4A	361	65	74.4
13	Sheffield	24			373	50	72.5
14	Leeds	22		5B	332	65	72.0
15	Salford	22		3aA	311	90	71.6
16	Oxford Brookes	23			362	90	71.5
17	Robert Gordon				453	95	71.2
18	St Andrews	E				75	71.1
19	Dundee	E	5*B		345	70	70.9

20	Edinburgh		4A		55	69.3
21	Glasgow	E		353	55	68.4
22	Queen Margaret College			434	90	67.6
23	East Anglia			386	100	66.0
24	Ulster			376	100	65.0
25	Hertfordshire		2D	346	95	64.7
26	West of England			371	100	64.5
27	Glasgow Caledonian			394	90	63.5
28	Bradford			361	100	63.4
29	Southampton			368	90	60.8
30	Keele			363	90	60.3
31	Leeds Metropolitan			354	90	59.3
32	Coventry			317	100	58.9
33	Sussex	22		338	65	57.0
34	East London			289	100	56.0
35	Queen's, Belfast	22		302	70	55.8
36	Teesside			268	100	53.8
37	Northampton UC	22			40	47.9
38	London South Bank	20	3aD		50	37.5
39	Abertay Dundee			210	65	36.2
40	Westminster	21		172		34.2

Employed in graduate job: 56%
Employed in non-graduate job: 15%
Studying, not employed: 19%
Average starting salary: £17,060

Employed in graduate job and studying: 5%
Employed in non-graduate job and studying: 1%
Unemployed: 4%
Teaching quality assessed 1998–2000

THE LETTERS THAT APPEAR IN THE RESEARCH QUALITY COLUMN INDICATE THE PROPORTION OF STAFF INCLUDED IN THE ASSESSMENT, A SHOWING THAT ALMOST ALL STAFF WERE INCLUDED AND F SHOWING THAT HARDLY ANY WERE.

Anthropology

Anthropology offers the best chance of a good degree in the social sciences, but the unemployment rate is also high, at 11 per cent. Almost one graduate in five goes on to take a higher degree or some form of postgraduate training, but more than a third take non-graduate jobs. Teaching grades were dropped from the table because the assessments took place up to a decade ago.

The top three are unchanged since last year, with Cambridge extending its lead over Oxford thanks to the highest entry scores in the table and a tie with St Andrews and Sussex for the best graduate employment record. The third-placed London School of Economics and University College London, in sixth, were the only institutions rated internationally outstanding for research, although all but four of those entering the last assessment exercise reached grade 5.

Anthropology was not assessed separately for teaching quality in Scotland or Wales. Oxford Brookes is the highest-placed of five new universities and one university college among the 22 institutions offering the subject. Outside Oxbridge, entry qualifications are more tightly bunched than for most subjects – only two institutions averaged less than

Anthropology CONT.

250 points and only one – the LSE – more than 400. Although still a minority taste, anthropology's popularity has been growing: there were almost 3,000 applications when the official deadline passed for full-time places on courses beginning in 2005, an increase of more than 15 per cent.

- **The Royal Anthropological Institute:** www.therai.org.uk

Anthropology		Research Quality/5	Entry Standards	Graduate Prospects %	Overall Rating
1	Cambridge	5A	484	75	100.0
2	Oxford	5A	467	65	95.8
3	London School of Economics	5*A	408	55	94.4
4	St Andrews	5A	377	75	93.2
5	Sussex	5A	322	75	89.6
6	University College London	5*B	369	60	89.3
7	Manchester	5B	364	65	85.5
8	Goldsmiths College	5A	293	55	81.5
9	Edinburgh	5B	396	45	81.3
10	Durham	5B	344	50	79.5
11	Queen's, Belfast	5B	328	50	78.5
12	SOAS	5B	320		78.4
13	Kent	5B	262	50	74.3
14	Oxford Brookes	4A	258	55	73.6
15	East London	4B		50	70.5
=16	Roehampton	5B	222		69.0
=16	Lampeter	3aA		55	69.0
18	Hull	3aB	283		59.8
19	Nottingham Trent		282	40	42.8
20	Southampton		268	40	41.9
21	West of England		287	30	39.9
22	Bath Spa UC		239	20	33.7

Employed in graduate job: 31%
Employed in non-graduate job: 35%
Studying, not employed: 16%
Average starting salary: £15,090

Employed in graduate job and studying: 4%
Employed in non-graduate job and studying: 3%
Unemployed: 11%

THE LETTERS THAT APPEAR IN THE RESEARCH QUALITY COLUMN INDICATE THE PROPORTION OF STAFF INCLUDED IN THE ASSESSMENT, A SHOWING THAT ALMOST ALL STAFF WERE INCLUDED AND F SHOWING THAT HARDLY ANY WERE.

Archaeology

Cambridge again tops the ranking for archaeology, with the highest entrance qualifications, the best graduate employment score and one of the three 5* research grades. Two of the teaching stars – Leicester and Exeter – move up from sixth and tenth respectively to fill the next places. Southampton, in fourth, and seventh-placed York are the other top-rated teaching universities, together with Cardiff and Lampeter in Wales.

Archaeology

		Teaching Quality/24	Research Quality/5	Entry Standards	Graduate Prospects %	Overall Rating
1	Cambridge	23	5*A	484	75	100.0
2	Leicester	24	5A	300	70	96.7
3	Exeter	24	5A	318	55	94.9
4	Southampton	24	5A	300	55	94.5
5	Durham	23	5A	385	70	94.0
6	Oxford	22	5*A	464		92.9
7	York	24	3aA	399	60	92.7
8	Cardiff	E	5A	326	40	92.3
9	Queen's, Belfast	23	5A	295	70	91.6
10	University College London	23	5A	355	55	90.9
=11	Reading	23	5*A	287	45	90.2
=11	Manchester	23	5B	306	70	90.2
=11	Lampeter	E	4A	231	60	90.2
14	Glasgow		4A	328		86.6
15	Edinburgh		3aA	419	55	85.7
16	Sheffield	22	5A	338	55	85.5
17	Liverpool	22	5A	305	50	83.9
18	Bristol	22	4B	364	60	83.0
19	Birmingham	22	4B	374		82.1
20	Bradford	22	5B	252	55	81.5
21	Nottingham	21	4A	344	65	79.6
22	Newcastle	21	3aB	305	70	75.6
23	Winchester UC		3aA	220	30	70.1
24	Bournemouth	22	3aC	184	25	68.7
25	Kent	22		285		65.7
26	Lincoln			241	65	62.8
27	Glamorgan			220	65	61.8

Employed in graduate job: 27%
Employed in non-graduate job: 30%
Studying, not employed: 24%
Average starting salary: £13,308

Employed in graduate job and studying: 2%
Employed in non-graduate job and studying: 5%
Unemployed: 11%
Teaching quality assessed 1996–98

THE LETTERS THAT APPEAR IN THE RESEARCH QUALITY COLUMN INDICATE THE PROPORTION OF STAFF INCLUDED IN THE ASSESSMENT, A SHOWING THAT ALMOST ALL STAFF WERE INCLUDED AND F SHOWING THAT HARDLY ANY WERE.

Reading and Oxford were the other top-rated research universities in the assessments, Oxford also running Cambridge close on A-level scores. Glasgow is the leading Scottish institution in a ranking which includes only three new universities. Outside Oxbridge, only Edinburgh averages more than 400 points on entry. At Lampeter, Bournemouth, Lincoln, Glamorgan and Winchester University College the average was below 250 points. The number of applications was up by more than 8 per cent, to 2,800, at the start of 2005. Assessors generally found high-quality teaching and a broad curriculum. Unemployment six months after graduation was relatively high, at 11 per cent. Less than a third of leavers were in graduate-level work within six month at Bournemouth or Winchester.

- **The Council for British Archaeology:** www.britarch.ac.uk

Architecture

Cambridge and Nottingham have swapped top places for architecture in each of the last three years, but both have been overtaken by Cardiff and Sheffield this time. Cardiff has the better employment record and entered a bigger proportion of academics in the last research

	Architecture	Research Quality/5	Entry Standards	Graduate Prospects %	Overall Rating
1	Cardiff	5A	414	95	100.0
2	Sheffield	5B	451	90	98.4
3	Cambridge	4A	504	85	97.9
4	Nottingham	4A	423	90	96.9
5	Bath	5B	393	90	96.5
6	University College London	4C	398	95	95.3
7	Newcastle	4C	376	95	94.6
8	Edinburgh	3aB	456	85	93.9
9	Manchester	4C	335	95	93.2
10	Liverpool	4B	314	90	92.3
11	Dundee	4B	306	85	90.4
12	De Montfort	4A	223	90	90.2
13	Northumbria	3bD	236	100	88.1
=14	Strathclyde	4C	382	75	88.0
=14	Oxford Brookes	4D	281	90	88.0
16	Westminster	4D	277	90	87.8
17	Robert Gordon	3bD	325	90	87.7
18	Queen's, Belfast	2B	341	85	87.0
19	Brighton	5B	290	70	86.4
20	Plymouth		266	90	83.3
=21	Leeds Metropolitan	3bD	238	85	83.1
=21	East London	4D	234		83.1
=23	Glamorgan	3bC		80	82.9
=23	Lincoln	3aD	204	85	82.9
25	Portsmouth	3aD	253	80	82.8
26	Manchester Metropolitan		341	80	82.4
27	Wolverhampton	3aB		70	81.6
28	Liverpool John Moores	3bC	244	75	81.0
29	Central England	2F	238	85	80.9
30	Sheffield Hallam	3aE	253		80.6
31	Kingston		241	75	77.4
32	Greenwich	3bE	245	70	77.3

Employed in graduate job: **57%**
Employed in non-graduate job: **8%**
Studying, not employed: **14%**
Average starting salary: **£15,075**

Employed in graduate job and studying: **16%**
Employed in non-graduate job and studying: **1%**
Unemployed: **4%**

THE LETTERS THAT APPEAR IN THE RESEARCH QUALITY COLUMN INDICATE THE PROPORTION OF STAFF INCLUDED IN THE ASSESSMENT, A SHOWING THAT ALMOST ALL STAFF WERE INCLUDED AND F SHOWING THAT HARDLY ANY WERE.

assessment exercise, although Sheffield's entrants were more highly-qualified. Third-placed Cambridge had the highest entry standards.

Only one university – Northumbria – saw all its leavers go straight into graduate-level jobs or postgraduate training, but De Montfort's superior research grade made it the top new university. No university was considered internationally outstanding for research, but Sheffield, Bath, Cardiff and Brighton all reached grade 5. Edinburgh is the top department in Scotland.

Architecture was among the first subjects to be assessed for teaching quality, so the grades have been dropped. A third of all undergraduates enter with qualifications other than A level, Highers or equivalents. There is a wide spread of entrance scores, from more than 500 points at Cambridge to less than 250 at East London, Lincoln, Liverpool John Moores, Central England, Kingston and Greenwich.

Unemployment on graduation is low: only five subjects have more 'positive destinations'. Nine out of ten graduates go on to complete their professional training, either with further study or within a job. The training is long, but the subject is regaining its popularity: there was a 17 per cent rise in applications in 2004 and a similar increase at the start of 2005.

- **The Royal Institute of British Architects:** www.architecture.com

Art and Design

Most courses in art and design are at new universities – often in former art colleges – but it is a clutch of old universities that head the ranking. Oxford remains in first position, with Brunel a new entrant in second. Oxford's traditional strength lies in A-level scores, but this year it is the only maximum score for teaching quality that secures top place. The assessors commented warmly on Oxford's studio-based course. Sixty undergraduates take the Fine Art degree at the Ruskin School of Drawing, almost 90 per cent of whom generally achieve a first or upper second. At third-placed University College London, students attend the equally famous Slade School of Fine Art, established over 100 years ago.

Art and design was one of the few areas to record poorer research grades in 2001 than in previous assessments – only Salford was rated internationally outstanding. UCL was one of six departments awarded grade 5. Fourth-placed Dundee was another top-scorer for teaching quality, rated Excellent under the separate Scottish system. UWIC, Cardiff has the third perfect teaching score, but Aberystwyth's higher entry grades and superior employment record make it the top university in Wales.

Brighton is the best-placed new university, in the top ten this year. Low entry grades and research scores count against many of the new universities and colleges, although most artists would argue that these are of less significance than in other subjects.

Perhaps inevitably, art and design has one of the highest unemployment rates, at 13 per cent, of all the subjects in these tables. Many graduates are prepared to persevere with part-time or irregular work while pursuing their vocation. The best employment record in this year's table is at Sunderland, where two thirds of the leavers went straight into graduate jobs or further training. The national prospects certainly do not seem to have deterred students from applying: the demand for design degree places had risen by 30 per cent at the start of 2005, while the smaller fine art area had seen an even bigger increase.

- **The British Institute of Professional Photography:** www.bipp.com
- **Skillfast UK:** www.skillfast-uk.org

Art and Design

		Teaching Quality/24	Research Quality/5	Entry Standards	Graduate Prospects %	Overall Rating
1	Oxford	24	4A			100.0
2	Brunel		4A	340	57	98.3
3	University College London	23	5B		57	97.2
4	Dundee	E	4B	332	48	96.4
5	Goldsmiths College	22	5B	305	61	95.4
6	Leeds	23	3aA	366	45	95.1
7	Loughborough	23	4C	292	58	94.8
8	City	23	5D			93.6
9	Brighton	22	5B	268	54	93.5
10	Aberystwyth		3aA	304	51	93.4
11	Lancaster	23	3aC	357	34	92.1
12	Salford	21	5*A	206	55	91.9
13	Oxford Brookes	23	3bB	244	51	91.7
14	UWIC, Cardiff	E	4D	233	43	91.2
=15	Sheffield Hallam	22	5C	265	42	90.5
=15	Sunderland	21	4C	240	66	90.5
17	University of the Arts, London	22	5D	254	49	90.3
18	Southampton	22	4C	268	41	89.6
=19	Kingston	21	4D	252	64	89.3
=19	Northumbria	22	4D	241	51	89.3
=19	Coventry	22	3aD	275	49	89.3
22	Nottingham Trent	22	3aE	295	51	89.1
23	Chichester UC	22	2A		47	88.5
24	Bournemouth	20	5D	300	61	88.5
25	Northampton UC	23	2E	213	48	88.2
=26	Staffordshire	22	4D	211	47	88.0
=26	Napier		3aD	255	52	88.0
=28	Newcastle	20	4B	324	41	87.7
=28	Bath Spa UC	22	3aD	233	45	87.7
=30	Central England	22	4E	273	42	87.6
=30	Robert Gordon	HS	3aD		37	87.6
=30	Manchester Metropolitan	22	4E	253	45	87.6
=33	Reading	19	5A	296	44	87.0
=33	Plymouth	21	3aC	243	47	87.0
=35	Hertfordshire	22	3aD	195	46	86.9
=35	De Montfort	21	4C	244	41	86.9
=37	Surrey Institute of Art and Design, UC	21	3aD	276	45	86.6
=37	Leeds Metropolitan	21	3aD	257	48	86.6
39	Central Lancashire	22	3bE	215	48	86.5
40	Middlesex	21	3aC	209	48	86.3
=41	Gloucestershire	21	3aC	268	37	86.1
=41	Luton	22		211	52	86.1
43	West of England	22	4D	193	36	86.0
=44	Anglia	21	3bA	218	42	85.8

=44	Westminster	21	4D	201	48	85.8
46	University of Wales, Newport	S	5E	223	47	85.6
47	Teesside	22		174	54	85.5
48	East London	21	4D	185	48	85.4
49	Huddersfield	21	3bF	247	49	84.6
50	Glamorgan			245	53	84.1
51	Buckinghamshire Chilterns UC	20	3aD	207	51	83.7
52	Ulster	19	5D	259	49	83.6
53	Lincoln	20	3aD	243	40	82.9
=54	Portsmouth	20	3aD	203	40	82.0
=54	Wolverhampton	21	3aF	200	38	82.0
=56	Liverpool Hope UC	20	2D		46	81.9
=56	Derby	20	3bD	198	44	81.9
58	Liverpool John Moores	19	3aC	212	46	81.8
59	Bolton	21	2E	191	33	81.2
60	Glasgow Caledonian			286	31	80.3
61	Roehampton	19		234	51	80.1
62	Canterbury Christ Church UC	19		283	42	79.9

Employed in graduate job: 36%
Employed in non-graduate job: 38%
Studying, not employed: 8%
Average starting salary: £13,760

Employed in graduate job and studying: 2%
Employed in non-graduate job and studying: 4%
Unemployed: 13%
Teaching quality assessed 1998–2000

THE LETTERS THAT APPEAR IN THE RESEARCH QUALITY COLUMN INDICATE THE PROPORTION OF STAFF INCLUDED IN THE ASSESSMENT, A SHOWING THAT ALMOST ALL STAFF WERE INCLUDED AND F SHOWING THAT HARDLY ANY WERE.

Biological Sciences

This year's guide includes a single table for biological sciences for the first time. Readers found the separate tables for molecular and organismal biosciences confusing, especially since some assessments were overlapping. Cambridge heads the combined ranking, as it did both tables last year. The highest entry qualifications and maximum points for both teaching and research give the university a clear lead over Oxford, with Bristol close behind in third place.

Bristol is one of three other English universities with top scores for both teaching and research. Sheffield and Newcastle complete the group, while Dundee managed the same feat under the separate Scottish system but still loses out to Edinburgh as the top university north of the border. More than a dozen of the 83 institutions in the table were awarded full marks for teaching in England, with another seven in Scotland and Wales also rated as Excellent. Research assessments improved out of all recognition in 2001, with ten universities rated internationally outstanding, compared with only three in the previous exercise.

UWIC registers the best employment score, with 96 per cent of leavers going straight into graduate jobs or further training. Its teaching quality was also rated as Excellent, but the decision not to enter the last Research Assessment Exercise cost the institute a place in the top 30. Nottingham Trent is the only new university to achieve that, while Cardiff is by some way the top university in Wales.

Biological Sciences CONT.

Although entrants to both Cambridge and Oxford average more than 500 points, entry standards elsewhere are more tightly bunched than in many other subjects. Only six other universities average more than 400 points and few institutions dip far below 200 points. There is a similar pattern in the employment column, with some universities towards the bottom of the table outscoring others near the top. Abertay, in 56th place, outperformed all but UWIC and Surrey on this measure. Nationally, graduate prospects are about average for all subjects.

Biology has not suffered the recruitment problems experienced by other sciences. Applications were up by 3.5 per cent at the start of 2005 and still well ahead of chemistry and physics. Two thirds of all entrants arrive with A levels or their equivalent and more than half of the undergraduates are awarded firsts or 2:1s. A third go on to take postgraduate courses.

- **The Biochemical Society:** www.biology4all.com
- **The Institute of Biology:** www.iob.org

Biological Sciences		Teaching Quality/24	Research Quality/5	Entry Standards	Graduate Prospects %	Overall Rating
1	Cambridge	24	5*A	542		100.0
2	Oxford	24	5A	503	76	97.1
3	Bristol	24	5*A	428	72	96.4
4	Newcastle	24	5*B	339	74	93.7
5	Bath	24	5B	386	76	93.6
=6	Sheffield	24	5*A	383	60	93.5
=6	York	24	5B	425	70	93.5
8	Durham	24	5B	429	66	92.9
9	University College London	24	5B	377	70	92.5
10	Edinburgh	E	5A	376	70	91.9
11	Dundee	E	5*B	300	74	91.3
12	Kent	24	4A	277	76	90.8
13	St Andrews	E	5B	387	66	90.5
14	Birmingham	24	5B	353	60	90.4
15	Cardiff	E	5A	353	62	90.1
16	Nottingham	23	5A	408	62	89.4
17	Manchester	23	5*B	352	66	89.3
=18	Warwick	23	5B	401	66	88.9
=18	Imperial College	22	5*B	451	72	88.9
20	Royal Holloway	24	5C	328	54	87.2
21	Glasgow	E	5B	349	50	87.1
22	Leeds	23	5B	331	62	86.8
23	Leicester	22	5*B	323	70	85.9
24	Essex	23	4B	273	70	85.6
25	Aberdeen	E	5C	288	58	85.5
26	Southampton	23	5B	344	50	85.2
=27	Salford	24	3aA	217	56	84.8

=27	Surrey	21	5*A	255	86	84.8
29	Swansea	E	3aA	277	52	83.9
=30	Nottingham Trent	24	5D	209	60	83.8
=30	Aberystwyth	E	3aA	273	52	83.8
32	Bangor	E	4A	290	40	83.7
33	Sunderland	24	3aB	184	56	83.5
=34	East Anglia	22	5B	341	60	83.3
=34	Kingston	24	3aC	166	64	83.3
=34	UWIC, Cardiff	E		194	96	83.3
=37	Ulster	22	5*A	192		83.0
=37	Exeter	22	4B	328	68	83.0
39	Sussex	22	5B	305	62	82.9
40	Heriot-Watt	HS	4A	283	58	82.3
41	Aston	23	3aC	299	58	81.7
42	Queen's, Belfast	21	4B	322	80	81.4
43	Oxford Brookes	23	3aA	213	56	81.3
44	Portsmouth	22	5A	198	54	80.3
45	Hull	23	4D	221	60	79.9
=46	King's College London	22	3aC	294	68	79.8
=46	Wolverhampton	23	3aC	189	60	79.8
=48	West of England	24		241	56	79.4
=48	Brighton	22	5C	217	62	79.4
50	Brunel	22	4C	256	60	78.8
51	Reading	21	4B	299	66	78.7
52	Keele	22	4C	291	54	78.6
=53	Lancaster	21	4B	314	60	78.0
=53	Queen Mary	22	4B	244	48	78.0
55	Napier	HS	4D	215	62	77.8
56	Abertay Dundee	HS		188	82	76.8
57	Liverpool John Moores	23		212	58	75.8
=58	Paisley	HS	3bC		46	74.9
=58	Westminster	21	3bC	163	82	74.9
60	Strathclyde	HS		305	54	74.8
=61	Central Lancashire	22	3bB	200	50	74.7
=61	Hertfordshire	21	3aC	179	72	74.7
63	Glasgow Caledonian	HS		292	54	74.5
64	Roehampton	23		199	46	73.6
65	Manchester Metropolitan	22	2D	248	52	73.5
66	Plymouth	22	3aE	288	44	73.4
67	Liverpool	19	5B	312	64	73.2
68	Derby	22		182	64	72.7
69	Luton	22	2D			72.6
70	Staffordshire	22		229	48	71.1
71	Sheffield Hallam	22		193		70.5
72	Liverpool Hope UC	21	3bC			70.1
73	Northumbria	21	2E	207	60	69.9
74	Greenwich	20	3aA	190	46	69.1
75	De Montfort	21		198	60	69.0

Biological Sciences CONT.

		Teaching Quality/24	Research Quality/5	Entry Standards	Graduate Prospects %	Overall Rating
76	Anglia	21		234	48	67.8
77	Bath Spa UC	21	3bE			67.3
=78	Leeds Metropolitan			234	48	65.8
=78	Glamorgan			202	52	65.8
80	Worcester UC	20	2D			62.4
81	Coventry	19	2C	180	46	61.6
82	London South Bank	20			38	60.3
83	East London	19	2D			57.3

Employed in graduate job: 28%
Employed in non-graduate job: 29%
Studying, not employed: 28%
Average starting salary: £14,279

Employed in graduate job and studying: 4%
Employed in non-graduate job and studying: 3%
Unemployed: 8%
Teaching quality assessed 1998–2000

THE LETTERS THAT APPEAR IN THE RESEARCH QUALITY COLUMN INDICATE THE PROPORTION OF STAFF INCLUDED IN THE ASSESSMENT, A SHOWING THAT ALMOST ALL STAFF WERE INCLUDED AND F SHOWING THAT HARDLY ANY WERE.

Building

Building is one of the most open of the tables because there is less correlation than normal between the top performers in teaching and research. Kingston was the only university to be awarded maximum points for teaching, but low entry grades and the absence of a research score in this category cost it a place in the top five. With Nottingham, last year's leader, dropping out of the ranking, Loughborough takes over at the top.

Loughborough is one of two universities rated internationally outstanding for research and in the top three for both employment and entrance qualifications. Second-placed Manchester has the most highly-qualified students, while Oxford Brookes, in fourth, and tenth-placed Salford both saw all their leavers go straight into graduate jobs or postgraduate training. Salford is the other research star, but a poor teaching score costs the university a higher place. Heriot-Watt is top in Scotland, while Glamorgan is the only Welsh representative.

Applications for building are on the rise, with a 16 per cent increase in 2004 and another 30 per cent at the start of 2005, perhaps because job prospects have been good in recent years. Three quarters of leavers were in graduate jobs after six months, and only one in 20 was unemployed.

Universities admit 44 per cent of students with qualifications other than A level. Those who do take the A-level route tend not to require the highest grades – only Loughborough, Manchester and Heriot-Watt registered an average of more than 300 points. Even fourth-placed Oxford Brookes averaged less than 200 points, as did several other new universities.

- **The Chartered Institute of Building:** www.ciob.org.uk
- **The Chartered Institute of Building Services Engineers:** www.cibse.org

Building

		Teaching Quality/24	Research Quality/5	Entry Standards	Graduate Prospects %	Overall Rating
1	Loughborough	22	5*B	324	95	100.0
2	Manchester	22	4C	330	95	97.5
3	Reading	21	5B	294	85	94.9
4	Oxford Brookes	23	4D	171	100	94.8
5	Nottingham Trent	22	3aB	224	95	94.6
6	Ulster	21	5A	239	85	94.1
7	University College London		4C	277		93.9
8	Plymouth	23	4E	282	80	93.7
9	Kingston	24		224	85	93.3
10	Salford	18	5*A	286	100	93.2
11	Westminster	22	3aD	232	90	92.6
12	Heriot-Watt	S	5B	302	85	92.5
13	De Montfort	20	4A		90	92.4
14	Northumbria	22	3bD	234	90	92.1
15	Coventry	22	3bC	217	85	91.5
=16	Sheffield Hallam	21	3aE	233	95	90.7
=16	Liverpool John Moores	22	3bC	216	80	90.7
18	Leeds Metropolitan	21	3bD	241	90	90.5
19	Wolverhampton	20	3aB			89.9
=20	Glamorgan		3bC		90	89.4
=20	Greenwich	21	3bE	224	90	89.4
22	Anglia	20	2B		90	88.6
23	Brighton	20	3bC	186	90	87.8
24	West of England	21		214	85	87.6
25	Central Lancashire	20	3aD		80	87.0
26	Robert Gordon	S	3bD	250	80	86.5
27	Napier	HS	3bD	193	70	86.2
28	Glasgow Caledonian	S	3aD	218	70	84.6
29	Northampton UC	19			90	84.4
30	Abertay Dundee	S		164	85	83.5
31	Teesside	19	2D			83.3
32	Bolton	19			80	82.5
=33	London South Bank	18	3bD		75	81.1
=33	Central England	18	2F	224		81.1
35	Staffordshire	17			75	77.2

Employed in graduate job: 73%
Employed in non-graduate job: 9%
Studying, not employed: 2%
Average starting salary: £19,217

Employed in graduate job and studying: 10%
Employed in non-graduate job and studying: 0%
Unemployed: 5%
Teaching quality assessed 1996–98

THE LETTERS THAT APPEAR IN THE RESEARCH QUALITY COLUMN INDICATE THE PROPORTION OF STAFF INCLUDED IN THE ASSESSMENT, A SHOWING THAT ALMOST ALL STAFF WERE INCLUDED AND F SHOWING THAT HARDLY ANY WERE.

Business Studies

Oxford retains the top place it has occupied since teaching grades were dropped from the business ranking because of the age of the original assessments, which were carried out more than a decade ago. Warwick, one of the two universities rated internationally outstanding for research, moves up to second, ahead of the London School of Economics. Eighth-placed Lancaster has the other 5* research grade. St Andrews is the top university in Scotland, having leapt 13 places up the table to fourth position overall. Cardiff remains the clear the leader in Wales.

Although Oxford's Said Business School is exclusively postgraduate, the colleges offer management in joint honours first-degree courses. London and Manchester business schools, like Cranfield and Cambridge's Judge School of Management, are also absent from the table because they do not offer first degrees.

Bradford boasts the best employment record, with 85 per cent of leavers going straight into graduate jobs or postgraduate training, but low entrance qualifications cost the university a place in the top 20. Both employment rates and entrance qualifications vary enormously in this, one of the largest tables in the *Guide*. More than half of the 98 institutions are new universities or university colleges, but only Bournemouth squeezes into the top 40. More than a dozen have average entry grades of less than 200 points, but at the majority of them fewer than half the leavers were in graduate jobs or postgraduate training within six months.

Applications for degrees in business and management seem to have reached their peak, with student demand and the number of places remaining roughly level in 2004 and 2005. However, business remains one of the most popular choices in higher education and job prospects are still good. Although one leaver in five starts off in a non-graduate job, only about one in 14 is unemployed six months after graduating.

- **The Chartered Management Institute:** www.managers.org.uk
- **The Institute of Management Consultancy:** www.imc.co.uk

Business Studies		Research Quality/5	Entry Standards	Graduate Prospects %	Overall Rating
1	Oxford	5A	501	78	100.0
2	Warwick	5*B	459	76	97.9
3	London School of Economics	5A	439	74	95.8
4	Bath	5A	383	77	94.1
5	St Andrews	4A	394	75	92.0
6	Nottingham	5B	424	68	91.9
7	Manchester	5A	392	66	91.1
8	Lancaster	5*B	392	64	91.0
9	King's College London	4B	354	80	90.7
10	City	5C	383	76	90.4
11	Imperial College	5B	405	65	90.1
12	Aston	5B	331	73	89.1
13	Leeds	5C	380	63	86.2
14	Royal Holloway	4B	324	69	85.8

=15	Cardiff	5B	354	58	85.5
=15	Birmingham	4D	379	72	85.5
17	Surrey	4C	301	77	85.4
18	Loughborough	4C	356	68	85.2
=19	Queen's, Belfast	4B	332	65	84.9
=19	Exeter	4C	363	66	84.9
21	Bradford	4C	226	85	84.5
22	Southampton	4B	358	59	84.2
23	Aberdeen	3aB	306	70	83.5
24	Sheffield	4B	384	50	82.6
=25	Strathclyde	4C	415	50	82.3
=25	Edinburgh	4B	417	44	82.3
27	Durham	3aD	382		81.1
28	Newcastle	3aC	350	60	81.0
29	Stirling	4B	324	53	80.8
=30	Glasgow	4C	366	52	80.6
=30	Essex	5C	275	61	80.6
32	Reading	5C	321	52	79.9
33	Leicester	3aB	291		79.3
34	Keele	4B	292	49	78.0
=35	Kent	3aC	263	63	77.8
=35	Swansea	3aD	282	65	77.8
37	Brunel	4C	282	53	77.0
38	Bangor	5B	257	45	76.9
39	Hull	4C	260	55	76.6
=40	Bournemouth	3aE	280	65	76.0
=40	Heriot-Watt	4D	364	44	76.0
42	Portsmouth	4C	212	60	75.9
43	Nottingham Trent	3bD	292	60	75.6
44	Aberystwyth	3bC	268	58	75.1
45	Ulster	3aD	281	56	74.8
46	Northumbria	3bF	270	68	74.7
47	Gloucestershire	3aD	246	60	74.5
48	Salford	3aB	264	47	74.3
49	Oxford Brookes	2F	275	65	73.8
50	East Anglia	3aC	287	46	73.6
51	Hertfordshire	3aC	209	56	73.1
52	Liverpool		314	55	72.3
53	De Montfort	3aC	220	50	71.7
54	Manchester Metropolitan	3aE	256	54	71.4
55	Plymouth	3bE	242	57	71.1
56	Liverpool John Moores	3bE	235	57	70.8
57	Central Lancashire	3bE	228	57	70.5
58	Brighton	3aE	262	50	70.4
59	Kingston	3aE	222	55	70.2
60	Robert Gordon	2F	272	53	69.9
61	Lincoln	3bD	225	51	69.6
=62	West of England	3aD	255	43	69.5

		Research Quality/5	Entry Standards	Graduate Prospects %	Overall Rating
=62	Liverpool Hope UC		207	62	69.5
64	Glamorgan	3bD	193	55	69.4
=65	Queen Margaret College	2C	215	52	69.3
=65	Napier	3bE	217	55	69.3
67	Sheffield Hallam	3bF	226	55	68.5
68	Glasgow Caledonian	3aE	266	42	68.1
69	Derby	2E	191	56	67.8
70	Sunderland	2F	218	54	67.7
71	Anglia	2D	227	47	67.5
72	Leeds Metropolitan	2F	263	46	67.2
73	Staffordshire	3bE	219	47	66.9
74	Westminster	3bE	244	43	66.8
75	Middlesex	3aE	163	53	66.7
=76	Abertay Dundee	3bE	187	51	66.6
=76	Canterbury Christ Church UC		246	47	66.6
=78	Teesside		171	58	66.5
=78	Huddersfield	3bE	197	49	66.5
=78	UWIC, Cardiff		218	51	66.5
81	London South Bank	3aE		44	66.2
82	Coventry	2E	205	46	65.3
83	Winchester UC		264	40	65.2
84	University of the Arts, London		235	43	64.8
85	Luton	3aE	193	41	64.4
86	Wolverhampton	3bF	193	46	64.2
87	Bath Spa UC		200	46	64.1
88	Greenwich	3bF	191	46	64.0
89	Central England	2F	204	44	63.8
90	Northampton UC	2E	196	41	63.3
91	East London	2E	184	42	63.1
92	Roehampton		218	40	63.0
93	Paisley	2E	206	38	62.8
94	University of Wales, Newport		165	46	62.4
95	Buckinghamshire Chilterns UC	2E	186	38	61.9
96	Worcester UC		187	40	61.6
97	Thames Valley		143	41	59.8
98	Bolton	1D	190	19	55.9

Employed in graduate job: 40%
Employed in non-graduate job: 38%
Studying, not employed: 7%
Average starting salary: £16,199

Employed in graduate job and studying: 5%
Employed in non-graduate job and studying: 3%
Unemployed: 7%

THE LETTERS THAT APPEAR IN THE RESEARCH QUALITY COLUMN INDICATE THE PROPORTION OF STAFF INCLUDED IN THE ASSESSMENT, A SHOWING THAT ALMOST ALL STAFF WERE INCLUDED AND F SHOWING THAT HARDLY ANY WERE.

Celtic Studies

There is no change in the top three for Celtic Studies. Aberystwyth extends its lead over Bangor, which also has maximum points for both teaching and research.

Third-placed Cambridge, which is also rated internationally outstanding for research, does not publish separate destinations data or entry grades for the subjects. Ulster overtakes Queen's, Belfast in the battle for top spot in Irish studies, with the other 5* research rating and maximum points for teaching quality.

Not surprisingly, universities in Wales and Northern Ireland dominate the table. There was no category of Celtic studies in the Scottish assessments of teaching quality, although Aberdeen joins the ranking this year.

The subjects have relatively small enrolments, but both Welsh and Irish studies have been attracting more applicants recently – there was a 10 per cent rise in 2004 and another of similar proportions at the start of 2005. Almost half of the graduates go on to further study – only law has a higher proportion in this category. Partly as a result, only a quarter go straight into a graduate-level job, but the 5 per cent unemployment rate is one of the lowest.

- **Dalriada Celtic Heritage Trust:** www.dalriada.co.uk
- www.celts.org/links.htm
- www.conjure.com/celtic

Celtic Studies		Teaching Quality/24	Research Quality/5	Entry Standards	Graduate Prospects %	Overall Rating
1	Aberystwyth	E	5*A	373	80	100.0
2	Bangor	E	5*A	299	60	93.0
3	Cambridge	23	5*A			92.1
4	Ulster	24	5*B		40	90.7
5	Queen's, Belfast	23	5A	307	70	88.3
6	Swansea		5A	273	80	87.9
7	Cardiff	S	5A	333	80	84.1
8	Aberdeen		4B		70	82.9
9	Lampeter	S	3bC			66.7

Employed in graduate job: 24%
Employed in non-graduate job: 24%
Studying, not employed: 41%
Average starting salary: £15,522

Employed in graduate job and studying: 4%
Employed in non-graduate job and studying: 3%
Unemployed: 5%
Teaching quality assessed 1996–98

THE LETTERS THAT APPEAR IN THE RESEARCH QUALITY COLUMN INDICATE THE PROPORTION OF STAFF INCLUDED IN THE ASSESSMENT, A SHOWING THAT ALMOST ALL STAFF WERE INCLUDED AND F SHOWING THAT HARDLY ANY WERE.

Chemical Engineering

Cambridge pips Imperial College at the top of the chemical engineering table for the fourth year in a row. Cambridge has the better teaching score and is the only university with a 100 per cent graduate employment record, but Imperial has the better rating for research (5*). Birmingham and University College London are also considered internationally outstanding for research, but their teaching scores keep them out of the top four.

Chemical Engineering CONT.

No university in England was awarded top marks for teaching, but Swansea was rated Excellent under the Welsh system. Heriot-Watt is the best-placed Scottish institution, with entrance qualifications second only to Imperial College – Cambridge does not publish separate data for the subject.

Chemical engineering is one of the smaller branches of engineering, with fewer than 6,000 applications by the start of 2005. But the appeal of the subject seems to be growing: this represented a 19 per cent increase, following a smaller rise in 2004.

Four out of five students have A levels or equivalent qualifications, and average entry grades are the highest for any engineering subject. This helps produce engineering's largest proportion of firsts and 2:1s. Almost six out of ten students go straight into graduate jobs, but the 9 per cent unemployment rate is higher than the average for all subjects. Assessors said the overall standard in English universities was high in relation to international competition, with most courses offering industrial placements in the final year and leading to Chartered Engineer status.

- **The Royal Society of Chemistry:** www.rsc.org
- **The Institution of Chemical Engineers:** www.icheme.org

Chemical Engineering		Teaching Quality/24	Research Quality/5	Entry Standards	Graduate Prospects %	Overall Rating
1	Cambridge	23	5A		100	100.0
2	Imperial College	22	5*A	454	75	95.5
3	Manchester	22	5A	360	80	91.2
4	Loughborough	22	4A	379	80	90.0
5	Birmingham	21	5*A	353	80	89.8
6	Swansea	E	4A	292		89.3
7	Newcastle	21	5B	366	85	87.9
8	Queen's, Belfast	21	4A	369	85	87.4
9	University College London	20	5*A	304	85	85.8
10	Bath	20	4A	386	85	85.0
11	Sheffield	21	4B	361	75	84.6
12	Nottingham	21	4B	376	60	82.8
13	Heriot-Watt	19	4A	449	70	81.8
14	Edinburgh	19	4C	417		78.3
15	Aston	19	5C	281	85	77.1
16	Strathclyde	20		377	60	71.8
17	Surrey	18	4B	286		71.3
18	Leeds	19	5C	246	50	70.5
19	London South Bank	18	3aE		60	64.1
20	Teesside	17	2D			58.0

Employed in graduate job: 48%
Employed in non-graduate job: 15%
Studying, not employed: 20%
Average starting salary: £21,049

Employed in graduate job and studying: 7%
Employed in non-graduate job and studying: 2%
Unemployed: 9%
Teaching quality assessed 1995–96

THE LETTERS THAT APPEAR IN THE RESEARCH QUALITY COLUMN INDICATE THE PROPORTION OF STAFF INCLUDED IN THE ASSESSMENT, A SHOWING THAT ALMOST ALL STAFF WERE INCLUDED AND F SHOWING THAT HARDLY ANY WERE.

Chemistry

The number of universities in the chemistry ranking has dipped below 50 for the first time following a much-publicised series of closures, most recently at Exeter. Yet applications continue to rise: a 7 per cent increase in 2004 was followed by one of almost 9 per cent at the start of 2005, bringing the total to almost 18,000. Forensic science has become an attractive alternative to the pure subject but, for many, chemistry remains the classic science.

A much-improved set of research assessments in 2001 produced challengers for Oxford and Cambridge for the first time, but the pair lead the ranking again. Both have the maximum research score and average entry grades of more than four As at A level. Durham, the other top research scorer, remains third, while Imperial College London, Bristol and University College London also boast 5* grades. Edinburgh retains top place in Scotland, while Cardiff takes over from Swansea (the scene of one of the closures) in Wales. However, Queen's, Belfast, is the top university outside England, having surged nine places up the table to fourth with the aid of the only full employment score for the subject.

Chemistry is old university territory, with only one former polytechnic – Manchester Metropolitan – in the top 30. Almost nine out of ten undergraduates have A levels or their equivalent, but entry requirements are not far above the average for all subjects. The unemployment rate, at 7 per cent, is on the average for higher education as a whole, and three-quarters of leavers either undertake further study or go straight into graduate-level jobs. Only two universities in the table had 'positive destinations' for less than 60 per cent of their graduates.

- **The Royal Society of Chemistry:** www.rsc.org

Chemistry		Research Quality/5	Entry Standards	Graduate Prospects %	Overall Rating
1	Cambridge	5*A	542		100.0
2	Oxford	5*A	521	80	92.1
3	Durham	5*A	435	80	88.3
4	Queen's, Belfast	4A	351	100	84.8
5	Warwick	5A	351	90	84.7
6	Sussex	5A	307	95	84.3
7	Imperial College	5*B	462	70	84.1
8	Bristol	5*B	415	75	83.6
9	Edinburgh	5A	406	75	82.5
10	University College London	5*B	353	80	82.4
11	Sheffield	5B	362	85	81.7
12	York	5A	364	75	80.6
13	Heriot-Watt	4A	347	85	80.0
14	Southampton	5A	368	70	79.2
15	Leeds	5B	365	75	78.7
16	Nottingham	5A	421	60	78.4
17	Strathclyde	4A	380	75	78.3
18	Liverpool	5A	307	75	78.1
19	St Andrews	5C	373	80	77.4
20	Manchester	5B	330	75	77.1

		Research Quality/5	Entry Standards	Graduate Prospects %	Overall Rating
21	Bath	4A	339	75	76.5
22	Hull	4C	291	95	76.3
23	Cardiff	4A	312	75	75.3
=24	Birmingham	5B	315	70	74.9
=24	Glasgow	4C	366	80	74.9
26	Leicester	4A	300	75	74.8
27	Surrey	3aA	260	90	74.7
28	Loughborough	4B	314	75	73.8
29	Manchester Metropolitan	4A	230	80	73.2
30	Reading	4A	225	80	73.0
31	Keele	3aA	331		72.5
32	Bradford	4B	249	75	70.9
33	East Anglia	5B	245	60	68.7
34	Northumbria	3bC	226	90	67.6
35	Huddersfield	4C	185	80	66.9
36	Newcastle	4C	299	55	64.2
37	Nottingham Trent	3aD	224	80	64.1
38	Brighton	5C	181		63.8
39	Plymouth	4C	221		63.2
40	Aston	5C		55	63.1
41	Coventry	4C	182	65	62.1
42	Bangor	3aA	273	30	56.6
43	Paisley	2C		65	55.0
44	Sheffield Hallam		174	75	54.5

Employed in graduate job: 32%
Employed in non-graduate job: 19%
Studying, not employed: 36%
Average starting salary: £16,670

Employed in graduate job and studying: 4%
Employed in non-graduate job and studying: 2%
Unemployed: 7%

THE LETTERS THAT APPEAR IN THE RESEARCH QUALITY COLUMN INDICATE THE PROPORTION OF STAFF INCLUDED IN THE ASSESSMENT, A SHOWING THAT ALMOST ALL STAFF WERE INCLUDED AND F SHOWING THAT HARDLY ANY WERE.

Civil Engineering

Cardiff holds onto top place in civil engineering, with maximum points for teaching and research, while Swansea slips from second after a comparatively poor year for graduate employment. Both were rated Excellent at teaching and were among five universities considered internationally outstanding for research. The others were second-placed Bristol, Imperial College and Southampton. Unusually, no university in England, Scotland or Northern Ireland gained full marks for teaching quality. Plymouth boasts the best score, with 23 points out of 24, but just loses out to Kingston as the top-placed new university. It was one of eight universities to be awarded 22 points for teaching, but none of the Scottish universities was rated better than Highly Satisfactory.

Bristol has the highest entry standards and is one of five universities with 100 per cent graduate employment scores. Of the others, Queen's, Belfast, Liverpool and Loughborough make the top ten, but Salford misses the top 20 in spite of its 5* research rating. Nationally, civil engineering has among the best job prospects: the 3 per cent unemployment rate is bettered only by medicine, dentistry, pharmacy and veterinary medicine, and three quarters of leavers go straight into graduate jobs.

There is a wide spread of entry scores, from more than 400 points at Bristol, Imperial, Southampton and Sheffield, to less than 200 at Abertay and Glasgow Caledonian. About a third of the universities offering civil engineering are former polytechnics, but only two make the top 20. Nearly four out of ten undergraduates are admitted with A levels or the equivalent, their grades close to the average for all subjects. The subject has been expanding: the 3,300 full-time degree places in 2004 represented a 24 per cent increase on the previous year. There were big increases in applications in both 2004 and 2005.

- **The Institute of Civil Engineers:** www.ice.org.uk

Civil Engineering

		Teaching Quality/24	Research Quality/5	Entry Standards	Graduate Prospects %	Overall Rating
1	Cardiff	E	5*A	364	90	100.0
2	Bristol	22	5*C	454	100	97.8
3	Queen's, Belfast	22	5B	376	100	96.6
4	Nottingham	22	5A	377	90	96.1
=5	Swansea	E	5*B	317	75	95.2
=5	Bath	22	5B	353	95	95.2
7	Imperial College	21	5*B	444	95	94.8
8	Liverpool	22	4A	321	100	94.6
9	Manchester	22	5B	388	85	94.5
10	Loughborough	22	4B	343	100	94.3
11	Southampton	21	5*B	412	85	92.4
12	Sheffield	21	5B	404	95	92.3
13	Surrey	22	4C	350	95	92.1
14	Dundee	HS	5A	305		90.6
15	Kingston	22	3aC		90	89.8
16	Plymouth	23	4E	221	90	88.9
=17	Heriot-Watt	HS	4A	361	75	87.7
=17	Birmingham	21	5C	323	90	87.7
19	Glasgow	HS	4C	319	95	87.4
20	Edinburgh	HS	5B	375	65	87.1
21	Aberdeen	HS	4C			85.9
22	Newcastle	20	5B	334	90	85.6
23	Strathclyde	HS	4C	336	80	85.4
24	Salford	19	5*A		100	85.1
25	Leeds Metropolitan	21	3aB		80	84.4
26	Bradford	20	4B		95	84.0
27	Napier	HS	4C	209	85	83.2
28	University College London	19	5A	316	90	82.1
29	Brighton	21	3bC			81.8

		Teaching Quality/24	Research Quality/5	Entry Standards	Graduate Prospects %	Overall Rating
30	Paisley	HS	3aC	220	80	81.5
31	Nottingham Trent	20	3aB	225	95	80.7
32	Ulster	19	5A	211	95	80.3
33	East London	21	2D			79.0
34	Greenwich	21	3bE			78.7
35	Portsmouth	20	3aC	235	75	76.6
36	Leeds	19	5D	308	80	75.3
=37	City	19	4B	220		74.7
=37	Abertay Dundee	HS		171		74.7
=39	Liverpool John Moores	20			90	74.2
=39	Bolton	20			90	74.2
41	Coventry	19	3bC	254	65	70.1
42	London South Bank	20			60	68.5
43	Glasgow Caledonian	S		198	55	65.9

Employed in graduate job: 67%
Employed in non-graduate job: 10%
Studying, not employed: 8%
Average starting salary: £19,388

Employed in graduate job and studying: 9%
Employed in non-graduate job and studying: 1%
Unemployed: 3%
Teaching quality assessed 1996–98

THE LETTERS THAT APPEAR IN THE RESEARCH QUALITY COLUMN INDICATE THE PROPORTION OF STAFF INCLUDED IN THE ASSESSMENT, A SHOWING THAT ALMOST ALL STAFF WERE INCLUDED AND F SHOWING THAT HARDLY ANY WERE.

Classics and Ancient History

Oxford and Cambridge have been locked together at the top of the classics table since it was first published two years ago, when their scores were identical. Cambridge edges ahead in the latest ranking because, although Oxford had higher entry standards, more of Cambridge's classicists went into graduate jobs or further study. Like third-placed King's College London, both universities have maximum points for teaching and research.

UCL matched the top three with a 5* research rating and nine of the remaining 20 universities reached grade 5. Six of the 18 universities in the teaching quality assessment for England achieved perfect scores – Birmingham, Manchester and Nottingham being the others – and only Leeds was awarded less than 21 points out of 24. Lampeter and Swansea were both considered Excellent in the older Welsh assessment. There was no separate category in Scotland, although Edinburgh and St Andrews have among the highest entry scores in Britain.

No new universities appear in the table, although some offer the subjects as part of a modular degree scheme. A-level grades in classics are among the highest for any group of subjects, but most universities teach the subject from scratch, as well as to more practised students.

Bristol registered the best-ever employment record for classics, with 95 per cent of leavers going straight into graduate jobs or postgraduate study, but it was not enough to secure a place in the top ten. The subjects' reputation for attracting analytical high-fliers helps in the

	Classics and Ancient History	Teaching Quality/24	Research Quality/5	Entry Standards	Graduate Prospects %	Overall Rating
1	Cambridge	24	5*A	473	85	100.0
2	Oxford	24	5*A	491	70	98.1
3	King's College London	24	5*A	357	60	88.8
4	Birmingham	24	5A	362	65	84.9
5	St Andrews		5B	444		82.5
6	Nottingham	24	4A	387	55	79.1
7	Manchester	24	5B	314	55	77.0
8	University College London	23	5*B	361	50	76.7
9	Swansea	E	4A	288		73.1
10	Warwick	23	5A	389	30	73.0
11	Royal Holloway	23	5A	324	40	71.4
12	Queen's, Belfast	23	4A			70.7
13	Bristol	21	5B	383	95	69.1
14	Exeter	22	5A	357	40	66.8
15	Durham	21	5B	440	65	66.4
16	Edinburgh		4B	419	40	64.2
17	Lampeter	E	3aC			62.5
18	Newcastle	22	3aA	351	55	59.0
19	Glasgow		4B	345		58.5
20	Reading	22	5A	271	20	58.2
21	Liverpool	22	4A	247	50	57.6
22	Leeds	19	4B	344	55	41.6
23	Kent	22		290	55	35.6

Employed in graduate job: 27%
Employed in non-graduate job: 32%
Studying, not employed: 26%
Average starting salary: £15,628

Employed in graduate job and studying: 4%
Employed in non-graduate job and studying: 4%
Unemployed: 8%
Teaching quality assessed 2000–01

THE LETTERS THAT APPEAR IN THE RESEARCH QUALITY COLUMN INDICATE THE PROPORTION OF STAFF INCLUDED IN THE ASSESSMENT, A SHOWING THAT ALMOST ALL STAFF WERE INCLUDED AND F SHOWING THAT HARDLY ANY WERE.

jobs market, but relatively few (31 per cent) go directly into graduate jobs. The 8 per cent unemployment rate six months after graduation is just above average for all subjects, but the proportion going on to postgraduate courses is high.

- www.classicspage.com

Communication and Media Studies

Although mainly the preserve of the new universities, eight of the top ten places are filled by older institutions. East Anglia is the third leader of the ranking in three years, taking over from Loughborough, although the two are difficult to compare. The only points of direct comparison are in research, where both score maximum points and entrance qualifications, where Loughborough is marginally ahead. East Anglia benefits from one of the best teaching scores, while Loughborough could not repeat last year's successes in graduate employment.

Communication and Media Studies CONT.

Chichester University College achieved England's only maximum score for teaching quality, although low graduate employment cost it a place in this year's top 20. Warwick, East Anglia and Westminster were only a point away on teaching, while Goldsmiths College was the other institution rated internationally outstanding for research. Westminster, the best-placed new university, was one of six institutions on grade 5.

Glasgow Caledonian is the top university in Scotland, Aberystwyth the leader in Wales, but neither makes the top ten. Fourth-placed Warwick is the only university to average more than 400 points at entry. Seven others average less than 200.

Controversy has raged over the subjects' currency in the employment market, and the division of jobs into graduate and non-graduate hits communication and media studies harder than any other group of subjects. Under the new classification introduced this year, only Leeds saw 70 per cent of leavers go straight into graduate jobs or further training. In ten institutions the proportion was below a third, sending the subjects to the bottom of the graduate employment table. Academics in the field argue that it is normal for students completing media courses to take 'entry level' work that is not classified as a graduate job.

Nevertheless, media studies continues to grow in popularity, with applications showing an annual increase of 19 per cent at the start of 2005. Assessors found that courses varied from conventional academic degrees to advanced vocational training. Their main concern was a shortage of resources in a fast-changing area of study.

- **The Broadcast Journalism Training Council:** www.bjtc.org.uk
- **The Institute of Scientific and Technical Communications:** www.istc.org.uk

	Communications and Media Studies	Teaching Quality/24	Research Quality/5	Entry Standards	Graduate Prospects %	Overall Rating
1	East Anglia	23	5*A	311		100.0
2	Loughborough		5*A	334	50	98.9
3	Royal Holloway		5B	370	58	98.1
4	Warwick	23	5B	415	40	97.0
=5	Goldsmiths College	22	5*C	347	62	95.0
=5	Leeds	22	4C	385	70	95.0
7	Sheffield		4C	395	60	94.8
8	Westminster	23	5D	348	58	93.8
9	Sussex	21	4A	364	48	90.7
10	Central Lancashire	22	3bC	305	66	89.6
11	Ulster	21	4B	293	58	89.2
12	Aberystwyth		5B	232		88.9
13	Liverpool	23		340	54	88.1
14	West of England	22	4C	286	40	87.4
15	Leicester	21	3aB	310	52	87.3
16	Cardiff	S	5B	371	46	87.2
17	Glasgow Caledonian	HS	3aB	324	42	86.3
18	Bournemouth	22		353	54	85.8
19	Stirling	HS	5C	351	24	85.5
20	Nottingham Trent	21	5D	307	46	85.4
21	Birmingham		3aC	378	34	84.9

22	Napier	HS	3aD	263	60	84.7
=23	Chichester UC	24		225	36	84.5
=23	London South Bank	20	4B			84.5
25	Plymouth	21	3aC			84.4
26	Sunderland	22	3aD	242	40	83.5
27	Liverpool John Moores	22	3bE	260	44	82.8
28	Luton	22	3aE	220		81.8
29	Salford	21		298	56	81.7
30	Glamorgan	E		212	34	80.1
31	Robert Gordon		3bD	272	50	79.9
32	De Montfort	20	3aB	259	30	79.7
33	Staffordshire	20	4D	250	42	79.5
34	Central England	21		287	42	79.3
35	University of the Arts, London	20		299	54	78.8
36	Queen Margaret College	S	2D	298	50	78.4
37	Oxford Brookes	21		242	44	78.2
38	Leeds Metropolitan	19	3aD	268	50	77.8
39	Canterbury Christ Church UC	20		258	52	77.3
40	City	19	3bD	338		77.1
41	Brunel	20		325	36	76.8
42	Gloucestershire	20		262	44	76.2
43	Greenwich	19	3bC	198	50	75.9
44	Northampton UC	21		192	34	75.2
45	Glasgow			381	26	75.1
46	Middlesex		3aD	217	36	74.8
47	Sheffield Hallam	19	3aE	276	32	73.9
48	Teesside		2A	183	36	73.0
49	Coventry	18	3bE	233	46	71.6
50	Winchester UC	18	3aD	247	30	71.4
51	Wolverhampton	19	2E	212	34	71.2
52	Lancaster			325	22	71.1
53	Thames Valley	18	1A	175	52	70.9
54	Anglia	18		232	50	70.8
55	Paisley			237	32	69.3
56	Surrey Institute of Art and Design, UC	17		298	32	67.3
57	Buckinghamshire Chilterns UC	18		188	32	66.7
58	East London	16	5D	188	34	66.6
59	Worcester UC			196	22	64.5
60	Essex			222	14	63.7

Employed in graduate job: 36%
Employed in non-graduate job: 43%
Studying, not employed: 6%
Average starting salary: £13,930

Employed in graduate job and studying: 3%
Employed in non-graduate job and studying: 2%
Unemployed: 10%
Teaching quality assessed 1996–98

THE LETTERS THAT APPEAR IN THE RESEARCH QUALITY COLUMN INDICATE THE PROPORTION OF STAFF INCLUDED IN THE ASSESSMENT, A SHOWING THAT ALMOST ALL STAFF WERE INCLUDED AND F SHOWING THAT HARDLY ANY WERE.

Computer Science

Computing is now the largest of our tables, with 98 institutions offering the subject at undergraduate level. However, troubles in the dotcom economy have had their effect on what was once seen as a guaranteed career path. Applications have been dropping – they were down by almost 20 per cent at the start of 2004, leading to a 12 per cent cut in full-time degree places. Although applications had steadied at the start of 2005, only one subject has a higher unemployment rate in the latest figures. The good news for computer scientists is that six out of ten leavers still go straight into graduate jobs or further training. The contrast is reflected in the ranking, which shows 94 per cent graduate employment at table-topping Oxford, but less than 50 per cent at the bottom five institutions.

With teaching grades dropped because of their age, employment has a considerable impact on the ranking. It made the difference between Oxford and Cambridge, which had higher average entry scores. Cambridge also has one of eight 5* research grades, although only Edinburgh, Surrey and Salford achieved this distinction while entering a full complement of academics for the 2001 Research Assessment Exercise. York, Manchester, Southampton and Imperial College were the other institutions to reach 5* with a more selective staff entry.

St Andrews widens its lead over Edinburgh as the top Scottish university, while Swansea overtakes Cardiff in Wales. Liverpool John Moores is the only new university in the top half of the table, squeezing in at 49th, just ahead of Nottingham Trent. Entry grades are largely responsible: ten universities in the upper reaches of the table average more than 400 points, while many of the former polytechnics average less than 200.

- **The British Computer Society:** www.bcs.org

Computer Science		Research Quality/5	Entry Standards	Graduate Prospects %	Overall Rating
1	Oxford	5A	543	94	100.0
2	Cambridge	5*B	564	88	99.4
3	Imperial College	5*B	487	82	94.6
4	York	5*B	490	80	94.1
5	University College London	5A	400	82	90.7
6	Bristol	5A	460	72	90.0
7	Surrey	5*A	331	82	89.8
8	St Andrews	5A	396		88.9
9	Bath	4A	380	84	88.7
10	Warwick	5B	483	66	87.8
11	Edinburgh	5*A	397	66	87.5
12	Southampton	5*B	405	68	87.0
=13	Swansea	5B	283	88	86.8
=13	Sheffield	5B	410	72	86.8
15	Lancaster	5A	331	76	86.2
16	Manchester	5*B	373	66	85.1
17	Cardiff	5A	321	72	84.5
18	Newcastle	5B	325	74	84.1
19	Nottingham	5B	364	68	83.8

20	Durham	4B	405	68	83.7
=21	Birmingham	5B	397	62	83.2
=21	Dundee	4A	301	76	83.2
23	Aberdeen	4C	288	86	83.1
24	Kent	4B	335	74	82.9
25	King's College London	4B	359	70	82.6
26	Royal Holloway	5B	301	72	82.5
27	Sussex	5A	316	66	82.4
28	Glasgow	5B	335	66	82.0
29	Queen's, Belfast	4A	325	68	81.6
30	Salford	5*A	277	60	80.9
31	City	4B	259	72	79.3
32	Loughborough	3aB	341	66	79.0
33	Aberystwyth	4A	279	64	78.6
34	Reading	4B	312	60	77.6
35	Leeds	5D	357	62	77.4
36	Brunel	5B	266	58	76.9
=37	Exeter	4B	337	54	76.7
=37	East Anglia	4B	335	54	76.7
=39	Stirling	3bC	284	74	76.6
=39	Heriot-Watt	4A	355	48	76.6
41	Liverpool	5B	258	58	76.5
42	Queen Mary	4B	265	62	76.4
43	Leicester	4B	274	60	76.2
44	Bangor	4B	242		75.7
=45	Hull	3aC	250	70	75.3
=45	Essex	4B	284	56	75.3
=47	Goldsmiths College	3bB	203	76	75.0
=47	Aston	5C	270	58	75.0
49	Liverpool John Moores	3aB	198	70	74.7
50	Nottingham Trent	3aE	243	76	74.0
51	Glamorgan	4D	219	70	73.6
=52	Bradford	4E	221	72	72.4
=52	Strathclyde	3aD	355	52	72.4
=52	Robert Gordon	3aD	244	66	72.4
55	West of England	3aC	244	58	71.4
56	Bournemouth	2E	244	70	71.0
57	Sunderland	3aC	216	60	70.9
58	Brighton	4E	208	68	70.7
59	Paisley	3aC	270	52	70.5
60	Keele	3bC	280	54	70.3
61	Hertfordshire	4C	195	56	70.2
=62	Ulster	4E	251	60	69.8
=62	Greenwich	4D	201	60	69.8
64	Gloucestershire	3aD	231	58	69.4
65	Kingston	3bD	190	66	69.3
66	Northumbria	3bC	216	58	69.0
67	De Montfort	4C	190	52	68.7

		Research Quality/5	Entry Standards	Graduate Prospects %	Overall Rating
68	Napier	3aD	196	60	68.6
69	Oxford Brookes	3bD	248	56	68.5
70	Sheffield Hallam	3bE	230	60	67.9
71	Abertay Dundee		260	60	67.6
72	Plymouth	5E	225	54	67.5
73	Derby		190	68	67.4
74	Liverpool Hope UC		174	70	67.3
75	Leeds Metropolitan	3bC	202	52	66.6
76	Manchester Metropolitan	3aD	231	48	66.3
77	Anglia		247	56	65.9
78	Central Lancashire		213	60	65.8
=79	Teesside	2F	189	62	65.6
=79	Portsmouth		223	58	65.6
81	Huddersfield	3aE	166	58	65.4
82	Canterbury Christ Church UC		279	50	65.3
83	Glasgow Caledonian	3bE	240	50	65.2
=84	Northampton UC		194	60	65.0
=84	Staffordshire		226	56	65.0
86	Central England		224	54	64.4
87	London South Bank	4D	166	46	64.0
88	Westminster	3aF	195	54	63.8
89	Luton		192	56	63.7
90	Coventry	2E	196	52	63.5
91	Wolverhampton	2F	163	56	62.8
92	Lincoln		199	52	62.7
93	University of Wales, Newport		150	56	62.1
94	Middlesex	3aE	147	44	60.3
95	Worcester UC		188	40	58.6
96	Roehampton		185	40	58.5
97	East London	2E	137	40	57.5
98	Buckinghamshire Chilterns UC		158	34	55.5

Employed in graduate job: 44%
Employed in non-graduate job: 26%
Studying, not employed: 10%
Average starting salary: £17,424

Employed in graduate job and studying: 4%
Employed in non-graduate job and studying: 3%
Unemployed: 13%

THE LETTERS THAT APPEAR IN THE RESEARCH QUALITY COLUMN INDICATE THE PROPORTION OF STAFF INCLUDED IN THE ASSESSMENT, A SHOWING THAT ALMOST ALL STAFF WERE INCLUDED AND F SHOWING THAT HARDLY ANY WERE.

Dentistry

Not even medicine can match dentistry's 98 per cent graduate employment rate. Applications are correspondingly buoyant: there was a 25 per cent rise in 2005 to follow a 14 per cent increase the previous year. But it is not a subject for academic slouches: entrants

Dentistry

		Teaching Quality/24	Research Quality/5	Entry Standards	Graduate Prospects %	Overall Rating
1	King's College London	24	5*C	428	100	100.0
2	Manchester	24	4B	419	100	99.0
3	Queen Mary	24	5B	366	100	98.4
4	Sheffield	23	5C	428	100	97.7
5	Newcastle	23	5D	468	100	97.4
6	Queen's, Belfast	24	3aC	429	100	97.3
7	Leeds	23	4C	401	100	95.9
8	Dundee	HS	5D	442		95.3
9	Birmingham	22	4D	439	100	94.4
10	Liverpool	21	4C	427	100	93.9
11	Glasgow	HS	3aD	423	100	93.7
12	Cardiff	E	4C	396	90	93.6
13	Bristol	19	5*D	417	100	90.7

Employed in graduate job: 81%
Employed in non-graduate job: 1%
Studying, not employed: 1%
Average starting salary: £26,236

Employed in graduate job and studying: 17%
Employed in non-graduate job and studying: 0%
Unemployed: 0%
Teaching quality assessed 1998–2000

THE LETTERS THAT APPEAR IN THE RESEARCH QUALITY COLUMN INDICATE THE PROPORTION OF STAFF INCLUDED IN THE ASSESSMENT, A SHOWING THAT ALMOST ALL STAFF WERE INCLUDED AND F SHOWING THAT HARDLY ANY WERE.

to all but two of the 13 undergraduate schools averaged more than 400 points on the UCAS tariff. Most demand chemistry and may give preference to candidates who also have biology A level.

One of the two 5* research ratings keeps King's College London at the top of the dentistry ranking. It was already one of four universities with full marks for teaching. Of the others, Manchester and Queen Mary move up – to second and third place respectively, while Queen's, Belfast drops to sixth. University College London is missing from the table because its Eastman Dental Institute has no undergraduates.

There are surprising variations in dentistry, judging by the indicators in our table. Although it entered a low proportion of academics for assessment, bottom-placed Bristol achieved the other top rating for research. By contrast, Queen's, Belfast, which has high entry grades and maximum points for teaching quality, has one of the two lowest grades for research. Newcastle, although not among the top scorers for teaching or research, has the highest entry grades.

No top grades were awarded in Scotland, although both Dundee and Glasgow were rated Highly Satisfactory for teaching. Cardiff, in the shape of the former University of Wales College of Medicine, offers the only dentistry degree in Wales and was awarded an Excellent teaching grade.

Most degrees last five years, although several universities offer a six-year option for those without the necessary scientific qualifications.

- **The British Dental Association:** www.bda-dentistry.org.uk

Drama, Dance and Cinematics

Five universities in England and one in Wales achieved maximum scores for teaching in this collection of performing arts, but it is the two research stars that dominate the table. Bristol retains top place, despite falling a point short of the maximum for teaching quality. It has the best employment record and among the highest entry standards. Second-placed Warwick was the other university rated internationally outstanding for research, as well as having one of the top teaching grades.

The remaining English universities with maximum points for teaching quality are Kent, Lancaster, Reading and Hull. There were no Excellent ratings in Scotland, but Glamorgan reached the standard in Wales. The top six places in the table remain unchanged from last year, but Bournemouth takes over as the leading new university.

This is another table where the gulf in entry standards between new and old universities is evident, with Birmingham and Warwick averaging over 400 points, compared with less than 200 points at several of those further down the ranking. The average tariff score is the lowest in any of the subject tables.

Employment scores also vary widely in a group of subjects where 8 per cent of graduates are without work six months after leaving university and more than 40 per cent are in non-graduate jobs. Only Goldsmiths, Northumbria and Queen's, Belfast, came close to Bristol's 80 per cent 'positive destinations', while none of those near the foot of the table reached 50 per cent. Freelancing and periods of temporary employment are common throughout the performing arts, but this does not seem to put off prospective students. Applications for dance were up by 34 per cent at the start of 2005 and those for the much larger pool of drama degrees by 20 per cent.

- **BBC:** www.bbc.co.uk
- **Metier:** www.metier.org.uk/php
- **SKILLSET:** www.skillset.org
- **The Stage:** www.thestage.co.uk

	Drama, Dance and Cinematics	Teaching Quality/24	Research Quality/5	Entry Standards	Graduate Prospects %	Overall Rating
1	Bristol	23	5*A	377	80	100.0
2	Warwick	24	5*B	403	60	99.1
3	Kent	24	5B	341	50	94.1
4	Reading	24	5B	339	50	94.0
5	Royal Holloway	23	5B	385	55	93.2
6	Lancaster	24	4A	396	35	92.7
7	Hull	24	4C	315	45	89.2
8	Loughborough	23	5C	375	40	88.6
9	Queen's, Belfast		3bA	313	75	87.5
10	Goldsmiths College	22	4A	349	45	87.0
11	Bournemouth	22	3bD	372	75	85.9
12	Brunel	23	3aB	288	45	85.5
13	Exeter	22	4B	348	40	85.2
14	Essex		4B	271	55	84.7
15	Glasgow	HS	4B	353		84.6

16	East Anglia	21	4A	372	35	83.2
=17	Manchester Metropolitan	23	3aD	264	50	82.7
=17	Northumbria	22	2C	268	75	82.7
=19	Surrey	20	4A	359	50	82.3
=19	Manchester	21	5C	385	35	82.3
21	Birmingham	21	4C	406	35	81.6
=22	Nottingham Trent		5C	271	45	81.4
=22	Roehampton	21	4B	265	50	81.4
24	Middlesex	22	3aD	264	60	81.3
25	Chichester UC	21	3aA	313	45	81.2
26	Ulster	22	3aB	209		80.8
27	Queen Margaret College	HS	3aD	307	65	80.6
28	Glamorgan	E	2C	235	55	80.3
29	De Montfort	22	3aC	228	45	79.4
30	Canterbury Christ Church UC	22		382	45	78.9
31	Aberystwyth	S	5B	295	40	78.1
32	Liverpool John Moores	21	2E	278	60	76.2
33	Sunderland	21	2D	248	60	76.0
34	Northampton UC	21	3bA	222	40	75.8
35	Salford	21		302	55	75.2
36	Leeds			312	60	74.2
37	Worcester UC		3aC	192	45	72.9
38	Queen Mary	21		300		72.8
39	Coventry			263	55	70.4
40	Plymouth	21		207	40	70.0
41	Westminster			248	55	69.6
42	Winchester UC	19	3bD	266	45	69.4
43	Bath Spa UC			231	55	68.8
44	Liverpool Hope UC	19		210	65	68.2
45	West of England			290	40	67.7
=46	Portsmouth			209	55	67.6
=46	Central Lancashire	20		250	35	67.6
48	Staffordshire	20		218	35	66.6
49	Wolverhampton	19		243	45	66.0
50	Sheffield Hallam	19		282	35	65.6
51	Bolton	20		152		64.0
52	Lincoln			240	35	63.9
53	East London	19		195		62.0
54	Buckinghamshire Chilterns UC			188	35	61.2
55	Huddersfield	17	3aD	213	30	60.5
56	Derby	18		207	30	59.7
57	Luton			192	25	58.7

Employed in graduate job: 31%
Employed in non-graduate job: 42%
Studying, not employed: 12%
Average starting salary: £13,387

Employed in graduate job and studying: 3%
Employed in non-graduate job and studying: 4%
Unemployed: 8%
Teaching quality assessed 1996–98

THE LETTERS THAT APPEAR IN THE RESEARCH QUALITY COLUMN INDICATE THE PROPORTION OF STAFF INCLUDED IN THE ASSESSMENT, A SHOWING THAT ALMOST ALL STAFF WERE INCLUDED AND F SHOWING THAT HARDLY ANY WERE.

East and South Asian Studies

The select group of universities offering East and South Asian Studies is back up to eight this year, with Nottingham offering new courses in Chinese. Student numbers are small – fewer than 1,000 students take the languages as their main subject, with Japanese still the largest recruiter – but the graduate employment record is generally good. Half the leavers go straight into graduate jobs and the unemployment rate is below average, at 6 per cent.

The subjects produced a high-scoring teaching quality assessment, although none was awarded maximum points. The last research grades were even higher, with both Oxford and Cambridge rated internationally outstanding. Cambridge retains top spot by virtue of that research record, with Nottingham entering the table in second place. Fifth-placed Oxford has by far the highest entry standards (in the absence of figures for Cambridge) but only three universities had enough graduates for prospects data to be compiled. Of these, London's School of Oriental and African Studies had by far the best record.

The subjects have not been assessed separately on teaching quality in Scotland, but Edinburgh holds onto fourth place, behind SOAS, which was one of the four top teaching centres in England. Cambridge, Leeds and Westminster – the only new university in the ranking – were the others.

Four out of five students enter with above-average tariff scores, so degree classifications are also high. Most undergraduates learn their chosen language from scratch, although universities expect to see evidence of potential in other modern language A levels.

- **The British Association for South Asian Studies:** www.basas.ac.uk
- **The Centre of South East Asian Studies:** www.soas.ac.uk/Centre/SouthEastAsia/aseasuk.html

East and South Asian Studies		Teaching Quality/24	Research Quality/5	Entry Standards	Graduate Prospects %	Overall Rating
1	Cambridge	23	5*B			100.0
2	Nottingham		5B	415		97.9
3	SOAS	23	5B	336	80	95.3
4	Edinburgh		5B	384		94.8
5	Oxford	22	5*B	496		88.3
6	Leeds	23	5C	314	50	86.4
7	Westminster	23	5E			83.7
8	Sheffield	22	4D	360	60	72.7

Employed in graduate job: 50%
Employed in non-graduate job: 24%
Studying, not employed: 11%
Average starting salary: £17,227

Employed in graduate job and studying: 7%
Employed in non-graduate job and studying: 2%
Unemployed: 6%
Teaching quality assessed 1996–98

THE LETTERS THAT APPEAR IN THE RESEARCH QUALITY COLUMN INDICATE THE PROPORTION OF STAFF INCLUDED IN THE ASSESSMENT, A SHOWING THAT ALMOST ALL STAFF WERE INCLUDED AND F SHOWING THAT HARDLY ANY WERE.

Economics

Average entry scores that are high even by its standards and the best graduate employment record keep Cambridge top of the economics ranking. Essex, University College London and second-placed Warwick all have perfect scores for teaching and research, although only UCL entered the maximum proportion of its academics for the last research assessment exercise. Essex comes lower in our table because of the relatively low tariff scores achieved by entrants – less than 300 points on average, compared with 518 at Cambridge.

A total of 15 English universities offering economics achieved maximum points for teaching quality. Among them were the new universities of Leeds Metropolitan, Oxford Brookes and Staffordshire, although low tariff scores prevented any of them breaking into the top 30. Controversially, the London School of Economics was not among them, dropping a point, despite being one of the four universities rated internationally outstanding for research and having the highest entry score after Oxbridge. It is also the only institution to get near to Cambridge's 90 per cent of leavers in graduate jobs or further study within six months of graduation.

St Andrews is the leading university in Scotland, although Aberdeen and Stirling also have Excellent ratings for teaching quality. Aberystwyth achieved the only Excellent teaching grade in Wales. Hertfordshire takes over as the leading new university, although not one of the top scorers for teaching quality.

Economics remains a popular option for undergraduates, with 34,000 applications at the start of 2005, although this represented a slight decline on the figure 12 months earlier. Employers look favourably because they see it as combining the skills of the sciences and the arts. But economics is not the sure-fire bet for a good job that many assume it to be: although two thirds of leavers are in graduate jobs or on postgraduate courses within six months, the 8 per cent unemployment rate is above average.

- **The European Economics Society:** www.eeassoc.org
- www.whystudyeconomics.ac.uk

Economics		Teaching Quality/24	Research Quality/5	Entry Standards	Graduate Prospects %	Overall Rating
1	Cambridge	24	5B	518	90	100.0
=2	Warwick	24	5*B	457	75	97.9
=2	University College London	24	5*A	432	70	97.9
4	London School of Economics	23	5*A	483	85	97.6
5	York	24	5A	429	70	96.1
6	Nottingham	24	5A	465	65	96.0
7	Bath	24	5B	371	80	95.4
8	Essex	24	5*B	287	80	95.2
9	Oxford	23	5B	500	80	94.3
10	Southampton	24	5A	377	60	93.4
11	Durham	24	4B	454	65	93.2
12	Bristol	23	4A	442	80	92.6
13	St Andrews	E	4B	408	65	91.8
=14	Lancaster		5*B	407	55	91.3
=14	Manchester	24	4B	363	65	91.3

		Teaching Quality/24	Research Quality/5	Entry Standards	Graduate Prospects %	Overall Rating
16	Stirling	E	4A	297	70	91.2
17	Queen's, Belfast	24	4B	307	65	90.2
18	Leicester	24	5B	316	50	89.5
19	Aberdeen	E	3aA	330	60	88.6
20	Birmingham	23	4B	395	65	88.3
21	Loughborough	23	3aB	343	70	86.5
22	Keele	23	3aA	295	70	86.2
23	Surrey	23	3aA	288	70	86.1
=24	Exeter	22	5B	388	65	86.0
=24	Newcastle	23	4C	358	65	86.0
26	Kent	23	4A	267	60	85.8
27	Royal Holloway	22	4B	346	75	85.2
=28	Aberystwyth	E	3bC	282	60	84.4
=28	Leeds	22	5C	400	65	84.4
=30	Edinburgh	S	4B	426	65	83.8
=30	Cardiff	S	5B	350	65	83.8
32	Hertfordshire	23	3aC			83.6
33	East Anglia	23	4B	300	45	83.1
34	Bangor	S	5B			82.4
35	Glasgow	S	4B	379	60	82.1
36	City	22	3aB	317	65	81.5
37	Swansea	S	4A	254	65	81.2
=38	Brunel	22	4A	292	50	81.0
=38	Liverpool	22	4B	296	55	81.0
=40	Oxford Brookes	24		258		80.8
=40	Queen Mary	21	5B	313	65	80.8
42	SOAS	21	4B	330	70	80.4
43	Hull	22	4C	292	60	80.1
44	Strathclyde	S	4C		65	79.4
45	Ulster	22	4C	240	60	79.1
46	Reading	21	5C	305	65	78.7
47	Leeds Metropolitan	24		246	45	78.2
48	Sheffield	21	3aB	373	60	78.1
49	Paisley	S	4C			77.8
50	Coventry	23		239	60	76.8
51	Sussex	21	4B	330	45	76.4
52	Heriot-Watt	S	4D	287	55	76.1
53	Portsmouth	21	4C	206	65	75.5
54	West of England	23		209	55	75.4
55	Northumbria	22	3bE	209	65	74.7
56	Nottingham Trent	22	3bD	237	50	73.9
57	Dundee	S	3aA	284	25	73.8
58	Salford	20	3aB	274	60	72.4

59	Plymouth		3bE	258	60	71.7
60	Wolverhampton	22	3bF			71.5
61	Liverpool John Moores	22		216		70.9
62	Manchester Metropolitan		3aC	216	40	70.5
63	Bradford	21	3bD	231		69.8
64	Anglia		2D		55	68.6
65	Middlesex	21		163	60	67.9
66	Kingston	21		171	50	66.4
67	East London	20	3aD			64.9
68	Greenwich	20	3bE	157	50	63.8

Employed in graduate job: 34%
Employed in non-graduate job: 27%
Studying, not employed: 16%
Average starting salary: £17,859

Employed in graduate job and studying: 10%
Employed in non-graduate job and studying: 4%
Unemployed: 8%
Teaching quality assessed 2000–01

THE LETTERS THAT APPEAR IN THE RESEARCH QUALITY COLUMN INDICATE THE PROPORTION OF STAFF INCLUDED IN THE ASSESSMENT, A SHOWING THAT ALMOST ALL STAFF WERE INCLUDED AND F SHOWING THAT HARDLY ANY WERE.

Education

There are big changes in the education ranking because of the use for the first time of Ofsted reports rather than the Quality Assurance Agency's teaching quality assessments. Academics have argued that Ofsted's more up-to-date judgments are a better reflection of teaching standards. The most obvious impact is to install Oxford at the head of the table – the absence of a QAA assessment had prevented it from appearing in previous versions of the ranking. It shares with Staffordshire the best teaching record, while its research grade is bettered only by Bristol and Cardiff.

Bristol was last year's leader but the university drops to fourth this time. Cambridge moves up to second, replacing Sheffield, which is the biggest casualty of the change of methodology, slipping out of the top ten. Three of the top four universities – and some further down the table – do not offer undergraduate teacher training, but qualify because they have assessments for both teaching and research. Their positions are a guide to the quality of PGCE courses, which are now the more popular route into teaching, especially for secondary education.

Third-placed Staffordshire is the only new university in the top 20, although it is joined by Canterbury Christ Church UC, which is soon to be a university itself. Hertfordshire is the only institution to boast immediate full employment (or further study) among its graduates. However, several others come close, even towards the foot of the table. The 3 per cent unemployment level is among the lowest for any subject, and more than 80 per cent of all those completing teacher training courses went into schools or postgraduate study.

Education remains one of the biggest subjects at degree level with more than 48,000 applications at the start of 2005 – an increase of 10 per cent. Entry grades have been creeping up – as the Teacher Training Agency has demanded – but the subject is still in the bottom five, with an average of only 250 points.

- **The Teacher Training Agency:** www.teach.gov.uk
- **The General Teaching Council for Scotland:** www.gtcs.org.uk
- **Learn Direct:** www.learndirect-advice.co.uk

		Teaching Quality/24	Research Quality/5	Entry Standards	Graduate Prospects %	Overall Rating
1	Oxford	4.0	5B			100.0
2	Cambridge	3.9	5B	396	96	97.7
3	Staffordshire	4.0	2B			94.9
4	Bristol	3.5	5*A			94.1
5	Aberdeen		5A	308	98	93.1
6	East Anglia	3.6	4B			92.4
7	Warwick	3.6	4B	338	86	92.0
8	Exeter	3.6	5C	299	94	90.7
9	Lancaster	3.4	5B	309		90.2
10	Newcastle	3.4	4B	342		89.6
11	Cardiff		5*A	304	62	88.8
12	Manchester	3.5	4C			88.6
13	Stirling		4C	317		88.5
14	Sheffield	3.2	5A			88.3
15	Sussex	3.3	5B			88.2
16	Bath	3.2	5B	311		88.0
17	King's College London	3.2	5B			87.3
18	Dundee		3aA	271	92	87.2
19	Canterbury Christ Church UC	3.4	3aE	328	96	86.7
20	Edinburgh		4D	307	92	86.4
21	Durham	3.2	5C	334	78	86.0
22	Aberystwyth		3aB	274		85.8
=23	Leeds	3.2	4B	304	82	85.6
=23	Birmingham	3.4	5B	273	60	85.6
25	Leicester	3.1	4B			84.4
26	Strathclyde		4E	311	88	84.3
27	Keele	3.2	3aB			84.2
=28	York	3.2	4B	314	58	83.9
=28	Brighton	3.3	3bD	252	96	83.9
30	Brunel	3.1	3aC	262	96	83.8
=31	Goldsmiths College	3.1	4C	253	92	83.7
=31	Nottingham	3.2	4C			83.7
33	Reading	3.1	3aC	276	96	83.6
34	Roehampton	3.5	3aE	213	84	83.3
35	Glasgow		4F	282	98	82.9
36	Sunderland	3.3	3aF	268	88	82.8
37	Paisley			302	94	82.5
38	Gloucestershire	3.2	3aE	275	82	82.4
39	London South Bank	3.0	4B			82.2
40	Manchester Metropolitan	3.2	4E	243	80	81.7
=41	Nottingham Trent	3.2	3bD	264	76	81.4
=41	Liverpool John Moores	3.3	3bF	237	82	81.4
43	West of England	3.1	3aE	264	88	81.2
=44	Southampton	3.0	4C			80.6

=44	Oxford Brookes	3.2	3bE	250	82	80.6
46	Liverpool Hope UC	3.2		221	90	80.4
47	Hertfordshire	3.0	3bE	230	100	80.3
48	Wolverhampton	3.2	2F	229	86	80.2
49	Central England	3.2	3bF	236	82	80.1
50	Winchester UC	3.1	3bE	258	80	80.0
51	UWIC, Cardiff			244	94	79.9
52	Plymouth	3.2	3aE	251	68	79.7
53	Bath Spa UC	3.3	2F	224	74	79.5
=54	Hull	2.9	3aD	253	86	79.1
=54	Luton	3.2			74	79.1
=54	Huddersfield	3.5	3bE	189	48	79.1
=54	Chichester UC	3.0	2D	223	94	79.1
58	Kingston	3.0		223	96	79.0
59	Northumbria	2.9	3bE	286	88	78.9
60	Sheffield Hallam	3.1	3aE	241	68	78.6
61	Central Lancashire		3bC	240	64	78.3
62	Anglia	2.9	3bD	238	84	78.2
=63	Bangor		3aF	241	80	78.0
=63	Worcester UC	3.1	3bD	221	66	78.0
65	University of Wales, Newport			212	84	76.9
66	Northampton UC	2.9	3bE	214	80	76.6
67	Greenwich	2.9	3aE	173	84	76.3
68	Leeds Metropolitan	2.8	3aE	253	72	76.1
69	Derby	2.9	3bD	218	64	75.8
70	De Montfort	2.8		198	94	75.7
71	Middlesex	2.6	2D	208	88	73.8
72	East London	2.7	3bD	163	72	72.8
73	Buckinghamshire Chilterns UC			171	40	68.0

Employed in graduate job: 70%
Employed in non-graduate job: 14%
Studying, not employed: 9%
Average starting salary: £17,548

Employed in graduate job and studying: 3%
Employed in non-graduate job and studying: 2%
Unemployed: 3%
Teaching quality assessed 2001

THE LETTERS THAT APPEAR IN THE RESEARCH QUALITY COLUMN INDICATE THE PROPORTION OF STAFF INCLUDED IN THE ASSESSMENT, A SHOWING THAT ALMOST ALL STAFF WERE INCLUDED AND F SHOWING THAT HARDLY ANY WERE.

Electrical and Electronic Engineering

Southampton again tops the table for electrical and electronic engineering with a perfect record in the teaching and research assessments. Imperial and Cambridge overtake Bristol to finish second and third respectively. Six universities were rated internationally outstanding for research in the last assessments, while ten English institutions achieved maximum points for teaching quality. Three Scottish universities and three in Wales were rated Excellent for teaching in their separate systems, although only Edinburgh was considered internationally outstanding for research. Huddersfield was the only new university among those with 24 points for teaching quality, while Glamorgan was rated Excellent in Wales.

Electrical and Electronic Engineering CONT.

Both entry standards and employment rates vary considerably among the 73 universities in the table. An impressive 95 per cent of leavers at Newcastle went straight into graduate jobs or further training, but at several universities the proportion dropped below half. Like computing, the subject has suffered from troubles in high-tech industries. Although half of the leavers nationally went straight into graduate jobs, the subjects have the highest unemployment rate of all, at 14 per cent. The gulf in entry standards is equally marked, with Imperial's entrants averaging nearly 500 points and several others less than 200. About half of the students – more in electrical engineering – come with qualifications other than A levels. Yet it is electrical engineering which has the higher proportion of firsts and 2:1s.

- **The Engineering Council (EC UK):** www.engc.org.uk
- **The Institution of Electrical Engineers:** www.iee.org

	Electrical and Electronic Engineering	Teaching Quality/24	Research Quality/5	Entry Standards	Graduate Prospects %	Overall Rating
1	Southampton	24	5*A	411	80	100.0
2	Imperial College	24	5B	494	75	98.1
3	Cambridge	23	5*A		90	97.7
4	Bristol	24	5A	401	80	97.0
=5	Queen's, Belfast	24	5A	376	75	94.9
=5	Sheffield	24	5*B	384	70	94.9
7	Surrey	23	5*A	313	85	93.2
8	York	24	3aA	384	80	91.1
9	Edinburgh	E	5*B	391	65	88.9
10	Loughborough	22	5B	386	85	88.2
=11	University College London	22	5A	392	75	88.1
=11	Hull	24	4C			88.1
13	Newcastle	21	5A	378	95	87.8
14	Essex	24	5B	246	70	86.9
15	Birmingham	24	5C	323	60	85.2
16	Manchester	22	5*B	347	65	84.8
17	Strathclyde	E	5B	366	60	84.5
18	Leeds	23	5*D	359	75	84.1
19	Nottingham	22	4A	352	70	82.8
20	Cardiff	E	5A	312	50	81.9
21	Warwick	21	5B	369	70	80.6
22	Liverpool	21	5A	295	75	80.3
23	Heriot-Watt	E	4B	362	50	80.0
24	Swansea	E	4C	263	80	79.7
25	Lancaster		4B	332	70	79.1
26	Reading	21	5B	320	60	76.6
27	Sussex	21	5B		60	76.1
28	Northumbria	22	3bC		80	75.5
29	Brunel	21	5B	312	55	75.2
30	Aston	21	5C	274	75	75.0
31	Kent	21	4C	286	75	73.6

32	Leicester		5A	303	40	73.4
33	Glasgow	S	5B	347	65	73.1
34	King's College London	20	5D	327	85	72.2
35	Huddersfield	24	3bF	246	60	71.8
36	Bath	20	4C	349	65	70.4
37	Queen Mary	21	3aB	266	55	68.8
38	City	21	3aC	179	75	67.4
39	Ulster	20	3bA	208	80	66.2
40	Bradford	21	4E	222	65	63.7
41	Westminster	21	4D	215	50	62.9
42	Aberdeen	S	4C		55	62.6
43	Brighton	20	3bC			59.9
44	Paisley	S	3aC	227	50	58.7
45	Robert Gordon	S	3bD	282	55	58.5
46	West of England	21		284	45	58.4
47	Teesside	21		181	65	58.3
48	Hertfordshire	20	3aD	198	55	58.2
49	Staffordshire	20	3bA	229	35	57.9
=50	Bangor	S	4B	212	25	57.1
=50	Glamorgan	E			20	57.1
=50	London South Bank	19	4D		55	57.1
=50	De Montfort	19	3aC			57.1
54	Nottingham Trent	20	3aE	245	50	57.0
55	Manchester Metropolitan	21		222	45	55.9
=56	Glasgow Caledonian	S	2C	236	45	54.3
=56	Portsmouth	20	2E	218	50	54.3
58	Dundee	S		298		54.1
59	Liverpool John Moores	18	3aD	206	65	53.1
60	Anglia	19	2C	205	50	52.1
61	Napier	S		189	60	52.0
62	Coventry	18	3aC			51.4
63	Greenwich	17	3aB	224	50	51.0
64	Bolton	20		117	60	50.9
65	Plymouth	18	4E		60	50.6
66	UWIC, Cardiff	S		188		48.8
67	Central England	19		205	50	48.7
68	Derby	19		227	45	48.5
69	Bournemouth	19		205		47.3
70	Sheffield Hallam	18		212	50	45.2
71	Leeds Metropolitan	17	3bC		35	41.9
72	Central Lancashire	15	3aE			28.1
73	East London	15	2D			27.3

Employed in graduate job: *42%*
Employed in non-graduate job: *24%*
Studying, not employed: *13%*
Average starting salary: *£18,085*

Employed in graduate job and studying: *5%*
Employed in non-graduate job and studying: *2%*
Unemployed: *14%*
Teaching quality assessed 1996–98

THE LETTERS THAT APPEAR IN THE RESEARCH QUALITY COLUMN INDICATE THE PROPORTION OF STAFF INCLUDED IN THE ASSESSMENT, A SHOWING THAT ALMOST ALL STAFF WERE INCLUDED AND F SHOWING THAT HARDLY ANY WERE.

English

Oxford is back on top of the English rankings after surrendering the lead to Cambridge for a year. Oxford boasted the best-qualified entrants and maximum points for research, and only two universities had a better graduate employment record. The margins are so slender at the top of the table that both York and Durham overtake Cambridge, partly because they entered a higher proportion of academics in the last research assessment exercise.

Teaching grades were dropped because of the age of assessments that took place over a decade ago, but the 2001 research assessments were generous. A total of 13 universities have 5* ratings for research, including all the top nine in our table. Cardiff is clearly the leading university in Wales, but St Andrews has taken over the top place in Scotland from Edinburgh.

No new university makes the top 20, but De Montfort's strong performance in the research assessment exercise and a relatively good employment score leave it ahead of the other former polytechnics in 28th place. The employment stars were Brighton – where an extraordinary 96 per cent of leavers went straight into graduate jobs or further study – and Derby where the proportion was still impressive at 74 per cent. Nationally, more than a third of those completing English degrees in 2003 were in non-graduate jobs six months later.

Entry standards remain high in most English departments: the average was 400 points or more at 14 universities and only two of the top 30 dropped below 300. However, it is still possible to win a place with 200 points at a handful of former polytechnics.

Competition is certain to remain intense. More than 54,000 applied for places at the start of 2005, an increase of 5 per cent on the previous year.

The proportion of English students gaining a first or 2:1, at seven out of ten, is among the highest in any subject. Almost a third of all graduates go on to further study, and the 7 per cent unemployment rate is no more than average for all subjects. But the table shows big variations, with a minority of students at 20 universities finding graduate jobs or study places within six months of graduation.

- **Book Careers:** www.bookcareers.com
- **The Publishers' Association:** www.publishers.org.uk
- **Teaching English as a Foreign Language:** www.eflweb.com
- **The Writers' Room:** www.bbc.co.uk/writersroom

English		Research Quality/5	Entry Standards	Graduate Prospects %	Overall Rating
1	Oxford	5*A	475	70	100.0
2	York	5*A	457	70	99.3
3	Durham	5*A	468	66	98.5
4	Cambridge	5*B	462	70	97.8
5	University College London	5*A	414	70	97.5
6	Leeds	5*A	424	62	95.5
7	St Andrews	5*B	429	62	94.0
8	Warwick	5*B	431	60	93.4
9	Edinburgh	5*A	415	56	93.3
10	Bristol	5C	450	70	92.8
11	Newcastle	5A	396	64	92.7

12	Cardiff	5*B	396	60	92.0
13	Sheffield	5B	422	60	91.1
14	Nottingham	5A	440	52	90.8
=15	Royal Holloway	5A	368	60	90.3
=15	Queen's, Belfast	5A	322	66	90.3
17	Leicester	5A	346	62	90.0
18	Liverpool	5*B	373	56	89.8
19	Manchester	5B	399	58	89.5
20	Southampton	5A	364	54	88.3
21	Queen Mary	5A	316	60	88.2
22	King's College London	4B	400	60	88.1
=23	Glasgow	5*B	357	50	87.3
=23	Exeter	5B	406	50	87.3
25	Sussex	5B	381	52	86.9
26	Birmingham	5C	391	58	86.7
27	Kent	5B	313	58	86.0
=28	Aberdeen	4B	299	64	85.2
=28	De Montfort	5A	229	62	85.2
30	Lancaster	5A	361	44	85.1
=31	Reading	5*B	328	46	84.9
=31	Swansea	4A	290	60	84.9
33	Brighton		272	96	84.1
34	Loughborough	5C	354	54	84.0
=35	East Anglia	5B	392	40	83.7
=35	London South Bank	4B		58	83.7
37	Keele	5B	342	46	83.5
38	Essex	4B	295	58	83.2
39	Nottingham Trent	5C	287	60	83.1
40	Hull	5B	281	52	82.8
=41	Salford	5A	287	42	81.5
=41	Strathclyde	5B	323	42	81.5
=43	Anglia	5C	231	62	81.4
=43	Oxford Brookes	5C	304	52	81.4
45	Roehampton	4B	232	60	81.3
=46	Aberystwyth	4B	306	50	81.2
=46	Gloucestershire	4A	216	58	81.2
=46	Northumbria	3aC	290	64	81.2
=49	Goldsmiths College	5A	311	36	80.6
=49	Liverpool John Moores	4C	250	62	80.6
51	Bath Spa UC	4B	282	50	80.2
52	West of England	4B	284	48	79.7
53	Sheffield Hallam	4B	287	46	79.2
54	Dundee	4A	298	40	79.0
55	Middlesex	4D	218	68	78.8
56	Sunderland	4C	207	60	78.2
=57	Brunel	3aB	276	50	78.0
=57	Stirling	5B	312	32	78.0
59	Hertfordshire	3aB	229	56	77.9

		Research Quality/5	Entry Standards	Graduate Prospects %	Overall Rating
60	Chichester UC	3aA	202	56	77.8
61	Central Lancashire	3aC	251	56	77.2
62	Kingston	3aB	228	52	76.6
63	Ulster	4C	223	52	76.4
=64	Plymouth	3aB	251	48	76.3
=64	Derby		247	74	76.3
66	Manchester Metropolitan	4C	242	48	76.0
67	Liverpool Hope UC	3bE	212	70	75.5
68	Worcester UC	3bC	247	56	75.4
69	Winchester UC	3aD	260	54	75.1
70	Glamorgan	4B	193	44	74.8
71	Lincoln		263	66	74.5
72	Bangor	4B	280	30	74.0
73	Portsmouth	4C	238	40	73.3
74	Wolverhampton		216	68	73.2
=75	Northampton UC	4C	231	40	73.1
=75	Greenwich		198	70	73.1
77	Central England	3aD	217	52	72.7
78	Teesside		190	66	71.5
79	Leeds Metropolitan		263	56	71.4
80	Westminster	3bD	253	44	70.6
81	Staffordshire	3aD	208	46	70.5
82	Canterbury Christ Church UC		246	46	67.7

Employed in graduate job: 28%
Employed in non-graduate job: 35%
Studying, not employed: 22%
Average starting salary: £14,177

Employed in graduate job and studying: 3%
Employed in non-graduate job and studying: 5%
Unemployed: 7%

THE LETTERS THAT APPEAR IN THE RESEARCH QUALITY COLUMN INDICATE THE PROPORTION OF STAFF INCLUDED IN THE ASSESSMENT, A SHOWING THAT ALMOST ALL STAFF WERE INCLUDED AND F SHOWING THAT HARDLY ANY WERE.

Food Science

Nottingham remains on top of the food science table, widening the gap slightly over King's College London. King's has the highest entry standards in the ranking, but Nottingham has the better employment record and entered more of its academics in the 2001 Research Assessment Exercise. The top two have the highest teaching ratings in England, although Robert Gordon and UWIC, Cardiff both achieved Excellent grades in the Scottish and Welsh systems.

Only third-placed Surrey and Leeds, which has dropped to eighth, managed 5* grades for research. Queen Margaret College in Edinburgh had the best employment score, with all its leavers finding graduate jobs or study places within six months. Most of the institutions

Food Science

		Teaching Quality/24	Research Quality/5	Entry Standards	Graduate Prospects %	Overall Rating
1	Nottingham	23	5A	308	90	100.0
2	King's College London	23	5B	353	70	98.1
3	Surrey	21	5*A	304	95	97.2
4	Reading	22	5A	283	80	95.3
5	Queen Margaret College	E			100	94.2
6	Robert Gordon	E	3bE		90	93.4
7	UWIC, Cardiff	E	3bC	255	80	91.7
8	Leeds	20	5*C	299	85	91.4
9	Queen's, Belfast	21	4C			90.7
10	Plymouth	22	3aE			90.4
11	Leeds Metropolitan		3bC	289	85	89.9
12	Ulster			283	90	87.3
13	Glasgow Caledonian	HS		275	80	87.0
14	Northumbria	21	2E		75	86.2
15	Sheffield Hallam			270	85	85.1
16	Newcastle			301	70	83.3
17	Huddersfield	20		182	85	81.9
18	Oxford Brookes	20			65	81.1
19	Manchester Metropolitan	19			70	79.4
20	Bath Spa UC			244	65	78.3
21	London South Bank	18	3aE			77.3
22	Teesside	17	2B			74.9

Employed in graduate job: 61%
Employed in non-graduate job: 15%
Studying, not employed: 12%
Average starting salary: £17,272

Employed in graduate job and studying: 5%
Employed in non-graduate job and studying: 2%
Unemployed: 4%
Teaching quality assessed 1996–98

THE LETTERS THAT APPEAR IN THE RESEARCH QUALITY COLUMN INDICATE THE PROPORTION OF STAFF INCLUDED IN THE ASSESSMENT, A SHOWING THAT ALMOST ALL STAFF WERE INCLUDED AND F SHOWING THAT HARDLY ANY WERE.

offering food science are new universities, with Robert Gordon, UWIC, Cardiff and Plymouth also making the top ten.

Entry standards are relatively low: only King's, Nottingham, Surrey and Newcastle average more than 300 points. Almost a third of entrants to food science courses arrive with alternative qualifications to A levels. Although there were only 1,600 applications at the start of 2005, this represented a rise of almost a third. The demand for places has grown substantially in each of the last three years.

Assessors in England were concerned at the high drop-out rate on more than half of the courses: more than 20 per cent of students failed to progress to the next stage of their degree. Career prospects are good, however, with 80 per cent of graduates going straight into graduate-level work or further study and only 4 per cent unemployed.

- **The Institute of Food Science and Technology:** www.foodtechcareers.org

French

Cambridge remains the top university for French, with Oxford now the only serious challenger. The ancient rivals were among seven universities awarded 5* research grades and three with the top employment scores but, while Oxford also has the highest entry standards, it loses out to Cambridge on teaching scores. The teaching assessments were among the toughest in any subject. No English university was awarded maximum points, but two former polytechnics – Westminster and Portsmouth – shared the best score with sixth-placed Queen Mary. Aberdeen and Glasgow have Excellent teaching grades from the Scottish system, but in Wales, none of the grades was better than Satisfactory.

French		Teaching Quality/24	Research Quality/5	Entry Standards	Graduate Prospects %	Overall Rating
1	Cambridge	22	5*A	475	80	100.0
2	Oxford	21	5*A	484	80	97.1
3	Glasgow	E	5B	388	70	94.5
4	Durham	22	5B	438	70	94.1
5	Aberdeen	E	5*A	366	45	93.2
6	Queen Mary	23	5A	264	65	92.7
7	St Andrews	22	4B	430	70	92.1
8	Liverpool	22	5A	339	65	91.7
9	Sussex	22	4A	362	70	91.2
10	Newcastle	22	4A	357	65	90.3
=11	University College London	21	5A	392	65	90.1
=11	King's College London	21	5A	362	70	90.1
13	Sheffield	21	5B	394	70	89.7
14	Oxford Brookes	22	5B	266	70	89.2
15	Bristol	20	5A	407	75	89.1
16	Exeter	22	4B	351	65	89.0
17	Leeds	22	4B	373	60	88.9
18	Warwick	21	5A	397	55	88.7
19	Edinburgh	HS	5C	418	65	87.6
20	Royal Holloway	21	5*A	328	45	87.1
21	Aston	22	5C	312	60	86.8
=22	Stirling	HS	5B	316		86.6
=22	Heriot-Watt	21	4B	458	50	86.6
24	Kingston	21	4A		55	85.4
25	Strathclyde	22	4C	394	45	85.3
26	Portsmouth	23	5C	232	45	85.2
27	Westminster	23	3aD	274		84.5
28	Cardiff	S	5A	350	65	84.3
29	Queen's, Belfast	20	4A	356	65	84.0
30	Salford	20	5A	325	55	83.5
31	Hull	21	4B	317	55	83.4
32	Northumbria	23	3bE	270	65	82.8

Oxford, Royal Holloway, Southampton, Birmingham and Manchester are the other institutions rated internationally outstanding for research. Bradford was the other top performer on graduate employment, with 80 per cent of leavers reporting 'positive destinations'. The subject still commands high entry grades, with nine universities averaging more than 400 points and only one less than 200.

French remains the most popular language for a first degree, with applications rising by 13 per cent at the start of 2005. Nine out of ten undergraduates enter with A levels or equivalents. Two thirds go on to graduate jobs or further study within six months and the

33	Swansea	S	4A	286	75	82.1
34	Bath	19	5A	346	60	81.8
35	Reading	21	5B	265	40	81.3
36	Lancaster	20	5C	392	50	81.2
37	Kent	19	4A	300	75	80.9
38	York	22		409		80.8
39	Central Lancashire	21	3bA		55	80.7
40	Aberystwyth	S	3aA	271	75	79.7
41	Birmingham	18	5*C	371	70	79.0
=42	Manchester	19	5*C	356	45	77.7
=42	Southampton	18	5*A	325	45	77.7
44	Ulster	20	4C	246	55	76.4
45	Brighton	20	5E		65	76.0
46	Nottingham	16	5A	422	60	74.6
47	Anglia	21	2C		40	74.0
48	Coventry	21		194	70	73.6
=49	Plymouth		3bA		55	73.4
=49	East Anglia	19	3bB	365	45	73.4
51	Leicester	19	3aB	273	50	73.3
52	Bradford	18	4D		80	73.1
53	Keele	20	2A		45	72.6
54	West of England	21		261	50	72.3
55	Wolverhampton	19	3aA		35	71.7
=56	Sheffield Hallam	21		258	45	71.4
=56	Roehampton	19	3aC			71.4
=58	Surrey	18	5C			70.9
=58	Manchester Metropolitan	21			40	70.9
60	Bangor	S	4D	286	25	69.3
61	Middlesex	19	3aD			68.9
62	Nottingham Trent	17	4B	227	55	68.4
63	Liverpool John Moores	19		209	60	66.2
64	Goldsmiths College	17	4C			64.2
65	Napier	19		244		63.9

Employed in graduate job: 34%
Employed in non-graduate job: 32%
Studying, not employed: 21%
Average starting salary: £15,054

Employed in graduate job and studying: 5%
Employed in non-graduate job and studying: 4%
Unemployed: 5%
Teaching quality assessed 1996–98

THE LETTERS THAT APPEAR IN THE RESEARCH QUALITY COLUMN INDICATE THE PROPORTION OF STAFF INCLUDED IN THE ASSESSMENT, A SHOWING THAT ALMOST ALL STAFF WERE INCLUDED AND F SHOWING THAT HARDLY ANY WERE.

French CONT.

5 per cent unemployment rate is below average for all subjects. The teaching assessments were carried out in 1995–96 and, at the time, assessors said that some universities had failed to think through the new teaching approaches that they were applying. However, some departments have changed radically in the intervening period.

- **CILT – The National Centre for Languages:** www.cilt.org.uk
- **The Institute of Translation and Interpreting:** www.iti.org.uk

General Engineering

Cambridge holds on to the top place it regained from Southampton last year, with the best graduate employment score. The top four all have 5* research grades, although Imperial entered a lower proportion of academics for assessment. Oxford takes second place with the highest entry standards.

General engineering produced another tough set of teaching assessments: no university was awarded maximum points. The top four all have 23 points out of 24, and the subject was not assessed separately in Scotland. Sheffield Hallam's 21 points represented the best teaching score in the new universities. It was enough to secure a place in the top 20, but not to catch Hertfordshire, Wolverhampton or Liverpool John Moores, which also held onto an exceptional grade 5 for research, but had among the lowest entry grades and teaching score.

As in the specialist branches of engineering, entry grades vary enormously, from over 500 points at Oxford and Cambridge to less than 100 at De Montfort. More than 10,000 undergraduates take general engineering courses, rather than specialising. Employment prospects are close to the norm for all engineering courses, with eight out of ten going straight into graduate jobs or further study, but the 10 per cent unemployment rate is well above average for all subjects. The assessors of teaching in England found that the courses nurtured the transferable skills required for later specialisation, but they worried about first-year dropout rates.

- **The Engineering Learning Information Portal:** www.elip.info
- **The Engineering Council (EC UK):** www.engc.org.uk

General Engineering		Teaching Quality/24	Research Quality/5	Entry Standards	Graduate Prospects %	Overall Rating
1	Cambridge	23	5*A	527	90	100.0
2	Oxford	23	5*A	539	85	98.9
3	Southampton	23	5*A			98.1
4	Imperial College	23	5*B	454		94.7
5	Durham	22	5B	458	80	87.6
6	Brunel	22	5B	297		82.4
7	Nottingham		4B	457		82.0
8	Warwick	21	5B	369	70	78.3
9	Strathclyde		5A	376	60	76.9
10	Leicester	20	5A			75.3

11	Lancaster	22	4B	305	55	75.0
12	Exeter	20	4C	290	65	66.7
13	Bradford	20	3bC			62.7
14	Hertfordshire	20	3aD	253		61.9
15	Wolverhampton	20	3aB	204	50	60.4
16	Cardiff			328	75	59.7
17	Liverpool John Moores	18	5A	131	65	59.2
18	Sheffield Hallam	21	3aF	133	60	58.8
19	Liverpool	20		301		58.4
20	Central Lancashire	20	3aE		50	55.8
21	Napier		4D	192		55.7
22	Central England	19	3bF	193	70	54.1
23	West of England		3bD	204	55	50.3
24	Queen Mary	19		181		49.5
25	Bournemouth	18	3bF	287	60	49.4
26	Greenwich	17	3aB			47.9
27	De Montfort	19		89		46.7
28	Coventry	18			55	44.1
29	Glamorgan			182	55	44.0
30	Leeds Metropolitan	17	3bC			43.2

Employed in graduate job: 48%
Employed in non-graduate job: 21%
Studying, not employed: 14%
Average starting salary: £19,327

Employed in graduate job and studying: 7%
Employed in non-graduate job and studying: 1%
Unemployed: 10%
Teaching quality assessed 1996–98

THE LETTERS THAT APPEAR IN THE RESEARCH QUALITY COLUMN INDICATE THE PROPORTION OF STAFF INCLUDED IN THE ASSESSMENT, A SHOWING THAT ALMOST ALL STAFF WERE INCLUDED AND F SHOWING THAT HARDLY ANY WERE.

Geography

There are big changes in the geography table this year, partly because it includes most of the scores previously listed under environmental science. It has become increasingly difficult to distinguish environmental courses from the rest of geography, and a single ranking was considered more representative of overall quality. The most obvious change is that Cambridge has moved up from third to first place, with the London School of Economics and Bristol also overtaking last year's leader, Durham. Cambridge has the highest entry standards and the best employment record, although it was not one of the six universities rated internationally outstanding for research.

The LSE also missed out on the 5* research grade, which went to Bristol, Durham, University College London, Edinburgh, Royal Holloway and Cardiff. Teaching grades have been removed from the ranking because of their age. Excellence in research helps Edinburgh retain the top place in Scotland, and Cardiff the same for Wales. While entries to seven of the top eleven universities average more than 400 points, even some old universities average less than 300 and the figure dips below 200 at a number of former polytechnics. None of the new universities makes the top 30 but Plymouth is the best-placed, just ahead of Sunderland, which has one of the best employment scores.

Geography CONT.

Geography and environmental sciences have been benefiting from rising interest in 'green' issues among potential students. Applications for physical geography and environmental sciences were up by another 9 per cent at the start of 2005, although demand for human geography declined for the second successive year.

In the latest survey, more than a third of graduates were in low-level jobs six months after completing their courses, but the unemployment rate was no higher than average for all subjects. Universities are more tightly bunched in this table than many others in terms of their graduates' success in the jobs market, but still less than half of those leaving some lowly-placed institutions went straight into graduate work or higher-level courses.

- **The Royal Geographical Society:** www.rgs.org
- **The British Ecological Society:** www.britishecologicalsociety.org

Geography		Research Quality/5	Entry Standards	Graduate Prospects %	Overall Rating
1	Cambridge	5A	490	88	100.0
=2	London School of Economics	5A	398	82	93.3
=2	Bristol	5*A	441	68	93.3
4	Durham	5*A	426	70	93.2
5	University College London	5*A	395	74	92.9
6	Oxford	4A	485	72	92.2
7	Nottingham	5B	426	74	90.7
8	Edinburgh	5*A	393	62	88.9
9	Newcastle	5A	343	76	88.6
10	East Anglia	4A	414	70	87.9
11	St Andrews	4B	420	70	87.0
12	Sheffield	5A	395	56	84.7
13	Royal Holloway	5*A	323	58	84.0
14	Loughborough	5B	346	64	83.3
15	Leeds	5B	355	62	83.2
16	Southampton	5A	367	52	82.0
17	Birmingham	4B	378	60	81.6
18	Reading	4A	346	60	81.2
19	Cardiff	5*A	334	46	80.7
20	Queen Mary	5A	257	62	79.7
21	Glasgow	4C	352	64	79.5
22	Exeter	4B	368	54	79.2
23	Aberystwyth	4A	296	58	78.1
=24	Sussex	4B	304	60	77.8
=24	Queen's, Belfast	4A	291	58	77.8
=24	Manchester	4B	354	52	77.8
27	King's College London	4A	312	54	77.5
28	Aberdeen	4B	300	58	77.0
=29	Hull	5B	292	52	76.7
=29	Swansea	4A	282	56	76.7

=29	Dundee	4A	244	62	76.7
32	Lancaster	4A	315	50	76.4
33	Liverpool	4A	301	50	75.7
34	Strathclyde	3aC	340	56	74.6
35	Plymouth	4B	268	54	74.1
36	Sunderland	3bC	205	76	72.6
37	Leicester	4B	287	46	72.4
38	Brunel	3aB	272	54	72.2
39	Liverpool Hope UC	3bC	193	76	72.0
40	Coventry	3aB	235	54	70.3
41	Hertfordshire	2B	221	68	70.0
42	De Montfort		257	74	69.9
43	Gloucestershire	3aC	246	56	69.8
44	Bradford	3bD	199	72	69.6
45	Nottingham Trent	3aB	239	50	69.2
46	Kingston	3bB	175	66	69.1
=47	Manchester Metropolitan	4C	232	50	68.8
=47	Canterbury Christ Church UC		312	62	68.8
=49	Brighton	3bB	224	56	68.3
=49	Bangor		276	66	68.3
51	Teesside		203	76	67.8
52	Keele	3aB	273	40	67.7
=53	Ulster	3bC	224	54	66.4
=53	Northumbria	3bD	239	56	66.4
55	Portsmouth	3aB	254	36	65.4
56	UWIC, Cardiff		175	72	65.1
57	Derby		229	62	64.6
58	Huddersfield	2B	203	54	64.5
59	Liverpool John Moores	3bC	221	48	64.3
60	Greenwich	3bE	147	68	64.2
61	Bath Spa UC	2A	205	48	63.2
62	Oxford Brookes		244	54	62.7
63	Worcester UC	2C	182	54	62.6
64	Bournemouth	2D	211	52	62.5
65	Staffordshire	3bC	226	40	62.0
66	Wolverhampton		188	52	59.2
67	Chichester UC		206	48	58.8
68	Northampton UC	2B	202	36	58.6
69	West of England	2D	234	36	58.5
70	Glamorgan		235	40	57.7
71	Stirling		308	20	54.9
72	Central Lancashire		194	24	50.4

Employed in graduate job: 32%
Employed in non-graduate job: 35%
Studying, not employed: 20%
Average starting salary: £14,722

Employed in graduate job and studying: 4%
Employed in non-graduate job and studying: 3%
Unemployed: 7%

THE LETTERS THAT APPEAR IN THE RESEARCH QUALITY COLUMN INDICATE THE PROPORTION OF STAFF INCLUDED IN THE ASSESSMENT, A SHOWING THAT ALMOST ALL STAFF WERE INCLUDED AND F SHOWING THAT HARDLY ANY WERE.

Geology

Slightly higher entry grades continue to keep Cambridge ahead of Oxford in geology. With the teaching grades dropped because of their age, the four 5* research grades assume added importance, their holders again filling the top four places. Bristol and Imperial College London, the other research stars, swap places but neither comes within 100 points of the exceptionally high entry grades at Oxbridge.

Ninth-placed Exeter has the best employment score – Cambridge does not publish separate data for geology – in a subject in which only two universities saw less than half of the leavers go straight into graduate jobs or further study. Edinburgh remains the top university in Scotland, as Cardiff does in Wales.

Geology		Research Quality/5	Entry Standards	Graduate Prospects %	Overall Rating
1	Cambridge	5*A	542		100.0
2	Oxford	5*A	521	75	96.2
3	Bristol	5*A	378	70	88.7
4	Imperial College	5*A	389	65	87.7
5	Liverpool	5A	326	75	85.3
6	University College London	5B	343	75	84.4
7	Leeds	5A	322	70	83.7
8	Edinburgh	5A	362	60	82.7
=9	Exeter	4B	285	85	82.5
=9	Durham	4B	415	65	82.5
11	Cardiff	5A	313	65	82.0
12	Southampton	5A	334	55	80.0
13	St Andrews	4B	375	60	79.3
=14	Royal Holloway	5B	310	60	78.8
=14	Glasgow	4B	361		78.8
16	Reading	3aB	372		76.1
17	Manchester	5B	302	50	75.6
18	Kingston	4B	225	65	74.3
19	Leicester	4A	257	50	72.8
20	Birmingham	3aC	335	55	72.1
21	Aberdeen	4C	302	50	71.1
22	Plymouth	4C	255	50	69.1
23	Keele	3aB	286	35	66.2
24	Portsmouth	3bA	231	45	65.2
25	Aberystwyth		270	55	62.4
26	Staffordshire		242	50	59.8

Employed in graduate job: 29%
Employed in non-graduate job: 31%
Studying, not employed: 27%
Average starting salary: £15,172

Employed in graduate job and studying: 2%
Employed in non-graduate job and studying: 2%
Unemployed: 8%

THE LETTERS THAT APPEAR IN THE RESEARCH QUALITY COLUMN INDICATE THE PROPORTION OF STAFF INCLUDED IN THE ASSESSMENT, A SHOWING THAT ALMOST ALL STAFF WERE INCLUDED AND F SHOWING THAT HARDLY ANY WERE

Only four new universities appear in the table, but Kingston makes the top 20 with a consistent set of scores. Oxbridge apart, there is less contrast in entry standards than in many other subjects. The average is well above 200 points at every university and above 300 in all but eight. Six out of ten geology students go on to graduate jobs or further study within six months of graduation, but the unemployment level is slightly above average for all subjects, at 8 per cent. Nevertheless, applications were down by 2 per cent when the official deadline passed for courses beginning in 2005.

- **The Geological Society:** www.geolsoc.org

German

Cambridge becomes the third different university in three years to top the ranking for German, despite dropping two points in the teaching assessment. Only Oxford, which dropped three points for teaching, has higher entry qualifications and just two universities boast a better employment record. Exeter, the only university in England to win full marks for teaching quality, regains second place, condemning last year's leader – University College London – to third.

Swansea was rated as Excellent for teaching under the Welsh system and is the leading university in the Principality, but was not among the ten universities rated internationally outstanding for research. Edinburgh, one of those with a 5* research grade, remains the leader in Scotland. All the top four also have maximum research ratings, as do King's College London, Manchester, Birmingham, Southampton and Royal Holloway. UCL, Warwick, Queen Mary and Northumbria all came close to maximum points for teaching quality. Kingston is the highest-placed new university and the only one in the top 20.

Almost 60 universities offer German, but the total number of students is now below 2,000, including certificate and diploma courses. However, there were signs of resurgence at the start of 2005, when applications were up by almost 20 per cent. Nine out of ten enter with A levels or equivalent qualifications, and entry standards are relatively high, especially at the leading universities. Only five of the top 20 averaged less than 350 points. Employment scores ranged from 90 per cent 'positive destinations' at Aston to only 30 per cent at Reading. But, as in other modern languages, career prospects are reasonable: although only two thirds of leavers go straight into graduate jobs or further study, the unemployment rate is below average.

Teaching assessments in England extended to Dutch and Scandinavian languages, as related languages, and the assessors were impressed with the general standard of provision. The main difficulty facing the subject is a shortage of A-level candidates, but most universities in the table teach it *ab initio* as part of a languages package.

- **CILT – The National Centre for Languages:** www.cilt.org.uk
- **The Institute of Translation and Interpreting:** www.iti.org.uk

German	Teaching Quality/24	Research Quality/5	Entry Standards	Graduate Prospects %	Overall Rating
1 Cambridge	22	5*A	475	80	100.0
2 Exeter	24	5*A	344	60	99.1
3 University College London	23	5*A	394	70	99.0

		Teaching Quality/24	Research Quality/5	Entry Standards	Graduate Prospects %	Overall Rating
4	Nottingham	22	5*A	434	65	96.1
5	Queen Mary	23	5A	301		94.6
6	Edinburgh	21	5*B	413	85	93.8
7	Oxford	21	5A	485	65	92.2
8	Durham	22	4A		75	92.1
9	Warwick	23	5A	398	40	91.9
10	Swansea	E	5A	268		91.7
11	Newcastle	22	4A			91.4
12	Bristol	21	5B	408	80	90.8
13	Aston	22	5C	304	90	90.1
14	Aberdeen	22	4A	341		89.4
15	King's College London	20	5*A	374	70	88.2
16	Glasgow	22	4C	364		86.5
17	Kingston	21	4A			86.3
18	Manchester	21	5*B	359	50	86.1
19	Leeds	22	4C	350	65	85.8
20	Heriot-Watt	21	4B	458	50	85.4
21	Sheffield	20	4A	399	70	84.7
22	Salford	20	5A			84.5
23	St Andrews	22	4C		55	84.2
=24	Birmingham	19	5*B	362	70	82.8
=24	Northumbria	23	3bE	282	75	82.8
26	Cardiff	S	5A	346	65	82.6
27	Aberystwyth	S	4A	317	70	80.3
28	Strathclyde	22	3bB		45	79.8
29	Lancaster	19	5C	343	80	79.5
=30	Bath	19	5A	349	55	79.3
=30	Hull	21	3aC		60	79.3
32	Portsmouth	21	5C		40	79.0
=33	Central Lancashire	21	3bA		55	78.6
=33	Liverpool	19	5A	328	55	78.6
35	Southampton	18	5*A	341	50	77.0
36	Stirling	20	4C			76.5
37	Oxford Brookes	19	4B		65	76.4
38	Bangor	S	3aA	331		76.3
39	Queen's, Belfast	19	4A			76.2
40	Royal Holloway	19	5*C	331	50	75.6
41	Kent	19	4B		60	75.4
42	Anglia	21	2C			74.5
43	Brighton	20	5E		65	73.5
44	Reading	20	4B	269	30	72.4
45	Keele	19	3aA		50	72.2
46	Sussex	17	4A	276	75	71.4
47	Coventry	21		194	70	70.6

48	West of England	21		261	50	69.3
49	Manchester Metropolitan	21			45	68.9
50	Surrey	18	5C			68.7
51	Ulster	19	3aC	246	50	68.1
52	East Anglia	19	3bB		45	67.7
53	Liverpool John Moores	19			65	64.9
54	Robert Gordon	19	3bD			64.7
55	Nottingham Trent	17	3aB	227	55	63.2
56	Wolverhampton	17	3aA			62.7
57	Sheffield Hallam	19		258	45	61.6
58	Goldsmiths College	17	4C			61.3
59	Napier	19		244		60.6

Employed in graduate job: 36%
Employed in non-graduate job: 30%
Studying, not employed: 20%
Average starting salary: £15,352

Employed in graduate job and studying: 6%
Employed in non-graduate job and studying: 4%
Unemployed: 5%
Teaching quality assessed 1995–96

THE LETTERS THAT APPEAR IN THE RESEARCH QUALITY COLUMN INDICATE THE PROPORTION OF STAFF INCLUDED IN THE ASSESSMENT, A SHOWING THAT ALMOST ALL STAFF WERE INCLUDED AND F SHOWING THAT HARDLY ANY WERE.

History

Cambridge is top again for history, with the best employment record and entry qualifications, as well as one of eight 5* research ratings. Another of the research stars went to Oxford Brookes, one of the few new universities to achieve this level in any subject in the 2001 Research Assessment Exercise. The accolade helps keep the university in the top 20, easily the best-placed new university.

Durham holds on to second place, while the London School of Economics moves up to third. Both are rated internationally outstanding for research, as are King's College London, the School of Oriental and African Studies and East Anglia. St Andrews remains the top university in Scotland, while Cardiff does the same in Wales. Swansea lost the benefit of the only Excellent teaching grade in Wales when the teaching scores were removed. History grades were among the first to be produced, almost a decade ago, and there have been big changes in many departments.

History remains one of the most popular subjects: it was in the top ten again in terms of total applications at the beginning of 2005, having registered another 9 per cent increase. Only two of the top 20 had average entry scores of less than 350 points and only three of the 81 institutions in the ranking dropped below an average of 200 points.

Career prospects are mixed: surveys have shown a strong representation of historians among business leaders, celebrities and senior politicians, but more than a third are in non-graduate jobs six months after completing courses. The unemployment rate is average for all subjects, but only law (where the profession requires further training) has a lower proportion of leavers going into non-graduate jobs.

- **The Royal Historical Society:** www.rhs.ac.uk

History

		Research Quality/5	Entry Standards	Graduate Prospects %	Overall Rating
1	Cambridge	5*A	481	84	100.0
2	Durham	5*A	440	76	96.1
3	London School of Economics	5*B	427	78	94.1
4	Oxford	5A	476	72	93.8
5	King's College London	5*A	387	66	91.1
6	Warwick	5A	429	62	89.1
7	York	5A	440	58	88.4
8	Bristol	4A	408	70	87.7
9	University College London	5A	384	62	87.2
10	St Andrews	5B	412	60	86.1
=11	SOAS	5*B	311	66	85.8
=11	Sheffield	5B	432	56	85.8
=11	Royal Holloway	5A	378	58	85.8
14	Leeds	5B	380	62	85.3
15	Nottingham	4A	420	58	84.9
16	Exeter	5A	377	54	84.6
17	Oxford Brookes	5*A	247	62	84.0
18	Newcastle	4A	380	60	83.8
=19	Glasgow	5B	368	58	83.7
=19	Cardiff	5A	353	54	83.7
21	East Anglia	5*B	377	48	83.6
22	Edinburgh	5B	395	52	83.2
23	Essex	5A	301	58	82.6
24	Birmingham	5B	380	52	82.5
25	Aberystwyth	4A	296	66	81.9
26	Hull	5A	293	56	81.7
27	Southampton	5A	341	48	81.5
28	Manchester	5B	367	50	81.4
29	Salford	5A	245	62	81.3
30	Sussex	4A	332	56	80.7
31	Queen's, Belfast	5B	320	54	80.5
32	Lancaster	4A	350	50	79.7
33	Leicester	5A	308	46	79.5
34	Aberdeen	4B	310	60	79.4
=35	Keele	5A	299	46	79.1
=35	Kent	4B	316	58	79.1
=35	Queen Mary	5B	286	54	79.1
38	Strathclyde	4B	330	54	78.6
=39	Liverpool	5B	331	44	78.2
=39	De Montfort	4B	255	64	78.2
=41	Dundee	5B	261	52	77.5
=41	Swansea	4A	283	52	77.5
43	Lampeter	4A	206	62	77.0
44	Roehampton	5B	222	54	76.4

=45	Stirling	5A	303	32	75.4
=45	Hertfordshire	5B	223		75.4
47	Sheffield Hallam	5B	261	42	74.7
48	Reading	4B	296	44	74.4
49	Liverpool Hope UC	3bC	210	78	74.0
50	Huddersfield	5A	239	36	73.8
51	Wolverhampton	4B	249		73.6
52	Ulster	4B	218	50	72.7
=53	Canterbury Christ Church UC	3aA	257	48	72.6
=53	Nottingham Trent	3aB	243	54	72.6
55	Bangor	4B	252	42	72.0
56	Central Lancashire	4A	213	40	71.2
57	Liverpool John Moores	4B	206	46	71.1
58	Chichester UC	3aA	244	44	71.0
59	Kingston	4B	239	40	70.9
60	Goldsmiths College	4B	260	36	70.7
61	Lincoln		270	76	70.6
62	Greenwich	3aA	223		70.1
63	Bath Spa UC	3bA	222	52	69.6
64	West of England	4B	253	32	69.3
65	Westminster	3aB	233		69.0
66	Northumbria	3aC	270	42	68.5
=67	Portsmouth	4C	211	44	68.4
=67	Winchester UC	4C	250	38	68.4
=67	Gloucestershire	3aC	255	44	68.4
70	Brunel	3aB	244	38	68.2
=71	Anglia	3aC	192	52	67.9
=71	Sunderland	4C	224	40	67.9
=73	Plymouth	3aC	258		67.7
=73	Manchester Metropolitan	3aC	265	40	67.7
75	Teesside	5C	170	40	67.5
76	Northampton UC	4B	207	30	66.7
77	Staffordshire	3bC	241	42	65.4
78	Glamorgan	3aC	208		64.6
79	Worcester UC	3aC	193		63.6
=80	Brighton		269	48	62.8
=80	Leeds Metropolitan	3aD	231		62.8

Employed in graduate job: 24%
Employed in non-graduate job: 36%
Studying, not employed: 25%
Average starting salary: £14,712

Employed in graduate job and studying: 3%
Employed in non-graduate job and studying: 5%
Unemployed: 7%

THE LETTERS THAT APPEAR IN THE RESEARCH QUALITY COLUMN INDICATE THE PROPORTION OF STAFF INCLUDED IN THE ASSESSMENT, A SHOWING THAT ALMOST ALL STAFF WERE INCLUDED AND F SHOWING THAT HARDLY ANY WERE

History of Art, Architecture and Design

London University's Courtauld Institute remains top of the table in Art History, with the only 5* rating in the last Research Assessment Exercise and a high teaching score. Second-placed UCL and London's School of Oriental and African Studies, in third, have the only maximum scores in Britain for teaching quality. Cambridge, which has slipped to fourth, has by far the highest entry standards, while York is just as far ahead on graduate employment. Its figure of 90 per cent in graduate jobs or further training is unprecedented.

St Andrews is the top university in Scotland, while Aberystwyth is Wales's only representative. Oxford Brookes, which was only one point off a perfect teaching score, remains the top new university and has broken into the top ten.

Nationally, the specialised nature of the jobs market makes for uncertain prospects immediately after graduation: unemployment is slightly above average for all subjects. Even some universities in the top 20 recorded 'positive destinations' for less than half their graduates in 2003.

Fewer than 4,000 undergraduates take full-time degrees in the history of art, although another 1,000 are registered on part-time courses. The majority of students are female. Outside Cambridge, entry standards range from 400 points at Birmingham and Edinburgh to less than 200 at Sheffield Hallam. Even in the bottom half of the table, however, most universities average around 300 points. Assessors in England found that most students were well supported, although about a third of libraries were under pressure.

- **The Gateway to Art, Design, Architecture and Media Information on the Internet (ADAM):** http://adam.ac.uk

History of Art, Archtecture and Design	Teaching Quality/24	Research Quality/5	Entry Standards	Graduate Prospects %	Overall Rating
1 Courtauld Institute	23	5*A	392		100.0
2 University College London	24	5B	378	60	97.4
3 SOAS	24	3aA			96.8
4 Cambridge	22	5A	470	70	95.5
5 Birmingham	22	5A	402		92.6
6 York	21	5A	352	90	90.7
7 Leeds	23	3aA	325	60	88.3
8 Oxford Brookes	23	3aA	291	60	87.2
9 Essex	22	5B		50	87.1
10 Nottingham	23	3bC	391	60	86.0
11 Plymouth	21	5A			85.8
12 St Andrews	HS	5A		55	85.4
13 Warwick	21	5A	392	45	84.9
14 Reading	23	4A	281	30	84.5
15 Kent	22	3aB		60	83.8
16 East Anglia	22	5B	285	40	83.0
17 Edinburgh	HS	4B	401	50	82.5
18 Glasgow	HS	5B	350	45	82.2
19 Sussex	20	5A	300	70	81.7

20	Brighton	21	5B	293	55	81.6
21	Leicester	22	4A	283	35	81.3
22	Middlesex	22	5	D		81.1
23	Manchester	21	5B	299	45	80.2
24	Aberdeen	HS	4C			77.3
=25	Bristol	20	3aB	389	60	77.2
=25	Manchester Metropolitan	22	4C	265	35	77.2
27	Southampton	20	4B	299	40	73.2
28	De Montfort	21	3bC			71.8
29	Northumbria	21	3aD			71.4
30	Loughborough		3aC	304		70.2
31	Goldsmiths College	19	3bA	304	65	69.8
32	Aberystwyth	S	3aA			69.5
33	Kingston	20	4D		40	67.3
34	Anglia	18	3bA			56.7
35	Sheffield Hallam	20		159		56.0

Employed in graduate job: 29%
Employed in non-graduate job: 35%
Studying, not employed: 20%
Average starting salary: £15,216

Employed in graduate job and studying: 3%
Employed in non-graduate job and studying: 4%
Unemployed: 8%
Teaching quality assessed 1996–98

THE LETTERS THAT APPEAR IN THE RESEARCH QUALITY COLUMN INDICATE THE PROPORTION OF STAFF INCLUDED IN THE ASSESSMENT, A SHOWING THAT ALMOST ALL STAFF WERE INCLUDED AND F SHOWING THAT HARDLY ANY WERE.

Hospitality, Leisure, Sport, Recreation and Tourism

This is one of the few areas to have seen a big increase in the number of universities offering courses: 11 more institutions qualify for inclusion in this year's table. Glasgow and Exeter both enter the ranking in the top five, but neither can prevent Liverpool John Moores (JMU) moving up to top place. It is the only university to register top scores for both teaching and research, and it also has the best employment record.

Although a number of old universities appear in the ranking, only Essex was awarded maximum points for teaching quality. The other top scorers all came from the new university sector, Sheffield Hallam and Westminster joining JMU on 24 points. No courses were rated Excellent for teaching in Scotland and the subjects were not assessed in Wales. Even in the research assessments, Manchester Metropolitan's 5* meant that former polytechnics accounted for two of the five top grades. Glasgow, Loughborough and Birmingham took the remainder.

The subjects are offered mainly by new universities, although only JMU, Westminster and De Montfort make the top ten. Third-placed Loughborough and Bath, in seventh – two of the universities with the best sports facilities and largest scholarship programmes – tie for the highest entrance standards. While they average close to 400 points, less than 200 points were needed to secure a place at many other institutions. The category covers a variety of courses, most directed towards management in the leisure and tourism industries.

Unemployment is below the average for all subjects, but almost half the 2003 leavers were

Hospitality, Leisure, Sport, Recreation and Tourism CONT.

in non-graduate jobs six months after completing their course. Nevertheless, sports science, in particular, has been growing in popularity: the number of applications for degree places was up by 14 per cent to more than 40,000 at the start of 2005. The smaller tourism area was also up, by nearly 20 per cent.

- **Springboard UK Ltd:** www.springboarduk.org.uk
- **English Institute of Sport:** www.eis2win.co.uk
- **British Association of Sport and Exercise Science:** www.bases.org.uk

	Hospitality, Leisure, Sport, Recreation and Tourism	Teaching Quality/24	Research Quality/5	Entry Standards	Graduate Prospects %	Overall Rating
1	Liverpool John Moores	24	5*B	274	86	100.0
2	Glasgow		5*A	334	60	98.9
3	Loughborough	23	5*C	387	62	94.6
4	Brunel	23	4B	292	84	94.1
5	Exeter		5C	356	60	92.8
6	Birmingham	22	5*A	369	54	92.6
7	Bath	23	3aC	387	60	91.0
8	Westminster	24	3aD			90.4
9	De Montfort	23	4B	194	68	88.9
10	Essex	24		271	68	87.9
11	Brighton	22	4A	212	74	87.8
12	Ulster	23	4D	293	54	86.8
13	Durham	23		381	60	86.6
=14	Stirling		4B	319	40	86.4
=14	Sheffield Hallam	24	4E	258	46	86.4
16	Leeds		3aC	309	58	86.2
17	Aberdeen		4B	240		86.0
18	Bangor		5A	261	32	85.5
19	Strathclyde	HS	4C	281	40	85.2
20	Surrey		4C	301	48	85.1
21	Hertfordshire	23	3aC	257	42	84.5
22	Manchester Metropolitan	22	5*C	220	48	84.2
23	Edinburgh		3aD	310	58	84.1
=24	Manchester	22	4C	284	48	83.9
=24	Nottingham Trent	22	3aC		60	83.9
26	Dundee	HS		344		83.5
27	London South Bank	22	3aD		60	82.4
=28	Leeds Metropolitan	22	3aD	269	50	81.4
=28	Plymouth	23	3aE	218	46	81.4
30	Chichester UC	21	3aC	213	60	79.1
31	Queen Margaret College	HS		218	46	78.9
32	Staffordshire	22	3aE			78.5
33	Luton		4C	186	44	78.2
34	Glamorgan		3bB	166	54	77.4
35	Canterbury Christ Church UC	21	3bC	240	48	77.1

		Entry standards	Research Quality			
=36	Oxford Brookes	22		237	46	76.9
=36	Bournemouth	22		227	48	76.9
38	Southampton			294	52	76.7
39	UWIC, Cardiff		3aF	238	60	76.6
=40	Kingston	22		181	54	76.4
=40	Napier	HS		202	32	76.4
42	Glasgow Caledonian	S	3aE	242	36	76.1
43	Central Lancashire	22		218	42	75.8
44	Roehampton	21	3bD	197	54	75.7
45	Robert Gordon	S		284	34	75.3
46	Gloucestershire	21	3bE	218	52	75.1
=47	Wolverhampton		3aE	188	54	74.7
=47	Huddersfield	22		200	38	74.7
49	Thames Valley	22		131	50	74.3
50	Lincoln	21		218	48	73.3
51	Northumbria	21		238	40	72.7
52	Derby	21		197	46	72.4
53	Coventry	21		202	44	72.2
54	Hull	20		236	58	71.9
55	Bolton	21			42	71.7
56	Portsmouth	21		206	36	71.2
57	Winchester UC	21		213	34	71.1
58	Buckinghamshire Chilterns UC	21	3bE	183	24	70.0
59	Sunderland	20	3bE			67.7
60	Greenwich	20		197	36	67.6
61	Liverpool Hope UC	19		170	64	67.5
62	Northampton UC	19		184	50	65.9
63	Salford	19		214	36	64.7
64	Anglia	18	2B		32	61.0

Employed in graduate job: 33%
Employed in non-graduate job: 43%
Studying, not employed: 12%
Average starting salary: £14,469

Employed in graduate job and studying: 3%
Employed in non-graduate job and studying: 4%
Unemployed: 6%
Teaching quality assessed 2000–01

THE LETTERS THAT APPEAR IN THE RESEARCH QUALITY COLUMN INDICATE THE PROPORTION OF STAFF INCLUDED IN THE ASSESSMENT, A SHOWING THAT ALMOST ALL STAFF WERE INCLUDED AND F SHOWING THAT HARDLY ANY WERE.

Iberian Languages

Cambridge remains well ahead of the field for Iberian languages, with the highest entry standards, the best employment score and one of six 5* ratings for research. The other research stars were Queen Mary, King's College London, Manchester, Southampton and Nottingham, the final two missing the top 20 because of low teaching grades. However, all of them are beaten to second place by St Andrews, which has the highest entry standards outside Oxbridge and a good graduate employment record.

A tough teaching assessment in England saw fourth-placed Hull awarded the only maximum score. Queen Mary and Northumbria were the only institutions to come close to

Iberian Languages CONT.

this mark, although Swansea was rated Excellent under the Welsh system. Oxford Brookes is the highest-placed new university and the only one in the top 20.

Spanish is growing in popularity as an alternative to French in schools, and is a common choice as an element of a broader modern languages degree. Applications rose by 15 per cent in 2004 and they were up by another 9.5 per cent when the official deadline passed for courses beginning in 2005. The table also includes Portuguese, which is still offered by about a dozen universities.

Unemployment is slightly below the average for all subjects, at 6 per cent, but the latest figures showed another 40 per cent in non-graduate jobs six months after completing courses. However, employment prospects appear to be more evenly spread than in many subjects: only six universities in the table saw less than half of their leavers go into graduate jobs or further training in 2003.

- **The Association for Contemporary Iberian Studies:** www.bton.ac.uk/languages/acis
- **CILT – The National Centre for Languages:** www.cilt.org.uk
- **The Institute of Translation and Interpreting:** www.iti.org.uk/

	Iberian Languages	Teaching Quality/24	Research Quality/5	Entry Standards	Graduate Prospects %	Overall Rating
1	Cambridge	22	5*A	475	80	100.0
2	St Andrews	22	5A	443	70	94.8
3	King's College London	22	5*A	368	65	93.7
4	Hull	24	4A	311	60	93.1
5	Birmingham	22	5A	380	65	91.8
6	Newcastle	22	5A	351	70	91.7
7	Oxford	21	5B	456	75	91.1
8	Edinburgh	21	5A	433	70	90.9
9	Bath		5A	380		90.7
10	Sheffield	21	5A	406	70	90.0
11	Bristol	22	4B	400	65	88.8
12	Swansea	E	5B	272	65	88.7
13	Leeds	22	4B	375	60	87.0
14	Queen's, Belfast	21	4A	343	75	86.5
15	Heriot-Watt	21	4B	458	50	84.5
=16	Queen Mary	23	5*A	258	15	84.4
=16	Oxford Brookes	22	3aC		70	84.4
18	Strathclyde	22	4C	382	55	84.2
19	Glasgow	22	3aB	373	55	84.0
=20	Liverpool	21	4A	333	60	83.4
=20	Manchester	20	5*A	349	50	83.4
22	Aberdeen	22	4D	352		81.8
23	Cardiff	S	5A	350	60	81.2
24	Salford	20	5A	293	55	80.0
25	Kent		4B	319	65	79.9
26	Lancaster	20	5C	333	65	79.1
27	Northumbria	23	3bE	261	60	78.4

=28	Aberystwyth	S	3aA	322	70	77.3
=28	Central Lancashire	21	3bA		55	77.3
=28	University College London	19	4A	386	55	77.3
31	Royal Holloway		4A	315	50	77.2
32	Exeter	20	4B	344	45	76.3
=33	Southampton	18	5*A	312	50	75.1
=33	Nottingham	17	5*A	414	50	75.1
35	Wolverhampton	20	4C			74.4
36	Paisley	19	4C			69.2
37	Coventry	21		194	70	69.0
38	Bradford	18	4D		75	67.8
39	West of England	21		261	50	67.6
40	Brighton	20			65	67.1
41	Roehampton	19	3aA	191		66.9
42	Surrey	18	5C			66.5
43	Plymouth		3bA		50	66.1
44	Manchester Metropolitan	21			40	65.9
45	Anglia	21	2C		20	65.3
46	Durham	16	4B		75	64.9
47	Stirling	20		304		64.6
48	Portsmouth	18	5C	228	30	62.3
49	Liverpool John Moores	19		209	65	61.7
50	Sheffield Hallam	19		258	45	59.7
51	Napier	19		244		58.0
52	Westminster	18	3bD			56.8
53	Ulster	18		246	50	56.7
54	Leicester			273	50	54.9
55	Nottingham Trent	17		227	55	53.5

Employed in graduate job: 33%
Employed in non-graduate job: 37%
Studying, not employed: 16%
Average starting salary: £15,004

Employed in graduate job and studying: 5%
Employed in non-graduate job and studying: 4%
Unemployed: 6%
Teaching quality assessed 1995–96

THE LETTERS THAT APPEAR IN THE RESEARCH QUALITY COLUMN INDICATE THE PROPORTION OF STAFF INCLUDED IN THE ASSESSMENT, A SHOWING THAT ALMOST ALL STAFF WERE INCLUDED AND F SHOWING THAT HARDLY ANY WERE.

Italian

Cambridge continues to lead a group of 37 universities offering Italian. It has by far the best employment record, as well as the highest entry standards, and is one of six universities rated internationally outstanding for research. Oxford is another of them, but it loses second place this year to Swansea, which was rated Excellent at teaching under the Welsh system. No university was awarded more than 22 points out of 24 for teaching quality in England or Scotland. Swansea is one of a number of universities in the table for which no data is published on entry qualifications or graduate destinations. In most cases, this is because the number of graduates was too small to compile valid scores.

Italian

		Teaching Quality/24	Research Quality/5	Entry Standards	Graduate Prospects %	Overall Rating
1	Cambridge	22	5*A	475	80	100.0
2	Swansea	E	4A			94.7
3	Oxford	21	5*A	466	65	93.0
4	Birmingham	22	5*B	354	50	89.8
5	Bristol	21	5A	387	70	89.1
6	St Andrews	22	4B			89.0
7	Warwick	21	5A	376	55	86.4
8	Edinburgh	21	4A	416	60	86.0
=9	Exeter	22	4B	339	50	85.2
=9	University College London	20	5*A	378	60	85.2
11	Strathclyde	22	4C		55	84.4
12	Glasgow	22	3bA			83.9
13	Hull	22	3aC		60	83.4
=14	Cardiff	S	5A	342	70	81.4
=14	Salford	20	5A			81.4
16	Royal Holloway	21	4A	314	45	80.6
17	Oxford Brookes	22			70	77.7
18	Central Lancashire	21	3bA		55	77.6
19	Bath	19	5A	332	55	76.4
20	Lancaster	20	5C	326		76.2
21	Leicester	20	4A	273	45	75.1
22	Reading	20	5*A	247	15	74.0
23	Kent	19	4B		65	73.3
24	Manchester	19	5B	355	40	73.2
25	Portsmouth	20	5C		40	73.1
26	Anglia	21	2C			72.0
27	Leeds	19	5*D	355	55	71.4
28	Coventry	21		194	70	69.8
29	Durham	20			75	68.3
30	Manchester Metropolitan	21			40	66.7
=31	Westminster	19	4C			66.4
=31	Brighton	20			65	66.4
33	Sussex	17	4A		70	65.4
34	Liverpool John Moores	19			65	61.2
35	Sheffield Hallam	19		258	45	59.0
36	Napier	19		244		56.6
37	Nottingham Trent			227	55	55.7

Employed in graduate job: 35%
Employed in non-graduate job: 38%
Studying, not employed: 15%
Average starting salary: £14,212

Employed in graduate job and studying: 4%
Employed in non-graduate job and studying: 3%
Unemployed: 5%
Teaching quality assessed 1995–96

THE LETTERS THAT APPEAR IN THE RESEARCH QUALITY COLUMN INDICATE THE PROPORTION OF STAFF INCLUDED IN THE ASSESSMENT, A SHOWING THAT ALMOST ALL STAFF WERE INCLUDED AND F SHOWING THAT HARDLY ANY WERE.

Italian CONT.

Cambridge was one of the eight top scorers for teaching, a group that includes sixth-placed St Andrews, the top university in Scotland. Oxford Brookes was another; it joins Central Lancashire as the only new universities in the top 20. The top research grades were widely spread in 2001, after a sharp improvement on the previous assessments. Oxbridge, Birmingham, UCL, Reading and Leeds were all awarded the 5* grade, although Leeds entered a relatively low proportion of its academic staff.

Fewer than 500 students take the language as a separate subject at degree level, although others include Italian in combined degree programmes. Assessors in England found some cases of overcrowding, but were satisfied with learning resources, which generally included satellite television. Most students have no previous knowledge of the language, but there is a high completion rate. The low numbers can make for mixed messages from the labour market: the unemployment rate is low, at 5 per cent, but over 40 per cent start off in non-graduate jobs.

- **CILT – The National Centre for Languages:** www.cilt.org.uk
- **The Institute of Translation and Interpreting:** www.iti.org.uk

Land and Property Management

Cambridge has a big lead, despite dropping two points out of 24 in the teaching assessment and missing the top grade for research. Its entry standards are in a different league to the other five universities with enough students for scores to be compiled, while its graduate employment score would top almost any table. Again, only five universities had enough leavers to calculate destinations scores, although De Montfort ran Cambridge close.

Second-placed Oxford Brookes shares with De Montfort the best teaching score in the table. Kingston was the only university to be awarded maximum points for teaching, but it did not enter academics in the relevant research category and had too few students graduating in 2003 to compile destinations or qualifications data.

Research grades improved significantly in 2001. Salford was the only university to be rated internationally outstanding but, since it shares the lowest teaching rating with the two lowest-ranked institutions, it still misses a place in the top ten.

All but five universities are former polytechnics. Entry standards are generally modest and completion rates tend to be higher at the universities with more demanding entrance requirements. Only about 2,000 students are taking the subject at degree or diploma level, although the subjects are often included in wider environmental programmes. Employment prospects inevitably depend to some extent on the state of the property market, but two thirds of those completing courses in 2003 went straight into graduate jobs – a higher proportion than in most subjects.

- **Royal Institution of Chartered Surveyors:** www.rics.org/

Land and Property Management	Teaching Quality/24	Research Quality/5	Entry Standards	Graduate Prospects %	Overall Rating
1 Cambridge	22	5B	480	95	100.0
2 Oxford Brookes	23	4C			91.1
3 Manchester	22	4B			86.1

		Teaching Quality/24	Research Quality/5	Entry Standards	Graduate Prospects %	Overall Rating
4	Reading	22	5B	327	65	85.3
5	Liverpool John Moores	22	3aA			83.3
6	Ulster	21	5A	256		80.7
7	West of England	22	3aB			80.6
8	De Montfort	23			90	76.1
9	Leeds Metropolitan	21	3aB			70.1
10	Plymouth	22	3aE			66.3
11	Northumbria	22		276	80	65.5
12	Portsmouth	20	3aB		75	63.2
13	Nottingham Trent	20	3aB			59.6
14	Salford	18	5*A			59.5
15	Sheffield Hallam	21	4D	225	45	57.1
16	Greenwich	21	3bE			54.0
17	City	19	3aC			44.8
18	Westminster	19	3aD	207		41.9
19	Anglia	19	2B			38.3
20	London South Bank	18	4D			32.4
21	Central England	18	3bE			22.5

Employed in graduate job: 55%
Employed in non-graduate job: 21%
Studying, not employed: 3%
Average starting salary: £16,745

Employed in graduate job and studying: 12%
Employed in non-graduate job and studying: 2%
Unemployed: 7%
Teaching quality assessed 1996–98

THE LETTERS THAT APPEAR IN THE RESEARCH QUALITY COLUMN INDICATE THE PROPORTION OF STAFF INCLUDED IN THE ASSESSMENT, A SHOWING THAT ALMOST ALL STAFF WERE INCLUDED AND F SHOWING THAT HARDLY ANY WERE.

Law

The top three in law are unchanged from last year, with Cambridge again producing the best scores of all 76 institutions on all three measures. Oxford, Durham, LSE, UCL and Keele also achieved 5* research ratings after entering a full complement of academics. Queen Mary, Southampton and Oxford reached the top grade with a more selective entry. But none could match Cambridge's average entry score of more than 500 points, or the 88 per cent of its leavers going into graduate jobs or further training.

In England, law was one of the first subjects to be assessed for teaching quality, and the grades are considered too dated. The employment data show that in all but a handful of the top 50 institutions in the table at least 70 per cent of leavers had 'positive destinations', even if not necessarily in the legal profession.

Competition is intense for the top position in Scotland, with Strathclyde, Glasgow and Aberdeen hot on the heels of Edinburgh, which stays ahead because of its high entry grades and employment record. Similarly, Cardiff emerges a fraction ahead of Aberystwyth in Wales. Of the new universities, only Oxford Brookes squeezes into the top 40.

Nine subjects have higher average entry scores than law, but only in medicine do so many universities make such testing demands. Almost 20 have average entry scores of more than 400 points. However, it is still possible to secure a place at some new universities with less than 200 points.

Applications were down slightly at the start of 2005, when there was an average increase of more than 9 per cent across higher education as a whole. But law still attracts more applications than any other single subject. The requirement for further professional training for solicitors and barristers means less than a quarter of students go straight into graduate jobs. Many opt for careers in other areas, but with six out of ten taking additional courses on graduation, the 5 per cent unemployment rate is still well below average.

- **The Bar Council:** www.barcouncil.org
- **The Law Society:** www.lawsociety.org.uk

Law

		Research Quality/5	Entry Standards	Graduate Prospects %	Overall Rating
1	Cambridge	5*A	512	88	100.0
2	Oxford	5*B	489	86	97.1
3	Durham	5*A	451	84	96.2
4	University College London	5*A	432	84	95.4
5	Manchester	5A	451	84	94.5
6	London School of Economics	5*A	455	78	94.3
7	Nottingham	5A	462	82	94.2
8	King's College London	5A	425	86	94.1
9	Edinburgh	5B	459	84	93.7
10	Leeds	5A	425	82	92.7
11	Strathclyde	5A	426	80	92.1
12	Glasgow	5B	448	80	91.9
13	Aberdeen	5B	418	82	91.4
14	Warwick	5B	445	78	91.1
15	Queen's, Belfast	5B	389	84	90.9
16	Bristol	5B	437	78	90.7
17	Kent	5B	338	88	90.2
18	SOAS	5A	357	80	89.3
19	Queen Mary	5*B	355	78	89.0
20	Newcastle	5C	429	78	88.6
21	Sheffield	5C	436	76	88.2
22	Birmingham	5C	434	74	87.5
23	Keele	5*A	320	74	87.4
24	Exeter	5C	414	76	87.3
25	Dundee	5B	367	76	87.2
26	Leicester	5A	386	70	87.0
27	East Anglia	5B	392	72	86.9
28	Brunel	5A	346	74	86.8
29	City	5B	338	76	86.1
30	Hull	5B	328	76	85.7

		Research Quality/5	Entry Standards	Graduate Prospects %	Overall Rating
31	Liverpool	4B	383	72	85.0
32	Southampton	5*B	392	62	84.9
33	Essex	5B	341	72	84.8
34	Reading	5B	355	70	84.7
35	Cardiff	5C	389	70	84.3
36	Sussex	4B	338	74	83.9
37	Aberystwyth	4B	317	76	83.7
38	Lancaster	5B	354	62	81.9
39	Surrey	5C	305		81.8
40	Oxford Brookes	4D	314	80	81.7
41	Ulster	5C	274	70	79.6
42	Swansea	3aB	281	70	78.7
43	Bournemouth	3aE	272	82	78.5
44	Leeds Metropolitan	3aE	296	78	78.1
45	Sheffield Hallam	3aF	288	80	77.1
46	Nottingham Trent	4F	313	76	76.9
47	Westminster	5F	294	76	76.3
48	Manchester Metropolitan		300	76	75.7
49	Central Lancashire	4E	250	74	75.3
50	Kingston		257	78	74.6
51	Hertfordshire	3aC	218	68	74.2
52	Lincoln		225	80	74.1
=53	Anglia	2B	216	72	73.7
=53	Northumbria		335	66	73.7
55	West of England	4F	295	68	73.4
56	Liverpool John Moores	3bC	244	64	72.7
57	Derby		207	78	72.6
=58	Teesside		201	78	72.4
=58	Central England		235	74	72.4
60	Glamorgan		227	74	72.1
61	Sunderland		198	76	71.6
=62	Huddersfield	3bE	212	68	70.7
=62	Napier	3aD	233	60	70.7
64	Staffordshire	3aF	228	68	70.5
65	Wolverhampton	3aE	187	68	70.2
66	Glasgow Caledonian	3bE	321	52	69.6
67	East London	3aE	167	68	69.4
68	Stirling		342	52	69.1
69	Greenwich	3bF	225	64	68.9
70	Plymouth	3bE	244	58	68.6
71	De Montfort	4E	233	54	67.8
72	Coventry		211	62	67.3
73	Luton		197	60	66.0
74	Middlesex		199	56	64.7

75	Northampton UC		203	44	60.7
76	Bangor		226	26	55.4

Employed in graduate job: 18%
Employed in non-graduate job: 21%
Studying, not employed: 46%
Average starting salary: £15,219

Employed in graduate job and studying: 5%
Employed in non-graduate job and studying: 6%
Unemployed: 5%

THE LETTERS THAT APPEAR IN THE RESEARCH QUALITY COLUMN INDICATE THE PROPORTION OF STAFF INCLUDED IN THE ASSESSMENT, A SHOWING THAT ALMOST ALL STAFF WERE INCLUDED AND F SHOWING THAT HARDLY ANY WERE.

Librarianship and Information Management

Loughborough's lead in librarianship and information management is the biggest in any of the subject tables, although teaching quality is the only indicator on which it has the best score. Second-placed UCL has the highest entry qualifications and easily the largest proportion of leavers in graduate jobs or further study within six months, while Sheffield, in third, is the only university rated internationally outstanding for research.

There are only 11 universities in the ranking – down from 14 last year because of low student numbers at some of the smaller providers. None of its rivals in England came within a point of Loughborough's maximum teaching score, but Aberystwyth was rated Excellent in the only assessment in Wales. The subjects were not assessed separately for teaching quality in Scotland.

More than half of the universities in the table are former polytechnics, Northumbria being the best-placed of them. Like Brighton, Northumbria scored 22 points out of 24 for

Librarianship and Information Management	Teaching Quality/24	Research Quality/5	Entry Standards	Graduate Prospects %	Overall Rating
1 Loughborough	24	5B	331	70	100.0
2 University College London	22	4A	369	85	87.6
3 Sheffield	22	5*A	330	60	86.3
4 Aberystwyth	E	3aB	259	35	82.4
5 City	21	5A			69.8
6 Northumbria	22	3bC	234		63.9
7 Brighton	22	3bD	251	50	63.5
8 Manchester Metropolitan	21	4C		35	56.7
9 Liverpool John Moores	S	3bE			54.4
10 Leeds Metropolitan		4E	174	50	51.2
11 Central England	20	3aB	151	30	43.8

Employed in graduate job: 33%
Employed in non-graduate job: 33%
Studying, not employed: 11%
Average starting salary: £17,034

Employed in graduate job and studying: 5%
Employed in non-graduate job and studying: 5%
Unemployed: 12%
Teaching quality assessed 2000–01

THE LETTERS THAT APPEAR IN THE RESEARCH QUALITY COLUMN INDICATE THE PROPORTION OF STAFF INCLUDED IN THE ASSESSMENT, A SHOWING THAT ALMOST ALL STAFF WERE INCLUDED AND F SHOWING THAT HARDLY ANY WERE.

Librarianship and Information Management CONT.

teaching quality, while Manchester Metropolitan achieved the best research grade among the new universities. As the small size of the table suggests, librarianship and information management are minority interests at degree level, and this makes the subjects vulnerable to swings in employment statistics. The latest figures show little more than half of those completing going straight into graduate jobs or onto postgraduate courses. The unemployment rate of 12 per cent is marginally down on last year but still one that is exceeded in only two subject categories.

- **The Chartered Institute of Library and Information Professionals:** www.cilip.org.uk/default.cilip

Linguistics

Queen Mary maintains its lead over Cambridge at the top of the table for linguistics, thanks to a superior teaching quality grade. Unusually, no institution achieved the maximum score for teaching, but Queen Mary and Lancaster came closest. The last research assessments produced four 5* ratings, with Oxford and University College London joining Cambridge and Queen Mary on the top grade.

All but three of the English universities in the table are within three points of each other in the teaching quality assessment, with Bangor rated Satisfactory under the separate Welsh system. The research grades improved dramatically in 2001, with more than half of the universities reaching the top two grades.

There was no separate assessment of teaching in linguistics in Scotland, but Edinburgh's high entry grades and research rating help secure a place in the top ten. Only Oxford's students have higher entry qualifications, although Cambridge does not publish separate data for this subject. Fourth-placed Sussex has the best graduate employment record, while Wolverhampton is the best-placed of seven new universities in the table. Portsmouth, Hertfordshire, Luton and Westminster also appear in the top 20.

Fewer than 2,000 students take linguistics at degree level, eight out of ten of them arriving with A levels. But there was a healthy 13.5 per cent increase in applications at the start of 2005. Immediate employment prospects are close to the average for all subjects, although the latest figures show four out of ten graduates in lower-level jobs six months after completing their courses.

- **The British Association for Applied Linguistics:** www.baal.org.uk

Linguistics		Teaching Quality/24	Research Quality/5	Entry Standards	Graduate Prospects %	Overall Rating
1	Queen Mary	23	5*A			100.0
2	Cambridge	22	5*A		80	94.7
3	York	22	5A	401	80	91.6
4	Sussex	22	4A		90	91.1
5	Oxford	21	5*A	465		90.0
6	Lancaster	23	5B	368	50	88.1
7	Newcastle	22	5A	360	60	86.6

8	Edinburgh		5C	453	60	83.5
9	University College London	22	5*C	374	50	82.9
10	Manchester	21	5B	346	40	76.4
11	Salford	20	5A			76.0
12	Essex	21	5B	283	50	75.9
13	Wolverhampton	21	3aA			75.6
14	Sheffield	22		384	60	73.3
15	Portsmouth		5C		50	72.0
16	SOAS	20	3aA			68.8
17	Hertfordshire	20	3aA	226	60	67.8
18	Westminster	20	5C	249		67.2
19	Luton	21	3aE			65.6
20	Reading	19	3aB	320	50	63.9
21	West of England	21		244	60	63.6
22	Bangor	S	3bB	342	30	61.4
23	Brighton	20	5E			61.0
24	East Anglia	19	3bB		50	59.6
25	Cardiff			360	50	57.5
26	Leeds	17	3aC	350	60	56.0
27	Leeds Metropolitan			256	40	47.9

Employed in graduate job: 26%
Employed in non-graduate job: 36%
Studying, not employed: 23%
Average starting salary: £13,760

Employed in graduate job and studying: 5%
Employed in non-graduate job and studying: 4%
Unemployed: 6%
Teaching quality assessed 1996–98

THE LETTERS THAT APPEAR IN THE RESEARCH QUALITY COLUMN INDICATE THE PROPORTION OF STAFF INCLUDED IN THE ASSESSMENT, A SHOWING THAT ALMOST ALL STAFF WERE INCLUDED AND F SHOWING THAT HARDLY ANY WERE.

Materials Technology

The top three for materials technology remain unchanged, with Cambridge staying ahead of Oxford on the strength of its students' unusually high entry grades. Both have 5* research grades – as do Sheffield, Manchester and Birmingham – and near-maximum scores for teaching quality. Third-placed Imperial College was the only institution in England to be awarded full marks for teaching.

With neither of the top two publishing separate destinations data, fourth-placed Swansea has by far the best graduate employment record. Swansea was rated Excellent at teaching under the Welsh system and nine out of ten leavers were in graduate jobs or further training within six months. Heriot-Watt is Scotland's only representative in the table.

Manchester Metropolitan narrowly denies Bolton the accolade of the highest-placed new university, with both appearing in the top ten. MMU did well on research and employment, while Bolton matched Oxford and Cambridge in the teaching assessments. Oxbridge and Imperial apart, there is less variation in entry standards than in many other subjects. Although student numbers are too small to compile scores for several institutions, none of the remainder has an average of less than 200 points.

The English courses assessed between 1996 and 1998 covered three distinct areas: materials science, mining and engineering; textiles technology and printing; and marine technology. More than three quarters of students go on to further study or graduate jobs

Materials Technology CONT.

within six months of graduating. Nationally, unemployment is above average, at 9 per cent, but more than 40 per cent go straight into graduate jobs.

- **The Institute of Materials, Minerals and Mining:** www.iom3.org
- **Materials Careers:** www.materials-careers.org.uk

	Materials Technology	Teaching Quality/24	Research Quality/5	Entry Standards	Graduate Prospects %	Overall Rating
1	Cambridge	23	5*A	542		100.0
2	Oxford	23	5*A	492		97.7
3	Imperial College	24	5A	374	70	92.9
4	Swansea	E	4A		90	87.8
5	Sheffield	22	5*A	337	65	81.5
6	Manchester Metropolitan	22	4A		70	78.7
7	Bolton	23	4D			77.7
8	Surrey	22	4B			76.9
9	Liverpool	21	5A			74.5
10	Manchester	21	5*B	307	70	73.4
11	Nottingham	21	5B	339	70	72.1
12	Birmingham	20	5*A	336	75	71.7
13	Sheffield Hallam	22	5D			71.0
14	Northampton UC	22	3aC			70.2
15	Loughborough	21	4B	315		67.1
16	Queen Mary	20	5B	289	75	65.3
17	Leeds	20	5C	308	65	61.0
18	Newcastle	20	4B			59.2
19	De Montfort	19	4A	333	55	56.1
20	University of the Arts, London	22		234	50	55.4
21	Heriot-Watt		3bB	294	45	52.6
22	Nottingham Trent	20	3bD	300	40	48.0
23	Buckinghamshire Chilterns UC		3bB	200	30	41.3
24	Plymouth	19	4E			38.0

Employed in graduate job: 37%
Employed in non-graduate job: 33%
Studying, not employed: 15%
Average starting salary: £16,861

Employed in graduate job and studying: 4%
Employed in non-graduate job and studying: 2%
Unemployed: 9%
Teaching quality assessed 1996–98

THE LETTERS THAT APPEAR IN THE RESEARCH QUALITY COLUMN INDICATE THE PROPORTION OF STAFF INCLUDED IN THE ASSESSMENT, A SHOWING THAT ALMOST ALL STAFF WERE INCLUDED AND F SHOWING THAT HARDLY ANY WERE.

Mathematics

Only two universities in England achieved maximum points for teaching quality in mathematics. One of them – Bath – had topped the table until last year, but Cambridge remains ahead with the best employment score, the highest entry standards and the best research record. Fifth-placed Birmingham was the other top scorer in the English teaching assessments. Edinburgh and St Andrews were rated Excellent under the Scottish system, St Andrews maintaining its position as the leader north of the border with a high employment score. Cardiff remains the leader in Wales, where no institution was rated better than Satisfactory at teaching.

Cambridge was the only university to be rated internationally outstanding for research in pure and applied mathematics and statistics, but it dropped a point in the teaching quality assessment. The three different research categories meant that 5* grades were sprinkled liberally among the leading universities, however. Bristol, Oxford, Warwick and Imperial College each achieved two top grades. Even Kent, in 51st place, has one.

Although 74 institutions qualify for inclusion in the ranking, only Coventry denies the traditional universities a clean sweep of the top 30 places. It was one of 11 English universities awarded 23 points out of 24 for teaching quality.

Despite the large number of students taking the subject, only medicine, dentistry and veterinary medicine have higher entry standards. No fewer than 16 universities average more than 400 points at entry and none of those for whom data is available drops below 200.

Although identified as one of the subjects most likely to lead to a high salary, graduate employment rates are not as high as for some vocational areas. Unemployment is above average, at 8 per cent and, although more than a quarter take postgraduate courses, less than four leavers in ten go straight into graduate jobs. However, good figures are scattered throughout the table: outside the top 50, Greenwich has a success rate of 80 per cent and both Hertfordshire and Liverpool Hope University College come close to that mark. Maths is still close to the top 20 subjects in terms of applications, which have recovered since a worrying downturn at the beginning of the decade. They were up by more than 11 per cent for the second year in a row when the official deadline passed for courses beginning in 2005.

- **Mathematics Resources on the Internet:** www.bham.ac.uk/ctimath/gateway/organ.htm
- http://pass.maths.org.uk

Mathematics

		Teaching Quality/24	Research Quality/5 Pure	Research Quality/5 Applied	Research Quality/5 Statistics	Entry Standards	Graduate Prospects %	Overall Rating
1	Cambridge	23	5*A	5*A	5*B	564	88	100.0
2	Bath	24	5A	5*B	5B	434	70	97.4
3	St Andrews	E	5B	5B	5A	419	80	96.4
4	Bristol	23	5B	5*A	5*A	465	62	94.5
5	Birmingham	24	5C	5B	4B	411	60	93.9
6	University College London	23	5B	5B	5B	420	74	93.7
7	Oxford	22	5*B	5A	5*C	538	76	93.5
8	Nottingham	23	5B	5B	5A	496	62	93.4
9	Warwick	22	5B	5*A	5*B	497	74	92.7
10	Newcastle	23	5C	4B	5A	392	72	92.5
=11	Imperial College	22	5*B	5*B	5B	479	72	92.2
=11	Edinburgh	E	5*A	5B	4C	456	42	92.2
13	London School of Economics	22			4B	461	78	90.5
14	City	23		4A	3aC	326	78	90.4
=15	East Anglia	23	5A	4B		381	54	90.3

Mathematics CONT.

		Teaching Quality/24	Research Quality Pure/5	Research Quality Applied/5	Research Quality Statistics/5	Entry Standards	Graduate Prospects %	Overall Rating
=15	York	22	5B	5A		436	66	90.3
17	Lancaster	22	4A		5*B	385	66	89.6
18	Sussex	23	4A	5B	4A	306	58	89.4
19	Leeds	22	5B	5B	5B	382	68	89.1
20	Liverpool	23	5B	5B	4A	317	52	89.0
21	Dundee	HS		5B		299		88.8
22	Exeter	22	4A	5A	4A	371	66	88.7
=23	Manchester	22	5A	5A	4B	380	60	88.6
=23	Durham	21	5B	5*B	4B	498	72	88.6
=25	Heriot-Watt	HS		5B	5C	428	54	88.5
=25	Aberdeen	HS	5C	4E	4A	376		88.5
27	Glasgow	HS	5D	5A	5A	369	62	88.4
=28	Loughborough	22		4B		342	74	88.0
=28	Coventry	23		3aC	3aE			88.0
30	Strathclyde	HS		5B	4C	375	52	87.2
31	Leicester	22	5B	5B		336	58	87.0
32	Reading	22	3aA	5A	4B	315	64	86.7
=33	Surrey	21		5A	5A	321	74	86.6
=33	Queen's, Belfast	22	3aC			373	76	86.6
35	Cardiff	S	5A			355	66	86.5
36	Keele	22	2C	5A	3aA	330	62	86.3
37	Hull	22	4B	4A		307	60	86.0
38	Brunel	22		5A	4B	258	60	85.7
39	Portsmouth	22		5C			56	85.5
40	Abertay Dundee	HS		3aA		236	62	85.1
41	Royal Holloway	22	5C			314	56	84.9
42	Sheffield	21	5B	4B	5C	385	64	84.5
43	Salford	21		3aA	5A			84.3
44	King's College London	21	5C	5B		360	62	84.2
=45	Oxford Brookes	22		3aB		229	66	83.9
=45	Aberystwyth	S	3bA	4A		389	60	83.9
47	Swansea	S	5C			303	70	83.8
48	Sheffield Hallam	23				242	74	83.6
49	Stirling	HS	3aA			304	40	83.2
50	Brighton	22		3aC		241	66	83.1
=51	Napier	HS			3bD			82.8
=51	Kent	21	3aC	5A	5*D	310	64	82.8
=51	Goldsmiths College	21	3aA		3aA		66	82.8
=54	Southampton	20	5C	5B	5A	377	64	82.0
=54	Glasgow Caledonian	HS		3bD		274	60	82.0
56	Queen Mary	21	5A	4B	5A	212	56	81.8
=57	Hertfordshire	21		4C		205	76	81.7

Rank	University						Jobs	Score
=57	Kingston	23					52	81.7
59	Ulster	22		4E				81.3
60	Paisley	HS		2C			40	79.4
61	Bangor	S	3aC			350	40	78.5
62	Essex	20	3aA	3aA			62	78.3
63	Nottingham Trent	21		3aC	3aD	223	58	78.0
=64	Northumbria	21		3aD		232	58	77.6
=64	West of England	21		3aC		263	46	77.6
=66	Greenwich	19			3aA	233	80	76.9
=66	Derby	21				241	72	76.9
=68	Plymouth	20	3bA	3aC	3aE	236	68	75.7
=68	De Montfort	20		3bA			56	75.7
70	Manchester Metropolitan	20					78	74.4
71	Liverpool Hope UC	21	1E					74.0
72	Westminster	20		3aC	3bC			73.8
73	Middlesex	20	3aF				66	73.0
74	Aston	19		5C				72.7

Employed in graduate job: 29%
Employed in non-graduate job: 26%
Studying, not employed: 25%
Average starting salary: £16,887

Employed in graduate job and studying: 10%
Employed in non-graduate job and studying: 3%
Unemployed: 8%
Teaching quality assessed 1998–2000

THE LETTERS THAT APPEAR IN THE RESEARCH QUALITY COLUMN INDICATE THE PROPORTION OF STAFF INCLUDED IN THE ASSESSMENT, A SHOWING THAT ALMOST ALL STAFF WERE INCLUDED AND F SHOWING THAT HARDLY ANY WERE.

Mechanical Engineering

The top two remain unchanged in the mechanical engineering table but a respectable graduate employment score (rather than last year's outstanding one) is not enough to keep Bradford in third place, or even in the top ten.

Imperial College London holds onto top place with the highest entry standards and among the best scores for research and graduate destinations. Second-placed Bath is one of six universities rated internationally outstanding for research. Like Liverpool and Southampton, it entered a full complement of academics for assessment. Teaching scores have been dropped because of their age.

It is Hull's turn to register the outstanding employment score, with every leaver in a graduate job or further training within six months, although low entry standards keep the university outside the top 20. Nationally, more than half go straight into graduate jobs, but the 10 per cent unemployment rate is well above average.

Cardiff remains the top university in Wales, but Strathclyde overtakes Glasgow to become the leader in Scotland. The majority of institutions offering mechanical engineering are old universities, which occupy all but one of the top 30 places. The exception is Robert Gordon, at 24th. The open access policies pursued by many of the new universities is reflected in the fact that more than a third of the entrants are admitted without A levels or equivalents. A handful have average entry standards of below 200 points.

Mechanical Engineering CONT.

Mechanical engineering now attracts more applications than any other branch of the wider discipline. The demand for places rose by more than 10 per cent in 2004 and there had been another small increase at the deadline for courses beginning in 2005.

- **The Institute of Mechanical Engineers:** www.imeche.org.uk
- **The Engineering Council (EC UK):** www.engc.org.uk

Mechanical Engineering

		Research Quality/5	Entry Standards	Graduate Prospects %	Overall Rating
1	Imperial College	5*B	462	85	100.0
2	Bath	5*A	410	80	97.1
3	Bristol	5A	429	80	95.3
4	Liverpool	5*A	311	85	92.5
5	Southampton	5*A	363	75	92.2
6	Queen's, Belfast	5*B	398	75	92.1
7	Nottingham	5B	433	75	91.7
8	Cardiff	4A	382	85	90.9
9	Sheffield	5A	404	65	88.1
10	Loughborough	5B	372	75	87.8
11	Strathclyde	5B	419	65	87.1
12	Leeds	5*B	344	70	86.8
13	Newcastle	4B	362	80	86.2
14	Surrey	4B	325	85	85.6
=15	Bradford	5B		70	84.6
=15	Aberdeen	4C		85	84.6
17	Heriot-Watt	4A	339	75	84.5
18	Manchester	5A	345	65	84.3
19	Birmingham	4C	391	75	83.5
20	Sussex	5B		65	81.9
21	Hull	4C	215	100	81.3
22	University College London	5B	318	65	80.5
23	Aston	5C		70	79.6
24	Robert Gordon	3bD	340	90	79.3
25	Glasgow	5B	367	50	78.2
26	Swansea	4A	324	60	78.0
27	Queen Mary	5B	254		77.5
28	Edinburgh	4C	383	60	77.4
29	Leicester	5A	311	50	76.6
30	Ulster	4A	203	70	73.9
31	King's College London	5C	268		73.8
32	Reading	5B	316	45	73.1
33	Brighton	3bC		75	72.5
34	De Montfort	4C		60	70.8
35	Coventry	3aC	249	70	70.2
36	Brunel	5C	279	50	69.2

37	Salford	3aA	229		68.7
38	Staffordshire	3bA	216	70	68.5
39	Manchester Metropolitan	3aA		50	67.3
40	Harper Adams UC		361	65	67.1
41	Exeter	4C	301	45	66.6
42	Portsmouth	4D	201	65	64.3
43	Oxford Brookes		308	65	63.7
=44	Kingston	3aC	216	55	62.5
=44	City	4D	234		62.5
46	Northumbria	3bD	202	65	61.2
47	Hertfordshire	3aD	255	50	60.7
48	Sheffield Hallam	3aF	202	70	59.6
49	Nottingham Trent	3bD	250		59.3
50	Paisley	2C		55	58.1
51	Central England		161	70	56.0
52	Greenwich	3aB		30	54.3
53	West of England	3bD		45	53.1
54	Huddersfield	4E	152	45	50.6
55	Napier		197	45	49.2

Employed in graduate job: 50%
Employed in non-graduate job: 22%
Studying, not employed: 11%
Average starting salary: £18,831

Employed in graduate job and studying: 5%
Employed in non-graduate job and studying: 2%
Unemployed: 10%

THE LETTERS THAT APPEAR IN THE RESEARCH QUALITY COLUMN INDICATE THE PROPORTION OF STAFF INCLUDED IN THE ASSESSMENT, A SHOWING THAT ALMOST ALL STAFF WERE INCLUDED AND F SHOWING THAT HARDLY ANY WERE.

Medicine

There is a tendency to assume that there is little to choose between Britain's medical schools, but both teaching and research assessments suggest otherwise. At a time when most teaching reviews saw traditional universities dropping only one or two points out of 24, medicine produced real variation. Three English universities achieved maximum points, all of which are in this year's top five, but the top two scored 'only' 21 each. Oxford regains the first place it lost last year, while Cambridge moves back up to second.

Such are the slim margins in medicine that Glasgow, which has one of three Excellent ratings in Scotland, has dropped from first to sixth. Dundee and Aberdeen have the other Excellent grades north of the border, while Cardiff achieved the same in the only Welsh assessment. However, Oxford was the only medical school to achieve 5* research grades with a full complement of academics in all three areas it entered. Only Cambridge's entrants were more highly-qualified in 2003, although no medical school averaged less than a fraction under 400 points. Newcastle is the only university with a 5* research element as well as perfect teaching scores, but it entered a relatively low proportion of academics in the research assessments.

The subject is a notoriously difficult one in which to win a place: Government quotas mean that candidates with three or four As at A level are frequently turned away. The establishment of the first new medical schools for more than 20 years was expected to ease this pressure, but the number of applicants has increased and some of the new courses cater for graduates and other mature students. Applications for courses beginning in 2005 were up by almost 10 per cent. Undergraduates have to be prepared to work long hours, particularly towards the end of the course. The latest survey shows no measurable unemployment, with all but three of the schools reporting every student completing training either finding a graduate job or taking on further study.

- **The British Medical Association:** www.bma.org.uk

Medicine

		Teaching Quality/24	Research Quality/5 Clinical Laboratory	Research Quality/5 Community	Research Quality/5 Hospital	Research Quality/5 Pre-Clinical	Entry Standards	Graduate Prospects %	Overall Rating
1	Oxford	21	5*A	5*A	5*A		521	100	100.0
2	Cambridge	21	5*A	5*B	5*B		554	99	99.3
=3	Southampton	24	5A	3aB	5B		442	100	99.1
=3	Liverpool	24	5B	4B	4B		464	100	99.1
5	Manchester	24	4B	5C	5C	5*B	464	100	98.9
6	Glasgow	E	5B	4C	5C		470	100	98.7
7	Newcastle	24	5*D	5C	5C		466	100	98.5
8	Edinburgh	HS		4B	5*C		504	100	98.3
9	Dundee	E	5*B	4D	5E		469	100	98.0
10	Imperial College	21	5*B	5B	5*B	5B	475	100	97.8
11	Cardiff	E	5C	4B	4B		424	100	97.4
12	Aberdeen	E	4B	5C	4B		457	99	97.2
13	Leicester	23	4B	3aB	4B		441	100	96.9
14	St George's Hospital	23	4A	4B	4A	5A	430	99	96.8
=15	King's College London	22	5C	4C	4B	5C	437	100	95.8
=15	University College London	21		4B	5B		434	100	95.8
17	Nottingham	21	3aB	3aC	4B	5A	491	100	95.3
18	Queen's, Belfast	22	4C	5E	3aC		454	100	94.7
=19	Bristol	20	5A	5*C	3aB		469	100	94.4
=19	Birmingham	20	5*B	4D	5C	5C	455	100	94.4
21	Queen Mary	21	3aB	3aB	4B		401	100	93.6
22	Peninsula			3aC	5A		397		93.5
23	Sheffield	19		4B	5C	5*C	466	100	93.4
24	St Andrews	HS					432	100	90.7
25	Leeds	18	5C	4C	4C		418	96	87.0

Employed in graduate job: 89%
Employed in non-graduate job: 0%
Studying, not employed: 8%
Average starting salary: £31,353

Employed in graduate job and studying: 2%
Employed in non-graduate job and studying: 0%
Unemployed: 1%
Teaching quality assessed 1998–2000

Note: A number of new medical schools have been established for which data is not yet available. East Anglia, Peninsula (Plymouth and Exeter) and Warwick medical schools admitted students for the first time in 2002, while Brighton and Sussex, Hull and York, and Keele recruited in 2003. In addition, a number of existing medical schools have introduced innovative new courses.

THE LETTERS THAT APPEAR IN THE RESEARCH QUALITY COLUMN INDICATE THE PROPORTION OF STAFF INCLUDED IN THE ASSESSMENT, A SHOWING THAT ALMOST ALL STAFF WERE INCLUDED AND F SHOWING THAT HARDLY ANY WERE.

Middle Eastern and African Studies

Edinburgh, which entered the ranking for Middle Eastern and African Studies in first place, has immediately dropped out again because its student numbers are too small to compile scores at entry or graduation. As a result, this year's top six have all moved up a place. The only other change in the order has seen Manchester move above Exeter and Leeds, while Westminster – the only new university to offer the subjects – has joined the table in tenth place.

None of the universities assessed for teaching quality was awarded full marks, although none scored less than 20 points out of 24 either. Birmingham and Cambridge came closest to the maximum with 23 points. In the absence of Edinburgh, Birmingham is also the only university rated internationally outstanding for research, and it has the highest entrance standards of the five institutions with entrance scores. Only Leeds and Durham fell below Grade 5 in the latest Research Assessment Exercise. There is no separate provision in Wales or Northern Ireland.

Middle Eastern Studies is the larger of two small subjects, in terms of student numbers. Fewer than 100 students were taking African languages, literature or culture at degree level in 1998, when the teaching assessments were carried out, compared with just over 500 for Middle Eastern subjects. The vast majority – all, in the case of African studies – come with A levels or their equivalent.

Completion rates are good, and a high proportion graduate with a first or 2:1. Student numbers are too low to compile valid employment scores at most of the universities in the table. But, while 10 per cent unemployment is high, the overall figures for positive destinations are better than average for all subjects.

- **The African Studies Association of the UK:** www.asauk.net
- **The British Society for Middle Eastern Studies:** www.dur.ac.uk/brismes
- **The European Association for Middle Eastern Studies:** www.eurames.de

Middle Eastern and African Studies		Teaching Quality/24	Research Quality/5	Entry Standards	Graduate Prospects %	Overall Rating
1	Birmingham	23	5*A	415		100.0
2	Oxford	22	5A			95.1
3	Cambridge	23	5C			94.5
4	Durham	22	4A	342	75	93.7
5	SOAS	22	5B	319	70	92.6
6	Salford	20	5A			89.2
7	Manchester	20	5B	269		88.0
8	Exeter	20	5B			87.9
9	Leeds	21	4C			87.1
10	Westminster	22		216		83.2

Employed in graduate job: 32%
Employed in non-graduate job: 23%
Studying, not employed: 27%
Average starting salary: £16,297

Employed in graduate job and studying: 2%
Employed in non-graduate job and studying: 5%
Unemployed: 10%
Teaching quality assessed 1996–98

THE LETTERS THAT APPEAR IN THE RESEARCH QUALITY COLUMN INDICATE THE PROPORTION OF STAFF INCLUDED IN THE ASSESSMENT, A SHOWING THAT ALMOST ALL STAFF WERE INCLUDED AND F SHOWING THAT HARDLY ANY WERE.

Music

Nottingham wins back the leadership of the music ranking by the narrowest of margins. The top three all have 5* research grades and identical employment scores. Cambridge, which has moved up to second, has the highest entrance standards but entered a lower proportion of academics than Oxford or Nottingham in the last Research Assessment Exercise. Unusually, Oxford suffers for its entrance standards. Nine universities were rated internationally outstanding for research, with Birmingham, Southampton, Manchester, Newcastle, Royal Holloway and City joining the top three. But only Ulster, in 30th place, comes close to Surrey's record of 90 per cent 'positive destinations' for its graduates. Edinburgh remains the top university in Scotland, while Cardiff replaces Bangor as the leader in Wales. Roehampton is the top new university and is joined by Canterbury Christ Church UC in the top 30. As in most subjects, the new universities suffer for their lower entry grade, although selection is as much a matter of musical ability as academic achievement.

Music		Research Quality/5	Entry Standards	Graduate Prospects %	Overall Rating
1	Nottingham	5*A	442	75	100.0
2	Cambridge	5*B	463	75	99.4
3	Oxford	5*A	422	75	98.7
4	King's College London	5A	421	80	97.7
5	Birmingham	5*B	422	75	96.7
6	York	5A	404	75	94.8
7	Sussex	5A		75	92.1
8	Surrey	3aA	359	90	91.7
9	Southampton	5*A	339	70	91.5
10	Durham	4A	395	70	89.8
11	Manchester	5*B	389	60	89.2
12	Queen's, Belfast	5B	302	75	86.4
13	Goldsmiths College	5A	279	70	84.8
14	Newcastle	5*A	261	65	84.6
=15	Bristol	5A	349	55	84.2
=15	Sheffield	5B	348	60	84.2
17	Royal Holloway	5*B	334	55	83.9
18	Keele	4A	313		83.6
19	Edinburgh	4B	388	55	82.6
20	City	5*C	311	65	82.5
21	Lancaster	4A	282	70	82.3
22	Cardiff	5C	317	65	81.0
23	Leeds	4C	345	65	80.8
24	Liverpool	4A	306	60	80.4
25	Hull	5B	263	65	80.3
26	East Anglia	4B	287		78.8

The 6 per cent unemployment rate in the latest survey was surprisingly low for a subject in which career prospects are notoriously uncertain, although more than a quarter of leavers were in non-graduate jobs six months after graduation.

Nevertheless, music has been growing in popularity as a degree subject. There was a 6 per cent increase in 2004 and, when the official deadline passed for courses beginning in 2005, there had been a rise of no less than 21 per cent. Nearly nine out of ten students come with A levels. There can be considerable variation in the character of courses, from the practical and vocational programmes in conservatoires to the more theoretical.

- **The Incorporated Society of Musicians:** www.ism.org
- **The Musicians Union:** www.musiciansunion.org.uk

27	Glasgow	4A	359	45	78.7
28	Roehampton	3aA	237	75	78.4
29	Canterbury Christ Church UC	3bA	275	70	76.5
30	Ulster	3aD	234	85	76.4
31	Huddersfield	5C	246	65	76.2
32	Bangor	5C	293	55	75.8
33	Central England	3aE	255	85	75.5
34	Salford	4A	256	50	73.6
35	Oxford Brookes	3aA	238	60	73.2
36	Bath Spa UC	3aC	251	65	72.7
37	Anglia	3bB	244	65	71.8
38	Westminster	4D	266	55	69.3
39	Kingston	3bC	217	65	68.6
40	Thames Valley	2A	213	65	67.9
41	Liverpool John Moores	2D		65	66.6
42	Hertfordshire	3bB	236		66.5
43	Wolverhampton		190	75	64.8
44	Napier	2C	285	45	64.1
45	Middlesex		181	70	62.4
46	Derby		232	60	62.3
47	Liverpool Hope UC	3bC	200		60.8
48	Chichester UC	1A	219	50	60.4
49	Brunel		255	50	60.3
50	Paisley		273	45	59.7
51	Staffordshire		244	40	56.1
52	Central Lancashire		221	40	54.6
53	Coventry		195	35	51.1
54	Buckinghamshire Chilterns UC		223	20	47.7

Employed in graduate job: 31%
Employed in non-graduate job: 29%
Studying, not employed: 26%
Average starting salary: £13,895

Employed in graduate job and studying: 4%
Employed in non-graduate job and studying: 4%
Unemployed: 6%

THE LETTERS THAT APPEAR IN THE RESEARCH QUALITY COLUMN INDICATE THE PROPORTION OF STAFF INCLUDED IN THE ASSESSMENT, A SHOWING THAT ALMOST ALL STAFF WERE INCLUDED AND F SHOWING THAT HARDLY ANY WERE

Nursing

Nursing has been one of the main growth points of higher education since becoming a graduate profession. A number of institutions have taken in nursing and midwifery colleges, sometimes at the expense of their normally high research grades. In the last assessments, Surrey registered the first 5* nursing grade, although the university still fails to make the top 20 because it has one of the lowest scores for teaching quality.

Manchester retains top place through all-round strength. Only second-placed Edinburgh has higher entrance standards and Manchester is one of almost 20 institutions where all the leavers were in graduate jobs or further study within six months. Only three of the 60 universities and colleges in the ranking reported a success rate of less than 90 per cent.

Nursing		Teaching Quality/24	Research Quality/5	Entry Standards	Graduate Prospects %	Overall Rating
1	Manchester	23	5B	341	100	100.0
2	Edinburgh	HS	3aB	358		97.8
3	Portsmouth	22	5A		100	97.7
4	Northumbria	24	3aC	260	98	97.4
5	Bradford	23	3bB			96.3
6	Central Lancashire	24	3bE	276	98	96.1
7	Nottingham	22	3aC	335	100	95.9
8	Plymouth	23	3bC		98	95.5
9	Kingston/St George's Hospital	22	3aA			95.3
10	Southampton	22	3bA	312	98	95.1
11	Anglia	23	3aD	245	100	94.9
12	Liverpool	22	3aB	294	96	94.8
=13	Glasgow	HS	3aD	319	96	94.6
=13	Reading	24			94	94.6
15	King's College London	21	4A	308	96	94.5
=16	York	21	5B			94.3
=16	Hertfordshire	23	4D	216	98	94.3
=18	Salford	22	3aA	233	96	93.7
=18	Bolton	24			90	93.7
20	Birmingham	22	3bD	314	96	93.5
21	Teesside	23			98	93.4
=22	West of England	22	3bC	245	100	93.2
=22	Swansea		3bB	242	100	93.2
24	Glamorgan		3bB	240	100	93.1
25	Buckinghamshire Chilterns UC	23			96	92.9
26	De Montfort	22	3aD	244	98	92.7
27	Glasgow Caledonian	HS	3aE	261	96	92.6
28	Queen Margaret College	HS		277	98	92.4
29	Leeds	20	4A	290		92.3
30	Cardiff	S	4D		100	92.2
=31	Surrey	19	5*A	285	96	92.1
=31	Ulster	22	4D	197	98	92.1

Northumbria and Central Lancashire were the only universities in the UK to be awarded full marks for teaching. Portsmouth has moved up to third, with a research grade to match Manchester's, to become the leading new university. Central Lancashire, Plymouth and Kingston (in partnership with St George's Hospital Medical School) are the other new universities in the top ten. Entry scores are more closely bunched than in many tables. Only Edinburgh averages more than 350 points and none of the institutions for which scores are available slipped more than a fraction below 200 points.

Almost two thirds of the students arrive without A levels, but there are more than five applicants to every place, mostly female. A quarter of those who join pre-registration programmes drop out, but the wastage rate is nearer 10 per cent thereafter. The demand for training is still growing rapidly: the 45,000 applications at the start of 2005 represented an increase of more than 30 per cent, and this followed a rise of 23 per cent in 2004.

- **The Royal College of Nursing:** www.rcn.org.uk

33	Canterbury Christ Church UC	22			100	91.7
34	Sheffield	21	5D			91.4
=35	City	20	4B	234	100	91.3
=35	Greenwich	23		211	94	91.3
37	Liverpool John Moores	21	3aC			91.2
38	Leeds Metropolitan	21	3bE	266	100	90.9
39	Queen's, Belfast	22			96	90.7
40	Brighton	22	2F			90.5
41	Thames Valley	20	3bA		100	90.3
42	Sheffield Hallam	21		260	100	90.1
=43	Wolverhampton	21		260	100	90.0
=43	Coventry	22		197	98	90.0
45	Keele	21	2E	286		89.9
46	Brunel	22			92	89.8
=47	Bournemouth	22	3bF	246	90	89.7
=47	Staffordshire	22		221		89.7
=47	Middlesex	22	3aF		90	89.7
=50	Northampton UC	22		215	94	89.6
=50	Luton	23			82	89.6
52	Manchester Metropolitan	21			100	89.5
53	Robert Gordon		2F		100	89.4
54	London South Bank	20	3aE		100	88.5
=55	Oxford Brookes	20	3bF	233	100	87.8
=55	Abertay Dundee	S		220		87.8
57	Central England	20	2E	251	96	87.7
58	Napier			232	86	84.3
59	Hull	17	3aE		100	82.0
60	Derby	19		208	76	80.5

Employed in graduate job: 86%
Employed in non-graduate job: 2%
Studying, not employed: 1%
Average starting salary: £19,333

Employed in graduate job and studying: 10%
Employed in non-graduate job and studying: 0%
Unemployed: 1%
Teaching quality assessed 1999–2000

THE LETTERS THAT APPEAR IN THE RESEARCH QUALITY COLUMN INDICATE THE PROPORTION OF STAFF INCLUDED IN THE ASSESSMENT, A SHOWING THAT ALMOST ALL STAFF WERE INCLUDED AND F SHOWING THAT HARDLY ANY WERE.

Other Subjects Allied to Medicine

The 'allied to medicine' category covers audiology, complementary therapies, counselling, health services management, health sciences, nutrition, occupational therapy, optometry, ophthalmology, orthoptics, osteopathy, physiotherapy, podiatry, radiography and speech therapy. Traditional universities monopolise the top ten, but big names such as Durham and Nottingham find themselves outside the top 40. Teaching scores were generally high, with all but two of the top 50 scoring at least 21 points out of 24.

Cardiff, rated Excellent at teaching under the Welsh system and internationally outstanding for research, retains top place in the table. It is also one of five institutions where every leaver was in a graduate job or further study within six months of graduation. City, Leeds, London South Bank and Northampton University College are the others.

Newcastle, one of six English universities with full marks for teaching, has moved up to second, overtaking Loughborough, a previous leader and another with that distinction. The other top teaching scores were at Loughborough, Leeds, Birmingham and Liverpool John Moores, while UWIC was rated as Excellent under the Welsh system. Glasgow Caledonian has a mixture of Excellent and Highly Satisfactory grades after separate assessments for occupational therapy, physiotherapy and radiotherapy. But it loses out to Strathclyde's high research grade in the race to be the top university in Scotland.

Birmingham and Newcastle have the highest entry standards, but no university averages 400 points. However, only a handful of those institutions for which data are available

Other Subjects Allied to Medicine	Teaching Quality/24	Research Quality/5	Entry Standards	Graduate Prospects %	Overall Rating
1 Cardiff	E	5*A	380	100	100.0
2 Newcastle	24	5A	388	92	99.0
3 Loughborough	24	4A			97.9
4 Manchester	23	5*B	366	98	94.8
5 University College London	24	5C	345	94	93.5
=6 Strathclyde		5A	348	86	92.5
=6 York		5A	294		92.5
8 Aston	23	5C	378	98	90.9
9 Bradford	23	5B	310	94	89.6
10 City	23	5C	329	100	89.0
11 Leeds	24	5D	264	100	88.1
12 King's College London	23	4B	328	80	86.0
13 Birmingham	24		388	92	85.8
14 Portsmouth	23	5A	232	82	85.4
15 Queen Margaret College	HS	4A	292	96	85.1
16 East Anglia	23	3bA	308	96	84.6
17 Glasgow Caledonian	E/HS	4C	323	92	84.5
18 Liverpool John Moores	24	4A	186	74	84.4
19 Surrey	21	5*A			83.1
20 Brighton	22	5C	291	98	82.2
21 Hull	23	4D	306	88	82.1

22	UWIC, Cardiff	E	3bD	277	94	82.0
23	Sheffield Hallam	23	4D	252	86	79.3
24	St George's Hospital Medical School	23	3aE	266	92	77.9
25	Nottingham Trent	23	5D	218	80	77.8
26	Salford	22	3aA	259	80	77.1
27	Northumbria	23		290	94	76.9
28	Westminster	23	3aC	202	80	76.6
=29	Manchester Metropolitan	22	3bD	330	90	76.5
=29	Leeds Metropolitan	23	3aE	293	76	76.5
31	Coventry	23	3aE	215	96	76.3
32	Sheffield	21	4B	359	70	76.2
33	Brunel	22	3aE	322	92	75.8
34	Canterbury Christ Church UC	22	2C	283	96	75.1
35	Teesside	22	3aC	198	96	74.4
36	Northampton UC	22	2C	247	100	74.2
37	Ulster	22	4F	311	92	73.7
38	Kingston	23	3aC	155	70	72.8
39	West of England	21	3aB	247	90	72.5
=40	Reading			355	92	72.3
=40	Derby	22		277	98	72.3
42	Durham	23		315	60	72.2
43	Central Lancashire	22	3bA	247	62	71.2
44	Liverpool	20	3aB	292	98	71.1
45	Queen Mary	22		309		70.4
46	Southampton	20	3aA	297	86	70.3
47	Aberdeen			369	80	69.9
48	Nottingham	21	3aC			69.2
49	Central England	22		244	86	68.7
50	Robert Gordon	HS/S	3bC	326	98	68.3
51	Wolverhampton	22	3aC	190	62	68.2
52	Hertfordshire	22	3bE	211	78	67.6
53	Glamorgan			275	94	66.6
54	London South Bank	21			100	66.5
55	Anglia	20	3bA	248	86	65.8
56	Middlesex	22		246	56	63.7
57	De Montfort	20	4C	214	70	62.7
58	Oxford Brookes	20		270	98	62.4
59	Kent	21		252		61.5
60	Plymouth	20	3bC			59.7
61	Roehampton	20	2F	214	64	54.2
62	East London	20	2C		30	49.9
63	Greenwich	18	3aA		42	47.8

Employed in graduate job: 68%
Employed in non-graduate job: 11%
Studying, not employed: 8%
Average starting salary: £16,806

Employed in graduate job and studying: 9%
Employed in non-graduate job and studying: 2%
Unemployed: 3%
Teaching quality assessment 1998–2000

The letters that appear in the Research Quality column indicate the proportion of staff included in the assessment, A showing that almost all staff were included and F showing that hardly any were.

average less than 200 points. Across the whole range of subjects, almost half of the students arrive without A levels. The demand for places is highest on professional courses such as optometry and physiotherapy, where graduate employment prospects are excellent. Nationally, only 3 per cent of graduates were unemployed in the last survey – one of the lowest figures in any set of subjects. Three quarters of those completing courses went straight into graduate jobs.

- **The Chartered Society of Physiotherapists:** www.csp.org.uk
- **The College of Occupational Therapists:** www.cot.co.uk
- **The General Chiropractic Council:** www.gcc-uk.org
- **The General Optical Council:** www.optical.org
- **The General Osteopathic Council:** www.osteopathy.org.uk
- **NHS Careers:** www.nhscareers.nhs.uk
- **The Royal College of Speech and Language Therapists:** www.rcslt.org
- **The Society of Chiropodists and Podiatrists:** www.feetforlife.org
- **The Society of Radiographers:** www.sor.org
- **The Health Professions Council:** www.hpc-uk.org

Pharmacology and Pharmacy

Cambridge retains top spot in the pharmacology and pharmacy ranking, with one of the six maximum scores for teaching at English universities and by far the highest entrance standards. Manchester moves up to second with another top teaching score and one of only two 5* research grades in pharmacy. The other went to sixth-placed Bath, while Dundee, UCL and Oxford achieved the same in pharmacology.

All but four of 23 English universities assessed for teaching quality achieved at least 22 points out of 24, but only Manchester managed top grades for both teaching and research. Cardiff and Strathclyde were both rated Excellent for teaching quality, helping them to top place for Wales and Scotland respectively.

Portsmouth is by far the top new university. Full marks for teaching and a grade 5 for research help earn it a place in the top five. Greenwich, Brighton and Robert Gordon are the other former polytechnics in the top 20.

Departments in England are evenly split between those specialising in pharmacy and pharmacology. Only four cover both. Since 1997, pharmacy degrees have been converted to the four-year MPharm, whereas pharmacology is available either as a three-year BSc or as an extended course. Applications were up by over 23 per cent at the start of 2005.

Career prospects are excellent, especially in pharmacy, with only 3 per cent unemployment across both subjects in the latest survey. Only medicine, dentistry, nursing and veterinary medicine had a higher proportion of 'positive destinations'. Four institutions reported full employment: London University's School of Pharmacy, Brighton, Liverpool John Moores and Robert Gordon, which did so for the third year in a row.

- **The British Pharmacological Society:** www.bps.ac.uk
- **The Royal Pharmaceutical Society of Great Britain:** www.rpsgb.org.uk
- **The National Pharmaceutical Association:** http://npa.co.uk

Pharmacology and Pharmacy

		Teaching Quality/24	Research Quality/5 Pharmacology	Research Quality/5 Pharmacy	Entry Standards	Graduate Prospects %	Overall Rating
1	Cambridge	24	5A		542		100.0
2	Manchester	24		5*B	396	92	94.5
3	Queen's, Belfast	24		4B	398	98	92.5
4	Nottingham	23		5A	432	98	91.3
5	Portsmouth	24	5A		270	94	90.9
=6	Bath	23		5*A	366	96	90.8
=6	Strathclyde	E		5B	402	90	90.8
8	Cardiff	E		5A	303	98	90.3
9	Bristol	23	4A		428	90	88.5
10	School of Pharmacy	23		5A	306	100	88.2
11	Aston	24		3aC	335	96	87.9
12	Greenwich	23	4A				86.3
13	Brighton	23	5C		278	100	84.7
14	Bradford	23		4B	281	96	84.5
=15	Leeds	23	5B		316	70	83.2
=15	Newcastle	24			342	92	83.2
17	King's College London	22		5B	327	88	81.4
18	Liverpool	22	5A		326	80	81.3
19	Robert Gordon	HS	3bC		382	100	81.0
20	Glasgow	E			343	82	79.7
21	Liverpool John Moores	23			319	100	79.1
22	Sunderland	22		3aB	286	94	78.3
23	Dundee	E	5*B		325	62	76.4
24	Oxford	21	5*B				75.5
25	University College London	20	5*A		338	70	72.7
26	Edinburgh		4A			50	72.2
27	Sheffield	21			372	80	68.5
28	Hertfordshire		3aC		195	66	66.9
29	Kingston		3aC		181	68	66.8
30	De Montfort	21		4C	257	88	66.5
31	Southampton				278	62	62.3

Employed in graduate job: 55%
Employed in non-graduate job: 8%
Studying, not employed: 12%
Average starting salary: £14,977

Employed in graduate job and studying: 21%
Employed in non-graduate job and studying: 1%
Unemployed: 3%
Teaching quality assessed 1998–2000

THE LETTERS THAT APPEAR IN THE RESEARCH QUALITY COLUMN INDICATE THE PROPORTION OF STAFF INCLUDED IN THE ASSESSMENT, A SHOWING THAT ALMOST ALL STAFF WERE INCLUDED AND F SHOWING THAT HARDLY ANY WERE.

Philosophy

Cambridge has lost top place in the philosophy ranking for the first time, thanks to Oxford's leadership in entrance qualifications and graduate employment. The top three all have top grades for teaching quality and research, although Oxford entered fewer academics in the last research assessments. Third-placed King's College London beat Cambridge on employment but the margin on entrance qualifications was too wide to make up the difference overall.

Only five universities were achieved 5* ratings in the 2001 research assessment exercise – the London School of Economics and Edinburgh were the others – but the teaching scores published in the same year in England were among the most generous for any subject, with 22 out of 33 universities achieving maximum points. In addition, Glasgow and Cardiff were rated Excellent under the separate Scottish and Welsh systems, although better scores on the remaining indicators leaves St Andrews as the highest-ranked university in Scotland.

Sixth-placed Brighton is by far the top new university, with a grade 5 for research to add to its full marks for teaching quality. None of the others make the top 20, although Hertfordshire, with maximum points for teaching, comes close. Middlesex did well to match Brighton's grade 5 in the research assessment exercise.

An 8 per cent unemployment rate is only just below the average for all subjects, but more than a third of all philosophers start work in low-level jobs. A minority of the universities for which employment scores could be compiled saw more than half of the leavers go straight into graduate jobs or further study. Nevertheless, the subject's popularity is growing, with 8,600 applications representing a 14 per cent increase at the start of 2005.

- **The Philosophical Society of England:**
  http://atschool.eduweb.co.uk/cite/staff/philosopher/philsocindex.htm

Philosophy		Teaching Quality/24	Research Quality/5	Entry Standards	Graduate Prospects %	Overall Rating
1	Oxford	24	5*B	504	80	100.0
2	Cambridge	24	5*A	488	65	99.0
3	King's College London	24	5*A	374	75	97.9
4	Sheffield	24	5A	406	60	94.1
5	Warwick	24	5B	440	60	93.4
6	Brighton	24	5B			92.8
7	Durham	24	5B	420	55	92.2
8	York	24	5B	414	55	92.1
9	Bristol	23	5A	421	70	91.1
10	Essex	24	5B	327	60	90.8
11	St Andrews	HS	5A	440	70	90.3
=12	Sussex	24	5B	343	50	89.6
=12	University College London	23	5B	383	75	89.6
14	Liverpool	24	4A	324	50	88.4
15	Manchester	24	4B	363	50	88.1
=16	Southampton	24	4A	337	45	87.9
=16	Leeds	24	5C	371	50	87.9
18	East Anglia	24	5B	285	45	87.5

19	Kent	24	4C	306	65	87.1
=20	London School of Economics	22	5*A	434		86.8
=20	Reading	24	5B	320	35	86.8
22	Keele	24	3aB	311		85.9
23	Bradford	24	4B	196		85.1
24	Hertfordshire	24	4B	191		85.0
25	Edinburgh	HS	5*C	397	55	84.8
26	Glasgow	E	4C	366	40	84.0
27	Cardiff	E	3aC	365	45	83.2
28	Stirling	HS	5B	284		82.7
29	Lancaster	24	3aB	305	35	82.4
30	Middlesex	23	5C			81.9
31	Nottingham	22	5B	411	50	81.5
32	Aberdeen	HS	3aB	290		78.1
=33	Manchester Metropolitan	23	3aC			77.1
=33	Bolton	23	3aC			77.1
35	Hull	22	4B	261	50	76.0
36	Staffordshire	23	3aC	200		75.1
37	Birmingham	21	4C	384	45	71.2
38	Lampeter	S	3aA			70.9
39	Dundee	S	3aB	254		70.5
40	Ulster	23		220		68.3
41	Queen's, Belfast	21	3aD	282		63.5
42	Greenwich	21	3bC	188		61.2

Employed in graduate job: 25%
Employed in non-graduate job: 34%
Studying, not employed: 23%
Average starting salary: £14,850

Employed in graduate job and studying: 4%
Employed in non-graduate job and studying: 5%
Unemployed: 8%
Teaching quality assessed 1998–2000

THE LETTERS THAT APPEAR IN THE RESEARCH QUALITY COLUMN INDICATE THE PROPORTION OF STAFF INCLUDED IN THE ASSESSMENT, A SHOWING THAT ALMOST ALL STAFF WERE INCLUDED AND F SHOWING THAT HARDLY ANY WERE.

Physics and Astronomy

Fractions of a point separate the top three in physics and astronomy, but last year's leader is not among them. A dip in its employment score has relegated Durham to fourth, with Oxford taking over at the top. Oxford and Cambridge have the same scores for teaching and research, and Cambridge entrants had marginally higher grades, but Oxford's high employment score carries the day. Only Surrey and Queen's, Belfast did better than 80 per cent 'positive destinations'.

Ten of the 39 universities whose teaching was assessed in England scored maximum points, and there were five more Excellent ratings in Scotland and Wales. Glasgow has overtaken St Andrews to assume the leadership in Scotland, while Swansea remains dominant in Wales. Northumbria is the top-placed new university, although Nottingham Trent is the one with a perfect teaching score.

In spite of the dearth of physicists going into teaching, the subjects command high entry grades in the traditional universities. Only four subjects averaged more than the 405 points recorded by physics and astronomy, although places could be secured at a small number of

Physics and Astronomy CONT.

new universities with 200 points. Applications had been declining, but the start of 2005 saw a 12 per cent increase. The total of almost 16,700 remained ahead of apparently more fashionable subjects such as marketing and journalism.

The profile of undergraduates is among the most traditional: only one in five is female and a similar proportion arrive without A levels or their equivalent. About 5 per cent transfer to other courses or drop out, usually at the end of the first year, but over half of those who remain get firsts or 2:1s. The 11 per cent unemployment rate is above average for all subjects, but two thirds find graduate jobs or go on to higher-level courses.

- **The Institute of Physics:** www.iop.org
- **The Association for Astronomy Education:** www.aae.org.uk

Physics and Astronomy		Teaching Quality/24	Research Quality/5	Entry Standards	Graduate Prospects %	Overall Rating
1	Oxford	23	5*A	531	80	100.0
2	Cambridge	23	5*A	542		99.6
3	Warwick	24	5A	460	75	99.5
4	Durham	24	5A	493	60	97.9
5	Leeds	24	5A	360	80	97.8
6	Manchester	24	5A	424	60	96.2
7	Queen's, Belfast	23	5A	403	85	95.1
8	Swansea	E	5A	314	80	94.5
9	Bristol	23	5A	439	75	94.4
10	Surrey	23	5A	360	85	94.0
11	Liverpool	24	5A	264	70	93.8
12	Glasgow	E	5B	369	75	93.4
13	Imperial College	22	5*A	494	70	92.8
14	York	24	4B	413	60	92.0
15	Nottingham	23	5A	465	55	91.8
16	St Andrews	E	5B	425	55	91.6
17	Bath	24	4A	357	55	91.2
18	University College London	23	5B	397	70	90.8
19	Edinburgh	E	5B	415	50	90.5
20	Reading	24	4B	311	65	90.2
21	Strathclyde	E	4A	334	65	90.0
22	Royal Holloway	23	5B	353	70	89.7
23	Birmingham	23	5B	373	65	89.4
24	Leicester	23	5A	369	55	89.3
25	Lancaster	23	5*A	321	35	87.4
26	Southampton	22	5*B	356	60	85.8
27	Sheffield	22	5B	400	60	84.7
28	Exeter	22	5A	334	60	84.6
29	Sussex	22	5A	325	55	83.6
30	Heriot-Watt	HS	4A	392	50	83.4
31	Salford	23	4A	228	50	82.5
32	Cardiff	S	5A	331	70	82.0

33	Loughborough	23	4C	317	50	81.0
34	Hull	23	4C	276	55	80.8
35	King's College London	22	4B	355	55	80.4
36	Queen Mary	21	5B	280	65	77.8
37	Northumbria	23	3aD			77.0
38	Aberystwyth	S	4A	242	65	76.5
39	Keele	22	3aB	306		76.4
40	Nottingham Trent	24	3aD	207	30	75.8
41	Kent	21	3aC	341	70	73.8
42	Hertfordshire	21	4B	192	55	71.7
43	Paisley	S	3aB			69.7
44	Dundee	HS		292		67.3
45	Staffordshire	22			40	63.1
46	Central Lancashire	19	4B			58.4

Employed in graduate job: 21%
Employed in non-graduate job: 24%
Studying, not employed: 36%
Average starting salary: £16,104

Employed in graduate job and studying: 6%
Employed in non-graduate job and studying: 2%
Unemployed: 11%
Teaching quality assessed 1998–2000

THE LETTERS THAT APPEAR IN THE RESEARCH QUALITY COLUMN INDICATE THE PROPORTION OF STAFF INCLUDED IN THE ASSESSMENT, A SHOWING THAT ALMOST ALL STAFF WERE INCLUDED AND F SHOWING THAT HARDLY ANY WERE.

Politics

Politics continues to enjoy a boom as a degree subject. Even after three years of substantial increases, applications were up by another 12 per cent at the start of 2005. Entry scores have been rising as a result, with a dozen universities averaging more than 400 points and only half a dozen registering averages of less than 200 points.

Oxford holds onto top place with by far the highest entry scores, maximum points for teaching quality and a 5* research grade. It is one of four English universities with perfect scores for teaching and research, although Oxford entered a lower proportion of academics than Essex, King's College London or Sheffield for the 2001 Research Assessment Exercise.

Aberystwyth has the other department rated internationally outstanding for research, as well as the only one in Wales to achieve an Excellent rating for teaching. St Andrews has pulled well clear of Strathclyde for the top place in Scotland, although the latter secured the only Excellent rating for teaching quality north of the border. The top nine universities in England were all awarded maximum points for teaching, an achievement matched by De Montfort, the leading new university in 24th place. No university received less than 21 points in England, or a Highly Satisfactory grade in Scotland.

Employment prospects varied widely in this ranking. While 95 per cent of those completing a course at the School of Oriental and African Studies were in graduate jobs or postgraduate training within six months, the proportion was only 35 per cent at a handful of universities. Nationally, the 8 per cent of leavers out of work after six months is close to the average for all subjects, but more than a third were in low-level employment.

- **The Political Studies Association:** www.psa.ac.uk/
- **The Politics Association Online:** www.politicsassociation.com

Politics

		Teaching Quality/24	Research Quality/5	Entry Standards	Graduate Prospects %	Overall Rating
1	Oxford	24	5*B	500	80	100.0
2	Warwick	24	5B	432	75	95.2
3	King's College London	24	5*A	395	55	95.1
4	Bath	24	5A	335	80	95.0
5	Sheffield	24	5*A	418	50	94.9
6	York	24	5A	427	60	94.3
7	St Andrews		5A	455	60	93.8
8	Essex	24	5*A	309	55	92.9
9	Birmingham	24	5B	367	70	92.7
10	Aberystwyth	E	5*A	313	55	92.3
11	Nottingham	24	4A	404	65	92.0
12	Cambridge	23	4A	456	85	90.7
13	Bradford	24	5B	260	70	89.9
14	Bristol	23	5A	407	70	89.5
15	Manchester	24	5B	376	45	89.0
16	Salford	24	5A	253	55	88.9
17	Keele	24	5A	282	40	87.3
=18	Newcastle	23	5B	345	75	87.1
=18	London School of Economics	22	5A	473	80	87.1
20	Strathclyde	E	5B	326	40	86.1
21	Southampton	24	4B	326	45	85.4
22	Queen's, Belfast	23	5A	331	55	85.2
23	Exeter	23	5B	355	60	85.0
=24	Leeds	23	4B	368	70	84.7
=24	De Montfort	24	5B	184	50	84.7
26	Hull	23	5A	271	60	84.4
27	Loughborough	23	5B	298	65	84.3
28	East Anglia	24	4B	323	35	83.8
29	Queen Mary	23	4A	295	65	83.3
30	Glasgow	HS	5B	386	50	82.8
31	Sussex	23	4A	325	55	82.5
32	SOAS	22	4B	326	95	81.7
33	Aberdeen	HS	4A	316	55	80.8
34	Liverpool	23	4A	316	45	80.7
35	Edinburgh	HS	4C	412	60	80.6
36	Lancaster	23	4B	331	50	80.5
37	Royal Holloway		4B	314		79.9
38	Durham	22	4C	428	70	78.2
39	Brunel	23	4B	232	50	77.9
40	Leicester	23	3aB	277	55	77.7
=41	Portsmouth	23	5C	204	55	77.5
=41	Cardiff	S	5A	342	55	77.5
43	Stirling	HS	3aB	316	55	77.3
44	Kingston	23	4A	183	45	77.2

45	Reading	22	5B	289	55	76.6
46	Dundee	HS	4B	273	35	75.2
47	Coventry	23	4C	170	55	74.9
48	Nottingham Trent	23	3aC	222	50	73.7
49	University College London	22	3aA	323		73.4
50	Ulster	22	3aB	259	65	73.0
51	Swansea	S	3aB	263	70	71.7
52	Oxford Brookes	22	3aA	264	45	71.0
53	Wolverhampton	23	3aD	196		70.4
54	Huddersfield	23	3aC	204	30	70.0
55	Leeds Metropolitan		3aA		35	68.5
56	Westminster	22	4C	208		68.4
=57	Kent	21	3aB	268	65	67.4
=57	Plymouth	22	3aC	233	45	67.4
59	Manchester Metropolitan	22	3aC		45	67.2
60	Central England		3aC	211	50	66.6
61	Northumbria	22	3aD	248	40	64.9
62	Middlesex	22	3bC			64.2
63	London South Bank	21	4B			64.1
64	Liverpool John Moores	22	3aD	198		63.5
65	Lincoln	22		232	60	62.9
66	West of England	21	4C	243		62.6
67	Staffordshire		3aC		35	61.6
68	Goldsmiths College	22		240	50	61.5
69	Greenwich	21		205		51.0
70	Northampton UC	21		182		50.3

Employed in graduate job: 30%
Employed in non-graduate job: 34%
Studying, not employed: 20%
Average starting salary: £15,525

Employed in graduate job and studying: 4%
Employed in non-graduate job and studying: 4%
Unemployed: 8%
Teaching quality assessed 2000–01

THE LETTERS THAT APPEAR IN THE RESEARCH QUALITY COLUMN INDICATE THE PROPORTION OF STAFF INCLUDED IN THE ASSESSMENT, A SHOWING THAT ALMOST ALL STAFF WERE INCLUDED AND F SHOWING THAT HARDLY ANY WERE.

Psychology

Only law had attracted more applications than psychology at the start of 2005: a slight downturn in the previous year had turned into another 9 per cent increase, renewing the upward trend that made the subject a higher education phenomenon in the 1990s. Most undergraduate programmes are accredited by the British Psychological Society, which ensures that key topics are covered, but the clinical and biological content of courses still varies considerably. Some universities require maths and/or biology A levels among an average of at least three Bs, but others are much less demanding. The contrast is obvious in the ranking, with 14 universities averaging more than 400 points but six dipping below 200 points.

Cambridge remains top of the table, with by far the highest entrance qualifications and maximum points for both teaching and research. All the top four have teaching and research maximums – St Andrews with an Excellent rating for teaching quality under the Scottish system. Oxford's entry score takes it into second place.

Psychology CONT.

Cardiff is the top university in Wales and St Andrews is the leader in Scotland, although Bangor and Glasgow also have Excellent grades for teaching quality and 5* ratings for research. A total of 14 English universities were awarded full marks for teaching in an unusually high-scoring assessment. None of the top 40 achieved less than 22 points out of 24. Of the three new universities in the top 40, Westminster and Sheffield Hallam scored top marks for teaching, while Plymouth has a grade 5 research rating. Central Lancashire also received full marks for teaching quality but is less competitive on the other indicators.

	Psychology	Teaching Quality/24	Research Quality/5	Entry Standards	Graduate Prospects %	Overall Rating
1	Cambridge	24	5*A	542		100.0
2	Oxford	24	5*A	487	70	98.5
3	York	24	5*A	452	56	95.4
4	St Andrews	E	5*A	404	70	95.1
5	Nottingham	24	5A	437	64	95.0
6	Bath		5B	379	76	94.3
7	Cardiff	E	5*A	414	60	93.7
8	Bristol	23	5*A	414	70	93.6
9	Royal Holloway	24	5A	382	58	92.9
10	Newcastle	24	5*C	415	60	92.6
11	Reading	24	5*B	363	52	91.8
12	Loughborough	24	4B	372	60	90.9
13	Lancaster	24	5A	374	46	90.8
14	Queen's, Belfast	24	4A	336	58	90.5
15	Leicester	24	4B	346	58	90.0
16	University College London	22	5*B	406	74	89.7
17	London School of Economics	23	5A			89.6
18	Swansea	E	4A	289	64	88.9
=19	Durham	23	5A	375	54	88.8
=19	Glasgow	E	5*C	371	52	88.8
21	Birmingham	23	5*C	406	56	88.4
=22	Exeter	23	5B	387	52	87.9
=22	Leeds	23	5C	409	58	87.9
24	Dundee	E	4B	278	62	87.7
25	Bangor	E	5*A	286	38	87.4
26	Sheffield	22	5A	424	58	87.2
27	Stirling	E	5A	318	38	86.8
28	Edinburgh	HS	5C	422	62	86.5
29	Manchester	22	5B	389	58	85.6
30	Aberdeen	HS	4B	312	68	85.4
=31	Surrey	22	5A	343	56	85.1
=31	Essex	22	5A	296	62	85.1
=31	Kent	22	4B	332	70	85.1
34	Aston	22	5C	323	70	84.6
35	Keele	23	4B	326	46	84.4

The last research grades showed considerable improvement on 1996, with a dozen universities rated internationally outstanding. Employment scores are more bunched than in many other tables. Thames Valley, in 77th place and with easily the lowest entry score, has the best destinations record, with 80 per cent of leavers going straight into graduate jobs or postgraduate training. Nationally, the unemployment rate is below average for all subjects, but half of all leavers are either in low-level jobs or without work six months after graduation.

- **The British Psychological Society:** www.bps.org.uk

36	Goldsmiths College	22	4A	292	66	84.3
37	Westminster	24	3aD	247	56	84.2
38	Sheffield Hallam	24	3bC	306	46	84.1
39	Hull	23	3aC	330	56	83.9
40	Plymouth	23	5C	284	46	83.2
41	Oxford Brookes	23	3aC	297		82.9
=42	Sussex	21	5A	330	62	82.5
=42	Southampton	21	5A	358	58	82.5
44	Hertfordshire	23	4B	228	46	82.2
45	Strathclyde	HS	4B	338	44	82.1
46	Warwick	21	5B	400	54	81.9
47	Brunel	22	4B	296	52	81.4
=48	Central Lancashire	24	3aE	267	42	81.3
=48	Liverpool	22	4C	360	50	81.3
50	Portsmouth	23	3aD	280	52	81.0
51	UWIC, Cardiff	E		261	56	80.4
52	Ulster	23	3aD	235	48	79.4
53	Northumbria	22	4D	282	54	78.8
54	City	21	4A	304		78.7
55	Staffordshire	23	3aD	247	40	78.4
56	Abertay Dundee	HS	3bB	216	52	78.3
57	East London	23	3aC	183	40	78.1
58	Bolton	24	3bD	179	30	77.9
59	Nottingham Trent	22	3aC	303	42	77.7
60	Liverpool Hope UC	22	2D	210	68	77.4
61	Greenwich	22	3bC	212	56	77.0
62	Paisley	HS	3aC	213	42	76.9
63	De Montfort	22	3aD	226	50	76.3
=64	London South Bank	20	4B		66	76.1
=64	Roehampton	22	3aE	228	56	76.1
=66	Manchester Metropolitan	22	3aD	292	36	75.4
=66	Anglia	22		248	58	75.4
68	Luton	22	2E	216	54	74.7
69	Lincoln	21	2D	254	64	74.4
70	Glasgow Caledonian	HS	4E	284	26	74.0
71	Derby	20	3aC	244	62	73.1
72	Bournemouth			224	64	73.0
73	Winchester UC	21	2B	275	44	72.7
74	Middlesex	21	3aD	182	50	72.0

		Teaching Quality/24	Research Quality/5	Entry Standards	Graduate Prospects %	Overall Rating
75	Wolverhampton	21	3bD	228	46	71.7
76	West of England	22		264	28	70.9
77	Thames Valley	20	1C	128	80	70.6
78	Bath Spa UC	21		223	50	70.3
79	Gloucestershire	21		235	48	70.2
80	Coventry	21	2D	233	36	69.5
81	Sunderland	20	3bD	229	48	68.7
82	Glamorgan			224	48	68.6
83	Buckinghamshire Chilterns UC	21		166	46	68.4
84	Teesside	20		202	60	68.1
85	Worcester UC	20	2D	239	44	67.6
86	Leeds Metropolitan	20		276	44	67.2
87	Huddersfield	20		222	46	66.3
88	Canterbury Christ Church UC	20		276		66.1
89	Liverpool John Moores	19		254	52	64.7
90	Kingston			197	36	64.3
91	Northampton UC	19		220	40	62.0

Employed in graduate job: 27%
Employed in non-graduate job: 39%
Studying, not employed: 17%
Average starting salary: £14,215

Employed in graduate job and studying: 6%
Employed in non-graduate job and studying: 5%
Unemployed: 6%
Teaching quality assessed 1998–2000

THE LETTERS THAT APPEAR IN THE RESEARCH QUALITY COLUMN INDICATE THE PROPORTION OF STAFF INCLUDED IN THE ASSESSMENT, A SHOWING THAT ALMOST ALL STAFF WERE INCLUDED AND F SHOWING THAT HARDLY ANY WERE.

Russian and Eastern European Languages

The top two remain the same but, for the first time in four years, there are changes in the upper reaches of the ranking for Russian and Eastern European languages.

Birmingham makes its debut in the table in third place, UCL slips to fourth and Oxford drops out of the top five. Sheffield has a commanding lead because it is the only university in Britain with maximum points for both teaching and research. Second-placed Cambridge has neither, but it boasts the highest entry standards and the best employment record.

No other university was awarded full marks for teaching, but Birmingham, Oxford and Bristol were also rated internationally outstanding for research. New universities make up almost a third of the ranking. Wolverhampton wins a place in the top ten with a teaching quality grade bettered by only four universities in England. Glasgow and Edinburgh are pipped to the leadership in Scotland by St Andrews, but there are no entries from Wales or Northern Ireland.

Small numbers mean that less than half the universities in the table have entry and employment scores. The entry scores that can be published range from less than 200 points at Coventry to 475 at Cambridge. Fewer than 700 students take Russian at degree level, and fewer than half of the universities assessed in England offered Russian as a single-honours degree. Most of the students were learning the language *ab initio*, and there was a high dropout rate from some universities, despite an 'excellent rapport' between staff and students. The small numbers make for exaggerated swings in employment prospects: only one subject had a higher unemployment rate in last year's guide, but this year's figure is exactly on the average. Two thirds were in graduate jobs or postgraduate study within six months of completing courses in 2003.

- **CILT – The National Centre for Languages:** www.cilt.org.uk
- **The Institute of Translation and Interpreting:** www.iti.org.uk

Russian and Eastern European Languages

		Teaching Quality/24	Research Quality/5	Entry Standards	Graduate Prospects %	Overall Rating
1	Sheffield	24	5*A		70	100.0
2	Cambridge	22	5A	475	80	93.8
3	Birmingham	23	5*B	369		93.1
4	University College London	23	5A	356	70	91.9
5	Queen Mary	23	5C			88.1
6	St Andrews	22	4A			86.1
7	Oxford	21	5*B			86.0
8	Bristol	20	5*A	380		84.8
9	Glasgow	22	4B			84.2
10	Wolverhampton	22	3aA			82.6
11	Edinburgh	21	4A			81.6
12	Nottingham	19	5A	408	70	81.2
13	Heriot-Watt	21	4B	458	50	80.9
14	Strathclyde	22	3aA		45	78.5
15	Exeter	20	5B			78.3
16	Leeds	20	4B	327	65	77.6
17	Northumbria	23	3bE			76.2
18	Bath	19	5A			76.1
19	Surrey	18	5A			71.6
20	Brighton	20			65	65.0
21	Coventry	21		194		63.3
22	Liverpool John Moores	19			65	61.3
23	Portsmouth	18	5D		40	60.2
24	Sussex	17	4D			54.9
25	Nottingham Trent	17		227	55	53.9

Employed in graduate job: 41%
Employed in non-graduate job: 27%
Studying, not employed: 17%
Average starting salary: £16,503

Employed in graduate job and studying: 6%
Employed in non-graduate job and studying: 3%
Unemployed: 7%
Teaching quality assessed 1995–96

THE LETTERS THAT APPEAR IN THE RESEARCH QUALITY COLUMN INDICATE THE PROPORTION OF STAFF INCLUDED IN THE ASSESSMENT, A SHOWING THAT ALMOST ALL STAFF WERE INCLUDED AND F SHOWING THAT HARDLY ANY WERE.

Social Policy

The London School of Economics maintains its lead at the top of the social policy ranking with one of the three maximum scores for research and among the highest scores in the other two indicators. But it is all change in the other leading places. Kent leaps from ninth to second thanks to the best employment score (jointly with Birmingham), practically

Social Policy		Research Quality/5	Entry Standards	Graduate Prospects %	Overall Rating
1	London School of Economics	5*A	357	70	100.0
2	Kent	5*A	271	80	98.0
3	Bristol	5A	342	70	96.9
4	Birmingham	4C	338	80	94.0
5	Sheffield	5B	335		93.5
6	Nottingham	4A	364	60	93.0
7	Queen's, Belfast	5A	311	60	92.4
8	Glasgow	4B	349	60	91.0
9	Manchester	5B	357	50	90.7
=10	Cardiff	5A	313	50	89.7
=10	Bath	5B	288	60	89.7
12	Loughborough	5*A	259	50	88.9
13	Liverpool	4B		60	88.6
14	York	5A	291	50	88.5
15	Newcastle	4B	306		88.1
16	Bangor	3aA		60	87.0
17	Leeds	5A	307	40	86.6
18	Hull	4B	210	70	86.2
19	Edinburgh	4B		50	84.3
20	Stirling	5B	288	40	84.0
21	Nottingham Trent	3aB	255	60	83.8
22	Keele	5B		40	83.1
23	Portsmouth	3aB		50	81.3
24	Sheffield Hallam	3aC		50	78.9
25	Salford	3aA		40	78.6
26	Ulster	4C	196	50	77.8
27	Brighton	3bC	234	50	76.6
28	Swansea	3aB	152	50	75.3
29	Aston		266	50	73.8
30	Lincoln	3aD	224		73.1
31	Anglia	3aD	206	40	72.0

Employed in graduate job: 36%
Employed in non-graduate job: 35%
Studying, not employed: 12%
Average starting salary: £15,850

Employed in graduate job and studying: 4%
Employed in non-graduate job and studying: 5%
Unemployed: 7%

THE LETTERS THAT APPEAR IN THE RESEARCH QUALITY COLUMN INDICATE THE PROPORTION OF STAFF INCLUDED IN THE ASSESSMENT, A SHOWING THAT ALMOST ALL STAFF WERE INCLUDED AND F SHOWING THAT HARDLY ANY WERE.

exchanging places with Bath, last year's top-scorer on employment. Bristol and Birmingham also move up from the fringes of the top ten to third and fourth respectively.

Teaching scores were removed because of their age – the assessments were published in 1995. Loughborough and Kent are the other research stars, while Nottingham has the highest entrance standards. Glasgow is the top university in Scotland, Cardiff the leader in Wales. There are only six new universities, led by Nottingham Trent, in the ranking, and none in the top 20.

Average entry standards are comparatively low, with no university averaging more than 370 points. Although two thirds of entrants come with A levels or their equivalent, some courses cater very largely for mature students. Not all institutions have entry scores but, of those that do, only two average less than 200 points. However, the proportion of students getting firsts or 2:1s is also low.

Demand for places in social policy had been dropping, but there had been a spectacular recovery when the official deadline passed for courses beginning in 2005. Applications were up by 21 per cent. Graduate unemployment is on the average for all subjects, but only about half of all leavers go straight into graduate jobs or postgraduate study.

- **The British Sociological Association:** www.britsoc.co.uk

Social Work

Social work used to be unusual for having more students taking certificate or diploma courses than degrees, but the diploma has now been withdrawn in the quest for an all-graduate profession. The new degree attracted almost double the number of applicants its predecessor managed when it was introduced in 2004, and then produced the biggest increase of any subject (73 per cent) at the start of 2005. Extra places at undergraduate level should ensure that entry requirements remain comparable. Up to now, almost two thirds of all students have been selected on qualities or qualifications other than A level.

Stirling jumped into first place last year, but has gone out of it again because there were too few students taking social work to compile scores at entry or graduation. Bristol, which has the highest entrance standards and the only 5* research grade, takes over at the top, leapfrogging Bath, which is one of four universities where every leaver went into a graduate job or further training. The others were Dundee, Nottingham Trent and Bradford.

The removal of teaching scores from the first round of assessments had already transformed the ranking. Almost half of the universities listed previously disappeared from the table because they run postgraduate courses only and do not have entry averages or graduate employment scores. Robert Gordon is the top new university, and is joined in the top ten by Nottingham Trent and Middlesex. Newport, at the bottom of the table, is the only representative from Wales.

Entry standards are lowest in any of the tables in this year's guide, with only Bristol averaging more than 300 points. Almost half of the other institutions registering separate grades average less than 200 points.

The vocational nature of the subject helps produce some of the best employment figures in higher education, however. The latest survey showed only 4 per cent unemployment six months after graduation. Only three universities had fewer than 70 per cent of leavers in graduate employment or further study.

- **Social Work Careers:** www.socialworkcareers.co.uk
- **The General Social Care Council:** www.gscc.org.uk

Social Work

		Research Quality/5	Entry Standards	Graduate Prospects %	Overall Rating
1	Bristol	5*C	309		100.0
2	Bath	5B		100	96.4
3	Dundee	4B		100	91.3
4	Southampton	3aB	289		88.8
5	Robert Gordon	3aA	243	95	86.5
6	Hull	3aB		95	84.0
7	Birmingham	4C	259	85	83.5
8	Nottingham Trent	3aB	200	100	81.9
9	Middlesex	4C		90	81.7
10	Bradford	4D		100	80.5
11	Huddersfield	5C	182	80	76.5
12	Salford	3aA	183	80	75.6
13	De Montfort	3aD		95	75.3
14	Ulster	3bD	222	90	73.4
=15	Anglia	3aD		90	73.1
=15	Brunel	3aD		90	73.1
17	Liverpool John Moores	3bC	236	75	72.7
18	Northumbria	3aB	192	70	71.9
19	Leeds		300	75	71.7
20	Durham	4A		50	71.4
21	Plymouth	4D		80	71.3
22	Oxford Brookes		248	85	69.4
23	Hertfordshire	3bE		95	69.0
24	Coventry	3bE		90	66.7
25	Lincoln		199	90	65.8
26	Sheffield Hallam		178	95	65.1
27	Wolverhampton		200	85	64.3
28	Manchester Metropolitan	3aE	209	65	63.3
29	Central Lancashire	3aD		65	61.6
30	Sunderland	3aB	165	45	61.4
31	Staffordshire	3bC		60	59.9
32	Canterbury Christ Church UC		180	60	54.5
33	University of Wales, Newport		153	55	50.2

Employed in graduate job: 63%
Employed in non-graduate job: 17%
Studying, not employed: 7%
Average starting salary: £19,177

Employed in graduate job and studying: 7%
Employed in non-graduate job and studying: 2%
Unemployed: 4%

THE LETTERS THAT APPEAR IN THE RESEARCH QUALITY COLUMN INDICATE THE PROPORTION OF STAFF INCLUDED IN THE ASSESSMENT, A SHOWING THAT ALMOST ALL STAFF WERE INCLUDED AND F SHOWING THAT HARDLY ANY WERE.

Sociology

The popular image of sociology may still be stuck in the 1960s, but it remains one of the largest of the social sciences. Although applications dropped slightly in 2004, there was a 4 per cent increase (to almost 20,000) by the official deadline for courses beginning in 2005.

Cambridge has regained the leadership that it lost to Warwick because it has the highest entrance standards and the best employment record in the table. Warwick, which was awarded one of only three maximum scores for teaching in England, pips Loughborough to second place. The other top teaching scores went to Sussex and Birmingham, with Edinburgh, Aberdeen, Stirling and Glasgow all rated Excellent under the Scottish system. Edinburgh overcomes one of the lowest employment scores in the table to beat Aberdeen to the leading place in Scotland. No Welsh university was rated better than Satisfactory, but Cardiff is best-placed in the table. Two new universities (Oxford Brookes and the West of England) are ahead of it, but neither makes the top 30.

Seven universities were rated internationally outstanding in the last research assessments, but only Loughborough and Essex make it to the top ten. The employment scores show wide variations, with 85 per cent of Cambridge graduates going straight into graduate jobs or higher-level courses, but only 25 per cent of Central England's doing the same. Entry qualifications are equally variable: from more than 450 points at Cambridge to less than 200 points at a dozen institutions.

Other subjects such as criminology, urban studies, women's studies and some communication studies were also covered in the teaching assessment, which included a large number of institutions where sociology is taught as part of a combined studies or modular programme. Although the unemployment rate is below average for all subjects, at 6 per cent, only four subject areas had a lower proportion of 'positive destinations' in 2003. Almost half those completing courses were in low-level jobs six months after graduation.

- **The British Sociological Association:** www.britsoc.co.uk

Sociology		Teaching Quality/24	Research Quality/5	Entry Standards	Graduate Prospects %	Overall Rating
1	Cambridge	23	5A	456	85	100.0
2	Warwick	24	5A	385	65	97.4
3	Loughborough	23	5*A	324	80	97.2
4	Sussex	24	4A	314	50	91.3
5	York	23	5A	362	45	91.1
=6	Bristol	21	5B	370	75	89.7
=6	Essex	22	5*A	289	55	89.7
=6	Edinburgh	E	5A	403	35	89.7
=9	Aberdeen	E	5A	290	55	89.5
=9	Newcastle		4B	321	75	89.5
11	Sheffield	E	5B	336	50	88.9
12	Manchester	21	5*A	346	55	88.7
13	Glasgow	E	4A	359	45	88.2
14	Brunel	22	5A	270		87.8
=15	Kent	21	5*A	279	60	87.6
=15	Birmingham	24	3aC	369	40	87.6

Sociology CONT.

		Teaching Quality/24	Research Quality/5	Entry Standards	Graduate Prospects %	Overall Rating
17	Goldsmiths College	21	5*A	255	60	86.9
18	London School of Economics	20	5A	413		86.6
19	Surrey	21	5*A	276	50	86.0
20	Nottingham	21	4A	363	55	85.8
21	Stirling	E	5B	304	35	85.7
22	Exeter	21	5B	305	60	85.5
23	Durham	21	4A	349	55	85.4
24	Keele	22	5B	311	40	85.1
25	Aston		5B	280	55	84.8
26	Southampton	21	5A	304	45	84.2
27	Bath	19	5B	311	80	83.6
28	Lancaster	21	5*B	289	40	83.5
29	Reading	22	3aB	296	50	83.1
30	Leeds	20	5A	344	45	82.8
31	Oxford Brookes	21	4A	245		81.8
32	West of England	23	3aB	235	35	81.6
33	Strathclyde	HS	3aB	340	45	81.2
34	Liverpool	21	4B	273	45	80.7
35	Cardiff	S	5A	331	35	79.6
36	Greenwich	23	3aB	162	35	79.5
=37	Sheffield Hallam	22		258	70	79.1
=37	Queen's, Belfast	19	5A	304	45	79.1
39	Northumbria	20	3aB	237	65	78.6
40	Liverpool Hope UC	22	2D	207	60	77.7
=41	Paisley	HS	3aC	200	55	77.5
=41	Salford	20	4A	219	45	77.5
43	Kingston	21	4A	175	35	77.2
44	Portsmouth	20	3aB	236	55	77.0
=45	Manchester Metropolitan	21	3aC	240	40	76.1
=45	City	19	4A	261	45	76.1
=45	Sunderland	21	3aB	221	35	76.1
=48	Hull	20	3aB	219	50	75.8
=48	Plymouth	20	4C	219	50	75.8
50	Bangor	S	3aA	232	50	75.6
51	Worcester UC	21	2C	237	50	75.2
=52	Bath Spa UC	22		223	50	75.0
=52	Glasgow Caledonian	HS	3aC	249	30	75.0
54	Roehampton	20	3aC	195	55	74.6
=55	East London	19	4B			74.0
=55	Leicester	19	4B			74.0
=55	Anglia	20	3aD	196	60	74.0
58	Nottingham Trent	19	3aB	249	45	73.3
59	London South Bank	19	4B	186	45	73.0
60	Teesside	19	3aC	168	50	70.5

=61	Middlesex	19	4C	158	40	69.9
=61	Wolverhampton	20		196	55	69.9
63	Coventry	21		186		69.6
64	Northampton UC	20	3bD	220	30	69.1
65	Huddersfield	20	2D			68.9
66	Canterbury Christ Church UC	20		294	30	68.8
=67	Gloucestershire	20		232	40	68.6
=67	Westminster	18	3aB	202	40	68.6
69	Brighton		3bC	222	40	68.4
70	Derby	18	2B	184	55	67.3
71	Central Lancashire	18	3bC	228	40	66.8
72	Liverpool John Moores	18		227	60	66.4
73	Glamorgan			221	50	64.9
74	Napier			218	50	64.8
75	Abertay Dundee			208	50	64.3
76	Ulster	17	3bD	211	45	63.5
=77	Staffordshire	17	3aD	205	35	62.6
=77	Leeds Metropolitan			201	45	62.6
=79	Bradford	17	4D			61.3
=79	Luton	18			40	61.3
81	Central England	18		206	25	60.3
82	East Anglia	16		293	35	59.2
83	De Montfort	17		196		57.5
84	Buckinghamshire Chilterns UC	16		154	40	56.0

Employed in graduate job: 28%
Employed in non-graduate job: 42%
Studying, not employed: 13%
Average starting salary: £14,601

Employed in graduate job and studying: 5%
Employed in non-graduate job and studying: 5%
Unemployed: 6%
Teaching quality assessed 1995–96

THE LETTERS THAT APPEAR IN THE RESEARCH QUALITY COLUMN INDICATE THE PROPORTION OF STAFF INCLUDED IN THE ASSESSMENT, A SHOWING THAT ALMOST ALL STAFF WERE INCLUDED AND F SHOWING THAT HARDLY ANY WERE.

Theology and Religious Studies

Oxford stays on top of the theology and religious studies table, having finally acquired a teaching score after an appeal against the original assessment. But Cambridge and Manchester, locked together in second place, are now only a whisker behind. Manchester has the best teaching score of the trio, while Cambridge boasts the best-qualified entrants, but Oxford's strength across the board carries the day.

Manchester heads a group of three universities with full marks for teaching quality. Lancaster and Sheffield are the other English universities to record maximum points for teaching, although Stirling and Bangor have top ratings in the Scottish and Welsh systems. Nevertheless, Glasgow, which was rated Highly Satisfactory for teaching quality, is the top university in Scotland and moves up to fourth overall with the only 100 per cent record for graduates going into high-level employment or postgraduate study.

Oxford, Manchester, Nottingham and Cardiff are considered internationally outstanding for research. Bath Spa University College, which matched Cambridge on both teaching and

Theology and Religious Studies CONT.

research scores, is the top alternative to a traditional university. Two other university colleges – Winchester and Liverpool Hope – also feature in this year's top 20. Entry qualifications are relatively high. Although only Oxford and Cambridge average more than 400 points, none of the 25 institutions with enough students to register a score slip below 220 points.

	Theology and Religious Studies	Teaching Quality/24	Research Quality/5	Entry Standards	Graduate Prospects %	Overall Rating
1	Oxford	23	5*B	453	75	100.0
=2	Cambridge	23	5A	471	70	99.3
=2	Manchester	24	5*B	300	70	99.3
4	Glasgow	HS	5B		100	98.2
5	Sheffield	24	5A	318	55	97.0
6	Durham	23	5B	391	70	95.5
7	Nottingham	23	5*A	380	50	95.4
8	St Andrews	HS	5A		75	95.1
9	Edinburgh	HS	5A	346	75	95.0
10	Stirling	E	5C	293		94.9
11	Lancaster	24	5A	292	45	94.7
12	Leeds	23	4A	321	80	94.2
13	Birmingham	23	5B	318	75	94.0
14	Bangor	E	4B	282	65	93.8
15	Aberdeen	HS	5B			92.6
16	Exeter	23	5A	326	55	92.5
17	Bath Spa UC	23	4A	236	75	90.8
18	Winchester UC	23	4B	291		90.2
19	Cardiff	S	5*A	332	65	89.7
20	Liverpool Hope UC	23	4A	228	65	89.0
21	Chichester UC	23	3bA			87.2
22	SOAS	22	5B	255	60	85.0
23	King's College London	21	5A	333	65	84.7
24	Canterbury Christ Church UC	22	3aA	339	45	82.6
25	Derby	22	3aB			81.8
26	Lampeter	S	5C			81.3
27	Bristol	20	5B	356	75	80.9
28	Roehampton	21	4A	226	75	81.0
29	Hull	23	3aD	232	50	80.8
30	Oxford Brookes	23	1D		55	79.6
31	Queen's, Belfast	22		270	75	77.3
32	Kent	20	3aD		50	65.2

Employed in graduate job: 28%
Employed in non-graduate job: 25%
Studying, not employed: 32%
Average starting salary: £14,765

Employed in graduate job and studying: 6%
Employed in non-graduate job and studying: 3%
Unemployed: 6%
Teaching quality assessed 2000–01

THE LETTERS THAT APPEAR IN THE RESEARCH QUALITY COLUMN INDICATE THE PROPORTION OF STAFF INCLUDED IN THE ASSESSMENT, A SHOWING THAT ALMOST ALL STAFF WERE INCLUDED AND F SHOWING THAT HARDLY ANY WERE.

Theology and religious studies have enjoyed substantial increases in popularity recently, with a 10 per cent rise in applications in 2004 and another 27 per cent by the official deadline for courses beginning in 2005. By no means all graduates go into the church, but the vocation helps the subjects to the upper reaches of the graduate employment table. Only 6 per cent of graduates are unemployed after six months, while more than 40 per cent go on to further study.

- www.prospects.ac.uk/links/signposts

Town and Country Planning and Landscape

There is no change in the top five positions for town and country planning and landscape studies, but Kingston's 100 per cent employment score gives it a place in the top six. Anglia matches Kingston's employment record, but not its maximum points for teaching quality. Cambridge remains top, largely thanks to the university's normal high entry standards. With no teaching assessment to draw on, Cambridge's overall score is derived from its performance on the other indicators.

Second-placed Cardiff is one of two universities rated internationally outstanding for research, the other being Leeds, which misses the top ten because of a low teaching score. Cardiff was also rated Excellent for teaching quality under the Welsh system.

Three other new universities turned the tables on their older-established peers in the English assessments of teaching quality, Oxford Brookes and Greenwich joining Kingston on maximum points. Oxford Brookes and the West of England also feature in the top ten. Aberdeen is the top university in Scotland, in 14th place.

Only 14 old universities offer degrees in a subject which was once available only at postgraduate level in most institutions. More than 5,000 students now take first degree courses, with almost another 1,000 taking certificate or diploma programmes. The size of departments varies from more than 500 students to less than 150, with about a third of the total postgraduates.

Fewer than half of the students are awarded firsts or 2:1s, but jobs prospects are good, with unemployment below average at 6 per cent and only one graduate in five in low-level work after six months. In the latest survey, only one university reported 'positive destinations' for less than 55 per cent of leavers.

- **The Royal Town Planning Institute:** www.rtpi.org.uk
- **The Landscape Institute:** www.l-i.org.uk

Town and Country Planning and Landscape		Teaching Quality/24	Research Quality/5	Entry Standards	Graduate Prospects %	Overall Rating
1	Cambridge		5B	480	95	100.0
2	Cardiff	E	5*A	304	95	90.5
3	Sheffield	23	5A	330	85	88.8
4	Reading	22	5B	372		85.5
5	Oxford Brookes	24	4C	258	75	81.5
6	Kingston	24			100	79.7
7	Liverpool	23	4A	266	65	79.4

		Teaching Quality/24	Research Quality/5	Entry Standards	Graduate Prospects %	Overall Rating
8	West of England	23	3aB	230	85	77.9
9	Queen's, Belfast	22	3bA	304	95	77.4
10	Newcastle	21	5B	282	80	75.4
11	Nottingham Trent		3aB	247	90	72.3
12	London South Bank	22	4D			71.9
13	Gloucestershire	21	4A	218	75	70.7
=14	Leeds	19	5*A			70.2
=14	Aberdeen	19	5B	334	85	70.2
16	Manchester	20	4B	300	80	69.6
17	University College London		4C	272		69.4
18	Sheffield Hallam	22	4D		55	66.7
=19	Dundee	21	3bD	225	90	64.7
=19	Greenwich	24		215	45	64.7
21	Leeds Metropolitan	21	3aB	214	60	63.8
22	Northumbria	21		276	80	61.4
23	Anglia	19	2B		100	59.3
24	Westminster	20	3aD			57.1
25	Central England	20	3bE	232	75	56.2
26	Manchester Metropolitan	20			85	55.7
27	Birmingham			359	55	53.8
28	Liverpool John Moores	18	3aA			52.0
29	Ulster			231	65	47.3

Employed in graduate job: 52%
Employed in non-graduate job: 18%
Studying, not employed: 16%
Average starting salary: £16,530

Employed in graduate job and studying: 6%
Employed in non-graduate job and studying: 3%
Unemployed: 6%
Teaching quality assessed 1996–98

THE LETTERS THAT APPEAR IN THE RESEARCH QUALITY COLUMN INDICATE THE PROPORTION OF STAFF INCLUDED IN THE ASSESSMENT, A SHOWING THAT ALMOST ALL STAFF WERE INCLUDED AND F SHOWING THAT HARDLY ANY WERE.

Veterinary Medicine

Only medicine itself compares with veterinary medicine for high entry standards: the number of applications has dropped slightly in each of the last two years, but still there were about 20 candidates for each place. This combined with the uncanny closeness of grades for both teaching and research, plus the virtual guarantee of a job for graduates who choose to practise, make it difficult to separate the six schools. Only the one point dropped in its teaching quality assessment prevents Cambridge from heading the table – it has the best employment record and the highest entry qualifications – but that single blemish relegates it to equal fifth place. Liverpool takes over at the top, as one of three English schools with maximum points for teaching. Both of those in Scotland were rated as Excellent under the separate assessment system there.

In research, all six schools were awarded grade 4 in 1996; in 2001 they had all moved up to grade 5, having entered similar numbers of academics. Bristol remains at the bottom of the ranking largely because, like the Royal Veterinary College, it entered a slightly lower proportion of staff than the rest in the last research assessment exercise.

Bristol, Cambridge and the Royal Veterinary College set applicants the specialist aptitude test also used by a number of medical schools in 2005. Vets' final qualifications are not classified, but between 5 and 15 per cent are awarded a commendation. The five-year courses have to meet the requirements of the Royal College of Veterinary Studies, but they vary in size from 65 to 155 students. Up to 10 per cent drop out, but those who complete the course are in high demand. Only medicine, dentistry and nursing have a lower unemployment rate.

- **The Royal College of Veterinary Surgeons:** www.rcvs.org.uk

Veterinary Medicine	Teaching Quality/24	Research Quality/5	Entry Standards	Graduate Prospects %	Overall Rating
1 Liverpool	24	5B	440	98	100.0
2 Edinburgh	E	5B	477	98	98.2
3 Royal Veterinary College	24	5C	445	98	97.1
4 Glasgow	E	5B	458	94	97.0
5 Cambridge	23	5B	531	100	96.6
6 Bristol	24	5C	464	78	95.2

Employed in graduate job: 70%
Employed in non-graduate job: 7%
Studying, not employed: 16%
Average starting salary: £20,765

Employed in graduate job and studying: 3%
Employed in non-graduate job and studying: 1%
Unemployed: 2%
Teaching quality assessed 1999–2000

THE LETTERS THAT APPEAR IN THE RESEARCH QUALITY COLUMN INDICATE THE PROPORTION OF STAFF INCLUDED IN THE ASSESSMENT, A SHOWING THAT ALMOST ALL STAFF WERE INCLUDED AND F SHOWING THAT HARDLY ANY WERE.

4 Applying to University

Once you have made your decisions about what you want to study and where, you can heave a huge sigh of relief because the really hard part is over. The next stage, making an application, is much easier. However, there are still enough issues and decisions to warrant a closer look at the process and how to go about it.

All applications to UK universities for full-time courses are made through UCAS, the Universities and Colleges Admissions Service. While *The Good University Guide* is only concerned with universities, many colleges of one sort or another also recruit through UCAS and so you will find over 300 institutions listed on the UCAS website. If you are interested in a part-time course you will need to contact universities individually to find out how to apply.

UCAS has announced its intention to move to all electronic applications for entry in 2006, using its online application procedure *ucasapply*. UCAS will work closely with schools, colleges, libraries and the agencies to ensure that all applicants will have access to this system. The big advantages will be that the systems have lots of built-in validation, which will reduce errors, and the processing at UCAS will be much faster. *Ucasapply* is available on the UCAS website (www.ucas.ac.uk) alongside details of all the courses available.

At the time of writing, the detailed procedures for 2006 entry had not been finalised, so do check for any changes from what is given here.

Filling in Your Application

The UCAS application may only be a few electronic screens or four A4 pages, but it still looks rather daunting. There is no substitute for reading the guidance and then going slowly and carefully through each section, checking back against the guidance as you go. For most applicants, what you (and your referee) say will be all the university uses to make a decision, so it is important to get it right.

Provided that you follow the guidance carefully, most of the application is straight-forward, but on the following pages are a few points about some of the more significant sections.

Address

This looks simple, and it is, but don't just fill in your current address and then forget about it. If your address changes, make sure you tell UCAS immediately. UCAS will automatically notify your university choices of the change. If you don't keep UCAS informed of your change of address you will find letters (which might be offers or a confirmation of a place) go to the wrong place. It is surprisingly common for applicants at a boarding school to put down their school address on the form but then forget to tell UCAS when they go home for the summer. They then find that the letter confirming a place at university goes to the school instead of to them at home.

Date of Birth

Apparently, getting the date of birth wrong is the most common error. It can make a difference if universities are scanning for mature students, so make sure you get it right.

Examination Results

Make sure you get the details of your examinations to be taken exactly right. If you are taking English Language and Literature, put the full title and not just English, even if everyone in your school or college calls it English. This is important because any mistakes could mean that UCAS cannot match your application with your examination results straightaway in the summer, resulting in a delay in universities making their decisions. Listing the full module details of a BTEC award is also important to avoid confusion over precisely what you have studied.

If you are taking the examinations of another country do not try to give a UK equivalent. Always state exactly what you are doing and let the university decide the equivalence so as to avoid any confusion. If the column headings on the form are inappropriate, then ignore them.

And be honest! Never be tempted to massage your results to make them look a little better. UCAS has some sophisticated fraud-busting techniques and admissions tutors are remarkably good at spotting dodgy applications. If you are found to be giving false or incomplete information, you will be promptly ejected from UCAS and lose any chance of a place at university that year. Even if you manage to slip through all the detection devices, you will probably be asked by the university to present your certificates. Any sign of tampering, or lame excuses about them having been eaten by the dog, will result in a check with the records of the examining board. When the board points out that the ABB on your form was really DDD, you will politely be shown the door.

Personal Statement

This is your chance to say anything you like, in your own words, to persuade admissions tutors that yours is the brightest and best application ever to have crossed their desk. You can write what you like, but the key areas probably include:

- why you want to study your chosen subject
- what particular qualities and experience you can bring to it
- details of any work experience or voluntary activity, especially if it is relevant to your course
- any other evidence of achievement, such as the Duke of Edinburgh award
- details of any sponsorship or placements you have secured or applied for
- your career aspirations
- any wider aspects of life that make you an interesting and well-rounded student
- if your first language is not English, describe any opportunities you have had to use English (such as an English-speaking school or work with a company that uses English).

Application Timetable

May – Sept	Research and make choices about universities and courses
1 Sept – 15 Oct	Apply for Cambridge or Oxford or medicine, dentistry or veterinary science/medicine in any university
1 Sept – 15 Jan	All other applications from the UK or elsewhere in the EU (except art and design route B)
1 Sept – 30 June	All other applications from outside the UK or elsewhere in the EU (except art and design route B)
1 Jan – 24 March	art and design route B
16 Jan – 30 June	Late applications from the UK or elsewhere in the EU considered at universities' discretion
18 Mar – 30 June	UCAS Extra
1 July onwards	Applications go straight into the Clearing procedure

Remember that for most admissions tutors an awful lot of applications will cross their desk. Many applicants will get advice about how to write the statement and see model examples. The result is a tendency for personal statements to be rather similar and, to a hard-pressed admissions tutor faced with a metre-high pile of UCAS forms, rather dull. Somehow you have to make it personal and stand out from the crowd. On the other hand, avoid being too wacky – not all admissions tutors will share your sense of humour and your form may be read by one who doesn't.

If there is anything about your application that is even slightly unusual, then explain why. If you want to defer your entry to the following year, say why and what you intend to do with your year out. If you are a mature student, explain why you want to enter higher education. In general, the more vocational the course, the more you need to emphasise your commitment to the profession and relevant experience you have gained. Conversely, the more academic the course, the more you need to enthuse about the subject and explain why you want to study it for several years.

As with examinations, be honest. If you say you are interested in philosophy and then get called for interview, you can almost guarantee that some learned professor will ask you about Plato's *Theory of Forms* or Spinoza's *Ethics*. If you can't talk sensibly about philosophy, you will look rather silly and will be unlikely to get an offer. Be specific in what you write. Don't just say you did some voluntary work; describe what you learned through the experience. Don't just say you are interested in reading – after all, students have to be interested in reading as they do a lot of it; describe what you like to read and why.

There is no ideal way to structure your statement, but it is a good idea to use paragraphs or sub-headings to make the presentation clear and easy for an admissions tutor to read. If you want to say more than there is space available, do not send additional papers to UCAS, as they will not automatically be passed on to your chosen universities. If you really can't make it fit, then send any additional material directly to the universities to which you have applied but wait until you have received your application number from UCAS, so that you can include this with your papers and make sure they are matched with the correct application.

Ucasapply will let you paste in your personal statement from another source. It is, therefore, a good idea to prepare it in advance and check it thoroughly before entering it into your application.

Choice of Courses

By the time you fill in your application, you should have your choice of courses ready. You are allowed six, but you don't have to use them all and many applicants don't – the average number of choices used is about five. (Indeed if you only use one choice there is a lower application fee.) If you want to apply for medicine, dentistry or veterinary science/medicine, you are only allowed to use four choices for these courses, though you can use the other two for different subjects if you wish. If you are using a paper application form, make sure you get the university and course codes exactly right. If they don't match up, your application will be delayed while UCAS sorts out what you ought to have put down.

Each university will only see details of its own application and so they will not know where else you have applied or whether all the courses in your application are the same.

In all sections of your application, make sure the grammar and punctuation are correct. It is a good idea to show it to someone else as a final check. Don't rely on a spellchecker – it won't pick up the difference between organic chemistry and orgasmic chemistry. When you have finally finished, print out a copy and arrange for your referee (usually someone from your school or college) to add their reference and follow the instructions about ways in which you can pay the fee (£15 for entry in 2005, or £5 if you only use one choice).

Your application can arrive at UCAS any time between 1 September and 15 January (or 15 October if Oxford or Cambridge or any medical, dental or veterinary course is among your choices – see the *Application Timetable* for this and other exceptions). In some circumstances there can be a small advantage in applying early (see below, *Should I Apply Early?*) but generally it will not make any difference. If you apply after the appropriate deadline your application will still be processed by UCAS but universities do not have to consider it. They can, if they wish, reject you on the grounds that they have received enough applications already. However, if you are applying for one of the less competitive courses or are applying from overseas you will probably find your application is treated just like those that arrived on time.

What Happens Next?

The first thing to happen after you have submitted your application to UCAS is the arrival of a confirmation of the courses and universities you have chosen and your application number. It is important to check this carefully to make sure there is no mistake and keep your application number safe as you will probably need it later. Then there is nothing to do but wait. Universities are increasingly aware that applicants don't like to be kept hanging around so you may find some decisions arriving fairly soon. However, if your application arrived at UCAS close to the main deadline it can take several weeks to make its way through UCAS processing and on to your universities. When any decisions do arrive, they will be one of the following:

Unconditional Offer (U): This means you have already met all the entry requirements for the course.

Conditional Offer (C): This means the university will accept you if you meet certain additional requirements, usually specified grades in the examinations you will be taking.

Should I Apply Early?

Universities are required by UCAS rules to treat all applications received by the appropriate deadline on an equal basis. This means that applying early or late should make no difference, as long as the deadline is met, and in practice this is the case for virtually all applicants. Indeed if you are applying for a low-demand subject you will probably get equal treatment even if your application arrives well after the deadline.

Occasionally a very popular university may experience a sudden increase in applications in very high-demand subjects such as medicine, English or law, which only becomes apparent after it has started making decisions. It will then be faced with a choice of either carrying on making offers in the same way and ending up with an intake way above target, or tightening up its criteria and admitting the right number. Neither of these outcomes is desirable: too many students means large classes and over-worked staff; tightening the criteria means being slightly tougher with some applicants. The university may choose the latter course, in which case a few of the later applicants might be rejected whereas, if they had applied earlier, before the increased number of applications was apparent, they might have received an offer. This situation is very rare, but the conclusion is that applying early never does any harm while applying later to high-demand subjects very occasionally might.

Rejection (R): This means that either you have not got, and are unlikely to get, some key requirement for the course, or that you have lost out in competition with other, better applicants.

If you receive an offer, you will almost certainly be invited to visit the university concerned. This is a good chance to find out much more about the course and university than you can through reading prospectuses and looking at websites. However, bear in mind that the occasion is designed to encourage you to accept the offer as well as to give you the opportunity to find out more. So, just like reading prospectuses, you have to be critical of what you are told and look for evidence for any claims that are made.

Sometimes you may be invited for an interview before a decision is made. This could be the normal practice for that particular course, or it could be because your application is unusual in some way and the university wants to check that you are really suitable (perhaps you are a mature student without the usual formal qualifications). In some cases interviews are not quite what they seem (see below, *When is an Interview not an Interview?*), but you can never be sure, so it is best to treat any interview as a real interview.

If you do get called for interview, then go – you are unlikely to be made an offer if you don't turn up – and be sure that you arrive on time. Prepare yourself in advance, particularly for the obvious questions such as why you want to study the subject and why you want to go to that university. Re-read the copy of your application form to remind yourself what is in your personal statement. And dress smartly. While it is not necessary to look as if you are going to a wedding, an interview is not the time to make a fashion statement.

All being well, particularly if you have chosen your universities carefully, you will get several offers. You can hold on to any offer you receive until all your chosen universities have made their decisions, but then you have to choose which ones you want to accept.

When is an Interview not an Interview?

Interviews come in two forms. Outwardly both look the same, but in fact they have very different purposes. The first type of interview is the 'real' interview, where a genuine attempt is being made to assess your suitability for the course and your performance in the interview will make a difference to your chances of being made an offer. The second type of interview is the 'psychological' interview. It looks like an interview, feels like an interview, but actually doesn't make any difference. The university has already decided to make you an offer and the interview is merely a psychologically clever way of encouraging you to accept the offer. If you travel half way across the country, answer some tough questions and then get made an offer of a place, it makes you feel good, both about yourself and about the university. Hence you are more likely to accept that offer in favour of one which just arrived in the post. At least that is the idea behind the psychological interview.

The problem for you is that it is hard to tell which type of interview you are facing. Generally speaking, interviews for medical and medically related professions and for education are real (though it is still common for 80 per cent or more of interviewees to be made an offer). Interviews at very competitive universities such as Oxford and Cambridge are also usually real, and interviews for applicants who have an unusual background or lack the usual qualifications are generally genuine attempts to assess suitability. However, interviews for less popular courses, such as chemistry or engineering, at anywhere other than the most competitive universities for these subjects are often the psychological type of interview.

Replies to Offers

You can accept one offer as your firm acceptance (often called your UF choice if the offer was unconditional or your CF choice if it was conditional). If your firm acceptance is CF, then you can accept a second offer as your insurance acceptance (often called your CI choice), but you must decline any others. Most applicants who have more than one conditional offer will accept as CF their first choice university and then a university which has made a lower offer as their CI choice.

You can, in fact, decline all your offers if you wish. Perhaps you have realised that you have made a dreadful mistake in your choice of subject and now wish to look for another subject in UCAS Extra or the Clearing procedure (see below). However, normally you will want to accept one offer as your firm acceptance.

Once you have done that, you and the university are bound together by the rules of UCAS. If you firmly accept an unconditional offer then you have a definite place at that university. If you firmly accept a conditional offer and then meet all the conditions, the university is obliged to accept you and you are obliged to go there. In making your firm acceptance, assuming you have conditional offers, you will have to balance your desire to attend a particular university against your estimate of whether you can meet the conditions. If you expect to get ABB at A level and the offers are all BCC or below, then it is easy: choose the place you want to go. If, however, you think you will get BCC and your offers are ABB, BBB, BCC and CDD, the decision is more difficult, especially if you really want to go to the university that offered ABB.

This is where the insurance acceptance comes in. If you want to, you can just have a firm acceptance and decline the rest. However, most applicants with more than one offer choose an insurance acceptance as well. If you are accepted by your firm choice then that is it, and

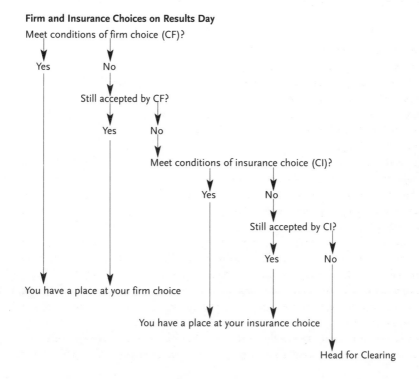

Firm and Insurance Choices on Results Day

Meet conditions of firm choice (CF)?
- Yes → You have a place at your firm choice
- No → Still accepted by CF?
  - Yes → You have a place at your firm choice
  - No → Meet conditions of insurance choice (CI)?
    - Yes → You have a place at your insurance choice
    - No → Still accepted by CI?
      - Yes → You have a place at your insurance choice
      - No → Head for Clearing

the insurance choice becomes irrelevant. However, if your firm choice turns you down because you don't meet their conditions, you might still be accepted by your insurance choice, so you get a second chance before heading for Clearing. Obviously, it makes sense to choose a lower offer for your insurance choice so as to maximise your chances of getting at least one of your two choices. However, make sure it is somewhere you would still like to go because, if that is where you are placed, the UCAS rules require you to go there. Remember that in some subjects, such as chemistry or electronic engineering, places in Clearing, even at prestigious universities, are easy to obtain, so you could be better off choosing just a firm choice rather than two choices, one of which you don't really want. In fact, holding an insurance offer just for the sake of it would delay your entry into Clearing. If all this sounds rather complicated, the flowchart above, *Firm and Insurance Choices on Results Day* may help. Finally, make sure you do reply to your offers. If you don't, and ignore the reminders UCAS will send you, you will be 'declined by default' and lose your offers.

You can track the progress of your application throughout the process using the *ucastrack* facility on the UCAS website. Your password will be sent to you with the acknowledgement of your application and the facility will give you an up-to-the-minute summary of where all your applications have got to. There is even a version for wap-enabled mobile phones.

UCAS Extra

If you are unlucky enough not to receive any offers from any of your choices, or you have a change of heart and decide to decline any offers you do have, UCAS Extra comes into play in mid-March. This, in effect, allows you to make a seventh choice of university. If you become eligible for UCAS Extra, UCAS will send you all the details you need, and courses at universities willing to consider UCAS Extra applications will be available on the UCAS website. You can then either use the UCAS website to make an application or contact a university directly. If you are made an offer, either unconditional or conditional, you can firmly accept or decline it just like any offer in the main UCAS scheme. If you don't get an offer (or decide to decline your offer), you can opt to make another UCAS Extra choice and so on, until either you get an offer or you run out of time (the scheme ends in July).

Once you have an offer and accept it, you become unconditional firm (UF) or conditional firm (CF) for that university (there is only one choice at any time in UCAS Extra so there is no question of an insurance choice). You are committed to it in exactly the same way as the main UCAS scheme. In its first two years, about 20,000 applicants were eligible for UCAS Extra, about 7,000 applied and 2,700 gained a place.

Results Day

If you accepted an unconditional offer, all you have to do is wait for the start of your course and roll up to register. However, most of you will be anxiously waiting for examination results before you find out whether you have been accepted. If you are taking Scottish Highers or an access course, then your results will usually come out before A levels in England. This can be helpful if you don't get accepted, as you will then have a chance to find a place somewhere else before the scramble for places after A-level results are published.

If you find that your results mean you have met all the conditions of your firm choice, congratulations! You have a place at your chosen university and you can relax, at least for now. Do check carefully though, especially if you have an offer expressed in terms of points rather than grades.

If you are sure you have met all the conditions, you don't have to do anything except to check *ucastrack* to make absolutely certain that your place has been confirmed. In a day or two you will receive confirmation of your place from UCAS, with a form to sign to confirm that you still want it, and details of when and where to register from your chosen university will follow a little while later. If you are not sure, or just need reassurance, you can ring the university to check, though bear in mind that several thousand others may be doing the same thing, so it may take a little while to get through. If you do ring, make sure you have your UCAS number handy.

Even if you have not met all the conditions, you may still find your place is confirmed and, again, *ucastrack* is the quickest and easiest way to check. The university may be short of applicants that year or the other offer-holders had worse results than you (see below, *What if I Just Miss My Grades?*). If you are just one grade down, your chances will often be quite good; more than that and your chances will be much less.

Clearing

If you find that you don't have a place then you will be eligible for the UCAS Clearing scheme, a way of matching universities without students to students without universities. Essentially, it is up to you to find a university that is prepared to accept you. The best way to do this is to ring a university and tell them what you want to do. Usually, if they have vacancies, they will take your details and either give you a decision straightaway or very soon afterwards. Just keep going until somewhere offers you a place. Here are some points to remember if you end up in this position:

- prepare in advance – unless you are very confident you will get the grades, do some contingency planning before results day. Make a list of possible courses and universities where you might be prepared to go in priority order. This will be easy to check against the Clearing vacancy lists when they are published
- be there – don't go on holiday at the critical time
- if you think you may not have a place, check with your firm and insurance choices as soon as possible
- check the Clearing vacancy lists in newspapers, the UCAS website, or the websites of individual universities to find where there are vacancies in your subject
- think about alternative courses (perhaps a joint course with another subject insteadof a single subject course) to maximise the choice available
- start ringing possible universities straight away (places at good universities can be filled very quickly)
- always ring yourself – universities are less impressed by people ringing on your behalf
- if you can't get through, keep trying, but also send an e-mail or fax.

What if I Just Miss My Grades?

Suppose you are offered BBC at A level and get BCC: will you still be accepted? This will depend on two main factors. First, did you drop a grade in a critical subject? If you were asked for a B in, say, chemistry and that was the subject where you got a C, this will reduce the chances of your being accepted. Second, what did everyone else with an offer for the course get? If the university has 50 places and 40 get the grades, they will look first for the extra 10 among those who just missed the offer and you will probably be accepted. However, if 60 get the grades, they will probably reject anyone who didn't meet the offer precisely, and you may well not be accepted. There is nothing you can do about this. Universities are financially penalised for admitting the wrong number of students, so they will always want to admit as near as possible to their target number.

There will be a few vacancies not listed in the official vacancy lists because the universities know they can fill them with speculative callers and do not need the extra calls generated by the vacancy lists. If there is somewhere you really want to go, it might just be worth ringing even if they are not in the lists. However, such vacancies will be taken within hours, at most within a day of A-level results being published.

Some applicants find that their results are much better than they expected and they are qualified for a much better university than the one where they accepted an offer, or for a high-demand course such as medicine for which they never thought they would be accepted. If you find yourself in this position, you can do one of three things:

1 Carry on with your existing choice, as long as you are sure that is still what you want to do.
2 Find an alternative university which is prepared to accept you and then negotiate with the university where you have been placed to be released into the Clearing scheme. The university is not obliged to do this, and will probably try to persuade you not to, but most will eventually give way if it is clear that you have genuinely thought through what you are doing. Once in Clearing your alternative university can accept you.
3 Withdraw completely from UCAS and apply again the following year.

If your results are much worse than you expected, the situation can be more difficult. If there were genuine extenuating circumstances (perhaps you were taken ill during your examinations or there was a bereavement in your family) your school should have told the examining board and university about this already. Neither will be impressed by being told about it after your low grades have been published. If the results are just plain surprising, you may wish to seek a re-mark by the examining board. If this brings to light an error, and your grades go up, the university will review its decision, though if you miss the deadline the university may say it can only accept you for the following year.

Trying to get a place in Clearing is not as difficult as it sounds. There is always a lot of talk about 'chaos' and 'scrambling', but in fact universities are getting much better at dealing with large numbers of enquiries very quickly. After all, they have a strong interest in signing up good students as they suffer financial penalties if they under-recruit by a large margin. And the range of courses available in Clearing is huge. In 2004, for example, there were a number of vacancies on courses in law and English, two very high-demand subjects. They may not have been precisely the right course or in an ideal part of the country, but they were there and anyone with the right grades who acted quickly could have obtained a place. If you wanted chemistry or engineering you could have had a choice of a number of prestigious universities, even with quite low grades in some cases.

Having said that, trying to find a place in Clearing is not much fun for anyone. The best way to avoid it is to be sensible and realistic early on in the application process. If you apply for courses and universities where you have a good chance of being made an offer and accept offers you have a good chance of achieving, then you will probably be able to avoid Clearing altogether. That is much better for both you and the universities.

Do I Apply This Year?

Some students take a year out between finishing at school or college and starting university, often known as a gap year. About 8 per cent of the applicants are accepted for deferred entry to the following year. In general, gap years are a good thing. It is possible to go trekking in Thailand, sailing in the Seychelles, teaching in Tanzania, on an adventure up the Amazon or even do drama in Stratford-upon-Avon. You can go for a few weeks or a full year and some opportunities will enable you to earn money to finance your degree course. If you choose your opportunity carefully, you will develop the kind of maturity and enterprise that will help with your studying and your future career. In particular, being able to demonstrate sustained commitment can be attractive to employers.

There are a number of reputable organisations that can help you organise your gap year. They have ready-made activities, take care of some of the practicalities and have a proper concern for safety and security.

On the other hand, a gap year means it will be one year later before you are in the job market and earning a salary. If your chosen course is a long one, this could be a consideration. In a few subjects it may take you a little while to get back into serious study – mathematics is notorious for being a bit harder to take up again after a year away from study – but most students soon catch up again.

If you are thinking about taking a gap year it is still best to apply during your final year at school or college as a 'deferred applicant'. When you fill in your application, you should put a D in the 'defer entry' column in section 3 of the application. This should mean that you get your university place sorted out before starting your job or travels and so don't have to worry about it during your gap year. Indeed, for the more adventurous travellers, trying to fill in a UCAS form on the back of a Mongolian yak or half way across the Australian desert is not recommended. Also, if things go badly wrong in your examinations and you don't get a place, you do get an opportunity to rethink your career options or resit your exams and still start at university when you planned to.

As a general rule, universities are happy to consider deferred applicants but, if the prospectus does not make a clear statement about the university's policy, it would be sensible to check.

Where to Live

5

After choice of university and course, the next most important decision is where to live. And here student demand is polarising. Some are seeking premium accommodation with fast internet connection and Sky, perhaps even a great view as standard, whilst others, more cash-strapped, are looking for the bare minimum. There might well be a bewildering number of options on offer; the National Union of Students (NUS) identifies 16 categories, ranging from deluxe en suite accommodation in a hall of residence with all meals provided to lodging in a family house or staying at home. No doubt we could even find a few students who live on houseboats or in caravans, but the majority of first-year students choose to live in university-owned accommodation as the table below shows.

University Halls and Houses

Most universities provide places for first-year students in their own halls of residence but here boundaries are becoming blurred with universities entering into partnerships with private sector organisations to build and manage private halls. These private halls still account for less than 5 per cent of the student bed spaces available, but their growing importance is highlighted by the fact that this figure has doubled in the last year. As well as providing halls specifically for a university, UNITE plc (www.unite-students.com), the biggest developer, and others offer students secure and flexible accommodation of their own with a wide range of payment options. This style of living can be somewhat more expensive but is purpose-built and of high quality. You might expect as standard for your room to be en suite with internet access, satellite TV and a phone line, and for your shared kitchen to have all mod cons. Nonetheless, we still have a long way

UNITE Student Experience Report 2005 Where Students Live	
Hall, en suite, with full board	3%
Hall, non en suite, with full board	11%
Hall, en suite, self-catering	12%
Hall, non en suite, self-catering	19%
University house or flat	7%
Private house or flat	12%
Living with parents	26%
Living in own house or flat	6%
Other	3%

to go to match some American universities where the more exotic offerings include in-room movies, bubble-jet tubs and personal trainers. One even invites parents to submit their offspring's favourite recipes to incorporate in their gourmet menus!

University halls of residence continue to be upgraded, often with one eye on the conference business in vacations, and new rooms coming on stream might well be similarly en suite with all mod cons. Paradoxically, at a time when there is much talk about student hardship, even poverty, these more expensive rooms are often in greatest demand. Perhaps students hope to balance the books by saving on food costs. Certainly, an increasing number are looking for the more independent lifestyle offered by self-catering. The universities and other providers have responded to this shift in demand by providing much more flexible eating arrangements rather than the traditional full-board package of accommodation and fifteen meals a week. Now many universities offer pay-as-you-eat as well as wholly catered and self-catering facilities in their residences. Halls can be mixed or, more rarely, single sex and might house up to 800 students. They are great places to make friends and be part of the social scene. They are also probably best for support, should you need it in those first few weeks and months away from family and friends. They can also be first-year student ghettos and are often rowdy well into the beginning of the academic year. In many universities you will be guaranteed accommodation if you firmly accept their offer by a given date in the summer, but not necessarily if you come through Clearing. However, private halls might still have some places available at Clearing time. You will generally be expected – and, most probably, will want – to move out to other accommodation at the end of your first year. There are exceptions, particularly in the collegiate universities, and it is quite common at Oxford or Cambridge to live in your college for a further year or two.

You will no doubt be asked to sign an agreement with the university and the average length of the contract is 40 weeks, including the Christmas and Easter vacations. With shorter term-time-only contracts you will be required to move out in the vacations, but there may be storage space to leave your belongings. If not, check if the university has a secure storage facility with a local company. Special arrangements are often made to enable international students to remain in residence in the short vacations. They might also experience life within a UK family home over a weekend or at Christmas under the auspices of www.hostuk.org and similar organisations.

If you possibly can, take full advantage of Open Days to see the accommodation for yourself. Opting for university accommodation often gives the distinct advantage that it can be arranged at a distance whereas much of the private housing requires you to be on the spot to secure it. The university cannot sign a tenancy agreement on your behalf. The University Accommodation or Housing Office will have literature describing the facilities in detail and many have excellent websites containing invaluable information on student housing provided by both the university and the private sector.

But wherever you decide to live, you may well be expected to pay a term's rent in advance. The information in the individual university profiles (see chapter 11) gives you a good idea of the weekly rent you might expect to pay for basic catered and self-catering university accommodation. As a general rule, accommodation and travel costs are highest in London, East Anglia and southeast England and least expensive in the Midlands, Wales and Northern Ireland.

You could also be asked to part with a deposit or bond (typically the equivalent of one month's rent) to cover breakages and damage. This could be about £150 (higher in London) in university-owned accommodation and as much as £200 in the private sector. This is returned, less any deductions, at the end of the contract and, at that stage, there is potential for dispute as to what constitutes fair wear and tear! In fact, disputes over the return of deposits is a real and recurring issue, particularly in the private sector, and the 2004 Housing Act (see below) has introduced a National Tenancy Deposit Scheme to protect students from unscrupulous landlords who withhold deposits for no good reason. Under this Scheme, deposits will be lodged with an independent body, not the landlord, and this will ensure that deposits are fairly returned with any disputes resolved quickly and cheaply.

Whilst the largest number of first-year students live in Halls, some prefer smaller, self-catering properties with shared kitchen, toilet, bathroom and possibly a lounge area. Unlike inclusive Hall costs, here you may find that you receive an additional bill for heating and lighting. But at least you are in control of the food bills and you might even be able to engage in a spot of discounted bulk buying with fellow residents and hence stretch the money further. University properties are often in or near the campus itself and so travel costs to and from the university are minimal. As a general rule, the older universities tend to have much more housing stock, but the scene is constantly changing with high rise cranes a regular feature of the university skyline.

Private Sector Accommodation

Some students will head for private sector accommodation because they have to or choose to, and we have already referred to the growth of some private sector building initiatives. In addition, there are legions of accommodation agencies and individual landlords in university towns and cities in response to the continuing growth in student numbers. Many have long since abandoned their cottage industry image and competition from some major property developers has created a much greater professionalism. It is illegal for them to levy a joining fee but they may charge a booking or reservation fee on an agreed property, and perhaps a fee for references or for drawing up the Tenancy Agreement. The University Accommodation Service will have an approved list and some are working closely with local councils to develop best practice for student housing in their areas through Student Accommodation Accreditation Schemes. This is timely, given a recent estimate that 14 per cent of full-time students living away from home do so in unsatisfactory conditions. Bear this statistic in mind when undertaking your own search for a roof over your head. These Schemes require the landlord to have current gas and electrical safety certificates and guarantee basic standards of security and safety.

Always take someone with you to view accommodation and do not rush to sign on the dotted line for the first one you see. Try to spend some time in the area, perhaps by staying at a Bed & Breakfast or a YHA hostel for a few days, preferably when students are in residence. Locations can look – and be – very different in the vacations and after dusk. How safe is the district? It is important, too, to check out public transport and the journey time to and from the university. What is the traffic flow (or chaos!) like at weekday peak times as compared with a quiet Sunday morning? For some students living in private accommodation, travel might mean not only time but also money. A recent survey of travel time between term-time accommodation and the university concluded that students fared best in Wales (86 per cent less than 30 minutes away) and, not surprisingly, worst in London (50 per cent more than 30 minutes away and 17 per cent more than an hour).

Make sure that you get yourself any discounted Student Travel Card and of any university or students' union transport system when returning to your accommodation late at night.

Houses in Multiple Occupation

As a result of the 2004 Housing Act, the licensing of Houses in Multiple Occupation (HMOs) in England and Wales, like Scotland and Northern Ireland, will no longer be discretionary. The Act defines an HMO as a house occupied by three or more unrelated residents and so it covers virtually all private houses occupied by students – although it specifically excludes all university-run accommodation. Compulsory licensing for those properties most at risk – where there are five or more unrelated residents and the house is three or more stories tall – will begin this year and take effect in 2006. In addition, local authorities can designate whole areas where **all** HMOs, including smaller houses, will have to be licensed, and there is no doubt that they will look to do this in some university city suburbs with large student populations. This may result in a reduced supply of privately rented properties or the additional costs associated with mandatory licensing being passed on by landlords to students.

It sounds complicated, but licensed HMOs give better property management, greater financial regulation, and added health and safety protection to student tenants so you need to understand all of this if the property that interests you is an HMO. In fact, it's worth asking if your house is covered by a Code of Standards drawn up by the University

Accommodation Office or local authority. These codes are models of good practice and act as a checklist of what constitutes decent standards and common sense responsibilities for both owner and student. Now that the Housing Act is law, it is likely that larger properties, even those administered by the universities themselves, will be encouraged to comply with the recently launched National Code of Standards.

The Paperwork

Once you have settled on the shared house, flat or bedsit you like, the next thing is to sort out the paperwork. You will almost certainly be asked to sign a Tenancy Agreement or lease offering perhaps an 'Assured Shorthold Tenancy'. This is a binding legal document so read it through carefully before signing. If you do not understand some of the clauses, do not sign but seek clarification, if needs be, from the University Accommodation Office or the Students' Union – they may well have model Tenancy Agreements – or from a local Citizens Advice Bureau or Law Advice Centre. It is much easier to agree terms at this early stage but almost impossible after you have signed and moved in. This is one of those occasions in your life when it pays (literally!) to read the small print. Where you are sharing with other students, beware that a joint tenancy implies joint liability so you might end up being responsible for the deeds and, more importantly, misdeeds of others. The same applies if you are asked to name, say, your parent as a guarantor to pay any charges not covered by you. Never part with money without getting a receipt and keep a copy of all documents. Remember that by law the landlord cannot increase the rent more than once a year unless your agreement contains a rent review clause.

What other paperwork might you expect?

- an Inventory and Schedule of Condition listing everything in the accommodation when you take it over and its condition. If you are given one, check it for accuracy and annotate any changes. If you are not, make one of your own, have it witnessed, send it to the landlord, and keep a copy yourself. Take photographs if necessary to record any initial damage.
- a Rent Book in the unlikely event that rent is payable on a weekly basis.
- a recent Gas Safety Certificate issued by a recognised CORGI engineer.
- a Fire Safety Certificate covering the furnishings.
- a record of current gas/electricity meter readings. If not, take your own readings as soon as you move in.

Water rates are usually included in the rent but clarify this and take meter readings if you are expected to pay separately for water.

You will not have to pay Council Tax if all the residents are full-time students. However, you may need to obtain an Exemption Certificate from the university to offer as proof. If, on the other hand, one of the inmates is not a full-time student then a reduced Council Tax will be levied.

The average length of the contract in private-sector accommodation is likely to be higher (45 weeks and often 52 weeks) than for university-owned property and deposits nearer £200 (higher in London) can be expected. The longer lease is becoming more popular and can, of course, be a distinct advantage for some students. You will not have to make way for conference delegates, can keep your belongings with you, stay to obtain vacation work in the university or nearby, and you might even get a rent discount, especially if you are staying in the property for a further year.

Sharing

Now, you cannot choose your family but you can choose your housemates, and you never know someone until you have lived with them. University accommodation officers can vouch for the problems they have to try and sort out as a result of student tenants falling out with each other over the state of the kitchen or the bathroom. Most reading this would be amazed (or would they?) at the depths of squalor to which some students can descend once away from the watchful eyes of parents. A quarter of students smoke – could you live with one? And what about a serial phone user? It is best to arrange at the outset for itemised billing and a number of providers (eg The Phone Co-op at www.thephone.coop) offer this facility. Or a nocturnal TV addict? It is a legal requirement to have a TV licence. Or a surrogate penguin who warms to the heating system left on all day every day? Remember fuel bills are not usually included in the rent.

Regardless of whether you are applying for university or private halls, always make sure you fill in the application forms as fully as you can. Universities and landlords will try to take your personal preferences and lifestyle into account when grouping tenants together in a flat or on a corridor.

Living at Home

A significant, and growing, number of first-year students, twice as many in London, live at home and the reasons advanced are many and varied. There are clearly pros and cons but one potential disadvantage is to treat university as a nine-to-five job and risk missing the whole university experience. Stay-at-home students are likely to make fewer friends and to feel rather detached from campus activities but there is no evidence that their academic work suffers. As a general rule, the new universities recruit many more local students. This being so, their students are twice as likely to opt for staying at home than those at the old universities.

Another feature of the current scene is 'buy to rent' – accommodation bought by parents to house the student member of the family. With mortgage interest rates still low, property prices and rents reasonably steady, and the stock market still in the doldrums some parents are opting to buy a small house or flat, perhaps defraying the expense by charging rent to fellow students. However, 'buy to rent' is not without its pitfalls, particularly in those university towns where 'areas of student housing restraint' are being introduced, where there is increasing competition from national developers of purpose-built student housing, and where the universities, themselves, are upgrading their own residences.

UNITE Student Experience Report 2005
Reasons for Living at Home

To save money or cut costs	32%
Just want to	28%
Cannot afford to live away	15%
For an easy life; to be looked after	6%
Near to university of choice	6%
Parents wanted me to	2%
To concentrate on my studies	2%
Other reasons	7%

Hostels and Lodgings

Some registered charities run small hostels, especially for students with particular religious affiliations or those who come from specific overseas countries. These are mainly in London and further details can be found in the British Council publication, *Studying and Living in the UK*.

Small numbers of students live in lodgings where they might share a home with the landlord and his family. A study bedroom and some meals are usually provided but other facilities might well be shared. Reports suggest that this integrated accommodation is preferred by some overseas students

We have deliberately devoted a complete chapter to where to live because it is often by far the biggest item of expenditure – rent alone could account for 70 per cent of weekly income. It is also crucially important to success at university so it is well worth giving time and effort to the various accommodation options available, making sure you maintain maximum flexibility within any arrangements. Leaving home, and perhaps your country, is a big move and it will all feel very strange at first. It is reassuring that the other first-year students are in the same boat. The trick is to survive, even thrive, to the Christmas vacation. Most who leave university do so in those first few months simply because they are lonely and feel isolated. If you are warm and well fed this will impact on your happiness and enjoyment and help you to settle in quickly. This, in turn, will have a positive effect on your studies and as a result you are likely to do well. It is false economy to cut corners when it comes to choosing your first accommodation.

Finally, a word on behalf of the neighbours! They were all young once and most welcome students. But whole areas of our major university towns and cities are now dominated by student housing in what has become known as 'studentification'. This has had some adverse effects, not only on the local people but also on students themselves. Living in such a community invites respect, tolerance and a bit of 'give and take' – work on it. Follow the Community Code: 'say hello, keep the peace and clean up'.

Safety and Security

It is better to be safe than sorry and a few basic precautions could go a long way to securing your wellbeing. Students are seen as rich pickings by some petty criminals who can pretty well guarantee that you have a mobile phone, portable television, CD or DVD, probably a laptop, digital camera or mp3, and maybe even a bike, a car or some designer gear. All are relatively easy to dispose of in the world they frequent. It is estimated that a third of students become victims of crime, mainly theft and burglary, but many could have been prevented. The trouble is most students are blissfully unaware of crime in our towns and cities until they fall prey to it. This is particularly true of freshers partying in their first few weeks at university who are not 'street-wise' about the local area.

The table below summarises crime rates in those 20 towns and cities – apart from London – with two or more universities profiled in chapter 12 and focuses on those issues most likely to affect students. We make no apology for publishing these figures together with the tips which follow on the basis that 'forearmed is forewarned'. They are compiled from police data published by the Home Office and, whilst not perfect, give a much more realistic picture than you might get from scare stories in the press or questionable claims about safety in the odd prospectus. If safety and security are significant factors in your choice of where to study then here are some hard facts for you to consider

Local statistics about crimes solely against students are not available but, after seeking expert advice, we have chosen three as likely to be the most relevant, namely burglary, robbery and assault. The data are rolling averages for the two years 2002–03 and 2003–04 per 1000 population. Definitions differ somewhat for Scotland and thus figures for the Scottish university cities are listed separately and should not be compared with the others.

These figures are also likely to over-represent crime levels. This is because they are based on resident populations and hence take no account of short-stay visitors and commuters.

Crime Levels in University Cities per 1000 population 2002-2004

City	Burglary	Robbery	Assault	Total
Brighton	7.8	1.5	0.5	9.9
Belfast	8.9	1.7	1.5	12.2
Cardiff	9.0	1.2	2.1	12.3
Oxford	9.7	2.1	0.7	12.5
Coventry	10.1	2.1	1.3	13.5
Newcastle	11.2	1.5	0.8	13.6
Cambridge	11.0	2.4	1.0	14.4
Sheffield	12.3	2.0	0.8	15.1
Leicester	11.5	4.1	1.9	17.5
Birmingham	12.2	5.7	1.2	19.1
Liverpool	14.3	3.2	2.7	20.3
Bristol	17.1	5.9	1.7	24.7
Leeds	21.0	2.9	1.0	24.9
Nottingham	28.1	6.8	1.1	35.9
Manchester	24.0	9.9	3.2	37.1
Edinburgh	4.0	1.4	0.9	6.3
Dundee	5.9	0.6	0.7	7.3
Aberdeen	9.9	1.0	0.9	11.8
Glasgow	6.5	2.8	4.0	13.4

The likelihood of your becoming a victim are therefore less in real terms than these figures might suggest. However, for the cities listed, this reporting problem is a common issue and hence the relative crime rates are still valid.

Don't let it happen to you.

- **Do** carry a personal alarm with you – many men see these as female accessories and somehow not macho. But figures show that male students stand a much higher risk of been attacked in the street.
- **Do** try to avoid walking home in the dark and make sure you are familiar with any late night transport provided. Keep to well-lit and busy streets and use designated safe walking routes where available.
- **Do** be aware of people crowding around you when using a cash machine and preferably draw out money during the day
- **Do** keep a record somewhere safe of plastic card details and the serial and model numbers of your expensive electrical equipment.
- **Do** mark your possessions with a UV pen – your student registration number plus th initials of your university is a unique number.
- **Do** remember dialling *#06# will give you your unique mobile registration (IMEI) number. Make a note and register it at www.immobilise.com. If your phone is then lost or stolen, a quick call to the immobilise hotline (08701 123 123) will result in your handset being blocked on all the networks. Mobiles are by far the most popular items stolen from young people.

- **Do** try to avoid using your mobile in isolated places. Texting can distract you from what is happening around you. When you are out and about switch your mobile to vibrate mode rather than a ring tone.
- **Do** consider installing security software on your laptop and always carry it hidden inside a sports bag rather than in its own obvious case. Nowadays, university IT and learning centres are open around the clock and many students could be leaving these places in the middle of the night.
- **Do** make sure the outside doors are fitted with a 'Yale' type lock and five lever mortise deadlock. Fit any vulnerable downstairs windows with key-operated locks. Students in private housing are twice as likely to be burgled than those in halls of residence, not least because their accommodation is often unoccupied for long periods of the day and night. You can give the impression of being at home by using timer switches on lights and radios.
- **Do** immobilise your car or lock your bike whenever you leave it even for a few minutes. Think about where you park. Stealing from vehicles is still a major problem and you should routinely remove your stereo and store it in a safe place.
- **Do** have adequate insurance – over half the students who fall prey to burglars are not insured.
- **Do** consider secure storage for expensive items if you are leaving these over the vacations. International students might find this service particularly helpful.
- **Do** get hold of your own free copy of the *Student Survival Guide* from www.good2bsecure.gov.uk or by phoning 0870-241 4680 quoting ref. SSG.

None of these simple precautions will cost you much in time or money. In fact, you will find that many universities or their students' unions, often working closely with the local police, distribute personal alarms, UV pens, etc, to new students. Many of the other items mentioned are not expensive so could be added to the birthday presents list! Don't act after the event when you or one of your friends has had something stolen. Imagine how you would feel if weeks of work on your lap-top was lost for ever – we all know of situations where that has actually happened. Better to be safe than sorry?

Sport at University

6

At a time when health and fitness clubs are springing up in every town and city, and obesity, particularly amongst young people, is high on the national agenda, it is hardly surprising that the universities are often leading players in their localities. Some are even sponsoring local teams. Sport is increasingly seen as a key element in the drive towards wider access to a university education and many universities offer state-of-the-art facilities to their students at a fraction of the real cost. The range of sports facilities is impressive and is likely to include a gym, squash and tennis courts, team pitches and a swimming pool as standard fare. A recent survey by Sport England summarised the following situation in the English universities:

Sports halls	139	Tennis courts (hard)	541
Fitness suites	145	Tennis courts (grass)	74
Free weights areas	125	Squash courts	296
Grass pitches (winter)	932	Swimming pools	41
Grass pitches (summer)	284		

Where such resources do not exist, there is likely to be a favourable arrangement with a local club. The university itself usually owns and manages the facilities which may well include a fully equipped Sports Centre for which there could well be a charge. However, charges do vary a lot, typically in the range £20 to £200, so check out the likely cost beforehand, The actual annual sporting calendar, on the other hand, is likely to be organised by a full-time dedicated students' union sabbatical officer elected by the student body. Sports often function under the umbrella of an Athletic Union for which there is usually a joining fee of the order of £5 to £50 plus a similar cost to pursue your particular sport and perhaps even a modest match fee. Some universities operate a 'pay as you play' system of charging, some by the term or on an annual basis, and a few, the best known being Bristol, by a lump sum for the duration of your course.

There has also been a significant growth in the number of degree courses in sport and sports science alongside sports research in subjects like medicine, physiology, psychology, biomechanics, sociology and management. The universities are by far the largest providers of advice and research on sports development.

University offers a whole new world of sporting opportunities. You will be able to participate at the level best suited to your interest, ability and commitment. At one end of the spectrum there are likely to be recreation or active lifestyles programmes offering taught classes, usually at beginner and improver levels, across a broad range of activities such as fitness, aerobics or dance, through 'learn to play' sports such as rackets, climbing or fencing, to more holistic classes like yoga, tai chi or pilates. These are ideal for those who aren't interested in formally joining a student sports club or competing for a university sports team. They provide university students with opportunities to try their hand – or foot – at new activities they may not otherwise have ever imagined.

Sitting between these taught recreation programmes and the national intervarsity competitions at the other end of the spectrum are the intramural leagues and competitions on your own university campus. These cover a good range of sports and are usually based on halls of residence, departments, faculties or little more than a group of friends deciding to get together to form a team. Intramural programmes are ideal for those who want to play competitive sport for fun without the commitment required at intervarsity level. They

BUSA UNIVERSITY CHAMPIONSHIP POINTS 2003–2004

1	Loughborough University	R.F. Kerslake Trophy
2	University of Bath	Sir Dennis Fellows Trophy
3	The University of Birmingham	Winifred Clarke Trophy

	University	Men's	Women's	Total
1	Loughborough	1512	1596	3108
2	Bath	765.5	759.5	1525
3	Birmingham	693	529	1222
4	Nottingham	617	487.5	1104.5
5	Cambridge	363	610	973
6	Exeter	568	357	925
7	UWIC	372.5	549.5	922
8	Edinburgh	356.5	551	907.5
9	Oxford	378.5	482.5	861
10	Durham	440.5	418.5	859
11	Manchester	335.5	301.5	637
12	Leeds	310.5	306	616.5
13	Bristol	261	296.5	557.5
14	Cardiff	268.5	276	544.5
15	Northumbria	240	290	530
16	Southampton	236	255	491
17	Sheffield Hallam	333	135	468
18	Stirling	328	93	421
19	Newcastle	251.5	164	415.5
20	Warwick	172.5	229	401.5
21	London Metropolitan	290	86	376
22	Brunel	196	163	359
23	London	167	176	343
24	Glasgow	118	221	339
25	Brighton	133	177	310
26	Aberdeen	121	185	306
27	Leeds Metropolitan	153	150	303
29	University College London	156	114	270
31	Nottingham Trent	135	130	265
32	Sheffield	148	104	252
32	St Andrews	160	92	252
34	Kent	117	125	242
35	London South Bank	110	131	241
36	Strathclyde	142.5	73.5	216
37	Oxford Brookes	144	56	200
38	Liverpool	75.5	122.5	198
40	LSE	42	132	174
42	Heriot Watt	140	28	168
43	Middlesex	165	1	166
44	Imperial College	114.5	45.5	160

	University	Men's	Women's	Total
45	Portsmouth	78.5	76.5	155
46	Liverpool John Moores	52	98	150
47	Reading	85.5	61	146.5
49	Gloucestershire	90	48	138
50	Swansea	125	12	137
51	Lancaster	91	44.5	135.5
52	York	100	34.5	134.5
53	Bournemouth	103	29	132
55	Dundee	66	61	127
56	Plymouth	101	6	107
57	East Anglia	64.5	40.5	105
57	Sussex	44	61	105
59	Central Lancashire	69.5	28.5	98
60	Aberystwyth	48	49	97
61	Coventry	52	37	89
62	Queen Mary College	52	34	86
62	Teesside	68	18	86
64	UMIST	53	32	85
66	Glamorgan	64	15.5	79.5
67	King's College London	35	38	73
69	Surrey	60	12	72
70	Staffordshire	30.5	37.5	68
72	Hull	18	48	66
73	Manchester Metropolitan	56	8	64
74	Hertfordshire	24	38	62
75	West of England	12	46	58
78	Queen's, Belfast	44	9	53
80	Sunderland	37	11	48
81	Robert Gordon	25.5	22	47.5
82	Kingston	43	1	44
84	Salford	4	38	42
85	Abertay	14.5	26	40.5
86	Lincoln	20	20	40
88	Glasgow Caledonian	35	2	37
88	Leicester	30	7	37
90	De Montfort	22	13	35
90	Essex	21	14	35
92	Derby	9	25	34
94	Bangor	16	14	30
94	Greenwich	28	2	30
96	Royal Holloway	11	18	29
97	Keele	9	16	25
98	Bradford	16.5	7.5	24
98	Napier	22	2	24

	University	Men's	Women's	Total
98	Ulster	9	15	24
104	Huddersfield	19.5	2	21.5
105	York St John	13	8	21
110	Roehampton	0	13	13
110	Wolverhampton	6	7	13
112	Central England	9	0	9
113	Bolton	8	0	8
114	Luton	5	1	6
114	Westminster	6	0	6
118	Aston	1	2	3
121	Anglia Polytechnic	1	0	1
123	City	0	0	0
123	Goldsmiths College	0	0	0
123	Lampeter	0	0	0
123	Newport	0	0	0
123	Paisley	0	0	0
123	SOAS	0	0	0

attract thousands of students playing sport every week across campuses up and down the country.

The British Universities Sports Association (BUSA) is the governing body of university student sport, and runs national competitions in 46 sports from athletics to windsurfing, and co-ordinates the Great Britain representative teams for the World University Games and World University Championships. The BUSA sporting programme involves some 90,000 students across the UK and over 3,500 teams are engaged in BUSA competitions on a typical sporting day. In fact, with over 600 leagues, it is the biggest sporting programme of its kind in Europe. Many past BUSA participants like Paula Radcliffe (Athletics), James Cracknell (Rowing), Stephanie Cook (Modern Pentathlon), Nasser Hussain (Cricket), Kate Howey (Judo) and Audley Harrison (Boxing) have gone on to achieve success in their chosen sport.

The introduction in 2004 of the Talented Athlete Scholarship Scheme (TASS) gives selected athletes access to grants of £3,000 to assist with training and competition costs, and enables many talented individuals to pursue their sport to the highest level whilst still continuing with their university studies. Most universities offer sports bursaries and these are likely to become more numerous from 2006 onwards. Centres of excellence for specific sports continue to be developed at numerous universities like Bath, Birmingham, Durham, Leeds Metropolitan, Loughborough, Northumbria, Stirling and UWIC. In addition, the regional hubs of the Institute of Sport in all four parts of the UK are located on university campuses.

The latest BUSA Championship Table gives the overall position for each university. Only those institutions with a profile in chapter 11 are listed and hence the occasional break in the rankings. Also listed for the same 2003–04 year are the top universities and colleges in specific team and individual sports.

BUSA UNIVERSITY WINNERS 2003–2004

Sport	Champion	Runner-up
Athletics, Indoor (women)	Loughborough	UWIC
Athletics, Indoor (men)	UWIC	Loughborough
Athletics, Outdoor (women)	Loughborough	UWIC
Athletics, Outdoor (men)	Loughborough	UWIC
Archery, Indoor	Edinburgh	York
Archery, Outdoor	Edinburgh	London
Badminton (men)	Loughborough	Birmingham
Badminton (women)	Loughborough	Bath
Basketball (men)	St Mark & St John	Worcester
Basketball (women)	Nottingham Trent	Brunel
Canoe Polo (women)	Liverpool	Warwick
Canoe Polo (men)	Nottingham	Cardiff
Canoe, White Water (men)	Durham	Loughborough
Clay Pigeon (women)	Harper Adams	Royal Agricultural College
Clay Pigeon (men)	Harper Adams	Royal Agricultural College
Climbing	Sheffield	Glasgow
Cricket (men)	Loughborough	Durham
Cricket (women)	Loughborough	Cambridge
Cross Country (women)	Loughborough	St Mary's
Cross Country (men)	Loughborough	Oxford
Cycling – Cyclo Cross (men)	Loughborough	
Cycling – Cyclo Cross (women)	Loughborough	
Cycling – Downhill (women)	Edinburgh	
Cycling – Downhill (men)	Birmingham	Manchester
Cycling – Cross Country (women)	Loughborough	
Cycling – Cross Country (men)	Loughborough	Cambridge
Cycling – 25m TT (women)	Cambridge	Loughborough
Cycling – 25m TT (men)	Oxford	Loughborough
Cycling – 10m TT (women)	Cambridge	Loughborough
Cycling – 10m TT (men)	Oxford	Birmingham
Equestrian	Cambridge	Royal Agricultural College
Fencing (men)	Cambridge	Northumbria
Fencing (women)	Northumbria	Oxford
Football (men)	Loughborough	Swansea
Football (women)	Loughborough	Bath
Gaelic Football	St Mary's	Liverpool Hope
GolfExeter	Birmingham	
Gymnastics (women)	Leeds Metropolitan	UWIC
Gymnastics (men)	UWIC	Loughborough
Hockey (men)	London Metropolitan	Bath
Hockey (women)	Loughborough	Exeter
Judo (women)	Bath	Ulster
Judo (men)	Loughborough	Bath
Karate (women)	Warwick	Edinburgh

Sport	Champion	Runner-up
Karate (men)	London	Edinburgh
Karate (overall)	Edinburgh	Bath
Korfball	Sheffield Hallam	UEA
Lacrosse	Loughborough	Edinburgh
Modern Biathlon (women)	Loughborough	Bath
Modern Biathlon (men)	Loughborough	Birmingham
Netball	Birmingham	Loughborough
Orienteering (women)	Edinburgh	Sheffield
Orienteering (men)	Edinburgh	Sheffield
Rifle, Small Bore	Southampton	Edinburgh
Rowing	Durham	Glasgow
Rugby League	Loughborough	Leeds
Rugby Sevens (women)	Bath	UWIC
Rugby Sevens (men)	Loughborough	Exeter
Rugby Union (men)	Durham	Exeter
Rugby Union (women)	Loughborough	UWIC
Sailing – Match Racing	Southampton	Southampton Institute
Sailing – Team Racing (women)	Southampton	London
Sailing – Yacht Racing	Southampton Institute	Southampton
Snooker	Glasgow	Warwick
Squash (men)	Birmingham	Loughborough
Squash (women)	UWIC	Loughborough
Surfing (women)	Aberystwyth	Cardiff
Surfing (men)	Plymouth	Cardiff
Swimming (women)	Loughborough	Birmingham
Swimming (men)	Loughborough	Bath
Table Tennis (men)	Middlesex	London South Bank
Table Tennis (women)	London South Bank	Nottingham
Tennis (men)	London Metropolitan	Loughborough
Tennis (women)	Loughborough	Bath
Ten Pin Bowling (women)	Hull	East Anglia
Ten Pin Bowling (men)	Portsmouth	Nottingham Trent
Trampolining	Brunel	Portsmouth
Volleyball (men)	Sheffield Hallam	Nottingham
Volleyball (women)	Loughborough	Edinburgh
Waterpolo (women)	Warwick	Cardiff
Waterpolo (men)	Bristol	London

Paying Your Way

7

The head of one university tells the story of a photographer at Graduation asking the student to place a hand on her parent's shoulder, only to hear the riposte from the parent, "Wouldn't it be more appropriate to have a hand in my pocket!" It is an apocryphal tale but one which will ring true for many parents, given the financial support required these days. Going to university can be an expensive family business and student debt, a bit like a house mortgage, has become an accepted fact of life. Indeed, it has not been uncommon for students to graduate with a debt of £5,000 or more, over and above their maximum student loan.

You will need to muster all the resources you can lay your hands on unless you are one of that small band who has a regular private income. The vast majority of students have to rely on loans, savings, earnings, overdrafts and the generosity of family and friends.

Any financial support from the public purse has been largely unchanged for a number of years but the new Labour Government has radical plans for students starting at English and Northern Irish universities from 2006. These are outlined below and are intended to shift the onus of responsibility from parents to students. At present, many families have to make advance, up-front payments of £1,200 maximum towards tuition fees but from next year most students will face annual fees of £3,000. However, they will be able to take out a Government loan under generous terms to cover these and will not have to start making repayments until after they graduate. Under this new system, debt is certain to increase for most students but there will be much more generous support for students from low-income families and, for these, grants and bursaries might well meet the total cost of any tuition fees.

UNITE Student Experience Report 2005 Sources of student debt	
Student loan	80%
Bank overdraft	48%
Credit card	20%
Parental loan	14%
Personal loan	5%
Unpaid bills	4%
Store card	3%
Car loan	2%
Friends	2%
Mail order	2%
Family loan	1%

Student Funding In 2006

More than any, this is the year when what UK country you live in and which one you plan to study in could have a marked effect on your pocket.

The picture is pretty clear for English students going to English universities, all of which can charge variable tuition fees up to a maximum of £3,000 (see chapter 13). The universities in N Ireland have yet to announce their full plans but are expected to follow the English model of charging variable tuition fees of up to £3,000 but with a more generous means-tested higher education maintenance grant of up to £3,200. Welsh universities, however, are committed to a much lower fixed tuition fee of £1,200 whereas the Scottish universities will continue their policy of charging no tuition fees at all for Scottish students. As this Guide went to press, the Scottish Parliament was still considering a range of options for Scottish students starting at English universities in 2006 but both it and the Welsh Assembly have flagged their intention to make sure that Scottish and Welsh students accepting places at English universities are not financially disadvantaged by the introduction of higher tuition fees there.

The Welsh Assembly has agreed to exercise its devolved powers over support for Welsh students, regardless of where they study in the UK. It has commissioned a study to report by June 2005 on the student funding arrangements for the academic year 2007–08 and beyond. The current system will remain essentially unchanged for entry to universities in 2006. This study, chaired by Professor Teresa Rees, and hence known as the Rees Review, is likely to recommend the introduction of variable top-up fees in Wales but with a National Bursary Scheme (NBS) alongside, rather than bursaries developed by the individual universities. The Assembly will have the option of adding funds to the NBS where it wishes to promote particular aspects of the Welsh economy or culture. The National Bursaries will be means-tested and available to Welsh and other UK students coming to Welsh universities but not to Welsh students going to English universities who will, of course, be eligible for bursaries offered by those universities. The Welsh universities will also be encouraged to use some of their tuition fee income to develop their own bursaries and scholarships. In addition, there is likely to be generous provision for part-time students in Wales.

Given these differences in policy towards tuition fees, there are Celtic concerns about increased migration across borders of would-be undergraduates seeking refuge from high fees. The Welsh and Scottish universities have a long tradition of welcoming scholars from elsewhere but are already net importers of students from the other UK countries. The Scots, already facing a shortfall in recruitment of home-grown medical staff, have a particular concern about the potential for increased numbers coming into their medical schools from south of the border. Expect, therefore, preferential financial treatment for students staying in their own country or the odd hurdle for individuals wanting to move country. These are likely to be in the form of means-tested grants and bursaries with a variety of names (eg Assembly Learning Grant in Wales, Young Students' Bursary in Scotland, Higher Education Bursary in Northern Ireland) which will not have to be repaid. These will be of particular interest to students from low-income families. Conversely, to make sure that there is no significant increase in students coming to Scotland and Wales, their universities will charge incomers a tuition fee at a rate which creates a level playing field. In Scotland, this is expected to be between £1,700 and £1,900, even higher for medical students.

Student loans administered by the Student Loans Company will continue to be available throughout all the UK countries in 2006.

As we have said, the new funding arrangements for students entering English and Northern Ireland universities in 2006 are far-reaching. They are also likely to prove more complex and confusing. And it is anticipated that some of the other countries will follow suit with variations of their own so be prepared for more confusion!

The full story is expected to unfold by December 2005 and we strongly advise you to consult the key country websites for the most up-to-date information. These are:

- England   www.dfes.gov.uk/studentsupport
- Wales   www.studentsupportwales.co.uk
- Scotland   www.saas.gov.uk
- Northern Ireland   www.delni.gov.uk/studentfinance

In our opinion, you cannot start this monitoring and research too early because there will be much to do. No sooner will you have completed your UCAS application then it will be time to apply for financial support. A timetable for this is summarised in *Countdown 2006* opposite. The fine detail has yet to be published and is not expected to become available until towards the end of 2005. However, it is likely to be very similar to the existing operation.

The Situation in England from 2006

Apart from those of you who have deferred entry from the previous year, new undergraduates starting on a full-time course at most **English** universities in autumn 2006 will be liable for the maximum **tuition fee** allowed of £3,000. Only three universities will charge less than the maximum amount: Leeds Metropolitan, £2,000; Greenwich, £2,500; and Thames Valley, £2,700. Although you, not your parents, will owe this fee, you will not have to pay it back before or during your studies. This is because you can take out a loan to cover it and need not start repaying the loan until after you have graduated. Students from low-income families will also be eligible for a Higher Education Grant from the Government and a bursary from the university to cover part or all of the tuition fees.

In summary, you **could** be eligible for the following bursary, grant and loans to help pay the tuition fee and other costs of going to university:

1	Bursary (non-repayable)	£300 (minimum)
2	Education Maintenance Grant (HEMG) (non-repayable)	£2,700 (maximum)
	Total	£3,000
3	Tuition Fee Loan (repayable) to cover any outstanding fee	
4	Maintenance Loan (repayable) to help with living costs	

Countdown 2006

Financial Planning for Student Loans, Grants and Bursaries

In summary, you will need funds to live now and to pay tuition fees later (not Scotland) but you will be entitled to help from the Government and maybe the university. Some things you know now: nearly all universities in England and Northern Ireland will charge tuition fees of £3,000, those in Wales £1,200 and those in Scotland no up-front fees at all; all of you will be eligible for student loans; many will be available for a Government grant or bursary; and many in England and Northern Ireland also a university bursary. At some universities, applications for this bursary will have to be made direct, whereas others have opted for this to be administered by the Student Loans Company under the proposed UUK/SLC model scheme (see chapter 13). **[THEY = LEA** (England and Wales); **SAAS** (Scotland); **ELB** (Northern Ireland)]

March onwards	**YOU** receive or request an Application Form for Student Support and any Guidance Notes. You can also apply online **YOU** read Booklet and return Application Form (keep a copy)
	↓
April/May/June	Within 6 weeks or so, the **STUDENT LOANS COMPANY (SLC)** will send you a letter confirming details of the financial help to which you are entitled, including how and when it will be paid. Scottish domiciled students will also receive an award notice from SAAS approximately 2 weeks before they get the letter from the SLC.
	↓
May/Early June	Deadline by which **YOU** must return your Application Form in order to guarantee that **THEY** will have your entitlement ready at the beginning of the academic year
	↓
September/October	Hopefully, **THEY** will have the first instalment of your loan waiting for you in your bank or building society account or, more rarely, for you to collect at university **YOU** can now start spending your loan or grant!

- It is anticipated that 30 per cent of students will receive a bursary and higher education grant to the full amount of £3,000.
- Loans will be arranged through the Student Loans Company (SLC) at a variable low-interest – not a commercial – rate linked directly to inflation. In effect, the money you repay will be the same in real terms as the money you borrowed.
- All of the higher education grant but only part of the loans (25 per cent) will be means-tested on individual or family incomes.
- The maintenance loan will be linked to average student expenditure and the amount will depend on three things: income, whether or not you continue to live in the family home, and whether or not the university is in London. The exact loan levels will be published nearer the time but will be highest for those studying in London and not living at home and lowest for those studying elsewhere but living at home.
- You need not start repaying loans until after you graduate and only then once you start earning more than £15,000. How much you repay each month will be determined only by your income, not by how much you owe.
- Loans will be repaid through the tax system at the rate of 9 per cent on that part of your annual income over £15,000. For example, the repayments for a graduate earning £20,000 would be:

£20,000 – £15,000 = £5,000 x 9%

$$= \text{£450 a year or £37.50 a month.}$$

- The Government proposes to write off all loan balances left unpaid after 25 years.
- This Government support will be supplemented by university bursaries and scholarships and by employer payments as part of their recruitment packages.

The table below *Financial Support and Family Income* gives a basic summary of your eligibility for the various components of the support package. The family income levels are indicative only; they will be finalised later this year.

Financial Support and Family Income

| | Family Income | | | |
| | Low | Medium | High | Highest |
Financial Support	Up To £16,000	£16,000-£33,000	£33,000-£43,000	£43,000 Plus
Full Maintenance Grant £2,700	Yes	No	No	No
Partial Maintenance Grant £1-£2,699	n/a	Yes	No	No
Full Bursary £300 Minimum	Yes	No	No	No
Partial Bursary £1-£299	n/a	Yes	No	No
Fees Loan £2,500-£3,000	Yes	Yes	Yes	Yes
Full Maintenance Loan or Loan+Grant	Yes	Yes	No	No
Partial Maintenance Loan	n/a	n/a	Yes	Yes
			99%-76%	75%

University Bursaries and Scholarships

The Government is strongly committed to a policy of fair access to a university education for all, regardless of family financial circumstances. To this end, it has set up the Office for Fair Access (OFFA) to monitor, amongst other things, the provision of bursaries and scholarships offered by each university. These are contained in their so-called Access Agreements which can be viewed in full on the OFFA website at www.offa.org.uk. Some are guaranteed and are based on your personal circumstances whilst others are available through open competition. More information is given in the summary grid at the back of this book. More information is given in the summary grid at the back of the book and in the individual university profiles.

Tuition Fees for Overseas Students

Overseas students normally resident in countries outside the EU and EEA pay full-cost tuition fees in all of the UK and these are likely to be in the range shown in the table below. Whilst many overseas students coming to Britain receive financial support from their home countries, it must be emphasised that UK scholarships, whether from the UK government, sponsors or the individual universities themselves are limited. The vast majority are for post-graduate study, although there are one or two schemes for which undergraduates can be considered in exceptional circumstances. Students from overseas are strongly advised, therefore, to make sure they have sufficient funds for the full tuition fees and all necessary living costs before leaving home. Indeed, you will almost certainly be asked to guarantee in writing that you have sufficient funds for the complete duration of your course. Estimates suggest that living costs alone could amount to £5,250 and considerably more in London. It is virtually impossible to arrange financial support once you have left your own country. The simplest way to transfer large sums of money is through a sterling bank draft. You should also make sure that you have some ready money or travellers' cheques with you for immediate use on arrival to cover food, travel and other essentials. In that context, a cash card with the Cirrus or Maestro signs allows you to draw money at a UK bank.

Your Likely Expenditure
Living costs

For all students the biggest expenditure items will be the regular living costs, such as accommodation, food and drink, travel and even, perhaps, some clothes. There is much evidence to suggest that most university entrants don't know what it costs to be a student and can seriously underestimate these items by as much as 50 per cent. An increasing number, particularly in London, are staying at home and travel daily to a nearby university and that is probably the cheapest option. Buy only what you need, including the occasional treat, and don't be tempted by 'two for the price of one' when you did not even want one in the first place. Local markets are good for fresh fruit and vegetables, charity shops like

---

Tuition Fees for Overseas Students

Subject	£ Sterling	$ US
Humanities and Social Sciences	£7,250–£8,108	$13,775–$15,405
Sciences and Engineering	£7,925–£10,500	$15,055–$19,950
Clinical Subjects	£18,990–£19,900	$36,080–$37,810

Conversion rate UK£1.00 to US$1.90

Oxfam for clothes, and the students' union for stationery. If you are sharing, you might even be able to engage in a spot of discounted bulk food buying with fellow residents and hence stretch the money further. There are travel costs, too, where most students rely on public transport, not just between home and university, perhaps two or three times a year, but also from your accommodation to the university every day. As a general rule, the cost of living is lower the further north and west you choose to study in the UK.

Apparently, a good third of students say they would rather spend more money on socialising than on a better roof over their heads! However, given the importance of day-to-day living, we have devoted chapter 5 to the issue of where to live.

Studying costs

Next come costs associated with course work and the essentials: books, stationery, equipment and perhaps fieldwork or electives, here and overseas. After all, you are at university to get a degree! Such additional course work is often compulsory, and whilst you might get some financial support for this it is unlikely to meet the full costs of a language year, medical elective, or archaeological dig overseas or a residential geography field trip away from the university. The recommended reading list might be long and expensive. You would be well advised not to rush out and buy the lot but rather get to know how to use the library at the earliest opportunity. Students' unions often organise second-hand book sales and access to the internet is easy and free via the university network. Are some textbooks you want available through these sources, at the very least to buy at discount prices? Or is it feasible to share books with a fellow student?

Other costs

But university most definitely shouldn't be all work. Again, the students' union will cater for play in all its guises at a fraction of the cost demanded by commercial providers. In fact, university is a great time – perhaps the only time – to pursue the most common or esoteric of interests at a price you can easily afford. However, expenditure on the social scene, whether it be the launderette, cinema or nightclub, drinking or occasional eating out, is still likely to be a significant cost for most students.

Phone bills can be another sizeable item, especially if you ring the old folks at home or that distant loved one for an hour or so every day and they happen to be in Tokyo or San Francisco! Competition for your custom is fierce and the students' union may well be able to advise on the best deals amongst a growing army of call providers. Selecting an appropriate package for your mobile from the many options available will also be important.

Insurance

Most students own desirable items like portable televisions, CD and DVD players, laptops, mobile phones and bikes, and a third of them fall victims of crime. Even so, recent surveys have shown that many students are uninsured or under-insured. Insurance cover is essential and might be possible under existing parental policies at home. If not, there are a number of insurance companies which tailor policies to student belongings and lifestyle. Premiums are usually linked to postal codes, and university residences often provide cheaper cover than private houses. It is worth the precaution of photographing expensive items and keeping serial numbers in a safe place. Some insurance companies offer a special policy for international students to cover goods in transit and emergency travel.

This, then, is a brief look at what you will need money for. Try looking at your own personal situation to draw up an annual expenditure list and return to it on a regular basis throughout the year to see how you are doing. In other words, begin to estimate an annual budget. This is shown in the chart of income and expenditure which appears later in this chapter on page 191.

Your Likely Income
Taking a gap year

One possible source of earnings to consider prior to coming to university is a gap year – another is sponsorship. Taking a year out is attractive to many students, whether to gain experience, to earn money or both. Circumstances might dictate that the opportunity to spend a year working whilst travelling may not come again and it is much easier to get a temporary work visa when you are young. Thanks to the House of Lords, those leaving school or college in 2005 and opting for a gap year have escaped the new tuition fees regime applying to other new students entering the universities with them in 2006.

There are essentially four main possibilities: cultural exchanges and courses, expeditions, volunteering, and structured work placements. These can be here in the UK or overseas and some could require considerable funding by you whilst others would pay a wage. You need to question, therefore, your own motives and means before embarking on a year out. The reasons for taking a gap year seem to be shifting from solely an opportunity for personal development to more one to boost the bank balance ahead of becoming a student. This understandable short-term expediency needs to be carefully measured against the somewhat longer-term but less tangible benefits of a placement, here or overseas, of real service to the community, but perhaps with less monetary reward. The Government wants to encourage voluntary work in local communities, particularly for gap year students, and has launched the Young Volunteer Challenge scheme (£60 a week plus expenses and a bonus on successful completion of £750).

These days, university selectors take careful note of extracurricular experience and interests alongside good exam grades and generally support a gap year but utter occasional reservations for those planning to study the mathematical sciences. Employers, too, operating increasingly in a global economy, look more and more to the development of self-reliance and teamwork skills and expertise beyond academic performance and class of degree, skills often developed through a gap year.

Work placements might be structured as, for example, with the 'Year in Industry Scheme' (www.yini.org.uk) or 'GAP Activity Projects' (www.gap.org.uk), or casual. Both provide invaluable experience to put on your CV. Sponsorship is available mostly to those wishing to study engineering or business and a good source for finding more information is www.everythingyouwantedtoknow.com.

Support from Government sources

The Access to Learning Fund (Financial Contingency Fund in Wales, Hardship Fund in Scotland) is a further source of modest government help to students on university courses and is allocated by the universities themselves to undergraduates in financial difficulties. This may simply be help with day-to-day study and living costs or to meet an unexpected or exceptional cost. The university decides which students need support and what the level of that support will be. Priority groups tend to be older or disadvantaged students and finalists. The Access to Learning Fund is a back-stop and is normally given as a non-repayable grant according to need. It can be available as a one-off sum or in the form of a bursary payable every year.

If you are ineligible for any of the above financial support, you may still be able to apply for a Career Development Loan, available through some major high street banks in partnership with the DfES. Students on a wide range of vocational courses can borrow from £300 to £8,000 at a fixed rate of interest to help you fund up to two years of learning and not pay anything back until you finish your studies.

Part-time work

Some firms, particularly the big supermarket chains, offer continuing part-time employment to their school employees when they go away to university. The last few years have also seen a significant growth in student employment offices on university campuses, no doubt a response, in part, to the introduction of fees and loans. Any income you earn by working will not normally affect your entitlement to loans and bursaries. About half of all undergraduates now have a part-time job bringing in an average of £83 for a 14-hour week. These offices act as agencies introducing employers with work to students seeking work, perhaps even in the university itself, throughout the academic year. They are also guardians of the student interest, abiding by Codes of Practice which regulate such things as minimum wages, maximum hours worked in term (typically 15 hours a week so as to avoid adverse effect on studies), non-discrimination, etc. Most universities now have a student employment office run by their careers

UNITE Student Experience Report 2005 Funds generated for university	
Full-time holiday job	26%
Part-time holiday job	20%
Long-term savings	15%
Part-time school job	15%
Gap year to save	13%
Monetary gifts	12%
Family loan	8%
Scholarship	6%
Bank loan	4%
Other grants and loans	9%
No funds	19%

service or the students' union and they make a welcome contribution to the local economy. This is hardly surprising given the enormous range of skills and knowledge residing in any student community. Some use their expertise to good effect as web designers, tutors or healthcare workers but most do casual work in retail stores, restaurants, bars and call centres. Many organisations are also interested in what students like and how they think and are willing to pay to find out. Others appoint brand managers on campus to promote their goods and services. Universities, too, frequently involve their students in market research, fundraising amongst their alumni or as ambassadors in schools and colleges.

Vacation work

Vacations, too, offer an opportunity to earn cash whilst developing skills for that CV. Such work experience can be casual, formalised in a scheme like the 'Shell Technology Enterprise Programme' (www.step.org.uk), or even as part of a sponsorship programme.

Banks

Finally, banks are well disposed to today's university students in the certain knowledge that many will be tomorrow's high-earning professionals. They are sympathetic to the student cause and will generally permit modest overdrafts on your account to ease cash flow problems without pain. It pays – literally – to shop around for the best offers when transferring or opening your account. Check to see if the bank offers a 24-hour service via the internet or telephone and make sure that its cash machines are free to users and accessible around the clock. Branches near universities often have dedicated student advisers to tell you about their latest tempting offers (interest-free overdrafts, travel cards, insurance, book discounts, CD and DVD vouchers, etc) all intended to lure you inside.

Your Annual Budget

You can now complete your estimated annual budget by listing all expected income, including any savings you will bring with you to university. See how this compares with expenditure in the hope that the balance sheet almost balances or, better still, that you are left with spare cash in the bank for doing what you've always wanted to do. However, budgeting accurately is never an easy process, and we have constructed this simple but realistic annual income and expenditure summary to make monitoring and controlling your finances easier. This is a budget for non-smokers and assumes the latest findings of an average weekly spend of £25 on food and £19 on drink. For the quarter of you who smoke, an additional outlay of almost £20 would be needed – is it worth it?

It can be difficult to predict accurately some variable expenses such as entertainment. Start by identifying bills which must be paid and include in this a small contingency fund. This will leave you with the 'flexible' part of your income to take weekly from the bank. Don't be too optimistic in your first budget, and do be aware of how much you actually spend. Budget for balls, birthdays and parties, or you may find yourself missing out on the

---

A typical budget for a student entering university in 2006

Income	£	Expenditure	£
Student loan	4,000	Rent	2,250
HEMG	2,700	Tuition fees	3,000
Bursary	300	Electricity, gas, water	200
Term time/vacation work	2,000	Mobile	230
		Insurance	100
		Food, drink	1,500
		Toiletries	200
		Laundry	100
		Books, stationery	250
		Clothes, shoes	350
		Travel, transport	300
		Going out	600
		Home entertainment	200
		Sports, leisure	200
		Holidays, presents	400
		Emergencies	250
Total income	9,000	Total expenses	10,130
		(Deficit)	(1,130)

In this example, we have assumed that the tuition fee is £3,000, that you are in receipt of the maximum Higher Education Maintenance Grant (HEMG) of £2,700 and minimum standard bursary of £300, and that you have taken out a £4,000 student loan. The deficit of £1,130 is in addition to the £4,000 loan from the Student Loans Company which will be carried forward as a debt to be repaid after you graduate.

best social events of the year. If there is a big gap between budget and actual, perhaps your spending habits need attention rather than your budgeting. Above all, remember to keep a check on your finances so that money worries do not detract from your studying and from enjoying university life. It has been suggested that women undergraduates are more likely to budget and, as a result, incur lower debt but, even so, tend to worry more about that debt! Clearly, your patterns of expenditure will differ significantly between term-time and vacations and you will need to allow for this.

Student Funding in 2005

We have already emphasised the changes and uncertainties facing university entrants in 2006. The student support system in England will be radically different and this will inevitably impinge on universities elsewhere in the UK. Earlier in this chapter, we outlined the story as best we could but have also decided here to give you an insight into the current system of loans and grants so that you can see how it operates. The figures will be different next year but the principles on which they will be based will be much the same.

Student loans (similar in 2006 but with higher loan rates)

Since October 1999, Government support for university students has been wholly through a loan, although grants in the form of NHS and GSCC Bursaries are available for students on most health-related and some social work degree courses. So for most UK students going to university in 2005 a significant source of income will be this student loan from the Student Loans Company. As with an application for contributions towards tuition fees, so with a student loan you must apply without delay in the first instance to your LEA or funding agency, and you should do this even if you feel you do not qualify for a government contribution towards your tuition fees.

You don't have to take out this loan – although more than 80 per cent of students do – but if and when you do, you will be entering into a legal contract to repay the loan in full after leaving university. When and what you repay will depend on your total income and will normally be deducted from your pay. You will repay nothing until your income exceeds £15,000 a year and some graduates might be exempt from repayment if, for example, they take up and remain teaching certain key shortage subjects in schools. The interest rate on the loan is linked to the rate of inflation so you will be asked to repay no more, in real terms, than you actually borrowed. Middle-class students are more likely to view debt (from what is essentially an interest-free student loan) as an investment – some have even been known to re-invest in ISAs – whereas many working-class students see it as a burden. It has been argued, therefore, that the current system encourages the development of a debt culture in some but dissuades others from coming to university.

The maximum annual loan rates for 2005–06, apart from the last year at university, are for living at home, £3,320 and for living away from home in London, £5,175, and elsewhere, £4,195. The amount of loan you can obtain depends, amongst other things, on how much you and your family will be expected to contribute to your living costs. However, 75 per cent (lower in Scotland) of the maximum loan is available regardless of family income. Only UK students can be considered for a student loan or any of the other support systems outlined.

New interactive online enquiry services have been introduced and these include an application form and an entitlement calculator. You can apply online or download an application form by logging onto the appropriate country website. You can also track your application by accessing the online service using a unique ID number.

Higher education grant for English students (higher in 2006)

This has been introduced for new full-time students from less affluent homes to help them with the costs of going to university. The maximum grant you could receive is £1,000 if your family income is £15,580 or less but if it is over £21,565 you are ineligible. It does not have to be repaid.

Student loans and bursaries for Scottish students (similar in 2006 but with increased support for students going to English universities)

For Scottish students starting courses in Scotland, a proportion of the student loan may be replaced by the Young Students' Bursary, a grant that does not have to be repaid. The maximum bursary is £2,395 for those students whose family income is less than £17,500, declining to zero when the family income exceeds £31,000. So, depending on family income, some of the total loan can be replaced by this bursary. An Additional Loan of up to £545 is also available to some students studying in Scotland who are in receipt of a bursary.

Scottish students studying elsewhere in the UK are eligible for a Young Students' Outside Scotland Bursary with a maximum of £545 where the family income is £16,590 or less. This is in addition to any student loan. Beyond income levels of £31,000 (studying in Scotland) and £19,730 (studying outwith Scotland), any financial support is entirely through the normal student loan. Whilst the maximum student loan rates are the same throughout the UK, the proportion assessed on the basis of family income is greater in Scotland. Full details of loans and bursaries are given on the SAAS website.

Assembly grants for Welsh students (similar in 2006 but with increased support for students going to English universities)

In 2002, the National Assembly for Wales introduced its new Assembly Learning Grant for Welsh students studying anywhere in the UK and this does not have to be repaid. The maximum grant is £1,500 for those whose family residual income is less than £5,350 declining to zero when the family income exceeds £16,065.

A similar grant or bursary of up to £2,000 is available to students ordinarily resident in Northern Ireland but with a more generous threshold of £10,500 and an upper limit of £21,000.

Tuition fees (higher in England in 2006 but with no up-front payment)

For many years now, full-time undergraduates whose homes are in the UK other than Scotland or in other EU and EEA countries have been liable to pay means-tested fees direct to the university (frequently by instalment), subject to the maximum for 2005–06 of £1,175 (£570 for students on full year sandwich/industry placements or studying abroad, except for EU exchange programmes such as SOCRATES and ERASMUS students.

However, most students can get a contribution towards these fees in the form of a Fee Remission Grant, the level of which is dependent on their – and their family's – income. In fact, it is estimated that almost half of all students are fully exempt from paying anything and only about a third pay the full fee. Any such state contribution towards tuition fees is not a loan and does not have to be repaid. English and Welsh students must apply through the Local Education Authority (LEA) where they normally live for assessment of any contribution. Scottish students must apply through the Student Awards Agency for Scotland (SAAS) and those in Northern Ireland to their local Education and Library Board (ELB). You should do so as soon as you have received an offer – even a conditional offer – of a university place. Other EU students are usually sent an application form by the university offering a place.

In 2000, the Scottish Parliament abolished fees for students ordinarily resident in Scotland who stay there to study and for mainland EU full-time students studying in Scotland (but not for other UK students studying in Scotland). However, those students who do not pay any tuition fees are expected after graduation to pay a fixed amount (currently £2,154), on essentially the same basis as repayment of a student loan (see page 192), into a Graduate Endowment Fund towards support for future generations of students. Students from Scotland who choose to study elsewhere in the UK will continue to pay income-assessed tuition fees to their universities.

Parental Contributions (not applicable in 2006)

For 2005 entrants, parental contribution towards university tuition fees and a student's living cost are means-tested and based on their so-called Residual Income. This is the gross income from all sources less certain defined allowances. Currently, below a Residual Income of £22,010 no parental contribution is expected. Above this figure, there is a sliding scale of contribution until at £32,745 your parents would be expected to pay the full tuition fee of £1,175. At higher income levels, your parents would also be expected to contribute towards part of your day-to-day living costs. If your parents no longer live together, then only the income of the one with whom you live will normally be assessed. Hitherto, on any remarriage without adoption, the income of a step-parent has not been considered when working out your financial support. From now on, however, if your parent has remarried or lives with a partner then the income of both of them will be taken into account. This includes a partner of the same sex if, as expected, a new law comes into force (other than in Scotland) in 2005–06.

Mature Students (applicable in 2006)

If you are over 25, are married, or have supported yourself for at least three years prior to becoming a student, you are assessed on your own income plus that of your spouse or partner (not Scotland) where appropriate. Your parents are not expected to contribute to either tuition fees or living costs. In addition, grants are available to students with adult dependants, for student parents for childcare, and for students who are single parents. Two new financial grants, the Parents' Learning Allowance and Child Tax Credit, have been introduced as further support for students with a family.

The information in this chapter was correct at the time of writing (May 2005) but the rules and regulations for all of these contributions towards tuition fees, student loans, grants and funds and other Supplementary Grants (for disabled students, students with dependants, single parent students, care leavers, and for some essential travel costs) are somewhat complicated and you should consult the relevant country website on student support (see page 184).

What Parents Need to Know

Many things in university life have changed in recent years and one of them is the increasing role of parents. Nowadays many are actively involved throughout the application process, a constant presence as universities are chosen, forms filled in and open days attended. One important reason for this is that parents are increasingly providing financial backing for their children's higher education. When you are paying for something, it is only natural to take a close interest in what is going on and seek to ensure you are getting value for money. On the whole this is a welcome development. Applying to university and surviving the examinations necessary to get there is a difficult time and young people need all the support they can get.

This chapter is aimed specifically at parents, offering a guide to what they will go through and some practical ways in which they can help. It focuses on areas specific to parents, so if you want to know about the application process in detail or how to choose a university, see the other chapters in this book. While this chapter generally refers to parents, it applies equally to guardians and other carers who may get involved in the process.

Practical Support for Applications

The single most important thing parents can do is relentlessly be positive about higher education. All the evidence is that, for most people, attending university is one of the most enjoyable and fruitful times of their lives. It is a time when they try a vast range of new experiences, form lifelong friendships and equip themselves for the world of work. If that isn't enough, the crude economics are telling: on average a graduate will earn much more in their

> **UNITE Student Experience Report 2005**
> 95% of students agree that going to university is worthwhile.
> 89% of students agree that the money they are spending on going to university is a good investment for their future.

working life than a non-graduate (the Government has estimated that it amounts to £120,000) and is much less likely to be unemployed. We all know of a few people who missed out on university but went on to be high-achievers, such as Richard Branson or the former Prime Minister John Major, but we know their names precisely because there are so few of them. Generally speaking, university is the gateway to success: the more you learn, the more you earn.

Having instilled the value of a university education sufficiently for your offspring to be making an application, it is time to get practical. A good school or college should provide plenty of practical support for their students through the application process (see chapter 4) but there are still some ways in which you can contribute:

- Help to gather all the necessary information. Provide stamps and surf time, and, if you borrowed this book, buy a copy!
- Read up about the things you are interested in, even if they are not at the top of the list of most applicants' priorities. For example, many parents are concerned about the safety of the university environment and many universities have information about this on their websites or in special publications. Don't just assume that big cities are bad and rural campuses good. Some city universities are in areas of their city with low crime rates; some campus universities may result in some students travelling home late at night to off-campus accommodation.

- Get to know the process so you can keep a check that UCAS deadlines are met (see chapter 4).
- Provide any information needed for LEA Assessment Forms.
- Offer a taxi service to university open days. Most universities now expect large numbers of parents to roll up for open days (both the big general open days and the specific departmental days held for applicants who have been made an offer) and make special arrangements. Far from being an embarrassing appendage, you will often get taken off for a parents' programme with sessions by university counsellors, safety officers and suchlike. If you have joined in the trip, you can help your son or daughter to be critical about what they have seen and heard. Open days are like prospectuses: they are designed to attract. A university that is unlucky with the weather can't hide the fact that it is a long walk in the rain from the lecture theatres to the Students' Union, but you can be sure that the lecture theatres you see are the most modern and up-to-date.
- If you move house, make sure UCAS is on your 'change of address' list.

A well-organised school and a well-organised student will cover most of this between them, but if either isn't quite on top of things then you can help to make sure that the process runs smoothly.

Advice

Offering advice to your children about their application is a fine and natural thing you will want to do. Parents can be an invaluable source of experience and good sense. If you happen to be a university admissions tutor or the head of recruitment for a large corporation, then you will be particularly well-placed to offer good advice about some (but probably not all) aspects of the process. However, if you are not as close to the heart of it as that, you do need to think carefully before you offer advice. Here are some of the common pitfalls:

- Basing your advice on your own experience of university 25 years ago. Universities and university life have changed since that time and you will almost certainly be out of date.
- Suggesting certain courses will always lead to a good job. Are you sure? See chapter 1 for the facts about graduate employment.
- Suggesting certain universities are good for a particular subject. Again are you sure? See chapters 2 and 3 for the facts about quality.
- Projecting your own desires onto your offspring. However much you love being a doctor or an advertising executive, it doesn't mean that they want to be, too. Students switching courses routinely comment that they never really wanted to do their initial subject but felt that it was expected by their family.

What a School Should Do

A good school or college will provide a programme of support for its students who are applying for higher education. This will include many or all of the following:

- A library of resources, including university prospectuses and UCAS publications
- A trip to a university open day
- A visit to a higher education fair with stands for many or all universities
- Talks by representatives of one or more universities
- A series of sessions giving advice about the UCAS process and how to fill in the UCAS application
- A member of staff responsible for all this and available to provide assistance.

So advice can be a tough one. You can offer all the usual sound, sensible stuff that kids never want (but always need) to hear. Read the prospectuses, take decisions slowly and carefully, don't apply for Aramaic & Offshore Engineering just because a best friend has done so, that sort of thing. One really helpful thing you can do is test the reasons for decisions. Check out that universities have been chosen for sensible reasons, such as the quality of a course, and not as a result of some dubious gossip. However, more specific advice needs to be watched: if you can't be sure you are accurate it may do more harm than good.

Examination Results

It's August. You've come through the application process together. You had a great time accompanying your son or daughter to an open day at your alma mater. They wisely ignored your romantic reminiscences and applied to six other universities instead. You were a rock when the first decision was a rejection and then provided the chocolates when the next one was an offer. Now things are tense as mid-August approaches.

After your important role in extolling the virtues of university life at the start of the process, Results Day is another time when your support can be crucial. The paramount thing is to remain calm and collected yourself. Whatever contortions your digestive system is engaged in there will be enough tension around already without your adding to it. If the right results come in, things are easy: just join in the celebration. But if they don't and disappointment reigns, don't add your own. No doubt you will feel disappointed, but your son or daughter will have enough to deal with already, not least the fact that many of their friends are probably celebrating. Now is the time to be a calm, comforting and constructive presence.

A few practical things are possible. First, be there, not on a Mediterranean beach. Moral support is not quite the same over a long-distance telephone call. Second, prepare for the possibility of Clearing by getting familiar with the procedure. Make sure you know how and when you can get access to the official vacancy lists and what needs to be done. Encourage clear and sensible thinking, so decisions are made carefully, and the first place available is not jumped at. They will have to do the leg-work, of course (universities much prefer to get the applicant on the phone), but sometimes it helps to be able to point them in the right direction. Third, be available as a long-distance taxi driver. Some universities run Clearing open days and some courses, even when recruiting in Clearing, will require an interview. Both of these possibilities will require transport.

Ten Dos and Don'ts

Do	be positive about higher education
Do	get to know the UCAS procedures
Do	stay calm in anxious times
Do	be there when they need you
Do	expect them to have changed when they come back home

Don't	expect them to follow in your footsteps
Don't	offer advice unless you are sure it is accurate
Don't	go on holiday in the middle of August or the end of September
Don't	expect them to tell you everything
Don't	convert their bedroom into your study without asking

Preparing to Leave

All being well, come September you will be preparing to drive off to university. In the last couple of weeks the doormat will have been dented by vast quantities of mail: confirmation of a place at university, details of registration, details of university accommodation and so on. Some of this may require forms to be filled in and returned. Assuming the university is not the local one, there is all the preparation for living in a completely different place that may be several hundred miles away.

Most students will get on and sort all this out without much help, but there are a few ways in which you can make it easier.

- Remember the boring things that are easy to forget, such as checking on insurance (many household insurance policies don't cover possessions taken to university), getting a licence if they have their own television, and arranging passport photographs.
- If they are self-catering, make sure they know a few simple recipes. There are plenty of books aimed at students cooking on a budget and a copy of one of those might be useful, too.
- Make sure they know how to operate a washing machine (but expect to run yours several times if they come home for a weekend).

The Empty Nest

Finally, all the tension of applications, interviews and examinations is over, the mass of form filling is complete, and you are driving away from a university leaving behind a slightly nervous-looking new student. For them the nervousness will soon evaporate as Freshers Week activities and the course get underway. If necessary, advice centres, tutors and counselling services will be on hand to provide help and support. In fact it may well be that you find the transition harder than they do. A new student is embarking on an exciting adventure that will lead to new experiences and new possibilities. It will be a new beginning for you, too, in some ways, but it will also be an ending and a reminder that time is passing, you are getting older and a new phase of life is beginning. Don't under-estimate how long it will take you to adjust.

Then, just as you are settling into a new routine, discovering new things to do as family life takes up less time, the Christmas vacation arrives and you are all together again. Your son or daughter is the same person, a few months older, back in the same bedroom and abandoning clothes in the same place on the landing. But they will have moved on and grown up in subtle ways. You, too, are the same person but you will have moved on as well, with that spot on the landing reserved for a nice Greek urn you bought on your first autumn holiday for 15 years.

Keeping in touch will help. It probably won't be you who is first to get in touch, but keep the contact going as the distractions of term-time mount. However, regardless of how long the phone calls and e-mails, and how frequent the text messages, you can't say everything that could be said. Indeed, one thing you can be sure of is that you won't get told everything. That is probably just as well – it would only make you worry about them even more. So, however hard you try, the chances are that both of you will behave as though the other hasn't changed a bit. They will expect their bedroom to be exactly as they left it and your routines to be the same as ever; you will expect them to behave just as they used to. You will almost certainly both be wrong and there will be another process of readjustment to go through. And the Greek urn will probably have a pair of dirty socks inside for months.

Coming from Overseas

9

It is difficult enough for individuals living in the UK when faced with the bewildering choice amongst the 100 or so universities. How much more so if you live on the other side of the world where, in addition, you will want to consider the varying costs of living and studying in another country. Take, for example, your accommodation. Will this be university-owned or in the private sector? How far is it from the university? Is it secure, safe and warm? Does it have access to an international telephone? Would you have to move out in the vacations? You will need a great deal of information – considerably more than is available within this chapter – but this and the other chapters will give you a good start and point you in the right direction.

The Country

The British Isles comprises two sovereign and independent states of the European Union (EU), the United Kingdom (UK) and the Republic of Ireland. Within the UK there are three further countries: England, Scotland and Wales – sometimes collectively called Great Britain – and the province of Northern Ireland. Of the 101 universities covered in *The Times Good University Guide*:

- 78 are in England
- 13 are in Scotland
- 8 are in Wales
- 2 are in Northern Ireland.

In the late 1990s, a Parliament in Scotland and an Assembly in Wales were established, each with devolved powers. These bodies are already having a positive impact on university education in these countries. For example, EU students at Scottish universities do not pay tuition fees, but do have to contribute after graduation to an endowment for future generations of disadvantaged students. In fact, Scottish universities have seen a surge in numbers of overseas applicants, no doubt as a result of such policy change. Some may also have benefited from Prince William's decision to study at St Andrews!

The Culture

Britain is a multicultural society which has become home to immigrants from the Indian subcontinent, the Middle East, Africa and the West Indies. In recent years, many mainland Europeans have made their homes here, and more are expected from the ten countries (mainly in eastern Europe) who joined the EU in May 2004. Travelling on the London underground, you are likely to hear a host of languages all around you.

The British have a reputation for tolerance and fair play. The media is independent and frequently critical and outspoken, and we strongly believe in justice, law and order. On the whole, British people are polite, often to an extreme that appears insincere. As a result, we tend to use indirect language when making a request or complaint. 'Please' and 'thank you' are among the first words a child is taught and these phrases are used liberally by everyone you meet. We also have a subtle sense of humour which is sometimes difficult to understand. And another thing (apart from the trains!), we try to keep to time. Lateness for a lecture or a doctor's appointment is considered rude but, oddly enough, you should avoid being the first to arrive as a guest at a social engagement. This might all sound rather strange but you will soon get used to us. Make the effort to get involved in sport, voluntary work or one of the many student societies on campus or perhaps as a mentor or a student representative. One of the many joys of living and studying in another country is to experience other ways of doing things, so take advantage of any opportunity to meet people. They will be interested in you and your culture and you will be made very welcome.

The Weather

Most students coming to the UK will find the climate different! Given its position west of the European mainland, Britain tends to have low humidity, warm summers and mild winters. Days are long and bright in June but short and grey in December and you will need to bring or buy a range of suitable clothing Although there are four distinct climatic seasons – spring, summer, autumn and winter – the weather is unpredictable and liable to change and change again in the course of a day. Rainfall is highest in and close to the hilly regions in the north and west – typically over 1,000 mm a year – whilst average daily temperatures range from 5 °C in January to 20 °C in July. Snow falls for a short time most winters and there is even a short skiing season in the Scottish Highlands. As a general rule, southeast England is relatively dry and sunny and northwest Scotland wet and cloudy.

Entry and Employment Regulations

There are four main receiving countries for university students in the English-speaking world – Australia, Canada, the UK and the US – and all have their distinctive characteristics but one thing in common – the need to apply early. All four have restrictions on entry and employment for foreign nationals and, since the attacks on the World Trade Center, reports suggest that visas for students from some countries might be harder to come by or, at very least, subject to greater scrutiny and long delays. Some US universities, for example, are planning to pay the visa fee to counter a perception that students are not welcome. Meanwhile, Australia has closed some of its student recruitment offices overseas to focus on the core Asian market. Developments are also taking place in other parts of the world with increased competition from the Singapore hub, universities in northern Europe offering courses taught in English, and new opportunities to stay and study in your home country.

In June 1999 the Prime Minister, Tony Blair, launched a worldwide campaign to encourage more overseas students to come to the UK's universities. As part of this initiative, the Government made the passage much easier by streamlining visa and entry procedures. In addition, overseas students can now work for up to 20 hours a week during the academic year and full-time in the vacations without the need for a work permit. Similarly, if you are staying in the UK for a year or more, then your spouse and children will be able to take paid employment even if they are here for a shorter period. You can also now apply to remain in the UK after graduation, perhaps for professional training, work experience or a graduate induction programme. This recent package of new measures on immigration and work experience is designed to make the UK a more attractive place to study. However, plans to increase the initial student visa fee have just been announced, and this plus a doubling of the fees for visa extensions has taken some of the shine off this policy. It has led to protests by the universities.

In Scotland, the so-called Fresh Start initiative has been established to attract inward migration because of its declining population, particularly among young people. Under this scheme, international students will be able to apply for an initial two-year extension to stay on after graduation to live and work. The scheme is expected to be operational from summer 2005 and the Scottish Parliament is also developing new scholarships that will allow graduates to combine a year of postgraduate study with work experience.

In addition to a valid passport, some students – called 'visa nationals' – coming to university in Britain will need to obtain a visa from the British Embassy or High Commission before arrival and this could take weeks to arrange. You should apply at least one month, but not more than six months, before coming to the UK. Non-visa nationals do not, as the name implies, require a visa for entry but it might be wise for you to submit your study documents to the British Consulate in your own country just to be on the safe side. In doing so, you can obtain an official entry certificate. Nationals of an EU country, Liechtenstein, Norway and Iceland and now Switzerland are free to travel to the UK without a visa to study or work.

How and When to Apply

Chapter 4 deals with this matter and you should read the information there in conjunction with what follows. If you are applying for a full-time first degree course you will need to fill in a UCAS application form and you can send for one through the UCAS website. You can even complete the form electronically and send it via the internet at some schools and British Council offices.

If you are applying from within an EU country, your application form must be received at UCAS by 15 January, otherwise you will be treated as a late applicant. Different, usually earlier, dates apply for Oxford and Cambridge, and for medical and art and design courses (see details in chapter 4). Prospective students from the ten new EU accession countries (Cyprus, Czech Republic, Estonia, Hungary, Latvia, Lithuania, Malta, Poland, Slovakia and Slovenia) are treated the same as applicants from the other member states. They are not listed in Table 1 because the figures given there pre-date their accession.

If you are applying from a non-EU country, you can submit your application to UCAS at any time between 1 September and 30 June preceding the academic year in which you plan to commence your studies. However, most students apply well before 30 June to make sure that places are still available and to allow plenty of time to make immigration, travel and accommodation arrangements.

British Universities

The UK universities have their origins in the ancient seats of learning at Oxford (1096), Cambridge (1209) and St Andrews (1411). They enjoy a world-wide reputation for the quality of their courses, teaching and research which are rigorously assessed by these independent bodies:

- Higher Education Funding Councils
- Quality Assurance Agency for Higher Education
- Office for Standards in Education.

The appointment of external examiners at each university also guarantees good standards. These, in turn, are reflected in high entry requirements, short and intensive courses of study, and high completion rates, the latter resulting from an infrastructure that offers strong student support. A degree from a British university is a well respected qualification throughout the world, not least because of an increasing emphasis on employability knowledge and skills.

Support for international students is more comprehensive than in most countries and begins long before students arrive in the UK. Most universities have advisers, even offices, in other countries and they are likely to put students in touch with current students or graduates and answer any queries. Then there may well be pre-departure receptions for students and their families and certainly full written pre-arrival information on all aspects of living and studying in Britain. On arrival in the UK, there are often arrangements to meet and greet students at the nearest coach or rail station or airport, a guarantee of warm and comfortable university accommodation, an orientation programme – often lasting several days – to meet friends and to help students adjust to their new surroundings, and courses in the English language for those who need them. But it's not all work. Each university has a students' union which organises social, cultural, religious and sporting clubs and events, including many specifically for overseas students, such as short visits to other European countries. Both the university and its students' union are most likely to have full-time staff whose sole purpose is to look after the welfare of overseas students.

And that's not all! Students receive free medical and subsidised dental and optical treatment under the National Health Service, full access to a professional counselling service and a university careers service network – with an enviable reputation throughout the world – to help you decide what to do on completion of your studies. The fact that degree courses here are more intensive, and thus shorter, than those in many other countries has an obvious financial advantage, not only in study and living costs, but also in the opportunity to enter, or re-enter, the employment market sooner.

Where Overseas Students Study

Most of what follows in this chapter refers to the tables within it. It must be emphasised that these are based solely on the numbers of overseas students attending a particular university and say nothing about the quality of that university. It is very important, therefore, that you

Table 1 Which countries do overseas students come from?

EU countries		%	Non-EU countries (Top 20)		%
Greece	9,941	25.4	China*	11,512	18.8
Germany	5,604	14.3	Malaysia	6,984	11.4
Republic of Ireland	5,522	14.1	Hong Kong	6,303	10.3
France	5,211	13.3	Singapore	2,640	4.3
Spain	2,610	6.7	Cyprus	2,177	3.6
Sweden	2,046	5.2	India*	2,163	3.5
Italy	1,671	4.3	United States	2,092	3.4
Belgium	1,255	3.2	Norway	2,027	3.3
Finland	1,239	3.2	Japan	1,795	2.9
Portugal	962	2.5	Kenya*	1,686	2.8
The Netherlands	891	2.3	Nigeria*	1,629	2.7
Denmark	728	1.9	Oman*	1,159	1.9
Austria	556	1.4	Sri Lanka*	945	1.5
Luxembourg	530	1.4	Pakistan*	945	1.5
Gibraltar	423	1.1	South Korea	943	1.5
All EU students	39,189		Mauritius	871	1.4
			Taiwan*	838	1.4
			Russia*	698	1.1
			Thailand*	622	1.0
			Zimbabwe	618	1.0
			All non-EU students	61,276	

*STUDENTS FROM THESE NON-EU COUNTRIES AND THE TURKISH REPUBLIC OF NORTH CYPRUS REQUIRE A VISA TO STUDY IN THE UK.

cross refer to the main ranking table in chapter 2 and the individual subject tables (chapter 3) which are concerned with quality.

The data are based on overseas students enrolling in all years of first degree courses at UK universities in 2002–03 and are the latest figures available. They exclude those students whose complete study programmes were outside the UK but include the majority of students taking part in European Union exchange programmes such as ERASMUS, TEMPUS and LINGUA at UK universities. Foundation degrees are relatively new and take two years. The traditional first degrees are mostly awarded at Bachelor level (BA, BEng, BSc, etc.) and last for three or four years. There are also some so-called 'enhanced' first degrees (MEng, MChem, etc.) which take four years to complete. Vocational courses like architecture, dentistry and medicine are one or two years longer. Some universities offer one-year courses, including English language tuition, to act as a bridge for overseas students whose qualifications are insufficient for direct entry to a degree course.

The Prime Minister's initiative to recruit an additional 50,000 university students from overseas by 2005 was achieved a year early. The demand is buoyant with significantly increased numbers, particularly from China and Hong Kong, and India but also from Pakistan, Nigeria and the USA. In many UK universities you could expect to have fellow students from over 100 countries across the world. The British university system is truly a global one and increasingly so with more than one in ten of its student population – a much higher figure than the USA – coming from countries overseas.

Which Countries Do Overseas Students Come From and *What Do Overseas Students Study* give a broad overview of overseas students in Britain. Greece and China are prominent as the major sending countries, and most students, regardless of where they come from, pursue courses of study which are strongly vocational. *Where Do Overseas Students Study* lists those

---

Table 2 What do overseas students study?

Subject group	EU	Non-EU	Total
Business and administrative studies	7,861	15,162	23,121
Engineering and technology	5,512	10,141	15,653
Social, economic and political studies	4,048	5,203	9,251
Computer studies	2,392	6,443	8,923
Creative arts and design	3,141	3,752	6,894
Languages	3,199	1,953	5,152
Biological sciences	2,980	2,134	5,114
Legal studies	1,399	3,574	4,949
Subjects allied to medicine	2,208	2,621	4,829
Architecture	1,160	1,751	2,911
Medicine and dentistry	563	2,233	2,796
Physical sciences	1,223	1,199	2,421
Librarianship and information science	1,162	1,040	2,202
Humanities	1,129	892	2,021
Mathematical sciences	388	1,457	1,844
Education	320	976	1,296
Combined studies	265	445	707
Agriculture	203	174	377
Veterinary science	36	126	161

*SUBJECTS ALLIED TO MEDICINE INCLUDE PHARMACY AND NURSING.

universities with large numbers of overseas students. Ulster owes much of its popularity to its close proximity to the Republic of Ireland. This pattern of distribution largely reflects chosen fields of study. As emphasised earlier, you must satisfy yourself about quality by going back to chapters 2 and 3.

Probably the most useful information is to be found in the series of tables *The Most Popular Subjects and Universities for Overseas Students* (opposite) which lists the universities by numbers of overseas students in the 25 most popular subjects, each of which has at least 1,000 overseas students. Use this information in conjunction with the tables that measure quality in the earlier chapters. The subjects are listed in order of popularity.

Advice and information on the UK universities are available through the British Council at its worldwide offices, its university exhibitions and its website (www.educationuk.org), where you can find details of their support services for overseas students. There is also information on course fees, living costs and English language requirements. UKCOSA, the Council for International Education, is another useful source of advice and information. Its website can be viewed at www.ukcosa.org.uk.

Table 3 Where do overseas students study?

Institution (Top 25)	EU students	Institution (Top 25)	Non-EU students
Ulster	1,220	Manchester	1,981
Portsmouth	1,074	University of the Arts, London	1,729
Lincoln	1,040	Nottingham	1,686
University of the Arts, London	981	Middlesex	1,647
Coventry	822	Leeds	1,596
Brighton	786	University College London	1,428
Anglia	751	Central Lancashire	1,353
Napier	747	Portsmouth	1,345
Edinburgh	733	London School of Economics	1,301
Westminster	690	Imperial College	1,217
Kent	673	Warwick	1,202
Kingston	638	Wolverhampton	1,074
Greenwich	630	Sheffield	1,066
University College London	610	Northumbria	1,001
Glamorgan	599	Oxford Brookes	997
King's College London	580	King's College London	976
Manchester Metropolitan	573	Hertfordshire	970
Sussex	572	Sunderland	838
West of England	564	Cambridge	831
Middlesex	553	Cardiff	824
Wolverhampton	522	Westminster	823
Manchester	517	Birmingham	813
Oxford Brookes	503	City	812
Salford	500	Greenwich	811
Aberdeen	485	Luton	810

Table 4 The most popular subjects and universities for overseas students

Business Studies	EU	Non-EU	Economics	EU	Non-EU
Lincoln	453	210	Manchester	32	341
Middlesex	93	408	London School of Economics	35	336
Westminster	246	227	Portsmouth	115	162
Northumbria	213	252	Anglia	251	25
Sunderland	97	359	University College London	50	218
Oxford Brookes	114	337	Essex	88	141
Luton	131	306	Leicester	12	151
Anglia	173	177	Warwick	52	108
Lancaster	225	110	Manchester Metropolitan	94	58
Brighton	183	137	Cambridge	31	112
All overseas students	6,517	9,418	**All overseas students**	1,990	3,390

Computer Science	EU	Non-EU	Art and Design	EU	Non-EU
Middlesex	56	537	University of the Arts	743	1529
Portsmouth	171	269	Surrey Institute	101	143
Hertfordshire	31	301	Middlesex	80	127
Manchester	35	235	Central England	30	139
Lincoln	63	196	Nottingham Trent	29	90
Luton	65	192	Wolverhampton	62	47
Westminster	48	193	Goldsmiths College	40	54
Northumbria	28	194	Coventry	42	52
Coventry	47	170	UWCN, Newport	60	31
Sunderland	48	161	Kingston	29	58
All overseas students	2,387	6,436	**All overseas students**	2,108	3,013

Electrical and Electronic Engineering	EU	Non-EU	Accounting and Finance	EU	Non-EU
Central Lancashire	10	338	London School of Economics	13	331
Sheffield	24	261	Middlesex	29	156
Manchester	34	188	Lancaster	8	160
Imperial College	46	171	Warwick	7	146
Portsmouth	90	112	City	47	97
Liverpool John Moores	52	149	Essex	15	128
Birmingham	20	177	Hull	4	138
Surrey	66	121	Portsmouth	16	121
Sheffield Hallam	21	133	Northumbria	8	123
Leeds	26	128	Kent	11	102
All overseas students	1,766	4,322	**All overseas students**	496	4,421

Table 4 The most popular subjects and universities for overseas students CONT.

Law	EU	Non-EU	Civil Engineering	EU	Non-EU
Wolverhampton	28	421	East London	95	57
King's College London	126	157	Portsmouth	83	68
Kent	106	142	Imperial College	31	98
Nottingham	6	177	Napier	110	3
Cardiff	13	170	Leeds	35	65
Sheffield	15	160	Nottingham	10	78
London School of Economics	24	151	Birmingham	22	61
Northumbria	17	143	University College London	15	65
Warwick	25	124	Brighton	66	9
Essex	69	76	Queen's, Belfast	55	17
All overseas students	**1,343**	**3,471**	**All overseas students**	**1,282**	**1,177**

Biological Sciences	EU	Non-EU	Mechanical Engineering	EU	Non-EU
Edinburgh	107	56	Imperial College	42	106
Imperial College	62	100	Liverpool John Moores	25	85
King's College London	52	64	Sheffield Hallam	10	98
University College London	42	69	Manchester	24	79
Aberdeen	76	26	Coventry	42	45
Leeds	27	41	Sheffield	6	78
Manchester	28	38	Bolton	47	31
Nottingham	17	46	Newcastle	43	30
Glasgow	39	18	Hertfordshire	21	51
Oxford	18	36	Nottingham	12	58
All overseas students	**1,362**	**1,199**	**All overseas students**	**904**	**1,515**

Medicine	EU	Non-EU	Hospitality and Tourism	EU	Non-EU
King's College London	63	147	Queen Margaret	12	211
Manchester	22	145	Oxford Brookes	86	109
University College London	29	116	Surrey	76	99
Imperial College	30	109	Thames Valley	27	113
Cambridge	33	99	Bournemouth	41	65
Nottingham	10	118	Leeds Metropolitan	41	38
Glasgow	17	110	Sheffield Hallam	23	56
Edinburgh	29	96	Brighton	44	22
Aberdeen	22	91	Manchester Metropolitan	23	43
Newcastle	17	91	Plymouth	30	28
All overseas students	**461**	**2,010**	**All overseas students**	**906**	**1,247**

Psychology	EU	Non-EU
Ulster	94	0
Middlesex	45	33
Goldsmiths College	45	29
Nottingham	11	63
Kent	48	24
Bangor	53	15
University College London	17	45
East London	29	27
Sussex	42	9
Luton	45	6
All overseas students	**1,280**	**757**

English	EU	Non-EU
Portsmouth	113	181
Central Lancashire	38	242
Kent	47	51
Wolverhampton	56	22
Warwick	9	36
St Andrews	12	31
Oxford	13	29
Salford	13	27
Kingston	30	8
Anglia	29	9
All overseas students	**849**	**1,039**

Communication and Media Studies	EU	Non-EU
Westminster	93	92
Thames Valley	87	69
Middlesex	47	69
Wolverhampton	81	10
Goldsmiths College	32	50
Sunderland	19	63
East London	47	29
Bournemouth	25	39
Glasgow Caledonian	49	12
University of the Arts	40	17
All overseas students	**1,056**	**896**

Mathematics	EU	Non-EU
City	9	154
Imperial College	26	117
University College London	14	115
Warwick	12	99
Cambridge	44	61
London School of Economics	15	83
Oxford	28	60
Manchester	9	78
Queen Mary	7	54
Heriot-Watt	8	43
All overseas students	**365**	**1,359**

Politics	EU	Non-EU
London School of Economics	66	137
Sussex	94	43
Kent	77	44
St Andrews	44	70
Oxford	27	50
Aberystwyth	43	25
Warwick	35	31
Edinburgh	38	24
Essex	29	31
Aberdeen	37	19
All overseas students	**1,026**	**922**

General Engineering	EU	Non-EU
Central Lancashire	13	315
Coventry	234	16
Warwick	18	134
Cambridge	29	123
Oxford	17	57
Portsmouth	23	19
Glamorgan	24	15
Brunel	19	16
Greenwich	9	23
Queen Mary	5	26
All overseas students	**608**	**1,008**

Table 4 The most popular subjects and universities for overseas students CONT.

Architecture	EU	Non-EU	Education	EU	Non-EU
Greenwich	64	59	Leeds	2	618
Nottingham	17	85	Middlesex	14	42
Oxford Brookes	46	42	Manchester	1	33
Manchester Metropolitan	21	53	Liverpool Hope	26	2
East London	31	39	Stirling	2	24
University College London	28	37	Nottingham	0	25
Cardiff	19	43	Surrey Roehampton	10	13
Dundee	51	9	Chichester	4	18
Liverpool	27	32	Greenwich	10	11
Westminster	35	22	Edinburgh	6	14
All overseas students	**781**	**731**	**All overseas students**	**320**	**976**

Other Subjects Allied to Medicine	EU	Non-EU	Aeronautical and Manufacturing Engineering	EU	Non-EU
Ulster	101	5	Coventry	44	103
Cardiff	31	69	Kingston	33	63
King's College London	27	55	Wolverhampton	0	91
Queen Margaret	44	31	Imperial College	32	55
Bradford	23	36	Nottingham	8	52
Middlesex	25	24	Hertfordshire	17	40
Glamorgan	43	3	Sheffield Hallam	1	55
Salford	29	17	Manchester	12	38
Bangor	43	1	Brunel	20	30
Westminster	21	21	City	18	25
All overseas students	**807**	**703**	**All overseas students**	**408**	**878**

Pharmacology and Pharmacy	EU	Non-EU	Nursing	EU	Non-EU
Strathclyde	11	206	Dundee	26	335
Sunderland	116	89	City	17	145
Robert Gordon	146	31	Ulster	103	6
Brighton	116	55	Napier	33	18
Nottingham	4	119	Thames Valley	27	4
Liverpool John Moores	42	78	Queen's, Belfast	31	0
King's College London	22	58	King's College London	14	16
Bradford	34	38	Luton	7	17
Portsmouth	22	38	Middlesex	5	17
Bath	9	47	Bournemouth	6	13
All overseas students	**581**	**903**	**All overseas students**	**427**	**755**

Building	EU	Non-EU		EU	Non-EU
Central Lancashire	4	143	Nottingham Trent	9	38
Wolverhampton	2	137	Greenwich	3	39
Sheffield Hallam	1	105	Napier	36	3
Northumbria	13	56	Salford	5	32
Glamorgan	47	5	Heriot-Watt	17	19
			All overseas students	**240**	**853**

Oxbridge

10

Oxbridge (as Oxford and Cambridge are called collectively) is another world when it comes to university admissions. Although part of the UCAS network, the two universities have different deadlines from the rest of the system, and applications are made through UCAS direct to colleges. There is little to choose between them in terms of entrance requirements, but a formidable number of successful applicants have the maximum possible UCAS tariff.

However, that does not mean the talented student should be shy about applying: both Oxford and Cambridge have fewer applicants per place than many less prestigious universities, and admission tutors are always looking to extend the range of schools and colleges from which they can recruit. For those with a realistic chance of success, there is little to lose except the possibility of a wasted space on the UCAS application. While a few universities are said to have looked askance at candidates who consider them second best to any other institution, UCAS no longer shows a chosen university the applicant's other choices.

Overall, there are about three applicants to every place at Oxford and Cambridge, but there are big differences between subjects and colleges. As the tables in this chapter show, competition is particularly fierce in subjects such as medicine and English, but those qualified to read metallurgy or classics have a high chance of success. The pattern is similar to that in other universities, although the high degree of selection (and self-selection) that precedes an Oxbridge application means that even in the less popular subjects the field of candidates is likely to be strong.

These two universities' power to intimidate prospective applicants is based partly on myth. Both have done their best to live down the *Brideshead Revisited* image, but many sixth-formers still fear that they would be out of their depth there, academically and socially. In fact, the state sector produces about half the entrants to Oxford and Cambridge, and the drop-out rate is lower than at many other universities. The 'champagne set' is still present and its activities are well publicised, but most students are hard-working high achievers with the same concerns as their counterparts on other campuses. A joint poll by the two universities' student newspapers showed that undergraduates were spending much of their time in the library or worrying about their employment prospects, and relatively little time on the river or in the college bar.

State School Applicants

Student organisations at both universities have put in a great deal of effort trying to encourage applications from state schools, and some colleges have launched their own campaigns. Such has been the determination to convince state school pupils that they will get a fair crack of the whip that a new concern has grown up of possible bias against independent school pupils. In reality, however, the dispersed nature of Oxbridge admissions discounts any conspiracy. Some colleges set relatively low-standard offers to encourage applicants from the state sector, who may reveal their potential at interview. Some admissions tutors may give the edge to candidates from comprehensive schools over those from highly academic independent schools because they consider theirs the greater achievement in the circumstances. Others stick with tried and trusted sources of good students. The independent sector still enjoys a degree of success out of proportion to its share of the school population.

Choosing the Right College

Thorough research to find the right college is therefore very important. Even within colleges, different admissions tutors may have different approaches, so personal contact is essential. The college is likely to be the centre of your social life, as well as your home and study centre for at least a year, so you need to be sure not only that you have a chance of a place, but that you want one at that college. Famously sporty colleges, for example, can be trying for those in search of peace and quiet.

The tables in this chapter give an idea of the relative academic strengths of the colleges, as well as the varying levels of competition for a place in different subjects. But only individual research will suggest which is the right place for you. For example, women may favour one of the few remaining single-sex colleges (St Hilda's at Oxford; New Hall, Newnham and Lucy Cavendish at Cambridge). Men have no such option.

Neither the Norrington Table, for Oxford, nor the Tompkins Table, for Cambridge, is published by the university concerned. Indeed, Oxford tried without success to make compilation impossible. However, both tables give an indication of where the academic powerhouses lie – information which can be as useful to those trying to avoid them as those seeking the ultimate challenge. Although there can be a great deal of movement year by year, both tables tend to be dominated by the rich, old foundations. Both tables are compiled from the degree results of final-year undergraduates. A first is worth five points, a 2:1 four, a 2:2 three, a third one point. The total is divided by the number of candidates to produce each college's average.

In both universities, teaching for most students is based in the colleges. In practice, however, this arrangement holds good in the sciences only for the first year. One-to-one tutorials, which are Oxbridge's traditional strength for undergraduates, are by no means universal. However, teaching groups remain much smaller than in most universities, and the tutor remains an inspiration for many students.

Cambridge The Tompkins Table 2004

College	2004	2003	College	2004	2003
Emmanuel	1	1	Robinson	16	23
Christs's	2	2	Downing	17	12
Trinity	3	8	Sidney Sussex	18	15
Clare	4	6	Churchill	19	9
Gonville and Caius	5	4	King's	20	9
Pembroke	6	3	Peterhouse	21	22
St Catharine's	7	11	Magdalene	22	18
Queens'	8	5	New Hall	23	24
Jesus	9	10	Homerton	24	25
Corpus Christi	10	7	Girton	25	17
Selwyn	11	14	Lucy Cavendish	26	26
Trinity Hall	12	19	Hughes Hall	27	24
Newnham	13	21	Wolfson	28	28
St John's	14	13	St Edmund's	29	29
Fitzwilliam	15	20			

Both Oxford and Cambridge give applicants the option of leaving the choice of college to the university. For those with no ready source of advice on the colleges, this would seem an attractive solution to an intractable problem, but it is also a risky one: a lower proportion succeeds in this way than by applying to a particular college and, inevitably, you may end up somewhere that you hate.

The Applications Procedure

Both universities have set a deadline of 15 October 2005 for entry in 2006. At the same time as your UCAS application is submitted, an Oxford Application Form or Cambridge Preliminary Application Form (PAF), which your school can obtain direct from the relevant university, must be sent direct to Oxford or Cambridge. You may apply to only one of Oxford or Cambridge in the same admissions year, unless you are seeking an Organ award at both universities. Interviews take place in September for those who have left school or applied early, but in December for the majority. By the end of October, the first group can expect an offer, a rejection or deferral of a decision until January. The main group of applicants to Oxford will receive either a conditional offer or a rejection by Christmas, while in Cambridge the news arrives early in the new year. There are other differences between the two universities, however. Some Cambridge colleges ask candidates to sit the university's Sixth Term Examination Papers. Oxford abolished its entrance examination because of claims that it favoured candidates from independent schools. Applicants are now given conditional offers in the normal way, although they may be asked to sit tests when they are called for interview. Oxford is more likely than Cambridge to make an offer as low as two E grades if it is sure that it wants the applicant, but the practice is no longer common.

For general information about Oxford and Cambridge universities, see each institution's profile in chapter 11.

Oxford The Norrington Table 2004

College	2004	2003	College	2004	2003
Merton	1	1	Lincoln	16	22
St John's	2	6	St Anne's	17	8
Balliol	3	5	Oriel	18	23
Hertford	4	19	St Hugh's	19	17
Magdalen	5	3	Christ Church	20	9
St Catherine's	6	16	Keble	21	21
Jesus	7	4	Pembroke	22	25
Wadham	8	2	Trinity	23	11
St Edmund Hall	9	20	Brasenose	24	13
St Peter's	10	18	University	25	4
New College	11	7	Queen's	26	27
Worcester	12	12	Lady Margaret Hall	27	29
Exeter	13	10	Harris Manchester	28	30
Corpus Christi	14	15	Mansfield	29	26
Somerville	15	28	St Hilda's	30	24

Oxford Applications and Acceptances by Course

Arts	Applications		Acceptances		% places to Applications	
	2004	2003	2004	2003	2004	2003
Ancient and Modern History	78	80	20	21	25.6	26.3
Archaeology and Anthropology	51	56	22	20	43.1	35.7
Classical Archaeology and Ancient History	86	85	24	19	27.9	22.4
Classics	262	228	114	114	43.5	50.0
Classics and English	30	34	8	12	26.7	35.3
Classics and Modern Languages	34	33	13	18	38.2	54.5
Economics and Management	608	563	84	89	13.8	15.8
English	1,098	1,088	247	265	22.5	24.4
English and Modern Languages	114	117	18	23	15.8	19.7
European and Middle Eastern Languages	25	17	12	6	48.0	35.3
Fine Art	150	132	19	18	12.7	13.6
Geography	247	302	78	83	31.6	27.5
History of Art	39	–	9	–	23.1	–
Law	1,105	1,106	211	222	19.1	20.1
Law with Law Studies in Europe	273	240	24	32	8.8	13.3
Mathematics and Philosophy	77	63	22	24	28.6	38.1
Modern History	813	875	243	270	29.9	30.9
Modern History and Economics	43	49	7	5	16.3	10.2
Modern History and English	88	97	12	15	13.6	15.5
Modern History and Modern Languages	96	86	22	24	22.9	27.9
Modern History and Politics	305	279	48	54	15.7	19.4
Modern Languages	409	453	178	167	43.5	36.9
Modern Languages and Linguistics	47	58	14	26	29.8	44.8
Music	146	148	60	61	41.1	41.2
Oriental Studies	110	107	44	44	40.0	41.1
Philosophy and Modern Languages	52	50	17	13	32.7	26.0
Philosophy and Theology	102	88	24	26	23.5	29.5
Physics and Philosophy	42	50	13	13	31.0	26.0
PPE	1,107	1,009	251	255	22.7	25.3
Theology	90	96	39	46	43.3	47.9
Total Arts	7,727	7,589	1,897	1,985	24.6	26.2

Sciences

	Applications		Acceptances		% places to Applications	
	2004	2003	2004	2003	2004	2003
Biochemistry	273	243	87	99	31.9	40.7
Biological Sciences	229	247	90	95	39.3	38.5
Chemistry	319	323	176	171	55.2	52.9
Computer Science	103	127	28	34	27.2	26.8
Earth Sciences (Geology)	55	69	35	30	63.6	43.5
Engineering Science	406	356	135	131	33.3	36.8
Engineering and Computer Science	35	36	2	5	5.7	13.9
Engineering, Economics and Management	92	87	12	20	13.0	23.0
Engineering and Materials	13	8	1	1	7.7	12.5
Experimental Psychology	251	217	42	39	16.7	18.0
Human Sciences	105	108	36	42	34.3	38.9
Materials Science and MEM	50	46	27	22	54.0	47.8
Mathematics	553	459	178	170	32.2	37.0
Mathematics and Computer Science	60	75	17	25	28.3	33.3
Mathematics and Statistics	105	80	31	26	29.5	32.5
Medicine	1,090	919	154	158	14.1	17.2
Physics	519	532	173	168	33.3	31.6
Physiological Sciences	49	62	17	17	34.7	27.4
PPP	201	210	38	43	18.9	20.5
Total Sciences	4,508	4,204	1,279	1,296	28.4	30.8
Total Arts and Sciences	12,235	11,793	3,176	3,281	25.9	27.8

NOTE: THE DATES REFER TO THE YEAR IN WHICH THE ACCEPTANCES WERE MADE.

Cambridge Applications and Acceptances by Course

Arts	Applications		Acceptances		% places to Applications	
	2004	2003	2004	2003	2004	2003
Anglo-Saxon, Norse and Celtic	57	64	30	27	52.6	42.2
Archaeology and Anthropology	165	141	67	56	40.6	39.7
Architecture	389	317	38	37	9.7	11.7
Classics	124	138	60	79	48.3	57.2
Classics (4 years)	29	9	8	5	27.5	55.6
English	1,000	883	204	225	20.4	25.5
Geography	324	318	97	97	29.9	30.5
History	806	801	198	221	24.5	27.6
History of Art	92	88	22	25	23.9	28.4
Modern and Medieval Languages	648	575	179	179	27.6	31.1
Music	192	167	67	70	34.8	41.9
Oriental Studies	147	118	40	40	27.2	33.9
Philosophy	322	261	54	43	16.8	16.5
Theology and Religious Studies	125	102	52	44	41.6	43.1
Total Arts	4,420	3,982	1,116	1,148	25.2	28.8

Social Science	2004	2003	2004	2003	2004	2003
Economics	1,027	1,035	151	171	14.7	16.5
Land Economy	177	165	34	48	19.2	29.1
Law	1,495	1,244	225	223	15.1	17.9
Social and Political Sciences	663	556	125	117	18.9	21.0
Total Social Sciences	3,362	3,000	535	559	15.9	18.6

Science and Technology	2004	2003	2004	2003	2004	2003
Computer Science	311	420	92	92	29.6	21.9
Engineering	1,245	1,206	281	306	22.6	25.4
Mathematics	1,060	967	238	244	22.5	25.2
Medical Sciences	1,591	1,408	282	288	17.7	20.5
Natural Sciences	2,002	1,994	583	605	29.1	30.3
Veterinary Medicine	419	459	59	78	14.1	17.0
Total Science and Technology	6,628	6,454	1,535	1,613	23.2	25.0
Education	272		107		39.3	
Total	14,682	13,436	3,293	3,320	22.4	24.7

NOTE: THE DATES REFER TO THE YEAR IN WHICH THE ACCEPTANCES WERE MADE.

MATHEMATICS INCLUDES THOSE APPLYING FOR MATHEMATICS, MATHEMATICS WITH COMPUTER SCIENCE, AND MATHEMATICS WITH PHYSICS.

THE TRIPOS COURSE AT CAMBRIDGE IN CHEMICAL ENGINEERING, LINGUISTICS, MANAGEMENT STUDIES AND MANUFACTURING ENGINEERING CAN ONLY BE TAKEN AFTER PART 1 OF ANOTHER TRIPOS. THE ENTRIES FOR THESE COURSES ARE RECORDED UNDER THE FIRST-YEAR SUBJECTS TAKEN BY THE STUDENT INVOLVED.

Oxford College Profiles

Balliol

Balliol College,
Oxford OX1 3BJ
T   01865 277748
E   admissions@balliol.ox.ac.uk
W   www.balliol.ox.ac.uk
Undergraduates: 410

Famous as the alma mater of many prominent postwar politicians, including Harold Macmillan, Denis Healey and Roy Jenkins, the university's last Chancellor, Balliol has maintained a strong presence in university life and is usually well represented in the Union. Academic standards are formidably high, as might be expected in the college of Wycliffe and Adam Smith, notably in the classics and social sciences. PPE in particular is notoriously oversubscribed. Library facilities are good and include a 24-hour law library. Balliol began admitting overseas students in the 19th century and has cultivated an attractively cosmopolitan atmosphere, of which the lively JCR (Junior Common Room) is a natural focus. Most undergraduates are offered accommodation in college for three years, while graduate students are usually lodged in the Graduate Centre at Holywell Manor. Centrally located with a JCR pantry that is open all day, Balliol is convenient as well as prestigious.

Brasenose

Brasenose College,
Oxford OX1 4AJ
T   01865 277510
E   admissions@bnc.ox.ac.uk
W   www.bnc.ox.ac.uk
Undergraduates: 361

Brasenose may not be the most famous Oxford college but it makes up for its discreet image with a healthy academic performance and an advantageous position in the centre of town. Brasenose was one of the first colleges to become co-educational in the 1970s, although men still take two thirds of the places. In its defence, the college prospectus points out that the major undergraduate office, President of the JCR, has been filled as often by a woman as a man. But BNC, as the college is often known, still has the image of a rugby haven. Named after the door knocker on the 13th-century Brasenose Hall, the college has a pleasant, intimate ambience which most find conducive to study. Law, PPE and modern history are traditional strengths and competition for places in these subjects is intense. Its library is open 24 hours a day and all undergraduate rooms have internet connections. Sporting standards are as high as at many much larger colleges and the college's rowing club is one of the oldest in the university. An annexe, the St Cross Building, means all undergraduates can live in. Most third years live in the Brasenose annexe at Frewin Court, just a few minutes' walk away.

Christ Church

Christ Church College,
Oxford OX1 1DP
T 01865 276181
E admissions@chch.ox.ac.uk
W www.chch.ox.ac.uk
Undergraduates: 426

The college founded by Cardinal Wolsey
in 1525 and affectionately known as The
House has come a long way since Evelyn
Waugh mythologised its aristocratic excesses
in *Brideshead Revisited*. The social mix is
much more varied than most applicants
suspect and the college has gone out of its
way recently to become something of a
champion of political correctness. Academic
pressure at Christ Church is reasonably
relaxed, although natural high-achievers
prosper and the college's history and law
teaching is highly regarded. The magnificent
18th-century library is one of the best in
Oxford. It is supplemented by a separate law
library. Christ Church has its own art
gallery, which holds over 2,000 works of
mainly Italian Renaissance art. Sport,
especially rugby, is an important part of
college life. The playing fields are a few
minutes' walk away through the Meadows.
The river is also close at hand for the
aspiring oarsman, and the college has good
squash courts. Accommodation for all three
years is rated by Christ Church students as
excellent and includes flats off Iffley Road as
well as a number of beautifully panelled
shared sets (double rooms) in college. The
modern bar adds to the lustre of a college
justly famous for its imposing architecture
and cathedral, the smallest in England.

Corpus Christi

Corpus Christi College,
Oxford OX1 4JF
T 01865 276693
E admissions.office@ccc.ox.ac.uk
W www.ccc.ox.ac.uk
Undergraduates: 239

Corpus, until recently Oxford's smallest
college, is naturally overshadowed by its
Goliath-like neighbour, Christ Church,
but makes the most of its intimacy, friendly
atmosphere and exquisite beauty. Like
The House it has an exceptional view across
the Meadows. Although the college has only
around 340 students including
postgraduates, it has an admirable library
open 24 hours a day. Academic expectations
are high and English, PPE and medicine are
especially well established. The college is
beginning to make the most of ties with its
namesake at Cambridge, establishing a joint
lectureship in history in 1999. Corpus is
able to offer accommodation to all its
undergraduates, one of its many attractions
to those seeking a smaller community in
Oxford.

Exeter

Exeter College,
Oxford OX1 3DP
T 01865 279648
E admissions@exeter.ox.ac.uk
W www.exeter.ox.ac.uk
Undergraduates: 320

Exeter is the fourth oldest college in the university and was founded in 1314 by Walter de Stapeldon, Bishop of Exeter. Nestling halfway between the High Street and Broad Street, site of most of the city's bookshops, it could hardly be more central. The college boasts handsome buildings, the exceptional Fellows' garden and attractive accommodation for most undergraduates for all three years of their university careers. Exeter's academic record is strong and the college is usually a high performer in the Norrington Table. It is, however, often accused of being rather dull. Given its glittering roll-call of alumni, which includes Martin Amis, J.R.R. Tolkien, Alan Bennett, Richard Burton, Imogen Stubbs and Tariq Ali, this seems an accusation that on the face of it at least is hard to sustain. College food is not rated highly by students although the bar is popular with students from other colleges.

Harris Manchester

Harris Manchester College,
Oxford OX1 3TF
T 01865 271009
E college.office@hmc.ox.ac.uk
W www.hmc.ox.ac.uk
Undergraduates: 102

Founded in Manchester in 1786 to provide education for non-Anglican students, Harris Manchester finally settled in Oxford in 1889 after spells in both York and London. A full university college since 1996, its central location with fine buildings and grounds in Holywell Street is very convenient for the Bodleian, although the college itself does have an excellent library. Harris Manchester admits only mature students of mostly 25 years and above to read for both undergraduate and graduate degrees, predominantly in the arts. There are also groups of visiting students from American universities and some men and women training for the ministry. Most of its members live in and all meals are provided, indeed the college encourages its members to dine regularly in hall. The college has few sporting facilities but its students do still manage to represent Harris Manchester in football, cricket, swimming and chess as well as playing on other college or university teams. Other outlets include the college Drama Society and also the chapel, a focal point to many there.

Hertford

Hertford College,
Oxford OX1 3BW
T 01865 279404
E admissions@hertford.ox.ac.uk
W www.hertford.ox.ac.uk
Undergraduates: 376

Though tracing its roots to the 12th century, Hertford is determinedly modern. It was one of the first colleges to admit women (in 1976). Hertford also helped set the trend towards offers of places conditional on A levels, which paved the way for the abolition of the entrance examination. It is still popular with state school applicants. The college lacks the grandeur of Magdalen, of which it was once an annexe, but has its own architectural trademark in the Bridge of Sighs. It is also close to the History Faculty library (Hertford's neighbour), the Bodleian and the King's Arms, perhaps Oxford's most popular pub. Academic pressure at Hertford is not high but the quality of teaching, especially in English, is generally thought admirable. Accommodation is improving, thanks in part to the Abingdon House complex, and the college can now lodge almost all of its undergraduates at any one time. Like most congenial colleges, Hertford is often accused of being claustrophobic and inward-looking – a charge most Hertfordians would ascribe simply to jealousy.

Jesus

Jesus College,
Oxford OX1 3DW
T 01865 279720
E undergraduate.admissions@jesus.ox.ac.uk
W www.jesus.ox.ac.uk
Undergraduates: 330

Jesus, the only Oxford college to be founded in the reign of Elizabeth I, suffers from something of an unfair reputation for insularity. Its students, whose predecessors include T.E. Lawrence and Harold Wilson, describe it as 'friendly but gossipy' and shrug off the legend that all its undergraduates are Welsh. Close to most of Oxford's main facilities, Jesus has three compact quads, the second of which is especially enticing in the summer. Academic standards are high and most subjects are taught in college. Physics, chemistry and engineering are especially strong. Rugby and rowing also tend to be taken seriously. Accommodation is almost universally regarded as excellent and relatively inexpensive. Self-catering flats in north and east Oxford have enabled every graduate to live in throughout his or her Oxford career. The range of accommodation available to undergraduates is similarly good and is available for the full length of any course. The college's Cowley Road development is described by the students' union as 'some of the plushest student housing in Oxford'.

Keble

Keble College,
Oxford OX1 3PG
T 01865 272711
E admissions@keb.ox.ac.uk
W www.keble.ox.ac.uk
Undergraduates: 435

Keble, named after John Keble, the leader of the Oxford Movement, was founded in 1870 with the intention of making Oxford education more accessible and the college remains proud of 'the legacy of a social conscience'. With around 420 undergraduates, Keble is one of the biggest colleges in Oxford, while its uncompromising Victorian Gothic architecture also makes it one of the most distinctive. Once famous for the special privileges it extended to rowers, the college is now academically strong, particularly in the sciences where it benefits from easy access to the Science Area, the Radcliffe Science Library and the Mathematical Institute. At the same time, the college's sporting record remains exemplary, providing a large number of rugby Blues in recent years. Undergraduates are guaranteed accommodation in their first two years and the college can also accommodate most undergraduates in their final year. Its library is open 24 hours a day and all rooms have internet connections. Students who live in must eat in Hall 30 times a year. The Starship Enterprise bar is a particular attraction.

Lady Margaret Hall

Lady Margaret Hall,
Oxford OX2 6QA
T 01865 274310/1
E admissions@lmh.ox.ac.uk
W www.lmh.ox.ac.uk
Undergraduates: 424

Lady Margaret Hall, Oxford's first college for women, has been co-educational since 1978 and is now equally balanced. For many students, LMH's comparative isolation – the college is three quarters of a mile north of the city centre – is a real advantage, ensuring a clear distinction between college life and university activities, and a refuge from tourists. Although the neo-Georgian architecture is not to everyone's taste, the college's beautiful gardens back onto the Cherwell river, which allows LMH to have its own punt house. The students' union describes academic life at the college as 'fairly lax' while commending its record in English, history and law. Accommodation is guaranteed for first and third years and for the great majority of second years. The college's two recent accommodation buildings have the remarkable attraction of private bathrooms in all their rooms. LMH shares most of its sports facilities with Trinity College though it has squash and tennis courts on site. Recently, it has become one of Oxford's dramatic centres.

Lincoln

Lincoln College,
Oxford OX1 3DR
T   01865 279836
E   admissions@lincoln.ox.ac.uk
w www.lincoln.ox.ac.uk
Undergraduates: 300

Small, central Lincoln cultivates a lower profile than many other colleges with comparable assets. The college's 15th-century buildings and beautiful library – a converted Queen Anne church – combine to produce a delightful environment in which to spend three years. Academic standards are high, particularly in arts subjects, although the college's relaxed atmosphere is justly celebrated. Accommodation is provided by the college for all undergraduates throughout their careers and includes rooms above The Mitre, a medieval inn. Students parade around Oxford in sub fusc (formal wear) on Ascension Day while choristers beat the bounds. Graduate students have their own centre a few minutes' walk away in Bear Lane. Lincoln's small size and self-sufficiency have led to the college being accused of insularity. Lincoln's food is outstanding, among the best in the university. Sporting achievement is impressive for a college of this size, in part a reflection of its good facilities.

Magdalen

Magdalen College,
Oxford OX1 4AU
T   01865 276063
E   admissions@magd.ox.ac.uk
w www.magd.ox.ac.uk
Undergraduates: 395

Perhaps the most beautiful college in Oxford or Cambridge, Magdalen is known around the world for its tower, its deer park and its May morning celebrations. The college has shaken off its public school image to become a truly cosmopolitan place, with a large intake from overseas and an increasing proportion of state school pupils. Magdalen's record in English, history and law is second to none, while its new science park at Sandford is bound to bolster its reputation in the sciences. Library facilities are excellent, especially in history and law. First-year students are accommodated in the Waynflete Building and allocated rooms in subsequent years by ballot. Undergraduates can be housed in college for the full length of their course. Sets in cloisters and in the palatial New Buildings are particularly sought after. Magdalen is also conveniently placed for the wealth of pubs and places to eat in east Oxford. The college bar is one of the best in Oxford and the college is a pluralistic place, proud of its drama society and choir. Enthusiasm on the river and sports field makes up for a traditional lack of athletic prowess.

Mansfield

Mansfield College,
Oxford OX1 3TF
T 01865 270982
E admissions@mansfield.ox.ac.uk
W www.mansfield.ox.ac.uk
Undergraduates: 191

Mansfield's graduation to full Oxford college status marked the culmination of a long history of development since 1886. Its spacious, attractive site is fairly central, close to the libraries, the shops, the University Parks and the river Cherwell. With just under 200 undergraduates, the community is close-knit, although this can verge on the claustrophobic. The male to female ratio is slightly better than for the university as a whole. Women may prefer the less intimidating atmosphere of Mansfield, perhaps helped by its strong representation of state-school students. First and third years live in college accommodation. Mansfield students share Merton's excellent sports ground and have numerous college teams although it is in drama that its students truly excel. Despite its former theological background, students are not admitted on the basis of religion and can read a wide variety of subjects. Mansfield is home to the Oxford Centre for the Environment, Ethics and Society (OCEES) and also the American Studies Institute, evidence of the strong links between Mansfield and the United States, which is reflected by some 70 visiting students annually.

Merton

Merton College,
Oxford OX1 4JD
T 01865 276329
E undergraduateadmissions@
   admin.merton.ox.ac.uk
W www.merton.ox.ac.uk
Undergraduates: 321

Founded in 1264 by Walter de Merton, Bishop of Rochester and Chancellor of England, Merton is one of Oxford's oldest colleges and one of its most prestigious. Quiet and beautiful, with the oldest quad in the university, Merton has high academic expectations of its undergraduates, often reflected in a position at the top of the Norrington Table, as in 2002, 2003 and 2004. History, law, English, physics and chemistry all enjoy a formidable track record. The medieval library is the envy of many other colleges. Accommodation is cheap, of a good standard and offered to students for all three years. Merton's food is among the best in the university; formal Hall is served six times a week. No kitchens are provided for students who live in college, however. Merton's many diversions include the Merton Floats, its dramatic society, an excellent Christmas Ball and the peculiar Time Ceremony, which celebrates the return of GMT. Sports facilities are excellent, although participation tends to be more important than the final score.

New College

New College,
Oxford OX1 3BN
T 01865 279551
E admissions@new.ox.ac.uk
W www.new.ox.ac.uk
Undergraduates: 420

New College is large, old (founded in 1379 by William of Wykeham) and much more relaxed than most expect when first confronting its daunting facade. It is a bustling place, as proud of its excellent music and its bar as of its strength in law, history and PPE. The college has been making particular efforts to increase the proportion of state school students, inviting applications from schools that have never sent candidates to Oxford. The Target Schools Scheme, designed to increase applications from state schools, is well established. Almost all undergraduates will be able to have college accommodation for three years. The college's library facilities are impressive, especially in law, classics and PPE. The sports ground is nearby and includes good tennis courts. Women's sport is particularly strong. A new sports complex, named after Brian Johnston, opened in 1997, at St Cross Road. The sheer beauty of New College remains one of its principal assets and the college gardens are a memorable sight in the summer. In spite of these traditional charms, the college has strong claims to be considered admirably innovative. Music is a feature of college life and the Commemoration Ball, held every three years, is a highlight of Oxford's social calendar.

Oriel

Oriel College,
Oxford OX1 4EW
T 01865 276522
E admissions@oriel.ox.ac.uk
W www.oriel.ox.ac.uk
Undergraduates: 304

In spite of its reputation as a bastion of muscular privilege, Oriel is a friendly college with a strong sense of identity and has adjusted rapidly to co-educational admissions (women were not admitted until 1985). The students' union describes the college as having 'a strong crew spirit' reflecting its traditions on the river. Academic standards are better than legend suggests and the college's well-stocked library is open 24 hours a day. But Oriel's sporting reputation is certainly deserved and its rowing eight is rarely far from the head of the river. Other sports are well catered for, even if their facilities are considerably farther away than the boathouse, which is only a short jog away. Accommodation is of variable quality but Oriel can provide rooms for all three years for those students who require them. Scholars and Exhibitioners chasing firsts in their final year are given priority in the ballot for college rooms. Extensive new accommodation has been completed one mile away off the Cowley Road and at the Island Site on Oriel Street. Oriel also offers a lively drama society, a Shakespearian production taking place each summer in the front quad.

Pembroke

Pembroke College,
Oxford OX1 1DW
T   01865 276412
E   admissions@pembroke.ox.ac.uk
W   www.pembroke.ox.ac.uk
Undergraduates: 418

Although its alumni include such extrovert characters as Dr Johnson and Michael Heseltine, Pembroke is one of Oxford's least dynamic colleges. Academic results are solid, and the college has Fellows and lecturers in almost all the major university subjects. Pembroke expects to accommodate all first years and most final-year undergraduates. The Sir Geoffrey Arthur building on the river, ten minutes' walk from the college, offers excellent facilities; in addition to 100 student rooms there is a concert room, computer room and a multigym. College food is reasonable, though some find formal Hall every evening rather too rich a diet. Rugby and rowing are strong, with Pembroke second only to Oriel on the river, and squash and tennis courts are available at the nearby sports ground.

Queen's

Queen's College,
Oxford OX1 4AW
T   01865 279167
E   admissions@queens.ox.ac.uk
W   www.queens.ox.ac.uk
Undergraduates: 304

One of the most striking sights of the High Street, Queen's has now shed its exclusive 'northern' image to become one of Oxford's liveliest and most attractive colleges. The college's academic record is good, although it fared badly in the 2004 Norrington Table. According to the students' union, 'the general attitude to work is fairly relaxed and seems to bring good results'. Modern languages, chemistry and mathematics are reckoned among the strongest subjects. Queen's does not normally admit undergraduates for the honours school of English language and literature or geography. The library is as beautiful as it is well stocked. All students are offered accommodation, first years being housed in modernist annexes in east Oxford. The college's beer cellar is one of the most popular in the university and the JCR's facilities are also better than average. An annual dinner commemorates a student who is said to have fended off a bear by thrusting a volume of Aristotle into its mouth.

St Anne's

St Anne's College,
Oxford OX2 6HS
T   01865 274825
E   enquiries@st-annes.ox.ac.uk
W   www.st-annes.ox.ac.uk
Undergraduates: 437

Architecturally uninspiring (a row of
Victorian houses with concrete 'stack-a-
studies' dropped into their back gardens),
St Anne's makes up in community spirit
what it lacks in awesome grandeur. One of
the largest colleges, it has a high proportion
of state school students. A women's college
until 1979, its academic standing is growing
after being in last place in the middle of the
last decade. The library is particularly rich
in law, Chinese and medieval history texts.
Opening hours are long. Accommodation is
guaranteed to all undergraduates and the
college is just to the north of the city centre.
Three new accommodation blocks contain
150 student rooms, including four for
disabled students, while the older rooms
have been refurbished.

St Catherine's

St Catherine's College,
Oxford OX13UJ
T   01865 271703
E   admissions@stcatz.ox.ac.uk
W   www.stcatz.ox.ac.uk
Undergraduates: 437

Arne Jacobsen's modernist design for 'Catz',
one of Oxford's youngest undergraduate
college and one of its largest, has attracted
much attention as the most striking contrast
in the university to the lofty spires of
Magdalen and New College. Close to the
university science area and the pleasantly
rural Holywell Great Meadow, St Catherine's
is nevertheless only a few minutes' walk
from the city centre. Academic standards are
especially high in mathematics and physics
though the college's scholarly ambitions
are far from having been exhausted. The
students' union prospectus used to
complain that Fellows were ' increasingly
eager to apply more academic pressure in
college'. The well-liked Wolfson library is
open till 1 am on most days. Rooms are
small but tend to be warmer than in other,
more venerable colleges. Accommodation is
available for first and third years, and plans
are underway to extend this to all three
years. Squash, tennis and netball courts
are all on the main college site. There is
an excellent theatre, and the college is host
to the Cameron Mackintosh Chair of
Contemporary Theatre. Recent incumbents
have included Sir Ian McKellen, Alan
Ayckbourn and Lord Attenborough. St
Catherine's has one of the best JCR facilities
in Oxford.

St Edmund Hall

St Edmund Hall College,
Oxford OX1 4AR
T   01865 279008
E   admissions@seh.ox.ac.uk
W   www.seh.ox.ac.uk
Undergraduates: 397

St Edmund Hall – 'Teddy Hall' – has one
of Oxford's smallest college sites but also
one of its most populous with nearly
400 undergraduates swarming through
its medieval quads. Some two thirds of
undergraduates are male, but the college
is anxious to shed its image as a home for
'hearties', and the authorities have gone
out of their way to tone down younger
members' rowdier excesses. Nonetheless,
the sporting culture at St Edmund Hall is
still vigorous and the college usually does
well in rugby, football and hockey.
Academically, the college has some impressive
names among its fellowship as well as a
marvellous library, originally a Norman
church. The students' union reports that
'a laid-back approach (to work) is the norm'.
Accommodation is reasonable and is
guaranteed to first and third years, though
most second-year students live out. Its
accommodation is being extended and it
will soon be able to provide rooms for all
three years. The college has two annexes,
one near the University Parks, the other in
Iffley Road, where many of the rooms have
private bathrooms. Hall food is better than
average.

St Hilda's

St Hilda's College,
Oxford OX4 1DY
T   01865 286620
E   college.office@st-hildas.ox.ac.uk
W   www.sthildas.ox.ac.uk
Undergraduates: 419 (women only)

With Somerville co-educational, St Hilda's is
now the last bastion of all-women education
in Oxford. How long the university will
allow it to remain that way is open to
question. In spite of its variable academic
record, the college is a distinctive part of
the Oxford landscape and is usually well
represented in university life. The 50,000-
volume library is growing fast and plans for
its extension are being considered. St Hilda's
also boasts one of the largest ratios of state
school to independent undergraduates in
Oxford. Accommodation is guaranteed to
first years and for one of the remaining two
years. The JCR has its own punts, which are
available free for college members and their
guests. Many of the rooms offer some of the
best river views in Oxford. Social facilities
are limited but the standard of food is high.

St Hugh's

St Hugh's College,
Oxford OX2 6LE
T   01865 274910
E   admissions@st-hughs.ox.ac.uk
W www.st-hughs.ox.ac.uk
Undergraduates: 419

One of Oxford's lesser-known colleges, St Hugh's was criticised by students in 1987 when it began admitting men. There are now fewer women than men at the college, although the male/female ratio is better balanced than at most Oxford colleges. Like Lady Margaret Hall, St Hugh's is a bicycle ride from the city centre and has a picturesque setting. It is an ideal college for those seeking a place to live and study away from the madding crowd, and is well liked for its pleasantly bohemian atmosphere. Academic pressure remains comparatively low, although the students' union says there are signs that this is changing. St Hugh's guarantees accommodation to undergraduates for all three years, although the standard of rooms is variable. Sport, particularly football, is taken quite seriously. The extensive grounds include a croquet lawn and tennis courts.

St John's

St John's College,
Oxford OX1 3JP
T   01865 277317
E   admissions@sjc.ox.ac.uk
W www.sjc.ox.ac.uk
Undergraduates: 404

St John's is one of Oxford's powerhouses, excelling in almost every field and boasting arguably the most beautiful gardens in the university. Founded in 1555 by a London merchant, it is richly endowed and makes the most of its resources to provide undergraduates with an agreeable and challenging three years. The work ethic is very much part of the St John's ethos, and academic standards are high, with English, chemistry and history among the traditional strengths, though all students benefit from the impressive library. It now has one of the highest number of state school students in Oxford, and the college compensates to some extent by offering generous hardship funds to those in financial difficulty. As might be expected of a wealthy college, the accommodation is excellent and guaranteed for three or four years. St John's has a strong sporting tradition and offers good facilities, but the social scene is limited.

St Peter's

St Peter's College,
Oxford OX1 2DL
T   01865 278863
E   admissions@spc.ox.ac.uk
W   www.spc.ox.ac.uk
Undergraduates: 390

Opened as St Peter's Hall in 1929, St Peter's has been an Oxford college since 1961. Its medieval, Georgian and 19th-century buildings are in the city centre and close to most of Oxford's main facilities. Though still young, St Peter's is well represented in university life and has pockets of academic excellence and rose to tenth in the Norrington Table in 2004. History tutoring is particularly good. There are no Fellows in classics at the college. Accommodation is offered to students for first and third years and about 60 per cent of second years. Student rooms vary from traditional rooms in college to new purpose-built rooms a few minutes' walk away. The college's facilities are impressive, including one of the university's best JCRs. St Peter's is known as one of Oxford's most vibrant colleges socially. It is strong on acting and journalism and has a recently refurbished bar.

Somerville

Somerville College,
Oxford OX2 6HD
T   01865 270629
E   secretariat@somerville.ox.ac.uk
W   www.somerville.ox.ac.uk
Undergraduates: 394

The announcement, early in 1992, that Somerville was to go co-educational sparked an unusually acrimonious and persistent dispute within this most tranquil of colleges. Protests were doomed to failure, however: the first male undergraduates arrived in 1994 and now account for half the students. Lady Thatcher was one of those who flocked to their old college's defence, illustrating the fierce loyalty Somerville inspires. The college's atmosphere appears to have survived the momentous change, although the culture of protest reappeared when a number of students refused to pay the government's tuition fees in 1998. Accommodation, including 30 small flats for students, is of a reasonable standard, and is guaranteed for first years and students sitting public examinations. Sport is strong at Somerville and the women's rowing eight usually finishes near the head of the river. The college's hockey pitches and tennis courts are nearby. The 100,000-volume library is open 24 hours a day and is one of the most beautiful in Oxford.

Trinity

Trinity College,
Oxford OX1 3BH
T   01865 279910
E   admissions@trinity.ox.ac.uk
W   www.trinity.ox.ac.uk
Undergraduates: 301

Architecturally impressive and boasting beautiful lawns, Trinity is one of Oxford's least populous colleges. It is ideally located, beside the Bodleian, Blackwell's book shop and the White Horse pub. Cardinal Newman, an alumnus of Trinity, is said to have regarded Trinity's motto as 'Drink, drink, drink'. Academic pressure varies, as the college darts up and down the unofficial Norrington Table of academic performance. Nonetheless, the college produces its fair share of firsts, especially in arts subjects. Trinity has shaken off its reputation for apathy, though the early gate closing times can leave the college isolated late at night. Members are active in all walks of university life and the college has its own debating and drama societies. The proportion of state school entrants has been rising. Accommodation is of a reasonable standard and most undergraduates can live in for three years if they wish.

University

University College,
Oxford OX1 4BH
T   01865 276601
E   admissions@univ.ox.ac.uk
W   www.univ.ox.ac.uk
Undergraduates: 420

University is the first Oxford college to be able to boast a former student in the Oval Office. Indeed, the college seems certain to benefit from its unique links with former President Clinton, a Rhodes Scholar at University in the late 1960s. The college is probably Oxford's oldest, though highly unlikely to have been founded by King Alfred, as legend claims. Academic expectations are high and the college prospers in most subjects. Physics, PPE and maths are particularly strong. That said, University has fewer claims to be thought a powerhouse in the manner of St John's, arguably its greatest rival. Accommodation is guaranteed to undergraduates for all three years, with third years lodged in an annexe in north Oxford about a mile and a half from the college site on the High Street. The students' union complains that facilities are poor. Sport is strong and University is usually successful on the river, but the college has a reputation for being quiet socially.

Wadham

Wadham College,
Oxford OX1 3PN
T 01865 277947
E admissions@wadham.ox.ac.uk
W www.wadham.ox.ac.uk
Undergraduates: 460

Founded by Dorothy Wadham in 1609, Wadham is known in about equal measure for its academic track record – the college generally ranks in the top third in examination performance – and its leftist politics. The JCR is famously dynamic and politically active, although the breadth of political opinion is greater than its left-wing stereotype suggests. And for somewhere supposedly unconcerned with such fripperies, its gardens are surprisingly beautiful. The somewhat rough-hewn chapel is similarly memorable. The college has a good 24-hour library. Accommodation is guaranteed for at least two years and there are many large, shared rooms on offer. Journalism and drama play an important part in the life of the college, although sport is there for those who want it. The College also includes the 18th-century Holywell Music Room, a historic concert hall.

Worcester

Worcester College,
Oxford OX1 2HB
T 01865 278391
E admissions@worc.ox.ac.uk
W www.worc.ox.ac.uk
Undergraduates: 417

Worcester is to the west of Oxford what Magdalen is to the east, an open, rural contrast to the urban rush of the city centre. The college's rather mediocre exterior conceals a delightful environment, including some characteristically muscular Baroque Hawskmoor architecture, a garden and a lake. Though academic pressure has been described as 'tastefully restrained', law, theology and engineering are among the college's strengths. The 24-hour library is strongest in the arts. Accommodation, guaranteed for two years and provided for the majority of third years, varies in quality from ordinary to conference standard in the Linbury Building. The ratio of bathrooms to students (one to four) is better than in many colleges. Sport plays an important part in college life, Worcester having enjoyed more success recently in rowing and rugby.

Cambridge Colleges

Christ's

Christ's College,
Cambridge CB2 3BU
T   01223 334953
E   admissions@christs.cam.ac.uk
W   www.christs.cam.ac.uk
Undergraduates: 395

Christ's prides itself on its academic strength, and it is also one of the few colleges still to offer places on two E grades at A level, meaning that the college is confident of its ability to identify potential high-flyers at interview and, in effect, prepared to circumvent A levels as the principal criteria for entry. The college has a 46:54 state-to-independent ratio and women make up a third of the students. Though the college has a reputation for being dominated by hard-working natural scientists and mathematicians, it has had good results for history and music. The atmosphere has been described as cosy, but some complain of short bar opening hours and a poor relationship between undergraduates and Fellows. Accommodation is guaranteed to all undergraduates in college, some of whom will be allocated rooms in the infamous New Court 'Typewriter'. The Typewriter houses the excellent New Court theatre, home to Christ's Amateur Dramatics Society and the adventurous student film society, Christ's Films. College sport has flourished in recent years, with teams competing to a good standard. The playing fields (shared with Sidney Sussex) are just over a mile away.

Churchill

Churchill College,
Cambridge CB3 0DS
T   01223 336202
E   admissions@chu.cam.ac.uk
W   www.chu.cam.ac.uk
Undergraduates: 440

Founded in 1960 to help meet 'the national need for scientists and engineers and to forge links with industry', Churchill has been rising again in the Cambridge league table and still has high standards. Maths, natural sciences, engineering and computer science are traditional strengths, but arts results have been disappointing recently. The college has some of the university's best computer facilities. Deferred entry is encouraged in all subjects. Churchill has an above average ratio of state to independent pupils (56:44) but one of the lowest proportions of women under-graduates: only one in three. Some are put off by Churchill's unassuming modern architecture and the college's distance from the city centre; others argue that the distance offers much-needed breathing space. One undeniable advantage is Churchill's ability to provide every undergraduate with a room in college for all three years. There are extensive on-site playing fields, and the college does well in rugby, hockey and rowing. The university's only student radio station (broadcasting to Churchill and New Hall) is based here.

Clare

Clare College,
Cambridge CB2 1TL
T   01223 333246
E   admissions@clare.cam.ac.uk
W   www.clare.cam.ac.uk
Undergraduates: 440

Though for many Clare's outstanding features are its gardens and harmonious buildings, hard-pressed undergraduates are just as likely to praise the rent and food charges, among the lowest in the university. Accommodation is guaranteed for all three years, either in college or nearby hostels. One of the few colleges which openly encourages applications from 'candidates of a good academic standard who have special talents in non-academic fields', Clare tends to feature near the top of the academic tables. Applicants are encouraged to take a gap year. Languages, social and political science and music are especially strong, but science results have been disappointing. The ratio of male to female students is better than many colleges (47:53), while systematic attempts to raise the proportion of state-educated students has left those from independent schools in a minority (37 per cent). Music thrives. The choir records and tours regularly, and Clare Cellars (comprising the bar and JCR) is a popular venue. Sporting emphasis is as much on enjoyment as competition. The women's teams have had outstanding success in recent years. The playing fields are little more than a mile away.

Corpus Christi

Corpus Christi College,
Cambridge CB2 1RH
T   01223 338056
E   admissions@corpus.cam.ac.uk
W   www.corpus.cam.ac.uk
Undergraduates: 250

The only college to have been founded by town residents, Corpus's size inevitably makes it one of the more intimate colleges. It prides itself on being a cohesive community, but some find the focus on college rather than university life excessive. Although small, it is traditionally broad based academically. The kitchen fixed charge is above average but the college is known for a good formal hall. Almost all undergraduates are allocated a room in college or neighbouring hostels. The library is open 24 hours. There is a fairly even social balance: the independent-to-state ratio is 49:51. The college bar has an enviable atmosphere. The sporting facilities, at Leckhampton (just over a mile away), are among the best in the university and include a swimming pool. The size of the college means that its sporting reputation owes more to enthusiasm than success, however. Drama is also well catered for, and the college owns The Playroom, the university's best small theatre.

Downing

Downing College,
Cambridge CB2 1DQ
T   01223 334826
E   admissions@dow.cam.ac.uk
W   www.dow.cam.ac.uk
Undergraduates: 410

Downing's imposing neo-Classical quadrangle may look more like a military academy than a Cambridge college but the atmosphere here is anything but martial. Founded in 1800 for the study of law, medicine and natural sciences, these are still the college's strong subjects. Indeed Downing is often called 'the law college', although recent results have been better in sciences than arts. A reputation for hard-playing, hard-drinking rugby players and oarsmen is proving hard to shake off. The college claims the best Cambridge boat club. But while sport undoubtedly enjoys a high profile, pressure to conform to the sporty stereotype is never excessive. Downing currently guarantees a place in college accommodation for three years and a significant proportion requiring a fourth year. The library, opened by Prince Charles in 1993, has won an award for its architecture. There is a 45:55 balance between students with state and independent school backgrounds. The student-run bar/party room has improved college social life following three candlelit formal dinners a week.

Emmanuel

Emmanuel College,
Cambridge CB2 3AP
T   01223 334290
E   admissions@emma.cam.ac.uk
W   www.emma.cam.ac.uk
Undergraduates: 483

Thanks in no small part to its huge and stylish, strikingly modern bar, Emmanuel has something of an insular reputation; although the students are active in university clubs and societies. Once a mid-table college, with no subject bias, Emmanuel has significantly raised its academic profile recently, gaining strength in medicine and social science, but particularly in English and taking top place in the Tompkins Table in 2003 and 2004. Deferred entry is greatly encouraged. A 54:46 state-to-independent ratio contributes to the college's unpretentious atmosphere and nearly half the undergraduates are women. All students are guaranteed accommodation. Second years are housed in college hostels. With self-catering facilities limited, most students eat in Hall. The college offers ten expedition grants to undergraduates every year, and has a large hardship fund. In the summer, the college tennis courts and open-air swimming pool offer a welcome haven from exam pressures. The duck pond is one of the most picturesque spots in Cambridge. The sports grounds are excellent, if some distance away.

Fitzwilliam

Fitzwilliam College,
Cambridge CB3 0DG
T 01223 332030
E admissions@fitz.cam.ac.uk
W www.fitz.cam.ac.uk
Undergraduates: 474

Based in the city centre until 1963, the college now occupies a large, modern site on the Huntingdon Road. What it may lack in architectural splendour, Fitzwilliam makes up in friendly informality. Around 60 per cent of its undergraduates come from the state sector, and about 40 per cent are women, though the college hopes 'significantly to raise this proportion in the coming years'. College accommodation is now available for all undergraduates with the completion of the Wilson Building. Fitzwilliam's academic record has been improving, with languages and geography the strongest subjects. Arts are generally stronger than sciences. Applications are also encouraged in archaeology and anthropology, classics, social and political sciences and music. As at Christ's, offers of places are sometimes made on the basis of two Es only at A level. On the extracurricular front, the badminton, hockey and football teams are among the best in the university. The playing fields are a few hundred yards away. The twice termly Ents (college entertainments) are exceptionally popular. Music and drama thrive.

Girton

Girton College,
Cambridge CB3 0JG
T 01223 338972
E admissions@girton.cam.ac.uk
W www.girton.cam.ac.uk
Undergraduates: 503

The joke about needing a passport to travel to Girton refuses to die. In fact, with the city centre a 15-minute cycle ride away, the college is closer than many hostels at other universities. But if comparative isolation inevitably encourages a strong community spirit, Girtonians still manage to participate in university life at least as much as students at more central colleges and are particularly active in university sports. On the other hand, since Girton stands on a 50-acre site and the majority of second-year students live in Wolfson Court (near the University Library), there is no question of over-crowding: rooms are available for the entire course. Some find that the long corridors remind them of boarding school. Since becoming coeducational in 1979, the college has maintained a balanced admissions policy. Just over half of the undergraduates are from state schools. Girton also has the highest proportion of women Fellows in any mixed college (50 per cent). The on-site sporting facilities, which include a swimming pool, are excellent. The college is active in most sports and particularly strong in football. The formal hall is excellent and popular, but held only once a week.

Gonville and Caius

Gonville and Caius College,
Cambridge CB2 1TA
T 01223 332447
E admissions@cai.cam.ac.uk
W www.cai.cam.ac.uk
Undergraduates: 489

Gonville and Caius College – to confuse the outsider, the college is usually known as Caius (pronounced 'keys') – is among the most beautiful of Cambridge's colleges, as well as one of the most central. It has an excellent academic reputation, especially in medicine and history, though maths and law are also highly rated. Recent results have been better in sciences than arts. Book grants are available to all undergraduates. The library has been refurbished and computer facilities improved.
Accommodation is split between the central site on Trinity Street and Harvey Court, a five-minute walk away across the river. Rooms are guaranteed for all first and third years. The majority of second years live in college hostels, none of which is more than a mile away. Undergraduates are obliged to eat in Hall at least 45 times a term, a ruling some find restrictive but which at least ensures that students meet regularly. The college has something of a Home Counties or public school reputation especially for its 'It' girls, society high-fliers. In 2002 acceptances for state-school pupils was around 46 per cent. However, Caius is 'eager to extend the range of its intake'. Caius tends to do well in rowing and hockey, but most sports are fairly relaxed. A lively social scene is helped by the student-run Late Night Bar.

Homerton

Homerton College,
Cambridge CB2 2PH
T 01223 507114
E admissions@homerton.cam.ac.uk
W www.homerton.cam.ac.uk
Undergraduates: 550

In August 2001 Homerton became the newest college of the university (formerly an 'Approved Society'), though its students had been university members for a quarter of a century. The college continues to specialise in education, including teacher training – through the BA degree and the postgraduate certificate in education (PGCE) courses offered by the Faculty of Education – but now admits students for many of the other courses offered by the university at both undergraduate and postgraduate level. All first years have rooms in college in new accommodation blocks. In the second year accommodation may be in college or in private rented houses, but final-year students can live in if they wish. There is a 73:27 state–independent split, with men, at the moment, making up around 24 per cent of undergraduates. The college's position, a mile from the city centre in its own large grounds, means that the onus is on Homerton students to take the initiative and get involved in university activities. Many do. Homerton is like the other undergraduate colleges in what it offers, and students can take advantage of Formal Hall, sport (there are on-site playing fields), music and drama.

Jesus

Jesus College,
Cambridge CB5 8BL
T   01223 339495
E   undergraduate-admissions@jesus.cam.ac.uk
W   www.jesus.cam.ac.uk
Undergraduates: 503

For those of a sporting inclination Jesus is perhaps the ideal college. Within its spacious grounds there are football, rugby and cricket pitches as well as three squash courts and no less than ten tennis courts, while the Cam is just a few hundred yards away. With these facilities, it is hardly surprising that sports, in particular rowing, rugby and hockey, rate high on many students' agendas. That said, sporting prowess is far from the whole story. The music society thrives, and has extensive practice facilities. Although Jesus lacks a theatre of its own, the college is active in university drama. On the academic front, the Fellows-to-undergraduates ratio is generous and, while philosophy and politics are among the college's strong suits, the balance between arts and sciences is fairly even. There is an excellent and stylish new library. Rooms in college are guaranteed for all first and third-year students. The majority of second years live in college houses directly opposite the college. Over half the undergraduates are state educated and the college is keen to encourage more applications from the state sector. The college grounds – particularly The Chimney walkway to the porter's lodge – are attractive.

King's

King's College,
Cambridge CB2 1ST
T   01223 331417
E   undergraduate.admissions@
     kings.cam.ac.uk
W   www.kings.cam.ac.uk
Undergraduates: 386

The reputation of King's as the most right-on place in the university has become something of an in-joke. It is true that the college has a 74:26 state-to-independent ratio and that it has banned Formal Hall and abandoned May Balls in favour of politically correct June Events. The college is involved in an initiative to increase the number of candidates from socially and educationally disadvantaged backgrounds, and is also keen to encourage applications from ethnic minorities and from women. The students' union is active politically. The college has fewer undergraduates than the grandeur of its buildings might suggest, one result being that accommodation is guaranteed, either in college or in hostels a few hundred yards away. With the highest ratio of Fellows to undergraduates in Cambridge, it is not surprising that King's has been one of the most academically successful colleges, although it has been falling down the Tompkins Table recently. No subjects are especially favoured, but recent results have been better in arts than sciences. Applications are not accepted in veterinary medicine and there are few law students. Sport at King's is anything but competitive. An extremely large bar/JCR is the social focal point, while the world-famous chapel and choir form the heart of an outstanding music scene.

Lucy Cavendish

Lucy Cavendish College,
Cambridge CB3 0BU
T   01223 330280
E   lcc-admissions@lists.cam.ac.uk
W   www.lucy-cav.cam.ac.uk
Undergraduates: 118 (women only)

Since its creation in 1965, Lucy Cavendish has given hundreds of women over the age of 21 the opportunity to read for Tripos subjects. A number of its students had already started careers and/or families when they decided to enter higher education. The college seeks to offer financial support to those with family responsibilities, though as yet it has no childcare facilities. Accommodation is provided for all who request it, either in the college's three Victorian houses or in its three modern residential blocks. The college's small size enables all students to get to know one another. Plans to increase the intake are unlikely to alter the intimate and informal atmosphere. Law is still the dominant subject in terms of numbers of students, but veterinary science is also strong and the college welcomes applications in the sciences and other disciplines. All the Fellows are women. For subjects not covered by the Fellowship, there is a well-established network of university teachers.

Magdalene

Magdalene College,
Cambridge CB3 0AG
T   01223 332135
E   admissions@magd.cam.ac.uk
W   www.magd.cam.ac.uk
Undergraduates: 337

As the last college to admit women (1988), Magdalene has still to throw off a lingering image as home to hordes of public school hearties. In fact, around 50 per cent of its undergraduates are from the state sector while over a third are women. That said, the sporty emphasis, on rugby and rowing in particular, is undeniable. The nearby playing fields are shared with St John's and the college has its own Eton fives court. Despite finishing closer to the foot of the academic league tables than its Fellows would wish, Magdalene is strong in architecture, law and social and political science. Students are heavily involved in university-wide activities from drama to journalism as well as sport. Accommodation is provided for all undergraduates, either in college or in one of 21 houses and hostels, 'mostly on our doorstep'. Living in is more expensive than in most colleges. Magdalene is proud of its river frontage, the longest in the university, which is especially memorable in the summer.

New Hall

New Hall,
Huntingdon Road, Cambridge CB3 0DF
T   01223 762229
E   admissions@newhall.cam.ac.uk
W   www.newhall.cam.ac.uk
Undergraduates: 370 (women only)

One of three remaining all-women colleges, New Hall enjoys a largely erroneous reputation for feminism and academic underachievement not helped by a much-publicised whitewash on University Challenge. Founded in 1954 to increase the number of women in the university, it occupies a modern grey-brick site next door to Fitzwilliam. Students are split 50:50 between state and independent schools. The college lays claim to certain paradoxes. While a rent strike early in the 1990s attested to a degree of political activism, tradition is far from rejected. The following year saw New Hall's first-ever May Ball, an event hosted jointly with Sidney Sussex. Its results regularly place the college near the bottom of the academic league, but it must be remembered that women's results lag behind men's throughout the university. Natural sciences, medicine, economics, and English are New Hall's strongest areas. The college is known for its unusual split-level bar, but many students choose to socialise elsewhere. Sport is a good mixture of high-fliers and enthusiasts, with grounds, shared with Fitzwilliam, half a mile away. The college is particularly proud of its collection of contemporary women's art.

Newnham

Newnham College,
Cambridge CB3 9DF
T   01223 335783
E   adm@newn.cam.ac.uk
W   www.newn.cam.ac.uk
Undergraduates: 401 (women only)

Newnham has long had to battle with a blue-stocking image. Its entry in the university prospectus used to insist that it 'is not a nunnery' and that the atmosphere in this all-women college is no stricter than elsewhere. It even has a 'Newnham Nuns' drinking club to make the point. With an 44:56 state–independent ratio, the college has not entirely cast off a reputation for public school dominance. Newnham is in the perfect location for humanities students, with the lecture halls and libraries of the Sidgwick Site just across the road. The college is, however, keen to encourage applications in engineering, maths and the sciences, and recent results in these subjects have been better than in the arts. All of the Fellows are women. Around 95 per cent of students live in for all three years. This is not to say that ventures into the social, sporting and artistic life of the university are the exception rather than the rule. Newnham students are anything but insular. As well as being blessed with the largest and most beautiful lawns in Cambridge, Newnham has its playing fields on site. The boat club has been notably successful, while college teams compete to a high standard in tennis, cricket and a number of minority sports.

Pembroke

Pembroke College,
Cambridge CB2 1RF
T 01223 338154
E admissions@pem.cam.ac.uk
W www.pem.cam.ac.uk
Undergraduates: 400

Another college with a reputation for public school dominance (but with a current state-to-independent ratio of around 55:45), Pembroke's image is changing. Rowing and rugby still feature prominently, but with a female population of about 50 per cent the heartiness is giving way to a more relaxed atmosphere. Around two thirds of all undergraduates live in college, including all first years. The rest are housed in fairly central college hostels, though the standards of these are variable. Academically, Pembroke is considered solid rather than spectacular. Engineering and natural sciences have the largest number of undergraduates, but the subject range is wide with history, classics and English recent strengths. The bar is inevitably the social focal point. The Pembroke Players generally stage one play a term in the Old Reader, which also doubles as the college cinema, and many Pembroke students are involved in university dramatics. The Old Library is a popular venue for classical concerts. Indeed music is a Pembroke strength. In a city of memorable college gardens, Pembroke's are among the best.

Peterhouse

Peterhouse,
Cambridge CB2 1RD
T 01223 338223
E admissions@pet.cam.ac.uk
W www.pet.cam.ac.uk
Undergraduates: 284

The oldest and among the smallest of the colleges, Peterhouse is another that has had to contend with an image problem. But while by no means as reactionary as its critics would have it, Peterhouse is certainly not overly progressive. There is a 2:1 male-female split, while the state-independent ratio is around 55:45. The college's diminutive size inevitably makes for an intimate atmosphere. But this does not mean that its undergraduates never venture beyond the college bar. Peterhouse is known above all as 'the history college'. But while history is indeed a traditional strength and results are excellent, there are in fact no more history students than there are taking natural science or engineering. Academically, the college is generally a mid-table performer, with a better record in arts than sciences, but has recently fallen down the Tompkins Table. The 13th-century candle-lit dining hall provides a fitting setting for what by common consent is the best food in the university. Rents are below average, and undergraduates live in for at least two years, the remainder choosing rooms in college hostels, most within one or two minutes' walk. The sports grounds are shared with Clare and are about a mile away. The college teams have a less than glittering reputation, not surprisingly, given its size.

Queens'

Queens' College,
Cambridge CB3 9ET
T   01223 335540
E   admissions@quns.cam.ac.uk
W   www.quns.cam.ac.uk
Undergraduates: 490

There is a strong case for claiming that Queens' is the most tightly knit college in the university. With all undergraduates housed in college for the full three years, a large and popular bar (open all day) and outstanding facilities, including Cambridge's first college nursery, it is easy to see why. Queens' also has the distinction of attracting an above-average number of applicants. The state-to-independent ratio is around 55:45, and more than a third of students are female. Though not to all tastes, the mix of architectural styles, ranging from the medieval Old Court to the 1980s Cripps Complex, is as great as any in the university. In addition to three excellent squash courts, the Cripps Complex is also home to Fitzpatrick Hall, a multipurpose venue containing Cambridge's best-equipped college theatre and the hub of Queens' renowned social scene. Friday and Saturday night bops are extremely popular. Queens' has perhaps the foremost college drama society and a thriving cinema. Law, maths, engineering and natural sciences are the leading subjects in a college with an enviable academic record across the board. Apart from squash, Queens' is not especially sporty. The playing fields (one mile away) are shared with Robinson.

Robinson

Robinson College,
Cambridge CB3 9AN
T   01223 339143
E   undergraduateadmissions@
    robinson.cam.ac.uk
W   www.robinson.cam.ac.uk
Undergraduates: 390

Robinson is the youngest college in Cambridge and admitted its first students in 1979. Its unspectacular architecture has earned it the nickname 'the car park'. On the other hand, having been built with one eye on the conference trade, rooms are more comfortable than most and the majority have their own bathrooms and online links to the university computer network. Almost all students live in college or in houses in the attractive gardens. The college is one of the few with rooms adapted for disabled students. Robinson has sometimes been close to the bottom of the academic tables, but it performed well in 2004. There is no particular subject bias, but recent results have been better in sciences than arts. One in four Fellows are women, the second highest proportion in any mixed college. Its youth and balanced admissions policy (43 per cent are from independent schools, and there is a 44 per cent female intake) ensure that Robinson has one of the more unpretentious atmospheres. The auditorium is the largest of any college and is a popular venue for films, plays and concerts. The college fields (shared with Queens') are home to excellent rugby and hockey sides, and the boat club is also successful.

St Catharine's

St Catharine's College,
Cambridge CB2 1RL
T   01223 338319
E   undergraduate.admissions@
    caths.cam.ac.uk
W   www.caths.cam.ac.uk
Undergraduates: 436

Known to everyone as 'Catz', this is a
medium-sized, 17th-century college
standing opposite Corpus Christi on King's
Parade. The principal college site, with its
distinctive three-sided main court, though
small, provides accommodation for all its
first years. The majority of second years live
in flats at St Chad's Court, a ten-minute
walk away. Catz was not considered one of
the leading colleges academically, but its
status is improving, having been halfway up
the Tompkins Table in 2003 and in seventh
position in 2004. It has a reputation as a
friendly place. Geography and law are
usually the strongest subjects. More than a
third of the students are women, and the
split between independent and state school
pupils is around 43:57. A new library and
JCR have improved the facilities
considerably, and there is a strong musical
tradition. College social life centres on the
large bar, which has been likened, among
other things, to a ski chalet or sauna. With
a reputation for being sporting rather than
sporty, Catz is one of the few colleges that
regularly puts out three rugby XVs, and also
has a good record in football and hockey.
The playing fields are a ten-minute walk
away.

St John's

St John's College,
Cambridge CB2 1TP
T   01223 338685
E   admissions@joh.cam.ac.uk
W   www.joh.cam.ac.uk
Undergraduates: 560

Second only to Trinity in size and wealth,
St John's has an enviable reputation in most
fields and is sometimes resented for it.
The wealth translates into excellent
accommodation in college for almost all
undergraduates throughout their three
years, as well as book grants and a 24-hour
library. First years are housed together,
which can hinder integration. There is no
particular subject bias and St John's has a
formidable academic record. English and
natural sciences have been recent strengths.
A reputation for heartiness persists and the
female intake is 40 per cent, slightly below
average. The state-to-independent split is
about 47:53. The boat club has a powerful
reputation, but rugby, hockey and cricket
are all traditionally strong. In such a large
community, however, all should be able to
find their own level. Extensive playing fields
shared with Magdalene are a few hundred
yards away and the boathouse is extremely
good. The college film society organises
popular screenings in the Fisher Building,
which also contains an art studio and
drawing office for architecture and
engineering students. Music is dominated
by the world-famous choir. Excellent as the
facilities are, some students find that the
sheer size of St John's can be daunting and
this makes it hard to settle into.

Selwyn

Selwyn College,
Cambridge CB3 9DQ
t   01223 335896
e   admissions@sel.cam.ac.uk
w   www.sel.cam.ac.uk
Undergraduates: 350

Described by one undergraduate as 'the least overtly intellectual college', Selwyn has a down-to-earth and relatively unpressured atmosphere with a regular mid-table performance in the Tompkins Table. Located behind the Sidgwick Site, it is in an ideal position for humanities students, and its academic prowess has traditionally been on the arts side although engineering is an emerging strength. One of the first colleges to go mixed (1976) now approaching half of Selwyn's undergraduates are female. Its state-to-independent ratio stands at about 54:46. Accommodation is provided for all students, either in the college itself or in hostels, all of which are close by. The college has been a leader in IT provision: all college rooms have online connections to the university computer network and there are two well-stocked computer rooms. As well as the usual college groups, the Music Society is especially well supported. The bar is popular if a little 'hotel-like'. In sport, the novice boat crews have done well in recent years, as have the hockey and badminton sides, but the emphasis is as much on enjoyment as achievement. The grounds are shared with King's and are three quarters of a mile away.

Sidney Sussex

Sidney Sussex College,
Cambridge CB2 3HU
T   01223 338872
E   admissions@sid.cam.ac.uk
w   www.sid.cam.ac.uk
Undergraduates: 346

Students at this small, central college are forever the butt of jokes about Sidney being mistaken for the branch of Sainsbury's over the road. All students are housed either in college or one of 11 nearby hostels. There are no shared rooms. Facilities range from an extensive library to a computer suite and a new multigym. Exam results generally place the college in the middle of the academic leagues. Engineering, geography and law are generally the strongest subjects. Sidney has a good social balance, with a 64:36 state-to-independent ratio, while around 50 per cent of the undergraduates are women. There is a large student-run bar, an active drama society (SADCO) and plenty of involvement in university activities. The sports grounds are shared with Christ's and are a 10-minute cycle ride away. Sidneyites are enthusiastic competitors, but the college does not have a reputation for excellence in any individual sports. Sidney's size means that the college is a tight-knit community. Some students find such insularity suffocating rather than supportive.

Trinity

Trinity College,
Cambridge CB2 1TQ
T   01223 338422
E   admissions@trin.cam.ac.uk
W   www.trin.cam.ac.uk
Undergraduates: 663

The legend that you can walk from Oxford to Cambridge without ever leaving Trinity land typifies Cambridge undergraduates' views about the college, even if it is not true. Indeed, the college is almost synonymous with size and wealth. Founded by Henry VIII, its endowment is almost as big as the other colleges' put together. However, the view that every Trinity student is an arrogant public schoolboy is less easily sustained. That said, it is true that only about 46 per cent of undergraduates come from state schools and 42 per cent of Trinity undergraduates are women. On the other hand, there is little obvious bias in the admissions policy. Being rich, Trinity offers book grants to every student as well as generous travel grants and spacious, reasonably-priced rooms in college for all first and third-year students as well as many second years. The college generally features in the top ten academically. Generally better for sciences than arts, the strongest subjects are engineering, maths and natural sciences. Trinity rarely fails to do well in most sports, with cricket in the forefront. The playing fields are half a mile away.

Trinity Hall

Trinity Hall,
Cambridge CB2 1TJ
T   01223 332535
E   admissions@trinhall.cam.ac.uk
W   www.trinhall.cam.ac.uk
Undergraduates: 359

The outstanding performance of its oarsmen has ensured the prevailing view of Trinity Hall as a 'boaty' college, but it is also known for its drama, music and bar. The Preston Society is one of the better college drama groups and stages regular productions. Weekly recitals keep the Music Society busy. The small bar is invariably packed. Not surprisingly, many undergraduates rarely feel the need to go elsewhere for their entertainment, although there has been considerable involvement in the students' union recently. The college is strong academically, returning to the top half of the Tompkins Table in 2004. Law is a traditional speciality and recently results have been excellent in modern languages. The college is strong in the arts, though the natural sciences are well represented. Almost half of the undergraduates are women and around 59 per cent are from state schools. All first years and approximately half the third years live in college, which is situated on the Backs behind Caius. The remainder take rooms either in two large hostels close to the sports ground, or in college accommodation about five minutes' walk away.

University Profiles

Some famous names are missing from our university listings: the Open University, the separate business and medical schools, Birkbeck College and Cranfield University among them. Their omission is no reflection on their quality, simply a function of their particular roles. The guide is based on provision for full-time undergraduates and the factors judged to influence this. The Open University (www.open.ac.uk), though Britain's biggest university, with 75,000 students, could not be included because most of the measures used in our listing do not apply to it. As a non-residential, largely part-time institution, Birkbeck College, London (www.bbk.ac.uk), could also not be compared in many key areas. Although Cranfield (www.cranfield.ac.uk), for example, offers undergraduate degrees in two of its campuses, it is primarily for graduate students. Manchester Business School (www.mbs.ac.uk) and London Business School (www.lbs.ac.uk) were excluded for the same reason. Similarly, specialist institutions such as the Royal College of Art (www.rca.ac.uk) and St George's Hospital Medical School (sghms.ac.uk) could not fairly be compared with generalist universities. A number of colleges with degree-awarding powers also do not appear because they have yet to be granted university status. However, at the end of the book, we list higher education colleges with their addresses and websites.

Each university profile includes some standard information, which is described below:

T   This is the telephone number for admission enquiries.
E   This is the e-mail address for admissions and prospectus enquiries.
W   This is the address of the main university website.
U   This is the website of the students' union

The Times rankings These figures are taken from the main League Table. See pages 33–43 for this table and the sources of the data. The headings used match those in the main League Table.

Undergraduates The first figure is for full-time undergraduates. The second figure (in brackets) gives the number of part-time undergraduates. The figures are for 2002–03, and are the most recent provided by HESA.

Postgraduates The first figure is for full-time postgraduates. The second figure (in brackets) gives the number of part-time postgraduates. The figures are for 2002–03, and are the most recent provided by HESA.

Mature students This figure is the percentage of First degree acceptances in 2003 who were over 21. The figures were compiled by UCAS.

Overseas students This figure is the number of undergraduate overseas students (both EU and non-EU) as a percentage of full-time undergraduates. All figures relate to 2002–03 and are based on HESA data.

Applications/place This figure is the number of applicants per place for 2004 as calculated by UCAS.

From state-school sector This figure gives the number of young full-time undergraduate entrants from state schools or colleges in 2002–03 as a percentage of total young entrants. The figures are published by HESA.

From working-class homes The number of young full-time undergraduate entrants in 2002–03 whose parental occupation is skilled, manual, semi-skilled or unskilled (Social Classes IIIM–V) as a percentage of total young entrants. The figures are published by HESA.

Teaching quality assessments The Quality Assurance Agency for Higher Education assessments published up to 2004. See page 35 for an explanation of the teaching assessment ratings. See opposite for the latest Scottish assessments.

Accommodation The information was obtained through a survey made of all university accommodation services, and their help in compiling this information is gratefully acknowledged.

Comments on campus facilities apply to the universities' own sites only. New universities, in particular, operate 'franchised' courses at further education colleges, which are likely to have lower levels of provision. Prospective applicants should check out the library and social facilities before accepting a place away from the parent institution.

The University of London

The University of London is a federal university composed of a number of institutions. In this profile section, the pages on the University of London (pages 354–55) outline the colleges of the university that are not listed separately in this guide. There are separate entries on the leading undergraduate colleges.

University of Wales

The University of Wales is also a federal university. General details are given below. Separate profiles can be found for the following institutions: Aberystwyth; Bangor; University of Wales Institute, Cardiff; Lampeter; University of Wales, Newport; and Swansea. Other member instituions are North East Wales Institute; Swansea Institute of Higher Education; Trinity College, Carmarthen; and the Royal Welsh College of Music and Drama. The University of Cardiff is no longer a member of the University of Wales.

Founded in 1893, it celebrated its centenary in 1993 and is second only to London, its federal counterpart in terms of full-time student numbers. Like London, it is surrendering more power to its colleges. At the same time, however, intercollegiate links have been increasing, especially in research. A new structure was introduced in 1996, bringing the former university colleges in Cardiff and Newport into the fold.

See www.wales.ac.uk.

Scottish Academic Review Reports since 2001

The outcomes are recorded in such a way that they cannot readily be incorporated into the subject tables (chapter 3) or the individual university profiles that follow. Details are given at www.qaa.ac.uk.

For the following the assessors expressed **confidence** in the *academic standards* and considered **commendable** the *teaching and learning, student progression* and *learning resources*:

Accountancy	Edinburgh, Napier, Paisley, Strathclyde
Anthropology	Edinburgh
Archaeology	Edinburgh
Architecture	Edinburgh, Robert Gordon, Strathclyde
Business studies	Edinburgh, St Andrews
Chemical engineering	Edinburgh, Heriot-Watt
Civil engineering	Edinburgh, Heriot-Watt
Classics and ancient history	Edinburgh, Glasgow, St Andrews
Computer science	Dundee, Heriot-Watt, Napier, St Andrews
Electrical and electronic engineering	Edinburgh, Heriot-Watt
Economics	Aberdeen, Abertay, Dundee, Edinburgh, Paisley, St Andrews, Stirling, Strathclyde
English	Dundee, Edinburgh, Strathclyde
Geography	Aberdeen, Dundee, Glasgow
Geology	Aberdeen
History	Dundee, Glasgow, Stirling, Strathclyde
Hospitality, leisure, sport and tourism	Robert Gordon
Law	Dundee, Glasgow, Strathclyde
Librarianship and information management	Robert Gordon
Mechanical engineering	Edinburgh, Heriot-Watt
Philosophy	Aberdeen
Politics	Edinburgh, St Andrews, Stirling
Social work	Stirling
Sociology	Edinburgh
Theology and religious studies	Aberdeen, Glasgow

For the following subjects the assessors expressed **confidence** in the *academic standards*, considered **commendable** the *teaching and learning* and *learning resources* and **approved** the *student progression*:

Chemical engineering	Paisley
Civil engineering	Abertay, Glasgow Caledonian, Paisley
Computer science	Glasgow Caledonian
Electrical and electronic engineering	Abertay, Glasgow Caledonian, Paisley
Environmental science	Abertay
Education	Strathclyde
Hospitality, leisure, sport and tourism	Strathclyde
Manufacturing engineering	Glasgow Caledonian
Mechanical engineering	Glasgow Caledonian, Paisley
Philosophy	Edinburgh

For the following subjects the assessors expressed **confidence** in the *academic standards*, considered **commendable** the *student progression* and *learning resources* and **approved** the *teaching and learning*:

Environmental science	Edinburgh, Stirling

For the following subjects the assessors expressed **confidence** in the *academic standards*, considered **commendable** the *teaching and learning* and *student progression* and **approved** the *learning resources*:

Economics	Glasgow
Law	Napier

For the following subjects the assessors expressed **confidence** in the academic standards and **approved** the *teaching and learning, student progression* and *learning resources*:

Business studies	Abertay
Environmental science	Glasgow Caledonian
Law	Abertay

University of Aberdeen

Aberdeen has benefited from a sharply improved performance in the last Research Assessment Exercise, when the number of internationally-rated departments shot up from two to ten. The relatively small French department achieved the only 5* rating, but other top grades were divided among the university's three colleges. These successes have been accompanied by record applications, including another small increase in 2004.

Previous research grades had been disappointing, but the university boosted its external research funds so successfully that it is now in the top 20 in the UK on this measure. It already enjoyed consistently good teaching scores, with only three subjects rated less than Highly Satisfactory in the initial round of inspections. French, biology, sociology and community-based medicine have top ratings for both teaching and research.

Aberdeen considers itself a 'balanced' university because roughly half of its students are men and half women, half study medicine, science or engineering, half the arts or social sciences. Most students are not even admitted to a particular department, allowing them to try out three or four subjects before committing themselves at the end of their first or even second year. The modular system, covering more than 620 first-degree programmes, is so flexible that the majority of students change their intended degree before graduation.

Medicine, law and divinity head Aberdeen's traditional strengths – the university established the English-speaking world's first chair in medicine and has produced its share of advances since. The Institute of Medical Sciences, which has brought together all Aberdeen's work in this area, was completed in 2002 with state-of-the-art laboratory facilities.

Biological sciences have developed considerably in recent years, becoming second only to the social sciences in terms of size. Biomedicine is particularly strong, and the university's links with the oil industry show in geology's high reputation. The university is also the main centre for agriculture in Scotland and part of a new European network for the subject.

Today's university is a fusion of two ancient institutions which came together in 1860. With King's College dating back to 1495 and Marischal College following almost a century later, Aberdeen likes to boast that for 250 years it had as many universities as the whole of England. The original King's College buildings are the focal point of an appealing campus, complete with cobbled main street and

---

King's College,
Aberdeen AB24 3FX
T   01224 272090/91
E   sras@abdn.ac.uk
W   www.abdn.ac.uk
U   www.ausa.org.uk

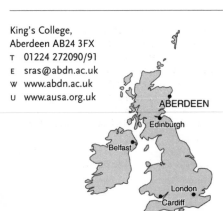

The Times Rankings
Overall Ranking: 28
(2005 ranking: =34)

Teaching assessment:	=14	(22.4)
Research assessment:	=42	(4.7)
Entry standards:	31	(339.8)
Student–staff ratio:	=26	(15.5)
Library/IT spend/student:	16	(£720)
Facilities spend/student:	=47	(£201)
Good honours:	=23	(67.5%)
Graduate prospects:	=15	(72.3%)
Expected completion rate:	=62	(82.6%)

some sturdily handsome Georgian buildings, about a mile from the city centre. Medicine is at Foresterhill, a 20-minute walk away, adjoining the Aberdeen Royal Infirmary. Buses link the two sites with the Hillhead residential complex, and there is a free late-night service. The Aberdeen arm of Northern College has now joined the fold, restoring the university's original involvement in teacher training, and forming its fifth faculty. The college will move to Old Aberdeen within the next year.

More than a third of the students come from the north of Scotland, but taking one in ten from outside Britain ensures a cosmopolitan atmosphere. Students from England and the 120 nationalities from further afield are generally prepared for Aberdeen's remote location and, although the winters are long, the climate is warmer than the uninitiated might expect. As the energy capital of Europe, transport links are good. Students find the city lively and welcoming but expensive, although its prosperity does provide a good selection of part-time jobs from the JobLink service.

Student facilities are good: there are first-class sports facilities and an NHS medical practice on campus. The students' union has closed but a new students' centre is being developed on the King's College campus. There is an impressive ICT network with over 1,000 computers for student use and a well-stocked library, whose replacement will be the next priority for one of the most successful fundraising campaigns at any British university. The institution's residential stock has been increased in recognition of the limited private market and all new undergraduates are guaranteed a place.

Accommodation

Number of places and costs refer to 2004–05
University-provided places: about 3,200
Percentage catered: 28%
Costs for catered accommodation:
£84.20–£99.50 (en suite) a week, 38-week let.
Costs for self-catered accommodation:
£51.50–£70.75 a week, 38-week let.
Policy for first-year students: accommodation is guaranteed. There are no restrictions for students whose homes are close to the university.
Policy for international students: accommodation is guaranteed.
Contact: m.d.irvine@abdn.ac.uk

Students

Undergraduates:	9,200	(1,060)
Postgraduates:	1,460	(1,945)
Mature students:	14.9%	
Overseas students:	11.7%	
Applications per place:	5.3	
From state-sector schools:	84.3%	
From working-class homes:	27.2%	

Teaching Quality Assessments
1993–98 Rated Excellent:
biological sciences; economics; French; geography; medicine; sociology
1993–98 Rated Highly Satisfactory: accounting; chemistry; civil engineering; English; geology; history of art; law; mathematics; mechanical engineering; philosophy; politics; psychology; theology.

See page 245 for recent assessments.

University of Abertay

Scotland's newest university doubled in size during the 1990s and has grown further since up-front tuition fees were abolished for Scottish students. Like several universities north of the border, Abertay saw a sharp drop in applications in 2004, but the number accepting offers went up and there are now more than 5,500 students, mainly in Dundee but with some as far afield as mainland Europe and even Malaysia. The former central institution has enjoyed a series of good teaching scores, although drop-out projections have been higher than the average for the subjects on offer. More than a quarter of the entrants from 2000 were expected to transfer to other courses or leave without a qualification. More than a third of the undergraduates come from socially deprived areas, considerably more than the average for the subjects offered. Almost all the students attended state schools and nearly four out of ten come from working-class homes.

The former Dundee Institute of Technology was made to wait for university status, which only came two years after the polytechnics were promoted. But the institute had already established its academic credentials, with teaching in economics rated more highly than in some of Scotland's elite universities. Subsequent assessments were solid, without living up to that early promise, but economics, engineering and environmental sciences were given the highest possible rating in later inspections.

Research is not being ignored. Abertay is proud of its record in establishing a series of specialist centres, in areas as diverse as wood technology, urban water systems and Chinese business. The university opened Europe's first research centre dedicated to computer games and digital entertainment and a major new environmental science centre is still being developed. The last research assessments showed a big improvement on 1996, doubling the average score, although only environmental sciences reached any of the top three grades.

Abertay plays to its strengths with a limited range of courses, and is not shy about its achievements. Among them is a high-tech approach that permeates all four of the university's schools. Until recently, its website offered prospective students 'better networking than Oxford', and its spending on libraries and computers is the second-highest per student in Britain in our League Table, providing one computer for every four students.

Based mainly in the centre of Dundee, all the university's buildings are within 15 minutes' walk of each other. The imposing

---

Bell Street, Dundee DD1 1HG
T 01382 308080
E siro@abertay.ac.uk
W www.abertay.ac.uk
U www.abertayunion.com

DUNDEE
Edinburgh
Belfast
London
Cardiff

The Times Rankings
Overall Ranking: 73
(2005 ranking: 66)

Teaching assessment:	=80	(20.8)
Research assessment:	=89	(2.0)
Entry standards:	86	(218.4)
Student–staff ratio:	50	(17.1)
Library/IT spend/student:	2	(£1,278)
Facilities spend/student:	96	(£111)
Good honours:	82	(49.6%)
Graduate prospects:	73	(57.6%)
Expected completion rate:	97	(66.9%)

Dudhope Castle dominates recruitment literature, although it is an economic research centre and the Tayside Institute of Health Studies. Other buildings are more modern and functional. New facilities are gradually being added, notably the £8-million library opened by the Queen. A £6-million student centre was scheduled for completion in February 2005 and a 500-bed student village is next on the list.

Entrance requirements have been rising, although for most courses they are still modest. Degrees are predominantly vocational, with more subjects being added every year. Forensic science, natural resources management and computer arts, games design and production are recent examples, as was a new degree in golf tourism. All courses can be taken on a part-time basis, and the aim is for new courses to offer students the chance to spend at least 30 per cent of their time in industry.

The university's revamped modular degree scheme means that undergraduates take a maximum of eight modules per year. First-year students are assessed by coursework alone in the first semester, with examinations at the end of the year. Students can complete a Certificate of Higher Education after one year, a diploma after two, an ordinary degree after three, or honours in four years.

With the student population still relatively small, that translates into a moderate social scene, particularly at weekends. However, Dundee has a large student population and is improving as a youth centre, and the cost of living is low. Over 28 per cent of the undergraduates are over 21 on entry, many living locally. This lifts the pressure on university-owned beds sufficiently to allow all first-years to be guaranteed accommodation.

Accommodation

Number of places and costs refer to 2004–05
University-provided places: 650
Percentage catered: 0%
Costs for catered accommodation: n/a
Costs for self-catered accommodation: £39–£65 a week inclusive of heat and light.
Policy for first-year students: places guaranteed for all first-year entrants who apply before 1 September in their year of study. No restriction on local students.
Policy for international students: first entrants guaranteed if apply by 1 September. Senior students allocated approx 15% of accommodation in designated halls on a first-come basis.
Contact: accommo@abertay.ac.uk

Students

Undergraduates:	3,485	(330)
Postgraduates:	365	(315)
Mature students:	22.1%	
Overseas students:	9.5%	
Applications per place:	4.9	
From state-sector schools:	97.2%	
From working-class homes:	37.7%	

Teaching Quality Assessments
1993–95 Rated Highly Satisfactory:
biological sciences; chemistry; civil engineering; mechanical engineering; mathematics and statistics; psychology.

See page 245 for recent assessments.

Aberystwyth, University of Wales

Although the oldest of the Welsh university colleges, Aberystwyth has long prided itself on a modern outlook. The modular degree system has been running since 1993, covering academic and vocational courses, and the principle of flexibility was established long before that. Uniquely in the UK, every student is offered the opportunity of a year's work experience in commerce, industry or the public sector, either at home or abroad. Students who have taken advantage of the scheme have achieved better than average degrees and enhanced their employment prospects. The college has expanded significantly in recent years, with a new School of Management and Business as well as a department of Sports and Exercise Science among the additions.

An attractive seaside location does the university no harm when the applications season comes around. A new £3.6 million centre for theatre, film and television studies and a purpose-built sports and exercise science centre are among the latest developments on the Penglais campus, which overlooks the town. A new £5 million building for the internationally-acclaimed International Politics Department will open in 2006. Aber is always heavily oversubscribed even though the number of places has increased. Almost a third of the students are from Wales. A new agreement to collaborate with the University of Wales, Bangor, in a range of subjects from business to science emphasises teaching in Welsh.

More than 90 per cent of the undergraduates come from state schools or colleges – a far higher proportion than the mix of subjects would imply – but less than 30 per cent come from working-class homes and not even than half that number hail from areas that send few students to higher education. However, the drop-out rate of less than 10 per cent is among the lowest in Wales and also lower than the funding council's 'benchmark' figure for the institution.

Merger with the Welsh Agricultural College produced a new Institute of Rural Sciences in 1995, allowing Aber to claim the widest range of land-related courses in the UK. The institute shares the Llanbadarn campus with information and library studies and a further education college. Teaching ratings have been impressive, especially in the arts and social sciences. Offers of places are made on the basis of the UCAS tariff, which not only recognises general studies as full A or AS levels, but also gives credit for Key Skills qualifications. Celtic studies and politics were rated internationally outstanding in the latest research assessments, while theatre, film and

Old College, King Street,
Aberystwyth, Ceredigion SY23 2AX
T 01970 622021
E ug-admissions@aber.ac.uk
W www.aber.ac.uk
U http://union.aber.ac.uk

The Times Rankings
Overall Ranking: 50
(2005 ranking: 49)

Teaching assessment:	=58	(21.4)
Research assessment:	50	(4.5)
Entry standards:	46	(290.6)
Student–staff ratio:	91	(21.8)
Library/IT spend/student:	50	(£536)
Facilities spend/student:	=29	(£249)
Good honours:	39	(62.6%)
Graduate prospects:	=79	(56.1%)
Expected completion rate:	31	(90.4%)

television studies reached the next rung of the ladder.

More than 40 entrance scholarships are available, worth up to £1,150 a year with a guarantee of university accommodation for three years. There are also £400 music awards and up to 200 merit awards of £400 are on offer to those who are not awarded scholarships. Candidates sit two papers in their schools or colleges, or on campus, in February. Poor performances are not held against those who pursue their applications. Aber boasts one of higher education's most informative websites and also publishes a 12-page guide for parents. There is 24-hour access to the computer network, and the four university libraries are complemented by the National Library of Wales.

The town of Aberystwyth is compact and travel to other parts of the UK slow, so applicants should be sure that they will be happy to spend three years or more in a tight-knit community. Most are: 94 per cent of first-year students responding to the annual satisfaction survey said they would make the same choice again. Applications have fluctuated over recent years, but were up again when the official deadline passed for entry in 2005. The students' guild is the largest entertainments venue in the region and the arts centre has been extended at a cost of £3.5 million.

The student-produced Alternative Prospectus describes the traditional seaside town of 25,000 people as the 'Welsh California'. They say it has 'plenty of life and vitality, and a certain *je ne sais quoi*'. It also offers plenty of out-of-season accommodation to supplement the university's 3,700 places, all of which are now online. Sports facilities are good for the size of institution, with 50 acres of pitches, a swimming pool, a climbing wall and specialist outdoor facilities for water sports.

Accommodation

Number of places and costs refer to 2004–05
University-provided places: 3,704
Percentage catered: 29%
Costs for catered accommodation: £68.48 (twin); £79.45–£83.16 (single) a week during term.
Costs for self-catered accommodation: £40.38 (twin); £51.83–£70.39 (single en suite) a week.
Policy for first-year students: all first years guaranteed accommodation in halls, including local residents and those coming through clearing.
Policy for international students: all international students are guaranteed accommodation in hall for the duration of their courses.
Contact: mew@aber.ac.uk
www.aber.ac.uk/residential

Students

Undergraduates:	6,070	(2,355)
Postgraduates:	895	(1,500)
Mature students:	9%	
Overseas students:	7.6%	
Applications per place:	4	
From state-sector schools:	93.1%	
From working-class homes:	29.4%	

Tuition fees 2006	£1,200

Teaching Quality Assessments
1993–95 Rated Excellent:
accounting and finance; biological sciences; Celtic studies; earth studies; economics; English; environmental science; geography; information and library studies; politics; Welsh.

Anglia Polytechnic University

The last university to retain the polytechnic title now finally seems set to discard it in order to avoid confusion among employers and overseas applicants. Having rejected a series of alternative names and decided to stay as it was, APU has been consulting on another set. No change is likely in time for the application process for courses starting in 2006, but a new identity is likely to be approved before those entrants graduate. The university has not been standing still, however: teacher training courses have been relocated to the 22-acre Rivermead campus in Chelmsford, where a new business school opened in 2003 and a new student centre and sports hall are on the way. Work is in progress, too, on the smaller Cambridge site.

An amalgamation of two well-established higher education colleges made Anglia the first regional polytechnic, but the twin bases in Chelmsford and Cambridge remain distinct. The two very different locations are far enough apart to ensure that there is little contact, although electronic networking and a central administration mean that key academic facilities are available throughout the university.

The regional ideal extends to a network of more than 20 partner colleges in Cambridgeshire, Essex, Norfolk and Suffolk, where 4,000 students take APU courses.

One, at Benfleet in Essex, has become a 'local campus' of the university. East Anglia has always lagged behind other parts of England for participation in higher education and although the university has continued to grow it has sometimes struggled to fill its places. Although more than a third of the undergraduates are from working-class homes, the proportion from areas of low participation is less than the national average for the subjects on offer.

Most teaching ratings were solid, rather than spectacular, although there was an improvement in the latter years of assessment. Nursing and theology (a postgraduate subject only) have produced the best scores, but the tourism and leisure course added to the low scores in 2001. The last research grades also showed improvement, but only one university submitted a lower proportion of academics for assessment, and only English made the top three categories. The introduction of a benchmarking system to take account of the mix of subjects at each university saw APU tumble down *The Times* League Table and it has not recovered.

The university has a strongly international outlook, encouraging students to take a language option and providing an unusually large number of exchange opportunities in Malaysia and China, as

Rivermead Campus: Chelmsford
Essex CM1 1SQ
Cambridge Campus: East Road
Cambridge CB1 1PT
T   0845-271 3333
E   answers@apu.ac.uk
W www.apu.ac.uk
U www.apusu.com

The Times Rankings		
Overall Ranking: 94		
(2005 ranking: 93)		
Teaching assessment:	=92	(20.3)
Research assessment:	=97	(1.5)
Entry standards:	78	(228.7)
Student–staff ratio:	86	(20.7)
Library/IT spend/student:	88	(£394)
Facilities spend/student:	=82	(£140)
Firsts and 2:1s:	=61	(54.9%)
Work and further study:	=44	(63.4%)
Expected completion rate:	70	(80.4%)

Edinburgh
Belfast
CAMBRIDGE
CHELMSFORD
Cardiff
London

well as Europe and the United States. Each undergraduate has an adviser to help compile a degree package which looks at the chosen subject from different points of view to maximise future job prospects.

Employers play a part in planning courses which are integrated into a modular system extending from degree level to professional programmes. Anglia is taking a leading role in the development of the Government's two-year foundation degrees, which are designed as partnerships between the academic and business worlds. They have been running since 2001, with computing, pop music and management the latest areas to be developed.

The university's cramped town-centre site in Chelmsford is due to close in 2005. Activities have been moving progressively to the more spacious and attractive Rivermead campus on the edge of town. The £6.5-million Ashcroft International Business School was named after the former Conservative Party Treasurer and alumnus, Lord Ashcroft, who met most of the cost. The new student union and leisure facilities will complete the campus.

The Cambridge site is also being redeveloped around a central pedestrian street, with a new student union building, catering facilities and music and performance areas. A new arts centre is planned to serve the both the student population and the local community. There is limited collaboration with Cambridge University, for example on a new cricket academy and a base for APU's rowing club.

The social scene inevitably varies between the two campuses. Cambridge students enjoy the advantages of a great university city, but have to shrug off the tag of attending the lesser institution. Essex students have found Chelmsford dull, but the social scene is said to be improving. Neither is far from London by train.

Accommodation
Number of places and costs refer to 2004–05
University-provided places: Cambridge, about 721; Chelmsford, 531
Percentage catered: 0%
Costs for catered accommodation: n/a
Costs for self-catered accommodation:
Cambridge: £54–£75 (shared houses); £65–£71 (shared communal facilities); £76.59 (en suite) a week.
Chelmsford: £55–£71 a week.
Policy for first-year students: approximately 80% of first years accommodated; restriction within 25-mile radius of Cambridge campus. 100% accommodated at Chelmsford campus.
Policy for international students: bed-spaces are divided between home and international students according to University allocations policy.
Contact : Cambaccom@anglia.ac.uk
essexaccom@apu.ac.uk

Students
Undergraduates:	9,985	(11,755)
Postgraduates:	710	(2,965)
Mature students:	30.4%	
Overseas students:	16.8%	
Applications per place:	4.5	
From state-sector schools:	96.7%	
From working-class homes:	34.4%	

Tuition fees 2006   £3,000
See chapter 13 for bursary details.

Teaching Quality Assessments
From 1995 (top score 24):
24 philosophy.
23 health subjects; nursing; theology.
22 psychology.
21 art and design; biological sciences; modern languages.
20 building and civil engineering; politics; sociology; electrical and electronic engineering; land management; politics; town planning.
19 education.
18 history of art; hospitality; media studies.

Aston University

Aston has always gloried in its role as a tight-knit, vocational, urban university, which has swum against the tide of British higher education over the past decade. Small and lively, set in the heart of Birmingham, it has remained resolutely specialist in science and technology, business and languages, concentrating on the sandwich degrees which have served its graduates so well in the employment market. Having rejected merger proposals from Birmingham and Central England universities, it is now having to chart a new course.

Despite some modest growth recently, the university still has fewer than 6,000 students. This has made for a bumpy ride financially – the funding council had to provide special help several times to avoid damaging budget cuts. But the strategy has paid off to some extent with encouraging rises in demand for places and big grants from industry, which have allowed the university to boost staffing in business, engineering and languages. Applications were up by 29 per cent at the start of 2005, a figure bettered by only one old university.

There were much-improved research grades at the end of 2001, with four of the five subject areas judged to be producing work of international quality. Business and management, languages and European studies, general engineering and neurosciences all achieved top scores, although the proportion of academics entered for assessment was low for a traditional university. Academic restructuring, designed mainly to break down barriers between departments, has reduced the number of schools to four.

As befits a one-time college of advanced technology, Aston's strengths are on the science side, although the business school is highly rated and accounts for almost half of the students. A £22-million extension to the business school, due to be completed in 2005, will allow its staff to rise from 80 to over 120. After a bruising introduction to the teaching quality assessments, in which none of the first six departments was considered excellent, ratings improved considerably. Aston achieved the first maximum score for pharmacy in 1999, building on high grades for optometry and biological sciences.

Subsequent assessments veered from a disappointing 19 points in mathematics and statistics to another maximum for business and management. There is a wide range of combined honours programmes for those who prefer not to specialise. Four out of five Aston graduates go straight into jobs, spurning the postgraduate courses and training programmes which have become

---

Aston Triangle
Birmingham B4 7ET
T   0121-359 6313 (admissions enquiries only)
E   prospectus@aston.ac.uk
W   www.aston.ac.uk
U   www.astonguild.org.uk

Edinburgh
Belfast
BIRMINGHAM •
Cardiff
London

the first port of call for many of their counterparts in the old universities. Often they are returning to the scene of work placements, which have become the norm for 70 per cent of Aston's undergraduates.

The university is flexible about entry requirements for mature students, but school-leavers are generally asked for at least the equivalent of a B and two Cs at A level. The actual entry grades are often even higher, and the rising demand for places is likely to prolong the trend. The drop-out rate has fluctuated, but the 10 per cent projection in the most recent set of figures is almost exactly the national average for the subjects on offer. Socially, the intake is diverse, with more than a third of the undergraduates coming from working-class homes.

The 40-acre campus, a ten-minute walk from the centre of Birmingham, is barely recognisable from the university's early days. Carefully landscaped, it is nearing the end of a £16-million building plan, which will see Aston's residential and academic accommodation concentrated on the same site. Almost half of the undergraduates live there, with places guaranteed for first years. New developments in sporting facilities have begun with the addition of a new gymnasium in 2002, and an £8-million Academy of Life Sciences, merging research with private practice in eye care and brain imaging, opened in 2004.

Aston was among the pioneers of 'smart cards', giving students access to university facilities and enabling them to make purchases on campus, once they have money in their accounts. There is plenty of opportunity to use them in a buzzing social scene, which most students find to their taste. The guild of students has always been among the most active both socially and politically.

Accommodation
Number of places and costs refer to 2005–06
University-provided places: 2,117
Percentage catered: 0%
Costs for catered accommodation: n/a
Costs for self-catered accommodation: £57.45 (standard); £89.80 (en suite) a week.
Policy for first-year students: all first years are guaranteed a place provided Aston is their first-choice university.
Policy for international students: international fee-paying students are guaranteed places for duration of course provided they apply each year.
Contact: accom@aston.ac.uk; www.aston.ac.uk/accommodation

Students

Undergraduates:	5,260	(160)
Postgraduates:	595	(1,570)
Mature students:	10.7%	
Overseas students:	8.1%	
Applications per place:	6.3	
From state-sector schools:	90.6%	
From working-class homes:	36.9%	

Tuition fees 2006   £3,000
See chapter 13 for bursary details.

Teaching Quality Assessments
From 1995 (top score 24):
24 business and management; pharmacy.
23 biological sciences; health subjects.
22 French; German; psychology.
21 electrical and electronic engineering.
19 chemical engineering; mathematics.

Bangor, University of Wales

Bangor's community focus dates back to a 19th-century campaign which saw local quarrymen putting part of their weekly wages towards the establishment of a college. The department of lifelong learning continues the tradition with courses across North Wales, but the college has also built a worldwide reputation in areas such as ocean sciences and environmental studies.

The last research assessments were an improvement on 1996, although only psychology and Welsh were rated internationally outstanding. Three-quarters of the researchers were placed in the top three categories of seven. Teaching assessments have been more impressive, with half of the subjects rated as excellent. As well as traditional strengths such as biology and forestry, the list includes social policy, placing Bangor at 16 in *The Times* ranking for the subject. There is a high proportion of small-group teaching and tutorials, as well as one of Britain's largest peer guiding schemes, which sees second and third-year students mentoring new arrivals. A range of scholarships worth at least £1,000, including new £1,500 awards for sport, are available to students in any subject, offsetting the cost of tuition fees.

Bangor merged with a nearby teacher training college, Colleg Normal, in 1996, and that site is now part of the university.

All departments are within walking distance of each other, apart from ocean sciences, which is two miles away near the Menai Bridge. Recent changes have seen departments coming together, for example with a School of Informatics encompassing electronic engineering, computer systems and mathematics.

An academic reorganisation brought together banking, accounting, economics, business and marketing with community development, tourism, leisure and heritage management in a School for Business and Regional Development focused on the needs of the Welsh economy. The theme continues through a combination of private funds and a £5-million European grant, which will produce a new Management Development Centre on a waterfront site. The latest development will see law taught at Bangor for the first time, capitalising on existing expertise in particular areas of the subject. A suite of degrees introduced in 2004 twin the subject with accounting and finance, business studies, criminal justice, environmental conservation and social policy, as well as offering single honours law. More recent innovations include journalism and media, and chemistry with biomolecular sciences.

Based little more than a stone's throw from Snowdonia with its attractions for

---

Bangor,
Gwynedd LL57 2DG
T 01248 382016
E admissions@bangor.ac.uk
W www.bangor.ac.uk
U www.undeb.bangor.ac.uk

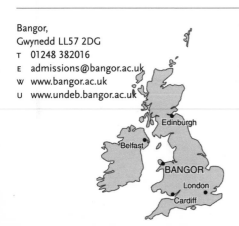

sports enthusiasts, Bangor is an expanding centre for Welsh-medium teaching, recently agreeing to collaborate with the University of Wales, Aberystwyth, to teach more subjects through the language. As well as a single honours degree in Welsh, some courses are only available in Welsh while others are offered in either English or Welsh. Although a majority of students come from outside Wales – there is a strong link with Ireland, for example – more than 10 per cent of the students speak the language and one of the seven halls of residence is Welsh-speaking. The college also has a flourishing international exchange programme, with some unusual partner institutions: Poland and Italy are favourite destinations for linguistics students, while biologists tend to head for Sweden or Norway. All biology, chemistry or engineering degrees carry the option of a year abroad. The university has also cut its fees by £1,000 for students from the world's poorest countries as part of a growing focus on overseas students.

Bangor does better than most traditional universities when judged against access benchmarks. More than nine out of ten students come from state schools or colleges, and almost one in three come from working-class homes. Overall, applications were up by more than 8 per cent in 2004 and an even bigger rise in 2005 was also above the national average. The 13 per cent drop-out rate is lower than at most universities with similarly diverse intakes – an achievement the college attributes to the priority it places on student support. The pioneering dyslexia unit, for example, offers individual and group support throughout students' courses.

Accommodation
Number of places and costs refer to 2004–05
University-provided places: about 2,150
Percentage catered: 34%
Costs for catered accommodation:
£76.51 (standard); £89.11 (en suite with internet access) a week.
Costs for self-catered accommodation: £47.25 (standard); £64.82 (en suite); £67.97 (en suite with internet access) a week.
Policy for first-year students: accommodation is guaranteed to all unaccompanied first years.
Policy for international students: international postgraduate students have priority.
Contact: aos017@bangor.ac.uk

Students

Undergraduates:	5,430	(1,995)
Postgraduates:	1,185	(640)
Mature students:	15.8%	
Overseas students:	6.9%	
Applications per place:	4.5	
From state-sector schools:	95.6%	
From working-class homes:	31.7%	
Tuition fees 2006	£1,200	

Teaching Quality Assessments
1993–98 Rated Excellent:
biological sciences; chemistry; forestry; music; ocean sciences; psychology; Russian; theology; Welsh.

University of Bath

Bath has recently completed a £70-million 'campus enhancement plan' and this year will see the addition of further facilities for science. But, for the moment, it remains a relatively small university of 11,000 students. The extra places will cater to some degree for the burgeoning demand at an institution which enjoys both an attractive location and a high academic reputation. Although applications dropped at the beginning of 2005, previous years' increases had resulted in entrance requirements rising by the equivalent of a full grade at A level. Bath's healthy showing in league tables may be one reason for its popularity – it has never been out of the top 20 in *The Times* League Table.

Students like the 'small and friendly' image the university projects, and one of the lowest drop-out rates in Britain suggests that they are well supported. The library is one of only two in the country to open 24 hours a day, seven days a week. Few can fail to be impressed by the magnificence of the city's architecture. The modern campus on the edge of Bath, with some undistinguished buildings dating from its origins as a technological university in the 1960s, offers an unfortunate contrast. But the 200-acre site has pleasant grounds and is functional, with academic, recreational and residential facilities in close proximity. New

teaching facilities for chemistry were added in 2003, followed by a £2.8-million physics facility, and 468 new study bedrooms have also been added recently. More lecture theatres and computer laboratories have eased the pressure on teaching space.

A campus in Swindon caters for 1,000 part-time students, bringing higher education to one of the few remaining counties without a university. The development is based in school premises, but plans for a new campus with 10,000 students have passed the first planning stage. There are also strong links with Bath Spa University College, which produced a successful joint bid for a New Technology Institute for the region.

Research is Bath's greatest strength, with applied mathematics, mechanical engineering and pharmacy all rated internationally outstanding in the last assessments. Teaching assessments have confirmed the university's excellence in science and technology, with biosciences achieving maximum points for teaching quality in 1999 and mathematics and statistics following in 2000. Arts and social science ratings have been mixed, but there were successes in economics and politics.

The latest academic developments have seen the establishment of a School of Health and an Institute for Contemporary

---

Claverton Down, Bath BA2 7AY
T   01225 323019
E   admissions@bath.ac.uk
W   www.bath.ac.uk
U   www.bathstudent.com

Edinburgh
Belfast
Cardiff
BATH   London

The Times Rankings
Overall Ranking: 13
(2005 ranking: 11)

Teaching assessment:	=51	(21.6)
Research assessment:	=10	(5.7)
Entry standards:	15	(375.1)
Student–staff ratio:	=23	(15.2)
Library/IT spend/student:	43	(£568)
Facilities spend/student:	3	(£407)
Good honours:	8	(74.8%)
Graduate prospects:	9	(76.7%)
Expected completion rate:	6	(96.7%)

Interdisciplinary Arts, both engaged in teaching as well as research. Most courses throughout the university have a practical element, and assessors have praised the university for the work placements it offers. The majority of students take sandwich courses or include a period of study abroad, which helps to produce consistently outstanding graduate employment figures.

The university's other great claim to fame lies in its sports facilities, which were already among the best in Britain before the recent addition of a £20-million training village, funded with Lottery money. The campus acquired an international-standard swimming pool by this route, to which it has added an indoor running track, a new sports hall and even a simulated bobsleigh start area. There is a strong tradition in competitive sports, with Team Bath hitting the headlines in 2002 as the first student team for 100 years to reach the first round of the FA Cup. The university pioneered sports scholarships more than 20 years ago, and they are now worth up to £12,000 a year for performers of international calibre. There are also courses to do the facilities justice, as recognised in a near-perfect score for teaching quality in sport and leisure in 2001.

Students – almost a fifth of whom were educated at independent schools – may find the campus quiet at weekends and struggle to afford some of Bath's attractions, but they value its location. When they tire of the beauty of Bath, the nightlife of Bristol is only a few minutes away. The two cities have a combined student population of more than 50,000. The students' union is active and there are regular community initiatives.

Accommodation

Number of places and costs refer to 2005–06
University-provided places: 3,066
Percentage catered: 0%
Costs for catered accommodation: n/a
Costs for self-catered accommodation:
£60–£75 (standard); £76.00–£84.50 (en suite) a week. Includes utility costs and data connection in every room.
Policy for first-year students: all first-year full-time full-degree undergraduates and new overseas fee-paying postgraduates are guaranteed university residence. No restrictions on local students.
Policy for international students: as above plus international exchange students are housed on a reciprocal pro-rata basis. Home/EU postgraduates are not guaranteed places, but priority is given to international postgraduates who apply by 1 July.
Contact:
www.bath.ac.uk/accommodation/enquiry/

Students

Undergraduates:	7,155	(2,425)
Postgraduates:	1,330	(2,850)
Mature students:	5.1%	
Overseas students:	11.6%	
Applications per place:	8.4	
From state-sector schools:	80.8%	
From working-class homes:	18.1%	

Tuition fees 2006   £3,000
See chapter 13 for bursary details.

Teaching Quality Assessments

From 1995 (top score 24):
24 biological sciences; economics; mathematics; physics; politics.
23 education; leisure management; pharmacy; sports science.
22 civil engineering.
20 chemical engineering; electrical and electronic engineering.
19 modern languages; sociology.

University of Birmingham

Birmingham set itself the target of becoming the 'Oxbridge of the Midlands', which may have been ambitious, but its position around the top 25 universities in *The Times* ranking is a good starting point. A consultants' report in 2004 found the university had a boring image, but it is addressing that. And, despite offering an unusually wide range of subjects, its teaching and research ratings seldom slip.

Students come to Birmingham from more than 100 countries, but the university enjoys particularly high prestige in its own region. Entry standards are high, averaging the equivalent of more than three Bs at A level. With seven applicants for each place, they are likely to remain so, but aspiring students still flock to the largest open days in Britain each spring. There is also an additional open day for upper sixth-formers in September.

The university's enduring reputation is based on its research, with two thirds of its departments considered nationally or internationally outstanding in the last assessments. A dozen 5* ratings tripled the number awarded in 1996, with languages doing particularly well: French, German, Italian and Russian all reached the top level.

Many of the teaching scores have also been impressive, with mathematics, biological sciences and physiotherapy following sociology and electrical and electronic engineering in recording maximum points. Economics only just missed out in 2001 and there was a string of Excellent verdicts in the early assessments.

Birmingham's highly regarded medical school was granted the biggest expansion in Britain when quotas for the subject were reviewed in 1999 and is about to open an £11.8-million student facilities building. Engineering has been reorganised, following a year-long review, to promote an inter-disciplinary approach, responding to employers' wish for more flexibility. Students can enter either a BA or BSc degree programme, combining Technology with subjects ranging from Latin or modern Greek to the management of floods and other natural disasters.

The 230-acre campus in leafy Edgbaston is dominated by a 300-foot clocktower, which is one of the city's best-known landmarks, and boasts its own station. Dentistry is located in the city, while the Centre for Lifelong Learning and part of the School of Education are in Selly Oak. Most of the halls and university flats are conveniently located in an attractive parkland setting nearby. There are more than 5,000 university-owned beds, following a ten-year programme costing £80 million, and private sector accommodation is also plentiful.

Edgbaston, Birmingham B15 2TT
T 0121-414 3374 (general admission enquiries)
E prospectus@bham.ac.uk
W www.bham.ac.uk
U www.bugs.bham.ac.uk

Edinburgh
Belfast
BIRMINGHAM ●
Cardiff
London

The Times Rankings
Overall Ranking: 23
(2005 ranking: 20)

Teaching assessment:	=20	(22.2)
Research assessment:	=25	(5.3)
Entry standards:	14	(382.7)
Student–staff ratio:	=42	(16.6)
Library/IT spend/student:	30	(£622)
Facilities spend/student:	45	(£208)
Good honours:	25	(67.4%)
Graduate prospects:	29	(67.3%)
Expected completion rate:	24	(92.1%)

The campus is less than three miles from the centre of Birmingham, but the area has plenty of shops, pubs and restaurants of its own. With its own nightclub among the facilities on campus, some students do not even stray that far, but the city is acquiring a growing reputation among the young, which is helping to make the university even more popular.

Pressure on teaching space was eased to some extent in 1999 with the creation of the Selly Oak campus, a joint venture with a Free Church college whose education and theology degrees the university had validated for many years. The site is used for part-time degrees and continuing education, as well as the existing college courses, under an agreement that saw the university take over the management of nine partner colleges. The campus is also to house the BBC Drama Village, following the agreement of a strategic alliance with the corporation.

Student facilities are on a par with the best in the country, with many restaurants and bars on campus, and an outdoor pursuits centre on Coniston Water, in the Lake District. Birmingham has always been concerned with the body as well as the mind; compulsory exercise was only abandoned in 1968. The Active Lifestyles Programme, the voluntary modern-day equivalent, attracts 4,000 students to 150 different courses. Tutors with national qualifications run classes from beginner to advanced level. In addition, Birmingham ranks in the top three universities in intervarsity competitions.

Accommodation
Number of places and costs refer to 2004–05
University-provided places: 5,470
Percentage catered: 31%
Costs for catered accommodation:
£96.40–£138.30 a week depending upon room size, en suite facilities and location.
Costs for self-catered accommodation:
£65.71–£89.60 a week depending upon room size, en suite facilities and location.
Policy for first-year students: a 'Freshers Guarantee Scheme' guarantees housing to all first years, subject to the terms and conditions of the scheme. Local students with postcodes of B1 to B98 are placed on a waiting list, with priority to those travelling furthest.
Policy for international students: First-year undergraduate and postgraduate international students are guaranteed university accommodation, subject to the terms and conditions of the guarantee.
Contact: ugradaccomm@bham.ac.uk (undergraduate enquiries)
pgradaccom@bham.ac.uk (postgraduate enquiries)
J.D.Lee@bham.ac.uk (private sector housing enquiries)

Students

Undergraduates:	15,975	(4,280)
Postgraduates:	5,140	(6,160)
Mature students:	8.3%	
Overseas students:	7.8%	
Applications per place:	7.0	
From state-sector schools:	78.9%	
From working-class homes:	22.1%	

Tuition fees 2006   £3,000
See chapter 13 for bursary details.

Teaching Quality Assessments
From 1995 (top score 24):
24 electrical and electronic engineering; health subjects; mathematics; politics; sociology.
23 biological sciences; economics; Middle Eastern and African studies; physics; psychology; theology.
22 American studies; dentistry; history of art; hospitality; Iberian languages; Italian; nursing; sport.
21 archaeology; business and management; chemical engineering; civil engineering; drama, dance and cinematics; education; philosophy.
20 mechanical engineering; materials science; medicine.
19 German; **18** French.

University of Bolton

The largest town in England finally got a university in 2005 after eight years of frustration. The former Bolton Institute was turned down by the Quality Assurance Agency and the Privy Council before eventually winning approval for university status. Mollie Temple, the Vice-Chancellor, has promised that the switch will not alter the vocational emphasis, but she recognises that it will help make the institution better known. It seems to have done that already: Bolton recorded the biggest increase in applications in the UK at the start of 2005, an unprecedented 35 per cent rise.

The new university traces its roots back as far as 1824 with the foundation of a mechanics institute in the town. Proposals to take the name of North Manchester or West Pennine have been rejected in order to stick with Bolton. There are already more than 8,000 students and there are no plans for dramatic growth, despite the new-found popularity. Based on two town-centre sites, the university sees itself as a regional institution, with three quarters of the students coming from the North West, many through partner colleges. But there is also an international dimension, with long-established links in Malaysia and a regular contingent of overseas students from 70 different countries.

Bolton has set itself the ambitious target of climbing into the top half of the university system within 15 years. Judged on our criteria, it has some way to go, but it is not unusual for brand new universities to make their debut near the foot of the table. In Bolton's case, this means 98th place. Even in its days as an institute of higher education, it was competitive in categories such as facilities and library spending, but it is dragged down by other indicators. Although teaching assessments under the old system in mechanical engineering and film and theatre studies were disappointing, newer assessments have been more encouraging. Education and nursing both achieved maximum points and the last seven assessments all produced more than 20 points out of 24. Not surprisingly, research grades were less impressive, but metallurgy and materials reached grade 4. A centre for research and innovation in materials which opened in 2003 is to be the first of a series of 'knowledge exchange zones'. Bolton is not one of the new breed of 'teaching-only' universities; it has been accredited for research degrees for several years and acquired its new status under the old rules. Nearly 3,000 of the students are postgraduates, taking qualifications up to and including PhDs.

Most development has taken place at the Deane campus, which houses the

---

Deane Road,
Bolton BL3 5AB
T   01204 900600
E   enquiries@bolton.ac.uk
W   www.bolton.ac.uk
U   www.bisu.co.uk

The Times Rankings
Overall Ranking: 98
(2005 ranking: –)

Teaching assessment:	=66	(21.2)
Research assessment:	=97	(1.5)
Entry standards:	100	(147.8)
Student–staff ratio:	78	(20)
Library/IT spend/student:	=63	(£498)
Facilities spend/student:	10	(£329)
Good Honours:	=89	(47.5%)
Graduate prospects:	97	(47.1%)
Expected completion rate:	99	(63.9%)

university's headquarters. A £6-million four-storey design studio opened in 2004, but there is more work to be done. The students' union building had to close in the same year because it did not meet national standards. The 700 reasonably-priced residential places go a long way in an institution with a high proportion of home-based students. About 60 per cent of the students are over the age of 20 on entry.

Bolton exceeds all the access measures designed to widen participation in higher education: nearly all the students are state-educated, almost half are from working-class homes and three in ten come from areas that produce low numbers of students. The downside – a big one – is that more than a third of the students are projected to leave without a qualification: by far the highest proportion in England.

The town of Bolton cannot compete with big university cities for nightlife, although it has a premiership football club and all the normal facilities, but Manchester is only 15 minutes away. The university has a multi-sport hall with climbing wall and gym, but is not overprovided with sports facilities.

Accommodation

Number of places and costs refer to 2004–05
University-provided places: 700
Percentage catered: 0%
Costs for catered accommodation: n/a
Costs for self-catered accommodation: £2,120 a year (single)
Policy for first-year students: all first years are generally accommodated.
Policy for international students: accommodation is secured for international students
Contact: accomm@bolton.ac.uk

Students

Undergraduates:	3,190	(2,630)
Postgraduates:	500	(840)
Mature students:	19.0%	
Overseas students:	15.8%	
Applications per place:	7.0	
From state-sector schools:	98.3%	
From working-class homes:	48.6%	

Tuition fees 2006 £3,000
See chapter 13 for bursary details.

Teaching Quality Assessments

From 1995 (top score 24):
24 education; nursing and health subjects; psychology.
23 materials; philosophy.
22 biological sciences.
21 art and design, history of art; leisure, tourism and sport.
20 civil engineering; electrical and electronic engineering; mathematics and statistics; film and theatre studies.
19 building; modern languages.

University of Bournemouth

Always an institution with an eye for the distinctive, Bournemouth's strategic plan declares that it will 'dare to be different and stand out from the crowd'. Study boundaries are set by areas of social or economic activity, rather than traditional academic disciplines, because the aim is to be a 'pre-eminent vocational university'. Thus, there is no Faculty of Arts but there is a School of Services Management.

Bournemouth's forte is in identifying gaps in the higher education market and then filling them with innovative programmes. Degrees in public relations, retail management, scriptwriting and tax law are among the examples. The university also boasts the National Centre of Computer Animation. The mix has been popular with students – the 22 per cent rise in applications at the beginning of 2005 was one of the largest at any university.

The university claims a number of firsts in its growing portfolio of courses, notably in the area of tourism, media-related programmes and conservation, which won a Queen's Anniversary Prize in 1994. It was no surprise to find the university among the successful bidders for the first Foundation Degrees – two-year highly vocational courses, which are at the heart of the Government's expansion plans for higher education. Now much expanded, the new courses are being delivered in further education colleges from Cornwall to Salisbury, supporting the needs of business in the creative arts, media and tourism. One example is an online foundation degree in business and management, taken over three years part-time and launched in partnership with Leeds Metropolitan University, which has already been adopted by the Army.

Many of Bournemouth's courses have an international focus and all students are encouraged to improve their linguistic ability. A majority of undergraduates take sandwich courses, and 70 per cent do work placements. The result is an employment rate which is the university's proudest achievement: four out of five graduates go straight into jobs. The Retail Management degree notched up eight successive years of full employment and is still running at over 90 per cent. The university puts its graduates' success down to the in-depth knowledge of the business world which they acquire.

Teaching ratings improved after a poor start, when student numbers doubled in four years and resources were stretched. Archaeology, television and video production, media studies and nursing all passed with flying colours. Media courses are a particular strength, with entry requirements well above the university's

---

Talbot Campus, Fern Barrow,
Poole, Dorset BH12 5BB

T   01202 524111
E   prospectus@
    bournemouth.ac.uk
W www.bournemouth.ac.uk
U www.subu.org.uk

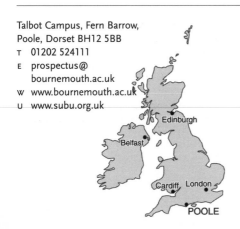

The Times Rankings
Overall Ranking: 85
(2005 ranking: 83)

Teaching assessment:	99	(19.5)
Research assessment:	=91	(1.9)
Entry standards:	51	(281.2)
Student–staff ratio:	=26	(15.5)
Library/IT spend/student:	99	(£360)
Facilities spend/student:	98	(£80)
Good honours:	=52	(57.3%)
Graduate prospects:	=47	(62.4%)
Expected completion rate:	=52	(84.7%)

modest average. State-of-the-art equipment includes a new Motion Capture facility for real-time animation, which will be used in teaching and be available for use by outside companies. Computer animation was the star performer in the 2001 research assessments, which saw much-needed improvement on 1996.

Bournemouth has come a long way since its days as a struggling college of education. University status arrived only two years after the success of a protracted battle to become a polytechnic. New teaching and residential accommodation has been added in recent years, with more to come. A multimillion-pound library opened in 2003. There are now two campuses – the original Talbot site in Poole and a dedicated campus in Bournemouth town centre – with associate colleges in Yeovil, Bournemouth and Poole, Cannington, Salisbury and Weymouth.

The southern seaside location and the subject mix attract more middle-class students than most new universities. Students are discouraged from bringing cars (which are banned within a mile of the town-centre campus) but many still do. The area has plenty to offer students during the summer season. Although it naturally becomes less lively in the winter months – party conferences apart – Bournemouth no longer shuts up when the tourists go home. The students' union's Old Fire Station bar is the favourite among many nightlife options. The university's Community Champions scheme is the centrepiece of an active volunteering programme, while competitive sport is also thriving. Bournemouth offers a wide range of accommodation, from university halls to bed and breakfast lets and shared houses.

Accommodation

Number of places and costs refer to 2005–06
University-provided places: about 2,350
Percentage catered: about 3% in privately-owned hotels and guest houses.
Costs for catered accommodation: £75–£95 a week (private hotels).
Costs for self-catered accommodation: £60–£80 a week for university-rented shared houses and halls of residence (includes utilities).
Policy for first-year students: the university expects to offer all first years a place to live. Halls places are not offered to students living within 15 miles, but university-shared houses are available.
Policy for international students: the university expects to offer all international students who request accommodation a place to live, mainly in halls of residence if key deadlines are met.
Contact: accommodation@bournemouth.ac.uk

Students

Undergraduates:	9,045	(3,455)
Postgraduates:	1,285	(1,130)
Mature students:	17.2%	
Overseas students:	7.2%	
Applications per place:	4.8	
From state-sector schools:	93.2%	
From working-class homes:	27.2%	

Tuition fees 2006 £3,000
See chapter 13 for bursary details.

Teaching Quality Assessments

From 1995 (top score 24):
22 archaeology; business; communication and media studies; nursing; television and video production.
20 agriculture; art and design; health subjects.
19 electrical engineering; food science.
18 mechanical engineering; modern languages.

University of Bradford

Plans to merge with the city's main further education college to create an institution spanning GCSE and postgraduate courses were shelved, leaving Bradford to plough a lone furrow as a university of less than 10,000 students. But the university is persevering with alliances with several institutions to help boost participation in a region where it is among the lowest in Europe. A ground-breaking foundation course run with Leeds University, for example, is intended to broaden the intake to clinical sciences and medicine. A BSc in clinical sciences was launched as part of the same initiative.

There are now ten foundation degrees, delivered in collaboration with local further education colleges, in areas such as public sector administration, metallurgy and enterprise in IT. Perhaps the best known is in health and social care, where the university was already expanding opportunities locally, bringing about a fourfold increase in nursing enrolments by young women from South Asian families.

Bradford has carved out a niche for itself with mature students, who now make up a third of all undergraduates. They relish the vocational slant and the accent on sandwich courses, which regularly place Bradford near the top of the graduate employment tables. Demand for places has recovered after a difficult period, and the older intake helped propel the university to one of the biggest increases in applications in Britain – almost 30 per cent – at the start of 2005. Admission requirements are modest compared with those in other old universities, especially in engineering, which still accounts for a significant share of the places and where applicants are notoriously thin on the ground.

The relatively small, lively campus is close to the city centre. Health students have their own building a few minutes' walk away, while the highly-rated management school is two miles away in a 14-acre parkland setting. The eventual aim is to develop a health and science quarter, with the School of Health Studies housed in its own building on campus. This is part of a £130 million plan to enhance the academic facilities and create more social space for students, beginning with improved laboratories for chemical and forensic science, more teaching accommodation and a new swimming pool.

Teaching assessments saw sudden and dramatic improvement after 1999, when no subject had been rated as excellent or amassed the 22 points regarded as its equivalent. Since then, nursing, pharmacy and other health studies have all managed 23 points out of 24, while politics and the

---

Richmond Road
Bradford BD7 1DP
T   01274 233081
E   enquiries@bradford.ac.uk
W   www.bradford.ac.uk
U   www.ubu.brad.ac.uk

Edinburgh
Belfast
BRADFORD
London
Cardiff

The Times Rankings
Overall Ranking: =47
(2005 ranking: 47)

Teaching assessment:	=72	(21.1)
Research assessment:	=51	(4.4)
Entry standards:	57	(260.9)
Student–staff ratio:	=42	(16.6)
Library/IT spend/student:	55	(£516)
Facilities spend/student:	22	(£274)
Good honours:	64	(53.8%)
Graduate prospects:	2	(81.5%)
Expected completion rate:	54	(84.5%)

interdisciplinary human studies programme, which combines philosophy with the study of psychology, literature and sociology, have been awarded full marks.

Research grades improved again in the latest assessment exercise, with European studies achieving the coveted 5* and archaeology, biomedical sciences, mechanical engineering and politics on the next rung of the ladder. Politics includes the university's best-known offering of peace studies, which has acquired an international reputation. A £6-million Institute of Pharmaceutical Innovation opened in 2003.

Almost a quarter of the undergraduates take sandwich courses, with health subjects now taking by far the biggest share of places overall. Elsewhere, the university has launched suites of ICT and media studies courses. Bradford was already offering courses in e-commerce and internet computing, alongside BScs in computer animation and special effects, and interactive systems and video games design. Computer-assisted learning is increasing in many subjects, making use of unusually extensive IT provision and a new wireless network. Some courses feature online assessment and the use of laptops in lectures.

More southerners are being attracted to Bradford's status as Britain's cheapest student city – it is even said to be possible to survive on the maximum student loan.

Almost 2,000 places in self-catering halls are reasonably priced. Many have been refurbished and more are promised by 2007. There is particularly good provision for disabled students, who account for 6 per cent of the university population. The university's senior management group includes a Dean of Students to ensure that the student voice is heard in future developments. The students' union operates a late-night 'safety bus' for those living within two miles of the campus.

Accommodation

Number of places and costs refer to 2005–06
University-provided places: 1,681
Percentage catered: 0%
Costs for catered accommodation: n/a
Costs for self-catered accommodation: £52.50–£76.50 a week.
Policy for first-year students: all first years placing the university as their first choice are guaranteed accommodation.
Policy for international students: all first-year international students are guaranteed accommodation.
Contact: halls-of-residence@bradford.ac.uk
www.brad.ac.uk/accommodation
www.unipol.bradford.ac.uk

Students

Undergraduates:	6,670	(1,705)
Postgraduates:	1,020	(2,555)
Mature students:	26.5%	
Overseas students:	16.2%	
Applications per place:	4.4	
From state-sector schools:	94.4%	
From working-class homes:	46%	

Tuition fees 2006   £3,000
See chapter 13 for bursary details.

Teaching Quality Assessments

From 1995 (top score 24):
24 philosophy; politics.
23 health subjects; nursing; pharmacy.
22 archaeology.
21 economics;
electrical and electronic engineering.
20 biological sciences; civil engineering; general engineering.
17 sociology.

University of Brighton

The 2003–04 academic year saw Brighton come of age, as one of the first new universities to be awarded a medical school. Run jointly with neighbouring Sussex University, the £28.5-million school is training 128 doctors a year and is already proving popular, registering big increases in applications in both years since it opened. Brighton was already heavily engaged in other health subjects such as nursing and midwifery. The medical school's head-quarters, on Brighton's Falmer campus, has also provided a new base for applied social sciences such as criminology and applied psychology, which are among the university's most sought-after degrees.

The two universities have been collaborating since Brighton was a polytechnic. There is a joint research building for science policy and management studies, and a joint accord guarantees the offer of a place to all suitably qualified applicants from the Channel Island of Jersey – Brighton does the same for applicants from Sussex. Almost a third of undergraduates now come through this route.

Only two new universities did as well as Brighton in the last Research Assessment Exercise, and only one entered such a high a proportion of its academics. Art and design, biological sciences and European studies were all rated nationally excellent, with some work of top international quality. Teaching ratings have also been consistently good, never dropping below 20 points out of 24, with philosophy registering a maximum score. The plaudits have not gone unnoticed: applications were up by almost 14 per cent by the official deadline in 2004 and there was another modest increase by the start of 2005. Fewer than one student in ten enters through clearing.

Brighton's acknowledged strengths in art and design and health subjects have been among the areas contributing to the university's rise, but there had been equally good scores in areas such as sport and hospitality, mathematics and pharmacy. The Design Council's national archive is lodged on campus, and the four-year fashion textiles degree has an international reputa-tion, with work placements in the United States, France and Italy, as well as Britain. The Faculty of Management and Information Sciences, launched in 2003, is now the largest in the university.

The modular course system gives students many options within their own faculty and sometimes across academic fields, and most undergraduates have a personal tutor, who will advise on combinations. Almost a quarter of the full-time undergraduates are over 21 on entry,

---

Mithras House, Lewes Road,
Brighton BN2 4AT
T   01273 642828
E   admissions@brighton.ac.uk
W   www.brighton.ac.uk
U   www.ubsu.net

Edinburgh

Belfast

Cardiff   London

BRIGHTON

The Times Rankings
Overall Ranking: 66
(2005 ranking: 63)

Teaching assessment:	=72	(21.1)
Research assessment:	=64	(2.9)
Entry standards:	66	(251.5)
Student–staff ratio:	75	(19.3)
Library/IT spend/student:	=70	(£465)
Facilities spend/student:	58	(£179)
Good honours:	63	(54.4%)
Graduate prospects:	57	(60.6%)
Expected completion rate:	=56	(83.6%)

often attracted by strongly vocational courses and the prospect of three years in 'London by the sea'.

Four sites house the five faculties. Art and design has the prime location opposite the Royal Pavilion, with sports science, service management and the health professions at Eastbourne and the other subjects on the outskirts of Brighton, at Falmer and Moulsecoomb, the university's headquarters.

The university has a cosmopolitan air, with more overseas students than most of the former polytechnics. Numerous European links give most courses an international flavour, often allowing a period of study on the Continent.

Over £100 million has been spent on new facilities and refurbishment since 1992. At Eastbourne there is a new library and extensive sports and leisure facilities, including a sports centre with three gymnasia and a dance studio, a refurbished swimming pool and fitness facilities. New sport-science laboratories followed and further grants have improved the learning resources centre, lecture theatres and refectory. The extensive modernisation of the Falmer campus continues, with extra accommodation, a library and a nursing and midwifery centre already added.

Students have taken to the 'managed learning environment', known as student central, an interactive service providing online access to teaching materials and other information. Most also like Brighton, although the cost of living is high despite hall rents that are the cheapest in the south of England. There is a lively social scene and part-time work is plentiful. Eastbourne is also surprisingly popular, and both towns offer plentiful accommodation to supplement the university's stock, and more residences are planned in Brighton and Eastbourne.

Accommodation
Number of places and costs refer to 2005–06
University-provided places: 1,950 in halls; 400 places in private sector university-managed houses or flats.
Percentage catered: 0%
Costs for catered n/a
Costs for self-catered accommodation: £57–£85 a week.
Policy for first-year students: only students holding unconditional offers by 30 June are guaranteed accommodation. Help and advice is provided and there is a web-based property database (Netlet) to assist students. Students living in East or West Sussex are not offered halls accommodation.
Policy for international students: accommodation guaranteed if an offer has been firmly accepted and the form is returned by 30 June.
Contact: accommodation@brighton.ac.uk
a.eastbourne@brighton.ac.uk

Students

Undergraduates:	10,705	(4,460)
Postgraduates:	1,170	(2,475)
Mature students:	23.3%	
Overseas students:	14.4%	
Applications per place:	5.8	
From state-sector schools:	92.4%	
From working-class homes:	26.6%	

Tuition fees 2006 £3,000
See chapter 13 for bursary details.

Teaching Quality Assessments
From 1995 (top score 24):
24 philosophy.
23 pharmacy.
22 art and design; biological sciences; health subjects; hospitality; librarianship and information management; mathematics and statistics; nursing.
21 civil engineering; education; history of art and design.
20 building; electrical and electronic engineering; modern languages.

University of Bristol

Bristol has long been a natural alternative to Oxbridge, favoured particularly by independent schools, whose pupils take at least three in ten places. But the university found itself at the centre of an admissions furore over long-established radical plans to widen its intake. Departments are encouraged to make lower offers to promising applicants from schools with poor records at A level, and some top schools have seen a link in the rejection of highly-qualified applicants. As the most popular university in Britain in terms of applications per place, Bristol has always turned away excellent candidates. But the policy led to fleeting talk of a boycott by leading independent schools – a 5 per cent drop in applications for courses beginning in 2004 had been reversed with interest when the official deadline passed for 2005.

The university has found it difficult to attract working-class teenagers, who fear that they would be out of place socially, if not academically. Less than one in eight came from a working-class home in 2003 – the lowest proportion outside Oxbridge. Tiny numbers are recruited from the thousands of schools in the bottom half of the A-level league tables. Bristol believes the controversy was worthwhile if previously untapped sources of bright students can be brought to the surface.

For most applicants, entry standards remain among the highest at any university. A modular course system is now well established, although the majority of students still take single or dual honours degrees.

The city is one of the most attractive in Britain, as well as possessing a vibrant youth culture. It is also prosperous, offering job opportunities to students and graduates alike. The university merges into the centre, its famous Gothic tower dominating the skyline from the junction of two of the main shopping streets. Departments dot the hillside close to the picturesque harbour area.

Bristol has no intention of aping the growth plans of some of its rivals, but there has been modest expansion and the university has continued to live up to expectations in assessments of teaching and research. A third of the staff assessed for research are in departments considered internationally excellent and three quarters saw their departments reach one of the top two grades. There are 30 Fellows of the Royal Society and similar numbers in other learned societies.

Research is Bristol's traditional strength. The 2001 assessments saw the university's tally of 5* subjects shoot up from one to 15, with another 21 subjects on the next of the

Senate House, Tyndall Avenue,
Bristol BS8 1TH
T   0117-928 9000
E   admissions@bris.ac.uk
W   www.bris.ac.uk
U   www.ubu.org.uk

Edinburgh
Belfast
Cardiff   London
BRISTOL

The Times Rankings
Overall Ranking: =10
(2005 ranking: 12)

Teaching assessment:	=34	(22)
Research assessment:	=10	(5.7)
Entry standards:	7	(423.7)
Student–staff ratio:	18	(14.5)
Library/IT spend/student:	13	(£726)
Facilities spend/student:	=24	(£263)
Good honours:	3	(81.3%)
Graduate prospects:	8	(76.8%)
Expected completion rate:	7	(96.5%)

seven grades. Only Cambridge, Oxford and University College London had more maximum scores. The 33 excellent teaching ratings also represent one of the largest totals in the university system, with veterinary medicine, molecular biosciences, anatomy, electronic engineering and, most recently, education all achieving perfect scores.

Bristol was given the best rating among the small group of universities seeking to demonstrate their creditworthiness to the money markets. A funding appeal which has raised more than £100 million has enabled the university to create new chairs and embark on a number of building projects. The highly-rated chemistry department, for example, moved into a well-appointed new centre in 2000, allowing new medical science laboratories to be constructed in the department's former premises. Dynamics engineering and neurology opened new buildings in 2004 and a new students' union is among the projects included in investment plans totalling £250 million. An impressive sports centre at the heart of the university precinct opened in 2002. The developments are much needed after 11 per cent growth in full-time undergraduate numbers over a five-year period when funding levels were reduced consistently.

Most students enjoy life in Bristol – a *New Musical Express* poll rated the social life the best at any university in 2004 – although some find the high cost of living a serious drawback, together with security concerns in some parts of the city. The drop-out rate is among the lowest in Britain. The current students' union is less of a social centre than in some universities, but it runs an evening bus service to the halls of residence, and there is a free late-night service for women from the library and the union to their homes.

Accommodation

Number of places and costs refer to 2005–06
University-provided places: about 4,500
Percentage catered: 40%
Costs for catered accommodation: £87–£93 (shared); £104–£122 (single) a week.
Costs for self-catered accommodation: £43 (shared); £61–£108 (single) a week.
Policy for first-year students: one offer of accommodation is guaranteed for new full-time undergraduate students during their first year of study provided they apply by 12 July, are aged 18 on 1 October of the relevant year, unaccompanied and live outside the Bristol area.
Policy for international students: accommodation is guaranteed for unaccompanied postgraduates paying overseas fees during their first year of study, who have accepted a place for a full academic year in Bristol, and who apply by 1 August.
Contact: Accom-office@bris.ac.uk

Students

Undergraduates:	10,575	(3,895)
Postgraduates:	2,615	(5,100)
Mature students:	5.5%	
Overseas students:	10.6%	
Applications per place:	10.5	
From state-sector schools:	63.8%	
From working-class homes:	13.7%	

Tuition fees 2006   £3,000
See chapter 13 for bursary details.

Teaching Quality Assessments

From 1995 (top score 24):
24 anatomy and physiology; biological sciences; education; electrical and electronic engineering; veterinary medicine.
23 drama, dance and cinematics; economics; mathematics and statistics; pharmacology; philosophy; physics; politics; psychology.
22 aeronautical engineering; archaeology; civil engineering; Iberian languages.
21 classics and ancient history; German; Italian; sociology.
20 French; history of art; medicine; Russian; theology.
19 dentistry.

Brunel University

Brunel celebrates 40 years as a university in 2006 and, in the run-up to this anniversary, has been investing in a £150-million plan to upgrade and centralise its teaching, research and sporting facilities, as well as making a large number of new academic appointments. For the first time since its early years, the whole university will be located on the main Uxbridge campus, as the last academic school moves into a new health and social care building. The move will see the closure of the old Borough Road College, which will bring its illustrious sporting traditions to the most modern surroundings. The building programme already includes a £6.5-million outdoor sports complex and a £7-million indoor athletics and netball centre, as well as a hugely extended university library. Other developments will see a big increase in residential accommodation, more catering and social amenities and enhanced teaching and research facilities.

There is plenty of scope for development. The university has quadrupled in size, with more than 12,600 students sharing a spacious but hitherto uninspiring main campus that has an isolated feel despite affording easy access to central London.

In recent years, Brunel has introduced more variety into a portfolio of degrees that was once given over almost entirely to sandwich courses. About half of all undergraduates still take four-year degrees with a work placement of six months or a year, but new developments have tended to be conventional three-year arts and social science programmes. There has also been significant growth in courses specialising in new technologies, such as multimedia design, interactive computing and mobile computing. Other innovations include creative music technology and motorsport engineering.

Work placements and the inclusion in degree courses of skills modules such as oral and written communication, business and computer literacy have helped maintain a consistently good record in the graduate employment market. Many courses are validated by professional institutions. The university is abandoning semesters and going back to a three-term year to give greater coherence to its programmes.

Teaching assessments were consistently good, with drama, education, sport science and politics producing the best scores. All the assessments since the millennium produced scores of at least 22 points out of 24. The last research assessments also showed further improvement, although only 61 per cent of the academics were entered and design lost its 5* rating. General and mechanical engineering, law,

Uxbridge, Middlesex UB8 3PH
T 01895 203214 (admissions office)
E admissions@brunel.ac.uk
W www.brunel.ac.uk
U www.brunelstudents.com

Edinburgh
Belfast
UXBRIDGE
Cardiff   London

The Times Rankings
Overall Ranking: 43
(2005 ranking: 43)

Teaching assessment:	=40	(21.9)
Research assessment:	=53	(4.3)
Entry standards:	49	(286.6)
Student–staff ratio:	=67	(18.6)
Library/IT spend/student:	47	(£555)
Facilities spend/student:	18	(£285)
Good honours:	31	(65.8%)
Graduate prospects:	58	(60.5%)
Expected completion rate:	39	(87.5%)

library and information studies and sociology all reached grade 5, and a £14-million investment in 60 more research posts should produce further progress. Sporting excellence is also being maintained, with double gold-medal-winning rower James Cracknell and heavyweight boxer Audley Harrison the best-known alumni of recent times.

Brunel was also among the first of the traditional universities to introduce access courses, run in further education colleges, to bring underqualified mature applicants up to the necessary standard for entry. Further efforts to widen access include plans for England's only university-run school, where the 800 sixth-formers will be taught by Brunel staff and mentored by its students. The level of applications to Brunel has fluctuated as the university has raised its entrance requirements, but the university recorded one of the biggest increases in places in 2004, taking an extra 500 students. The projected total of 12 per cent leaving without a qualification is significantly lower than the UK average for the subjects on offer.

Student union facilities are good and students like Brunel's intimacy. The university's residential stock has been increased in recent years and new undergraduates have normally been offered accommodation on campus. The policy for entrants in 2006, when the pressure on facilities will be increased with the concentration on Uxbridge, has yet to be confirmed.

Accommodation
Number of places and costs refer to 2004–05
University-provided places: 3,541
Percentage catered: 0%
Costs for catered accommodation: n/a
Costs for self-catered accommodation: £60.06 (shared); £62.09 (single); £76.02 (en suite); £93.17 (studio flat) a week.
Policy for first-year students: all new first-year students are eligible for on-campus accommodation irrespective of home address.
Policy for international students: all new international students are given on-campus accommodation.
Contact: accom-uxb@brunel.ac.uk (Uxbridge and Runnymede)
accom-twic@brunel.ac.uk (Twickenham and Osterley)

Students
Undergraduates:	9,715	(1,050)
Postgraduates:	1,625	(2,750)
Mature students:	17.7%	
Overseas students:	7.4%	
Applications per place:	6.7	
From state-sector schools:	91.8%	
From working-class homes:	35.8%	

Tuition fees 2006	£3,000

See chapter 13 for bursary details.

Teaching Quality Assessments
From 1995 (top score 24):
23 drama and dance; education; politics; sports science.
22 biological sciences; economics; general engineering; health subjects; mathematics; nursing; psychology; sociology.
21 American studies; electrical and electronic engineering.
20 materials science; mechanical engineering; media studies.

University of Buckingham

Britain's only private university is its smallest by far, but no longer the youngest. Nor, it claims, even before the advent of top-up fees elsewhere, was it any more expensive than other universities, especially if you are well qualified. Its intensive two-year degrees cut maintenance costs, and a discount scheme reduces the £12,000-a-year fees by more than £4,000 for applicants with the 300 points at A level, or the equivalent. The threshold is reduced to 240 points for those who go to school or live in Buckinghamshire and the surrounding counties of Bedfordshire, Berkshire, Hertfordshire, Northamptonshire and Oxfordshire. In addition, students of 25 or more at the start of their course can apply for bursaries of £1,200 a term and there are two smaller schemes offering full-fee scholarships for local students.

The university, which celebrated its 25th anniversary in 2001, has no ambitions to follow its peers into the mass higher education market: it values the personal approach that comes with having only ten students to each member of staff, when the UK average is 17. One-to-one tutorials, which have all but disappeared outside Oxbridge and are by no means universal there, are common at Buckingham. The average teaching group contains about six students.

The scholarship initiative, which is open to British and foreign students, could bring modest growth and breathe new life into the university. A Conservative-backed experiment of the 1970s, Buckingham had to wait almost ten years for its royal charter, but is now an accepted part of the university system. Although in 1992 it installed Baroness Thatcher as Chancellor, the university has no party political ties. Dr Terence Kealey, a biochemist from Cambridge University, became the latest Vice-Chancellor in April 2001, declaring an ambition for Buckingham to 'one day' challenge the cream of American higher education. He has recruited a number of high-profile libertarians, including Chris Woodhead, the former Chief Inspector of Schools.

Buckingham's private status excludes it from the funding councils' assessment of teaching and research, making it impossible to place in our league table. However, the university commissioned its own audit of teaching standards from the Quality Assurance Agency, which gave it a clean bill of health in 2004. The university's degrees carry full currency in the academic world and teaching standards are high. Law and business are particularly popular.

The university runs on calendar years, rather than the traditional academic variety,

---

Hunter Street,
Buckingham MK18 1EG
T 01280 824081 (admissions)
E admissions@
   buckingham.ac.uk
W www.buckingham.ac.uk
U student.union@
   buckingham.ac.uk

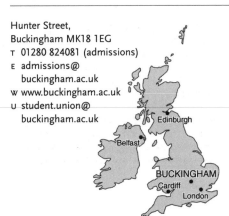

The Times Rankings
not applicable

although law students have the option of entering in July. Between October and December, students taking degrees including French are offered a ten-week course in Lille. Degree courses run for two 40-week years, minimising disruptive career breaks for the many mature students. Students have the option of a three-year degree in the humanities and soon the university will house the UK's first private medical school, in partnership with Brunel University. About three quarters of the students are from overseas, but the proportion from Britain has been growing.

Even before the QAA audit, the two-year degree had been fully assessed by Professor John Clarke, a founder member of the university staff. Although hardly neutral, he concluded that the individual tuition given to Buckingham students, made possible by unusually generous staffing levels, allowed the system to succeed. However, he acknowledged that 'undercapitalisation' has prevented the university achieving as much as it hoped.

Recent additions to the subjects on offer included multimedia journalism and media communications, both paired with English. The university is also focusing on e-commerce, with a Certificate in Internet Technologies and an MSc in e-business.

Campus facilities have improved considerably in recent years, although they cannot compare with those available at traditional universities. Buckingham operates on three sites, all within easy walking distance of each other, including a business school which opened in 1996. An academic centre containing computer suites, lecture theatres and student facilities provides a focal point that was missing previously.

The social scene is predictably quiet, given the size of the university and the workload, especially at weekends. The town is pretty and has its share of pubs and restaurants. Milton Keynes or Oxford are near, except that Buckingham has no station.

Accommodation

Number of places and costs refer to 2004–05
University-provided places: 446
Percentage catered: 0%
Costs for catered accommodation: n/a
Costs for self-catered accommodation:
£69–£114 a week; 50% weekly reduction during vacation (students may stay in their allocated room during vacation).
Policy for first-year students: all students are guaranteed accommodation for one year but may opt for six months.
Policy for international students: same as for first-year students.
Contact: admissions@buckingham.ac.uk

Students

Undergraduates:	468	(40)
Postgraduates:	131	(18)
Mature students:	37%	
Overseas students:	70%	
Applications per place:	6.3	
From state-sector schools:	n/a	
From working-class homes:	n/a	

Teaching Quality Assessments

The Higher Education Funding Council has no jurisdiction. The university commissioned its own audit of teaching standards from the Quality Assurance Agency, which were satisfactory.

Main subject areas: accounting; business studies; computer science; English; history; history of art and heritage management; hotel management and economics; law; politics; psychology.

University of Cambridge

Until 2001, Cambridge had enjoyed an unbroken run at the top of *The Times* League Table, and even now it is practically inseparable from first-placed Oxford. The university has the best record in the teaching and research assessments. Traditionally supreme in the sciences, where it was ranked best in the world by *The Times Higher Education Supplement* in 2004, the university boasts an array of subjects with top ratings for teaching and research. But the arts and social sciences have also been strengthened. The Centre for Research in the Arts, Social Sciences and Humanities, designed to compete with similar institutes in Australia, Germany and the United States, has been one example, while the Judge Management School is also well established now.

All but one of the subjects assessed in the first rounds of teaching quality assessment were considered excellent and none dropped more than two points out of 24 under the later system. Classics and economics were added to the subjects on full marks in 2001. Almost three quarters of the academics entered for research assessment were in subjects rated internationally outstanding, and only three subjects failed to reach the next-highest grade. The tripos system was a forerunner of the currently fashionable modular degree, allowing students to change subjects (within limits) midway through their courses. Students receive a classification for each of the two parts of their tripos degree.

More students now come from state schools than the independent sector – a trend the university is keen to continue – but the proportion of working-class undergraduates remains low, at only 11 per cent. Summer schools, student visits and, in some colleges, sympathetic selection procedures, are helping to attract more applications from comprehensive schools. Cambridge escaped largely unscathed from the controversy over Laura Spence's rejection at Oxford, although the university acknowledged that it could just as easily have been the centre of attention. Instead, it has been the appointment of Alison Richard as the first woman to head the university since the Vice-Chancellorship became a permanent post that has trained the spotlight on Cambridge once more.

A lively alternative prospectus, available from the students' union, says there is no such thing as Cambridge University, just a collection of colleges. Where applications are concerned, this is true, as it is to some extent socially. Making the right choice of college is crucial, both to maximise the chances of winning a place and to ensure an enjoyable three years if you are successful.

Kellet Lodge, Tennis Court Road,
Cambridge CB2 1QJ
T 01223 333308
E ucam-undergraduate-admissions@lists.cam.ac.uk
W www.cam.ac.uk
U www.cusu.cam.ac.uk

Edinburgh
Belfast
CAMBRIDGE
Cardiff
London

The Times Rankings
Overall Ranking: 2
(2005 ranking: 2)

Teaching assessment:	5	(22.9)
Research assessment:	1	(6.6)
Entry standards:	1	(510.6)
Student–staff ratio:	6	(11.5)
Library/IT spend/student:	4	(£1,161)
Facilities spend/student:	=20	(£281)
Good honours:	1	(90.4%)
Graduate prospects:	1	(85.4%)
Expected completion rate:	1	(98.5%)

However, teaching is university-based, especially in the sciences, and a shift of emphasis towards the centre has been taking place with the aid of a £250-million funding appeal. Applicants can take pot luck with an open application if they prefer not to opt for a particular college. But, though the statistics show that this route is equally successful, only a minority take it.

The university's leading place in British higher education was underlined by its success in attracting Microsoft's first research base outside the United States. This is one of a series of technological partnerships with the private sector, several of which benefit undergraduates as well as researchers. Cambridge was also chosen for a Government-sponsored partnership with the Massachusetts Institute of Technology to promote entrepreneurship.

Such is the scale of development that almost £500 million worth of building is either planned or under construction. The medical school's facilities are being upgraded at Addenbrooke's Hospital but, with the city choking with traffic and short of sites for development, the university is looking to the outskirts to expand. The West Cambridge site will take a mixture of teaching and research buildings, and there are plans for more on green-belt land further north. In the long term, up to three new colleges could be built but there will be few extra places in the foreseeable future.

For the moment, therefore, entrance requirements will remain the toughest in Britain. With fewer than four applicants for each place – fewer still if you choose your subject carefully – the competition for places appears less intense than at the popular civic universities. The difference is that nine out of ten entrants have at least three A-grade A levels. The pressure does not end there: the amount of high-quality work to be crammed into eight-week terms can prove a strain, although the 1 per cent drop-out rate is the lowest in Britain.

The college system ensures that student facilities are among the best, especially for sport. Students do not pick Cambridge for the clubbing, which is just as well. With two universities within its boundaries, the city caters well for students in many respects, but it is never going to be among the leading lights for its youth scene.

Accommodation

See Chapter 10 for information about individual colleges.

Students

Undergraduates:	11,955	(4,595)
Postgraduates:	5,210	(3,675)
Mature students:	3.5%	
Overseas students:	11.9%	
Applications per place:	4.5	
From state-sector schools:	57.6%	
From working-class homes:	11.3%	

Tuition fees 2006	£3,000

See chapter 13 for bursary details.

Teaching Quality Assessments

From 1995 (top score 24):
24 biological sciences; classics and ancient history; economics; pharmacy; philosophy; psychology.
23 anatomy and physiology; archaeology; Celtic studies; chemical engineering; education; general engineering; materials science; mathematics; Middle Eastern and African studies; physics; politics; sociology; theology; veterinary medicine.
22 history of art; land management; linguistics; modern languages.
21 medicine.

University of Cardiff

Cardiff has established itself as the front-runner in Welsh higher education and is bracing itself for a further influx from England when top-up fees are introduced in 2006. It has now left the University of Wales, believing that only full independence would enable it to compete with other top universities, although some health courses still lead to degrees from the federal university. After 75 years of partnership, Cardiff has also merged with the University of Wales College of Medicine with the backing of £60 million from the Welsh Assembly and other sources. The new venture has already attracted brain imaging facilities worth £10.8 million.

With more than 22,000 students and 5,000 staff, the university is a match for most rivals in teaching and research. A third of the students come from Wales, but the 3,000 from overseas testify to Cardiff's international reputation. Seven subjects – city and regional planning, civil engineering, education, English, optometry, psychology and theology – were rated internationally outstanding in the latest research assessments. Almost nine out of ten researchers were placed in the top two of the seven categories, one of the best ratios in Britain.

Research income is healthy, too, with industrial collaboration by the Manufacturing Engineering Centre winning a Queen's Anniversary Prize in 2001. Teaching quality is also highly rated. The 21 subjects graded as excellent represent more than half of the university. An overall audit by the Quality Assurance Agency complimented the university on its 'powerful academic vision and well-developed and effectively articulated mission to achieve excellence in teaching and research'. Student support services, including counselling facilities and the help offered to dyslexics, were among the features singled out for praise.

Humanities and social sciences take the largest share of places. A partial reorganisation has created two 'super schools' of biosciences and social sciences, while a new Centre for Lifelong Learning co-ordinates 700 courses, which are offered at 100 regional centres. Many full-time degrees share a common first year, and the introduction of a modular system has made undergraduate study more flexible.

The university enjoys a central location in the Welsh capital, occupying a significant part of the civic complex around Cathays Park. In recent years, more than £200 million has been invested in new buildings and equipment, and extensive refurbishment. The flagship projects involved a £30-million centre for

---

PO Box 921,
Cardiff CF10 3XQ
T   029-2087 4839
E   admissions@cardiff.ac.uk
W   www.cardiff.ac.uk
U   www.cardiffstudents.com

The Times Rankings
Overall Ranking: 22
(2005 ranking: 21)

Teaching assessment:	=34	(22.0)
Research assessment:	=22	(5.4)
Entry standards:	22	(361.1)
Student–staff ratio:	=19	(14.7)
Library/IT spend/student:	22	(£667)
Facilities spend/student:	39	(£216)
Good honours:	18	(69.5%)
Graduate prospects:	20	(69.7%)
Expected completion rate:	29	(90.7%)

Edinburgh
Belfast
London
CARDIFF

engineering, physics and computer science, with facilities comparable with the best in Britain, and a £3.5-million refurbishment of the chemistry department. The latest phase of the programme has seen the opening of a £3.5-million resource centre alongside the business school and a £14-million life sciences building, with optometry and vision sciences the next to benefit.

The medical school is a mile away at Heath Park, where the five healthcare schools share a 53-acre site bordering parkland and fields with the University Hospital of Wales. Between the two campuses the university is building student accommodation containing 511 en suite study bedrooms, adding to the 4,700 beds already available. Two thirds of those are also en suite, and most are within walking distance of lectures. Rents are among the lowest in the UK, according to a National Union of Students survey.

Entry requirements have been rising, despite recent expansion, and the graduate employment record is good. A 15 per cent rise in applications for courses beginning in 2005 was one of the largest at a leading university and the absence of top-up fees may see that trend accelerate in 2006. One undergraduate in six comes from an independent school, but still almost 30 per cent have a working-class background. The 6 per cent dropout rate is the lowest in Wales and among the lowest in Britain.

The city of Cardiff is popular with students, offering all the attractions of a large conurbation without such high prices as students experience elsewhere. The main residential site at Talybont boasts a 'sports village', with three multipurpose sports halls, a fitness suite and outdoor pitches. There is also a city-centre fitness suite and a sports ground that was used as a training facility for the rugby union World Cup.

Accommodation
Number of places and costs refer to 2004–05
University-provided places: about 4,983
Percentage catered: 11%
Costs for catered accommodation: £60–£69 a week.
Costs for self-catered accommodation: £42–£65 a week.
Policy for first-year students: a guarantee of accommodation is given to all first years entering through the normal admissions cycle. No restrictions are placed on those who live locally.
Policy for international students: as above for first-year students. They are also guaranteed accommodation for the duration of their course.
Contact: residences@cardiff.ac.uk

Students		
Undergraduates:	13,035	(4,005)
Postgraduates:	3,845	(1,865)
Mature students:	5.3%	
Overseas students:	9.4%	
Applications per place:	5.9	
From state-sector schools:	85.2%	
From working-class homes:	22.6%	
Tuition fees 2006	£1,200	

Teaching Quality Assessments
1993–95 Rated Excellent:
accounting and finance;
anatomy and physiology; archaeology;
architecture; biochemistry; biological sciences;
chemistry; civil engineering; dentistry;
education; environmental engineering;
English language;
electrical and electronic engineering;
maritime studies; mechanical engineering;
medicine; optometry; pharmacy; philosophy;
psychology; town planning.

Cardiff, University of Wales Institute (UWIC)

UWIC has an international reputation for sport, but is no slouch in some academic fields either, as the second highest-placed new university in *The Times* League Table. The combination has been attracting record numbers of applicants: a 4.5 per cent increase at the start of 2005 was below the national average, but big increases earlier in the decade meant demand was still buoyant.

Extra places have been added, but plans for UWIC to become part of a much larger university through a merger with neighbouring Glamorgan were abandoned in 2003. Instead, the Institute has been exploring the possibility of a closer relationship with the University of Wales, Newport. Two thirds of UWIC's 9,000 students are Welsh, half of them from Cardiff or the Vale of Glamorgan. Nearly 95 per cent attended state schools and 30 per cent come from working-class homes. The 17 per cent who come from areas sending few students to higher education is ahead of the 'benchmark' set according to the mix of courses. The drop-out rate is lower than the average for new universities.

UWIC is one of Britain's leading centres for university sport, with team performances to match some excellent facilities. The Institute has had British university champions in gymnastics, trampolining, athletics, rugby union, rugby league, boxing, squash, archery, weightlifting and judo. More than 240 past or present students are internationals in 28 sports, world and Olympic champions among them. The £7-million national indoor athletics centre is UWIC's's pride and joy, but other facilities are also of high quality.

Academically, art and design is the star performer, with teaching in ceramics, fine art and interior architecture rated excellent, and the whole area considered nationally excellent for research. All six teacher training courses are rated excellent for teaching and there have been top scores in several sciences, but less than one academic in five was entered for the last Research Assessment Exercise, leaving UWIC near the bottom of the research table in terms of average grades per member of staff.

Entrance requirements are generally modest, but the menu of largely vocational courses means that many students come with qualifications other than A levels. About a fifth are mature students and there is a relatively high proportion from overseas.

UWIC has four sites, all within three miles of the centre of Cardiff. The Cyncoed campus, which houses education and sport, is the centre of activity, particularly for first-year students. The national athletics centre

Western Avenue,
Cardiff CF5 2YB
T   029-2041 6070
E   uwicinfo@uwic.ac.uk
W   www.uwic.ac.uk
U   www.uwicsu.co.uk

The Times Rankings

Overall Ranking: 51

(2005 ranking: 45)

Teaching assessment:	=51	(21.6)
Research assessment:	=72	(2.7)
Entry standards:	75	(232.9)
Student–staff ratio:	=67	(18.6)
Library/IT spend/student:	84	(£408)
Facilities spend/student:	2	(£445)
Good honours:	86	(48.5%)
Graduate prospects:	39	(65.1%)
Expected completion rate:	60	(83.3%)

is there, together with a multitude of outdoor facilities and also the Welsh Sports Centre for the Disabled. Student facilities, including the Institute's largest bar, have been upgraded recently. A new IT suite has 250 computers available 24 hours a day.

Howard Gardens is the home of fine art, while the Llandaff campus hosts design, engineering, food science and health courses. Llandaff has a new £3-million student centre, which includes a dyslexia support unit among a number of advice and representation services, and a learning centre with more than 300 computers opened in 2003. Business, hospitality and tourism are taught at the Colchester Avenue campus.

Students tend to like Cardiff as a city, and UWIC's enterprising union does its best to make their time there as lively as possible. It owns a nightclub and bar in the city centre to add to the campus choices. Before the recent expansion, all first years were guaranteed accommodation, and 90 per cent still live in halls. UWIC is the only university to have been awarded the government's Charter Mark three times, the judges commenting particularly on the level of satisfaction among students.

Accommodation

Number of places and costs refer to 2005–06
University-provided places: 1,183 (21% supplied under the UNITE scheme)
Percentage catered: 33%
Costs for catered accommodation: £88.50–£95.50 a week.
Costs for self-catered accommodation: £62–£80 (standard); £66–£72 (en suite) a week.
Policy for first-year students: There are no guarantees for any students, whether first years or returners. Halls are allocated on a distance from Cardiff and date order basis.
Policy for international students: accommodation is reserved for international students, subject to availability and a deadline for applications, through the International Office.
Contact: accomm@uwic.ac.uk
www.uwic.ac.uk

Students		
Undergraduates:	6,080	(1,420)
Postgraduates:	715	(875)
Mature students:	17.4%	
Overseas students:	6.8%	
Applications per place:	4.7	
From state-sector schools:	94.5%	
From working-class homes:	29.5%	
Tuition fees 2006	£1,200	

Teaching Quality Assessments
1993–95 Rated Excellent:
art and design; biological sciences; environmental health; nutrition; podiatry; psychology; speech therapy.

University of Central England in Birmingham

UCE describes itself as 'the responsive university', emphasising its willingness to act on students' wishes as well as serving the needs of the Second City. The annual satisfaction survey goes to half of the student body, in a model that will soon be part of a national system of quality assurance and has already been adopted by other universities in Britain and abroad. The results are taken seriously: more than £1 million was spent on library stock after one survey, and a more recent exercise has led to the introduction of internet tutorials in engineering and new help with research for undergraduates in law and social science. The longstanding initiative is just one of the activities of the influential Centre for Research into Quality, which is headed by one of the university's most senior academics.

The university has a proud record of extending access to higher education: 42 per cent of its students come from working-class homes and 97 per cent attended state schools. Around one in five drop out, but this is only slightly more than the funding council forecast, given the subject mix and entry qualifications. About half of the full-time students come from the West Midlands, many from ethnic minorities. UCE also has one of the largest

programmes of part-time courses in Britain, making it the biggest provider of higher education in the region. Students also enter through the network of 15 associated further education colleges, which run foundation and access programmes. Demand for places was up by 13 per cent at the start of 2005.

One of the university's best-known features is its Conservatoire, housed in part of Birmingham's smart convention centre. Courses from opera to world music have given it a reputation for innovation, which was recognised in an excellent rating for teaching. Most other teaching ratings were mediocre, however, although the teacher education courses produced the best scores among the former polytechnics in the Teacher Training Agency's performance indicators. Those for secondary teachers were bettered only by Oxford and Cambridge.

Art and design, education and health subjects registered the best scores for teaching quality. The university has been building up its portfolio of high-tech courses with degrees in communications and network engineering, electronic commerce, electronic systems and mechanical engineering systems.

UCE opted out of the first research

Perry Barr, Birmingham B42 2SU
T   0121-331 5595
E   recruitment@uce.ac.uk
W www.uce.ac.uk
U www.unionofstudents.com

The Times Rankings
Overall Ranking: 78
(2005 ranking: 87)

Teaching assessment:	96	(19.9)
Research assessment:	=84	(2.2)
Entry standards:	74	(235.6)
Student–staff ratio:	=38	(16.3)
Library/IT spend/student:	68	(£481)
Facilities spend/student:	=20	(£281)
Good honours:	50	(58.2%)
Graduate prospects:	60	(60.1%)
Expected completion rate:	76	(78.9%)

Edinburgh
Belfast
BIRMINGHAM •
Cardiff
London

assessment exercise – the only university to do so – as a statement of its priority for teaching. The last assessments showed improvement on 1996, but only art and design reached any of the top three grades. However, income from research contracts has been healthy throughout.

Seven campuses straggle across the city, but the majority of students are concentrated on the modern Perry Barr site three miles north of the city centre. The large teacher training centre moved there from the southern suburb of Edgbaston in 2001, and the university bought an adjacent 43-acre site to improve sporting provision, which was poorly positioned and inadequate for 25,000 students. The pavilion has added £4.5 million of sports and conference facilities.

A £21-million development is providing new teaching facilities for the Faculty of Health and Community Care and the Royal Centre for Defence Medicine. UCE has also joined with the Birmingham Children's Hospital to provide training for staff, from consultants to domestics, in the care of sick children.

The Institute of Art and Design, refurbished at a cost of £20 million, spreads further south to Bourneville, where it occupies part of the Cadbury village. It is the largest in Britain, and includes a school of jewellery in the city centre. The recent relocation of engineering and computing to the city's Millennium Point high-tech development provided a new focus for the university. Facilities in the £114-million Lottery-funded centre are open to the public.

University-owned accommodation is only guaranteed for some first years. But the high proportion of locally-based mature students and the relatively cheap and plentiful private sector housing make this less of a problem. Students have been critical of the union facilities, but the city's youth scene is highly rated.

Accommodation
Number of places and costs refer to 2005–06
University-provided places: 2,146
Percentage catered: 6.3%
Costs for catered accommodation: £71–£73 a week.
Costs for self-catered accommodation: £50–£80 a week; 75% of rooms under £66 a week.
Policy for first-year students: all first-years who have firmly accepted an offer by 31 May will be allocated a room in halls. Students living within relatively close commuting distance are excluded from this guarantee, but if sufficient places remain they will normally be allocated a room.
Policy for international students: guaranteed a room in the halls of residence for the duration of their course.
Contact: Accommodation@uce.ac.uk

Students

Undergraduates:	11,915	(6,660)
Postgraduates:	1,540	(2,415)
Mature students:	21.6%	
Overseas students:	9.2%	
Applications per place:	5.5	
From state-sector schools:	97.1%	
From working-class homes:	42.6%	

Tuition fees 2006 £3,000
See chapter 13 for bursary details.

Teaching Quality Assessments
From 1995 (top score 24):
22 art and design; education; health subjects.
21 business; economics.
20 architecture;
librarianship and information management;
nursing; town planning.
19 agriculture;
electrical and electronic engineering;
mechanical engineering.
18 building; land and property management;
sociology.

University of Central Lancashire

A big university at the heart of England's newest city, Central Lancashire does not dominate Preston to the extent that Cambridge or Durham do their cities, but students account for a sixth of the population during term time. The balance will shift much further in their favour if the university succeeds in its aim of expanding to 50,000 students by the end of the decade. The modern, town-centre campus has seen considerable development, as the university has doubled in size, and still the building continues. A £12-million Lottery-funded sports centre opened in 1999 followed by a 'knowledge park' for technology transfer the following year. A new computing and technology building opened in 2003 and £6 million is being spent on extending and refurbishing the students' union.

Amid the expansion, the university has revamped its pioneering credit accumulation and transfer system, allowing undergraduates to mix and match from a menu of more than 3,000 courses. Electives are used to broaden the curriculum, so that up to 11 per cent of students' time is spent on subjects outside their normal range. There is particular encouragement to include a language as part of the package, and more than 2,000 students do so. A growing proportion also take advantage of the numerous international exchange programmes, which are available in all subject areas. The university's website is even available in Chinese.

The former polytechnic has acquired a high reputation in some apparently unlikely fields. American studies and psychology both achieved perfect scores for teaching quality, followed more recently by education and nursing. Journalism, which also scored well, is sufficiently popular to be able to demand the equivalent of three Bs at A level. Astrophysics benefits from two observatories, including Britain's most powerful optical telescope. Although its teaching quality score was disappointing, it was one of the successes of the last research assessments. These were a definite improvement on 1996 but, apart from physics and astronomy, only history and law rated in the top three categories. New courses have been springing up in all areas, with recent examples including event management, television production and retail design.

The university took in an agricultural college at Newton Rigg, in Cumbria, in 1998 – its first excursion beyond Preston – and it is now involved in plans to bring more higher education to the county, which has never had a university of its own. Further education in land-based subjects is continuing at Newton Rigg and new

---

Preston PR1 2HE
T   01772 201201
E   cenquiries@uclan.ac.uk
W   www.uclan.ac.uk
U   www.yourunion.co.uk

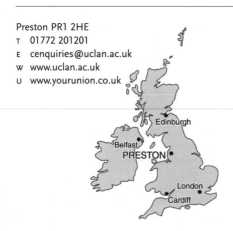

The Times Rankings
Overall Ranking: 86
(2005 ranking: 79)

Teaching assessment:	=78	(20.9)
Research assessment:	=84	(2.2)
Entry standards:	67	(249)
Student–staff ratio:	94	(22.8)
Library/IT spend/student:	86	(£406)
Facilities spend/student:	38	(£217)
Good honours:	=67	(52.8%)
Graduate prospects:	=77	(56.5%)
Expected completion rate:	=90	(73.3%)

programmes across a broader curriculum are being developed at degree and postgraduate level. A £3.5-million learning resources centre has been added and there are plans for an all-weather sports facility, a Centre for Outdoor Management and Training and a new building for the National School of Forestry.

A high proportion of Central Lancashire's students are local people in their twenties or thirties, many of whom come through the well-established lifelong learning networks run in colleges throughout the North West. No fewer than 14 per cent of the university's students are taught in colleges but, unlike some institutions involved in 'franchising', Central Lancashire has carried out a thorough review of the quality of its external programmes. Applications have been low for the number of places on offer, but there have been improvements recently, with another 8 per cent rise at the start of 2005. Even so, a quarter of all under-graduates enter through clearing. More than a third of the students come from working-class homes but over a quarter are projected to leave without a qualification – significantly more than the average for the subjects on offer.

The social scene in Preston may not compare with Manchester or Liverpool, but neither do the security risks and the cost of living is low. Both cities are within easy reach, and the student union's 'Feel'

club nights have won national recognition. Although still not the most fashionable university, Central Lancashire commands great loyalty among its students.

Rents for the 1,500 places in university accommodation are among the lowest in Britain and the new 60-acre Preston Sports Arena, built in partnership with the local authority, is among the best in any higher education institution. Three miles from the main campus, the centre is available to clubs throughout the region but there are reserved periods for students, who can also book at peak times.

Accommodation
Number of places and costs refer to 2005–06
University-provided places: 1,450
Percentage catered: 0%
Costs for catered accommodation: n/a
Costs for self-catered accommodation: £47–£70 a week.
Policy for first-year students: the Student Accommodation Service guarantees to help all first years find suitable accommodation either in university-managed housing or in the private sector. No restrictions for local students.
Policy for international students: as above.
Contact: saccommodation@uclan.ac.uk

Students

Undergraduates:	15,490	(10,010)
Postgraduates:	680	(2,025)
Mature students:	20.1%	
Overseas students:	13.5%	
Applications per place:	4.1	
From state-sector schools:	96.6%	
From working-class homes:	36.2%	

Tuition fees 2006 £3,000
See chapter 13 for bursary details.

Teaching Quality Assessments
From 1995 (top score 24):
24 American studies; education; nursing; psychology.
22 art and design; biological sciences; business; health subjects; linguistics; media studies; politics; tourism and leisure.
21 modern languages.
20 building; drama, dance and cinematics; general engineering.
19 history of art; mathematics; physics and astronomy.
18 agriculture; sociology.
15 electrical and electronic engineering.

City University

Once a college of advanced technology, a third of City students now study business, a third health subjects and a third study law, computing, engineering, journalism, and the arts. But the university has maintained its links with business, industry and the professions, reaping the benefits with consistently good graduate employment figures. Courses have a practical edge, and many of the staff hold professional, as well as academic, qualifications.

The university is still comparatively small despite consistent growth in the last five years, which has seen student numbers pass 13,000, including large contingents of postgraduates and part-timers. Numbers doubled during the 1990s, partly due to the incorporation of a nursing and midwifery college at nearby St Bartholomew's Hospital and the Charterhouse College of Radiography. Applications were up by almost 16 per cent at the start of 2005.

Development has taken place at the university's headquarters, on the borders of the City of London, but the most ambitious project has been a new £42-million home for the business school, in the financial district of the City of London. Opened in 2002, the new building, spread over eight floors, has doubled the school's usable space, enabling it to expand its academic activity and executive programmes. Another £20 million has gone into an impressive new building for the School of Social Sciences.

The business school is, not surprisingly, one of City's great strengths. It was the first Western university to forge links with the Bank of China, running an Executive MBA programme in Shanghai as the first step to a wider role in business education throughout southeast Asia.

The university had already boosted its legal provision by incorporating the Inns of Court School of Law. The new Institute of Law, which includes the university's original department, offers London's only 'one-stop shop' for legal training, from undergraduate to professional courses. City is also working with Queen Mary, University of London, in a range of subjects, starting with medicine and other health subjects, journalism and engineering.

City has a particularly high reputation in music, where it is associated with the Guildhall School of Music and Drama, with its teaching rated as excellent and research internationally outstanding. The subject achieved the university's only 5* rating in the 2001 Research Assessment Exercise, but arts policy, business, information science, law and optometry all reached the next grade.

Early teaching assessments were

Northampton Square,
London EC1V 0HB
T 0207-040 5060
E ugadmissions@city.ac.uk
W www.city.ac.uk
U www.cusuonline.org

The Times Rankings
Overall Ranking: 56
(2005 ranking: 55)

Teaching assessment:	=82	(20.7)
Research assessment:	=51	(4.4)
Entry standards:	43	(301.4)
Student–staff ratio:	=48	(17.0)
Library/IT spend/student:	83	(£415)
Facilities spend/student:	=71	(£157)
Good honours:	46	(59.3%)
Graduate prospects:	4	(79.7%)
Expected completion rate:	40	(86.9%)

Edinburgh
Belfast
Cardiff
LONDON

disappointing. The university's response was to establish an educational development unit to enhance the quality of teaching and launch a review of the effectiveness of personal tutoring. It set a target of 22 points out of 24 for each teaching assessment, a mark that has since been met by all but two subjects, which only narrowly missed out. There have been near-perfect scores in business and management, maths and statistics, and health subjects (language and communication science, optometry and radiography).

Recent additions to the portfolio of degrees include environmental engineering and Anglo-American law, while the journalism department is well regarded. There is also a flourishing sub-degree programme for adults, which ranges from sitcom writing to e-business. The changes have maintained City's position among the most popular universities in London, with nine applications per undergraduate place

Official performance indicators for higher education have brought mixed news: the drop-out rate has been falling but 13 per cent is still high for a traditional university. City has a good record among its peers for widening participation in higher education, with a third of all undergraduates from working-class homes. Students tend to be more concerned about their inability to afford the attractions of a trendy part of London. Most fall back on the extended

students' union, but this is usually shut at weekends for lack of demand for its facilities.

Accommodation

Number of places and costs refer to 2004–05
University-provided places: 1,191
Percentage catered: 0%
Costs for catered accommodation: n/a
Costs for self-catered accommodation: £89–£103 a week.
Policy for first-year students: guaranteed if an offer has been firmly accepted and accommodation has been applied for by 15 May, and the student is normally resident outside the Greater London area and is aged over 18 at time of residency.
Policy for international students: preference is given to overseas students arriving in the UK for the first time, but halls will have a mix of UK and international students.
Contact: accomm@city.ac.uk
www.city.ac.uk/accommodation

Students

Undergraduates:	6,200	(6,955)
Postgraduates:	3,045	(5,225)
Mature students:	17.9%	
Overseas students:	22.4%	
Applications per place:	7.9	
From state-sector schools:	99.5%	
From working-class homes:	33.2%	

Tuition fees 2006   £3,000
See chapter 13 for bursary details.

Teaching Quality Assessments
From 1995 (top score 24):
23 art and design; business and management; health subjects; mathematics.
22 economics.
21 electrical and electronic engineering; librarianship and information management; psychology.
20 nursing.
19 civil engineering; land management; mechanical engineering; media studies; sociology.

Coventry University

Coventry's origins go back to the foundation of the College of Design in 1843 and its links with the motor industry of the Midlands were reflected in its earlier title of Lanchester Polytechnic, named after a leading engineering figure. The campus of the university is close to the city centre, with all its departments within walking distance of each other. There has been an ambitious building plan after a decade in which student numbers doubled, reaching 20,000 in 2004 with 17,000 in Coventry itself. A new library, media and arts centre, technology park and enhanced student facilities, including additional accommodation and a second students' union building, are transforming the university.

The university's financial base is sound, its income more than doubling in the 1990s, but not all its recruitment targets were met. After recording its first deficit in 2000, the position was turned around the following year and the position has improved since. Although some class sizes increased, students have been benefiting from an innovative approach to computer-assisted learning, supported by an expanded computer network and the £20-million showpiece library, almost entirely naturally ventilated and lit. The old library has been renovated for nursing, midwifery, social work and health sciences staff. The university was chosen to house national centres of excellence in teaching for e-learning in health and social care, as well as in transport and product design. Degrees in automotive engineering and design courses have been developed in collaboration with the motor industry, both in Coventry and further afield.

A £7-million arts centre and the conversion of a former working men's club provides much needed space for the students' union with dedicated facilities for mature and international students. A £3.6-million centrally-located sports complex opened in January 2004. The university put £50,000 into sports scholarships for 56 students that year.

Its predominantly vocational curriculum has a strong sense of direction, and its IT and engineering courses have proved particularly popular with overseas students. A rough balance is maintained between arts, technology, business and health studies in order to preserve an all-round educational environment. The majority of students exercise their right to take 'free choice modules' that cover the full range of university provision, with IT skills and languages particularly popular. Coventry has been building up its portfolio of courses, having introduced eye-catching degrees in subjects such as disaster

---

Priory Street, Coventry CV1 5FB
T   024-7688 7688
E   info.reg@coventry.ac.uk
W   www.coventry.ac.uk
U   www.cusu.org

The Times Rankings
Overall Ranking: 88
(2005 ranking: 82)

Teaching assessment:	=82	(20.7)
Research assessment:	88	(2.1)
Entry standards:	=79	(226.6)
Student–staff ratio:	=81	(20.3)
Library/IT spend/student:	58	(£503)
Facilities spend/student:	37	(£219)
Good honours:	96	(42.9%)
Graduate prospects:	59	(60.3%)
Expected completion rate:	64	(81.7%)

management, forensic chemistry, criminology and boat design. The vocational slant of its courses ensures that the university always enjoys a healthy graduate employment rate.

Teaching ratings were good, with history and politics, economics, health subjects and mathematics achieving near-perfect scores, following early successes for geography and mechanical engineering. Business and art and design, two of the biggest areas of the university, were close behind, as was the growing field of nursing. Research grades improved considerably in the 2001 assessment exercise, but only design, materials and politics reached any of the top three categories. Design should benefit further from a revolutionary £1.6-million digital modelling workshop, sponsored by the Bugatti Trust, which will provide full-scale vehicle modelling facilities for undergraduates as well as researchers.

Dr Mike Goldstein, the last Vice-Chancellor, claimed that a 'quiet revolution' had taken place in recent years, and the university was highly confident in taking new initiatives. As well as the bricks and mortar, this has meant measures such as the introduction of tangible rewards for excellent teaching and further development of electronic learning. Almost 40 per cent of the undergraduates have working-class backgrounds and the 18 per cent projected dropout rate is better than the benchmark figure for the university, which takes account of entry qualifications and the mix of subjects.

More than most universities, Coventry is a creature of its city, and the civic-minded approach of the university has created many town–gown links. The main buildings open out from the ruins of the bombed cathedral, as university and public facilities mingle in the city. Student residences are within easy walking distance of the campus and city centre. Students welcome the relatively low cost of living in Coventry, and, as at most new universities, the student body encompasses a wide range of ages.

Accommodation

Number of places and costs refer to 2005–06
University-provided places: 2,357
Percentage catered: 25.5%
Costs for catered accommodation: £86 a week (10 meals).
Costs for self-catered accommodation: £47.00–£79.50 a week.
Policy for first-year students: guaranteed offer of accommodation to all first years, in university-owned or managed accommodation, on condition that Coventry is first choice (CF or UF on UCAS form), and that the application is submitted by 31 May.
Policy for international students: international students are given priority.
Contact: accomm.ss@coventry.ac.uk
www.coventry.ac.uk/accommodation

Students

Undergraduates:	10,920	(4,605)
Postgraduates:	1,235	(1,600)
Mature students:	21.9%	
Overseas students:	15.6%	
Applications per place:	4.8	
From state-sector schools:	95.7%	
From working-class homes:	39.5%	

Tuition fees 2006 £3,000
See chapter 13 for bursary details.

Teaching Quality Assessments

From 1995 (top score 24):
23 economics; health subjects; history; mathematics; politics.
22 art and design; building; business and management; nursing.
21 agriculture; hospitality; modern languages; psychology; sociology.
19 biological sciences; civil engineering; town planning.
18 electrical and electronic engineering; media studies; aeronautical and manufacturing engineering.

De Montfort University

Like the 13th-century Earl of Leicester, after whom the university is named, De Montfort had a fiefdom of sorts: in this case a network of campuses in a 50-mile radius. Based on what was Leicester Polytechnic, the new university spread ever outwards, making it the biggest in the region. But the closure of the Milton Keynes outpost in 2003, following the transfer of campuses in Lincolnshire to Lincoln University, signalled an unexpected end to the process. DMU is now putting £50 million into consolidating a more manageable estate.

There will soon be only three campuses: one in Bedford and two in Leicester, following the relocation of health and life sciences to the university's Leicester headquarters. Bedford's Polhill campus will house the Faculty of Education and Contemporary Studies, adding sports science, management, performing arts and social work to its traditional teacher training and physical education. Another 12 colleges are associates, linked into the university's network and offering its courses. A formal agreement commits the colleges, which stretch from North Oxfordshire to Grantham, to work with each other as well as with De Montfort.

The university has an uncompromisingly vocational emphasis in its courses, but has also invested in research. The approach paid off in the 2001 Research Assessment Exercise, when DMU registered the highest proportion of subjects of any new university in the top three categories. Politics and English were only one grade off the top of the seven-point scale, while the total of 11 subjects on the next grade was easily the highest among the former polytechnics.

Teaching ratings were patchy in the early rounds of assessment, with only one excellent grade in the first 11 attempts. But there was marked improvement in the later years of the system, with politics and international studies achieving full marks and the sport and leisure courses only one mark short of the maximum. The professional accounting courses were awarded 'premier' status in a worldwide accreditation scheme and the university has been chosen to house a national teaching centre for drama, dance and theatre studies.

De Montfort's range of programmes has been expanding and student enrolments are healthy but the drop-out rate remains high, with more than a quarter of students projected to transfer to other courses or leave without a qualification in the last published figures. The university is abandoning semesters and going back to a three-term year, partly because it believes the prospect of imminent assessment

---

The Gateway,
Leicester LE1 9BH
T   0645 454647 (Enquiry Centre)
E   enquiry@dmu.ac.uk
W   www.dmu.ac.uk
U   www.mydsu.com

The Times Rankings
Overall Ranking: 89
(2005 ranking: 81)

Teaching assessment:	=78	(20.9)
Research assessment:	60	(3.1)
Entry standards:	82	(225)
Student–staff ratio:	71	(18.8)
Library/IT spend/student:	59	(£501)
Facilities spend/student:	90	(£126)
Good honours:	100	(39.7%)
Graduate prospects:	72	(57.7%)
Expected completion rate:	=82	(77%)

encouraged some students to give up at Christmas in their first year. De Montfort has a proud record for widening access to higher education with 43 per cent of students coming from working-class homes. It was one of the first to set up an employment agency to help students find part-time work during their course of study, as well as find careers upon graduation. There are strong links with local business and industry, which manifest themselves in courses such as the BSc in media production, produced in conjunction with the BBC.

Inevitably, the quality of student life varies widely among the different campuses, but technology ensures that everyone has access to the same academic support and resources. Not surprisingly, Leicester, which has by far the largest concentration of students, also has the best facilities. Over £100 million is being spent on the main campus area, some of it by the city council and local businesses. The investment includes a £9 million campus centre, which opened in September 2003, incorporating a new students' union, music venue and other facilities. Part of the ring road is being diverted to allow the university to open up the 15th-century Magazine Gateway building, which will become the focal point of a university quarter with public open spaces and new links to the city centre.

A £6-million library opened in Bedford in 2001, and redevelopment there will include more residential accommodation, a campus centre building and two gyms. Students should find it easier to relate to the reduced scale of De Montfort. Accommodation difficulties have been addressed, with five new halls of residence opening in 2003. All first years, apart from locals, are now guaranteed a residential place.

Accommodation
Number of places and costs refer to 2004–05
University-provided places: 2,514 (Leicester), 361 (Bedford)
Percentage catered: 0% (Leicester), 79% (Bedford)
Costs for catered accommodation: £76 for meals Monday to Friday (Bedford).
Costs for self-catered accommodation: £67.50–£82.00 (Leicester) and £65 (Bedford) a week.
Policy for first-year students: First years are guaranteed accommodation. First years having a home address with local postcodes for either Leicester or Bedford or who are over 23 are not allocated housing, but can apply if there are exceptional circumstances.
Policy for international students: guaranteed accommodation.
Contact: studenthousing@dmu.ac.uk

Students

Undergraduates:	13,910	(4,280)
Postgraduates:	1,205	(2,710)
Mature students:	15.2%	
Overseas students:	5.2%	
Applications per place:	4.7	
From state-sector schools:	96.5%	
From working-class homes:	43.0%	

Tuition fees 2006	£3,000

See chapter 13 for bursary details.

Teaching Quality Assessments
From 1995 (top score 24):
24 politics.
23 hospitality, leisure and tourism; land management; sports science.
22 drama, dance and cinematics; nursing; psychology.
21 art and design; biological sciences; history of art; pharmacy; town planning.
20 building; education; health subjects; mathematics and statistics; media studies.
19 electrical and electronic engineering; general engineering; materials technology.
17 sociology.

University of Derby

Derby sees itself as a prototype for the modern university, providing courses at all levels from the age of 16 into retirement. Although not as extensive as the original plans for spanning further and higher education in the same institution, a merger with High Peak College and the subsequent creation of the University of Derby College Buxton have stayed true to the model. While accepting that Derby will never scale the heights in league tables such as ours, the university set itself the target of becoming the pre-eminent university of its type by 2020. Its yardsticks are student satisfaction, employability and cost-effectiveness.

As the only higher education college promoted to university status with the polytechnics, Derby had to run to keep up with its peers in its early days. Student numbers doubled in four years, the residential stock increased fivefold and extra teaching space was built. The pace of expansion inevitably imposed strains, and at one time Derby was the only university with two Unsatisfactory verdicts in the teaching assessments. Although still not spectacular, scores improved subsequently. Indeed, a failure in pharmacy turned into maximum points on re-inspection after provision was rationalised. Business and theology also scored well, as did biosciences and other health subjects before them.

The university takes pride in its record for widening access: almost all the undergraduates are state-educated and four in ten are from working-class homes. The 20 per cent projected dropout rate is lower than in previous years and slightly better than the national average for the subjects and entry qualifications found at Derby.

Development is still continuing, with an £8-million art and design campus due to open in September 2005, bringing together courses presently spread around three different sites. The college already has a new home in the centre of Buxton, where the purchase of the Devonshire Royal Hospital for a nominal fee has provided an ideal centre for courses in tourism and hospitality management, as well as further education programmes. The landmark building, which has a bigger dome than St Paul's Cathedral, will house a 4-star training hotel and health spa, in addition to academic facilities.

There were six sites already – the legacy of a series of mergers in the 1970s and 1980s. The Kedleston Road site, two miles north of the city centre, is the largest, catering for most of the main subjects as well as the students' union headquarters. The Mickleover campus, which specialises in education and health, is also in a suburban location, while art and design

---

Kedleston Road,
Derby DE22 1GB
T   01332 622289
E   admissions@derby.ac.uk
W   www.derby.ac.uk
U   www.udsu-online.co.uk

Edinburgh
Belfast
DERBY
London
Cardiff

The Times Rankings
Overall Ranking: 96
(2005 ranking: 95)

Teaching assessment:	97	(19.8)
Research assessment:	=97	(1.5)
Entry standards:	90	(207.8)
Student–staff ratio:	79	(20.1)
Library/IT spend/student:	=38	(£576)
Facilities spend/student:	=82	(£140)
Good honours:	81	(50.4%)
Graduate prospects:	61	(60.0%)
Expected completion rate:	75	(79.2%)

have had smaller, more central sites. There are plans for a multifaith centre on the Kedleston Road campus, which has attracted the support of the Prince of Wales.

Courses are modular and a foundation programme allows students to begin work at a partner college before transferring to the university. Distance learning is a growth area either online or through Derby's nine regional centres. Prospective students can even sample a virtual open evening. Business and management is by far the biggest academic area, but work placements are encouraged in all subjects. The accent on employability continues with an eight-week course on key skills such as CV preparation and interview technique. Derby has also been in the forefront of the adoption of new teaching methods, pioneering the use of interactive video for a national scheme. A variety of courses, from foundation degrees to postgraduate qualifications, are available online.

The university has spent £30 million in five years to maintain its guarantee of accommodation for all first years. Students seem to appreciate the university's efforts because it comes out well in satisfaction surveys. There was a 6 per cent increase in applications at the start of 2005, although the decline in the previous year was one of the largest at any university.

Accommodation
Number of places and costs refer to 2004–05
University-provided places: 2,350
Percentage catered: 0%
Costs for catered accommodation: n/a
Costs for self-catered accommodation: £38.71 (twin room); £39.83 (standard single, 5-day option); £54.18–£61.60 (standard single); £73.50 (en suite single) a week; all costs inclusive of utilities and energy costs based on 39-week agreements.
Policy for first-year students: all new students who wish to live in halls will be accepted; priority is given to international students or those with special needs.
Policy for international students: policy as above; priority given to new students.
Contact: Accommodation@derby.ac.uk

Students

Undergraduates:	8,360	(2,505)
Postgraduates:	490	(1,820)
Mature students:	24.2%	
Overseas students:	4.9%	
Applications per place:	5.8	
From state-sector schools:	97.2%	
From working-class homes:	40.5%	

Tuition fees 2006	£3,000

See chapter 13 for bursary details.

Teaching Quality Assessments
From 1995 (top score 24):
24 pharmacy.
22 biological sciences; business; education; health subjects; theology and religious studies.
21 American studies; hospitality; mathematics; psychology.
20 art and design.
19 civil engineering; electrical and electronic engineering; history of art; nursing.
18 drama, dance and cinematics; modern languages; sociology.
17 media studies.

University of Dundee

Dundee describes itself as 'Scotland's most enterprising university' and, while there would be other claimants to that title, it has certainly been among the liveliest in recent years. The message appears to be getting through to prospective students: there was a 17 per cent increase in applications at the start of 2005, building on rises of more than 10 per cent in each of the previous two years. Already on a roll after a series of good quality ratings and the acquisition of education, nursing and art colleges, which increased its scope and size, the university has also extended its horizons by going into partnership with St Andrews. Merger is not on the agenda, but the pooling of areas of excellence has begun with two postgraduate programmes and a joint degree in microelectronics and photonics. Working groups are examining the potential for collaboration in five areas, from engineering to art history, with the intention of developing more teaching and research links over the next two years.

The initiative predated the arrival of a new Principal, Sir Alan Langlands, who is equally determined to build up Dundee's industrial links. Dundee has doubled its student population in recent years and is challenging Scotland's elite universities in a growing number of areas. The university now has 17,000 students, including a healthy number from overseas, and is looking outwards to achieve the 'critical mass' which experts regard as essential to break into the higher education elite.

Dundee is best known for the life sciences, where research into cancer and diabetes is recognised as world-class. The university is leading an international initiative with the other Scottish medical schools aiming to take advantage of new technology and e-learning in the training of future doctors. The medical school won a Queen's Anniversary Prize in 1998, as well as an excellent rating for teaching and a 5* research grade for clinical laboratory sciences in the latest research assessments. Work on a new clinical research centre began in 2004. Set in 20 acres of parkland, the medical school is the one of several components of the university outside the compact city-centre campus – some of the nursing and midwifery students are 35 miles away in Kirkcaldy, and education and social work are located at the former Northern College campus, two miles outside the centre.

Biochemistry is the flagship department, moving into the £13-million Wellcome Trust Building in 1997. Its academics were the first in Britain to be invited to take part in Japan's Human Frontier science programme and are now the most-quoted

---

Nethergate,
Dundee DD1 4HN
T 01382 344160
E srs@dundee.ac.uk
W www.dundee.ac.uk
U www.dusa.dundee.ac.uk

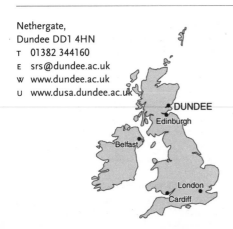

The Times Rankings		
Overall Ranking: 25		
(2005 ranking: 28)		
Teaching assessment:	1	(23.5)
Research assessment:	=34	(5.1)
Entry standards:	35	(324.1)
Student–staff ratio:	=13	(13.5)
Library/IT spend/student:	69	(£478)
Facilities spend/student:	67	(£162)
Good honours:	38	(63.3%)
Graduate prospects:	23	(68.7%)
Expected completion rate:	=86	(76.2%)

researchers in their field. The biological sciences won Dundee's other 5* research rating, while six more subjects were on the next rung of the research assessment ladder, leaving half of the university's researchers in departments rated in the top two categories.

Teaching ratings have been almost uniformly impressive, with only philosophy judged less than Highly Satisfactory. Vocational degrees predominate, helping to produce the university's consistently good graduate employment record. The law department is the only one on either side of the border to offer both Scots and English law. The highly-rated design courses are taught at the former Duncan of Jordanstone College of Art.

There has been an emphasis on opportunities for women ever since Dundee's separation from St Andrews University in 1967. The incorporation of Northern College's local arm will increase the female majority in the university, adding teacher education to the portfolio of courses. The Royal Bank of Scotland is funding a more general access initiative, which enables 100 students from poor backgrounds to attend a university summer school and provides 25 of them with £1,000-a-year bursaries.

Two thirds of Dundee's students are from Scotland and nearly one in ten from Northern Ireland. More than 20 per cent come from an area with little tradition of higher education and almost 34 per cent from working-class homes – both figures much higher than the UK average for the subjects on offer. They enjoy a welcoming atmosphere and a cost of living which is lower than in most university cities. Private accommodation is plentiful for those who are not housed by the university. New students even have their own website. The city is profiting from recent regeneration programmes and becoming more fashionable. Spectacular mountain and coastal scenery are close at hand, but social life tends to be concentrated on the students' union, which is one of the largest in Scotland.

Accommodation
Number of places and costs refer to 2005–06
University-provided places: 1,293
Percentage catered: 0%
Costs for catered accommodation: n/a
Costs for self-catered accommodation: £47.25–£94.01 a week.
Policy for first-year students: entrant students guaranteed accommodation if they apply by 31 July for 10 September entry. No restrictions for local students.
Policy for international students: entrant students guaranteed accommodation if they apply by 31 July for 10 September entry.
Contact: residences@dundee.ac.uk
www.dundee.ac.uk/residences

Students

Undergraduates:	8,685	(3,650)
Postgraduates:	940	(3,185)
Mature students:	18.5%	
Overseas students:	15.3%	
Applications per place:	5.5	
From state-sector schools:	91.7%	
From working-class homes:	33.9%	

Teaching Quality Assessments
1994–97 Rated Excellent:
biological sciences; English;
finance and accounting;
graphic and textile design; medicine;
psychology.
1994–97 Rated Highly Satisfactory:
civil engineering; dentistry;
environmental science; fine art; history;
hospitality studies; law; mathematics; physics;
politics; social work; statistics.
From 1998:
21 planning and landscape.

See page 245 for recent assessments.

University of Durham

Long established as a leading alternative to Oxford and Cambridge, Durham even delays selection to accommodate those applying to the ancient universities. A collegiate structure and picturesque setting add to the Oxbridge feel, attracting a largely middle-class student body. However, although a third of undergraduates come from independent schools, the university is attracting more applicants from non-traditional backgrounds. Those who receive offers without interview are invited to a special open day to see if Durham is the university for them. Since around 80 per cent come from outside the North East of England, most are seeing the small cathedral city for the first time. The proportion of regional students is much higher at the Stockton campus.

Applications are made to one of the 14 colleges, all of which are mixed since the decision of St Mary's to abandon its women-only tradition from 2004. They range in size from 300 to 900 students and are the focal point of social life, although all teaching is done in central departments. A new 400-bed college is due to open in 2006. There are significant differences in atmosphere and student profile, ranging from the historic University College, in Durham Castle, to modern buildings on the outskirts of the city.

Winning a place is far from easy – entrance requirements are among the highest in Britain – but the dropout rate of 2 per cent is also among the lowest in any university. Six subjects (chemistry, applied mathematics, geography, law, English and history) reached the pinnacle of the last research assessment exercise, and 14 others were considered nationally outstanding. Most of the teaching ratings have also produced high scores. Biological sciences, physics and chemistry are particularly strong on the science side; history, philosophy, economics and theology among the stars of the arts. A £3-million grant to establish a centre for fundamental physics should place Durham at the forefront of world research on the structure of the universe.

Durham is generally quite traditional. Wherever possible, teaching takes place in small groups and most assessment is by written examination. However, the establishment of the Queen's Campus, in Stockton-on-Tees, broke the mould of tradition. Initially a joint venture with Teesside University, Stockton is now Durham's own venture into community education. Entry standards are 240 points at A level, compared with an average of 320 for the main university, and subjects such as business, primary education and psychology

University Office,
Old Elvet, Durham DH1 3HP
T   0191-374 2000
E   admissions.office@durham.ac.uk
W   www.durham.ac.uk
U   www.dsu.org.uk

The Times Rankings
Overall Ranking: =10
(2005 ranking: 8)

Teaching assessment:	=20	(22.2)
Research assessment:	=10	(5.7)
Entry standards:	6	(426.1)
Student–staff ratio:	=31	(15.6)
Library/IT spend/student:	14	(£724)
Facilities spend/student:	11	(£313)
Good honours:	12	(72.3%)
Graduate prospects:	=24	(68.6%)
Expected completion rate:	3	(97.7%)

have helped broaden the university's intake.

The Stockton campus has also seen the fulfilment of Durham's long-held ambition to restore the medical education it lost when Newcastle University went its own way more than 35 years ago. In another joint project, this time with Newcastle, 95 students will do the first two years of their training on Teesside, concentrating on community medicine before transferring to Newcastle to complete their training.

Medicine has added to the 80 subjects available at degree level. Undergraduates are also offered a variety of generalist 'free elective' modules, such as environmental economics and personal language learning. The aim is to make Durham graduates even more employable.

The university dominates the city of Durham to an extent to which sometimes causes resentment, but adds considerably to the local economy. For those looking for nightlife, or just a change of scene, Newcastle is a short train journey away. Sports facilities are excellent, and Durham is among the premier universities in national competitions. The university's teams were champions in cricket, rowing and rugby union in 2004. Among the alumni are the former England cricket captain, Nasser Hussain, and rugby World Cup winner, Will Greenwood. The university hosts one of England's centres for cricketing excellence.

Accommodation

Number of places and costs refer to 2005-06
University-provided places: 5,689
Percentage catered: 88%
Costs for catered accommodation: £3,552
(3 terms, Durham)
Costs for self-catered accommodation: £2,442
(3 terms, Stockton).
Policy for first-year students: all full-time students become a member of one of the university's colleges or societies. St Cuthbert's Society may offer membership without accommodation. No restrictions based on home address.
Policy for international students: normally all first-year and final-year international students are offered a place in college-owned accommodation.
Contact: admissions@durham.ac.uk

Students

Undergraduates:	10,380	(385)
Postgraduates:	2,190	(2,360)
Mature students:	4.7%	
Overseas students:	4.8%	
Applications per place:	6.9	
From state-sector schools:	68.4%	
From working-class homes:	15.1%	

Tuition fees 2006 £3,000
See chapter 13 for bursary details.

Teaching Quality Assessments

From 1995 (top score 24):
24 biological sciences; economics; philosophy; physics.
23 archaeology; education; health subjects; psychology; theology.
22 engineering; French; German;
Middle Eastern and African studies; politics.
21 classics and ancient history;
mathematics and statistics; sociology.
20 Italian; Russian.
16 Iberian languages.

University of East Anglia

UEA is best known for its star-studded creative writing course and extensive art collections, but some of the broad subject combinations which the university pioneered from its origins in the 1960s are equally highly regarded in the academic world. Development studies and environmental sciences are two such areas, which have attracted top ratings for teaching and research.

The university is engaged in an ambitious building programme, which will allow its residential stock to keep pace with the expansion in student numbers and has added extensive new sports facilities. Other recent developments on the 320-acre campus just outside Norwich have included 400 more en suite student bedrooms and academic buildings for the new School of Medicine, Health Policy and Practice. Health studies have been among UEA's fastest-developing areas, and the university has achieved its ultimate ambition with the establishment of one of the first new medical schools for 20 years. More than 110 students were in the first intake in September 2002 and demand for places has continued to rise. The addition of a pharmacy degree is the latest element of the health blueprint.

With successive 5* ratings for research and an excellent teaching grade, environmental sciences is the flagship school. The Climatic Research Unit is among the leaders in the investigation of global warming, and UEA also hosts the Government-funded Tyndall Centre for Climate Change Research, which brings together scientists, economists, social scientists and engineers in nine institutions. History and film studies added to the 5* research grades in 2001.

Philosophy and politics joined American studies as the top performers in the teaching assessments. Like the English degrees, one of which includes creative writing, American studies is heavily oversubscribed. With authors Michelle Roberts and Patricia Duncker taking up where Andrew Motion, the Poet Laureate, and the late Malcolm Bradbury left off, the attraction of creative writing for both undergraduates and postgraduates remains undimmed. Art history is another strong subject, aided by the presence of the Sainsbury Centre for the Visual Arts, perhaps the greatest resource of its type on any British campus. The centre houses a priceless collection of modern and tribal art, in a building designed by Lord (Norman) Foster.

Almost nine out of ten undergraduates come from state schools or colleges, but only just over one in five has a working-

---

University Plain
Norwich NR4 7TJ
T 01603 592216
E admissions@uea.ac.uk
W www.uea.ac.uk
U www.stu.uea.ac.uk

Edinburgh

Belfast

NORWICH
London

Cardiff

class background. Since 1999, most have had the opportunity of work experience as part of their course. An academic adviser guides students on their options under the modular course system and monitors their progress right through to graduation.

Most UEA students come from outside the region, despite the presence of unusually large numbers of mature students for a traditional university. However, the university reaches some 3,500 local people with its programme of evening and day courses at 50 locations in Norfolk and Suffolk. A blip in the projected dropout rate was more than reversed in the latest official figures. Only 7 per cent of students who started courses in 2001 are expected to leave without the qualification they originally sought – significantly less than the national average for the subjects on offer.

The number of university-owned beds has increased considerably in recent years, ensuring that most first years can still be guaranteed accommodation. Sporting facilities are excellent: a £17.5-million sports park, with an Olympic-size swimming pool and climbing wall, opened in 2000, and the university was chosen as the base for the English Institute of Sport in the East, developing a sports science network for the region.

The university is situated in parkland, formerly a golf course, on the outskirts of the medieval city of Norwich, which can boast a pub for every day of the year. Rail links to London can be slow but have been improving, while Norwich airport offers flights through Amsterdam to worldwide connections.

Accommodation

Number of places and costs refer to 2005–06
University-provided places: 3,400
Percentage catered: 0%
Costs for catered accommodation: n/a
Costs for self-catered accommodation: £50.19 and £54.39 (standard single); £70.56 and £81.69 (en suite single); £73.22 (two-person flat) a week.
Policy for first-year students: all home and EU first-year students guaranteed accommodation for one academic year if the offer of a place has been accepted by the deadline date. Those living within 12 miles of UEA are not offered a place until all guaranteed students accepting accommodation have been housed.
Policy for international students: overseas for fees students are guaranteed accommodation for the whole of their course provided they apply each year when requested to do so.
Contact: accom@uea.ac.uk
www.uea.ac.uk/accom

Students		
Undergraduates:	6,905	(3,805)
Postgraduates:	2,010	(1,430)
Mature students:	15.7%	
Overseas students:	9.9%	
Applications per place:	5.6	
From state-sector schools:	88.5%	
From working-class homes:	21.4%	

Tuition fees 2006 £3,000
See chapter 13 for bursary details.

Teaching Quality Assessments
From 1995 (top score 24):
24 American studies; philosophy; politics.
23 business and management; economics; mathematics and statistics; communication and media studies; health subjects.
22 biological sciences; history of art.
21 drama, dance and cinematics.
19 education; electrical and electronic engineering; modern languages.
18 nursing.
16 sociology.

University of East London

East London's £40-million Docklands campus, which opened in 1999, offered a new lease of life to a university which had struggled to recapture the sparkle it had as a pioneering polytechnic. It should be complete by 2006, with student residences and recreational facilities side by side with academic buildings in a prize-winning waterside development for more than 7,000 students. The campus has helped UEL to 7 per cent increases in both 2004 and 2005.

The capital's first new campus for 50 years, which borders on London City Airport, has given the university a new focal point, with its modern version of traditional university features like cloisters and squares. Students of fashion, fine art, graphic design, product design, media and cultural studies were first into the futuristic premises near the Thames, which also houses a technology centre promoting links with local business and industry. UEL's highly-rated School of Architecture and the Visual Arts moved to the site in 2004 and were to be joined by electrical and manufacturing engineering in 2005.

The university's original campus in Stratford is also being redeveloped, with a new Learning Resource Centre, science labs, and facilities for part-time and evening courses. The London Foot Hospital, housing the university's podiatric students,

was due to open in 2005, with student residences and a computer centre next on the development plan. The Barking campus will close in 2005 to be replaced by a lifelong learning centre run in partnership with the neighbouring further education college and local council. Courses currently based at Barking will move to the Stratford or Docklands campuses.

With research in media studies judged to be nationally outstanding and sociology and art and design on the next grade, UEL was among the leading new universities in the latest research assessments. However, teaching assessments were patchy, largely accounting for the university's low position in our rankings, despite a requirement for all new lecturers to take a teaching qualification if they do not already have one. Psychology did well, and both English and architecture achieved excellent ratings in the early rounds of assessment, but communication and media studies and electrical and electronic engineering both registered unusually low scores. Electrical and electronic engineering did better in a more recent assessment, when environmental sciences and law were also highly rated. Teacher training courses, too, were given good marks by the Office for Standards in Education.

UEL's mission is more concerned with

Romford Road,
London E15 4LZ
T 020-8223 2835
E admiss@uel.ac.uk
W www.uel.ac.uk
U www.uelsu.net

The Times Rankings
Overall Ranking: 99
(2004 ranking: 98)

Teaching assessment:	100	(19.3)
Research assessment:	=76	(2.5)
Entry standards:	97	(181.1)
Student–staff ratio:	85	(20.6)
Library/IT spend/student:	42	(£570)
Facilities spend/student:	9	(£337)
Good honours:	97	(42.2%)
Graduate prospects:	=91	(53.4%)
Expected completion rate:	98	(65.1%)

extending access to higher education than competing with the elite universities. Barely more than half of the new first year intake now arrive with A levels and a majority are over 21 on entry – many choosing to start courses in February, as 800 students did in 2004. Most degrees are vocational and employers are closely involved in course planning. The university has pioneered a work-based learning initiative, offering accredited placements with local employers.

More than four out of ten UEL students come from working-class homes, many from the area's large ethnic minority population. A successful mentoring scheme for black and Asian students has become a model for other institutions. A Widening Participation Unit provides advice and guidance sessions for people considering returning to education. The university is also strong on provision for disabled students, who can share their experiences with others worldwide through the new Rix Centre for Innovation and Learning Disability. However, only two universities had a worse projected dropout rate in the funding councils' most recent survey, with almost three out of ten not expected to finish their degree. Graduate employment rates have also been relatively poor, but the university is working to improve both retention and employability through its innovative Skillzone programme.

University-owned accommodation is not plentiful for the number of students but it represents good value for London and, because many choose to live at home, all first years who request accommodation are housed. The social mix means that UEL has not been the place to look for the archetypal partying student lifestyle, although the new campus is beginning to change this. A new students' union facility, housed in a restored Victorian building opened in 2003. There are some sports facilities on all three campuses, including a 30-metre swimming pool at Barking, where full membership of the centre costs students £108 a year.

Accommodation
Number of places and costs refer to 2004–05
University-provided places: 1,500
Percentage catered: 0%
Costs for catered accommodation: n/a
Costs for self-catered accommodation:
51.50–£82.00 a week.
Policy for first-year students: Accommodation guaranteed to first year students provided that the application, together with any required fees, is received by 1 September.
Policy for international students: same as for first years.
Contact: Docklands Campus 020 8223 5093/4
Stratford Campus 020 8223 5524/5525.

Students

Undergraduates:	7,540	(2,625)
Postgraduates:	1,410	(2,730)
Mature students:	50.1%	
Overseas students:	15.4%	
Applications per place:	3.8	
From state-sector schools:	97.4%	
From working-class homes:	43.3%	

Tuition fees 2006   £3,000
See chapter 13 for bursary details.

Teaching Quality Assessments
From 1995 (top score 24):
23 psychology.
21 art and design; civil engineering.
20 economics; health subjects.
19 biological sciences;
drama, dance and cinematics; education;
pharmacy; sociology.
18 mechanical engineering;
modern languages.
16 media studies.
15 electrical and electronic engineering.

University of Edinburgh

Edinburgh retains a special status in Scotland, where the university is regarded as the nearest thing to Oxbridge north of the border. The university dropped out of our top ten for the first time last year, but it has now regained its previous position. The inclusion of new teaching scores has helped win a top five place, overtaking St Andrews to become the top university in Scotland.

Like Oxbridge, Edinburgh has been trying to widen its intake, especially since the arrival of Professor Tim O'Shea as Principal, the first non-Scot to hold the office in modern times. More than £1 million is going into access bursaries of £1,000 a year, with hopes of increasing the number beyond the initial 100 awards in due course. Other measures include an eight-week summer school for teenagers from Lothian schools and a mentoring programme. The university has always attracted a high proportion of middle-class candidates – many from England – and is a favourite in independent schools, whose students take about a third of the places. New selection guidelines aim to look more broadly at candidates' potential, reducing minimum entry requirements and placing more weight on references and personal statements. The measures appeared to have an instant impact, with a 14 per cent increase in applications – among the biggest at any university – by the start of 2004. There was almost as big a rise 12 months later, when several Scottish universities saw applications decline. There are plans for a 40 per cent increase in overseas students, who already number more than 2,000, testifying to Edinburgh's reputation.

The university raised a £40 million investment bond to ensure long-term financial stability, and carried out limited restructuring, abandoning some subjects and cutting staff, but making investment in new buildings and extra posts in selected areas. First to go were degree courses in agriculture, which transferred to Aberdeen. The university has also stepped up its fundraising activities, which have already produced a new Medical Research Centre. A second review was launched early in 2005.

The incorporation of Moray House, whose Holyrood site houses education, made Edinburgh the largest university in Scotland, now with more than 21,000 students. Yet, despite the new approach to selection, entry standards remain among the highest in Britain, whether in A levels or Highers. The university's buildings are scattered around the city, but most border the historic Old Town. The science and engineering campus is two miles to the south.

Old College, South Bridge,
Edinburgh EH8 9YL
T 0131-650 4360
E rals.enquiries@ed.ac.uk
W www.ed.ac.uk
U www.eusa.ed.ac.uk

The Times Rankings
Overall Ranking: 5
(2005 ranking: 13)

Teaching assessment:	4	(23.0)
Research assessment:	=16	(5.6)
Entry standards:	11	(403.6)
Student–staff ratio:	=15	(14.0)
Library/IT spend/student:	8	(£901)
Facilities spend/student:	33	(£231)
Good honours:	6	(77.2%)
Graduate prospects:	=31	(66.9%)
Expected completion rate:	21	(92.4%)

EDINBURGH

Belfast

London

Cardiff

The last research assessments showed a big improvement on a disappointing outcome in 1996, when only two subjects reached the top grade. This time, nine were awarded the coveted 5* and another 19 achieved grade 5, accounting for three quarters of those entered for the exercise. The 15 subjects rated as Excellent for teaching already amounted to the biggest haul in Scotland. Despite having to settle for Highly Satisfactory in its teaching assessment, medicine is a traditional strength and the law faculty is the largest north of the border. The university enjoys a reputation for high quality across the board.

Departments organise visiting days in October for those thinking of applying and in the spring for those holding offers. There is also an annual open day in June. New students join one of three Colleges, which are divided into 21 Schools, and generally take three subjects in both their first and second years. Every student has a Director of Studies to help them narrow down the selection of a final degree and give personal advice when necessary.

Considerable sums have been spent making the university more accessible to the 1,200 disabled students, who can also call on the services of a disability office. All students are issued with a smart card for access to university facilities, which can be loaded with money to pay for a variety of goods and services. The students' union operates on several sites and sports facilities are excellent.

The city is a treasure-trove of cultural and recreational opportunities, even away from the Festival period. Most students thrive on Edinburgh life, even though the cost of living can make it difficult to do it justice. Some scientists complain of isolation, although there is a regular bus link with George Square. The plentiful stock of residential accommodation was increased in 2003 with the addition of 526 rooms, which are not only en suite, but come with their own television.

Accommodation
Number of places and costs refer to 2005–06
University-provided places: about 5,750
Percentage catered: about 33%
Costs for catered accommodation: £120–£140 a week.
Costs for self-catered accommodation: £70–£78 a week.
Policy for first-year students: first years are guaranteed accommodation providing they have submitted an accommodation form by 16 August, are confirmed by UCAS by 30 August, and do not reside within the City of Edinburgh.
Policy for international students: visiting undergraduates on formal exchanges are guaranteed if they have applied by 16 August. Visiting non-EU undergraduates are also guaranteed if they apply by 16 August.
Contact: www.accom.ed.ac.uk

Students

Undergraduates:	15,095	(1,055)
Postgraduates:	3,275	(2,670)
Mature students:	10.3%	
Overseas students:	11.0%	
Applications per place:	8.4	
From state-sector schools:	65.7%	
From working-class homes:	17.8%	

Teaching Quality Assessments
1993–98 Rated Excellent:
biological sciences; chemistry; computing; electrical and electronic engineering; finance and accounting; geology; history; mathematics and statistics; physics; social policy; social work; sociology; veterinary medicine.
1993–98 Rated Highly Satisfactory:
architecture; civil engineering; English; French; geography; history of art; law; medicine; music; nursing; philosophy; politics; psychology; theology.
From 1998 (top score 24):
21 European languages.
19 chemical engineering.

See page 245 for recent assessments.

University of Essex

Essex has long since moved out of the shadow of its radical past, acquiring a reputation for high-quality research, especially in the social sciences. It did well in the last research assessments and is in the top 10 in our League Table for teaching. The university's small size and arts bias held it back in previous university rankings. There has been some recent growth but plans for a 20 per cent increase in student numbers by 2005 were not fulfilled.

Law was top-rated in the early teaching quality assessments and sociology is among the leading departments in Britain, attracting a series of prestigious research projects as well as a high score for teaching. Both sociology and government achieved their second successive 5* grades in the latest research assessments, with economics joining them on the top grade. With eight subjects on grade 5, three quarters of the researchers are in departments where most work is judged to be of international quality.

The sciences have been growing in strength and the biological and chemical sciences department is one of the university's largest. Electronic engineering recorded a perfect score for teaching quality to add to an improved research rating, and biosciences almost repeated the feat. Computer science is also strong and a BSc

in computer games and internet technology shows Essex keeping pace with changing demands in graduate employment. The last four teaching assessments – for sports science, economics, philosophy and politics – have all seen full marks.

But improvements in the university's academic performance could not disguise the fact that the glass and concrete campus, set in 200 acres of parkland on the outskirts of Colchester, was showing distinct signs of a quarter of a century's wear and tear. The university has been carrying out a programme of refurbishment at the same time as expanding student facilities. Teaching and administration blocks, which cluster around a network of squares, are gradually being transformed and extra catering and residential facilities added.

The newest development, University Quays, added a further 750 en suite bedrooms in 2004. All accommodation is now networked to the university IT system. More office and teaching accommodation for history, accounting and management became available in 2002. The library has been extended to provide 1,100 reader spaces and is open for over 84 hours a week.

Essex was originally expected to grow rapidly to become a medium-to-large university, but Government cuts intervened and it has remained among the smallest.

Wivenhoe Park, Colchester,
Essex CO4 3SQ
T   01206 873666
E   admit@essex.ac.uk
W www.essex.ac.uk
U www.essexstudent.com

The Times Rankings
Overall Ranking: 29
(2005 ranking: 27)

Teaching assessment:	=10	(22.5)
Research assessment:	=16	(5.6)
Entry standards:	44	(296.5)
Student–staff ratio:	=26	(15.5)
Library/IT spend/student:	24	(£649)
Facilities spend/student:	17	(£294)
Good honours:	65	(53.5%)
Graduate prospects:	63	(59.7%)
Expected completion rate:	=48	(85.3%)

There are still only 7,400 full-time students, with the incorporation of the East 15 acting school, in Loughton, adding another 130 places. The arrangement had more to do with enhancing the university's provision in theatre studies, but it was the university's first venture beyond Colchester. Students also take Essex degrees at Writtle College in Chelmsford, and South East Essex College in Southend, where work has started on a £75-million joint campus.

Essex champions academic breadth, and in each of the four schools of study, undergraduates follow a common first year before specialising. They may take four or five different subjects before committing themselves to a particular degree. Essex's student population is also unusually diverse for a traditional university, with high proportions of mature and overseas students. More than a quarter of the undergraduates are from working-class homes and 96 per cent went to state schools or colleges – a significantly higher proportion than the subject mix would suggest.

Social and sporting facilities are good, the more so following an extension of the Sports Centre and the refurbishment of the student union bars. There are now four bars, a nightclub and numerous cafés on campus. Some 40 acres of land are devoted to sports facilities, used extensively by individual students and over 40 university sports clubs. Town–gown relations in the garrison base of Colchester have not always been smooth, but the university insists that they have improved in recent years. The campus can be bleak in winter and tends to empty at weekends, but there is a strong community atmosphere.

Accommodation

Number of places and costs refer to 2004–05
University-provided places: 3,996
Percentage catered: 0%
Costs for catered accommodation: n/a
Costs for self-catered accommodation: £45.78 (off campus); £49.77 (on campus, shared facilities); £75.18 (on campus, en suite) a week.
Policy for first-year students: new undergraduates are guaranteed accommodation provided that forms are submitted before the closing date given.
Policy for international students: new students are guaranteed accommodation, provided that forms are submitted before the closing date given; priority given to students in 2nd and 3rd year.
Contact: admit@essex.ac.uk (undergraduates)
pgadmit@essex.ac.uk (postgraduates)

Students

Undergraduates:	5,480	(1,815)
Postgraduates:	1,840	(1,850)
Mature students:	10.1%	
Overseas students:	23.6%	
Applications per place:	6.2	
From state-sector schools:	95.8%	
From working-class homes:	27.8%	

Tuition fees 2006   £3,000
See chapter 13 for bursary details.

Teaching Quality Assessments

From 1995 (top score 24):
24 economics;
electrical and electronic engineering;
hospitality, sport, leisure and tourism;
philosophy; politics.
23 biological sciences.
22 history of art; psychology; sociology.
21 linguistics.
20 mathematics and statistics; nursing.

University of Exeter

Exeter is one of Britain's most popular universities in terms of first-choice applications, not only in its traditional strong suit, the arts, but increasingly in the sciences and social sciences. A third of the undergraduates come from independent schools – a much higher proportion than the national average for the subjects Exeter offers, and one that places the university among the dozen with the lowest state-school intake. Professor Steve Smith, the Vice-Chancellor, has put broadening the social mix at the top of his agenda, particularly targeting schools and colleges in the rural South West.

Location is partly responsible for the relatively rarified social mix. There is no large industrialised centre of population to draw on and, however lively, cathedral cities in the South West are not what every teenager is looking for. However, the academic reputation is strong and there have been exciting developments recently. Chief among them is the establishment of the Peninsula Medical School, in association with Plymouth University. It opened in October 2002 with 127 students and is the first in the region. Recruitment has been strong, with applications doubling in the school's first year of operation and continuing to grow.

More recently, Exeter was the subject of national controversy after deciding to close the chemistry and music departments as part of a rationalisation exercise ahead of the next research assessment exercise. The last assessments were an improvement on 1996: only German was considered internationally outstanding, but another 18 areas reached the next highest grade. However, the university decided that research funding was too low in other subjects to keep all the more expensive departments open.

Arabic and Islamic studies have benefited from support from the Middle East and a £20-million programme for new research centres is nearing completion. A longstanding international focus is exemplified by the popular European Law degree. All students are offered tuition in foreign languages and even some three-year degrees include the option of a year abroad. Language degrees scored well in the teaching assessments, with German achieving a perfect score. Education and archaeology also achieved full marks for teaching quality. Every subject assessed since 1996 has registered top marks for student support and guidance.

English literature, drama, law, psychology and history are among the most heavily subscribed courses in their fields, and only 5 per cent of students starting courses

---

Northcote House
The Queen's Drive, Exeter EX4 4QJ
T   01392 263035
E   admissions@exeter.ac.uk
W www.exeter.ac.uk
U http://xnet.ex.ac.uk

The Times Rankings
Overall Ranking: 34
(2005 ranking: =31)

Teaching assessment:	=34	(22.0)
Research assessment:	=30	(5.2)
Entry standards:	25	(359)
Student–staff ratio:	41	(16.5)
Library/IT spend/student:	=38	(£576)
Facilities spend/student:	94	(£120)
Good honours:	21	(68.5%)
Graduate prospects:	65	(59.5%)
Expected completion rate:	12	(95.1%)

anywhere in the university in 2004 came through clearing – the lowest ever at Exeter. A modular system allows students to build a degree from a wide range of courses at the end of their first year. Career management skills are built into degree programmes and students can gain work experience through the university's employability and business project programmes. Web-based learning is used in all academic areas.

Some £38 million has been invested in residential accommodation over the past 15 years. As much again will go on the replacement of substandard stock, increasing the range of self-catering options. There has also been a substantial investment in sports facilities, the latest of which saw a high-quality tennis centre open in 2004, and the establishment of a sports scholarship scheme.

The main Streatham Campus, close to the centre of Exeter, is one of the most attractive in the country. The highly-rated schools of education, sport and health studies are a mile away in the former St Luke's College. The university is also part of the Combined Universities in Cornwall (a partnership with Falmouth College of Arts, Plymouth University and FE colleges in Cornwall). A new £50-million campus has opened outside Falmouth, and the Camborne School of Mines, now part of the university, is moving there. A distinctive range of new degrees in geography,

conservation biology and environmental fields has been developed to tempt students west, as well as catering for Cornish demand.

Exeter has a growing number of pubs and clubs catering for students and millions of pounds are being spent on the guild of students and other campus facilities. There is a lively social scene on campus, the students being kept informed by thriving print and broadcast media. The Northcott Theatre, at the heart of the campus, is one of the cultural centres of the region, and the area's beautiful countryside and enticing beaches are within easy reach.

Accommodation

Number of places and costs refer to 2005–06
University-provided places: 4,099
Percentage catered: 46.6%
Costs for catered accommodation:
£99.96–£129.99 a week (21 meals, 31-week let).
Costs for self-catered accommodation:
£57.47–£89.46 a week (options for 40 or 51-week lets).
Policy for first-year students: all first years are guaranteed accommodation. There are no restrictions for local students.
Policy for international students: accommodation is currently provided for all unaccompanied international (non-EU) postgraduates.
Contact: Hallaccommodation@exeter.ac.uk
Selfcateringaccommodation@exeter.ac.uk

Students

Undergraduates:	7,715	(1,655)
Postgraduates:	2,010	(1,770)
Mature students:	7.9%	
Overseas students:	5.4%	
Applications per place:	7.8	
From state-sector schools:	67.1%	
From working-class homes:	15.0%	

Tuition fees 2006   £3,000
See chapter 13 for bursary details.

Teaching Quality Assessments

From 1995 (top score 24):
24 archaeology; education; German.
23 politics; psychology; theology.
22 biological sciences; business and management; classics and ancient history; drama, dance and cinematics; economics; French; Italian; mathematics and statistics; physics.
21 materials technology; Middle Eastern and African studies; sociology; education.
20 general engineering; Iberian languages; Russian.
16 linguistics.

University of Glamorgan

Wales's second university had been planning to become the senior partner in one of the largest institutions in Britain, by merging with nearby UWIC to form a modern university of more than 30,000 students. But the plan has been shelved and Glamorgan will continue increasing numbers on campus and franchising courses to colleges at home and abroad. Twinning programmes operate in five overseas centres, while in Wales a growing number of further education colleges offer the university's courses. Four have become associate colleges, guaranteeing places on degree courses if students fulfil set conditions.

The university's own campus is 20 minutes by train from Cardiff in Treforest, overlooking the market town of Pontypridd. Originally based in a large country house, Glamorgan now has purpose-built premises for the science and technology departments. There has also been a £5-million refurbishment of teaching accommodation for mathematics and computing. The law, nursing and midwifery schools are in Glyntaff, a short walk from the campus. They are housed in new buildings and specially restored tramsheds, a reminder of the industrial past of the area. The Institute of Chiropractic is the only university-based centre for training chiropractors in the UK, while the new Film Academy for Wales is another unique development, built on a successful range of film-related courses.

Glamorgan is committed to retaining its vocational slant, tailoring a diploma in management to the needs of the Driver and Vehicle Licensing Agency, for example. The business school is the largest in Wales, and the university was among the first providers of the two-year foundation degree, focusing on human resources management and marketing, business and accounting. The range of courses has since expanded rapidly, covering subjects as diverse as turf management and product design.

The vocational approach pays dividends for graduate employment, which is consistently good, although the dropout rate is also the highest among the university institutions in Wales. The funding council expected a quarter of the students starting degree courses in 2002 not to complete their course in the normal period. The dropout rate reflects an intake which is more socially diverse than elsewhere in Wales. Four out of ten undergraduates come from working-class homes and three in ten are from areas with no tradition of higher education – one of the highest figures at any UK university. Applications were up by 7 per cent when the official

Llantwit Road, Treforest,
Pontypridd,
Mid Glamorgan CF37 1DL
T 01443 480480
E enquiries@glam.ac.uk
W www.glam.ac.uk
U www.glamsu.com

The Times Rankings
Overall Ranking: 71
(2005 ranking: =61)

Teaching assessment:	=40	(21.9)
Research assessment:	=80	(2.4)
Entry standards:	89	(209.9)
Student–staff ratio:	80	(20.2)
Library/IT spend/student:	80	(£426)
Facilities spend/student:	=49	(£194)
Good honours:	=87	(48.1%)
Graduate prospects:	71	(58.2%)
Expected completion rate:	89	(73.7%)

deadline passed for courses starting in 2005.

Glamorgan was one of the top scorers among the former polytechnics in teaching quality assessments: 12 subjects have been rated as Excellent at degree level, and there have also been awards for the remaining further education course provision. The best-known courses are in engineering and professional studies, but new offerings in 2005 ranged from astrobiology to foundation degrees in surveying and estate agency. The success of the English and creative writing programmes is reflected in the establishment at the university of the National Centre for Writing, which opened in 2002. The School of Technology has been designated a centre of excellence for Wales, while three National Partnership awards testify to high standards in course design and delivery.

Many of the 9,000 full-time under-graduates live around Pontypridd, while others choose Cardiff, which is both livelier than Pontypridd and a better source of accommodation. However, the campus has been developing, with the addition of a recreation centre and an extension to the students' union, which is the focus of social life. Its bars are the only part of the university where smoking is allowed.

The sports facilities are good enough for Glamorgan to have been awarded the 2001 British University Games and to become one of six centres of excellence in cricket.

The university is successful in student competitions, especially in rugby, and offers a number of sports bursaries for students with international potential. But there is also a wide range of health and fitness classes for those with lower aspirations.

Accommodation

Number of places and costs refer to 2005–06
University-provided places: 1,108
Percentage catered: 6%
Costs for catered accommodation: £77.50 (shared facilities); £90.00 (en suite). All catered students still have access to kitchen facilities.
Costs for self-catered accommodation: £52.50 (shared facilities); £65.00 (en suite) a week all based on a full 37-week academic year.
Policy for first-year students: no restrictions except for those living in the immediate locality.
Policy for international students: all international students are guaranteed accommodation, which could be either on or off campus depending on availability.
Contact: accom@glam.ac.uk

Students

Undergraduates:	9,380	(7,240)
Postgraduates:	845	(2,355)
Mature students:	27.4%	
Overseas students:	10.6%	
Applications per place:	3.9	
From state-sector schools:	97.9%	
From working-class homes:	39.7%	

Tuition fees 2006	£1,200

Teaching Quality Assessments
1993–98 Rated Excellent:

accounting and finance; biological sciences; business studies; creative writing; drama; earth studies; electrical and electronic engineering; English; information and library studies; media; mining surveying; public sector schemes; Welsh.

University of Glasgow

Glasgow enjoys the rare distinction of having been established by Papal Bull, and began its existence in the Chapter House of Glasgow Cathedral in 1451. Since 1871 it has been based next to Kelvingrove Park in the city's fashionable west end on the Gilmorehill campus, with its many listed buildings. The latest addition, to house the prestigious medical school, opened in 2002.

The university has taken in St Andrew's College to form a new faculty of education, which has been based on the Park campus, between Gilmorehill and the city centre, since summer 2002. The campus, formerly the Queen's College, has been acquired from Glasgow Caledonian University, and provides the extra teaching accommodation needed to locate the education faculty close to the main campus. The Vet School and outdoor sports facilities are located at Garscube, a few miles away, while the innovative Crichton College campus in Dumfries is taking higher education to southwest Scotland with three-year degrees.

More distinctively Scottish than its rivals in Edinburgh or St Andrews, almost half of the students come from within 30 miles of Glasgow and three quarters are from north of the border. There was a high proportion of home-based students long before the city became fashionable, but it also attracts students from some 80 countries.

The university has adopted an increasingly outward-looking style in recent years, marked by two Queen's Anniversary prizes for opening up artistic, scientific and cultural resources and taking computing to local communities. A 'synergy' agreement with neighbouring Strathclyde University has led to the development of teaching and research partnerships, the latest establishing a single department of naval architecture and marine engineering. Not that Glasgow is a stranger to innovation: it was the first university to have a school of engineering, for example. The huge science faculty – the biggest outside London – is strong, having received top ratings for teaching in six subjects. Applications for science degrees reflect this quality, having risen by 25 per cent since the mid-1990s. Overall, a 6.6 per cent increase in applications for courses starting in 2005 was one of the highest in Scotland. Among other sources, the university has seen a steady flow of applicants from schools taking part in the university's access scheme.

The last research assessments were an improvement on a disappointing set of results in 1996, with arts and social sciences leading the way. Four subjects were rated internationally outstanding – English, European studies, psychology and sports science – a further 19 achieving grade 5 and

---

University Avenue,
Glasgow G12 8QQ
T 0141-339 8855 (main switchboard)
E sras@gla.ac.uk
W www.gla.ac.uk
U www.glasgowstudent.net

GLASGOW
Edinburgh
Belfast
London
Cardiff

The Times Rankings
Overall Ranking: 20
(2005 ranking: =22)

Teaching assessment:	=7	(22.7)
Research assessment:	=30	(5.2)
Entry standards:	16	(373.9)
Student–staff ratio:	=13	(13.5)
Library/IT spend/student:	21	(£682)
Facilities spend/student:	43	(£211)
Good honours:	16	(70.2%)
Graduate prospects:	40	(65%)
Expected completion rate:	51	(85%)

95 per cent of researchers were in the top three categories. The university has opened an office in California's Silicon Valley in order to make the most of its research successes.

Overseas recruitment has remained strong, especially in engineering. Glasgow is also taking an active role in the Universitas 21 worldwide group of universities, involving partnerships on five continents. But the home market has not been overlooked: the Century 21 Club has enrolled 20 firms to sponsor under-graduates at £1,000 a year, as part of an arrangement to forge closer links with local business. Another ten scholarships for students from poor backgrounds commemorate the life of Donald Dewar, Scotland's late First Minister. The scheme is the first of a number of memorials planned for one of the university's best-known graduates.

Over a fifth of the students are from working-class homes, one in six from an area without a tradition of higher education. Most like the combination of campus and city life, with the relatively low cost of living an added attraction, but the dropout rate of 15 per cent is above the average for the subjects on offer and entry qualifications. Undergraduates have the choice of two student unions, plus a sports union supporting 50 different clubs and activities.

Accommodation
Number of places and costs refer to 2005–06
University-provided places: 3,262
Percentage catered: 7%
Costs for catered accommodation: £98.63 (standard); £112.84 (en suite).
Costs for self-catered accommodation: £64.47 (standard); £79.87 (en suite); 85% of rooms have internet access.
Policy for first-year students: first years living beyond commuting distance are guaranteed accommodation if they apply by 22 August in their year of entry. Those living in and around Glasgow have to commute in the first instance until places become available.
Policy for international students: first years are guaranteed accommodation if they apply by 22 August.
Contact: accom@gla.ac.uk

Students

Undergraduates:	14,815	(4,565)
Postgraduates:	2,510	(2,570)
Mature students:	10.7%	
Overseas students:	6.2%	
Applications per place:	6.0	
From state-sector schools:	89.2%	
From working-class homes:	22.9%	

Teaching Quality Assessments
1993–98 Rated Excellent:
biological sciences; chemistry; computing science; English; French; geography; geology; medicine; physics; philosophy; psychology, social policy; sociology; veterinary medicine.
1993–98 Rated Highly Satisfactory:
civil engineering; dentistry; drama; finance and accounting; history; history of art; mathematics and statistics; mechanical engineering; music; nursing; politics; social work.
From 1998 (top score 24):
22 European languages.

See page 245 for recent assessments.

Glasgow Caledonian University

Glasgow Caledonian has spent more than £50 million transforming previously mediocre facilities into a single campus that does justice to a modern university of more than 14,000 students. Only Edinburgh and Glasgow universities are bigger north of the border. Over 80 per cent of the buildings are new or have been upgraded, and improvements are still being made. The new health building brings together teaching and research facilities and includes a virtual hospital, where students can hone their clinical and interpersonal skills. Work has started on a new learning centre, which will bring all library and computing centres together for the first time.

With the accent firmly on widening participation in higher education, the university will always struggle in league tables such as ours, but it is well-regarded by employers and applications were up by more than 5 per cent at the beginning of 2004.

Caledonian is in the top four UK universities for attracting students from areas without a tradition of higher education, and more than a third of its undergraduates come from working-class homes. The university has argued forcefully that extending access should be rewarded more generously if such students are to receive the support they need to make a success of higher education.

The latest performance indicators suggested that one undergraduate in six would fail to complete the degree they embarked upon. However, this projection represented another improvement on previous years and was only marginally worse than the UK average for Caledonian's subject mix and entrance qualifications. The university introduced a series of measures designed to improve retention. Telltale signs are monitored, such as non-attendance at lectures, and better academic, social and financial support offered to those at risk of dropping out.

Consolidated on its city-centre campus, Caledonian's original two sites have now been reduced to one with the sale of the Park Campus, in the west end of the city, to Glasgow University. The latest improvements have included leisure facilities and a new building for the health faculty, opened by Thabo Mbeki who named it in honour of his father. Physiotherapy is the only subject since chemistry's success in 1993 to be rated Excellent for teaching, and Caledonian now boasts among the most extensive health programmes in Britain.

A string of other subjects (mainly on the science side) are considered Highly Satisfactory. Business is the other big area,

City Campus, 70 Cowcaddens Road, Glasgow G4 0BA
T 0141-331 3000
E admissions@gcal.ac.uk
W www.caledonian.ac.uk
U www.caledonianstudent.com
GLASGOW

The Times Rankings		
Overall Ranking: 74		
(2005 ranking: =76)		
Teaching assessment:	=58	(21.4)
Research assessment:	=76	(2.5)
Entry standards:	52	(278)
Student–staff ratio:	=83	(20.5)
Library/IT spend/student:	=90	(£388)
Facilities spend/student:	99	(£72)
Good honours:	47	(59.2%)
Graduate prospects:	=88	(54%)
Expected completion rate:	=65	(81.6%)

the Caledonian Business School boasting more undergraduates than any other institution in Scotland, with over 1,000 in each year group. The university pioneered subjects such as entrepreneurial studies and risk management – the only university in the country to do so – and offers highly specialist degrees, such as tourism management, fashion marketing, leisure management and consumer protection.

Degrees in all areas are strongly vocational, and are complemented by a wide portfolio of professional courses. A high proportion of students choose sandwich courses, and the university operates on a modular system. REAL@Caledonian is a new student facility combining enhanced learning technology with a informal cyber-café atmosphere.

The legacy of Queen's College, which catered mainly for women, has ensured that the proportion of female students is the highest of any university in Britain. Sports and social facilities have been among the priorities in the building programme, and the library has been extended and upgraded recently. Some students find that the high proportion of their peers living at home detracts from the social scene, but Glasgow is a very lively city with a large student population.

Accommodation
Number of places and costs refer to 2005–06
University-provided places: 660
Percentage catered: 0%
Costs for self-catered accommodation: £69.00 (standard); £79.60 (en suite) a week.
Policy for first-year students: priority for students under 19 living outside the Glasgow area.
Policy for international students: priority for non-EU international students applying before August.
Contact: accommodation@gcal.ac.uk

Students
Undergraduates:	10,610	(2,305)
Postgraduates:	905	(1,360)
Mature students:	23.8%	
Overseas students:	3.8%	
Applications per place:	6.1	
From state-sector schools:	97.2%	
From working-class homes:	35.2%	

Teaching Quality Assessments
1993–98 Rated Excellent:
chemistry; physiotherapy.
1993–98 Rated Highly Satisfactory:
biological sciences; consumer studies; finance and accounting; mathematics and statistics; mass communications; nursing; nutrition and dietetics; occupational therapy; physics; psychology; social work; sociology.

See page 245 for recent assessments.

University of Gloucestershire

One of the most recent additions to the list of English universities, Gloucestershire is also the first for more than a century to have formal links with the Church of England. Although its religious origins have been played down in recent years, the university will maintain an association that includes church appointees on its governing body and Lord Carey, the former Archbishop of Canterbury, as the first Chancellor. However, this has not prevented it dropping theology, its top-rated subject with good scores for both teaching and research, at first degree level. Along with religious studies, it was one of 14 degrees to go in a curriculum review that has seen an expansion of leisure and tourism, social work and journalism.

Cheltenham and Gloucester College of Higher Education had been pressing for university status almost since it came into existence in 1990. The product of a merger between a church college and the higher education wing of a college of arts and technology, it had the breadth of study necessary to meet the Government's exacting criteria for promotion, including the power to award doctorates as well as first degrees.

Teaching ratings were good enough to satisfy the assessors, without being spectacular, and the latest research grades suggested that Gloucestershire would not be out of place in the university system. More than 40 per cent of academics were entered for the 2001 Research Assessment Exercise – a figure exceeded by only four former polytechnics – and the average score per member of staff placed the new university seventh among that group for research. English matched theology's grade 4, denoting national excellence in virtually all of the work submitted.

After considerable expansion during the 1990s, there are now almost 10,000 students, including 3,300 part-timers, and 1,000 academic and support staff. The main subject areas are management and IT, the arts, media and design, humanities, the environment, teacher education, leisure and tourism, social sciences and sport. The university prides itself on a good range of work placements, which include British Aerospace and Disneyworld.

The main campus is on the attractive site of the former College of St Paul and St Mary, a one-time botanical garden a mile outside Cheltenham, but a new base is being developed in Gloucester on the site of a former domestic science college which became part of the university in 2002. Although middle-class Cheltenham is a world away from more working-class Gloucester socially, the two campuses are

---

The Park Campus, PO Box 220,
The Park, Cheltenham GL50 2QF
T   01242 543477 (prospectus)
E   admissions@glos.ac.uk
W   www.glos.ac.uk
U   www.ugsu.org

The Times Rankings
Overall Ranking: 87
(2005 ranking: =90)

Teaching assessment:	=82	(20.7)
Research assessment:	=61	(3.0)
Entry standards:	69	(241.9)
Student–staff ratio:	55	(17.5)
Library/IT spend/student:	93	(£385)
Facilities spend/student:	61	(£173)
Good honours:	98	(41.1%)
Graduate prospects:	86	(54.3%)
Expected completion rate:	80	(77.6%)

only seven miles apart and students will not be as isolated as they are in some split-site institutions. There are also two smaller sites in Cheltenham: Pittville for art and design, and Francis Close Hall for a range of subjects, including sport and social sciences. The latter will also house a national centre of excellence in the teaching of geography, environment and related disciplines.

Gloucestershire's intake is as diverse as its locations, with 94 per cent of under-graduates from state schools and 31 per cent from working-class homes. But the latest projected dropout rate, although an improvement on the previous year at 21 per cent, was still significantly higher than the national average for the subjects offered and the students' entry qualifications. The new sport-oriented Oxstalls campus, in Gloucester, where participation in higher education has always been low, will focus particularly on access initiatives.

Sports facilities include a swimming pool, sports hall and tennis courts, but are not extensive for a university of 10,000 students. Likewise accommodation: with around 1,100 beds, students need to be quick off the mark at the start of the academic year, although first years are given priority in the allocation of places. However, 'enhancement of the student experience' is one of the priorities in the university's strategic plan. Another 104 rooms became available in September 2004. Although Cheltenham and Gloucester are not clubbers' paradises, neither is dull and facilities are improving.

Accommodation

Number of places and costs refer to 2005–06
University-provided places: 1,174
Percentage catered: 0%
Costs for catered accommodation: n/a
Costs for self-catered accommodation: £64–£85 a week.
Policy for first-year students: all places are reserved for first-year students.
Policy for international students: first-year international students are given priority if they request a place in residence.
Contact: accommodation@glos.ac.uk

Students

Undergraduates:	5,815	(1,865)
Postgraduates:	525	(1,010)
Mature students:	19.7%	
Overseas students:	4.4%	
Applications per place:	4.8	
From state-sector schools:	94.3%	
From working-class homes:	31.2%	

Tuition fees 2006 £3,000
See chapter 13 for bursary details.

Teaching Quality Assessments
From 1995 (top score 24):
21 art and design; hospitality and leisure; psychology; town and country planning.
20 media studies; sociology.

Goldsmiths College, University of London

Dubbed the 'campus of cool', Goldsmiths has long been Britain's leading university of the creative arts because of the range of excellence it encompasses, although it now has competition for that title with the upgrading of the London Institute. The nickname, which the college is more than happy to encourage, comes from the inclusion of Goldsmiths alongside MTV, Apple and the Tate among 50 'cool brandleaders' identified by the Brand Council in 2004. Its alumni include Mary Quant and Damien Hirst among many other famous names, such as Malcolm McLaren and Linton Kwesi Johnson. Graduates of the college won the Turner Prize no fewer than five times during the 1990s and accounted for three of the four nominees in 2002. Former Goldsmiths students were also in evidence in the 2003 and 2004 prizes.

There is another side to Goldsmiths, however, in its long history of community-based courses. Evening classes are still as popular as conventional degree courses and many subjects can be studied from basic to postgraduate levels. A history of providing educational opportunities for women is reflected in the largest proportion of female students in the British university system – over two thirds at the last count.

Determinedly integrated into their southeast London locality, the college precincts have a cosmopolitan atmosphere. Nearly 40 per cent of all undergraduates are over 21 on entry (half of them over 30), many coming from the area's ethnic minorities, and there is a growing proportion of overseas students. The age profile helped boost applications by more than 20 per cent when the official deadline passed for courses beginning in 2005, as the prospect of top-up fees in 2006 helped concentrate minds.

The older premises have been likened to a grammar school, with their long corridors of classrooms. But the Rutherford Information Services Building, opened in 1997, won an award from the Royal Institute of British Architects, and a former baths building has been converted to provide more space for research and art studios. A new arts complex opened in 2005, with state-of-the-art facilities and two multidisciplinary centres for interaction between the arts and social sciences, all housed in a unique building that features a dramatic metal 'scribble' by the acclaimed architect Will Alsop. Goldsmiths describes itself as specialising in the study of 'creative, cognitive, cultural and social processes', making room for computing and psychology in the arts-dominated portfolio of courses. A newly-established Department

---

Lewisham Way, New Cross,
London SE14 6NW
T   0207-919 7766
E   admissions@gold.ac.uk
W   www.goldsmiths.ac.uk
U   www.gcsu.org.uk

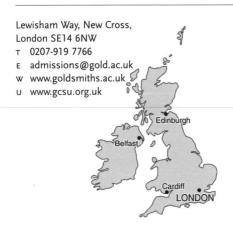

The Times Rankings
Overall Ranking: 54
(2005 ranking: =59)

Teaching assessment:	=92	(20.3)
Research assessment:	=25	(5.3)
Entry standards:	48	(288.3)
Student–staff ratio:	=36	(16.2)
Library/IT spend/student:	56	(£509)
Facilities spend/student:	=65	(£163)
Good honours:	37	(63.6%)
Employment prospects:	=55	(60.8%)
Expected completion rate:	=46	(85.6%)

of Visual Cultures teaches history of art as well as visual culture. Both media and communications and sociology were rated internationally outstanding in the last research rankings, which were a spectacular success for the college. Anthropology, art and design, music and English and comparative literature were close behind, leaving more than a third of the academics entered for assessment in the top two of seven categories. The research scores have helped transform Goldsmiths' financial position, allowing more investment in teaching. Art and design, economics, politics and psychology have joined music, media studies and drama as the college's best performers for teaching scores so far, but education is also well regarded, especially for primary teacher training.

Employment prospects are good, especially for a college with such a high proportion of students taking performing arts subjects, where a period of unemployment after graduation is commonplace. Indeed, on postgraduate courses, recent success rates have been among the best in Britain.

Student politics has survived at Goldsmiths to an extent not seen at many universities – the union building was given the name Tiananmen – while a college in which Alex James, from Blur, and Graham Coxon are just two of a number of successful rock alumni cannot fail to have a thriving music scene. The surrounding area is enjoying a mini-boom as a prime location for loft apartments. Although sky-high prices put them way beyond the reach of the student housing market, there are plenty of more reasonably-priced options in the vicinity. Most first years are allocated one of the 1,039 residential places within walking distance of the campus and overseas students can be housed throughout their course. Sports enthusiasts are less well provided for. Although there is a swimming pool and indoor complex in Deptford, the main pitches are eight miles away.

Accommodation
Number of places and costs refer to 2004–05
University-provided places: 1,039 (college halls).
Percentage catered: 0%.
Costs for catered accommodation: n/a
Costs for self-catered accommodation: £72.50–£93.50 a week.
Policy for first-year students: priority is given to new full-time students living outside Travelcard Zone 6. Students living within Travelcard Zone 6 are placed on a waiting list.
Policy for international students: overseas (non-EU) students are guaranteed a place in College accommodation (subject to conditions).
Contact: accommodation@gold.ac.uk
0207-919 7130
www.goldsmiths.ac.uk/accommodation

Students

Undergraduates:	3,560	(1,255)
Postgraduates:	1,375	(1,030)
Mature students:	40%	
Overseas students:	13.9%	
Applications per place:	6.0	
From state-sector schools:	90.5%	
From working-class homes:	25.5%	

Tuition fees 2006	£3,000

See chapter 13 for bursary details.

Teaching Quality Assessments
From 1995 (top score 24):
22 art and design;
drama, dance and cinematics; economics; media studies; politics; psychology.
21 mathematics; sociology.
19 history of art.
17 French; German.

University of Greenwich

Greenwich's move into the former Royal Naval College buildings designed by Sir Christopher Wren at last gave the university a campus worthy of one of the most desirable titles in the higher education world. Its name has always conjured up images of history and science in equal measure. Following a £45.8-million programme of restoration and conversion the entire Maritime Greenwich campus is now complete and open to the public. The last building, Queen Mary Court, opened in 2002, and the campus is a World Heritage site.

Wren's baroque masterpiece is now being used, with the former Dreadnought Hospital, to teach over half the university's students humanities, business, law, computing, maritime studies and maths. A former nurses' home nearby has been converted into a hall of residence and conference centre, one of three halls providing 760 beds close to the campus. Another 600 rooms became available in 2004.

Now under the leadership of Baroness Blackstone, the former Higher Education Minister, Greenwich has dropped the soubriquet of 'regional university' but still draws primarily from southeast London and Kent, a populous county with only one university of its own. The main investment is in the Medway campus, centred on the former HMS Pembroke naval base at Chatham, which is being developed in partnership with the University of Kent. Some £20 million is going into one of the first new schools of pharmacy for 20 years, as well as the School of Science, the Medway School of Engineering and the Natural Resources Institute, nursing and some business courses. A joint learning resources centre will serve Chatham Maritime and the University of Kent's neighbouring premises. The range of courses is expanding as the campus moves towards its target of 6,000 students by 2006.

Other departments are situated at Avery Hill, a Victorian mansion on the outskirts of southeast London, which also has a student village of 1,300 rooms in its grounds. The campus is home to health and social care, the social sciences, and the large education faculty, one of the few teacher training centres to offer both primary and secondary education courses. Architecture, landscape and construction students have also transferred there from Dartford.

Most teaching assessments have been favourable, with pharmacy and pharmacology, town planning, sociology and nursing the star performers. Where scores have been low, it has generally been the quality assurance procedures that have

---

Old Royal Naval College, Park Row,
Greenwich, London SE10 9LS
T   0800 005006
E   courseinfo@greenwich.ac.uk
W www.gre.ac.uk
U www.suug.co.uk

The Times Rankings		
Overall Ranking: 97		
(2005 ranking: 94)		
Teaching assessment:	=90	(20.5)
Research assessment:	=76	(2.5)
Entry standards:	93	(198.9)
Student–staff ratio:	98	(24.5)
Library/IT spend/student:	72	(£463)
Facilities spend/student:	84	(£138)
Good honours:	=89	(47.5%)
Graduate prospects:	=68	(58.9%)
Expected completion rate:	88	(75.8%)

been found wanting. The university also achieved some respectable results in the latest research assessment exercise, with computing, German and materials leading the way, although less than a third of the academic staff entered. Greenwich does not shy away from assessment, however. It was among the first British universities to be rated by investment analysts, who pored over its academic, administrative and financial standing. A fifth of its income is from research and consultancy – the largest proportion at any former polytechnic.

Greenwich has celebrated two successive Queen's Anniversary Prizes for Higher and Further Education, the latest for developing computer software that simulates evacuations from buildings or vehicles during emergencies.

Strong links with institutions in Europe and further afield provide a steady flow of overseas students – mainly from China, India and Greece – as well as exchange opportunities for those at Greenwich. Seven associated colleges in Kent and London teach the university's courses. Applications were up by almost 9 per cent at the start of 2004 and by 15 per cent at the start of the following year.

A commitment to extending access to higher education has led to low entrance requirements in many subjects and a relatively high proportion of mature students. More than 95 per cent of students are state-educated, with 42 per cent coming from working-class homes. Both figures are significantly higher than the benchmark, which takes account of the subject mix and entrance qualifications. The downside is a projected dropout rate of almost 24 per cent, with less than two thirds of those starting a degree in 1999 expected to complete the course they started at Greenwich.

Accommodation
Number of places and costs refer to 2004–05
University-provided places: 2,300
Percentage catered: n/a
Costs for catered accommodation: n/a
Costs for self-catered accommodation: £65.50–£129.57 a week.
Policy for first-year students: first years are guaranteed a place. Priority given to disabled students throughout all years of their study.
Policy for international students: as new students they would get priority; in later years they are treated as home students.
Contact: accommodation-AH@gre.ac.uk (for Avery Hill campus),
accommodation-GM@gre.ac.uk (for Maritime Greenwich campus),
accommodation-ME@gre.ac.uk (for Medway Campus),
http://accommodation.gre.ac.uk

Students
Undergraduates:	10,605	(4,070)
Postgraduates:	2,285	(3,240)
Mature students:	30.1%	
Overseas students:	16.2%	
Applications per place:	6.6	
From state-sector schools:	97.1%	
From working-class homes:	42.1%	

Tuition fees 2006 £2,500
See chapter 13 for bursary details.

Teaching Quality Assessments
From 1995 (top score 24):
24 town and country planning.
23 nursing; pharmacy; sociology.
22 psychology.
21 building; civil engineering; land and property management; philosophy; politics.
20 biological sciences; agriculture; business and management; economics; education.
19 mathematics and statistics; media studies.
18 health subjects.
17 electrical and electronic engineering; general engineering.

Heriot-Watt University

Concentration on technology, languages and business is fitting for a university which commemorates James Watt, the pioneer of steam power, and George Heriot, financier to King James VI. Still evolving 35 years after attaining university status, in many ways Heriot-Watt is Scotland's most unconventional university. The main campus, on the outskirts of Edinburgh, was completed only in 1992, and is among the most modern in Britain. Still small in terms of full-time students, the primarily technological university is aiming to double its numbers over 20 years. It already has 10,000 students taking distance learning courses and expects to add more. The new Interactive University launched with Scottish Enterprise will help higher education institutions throughout Scotland to market and deliver degrees around the world

For many years, Heriot-Watt's main claim to fame outside the academic community lay in its degree in brewing and distilling. But the university has a wide variety of vocational programmes, as well as more conventional degrees. Research in petroleum engineering is rated internationally outstanding, while modern languages are a more unexpected strength. Actuarial mathematics and statistics is one of only two centres in the UK, and

photonics and optoelectronics is highly regarded. The new School of the Built Environment integrates civil and building engineering and surveying, with the former School of Planning and Housing at Edinburgh College of Art.

Only electrical and electronic engineering achieved the maximum score for teaching under the original assessment system, although there was a succession of Highly Satisfactory ratings. However, computer sciences and chemical, electrical and electronic, mechanical and petroleum engineering all achieved the top Commendable grades in 2002.

Science, engineering, management and languages are located on the main campus at Riccarton, which saw £100 million of investment in the 1990s. The university has also been investing in people: a five-year programme has seen £3.7 million worth of new appointments. There is a postgraduate campus in the Orkneys, but in the current decade the focus has been on the Borders, where higher education provision has always been scarce. The Scottish Borders Campus is situated in Galashiels, 35 miles south of Edinburgh, where the university took over and upgraded the Scottish College of Textiles. There are plans to develop a new campus in the town by linking with Borders College,

Riccarton,
Edinburgh EH14 4AS
T   0131-451 3376/77/78
E   admissions@hw.ac.uk
W   www.hw.ac.uk
U   www.hwusa.org

EDINBURGH

Belfast

London

Cardiff

The Times Rankings
Overall Ranking: 36
(2005 ranking: 46)

Teaching assessment:	=10	(22.5)
Research assessment:	=42	(4.7)
Entry standards:	21	(362.7)
Student–staff ratio:	17	(14.4)
Library/IT spend/student:	53	(£526)
Facilities spend/student:	32	(£232)
Good honours:	78	(50.9%)
Graduate prospects:	76	(56.6%)
Expected completion rate:	67	(81.5%)

supplementing this with community centres throughout the region.

The university has long been a leader in the use of information technology for teaching, thanks partly to a huge research and development programme. Heriot-Watt is also one of the most commercially diversified universities in Britain, with the share of private research funding consistently among the highest in the UK per member of academic staff. About 45 per cent of Heriot-Watt's income, more than £35 million, comes from research, training and commercial services.

The subject mix also serves graduates well in the jobs market: Heriot-Watt is seldom far from the top of the employment league tables. But the new acquisitions have altered the student profile, with the proportion of women creeping up to 38 per cent. The latest projected dropout rate, at almost 18 per cent, is higher than the average for other universities offering the same subjects. But this may turn out to be a blip since the university has had a consistently good record for retention since official figures were first published. Over a quarter of the students are from overseas, a proportion that has risen sharply in recent years and one that produces a cosmopolitan atmosphere on campus. Around 55 per cent are from Scotland, and 20 per cent from other parts of Britain.

Heriot-Watt has an attractive parkland setting, with the students' union at its heart and halls of residence conveniently placed. Students at Riccarton have complained that the six-mile journey to the city centre leaves them isolated, but transport links have improved, with buses about every ten minutes. Sports enthusiasts are well provided for, and representative teams do well. Hearts, one of Edinburgh's two Premier League clubs, have chosen the campus as the site for their sports academy, which will be used by students and local people as well as the young professionals. Music also thrives: there is a professional musician-in-residence and a number of scholarships, as well as a varied programme of events.

Accommodation

Number of places and costs refer to 2005–06
University places provided: 1,619
Percentage catered: 19%
Costs for catered accommodation: £80–£87 a week, with flexibility for food.
Costs for self catered accommodation: £49–£53 a week (self-catering flats); £58 a week (standard halls); £70 a week (self-catering halls with en suite facilities).
Policy for first year students: all new first-years who apply by 1 September are guaranteed accommodation provided they have firmly accepted an unconditional offer at this stage.
Policy for international students: as above.
Contact: AO@hw.ac.uk

Students

Undergraduates:	4,905	(225)
Postgraduates:	1,200	(1,865)
Mature students:	14.7%	
Overseas students:	17.3%	
Applications per place:	5.0	
From state-sector schools:	92.0%	
From working-class homes:	29.0%	

Teaching Quality Assessments
1993–95 Rated Excellent:
electrical and electronic engineering.
1993–98 Rated Highly Satisfactory:
biological sciences; chemistry;
civil engineering; computer studies;
finance and accounting;
mathematics and statistics;
mechanical engineering; physics.
From 1998 (top score 24):
21 modern languages.
19 chemical engineering.

See page 245 for recent assessments.

University of Hertfordshire

Hertfordshire opened a purpose-built £120 million campus in September 2003 close to the existing Hatfield headquarters, bringing the university together for the first time and promising outstanding facilities. There is a 24-hour resources centre, £15-million sports complex and 1,600 networked, en suite residential places. The two sites are linked by cycle-ways, footpaths and shuttle buses. The blaze of publicity that accompanied the opening contributed to the biggest rise in applications (22 per cent) at any UK university. That was a hard act to follow but there was another rise of 12.5 per cent at the start of 2005.

The new de Havilland campus, named after the aircraft manufacturer which once occupied the site, houses business, education and the humanities. The Hertford and Watford campuses have closed, but law will remain in its current base in the centre of St Albans.

As Hatfield Polytechnic, the university's reputation was built on engineering and computer science, but health subjects now account for by far the largest share of places. An innovative degree in Paramedic Science is Britain's first, and the university is still hoping for a medical school, although its last bid was unsuccessful. The announcement of a £500 million hospital and cancer centre in Hatfield should strengthen the university's case, as should the launches of a new School of Pharmacy and a postgraduate medical school. The latter is a collaboration with Cranfield and Luton universities and the Bedfordshire and Hertfordshire health authority. Art and design is also growing, particularly the multimedia courses. In 2005, the university will launch a new School of Film, Music and New Media. The College Lane campus, where another 1,400 residential places are planned, includes the largest art gallery in the eastern region, which mounts regular public exhibitions. A new 460-seat auditorium will enhance the cultural programme. An Automotive Centre has upgraded teaching facilities for that branch of engineering, as well as boosting interaction with industry.

Average grades for A-level entrants rose under the previous Vice-Chancellor, who called for a 'tougher and more rigorous' academic style and declared a desire to propel Hertfordshire up the league tables. Professor Tim Wilson, the present incumbent, retains this ambition but is also trying to widen the university's base further through collaboration with the county's further education colleges. The intake is more diverse than the funding councils expected, given the location and subject mix: 97 per cent of undergraduates are

College Lane, Hatfield,
Herts AL10 9AB
T   01707 284800
E   admissions@herts.ac.uk
W   www.herts.ac.uk
U   www.uhsu.herts.ac.uk

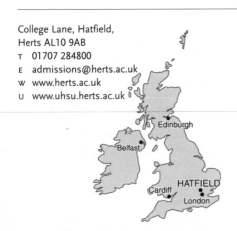

Edinburgh
Belfast
HATFIELD
Cardiff
London

The Times Rankings
Overall Ranking: 60
(2005 ranking: =59)

Teaching assessment:	=20	(22.2)
Research assessment:	=76	(2.5)
Entry standards:	85	(221.9)
Student–staff ratio:	54	(17.4)
Library/IT spend/student:	52	(£530)
Facilities spend/student:	=74	(£154)
Good honours:	79	(50.8%)
Graduate prospects:	54	(61.2%)
Expected completion rate:	72	(79.7%)

state-educated and 42 per cent come from working-class homes. A 16 per cent drop-out rate is better than the funding council's benchmark but, still more than a quarter of students do not complete the course they entered in the expected time.

Many students include work placements in their degrees, the close links with employers sometimes bringing in valuable research and consultancy contracts, and contributing to a consistently good graduate employment record. Hertfordshire is one of the few universities in a rural setting, many students commuting from towns and villages in the area, using the most extensive university bus network in Britain. For those looking for more sophisticated nightlife, London is only a short train journey away.

In previous years, Hertfordshire has suffered in *The Times* League Table for indifferent grades in the early years of teaching assessment, when only environmental studies was rated Excellent. Later in the process, philosophy achieved a perfect score, with business and management, psychology and nursing close behind. Grades in the last research assessment exercise showed considerable improvement on 1996, with history rated nationally outstanding and computing, nursing, physics and psychology all in the next category.

Even before the opening of the new campus, students were well served in terms of information technology. The award-winning library and resource centre on the main campus is Britain's biggest, offering 24-hour access to hundreds of computer workstations. A second centre on the de Havilland campus will provide another 1,000 workstations by 2006. The StudyNet information system has been a leader in its field, giving all staff and students their own storage space. Students can use it for study, revision or communication, as well as to access university information.

Accommodation

Number of places and costs refer to 2004–05
University-provided places: 3,400
Percentage catered: 0%
Costs for catered accommodation: n/a
Costs for self-catered accommodation: £56–£84 a week.
Policy for first-year students: first years are guaranteed accommodation if they apply before A-level results are published and accept course places by 31 August. No restrictions on geographical location.
Policy for international students: overseas students are guaranteed accommodation if they apply before 6 September.
Contact: Accommodation@herts.ac.uk

Students

Undergraduates:	13,465	(3,545)
Postgraduates:	1,655	(2,230)
Mature students:	14.5%	
Overseas students:	12.3%	
Applications per place:	4.3	
From state-sector schools:	96.8%	
From working-class homes:	41.8%	

Tuition fees 2006 £3,000
See chapter 13 for bursary details.

Teaching Quality Assessments

From 1995 (top score 24):
24 philosophy.
23 business and management; economics; hospitality; nursing; psychology.
22 art and design; education; health subjects; mechanical and aeronautical engineering.
21 biological sciences; mathematics and statistics; physics.
20 electrical and electronic engineering; general engineering; linguistics.

University of Huddersfield

Official performance indicators for higher education have shown Huddersfield living up to its mission to help produce a more diverse student population. Four out of ten full-time students are from working-class homes and almost a quarter are from areas without a strong tradition of higher education. The downside of this open access approach is that 22 per cent are not expected to complete their degrees – a lower proportion than in previous years but still marginally more than the funding councils' benchmark for the university, which takes account of the courses on offer. Nevertheless, Huddersfield achieved the highest possible score in an audit by the Quality Assurance Agency in 2004.

Imaginative conversion and new buildings have finally allowed the university to come together on one town-centre campus. The Holly Bank site, where the School of Education and Professional Development was based, was sold and the transfer of the School of Music and Humanities will complete the process.

The university has capitalised on Huddersfield's industrial past to ease the strain on facilities that were struggling to cope with expansion which reached 13 per cent a year at its peak. Canalside, a refurbished mill complex, has provided new space for mathematics and computing, and

education occupies another mill site – this time a £4-million recreation of the original. The university is even creating 'pocket parks' and a landscaped area along the reopened Narrow Canal to provide additional green space. Human and health sciences have also acquired new premises, and £4 million has been spent on a new students' union, allowing drama courses to take over the existing union complex. The new union includes alcohol-free social areas to encourage participation by those overseas students and ethnic minorities who would otherwise avoid the facilities.

A tradition of vocational education dates back to 1841, and the university has a long-established reputation in areas such as textile design and engineering. But there are less obvious gems such as music and social work, both of which were rated excellent for teaching and nationally outstanding for research. Teaching assessments ranged from the sublime (maximum points for electrical and electronic engineering) to the ridiculous (only 15 out of 24 for the now discontinued modern languages). Later results were consistently good, the last seven assessments all producing either 21 or 22 points. The university's satisfaction surveys suggest that students value the friendliness and helpfulness of staff.

The university adopted a much more

Queensgate, Huddersfield,
West Yorkshire HD1 3DH
T 01484 422288
E admissions@hud.ac.uk
w www.hud.ac.uk
U www.huddersfield
   student.com

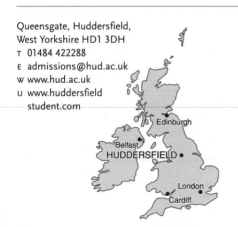

Edinburgh
Belfast
HUDDERSFIELD
London
Cardiff

The Times Rankings
Overall Ranking: 72
(2005 ranking: 80)

Teaching assessment:	=20	(22.2)
Research assessment:	=80	(2.4)
Entry standards:	88	(210.9)
Student–staff ratio:	=62	(18.2)
Library/IT spend/student:	94	(£384)
Facilities spend/student:	87	(£132)
Good honours:	95	(45.3%)
Graduate prospects:	=91	(53.4%)
Expected completion rate:	81	(77.5%)

selective approach to the last research assessments, entering half the number of academics it did in 1996. History matched social work and music's grade 5, with mechanical engineering in the next category. A flourishing relationship with industry produces more private income than is achieved in many larger institutions, as well as influencing courses.

The most popular courses are in human and health sciences. Many arts and social science courses have a vocational slant. Politics, for example, includes a six-week work placement, which often takes students to the House of Commons. A third of the students in all subjects take sandwich courses, one of the highest proportions in Britain, and more than 4,000 have some element of work experience. The approach pays off with consistently good graduate employment figures and rises of more than 12 per cent in applications for 2004 courses and nearly twice that a year later.

Additional accommodation is available at Ashenhurst, just over a mile from the campus, but most residential accommodation is now concentrated in the Storthes Hall Park student village. Despite recent developments, the 1,712 residential places are not enough to guarantee accommodation to first years. Private housing is cheap in Huddersfield, but many students commute from Leeds or Manchester. Students are also encouraged to follow a structured fitness programme at the upgraded campus sports centre. Town–gown relations are good and the cost of living low. Most students like the town's friendly atmosphere, although they tend to base their social life on the students' union. It is not far to Leeds for those in search of serious clubbing.

Accommodation

Number of places and costs refer to 2004–05
University-provided places: 1,712 in privately-owned halls
Percentage catered: 0%
Costs for self-catered accommodation: £54.95 (shared); £69.95 (single) a week.
Policy for first-year students: a place is guaranteed in halls for any first years who have made Huddersfield their firm choice, no matter where they live, provided they apply before 30 June and return contracts, deposits and booking fee after exam results are known.
Policy for international students: all international students who choose to go into university halls accommodation are allocated places, provided the application form arrives in time.
Contact: info@campusdigs.com;
www.campusdigs.com

Students

Undergraduates:	9,600	(5,150)
Postgraduates:	1,030	(2,610)
Mature students:	21.6%	
Overseas students:	6.6%	
Applications per place:	4.8	
From state-sector schools:	97.8%	
From working-class homes:	40.4%	

Tuition fees 2006 £3,000
See chapter 13 for bursary details.

Teaching Quality Assessments

From 1995 (top score 24):
24 electrical and electronic engineering.
23 politics.
22 biological sciences; education; health subjects; hospitality, leisure and tourism; nursing.
21 art and design; materials technology; mathematics.
20 food science; psychology; sociology.
18 media studies.
17 drama, dance and cinematics.

University of Hull

After years of relative stability, Hull has been expanding rapidly, both on its spacious home campus and through mergers. First it added nursing to its portfolio of courses with the acquisition of the former Humberside College of Health, then it took in University College Scarborough in 2000 and finally the university bought the adjacent campus of the former Humberside University, turning it into the Faculty of Health There are now more than 16,500 students, including part-timers. Applications were up 14 per cent – one of England's biggest rises – at the start of 2004, although they were down fractionally a year later.

The main academic development has been the establishment of a medical school in conjunction with York University. Hull's patient development, in collaboration with the local health authority, of a postgraduate medical school was rewarded with the award of a traditional school housed in a landmark building on the former college campus. The original 94-acre main campus has also seen considerable development, with new buildings for languages and chemistry, a Graduate Research Institute and a state-of-the-art sport, health and exercise science laboratory. The campus, with its art gallery and highly automated library, is less than three miles from the centre of Hull. The Scarborough campus has also seen investment in new laboratories for music technology and digital arts.

The modest cost of living and ready availability of accommodation have much to do with Hull's popularity with students, who can expect to pay less than £2,000 a year in rent, but the quality of courses is also high. Although neither would be considered fashionable, both the city and the university inspire strong loyalty among students. Teaching has been rated excellent in most subjects, with drama, electronic engineering and Iberian languages all achieving perfect scores. Politics and theology almost repeated the feat in 2001, but nursing recorded an unusually low score the previous year, with criticism of student support and quality management on the course. These issues have been addressed, and new nursing facilities provided. Strength in politics – confirmed by one of three grade 5 assessments for research, as well as the teaching quality success – is reflected in a steady flow of graduates into the House of Commons. A longstanding focus on Europe shows in the wide range of languages available at degree level, with the purpose-built Language Institute heavily used by students of all subjects. But the university was criticised for deciding in 2004 to close maths

---

Cottingham Road, Hull HU6 7RX
T 0870-126 2000
E admissions@admin.hull.ac.uk
W www.hull.ac.uk
U www.hullstudent.com

Edinburgh
Belfast
HULL
London
Cardiff

The Times Rankings
Overall Ranking: =47
(2005 ranking: 52)

Teaching assessment:	=20	(22.2)
Research assessment:	=53	(4.3)
Entry standards:	50	(283.8)
Student–staff ratio:	73	(19.1)
Library/IT spend/student:	81	(£422)
Facilities spend/student:	=63	(£165)
Good honours:	=57	(56.3%)
Graduate prospects:	=51	(61.9%)
Expected completion rate:	=48	(85.3%)

following poor recruitment to the honours degree.

No subject was rated internationally outstanding in the last research assessments, but law and geography joined politics in the next category. Social work collected a Queen's Anniversary Prize and was also rated excellent for teaching. An Institute for Learning tries to put research findings into practice, developing training courses for lecturers and encouraging the university's interest in lifelong learning.

Hull has always maintained a roughly equal balance between science and technology and the arts and social sciences, believing that this promotes a harmonious atmosphere, although the Scarborough campus has tipped the scales towards the arts.

Only one traditional university in England has a higher proportion of state-educated students than Hull's 93 per cent. Almost three in ten are from working-class homes and although the projected drop-out rate had risen to 13 per cent in the latest survey, it is still below the funding council's benchmark for the subjects offered. In an effort to broaden its intake further, the university is offering conditional places to local 16-year-olds if they take part in a Science Experience Programme. Many of the youngsters have been attending a university science club once a month since the age of 11 or 12, and have access to the library and computer facilities. The initiative, which has drawn praise from Tony Blair, should help to raise participation in higher education in an area where it has traditionally been low.

Student leisure facilities, which were always good but becoming crowded, have been upgraded as part of the campus building programme. The students' union, which was rated the best in Britain in one survey, has been refurbished and opened the popular Asylum nightclub.

Accommodation

Number of places and costs refer to 2004–05
University-provided places: 2,597 (owned stock); 295 (leased/associated stock)
Percentage catered: 41%
Costs for catered accommodation: £95.62 a week (31 weeks); £75.25 a week (semi-catered; 31 weeks).
Costs for self-catered accommodation: £55.93 a week (student houses; 42 weeks); £56.91 a week (self-catered halls; 31 weeks); £73.08 a week (on-campus en suite flats; 50 weeks).
Policy for first-year students: accommodation for unaccompanied first years is guaranteed, excepting late applicants.
Policy for international students: accommodation for new unaccompanied undergraduate and postgraduate international students is guaranteed, excepting late applicants.
Contact: rooms@hull.ac.uk

Students

Undergraduates:	9,615	(8,110)
Postgraduates:	1,775	(2,440)
Mature students:	19.9%	
Overseas students:	10.9%	
Applications per place:	4.7	
From state-sector schools:	93.0%	
From working-class homes:	28.2%	

Tuition fees 2006   £3,000
See chapter 13 for bursary details.

Teaching Quality Assessments

From 1995 (top score 24):
24 drama; electrical and electronic engineering; Iberian languages.
23 biological sciences; American studies; physics; politics; psychology; theology.
22 economics; Italian; mathematics and statistics; philosophy.
21 French; German.
20 anthropology; Dutch; education; sociology.
19 Scandinavian.
17 nursing.

Imperial College of Science, Technology and Medicine

After years of running Oxford close in *The Times* rankings, London's specialist college of science, engineering and medicine briefly moved ahead in 2000 but is now back in third place. Over 5,000 academic staff include Nobel prizewinners and 57 Fellows of the Royal Society. Three quarters of the academics entered for assessment in the latest research assessment exercise were in departments considered internationally outstanding – the highest proportion in any university – and almost all were in one of the top two categories.

Teaching scores have been up to the same high standard, with electrical and electronic engineering and materials science achieving maximum points. Subsequent grades have not quite reached that level, but physics and mathematics both scored 22 points out of 24, and medicine also did well. Imperial is not recommended for academic slouches, but tough entrance requirements ensure that they are a rare breed in any case. The dropout rate of only 3.6 per cent is one of the lowest in the country. Such is the level of competition that applications had been dropping, although there was a 10 per cent increase when the official deadline passed for courses beginning in 2004. Even though many of the subjects struggle for candidates elsewhere, entrants average better than an A and two Bs at A level. More than a third of the undergraduates are from independent schools – one of the highest proportions at any university.

Engineering courses last four years and lead to a Masters qualification. Almost all branches of engineering achieved the coveted 5* rating for research. The college has been expanding its range of European exchanges, with a variety of prestigious technological institutions available for courses such as the MSc in physics.

Medicine was the main area of development in the 1990s: mergers with the St Mary's, Charing Cross and Westminster teaching hospitals producing one of the biggest medical schools in the country. Top ratings for research in clinical medicine were a source of pride, given its size. Further mergers in 2000 brought in the Kennedy Institute of Rheumatology and Wye College, in Ashford, Kent, which specialised in agriculture and now has 400 full-time students and another 1,000 taking distance learning courses.

Facilities on the main campus, in the heart of South Kensington's museum district, have been expanded with the construction of a new biosciences building.

Exhibition Road,
South Kensington,
London SW7 2AZ
T 0207-594 8014
E admissions@ic.ac.uk
W www.ic.ac.uk
U www.union.ic.ac.uk

Edinburgh
Belfast
Cardiff
LONDON

The Times Rankings
Overall Ranking: 3
(2005 ranking: 3)

Teaching assessment:	=17	(22.3)
Research assessment:	=3	(6.4)
Entry standards:	3	(467.8)
Student–staff ratio:	2	(9.3)
Library/IT spend/student:	5	(£1,138)
Facilities spend/student:	1	(£473)
Good honours:	11	(72.7%)
Graduate prospects:	5	(78.9%)
Expected completion rate:	8	(96.4%)

There are also fieldwork facilities and more laboratories at Sillwood Park, near Ascot.

A growing business school, rated excellent for teaching, is the main concession to the academic world beyond science and technology. Dr Gary Tanaka, an Imperial graduate and successful technology investment manager, donated £25 million to provide a new home for the school. The gift is the largest personal donation in the history of the college.

The Undergraduate Research Opportunities Programme provides opportunities for 'hands-on' experience of the research activities of college staff and postgraduates. A voluntary scheme open to all undergraduates, it is especially popular in the summer vacation, when students can be paid bursaries and international undergraduates can participate without needing a work permit. There is also a vacation placement scheme during the summer for undergraduates to acquire work experience.

Imperial's specialisms have the effect of making it the most male-dominated university institution in Britain, although the number of female students doubled during the 1990s and now stands at more than a third. The imbalance shows in a social scene which many students find limited, despite the impressive selection of clubs and societies on offer. Outdoor sports facilities are remote, but Wednesday afternoons are left free to encourage students to make the effort to exercise.

Accommodation

Number of places and costs refer to 2004–05
University-provided places: 3,100
Percentage catered: 10%
Costs for catered accommodation: £81 (twin); £117 (single) a week.
Costs for self-catered accommodation: £55 (triple); £127 (single en suite) a week.
Policy for first-year students: first years are guaranteed accommodation provided that they have accepted an unconditional academic offer and have completed and returned their application for residence form by 15 September; will be attending for the full academic year; and have not previously had a place in university or college accommodation while attending a full-time course in the UK.
Policy for international students: for undergraduates, as above; postgraduates are given high priority (with the same provisos as above).
Contact: student.accom@ic.ac.uk

Students

Undergraduates:	7,365	(0)
Postgraduates:	3,165	(1,210)
Mature students:	2.6%	
Overseas students:	31.1%	
Applications per place:	5.4	
From state-sector schools:	62.8%	
From working-class homes:	17.9%	

Tuition fees 2006 £3,000
See chapter 13 for bursary details.

Teaching Quality Assessments

From 1995 (top score 24):
24 electrical and electronic engineering; materials science.
23 general engineering.
22 aeronautical engineering; agriculture; biological sciences; chemical engineering; mathematics; physics.
21 civil engineering; medicine.

University of Keele

The broad foundation course and four-year degree that made Keele's name is a fading memory, but the university remains committed to breadth of study and has set itself the target of being the leading interdisciplinary institution in Britain. Nine out of ten students take more than one subject for their degree, usually taking a subsidiary from the other side of the arts–science divide in the first year, and the range of options is still widening. Among the more outlandish combinations are astrophysics and criminology, or music technology and environmental management. Most programmes provide the opportunity of a semester abroad, which the university would like a quarter of all undergraduates to take.

American studies, education, philosophy and politics have all produced perfect scores in teaching assessments, but the many dual honours programmes – especially those featuring politics or music – and international relations are the university's traditional strengths. Law was the only subject to be rated internationally outstanding for research, but seven more reached grade 5. The improvement on the previous assessments, in 1996, has helped propel Keele up our League Table – it jumped 13 places last year, almost into the top 30, but slipped bak a little this year.

Science subjects have been gaining ground: biosciences and physics both scored well in recent teaching assessments. However, it is in health subjects that the main development has been focused. First degrees in physiotherapy, medicines management and nursing and midwifery were added to the well-established postgraduate medical school. Now collaboration with Manchester University has brought undergraduate medicine to Keele. Initially, students have been spending their first two years in Manchester, with the choice of completing their training there or moving to the Potteries. But, since 2003, it has been possible to take an entire medical degree at Keele, which will eventually train more than 600 student doctors each year. New buildings have been springing up at the North Staffordshire Hospital site, while a second undergraduate medical school (UGMS2) has opened on the main campus.

All Keele's courses are modular, with the academic year divided into two 15-week semesters, with breaks at Christmas and Easter. The university remains small by modern standards – less than 6,000 full-time students – despite 75 per cent growth during the 1990s. The proportion of postgraduates has also been growing, with a third of the students now taking higher degrees. Further growth is likely after the

---

Keele, Staffordshire ST5 5BG
T 01782 584005
E undergraduate@keele.ac.uk
w www.keele.ac.uk
u www.kusu.net

The Times Rankings
Overall Ranking: 35
(2005 ranking: =31)

Teaching assessment:	=34	(22.0)
Research assessment:	=48	(4.6)
Entry standards:	41	(306.8)
Student–staff ratio:	=31	(15.6)
Library/IT spend/student:	=76	(£451)
Facilities spend/student:	=74	(£154)
Good honours:	60	(55.2%)
Graduate prospects:	=15	(72.3%)
Expected completion rate:	9	(95.8%)

conclusion of an institutional review. With applications up by more than a quarter at the beginning of 2005, finding suitable candidates should not be a problem.

Keele is among the top universities for retaining students: the 4 per cent dropout rate is among the lowest in the UK and barely more than a third of the national average for the subjects on offer, despite a mixed intake. Nine out of ten undergraduates are state-educated, a figure exceeded by only two traditional universities in England, and a quarter come from working-class homes. Keele has been proactive in trying to broaden its intake, targeting 12 and 13-year-olds with a special website, as well as running masterclasses in local schools and hosting a summer school at the university.

The attractive 617-acre campus near the M6 outside Stoke-on-Trent is the largest in England and could take many more students. Nearly half of all undergraduates and many staff live on campus, which inevitably dominates the social scene as well as providing part-time employment for hundreds of students. The students' union has been refurbished recently, and now boasts two restaurants and a host of clubs and societies. Further improvements are planned under a five-year restructuring. Sports facilities are good for those seeking a more active lifestyle. Although the cost of living is relatively low in the Potteries, it is not an area famous for youth culture. The normal overstated section on the attractions of the locality is noticeably absent from the prospectus.

Accommodation

Number of places and costs refer to 2005–06
University-provided places: 3,200
Percentage catered: 0%
Costs for self-catered accommodation: £53, £62, £86 a week.
Policy for first-year students: first years holding Keele as a firm choice are guaranteed accommodation on campus. No restrictions on those living locally.
Policy for international students: guaranteed accommodation for the duration of the course.
Contact: hpa09@keele.ac.uk

Students

Undergraduates:	4,905	(4,795)
Postgraduates:	1,055	(2,130)
Mature students:	9.3%	
Overseas students:	6.8%	
Applications per place:	5.2	
From state-sector schools:	91.0%	
From working-class homes:	25.2%	

Tuition fees 2006 £3,000
See chapter 13 for bursary details.

Teaching Quality Assessments

From 1995 (top score 24):
24 American studies; education; philosophy; politics.
23 economics; psychology.
22 mathematics and statistics; physics; sociology.
21 biological sciences; business; nursing.
20 French; health subjects; Russian.
19 German.

University of Kent at Canterbury

Kent has capitalised sensibly on its position near the Channel ports, specialising in international programmes, as well as the flexible degree structures that have been the hallmark of most 1960s universities. Interdisciplinary study is encouraged, and many courses include the option of a year spent elsewhere in Europe or in the United States. The process should accelerate with the establishment of the Transmanche University with four counterparts in northern France, which will take its first undergraduates in 2006. The project, backed by both governments, will involve joint courses at a variety of levels and research collaboration. Almost a quarter of Kent's undergraduates take a language for at least part of their degree, and European studies are among the most popular subject combinations.

The university is broadening its horizons at home as well, however, assuming a regional role. Access courses throughout the county allow students to upgrade their qualifications to university standard, but the main focus is on the Medway towns, where Kent is involved in ambitious projects with Greenwich University and Mid-Kent College. The Chatham Maritime campus, based in the old dockyard is intended to cater for 6,000 students by 2010, with a new School of Pharmacy among the main

features of a £50-million development. The first intake of pharmacists was 50 per cent larger than planned and the school is eventually expected to take 430 students. Mid-Kent's degree courses will transfer to the university, while further education programmes continue under the aegis of the college.

The original low-rise campus, set in 300 acres of parkland overlooking Canterbury, is tidy rather than architecturally distinguished. A new psychology building opened in 2000, while the EC Jean Monnet Centre of Excellence co-ordinates European research in Kent and beyond. Among other recent developments is a long-desired student centre with a nightclub big enough to attract big-name bands. A university centre serves 1,400 part-time students in Tonbridge, and a series of associate colleges also offer university courses.

Entry grades are variable, with offers pitched according to the UCAS points tariff, although those taking A levels are expected to pass at least three subjects (one of which may be general studies). A period of declining applications has been reversed in the last four years, with a 22 per cent increase at the start of 2005, largely thanks to the Medway development.

Kent is strongest in the social sciences, although biosciences, philosophy and

---

Canterbury, Kent CT2 7NZ

T   01227 827272
E   recruitment@ukc.ac.uk
W   www.kent.ac.uk
U   www.kentunion.co.uk

The Times Rankings
Overall Ranking: 46
(2005 ranking: 44)

Teaching assessment:	=66	(21.2)
Research assessment:	=39	(4.8)
Entry standards:	42	(305.8)
Student–staff ratio:	=64	(18.3)
Library/IT spend/student:	40	(£575)
Facilities spend/student:	=77	(£150)
Good honours:	48	(58.8%)
Graduate prospects:	33	(66.8%)
Expected completion rate:	38	(87.8%)

drama, dance and theatre studies have taken pride of place in the teaching assessments, each registering a maximum score. The university takes teaching standards seriously, encouraging all academics to take a Postgraduate Certificate in Higher Education. Social policy and statistics were rated internationally outstanding in the last research assessments, which showed marked improvement on the disappointing grades in 1996.

Kent, which has taken to using the acronym UKC, has been trying to build up its science departments, among which computing is particularly well regarded. But still two thirds of the students take arts or social sciences. Graduates of all disciplines fare well in the employment market – a jobless rate below 4 per cent is impressive for an arts-dominated institution.

The university has a more mixed intake than many in the south of England: nine out of ten undergraduates are from state schools and almost a quarter come from working-class homes. Significant numbers of American and European students give the university a cosmopolitan feel, but some complain that the campus is empty at weekends, while Canterbury itself is expensive and limited socially.

Students are attached to one of four colleges, although they do not select it themselves. The colleges act as the focus of social life, and include academic as well as residential facilities. They provide accommodation for all first years. Among £100 million of completed or planned capital developments has been an expansion of sports facilities and the addition of 500 rooms at the Parkwood student village. When it comes to moving out, private housing in Canterbury is limited, but the seaside towns of Whitstable and Herne Bay are fertile ground.

Accommodation
Number of places and costs refer to 2005–06
University-provided places: 4,032
Percentage catered: 33%
Costs for catered accommodation: from £77.91; from £93.52 (en suite) a week, bed and breakfast.
Costs for self-catered accommodation: from £65.94; in new halls from £95.13 a week.
Policy for first-year students: first years are guaranteed accommodation provided they return completed application before 31 July in the year of entry.
Policy for international students: all international fee-paying students are guaranteed accommodation provided they return a completed application form before 31 July.
Contact: accomm@ukc.ac.uk
www.kent.ac.uk/hospitality

Students

Undergraduates:	8,165	(3,370)
Postgraduates:	1,075	(1,415)
Mature students:	12.9%	
Overseas students:	19.6%	
Applications per place:	4.5	
From state-sector schools:	90.1%	
From working-class homes:	24.6%	

Tuition fees 2006   £3,000
See chapter 13 for bursary details.

Teaching Quality Assessments
From 1995 (top score 24):
24 biological sciences;
drama and theatre studies; philosophy.
23 economics.
22 archaeology; classics and ancient history; history of art; psychology.
21 American studies;
business and management;
electrical and electronic engineering;
health subjects; mathematics; physics;
sociology.
20 media studies; theology.
19 modern languages.

King's College London

The second largest of London University's colleges, King's has completed an extended period of renewal, leading to concentration on three campuses close to the Thames. Most departments are now within walking distance of each other, on the original Strand site or the new Waterloo campus, with medicine and dentistry based not far away at London Bridge as well as at Denmark Hill, in south London. Students seem to like the outcome: King's registered a 13 per cent increase in applications for courses beginning in 2004 and topped that the following year. An institutional audit by the Quality Assurance Agency gave King's the highest mark, stressing the excellence of the student support services.

Medical subjects have been the main growth point. Two nursing schools were amalgamated, building on the college's longstanding BSc in nursing studies, while the merger in 1998 with the United Medical and Dental Schools of Guy's and St Thomas's Hospitals made King's a major centre for medical and dental education. Among more than 2,500 students training to become doctors or dentists are mature students on a new course designed to provide more variety in the medical profession.

A £400-million transformation of the college estate is still in progress. So far, it has produced two well-equipped campuses, with 2,000 health and life sciences students occupying the largest university building in London, near Waterloo Station, while biomedical sciences, medicine and dentistry have acquired purpose-built facilities on the Guy's Campus. There is to be further development of the St Thomas's site for medical education and hospital use, although the college was tempted to accept a much more substantial bid from the Aga Khan's foundation.

Another property deal has created the largest new university library in Britain since World War II at the former Public Record Office in Chancery Lane. A £4-million donation by a graduate has underwritten the spectacular new Maughan Library with 330 networked reader places. The next phase of the college's plans involves the £40-million restoration of the main building on the Strand Campus.

Once known primarily for science, King's now excels in a wide range of subjects in ten schools of study, including such unusual features as Britain's only department devoted entirely to Portuguese – one of four language departments rated internationally outstanding in the latest research assessments. War studies, developmental biology, dentistry, history, philosophy and psychiatry completed the college's

---

Strand, London WC2R 2LS
T 0207-848 2929
E ceu@kcl.ac.uk
W www.kcl.ac.uk
U www.kclsu.org

Edinburgh

Belfast

Cardiff

LONDON

The Times Rankings
Overall Ranking: =16
(2005 ranking: 16)

Teaching assessment:	=20	(22.2)
Research assessment:	=18	(5.5)
Entry standards:	18	(368.5)
Student–staff ratio:	5	(11.4)
Library/IT spend/student:	9	(£870)
Facilities spend/student:	56	(£183)
Good honours:	15	(70.6%)
Graduate prospects:	3	(79.9%)
Expected completion rate:	19	(93%)

impressive haul of 5* grades and won a Queen's Anniversary Prize in 2002. Almost one in three of those entered for the exercise were in starred departments. A further 14 departments achieved a 5 grade.

Classics, dentistry, war studies and philosophy are all top-rated for teaching. Medicine scored 22 points out of 24, which was more of an achievement than in areas where grading was more lenient. Throughout the college, scientists remain in a majority, and are now offered a wide range of interdisciplinary combinations, such as War Studies and philosophy, or French and mathematics. But the famous chemistry department is to cease teaching undergraduates.

King's was one of the two founding colleges of London University, but has tended to be the forgotten member of the capital's academic elite. The full extent of the college's ambitions is clear from its mission statement, which includes having all its departments rated excellent for both teaching and research. The college was among the first to follow the example of American universities by submitting to a credit rating, which took account of its academic and financial standing. The 'AA minus' result was better than many big cities have achieved.

King's is also a solid bet for a good degree for those who satisfy its demanding entry requirements, with over 70 per cent reaching the first or 2:1 classification. Every student is allocated a personal tutor, and much of the teaching is in small groups. There are more than 2,650 residential places, and the college also has access to 545 places in the intercollegiate halls of London University. Some of the outdoor sports facilities are rather dispersed.

Accommodation

Number of places and costs refer to 2005–06
University-provided places: 2,659 (college); 545 (intercollegiate)
Percentage catered: 18% (college); 100% (intercollegiate)
Costs for catered accommodation: £97.86 (King's) for 40-week let; £91.70–£121.10 (intercollegiate) a week for 36–40 week let.
Costs for self-catered accommodation: £56.21 (twin); £82.39 (single); £98.42 (single en suite) a week.
Policy for first-year students: all new full-time students, on at least a 2-year programme, are guaranteed one year. Students who have firmly accepted a conditional or unconditional offer, and submit their completed application by 30 June, will receive an offer of a place in residence for their first year.
Policy for international students: within the quotas, priority for vacancies is given to intending overseas applicants who have not previously lived or studied in the UK.
Contact: 0207-848 2759;
www.kcl.ac.uk/accomm

Students

Undergraduates:	11,915	(2,430)
Postgraduates:	2,910	(3,220)
Mature students:	15.0%	
Overseas students:	18.8%	
Applications per place:	8.4	
From state-sector schools:	70.3%	
From working-class homes:	22.8%	

Tuition fees 2006	£3,000

See chapter 13 for bursary details.

Teaching Quality Assessments

From 1995 (top score 24):
24 classics and ancient history; dentistry; philosophy; war studies.
23 education; health subjects; Portuguese.
22 anatomy and physiology; biological sciences; medicine; pharmacy; physics and astronomy; Spanish.
21 French; Institute of Psychiatry; mathematics and statistics; nursing; theology.
20 electrical and electronic engineering; German.

Kingston University

Having established itself as one of the leading new universities, with 18,500 students, Kingston is hoping for a location to match. The university is planning to take over the headquarters of Surrey County Council, in the town centre, to provide a focal point and give it more flexibility. But it is not waiting for the go-ahead to pursue new developments. There is already a joint faculty with St George's Hospital Medical School and new buildings are planned at Penrhyn Road, the current main campus.

No department scored less than 20 points out of 24 in the final rounds of teaching assessment. The university has been trying to spread the message more widely to reduce what had been surprisingly large numbers recruited through clearing. It seems to be succeeding: Kingston has been bucking the trend among the few former polytechnics by registering regular increases in applications. A 17 per cent rise for courses beginning in 2004 was bettered by only one university in England and the same was true of the impressive 32 per cent rise registered at the start of 2005.

For the moment, the university has four campuses in southwest London: two close to Kingston town centre, another two miles away at Kingston Hill and the fourth in Roehampton Vale, where a new technology block occupies a site once used as an aerospace factory. A flight simulator and the university's own Learjet continue the tradition and a foundation degree in aeronautical engineering is ministers' favourite example of the two-year course. An unusually extensive, 1,600-terminal computer network links them all. Information technology plays an important role in student life, with the university's Blackboard system giving 24-hour online access to lecture notes and presentations, as well as chat rooms and bulletin boards. Seven more foundation degrees were added in 2004, including construction engineering and early years learning.

Over the last decade Kingston has invested more than £65 million in new buildings, which include facilities such as a 300-seat lecture theatre, additional teaching space and a high-tech learning resources centre. At the Penrhyn Road campus, recent development has featured a £9.8-million science building which has provided additional laboratory space with an electron microscope for the biomedical sciences and spectrometers for pharmaceutical subjects. Earlier phases of the development provided state-of-the-art computing facilities and increased library space.

Research grades in the last assessment exercise showed improvement, with European studies, history and history of art

---

Kingston upon Thames,
Surrey KT1 1LQ
T   0208-547 2000
E   admissions-info@
    kingston.ac.uk
W   www.kingston.ac.uk
U   www.kingston.
    ac.uk/guild

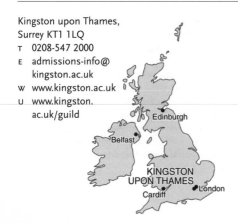

The Times Rankings
Overall Ranking: 61
(2005 ranking: 65)

Teaching assessment:	=17	(22.3)
Research assessment:	=72	(2.7)
Entry standards:	87	(214.3)
Student–staff ratio:	=92	(21.9)
Library/IT spend/student:	=62	(£498)
Facilities spend/student:	81	(£144)
Good honours:	=61	(54.9%)
Graduate prospects:	=47	(62.4%)
Expected completion rate:	69	(80.7%)

scoring well, but teaching scores have shown Kingston's real strength. The School of Life Sciences joined building and mechanical, aeronautical and manufacturing engineering in recording perfect scores, following on from some good performances under the original quality system. Politics almost joined the club in 2001, when nursing also produced a good result. Nursing is part of the Faculty of Health and Social Care Sciences, the successful collaboration with St George's Hospital Medical School. Pharmacy is the latest subject to be added to the faculty's portfolio of courses.

Private research income is healthy, with all academics encouraged to extend their interests beyond teaching. The business school has been especially successful with its services for small firms, and the university has also become a world leader in GIS – geographical information systems. The successful work-based MSc has allowed, for example, employees from the satellite company Astrium to embark on a series of projects, in this case to reduce production lead-times, and earn postgraduate degrees.

Nearly a third of Kingston's places go to mature students and a similar proportion to those from working-class families – both groups with low completion rates nationally. The latest projected dropout rate is 19 per cent, but this is no more than the national average for the subjects on offer. To make the university more responsive to its students, it provides a 'one-stop shop', which deals with student issues ranging from careers and accommodation to complaints and internal discipline, while the Dean of Students is a member of the university executive. Over £20 million has been spent on halls of residence in recent years, most recently with extensions and refurbishment of the two largest halls, which now have almost 1,400 beds. Students like the location, on the fringe of London, although complaints about the high cost of living are common.

Accommodation
Number of places and costs refer to 2005–06
University-provided places: 2,437
Percentage catered: 0%
Costs for self-catered accommodation: £79.50–£94.75 a week.
Policy for first-year students: first years are offered places provided an application is received by 26 August. Priority is given to those who make Kingston their firm choice. Students must be studying at Kingston for the first time for at least one academic year and their home must be more than 10 miles from Kingston station.
Policy for international students: the same policy applies for international students studying for at least one academic year.
Contact: Accommodation@kingston.ac.uk

Students

Undergraduates:	12,675	(1,880)
Postgraduates:	1,215	(2,835)
Mature students:	22.2%	
Overseas students:	11.8%	
Applications per place:	4.9	
From state-sector schools:	93.9%	
From working-class homes:	39.2%	

Tuition fees 2006 £3,000
See chapter 13 for bursary details.

Teaching Quality Assessments
From 1995 (top score 24):
24 biological sciences;
building and land management;
mechanical and aeronautical engineering;
town and country planning.
23 health subjects; mathematics; politics.
22 civil engineering; nursing; sports science.
21 art and design; economics;
electrical and electronic engineering;
modern languages; sociology.
20 history of art.

Lampeter, University of Wales

In the whole of England and Wales, only Oxford and Cambridge were awarding degrees before Lampeter. Yet only Buckingham University is smaller today. In fact, Lampeter claims to be the smallest publicly-funded university in Europe, making a virtue of its size by stressing its friendly atmosphere and intimate teaching style. It remains to be seen whether small remains beautiful when the recommendations of the Welsh Assembly review of higher education are implemented, however. The politicians favour collaboration between the Principality's small higher education institutions and some administrative tasks are already carried out jointly with Trinity College, Carmarthen.

Based on an ancient castle and modelled on an Oxbridge college, St David's College (as it was originally known) was established to train young men for the Anglican ministry. That title receded into the small print, as the University of Wales allowed its member institutions to drop their college titles. But the original quadrangle remains and the chapel is in daily use.

There have been significant changes in the last few years – notably a big expansion in distance learning and the introduction of such subjects as anthropology, IT, management, and film and media studies.

There are now 300 course combinations available in the joint honours programme. Victorian studies and medieval studies are unusual constructs, while Chinese studies, creative writing and media production are among the new arrivals. However, there is no immediate aim to go beyond 2,000 students, itself almost double the numbers taken a decade ago.

Lampeter remains an arts-dominated haven in rural Wales. Even IT leads to a BA, and the Bachelor of Divinity is the only other undergraduate degree. Lampeter is best known for theology, one of the two top-rated research departments, the other being English. The small campus includes a mosque for the growing number of Muslim students attracted by a well-endowed programme of Islamic studies. But students are opting increasingly for broad courses such as medieval studies, which includes archaeology, classics and theology, as well as history, English and Welsh. Media studies, which benefits from a well-equipped media centre for film and television students, is also growing in popularity. The university won a Queen's Anniversary Award for a degree in voluntary sector studies, developed from a series of sub-degree courses.

Modular degrees have been introduced, but degrees are still divided into two parts,

---

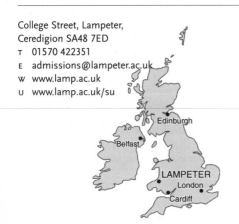

College Street, Lampeter,
Ceredigion SA48 7ED
T   01570 422351
E   admissions@lampeter.ac.uk
W www.lamp.ac.uk
U www.lamp.ac.uk/su

Edinburgh
Belfast
LAMPETER
London
Cardiff

The Times Rankings
Overall Ranking: 52
(2005 ranking: =61)

Teaching assessment:	=10	(22.5)
Research assessment:	=42	(4.7)
Entry standards:	76	(231)
Student–staff ratio:	=96	(23.8)
Library/IT spend/student:	79	(£427)
Facilities spend/student:	76	(£151)
Good honours:	43	(60.1%)
Graduate prospects:	=55	(60.8%)
Expected completion rate:	33	(89.8%)

with the first year designed to ensure breadth of study. Undergraduates are encouraged to try a new language, such as Arabic, Greek or Welsh. Part two normally takes a further two years, although philosophy takes three. From 2005, most courses will offer the option of a January start.

Lampeter is deep in Welsh-speaking West Wales, and both the university and the students' union have strong bilingual policies. The university is also taking Welsh to a wider audience, with the only university course teaching the language over the internet.

Although only four hours from London and two from Cardiff, Lampeter's geographical position could be a problem for the unprepared. The town has only 4,000 inhabitants, with among the lowest crime rates in Britain, and the nearest station is more than 20 miles away at Carmarthen. A high proportion of the students run cars. The students' union is the centre of social life – not surprising when the university's guide to the town lists its attractions as 'cafés, pubs, a curry house and a French patisserie'. Most students have made a deliberate choice to avoid the bright lights, and many would like to remain in the area after graduation, although jobs are scarce. The location helps to produce a relatively high proportion of students from areas with little tradition of higher education and, more surprisingly, more than a quarter come from working-class homes. The college's size can make for big fluctuations in the various published indicators. The projected dropout rate, for example, doubled in the funding councils' 2002 estimates, reaching 26 per cent, but it has now dipped below 10 per cent and is much better than the UK average for the subjects available.

Accommodation

Number of places and costs refer to 2004–05
University-provided places: 600
Percentage catered: 10%
Costs for catered accommodation: £70.00 a week (18 meals).
Costs for self-catered accommodation: £45.67 (standard); £52.70 (en suite) a week.
Policy for first-year students: all first years who wish to live in can be accommodated. No restriction on those living close to the university.
Policy for international students: all international students who apply can be accommodated in the university.
Contact: p.thomas@lampeter.ac.uk

Students

Undergraduates:	875	(5,185)
Postgraduates:	180	(870)
Mature students:	35.9%	
Overseas students:	15.4%	
Applications per place:	3.4	
From state-sector schools:	91.6%	
From working-class homes:	26.4%	

Tuition fees 2006	£1,200

Teaching Quality Assessments
1993–95 Rated Excellent:
archaeology; classics and ancient history.

Lancaster University

Having celebrated its 40th birthday, Lancaster is well under way with a £160-million makeover for its campus to give it a more modern feel and increase its capacity by up to 50 per cent. Still a relatively small institution, the aim is to break into the leading group of research universities and contribute more to the local economy. An assessment by investment analysts, who examined educational and financial issues, gave Lancaster a good rating, confirming that the university had recovered from funding problems in the mid-1990s. The process placed Lancaster among the top dozen universities for research and in the top 20 for teaching, as well as pronouncing it financially sound and capable of competing for students and research funds nationally and internationally. Official assessments place the university higher still: its last research grades were in the top ten and teaching ratings have been consistently excellent. An audit by the Quality Assurance Agency in 2000 gave top marks to all teaching areas.

Results from the 2001 Research Assessment Exercise were an improvement on an already strong performance five years earlier. Business and management, physics, sociology and statistics were all rated internationally outstanding and, with another ten subjects achieving grade 5, more than 70 per cent of the academics were in departments placed in the top two categories.

A £12-million environment centre to be shared with the Natural Environment Research Council opened in 2003, reinforcing the university's strength in environmental science. A £15-million centre of excellence in information communication technology, Infolab 21, was launched in 2005, providing a new research, computing and communications centre on campus. It will act as a technology transfer and incubation facility and house a training facility for high-tech businesses. The highly-rated Management School is also acquiring a £9.5-million extension.

Social work, which has a dozen applications for every place, attracted one of a number of glowing reports for teaching. Education, philosophy and theology joined psychology and drama, dance and cinematics on maximum scores in 2001. With politics also recording a near-perfect score, Lancaster departments had gone more than two years without dropping more than one point out of 24 in teaching assessments. Nevertheless, Lancaster is not just a ratings factory. Provision for students with special needs was rewarded with a Queen's Anniversary Prize.

Lancaster is another of the campus

Bailrigg, Lancaster LA1 4YW
T   01524 65201
E   ugadmissions@lancaster.ac.uk
W   www.lancaster.ac.uk
U   www.lusu.co.uk

The Times Rankings
Overall Ranking: 30
(2005 ranking: 24)

Teaching assessment:	=28	(22.1)
Research assessment:	=7	(5.8)
Entry standards:	28	(345.7)
Student–staff ratio:	76	(19.7)
Library/IT spend/student:	23	(£654)
Facilities spend/student:	=26	(£262)
Good honours:	34	(65.2%)
Graduate prospects:	93	(53.2%)
Expected completion rate:	14	(94.1%)

Edinburgh
Belfast
LANCASTER
London
Cardiff

universities of the 1960s which has always traded on its flexible degree structure. Most undergraduates can broaden their first-year studies by taking a second or third subject. The final choice of degree comes only at the end of that year. Combined degree programmes, with 200 courses to choose from, are especially popular. Some offer 'active learning courses', in which outside projects count towards final results.

The dropout rate has fluctuated but, at less than 6 per cent, the latest figure is much lower than the average for the subjects on offer. Lancaster has exceeded the funding council's expectations for the recruitment of students from state schools, but the proportion from working-class homes and disadvantaged areas are both significantly below the benchmark for the university's courses.

The previously uninspiring campus has benefited from recent developments, which have included refurbished lecture theatres, sports facilities and residences. The university is a ten-minute bus ride from Lancaster, three miles away. Students join one of nine residential colleges, which run their own 'freshers' weeks' and become the centre of most students' social life. Most house between 400 and 600 students in self-catering accommodation. Some 3,400 new and updated residential places came on stream in 2005, paving the way for the demolition of three existing accommodation blocks and their replacement by two new ones. The development has enabled Cartmel and Lonsdale colleges to transfer to the New Alexandra Park area of the campus with enhanced social facilities.

The campus has a reputation for being one of the safest in the UK. Sports facilities are good and conveniently placed. For those who want the outdoor life, the Lake District is within easy reach. Road and rail communications are good but, while Manchester and Liverpool are within easy reach, some students still find the immediate location more isolated than they expected.

Accommodation

Number of places and costs refer to 2004–05
University-provided places: 5,600
Percentage catered: 0%
Costs for self-catered accommodation:
£46–£54 (single); £71–£74 (en suite) a week.
Costs for meals: by joining the Campus Dining Club students can eat at university restaurants at reduced rate.
Policy for first-year students: all first years are normally accommodated, but insurance, clearing and very late applicants are not guaranteed places.
Policy for international students: international students are guaranteed accommodation throughout their studies.
Contact: CRO@lancaster.ac.uk

Students

Undergraduates:	7,510	(6,005)
Postgraduates:	1,510	(1,705)
Mature students:	5.0%	
Overseas students:	11.3%	
Applications per place:	6.3	
From state-sector schools:	90.7%	
From working-class homes:	19.0%	

Tuition fees 2006   £3,000
See chapter 13 for bursary details.

Teaching Quality Assessments

From 1995 (top score 24):
24 drama, dance and cinematics; education; philosophy; psychology; theology.
23 art and design; linguistics; physics; politics.
22 general engineering; mathematics.
21 biological sciences; health subjects; sociology.
20 French; Italian; Spanish.
19 German.

University of Leeds

The rise of Leeds as a clubbing mecca to rival Manchester has added to the attractions of a university which has long been one of the giants of the higher education system. It regained its position as the most popular university in Britain in 2003, retained that title a year later and was second only to the newly-merged Manchester University at the start of 2005. An unusually wide range of degrees gives applicants more than 700 undergraduate programmes to choose from, with over 1,300 academic staff teaching more than 31,000 students.

The university occupies a 140-acre site, two thirds of which is designated a conservation area, close to Leeds Metropolitan University and within walking distance of the city centre. The buildings are a mixture of Victorian and modern, the latest of which have extended the library, provided more space for biology and moved the business school into new £10-million premises.

The university had begun to spread its wings with a merger with Bretton Hall College, near Wakefield, with its sculpture park and established reputation in the performing and visual arts. But it has already been decided to close the campus in 2007 and bring the new Faculty of Performing Arts and Cultural Industries back to Leeds, where there will be a £1.5-million development including a theatre, performance design studio and rehearsal space. Nine other colleges in various parts of the county offer Leeds courses, but handle their own admissions.

Further afield, Leeds is also part of a 'worldwide network' which brings together four American and four British universities to collaborate initially on research, postgraduate degree programmes and continuing professional development. There was already a thriving European programme involving more than 100 Continental partners and a flow of students in both directions. A free-standing language unit caters for casual learners as well as specialists.

Leeds has followed the fashion for modular courses, enabling its students to take full advantage of a growing range of interdisciplinary degrees. Almost a quarter now take dual honours or combinations such as communications, women's studies or international studies. The university has been chosen to house a national centre of excellence in interdisciplinary teaching and another in assessment and learning in medical practice settings. Business and management is also increasingly popular, the business school having moved into the former Leeds Grammar School site.

Leeds, West Yorkshire LS2 9JT
T 0113-233 2332
E admissions@leeds.ac.uk
W www.leeds.ac.uk
U www.luuonline.com

The Times Rankings
Overall Ranking: 38
(2005 ranking: =34)

Teaching assessment:	=55	(21.5)
Research assessment:	=25	(5.3)
Entry standards:	20	(364)
Student–staff ratio:	=57	(17.8)
Library/IT spend/student:	44	(£563)
Facilities spend/student:	79	(£148)
Good honours:	26	(67.3%)
Graduate prospects:	34	(66.6%)
Expected completion rate:	=17	(93.4%)

Electrical and mechanical engineering, English, food science, Italian and town planning were all rated internationally outstanding for research in 2001, when Leeds had among the largest number of academics in the national assessment exercise. Teaching ratings were generally good, if sometimes less than outstanding. Education and philosophy joined physics and healthcare studies on maximum points for teaching, but 18 points out of 24 was disappointing for medicine and the assessment of classics highlighted student dissatisfaction with some aspects of the courses.

Student facilities are generally first-rate. Leeds teams regularly excel in competition and the university has been awarded one of five centres of cricketing excellence. The 8,000 computer workstations are among the most at any university and the library one of the biggest. It all contributes towards a low dropout rate of 6 per cent.

The already large students' union, famous for its long bar and big-name rock concerts, has been extended to cope with the latest phase in the university's expansion. A £4-million upgrade provided a new venue, more shops and catering facilities. Most students like the broad mix of backgrounds within the university, where nearly a quarter of the undergraduates come from independent schools. However, official performance tables have shown a surprisingly low proportion of working-class students and even fewer than the funding council expected from state schools and colleges.

Town–gown relations are generally good, but there has been concern about student domination of some areas. The university has over 7,800 residential places of its own, allowing it to guarantee accommodation to first years and overseas students.

Accommodation

Number of places and costs refer to 2005–06
University-provided places: 7,863
Percentage catered: 26%
Costs for catered accommodation:
£72.58–£109.68 a week (single room) for a 31-week contract.
Costs for self-catered accommodation:
£31.25–£85.00 a week (single room) for 40-week contract.
Policy for first-year students: single first years submitting an application by 21 June and not coming through clearing are guaranteed a place. No restrictions for local students
Policy for international students: full fee-paying undergraduates are guaranteed accommodation provided they submit applications by the required deadlines. New postgraduates are guaranteed accommodation until the end of the academic session in which they arrive.
Contact: accom@adm.leeds.ac.uk
www.unipol.leeds.ac.uk

Students

Undergraduates:	21,130 (4,555)
Postgraduates:	5,920 (3,960)
Mature students:	7.1%
Overseas students:	10.4%
Applications per place:	7.3
From state-sector schools:	76.7%
From working-class homes:	19.9%

Tuition fees 2006 £3,000
See chapter 13 for bursary details.

Teaching Quality Assessments

From 1995 (top score 24):
24 education; health subjects; philosophy; physics.
23 art and design; biological sciences; dentistry; E and S Asian studies; electrical and electronic engineering; history of art; pharmacy; politics; psychology; theology.
22 anatomy and physiology; business; drama; economics; French; German; media studies; Iberian languages; mathematics and statistics.
21 art and design; Middle Eastern and African studies.
20 agriculture; food science; materials technology; nursing; Russian; sociology.
19 chemical engineering; civil engineering; classics and ancient history; Italian.
18 medicine; **17** linguistics.

Leeds Metropolitan University

Leeds Met took the bold step of becoming the first university to set fees below the £3,000-a-year maximum allowed in 2006. Professor Simon Lee, the Vice-Chancellor, admitted that some of his colleagues considered him 'crazy' for opting for £2,000 because students might think the university's degrees were of lower quality than its competitors', but the move made a mark in a crowded market. The rate inevitably limited scope for bursaries for students from poor backgrounds, but was bound to attract middle-class students, who would not qualify for bursaries.

The university already had a reputation for widening participation in higher education: it is one of the largest providers of foundation degrees and has more than 40,000 students since the incorporation of a large further education college in Harrogate. Partnerships with two other FE colleges, in Leeds and Bradford, have produced a 'comprehensive' post-school institution, in which students can take courses from diplomas to doctorates. Four out of ten of its students come from the Yorkshire and Humberside region, and over half are over 21 on entry. More than nine out of ten are state-educated, although the proportions of working-class students and those from areas without a tradition of higher education are both lower than the national average for the subjects offered and entry qualifications.

Applications were up by more than 11 per cent when the official deadline passed for courses beginning in 2005, with the university remaining a popular choice for students at home and abroad. More than 3,500 students come from 120 countries outside the UK. Just over half are taking conventional full-time degrees, such is the popularity of sandwich and part-time courses. The projected dropout rate of 17 per cent is still below the official benchmark. As part of its efforts to widen access, LMU runs a course for sixth-formers from the region, awarding UCAS points for those who complete successfully. There is also a wide range of summer schools, including one for Asian women and one for Afro-Caribbean boys. Even before the advent of top-up fees, the university offered a range of scholarships for students from non-traditional backgrounds.

There are two campuses in Leeds: the main site close to the city centre and Leeds University, and Beckett Park, a former teacher training college three miles away in 100 acres of park and woodlands. The latter boasts outstanding sports facilities, including the £2 million Carnegie Regional Tennis Centre, as well as teaching

---

City Campus, Leeds,
West Yorkshire LS1 3HE
T   0113-283 3113
E   course-enquiries@lmu.ac.uk
W   www.lmu.ac.uk
U   www.lmusu.org.uk

The Times Rankings
Overall Ranking: 90
(2005 ranking: 75)

Teaching assessment:	=82	(20.7)
Research assessment:	=84	(2.2)
Entry standards:	65	(251.6)
Student–staff ratio:	99	(25.2)
Library/IT spend/student:	75	(£453)
Facilities spend/student:	=91	(£122)
Good honours:	70	(52.7%)
Graduate prospects:	81	(56%)
Expected completion rate:	61	(83%)

accommodation for education, informatics, law and business. Over 7,000 students take part in some form of sporting activity, and there is a range of £1,000 sports scholarships. The city campus is the subject of a £100 million development programme, beginning with the opening in 2005 of new premises for the film school.

Teaching scores improved after a poor start and it took until 2001 for business, management and economics to record the first perfect scores. Education and the large School of Health Sciences, with its 1,200 students, were close behind. Only 12 subjects were entered for the last research assessment exercise, with librarianship and information management the only one to reach the top three categories of seven. However, an institutional audit by the Quality Assurance Agency in 2004 praised the university for 'placing the student experience at the heart of the enterprise.'

Students are included on the committees that design and manage courses. There is a growing emphasis on educational technology, which was enhanced by a £20-million learning resources centre. More than 400 computers, audio-visual presentation studios and study areas are available all hours. Contacts with small and medium-sized businesses have been carefully fostered as part of the university's successful attempts to maintain a good record in graduate employment. The links

even attracted a Queen's Anniversary Prize in the last set of awards. Most undergraduate courses are determinedly vocational, although the modular system gives students considerable control over the content of their degree. Like its older neighbour, Leeds Met is benefiting from the city's growing reputation for nightlife. But it is making its own contribution with a famously lively entertainments scene. Young and mature students seem to mix well socially.

Accommodation
Number of places and costs refer to 2004–05
University-provided places: 2,300
Percentage catered: 0%
Costs for self-catered accommodation:
£60–£79 a week.
Policy for first-year students: allocations are mainly for first years or for students new to Leeds.
Policy for international students: international students are guaranteed accommodation if they apply by 31 July.
Contact: accommodation@leedsmet.ac.uk

Students
Undergraduates:	14,280	(8,180)
Postgraduates:	1,195	(3,180)
Mature students:	5.0%	
Overseas students:	2.7%	
Applications per place:	4.9	
From state-sector schools:	93.7%	
From working-class homes:	31.7%	

Tuition fees 2006	£2,000

See chapter 13 for bursary details.

Teaching Quality Assessments
From 1995 (top score 24):
24 business and management; economics.
23 education; health subjects.
22 cinematics; hospitality.
21 art and design; building;
civil engineering;
land and property management; nursing;
town planning.
20 psychology.
19 media studies; modern languages.
17 electrical and electronic engineering;
mechanical engineering.

University of Leicester

Leicester is beginning to take off, after many years living in the shadow of the big city universities. A string of excellent assessments for teaching and research have coincided with rising student enrolments and a £300-million campus development programme – one of the biggest in Britain – that has produced a buzz around the university. Rising demand has led to many subjects raising their entrance requirements – even chemistry (in the doldrums elsewhere) increased by 45 per cent.

Though the university celebrated its 80th anniversary in 2001, it is only now approaching the size of most of its traditional counterparts after growing by more than 60 per cent in recent years. Less than half of the 19,000 registered students are full-time campus-based undergraduates, but Leicester has the largest number of taught postgraduates in Britain and more than 6,000 distance learners, many of them overseas. Professor Robert Burgess, the Vice-Chancellor, is focusing on strengthening research and has scaled down the university's initial enthusiasm for two-year foundation degrees. But efforts continue to broaden Leicester's intake, for example through a summer school for local teenagers. Almost nine out of ten undergraduates come from state schools and more than a quarter come from working-class homes.

Teaching ratings improved considerably after a sound, rather than spectacular, start. The last dozen assessments all produced at least 22 points out of 24, with archaeology, ancient history, economics, education, museum studies and psychology recording full marks. Close behind are history of art, maths and statistics, American studies, politics, medicine and physics and astronomy – a predictable success for a leader in space science and the recipient of a Queen's Anniversary Prize. Leicester has Europe's largest university-based space research facility, including the £52-million National Space Centre, and was heavily involved in the Beagle 2 mission to Mars. By contrast, the university has also been chosen to promote good teaching practice in archaeology.

The medical school registered one of the best teaching quality scores for the subject. It has developed a new style of medical degree with Warwick University, allowing graduates in the health and life sciences to qualify in four years. The school has among the most modern facilities in Britain, and the siting of a medically-based interdisciplinary research centre at the university was another indication of growing strength. Genetics, which won the university a second Queen's Anniversary

---

University Road,
Leicester LE1 7RH
T   0116-252 5281
E   admissions@le.ac.uk
W   www.le.ac.uk
U   www.leicester
    student.org

The Times Rankings
Overall Ranking: 24
(2005 ranking: 29)

Teaching assessment:	=17	(22.3)
Research assessment:	=36	(5.0)
Entry standards:	34	(330.2)
Student–staff ratio:	=46	(16.9)
Library/IT spend/student:	49	(£545)
Facilities spend/student:	4	(£394)
Good honours:	30	(66.8%)
Graduate prospects:	46	(62.5%)
Expected completion rate:	26	(91.7%)

Prize in 2002, achieved the only 5* rating in the last research assessments. But a dozen subjects in the next category enabled Leicester to outperform a clutch of civic universities in terms of average grades per member of staff.

Other than clinical medicine at the city's three hospitals, all teaching and much residential accommodation is concentrated in a leafy suburb a mile from the city centre. Its location, adjacent to one of Leicester's main parks, is an attraction to students. A new biomedical sciences building opened in 2004 and a £25-million library extension, doubling its size and expanding its capacity to 1,500 seats, is scheduled for completion in 2007. The Richard Attenborough Centre has given the university a particular reputation for catering for disabled students.

Among a number of areas to have been refurbished recently is the students' union, which has spruced up its main bar areas and runs one of the most popular university nightclubs, the Venue. Extensive residential accommodation includes a £20-million 600-bed en suite development, with another 580 rooms due to be refurbished by September 2006. First-years are guaranteed a residential place and many second and third-year students also live in hall, although the majority choose to live in the reasonably-priced private accommodation available nearby. The main sports facilities are conveniently located; in 2004–05, students paid £45 a year to use them.

Accommodation
Number of places and costs refer to 2004–05
University-provided places: 4,404
Percentage catered: 32%
Costs for catered accommodation: £88.48 a week (14 meals) for a 30-week contract; includes telephone rental, cleaning, linen and JCR fee.
Costs for self-catered accommodation: £54.10 a week for a 39-week contract; includes telephone rental and JCR fee.
Policy for first-year students: a guarantee is offered to all first-year students.
Policy for international students: a guarantee of university accommodation is offered to all new international students with priority to those returning in subsequent years.
Contact: accommodation@le.ac.uk

Students
Undergraduates:	7,575	(1,635)
Postgraduates:	1,870	(4,835)
Mature students:	15.3%	
Overseas students:	11.0%	
Applications per place:	6.8	
From state-sector schools:	87.6%	
From working-class homes:	26.4%	

Tuition fees 2006   £3,000
See chapter 13 for bursary details.

Teaching Quality Assessments
From 1995 (top score 24):
24 archaeology; ancient history; economics; education; museum studies; psychology.
23 American studies; medicine; physics and astronomy; politics.
22 biological sciences; history of art; mathematics.
21 media studies; German.
20 general engineering; Italian.
19 French; sociology.

University of Lincoln

The opening of an impressive purpose-built campus alongside a marina in the centre of Lincoln brought about the most dramatic transformation of any university in recent times. Humberside University, as it then was, even gave its new location pride of place in its title. Now it has gone a step further, selling the previous headquarters campus and securing the approval of the Privy Council to become plain Lincoln University. While not moving out of Hull entirely, the university is concentrating its activities on a much smaller city-centre site.

The switch has paid undoubted dividends, helping to attract high-quality academics. The number of professors has grown from eight to almost 60 in three years. Student applications have increased for five years in a row, although only one new university in England had a smaller rise at the start of 2005. Rising entry grades in a number of the more popular courses may have put some applicants off.

New science laboratories and sports facilities brought the cost of the development in Lincoln to more than £75 million. Extra teaching and office accommodation has been added and a new £10-million architecture, media and communications building opened in 2003. A derelict warehouse on the edge of the campus has since been converted into a £5-million library, winning a nomination for a Civic Trust award. The campus now has just over 1,000 beds and there are plans for a dedicated students' union and event venue.

Despite the change of name, the university remains effectively two institutions 40 miles apart, although a broadband telecommunications network links the sites – part of the impressive IT provision, which runs to 1,200 computers. A further rationalisation of courses has left Hull with health and social care, applied computing, art and design and management, with £4 million being invested over five years in a site that now takes 2,000 students.

Lincoln initially concentrated on social sciences, accentuating the university's bias in favour of the arts, but has been building up a wider range of courses. The School of Architecture, for example, now has over 400 students. The 40-acre campus attracted architectural as well as educational interest, and represented the end of a saga. The cathedral city had been seeking a university presence for several years, but previous negotiations came to nothing. Following the acquisition of former art and design and agriculture colleges from De Montfort University in 2001, the university now has more than 8,000 students in and around Lincoln. Art and design is based in the

---

Brayford Pool, Lincoln LN6 7TS
T 01522 882000
E marketing@lincoln.ac.uk
W www.lincoln.ac.uk
U www.lincolnsu.com

Edinburgh
Belfast
LINCOLN
London
Cardiff

former college campus in the city centre, while agriculture and equine studies are at Riseholme Park, a 1,000-acre site ten minutes outside Lincoln.

Poor performances in both teaching and research assessments account for Lincoln's low position in *The Times* ranking, although results improved in the later years of the cycle and two recent institutional audits have been complimentary. Education achieved the university's first perfect score for teaching quality, while politics and international relations managed 22 points out of 24. Only 21 per cent of the academics were entered for the last research ratings, but still none reached the top three categories of seven.

All students take the Effective Learning Programme, which uses computer packages backed up by weekly seminars to develop necessary study skills and produce a detailed portfolio of all their work. Research into teaching and learning methods has been aided by a £1-million fund provided by BP. Some degrees can be taken as work-based programmes, with credit awarded for relevant aspects of the jobs.

Lincoln was the first university to win a Charter Mark for exceptional service, but the student experience inevitably differs between sites. More than a third of the undergraduates come from working-class homes and, although the projected dropout rate is 22 per cent, that is no more than the average for the subjects on offer, given the entry standards. Lincoln is adapting to its new student population with new bars and clubs, but will always be quieter than Hull, where a lively waterfront area means the city is no longer known just for the low cost of living.

Accommodation

Number of places and costs refer to 2004–05
University-provided places: Hull, 200; Lincoln, 1,037
Percentage catered: 0%
Costs for catered accommodation: n/a
Costs for self-catered accommodation: £77–£69 a week.
Policy for first-year students: priority given to students living more than 25 miles away.
Policy for international students: given detailed information and assistance.
Contact: mball@lincoln.ac.uk

Students

Undergraduates:	7,875	(5,235)
Postgraduates:	985	(1,220)
Mature students:	20.4%	
Overseas students:	21.4%	
Applications per place:	3.8	
From state-sector schools:	97.4%	
From working-class homes:	34.9%	

Tuition fees 2006 £3,000
See chapter 13 for bursary details.

Teaching Quality Assessments

From 1995 (top score 24):
24 education management.
22 politics and international relations.
21 health subjects; tourism; psychology.
20 art and design

University of Liverpool

Liverpool is investing £85 million to improve its 100-acre precinct for a student population that has reached 22,000 and will continue to grow despite a temporary drop in new entrants in 2004. An extended and renovated sports centre opened that year, refurbishment of the engineering facilities began in 2005 with the addition of an active learning laboratory, and a new small animal teaching hospital will follow in 2006, bringing all veterinary science clinical teaching onto one site. A £40-million fundraising drive is aimed at establishing world-class centres of excellence in management, law, medicine, engineering, veterinary science and architecture.

The university has already modernised its portfolio of courses while preserving a well-established reputation for research. The introduction of flexible, part-time degrees, with the option of day or evening classes, was the first step in the expansion programme. Applications rose by 12 per cent in 2004, although an increase of less than 1 per cent at the beginning of the following year was well below the national average.

Liverpool is been among the top 15 recipients of research funds, with outside income increasing dramatically in recent years. And there has been substantial investment in new educational technology, helping to cope with the demands of extra undergraduates. Students arriving in 2006 will benefit from a newly-extended main library and the top-rated medical school has also being expanded. Full-time numbers are almost exactly balanced between the sexes.

A series of excellent ratings in the early teaching assessments took time to repeat, but philosophy joined veterinary science, medicine and physics on perfect scores, while media studies and politics, mathematics and town planning all went close to emulating the feat. Nursing came through a re-inspection successfully with a score of 22 points out of 24. Physiology, mechanical engineering and English recorded 5* ratings for research in the last assessments, when more than half of the academics entered for research assessment were in departments placed in one of the top two categories.

The university prides itself on strength across the board. New courses include avionic systems with pilot studies and wireless communications with 3G technology. Most undergraduate courses are divided into eight units per two-semester year, many with examinations at the end of each semester which count towards the final degree. The university has withdrawn from teacher training, but it still claims that an unusually high proportion of teaching and research relates to the profession.

Liverpool L69 3BX
T 0151-794 5928
E ugrecruitment@liv.ac.uk
W www.liv.ac.uk
U www.liverpool
   guild.org.uk

The Times Rankings
Overall Ranking: 41
(2005 ranking: 41)

Teaching assessment:	=40	(21.9)
Research assessment:	=30	(5.2)
Entry standards:	33	(332.7)
Student–staff ratio:	=23	(15.2)
Library/IT spend/student:	60	(£500)
Facilities spend/student:	68	(£160)
Good honours:	41	(61.8%)
Graduate prospects:	38	(65.6%)
Expected completion rate:	27	(91.4%)

Liverpool was among the first traditional universities to run access courses for adults without traditional academic qualifications, but the projected dropout rate of less than 9 per cent is still better than the benchmark set by the funding council. Even before the introduction of top-up fees, the university was awarding record numbers of scholarships and bursaries to widen opportunities further. They include five in memory of the Hillsborough disaster victims and 34 in memory of John Lennon, mainly for Merseyside residents. Other access initiatives include a week-long summer school and the opening of a purpose-built children's centre to help mature students and staff, with 68 subsidised places. The proportion of state-educated students is higher than at the other civic universities and a quarter of the undergraduates are from working-class homes.

The university campus is only half a mile up the hill from the city centre. Other recent developments have included a £29-million biosciences centre, a £20-million cancer research centre and a £9-million management school with courses from undergraduate level to MBA. Both the university and the city have a loyal following among students, and Liverpool's status as Capital of Culture for 2008 should add to the attractions. The 3,350 places in halls of residence, self-catering flats and houses are more than enough to guarantee accommodation to all first years. The suburban setting of the main halls complex and the focus of social life on the guild of students means that there is less integration than at some other civic universities, but there is no shortage of nightlife.

Accommodation

Number of places and costs refer to 2005–06
University-provided places: 3,350
Percentage catered: 62%
Costs for catered accommodation:
£91.84–£103.95 a week.
Costs for self-catered accommodation:
£64.75–£77.35 a week.
Policy for first-year students: students offered and firmly accepting a place who apply by 26 August are guaranteed accommodation. The guarantee is not affected by a student's home address.
Policy for international students: the accommodation guarantee applies to all categories of international student provided application received before 26 August.
Contact: accommodation@liverpool.ac.uk
www.liv.ac.uk/accommodation

Students

Undergraduates:	12,500	(4,265)
Postgraduates:	2,225	(3,165)
Mature students:	11.0%	
Overseas students:	9.2%	
Applications per place:	7.1	
From state-sector schools:	86.2%	
From working-class homes:	25.2%	

Tuition fees 2006 £3,000
See chapter 13 for bursary details.

Teaching Quality Assessments

From 1995 (top score 24):
24 medicine; philosophy; physics; veterinary medicine.
23 physiology; business; mathematics; media studies; politics; town planning.
22 archaeology; civil engineering; classics; economics; French; nursing; pharmacy; psychology.
21 dentistry; electrical and electronic engineering; Iberian languages; materials technology; sociology.
20 health subjects; mechanical engineering.
19 biological sciences; German; **17** building.

Liverpool John Moores University

Naming itself after a football pools millionaire was just the start for one of the most innovative of the new universities. JMU was once accused of marketing itself more as a fun factory than a seat of learning, but the former polytechnic prefers to portray itself as 'forward-thinking'. Among the initiatives to its credit was the launching of Britain's first student charter, which became a template for others. It also launched the first degree in criminal justice and the first distance learning degree in astronomy.

Before university status had even been confirmed, it set about transforming itself into a huge, futuristic multimedia institution. The two learning resource centres serving different academic areas and a state-of-the-art media centre are open all hours. Many lectures have been replaced by computer-based teaching, freeing academic staff for face-to-face tutorials. Student numbers have soared, although there was a slight drop in new entrants in 2004.

Mainly concentrated in an area between Liverpool's two cathedrals, the university is now one of Britain's biggest with more than 21,000 students. Arts and science courses occupy separate sites within easy reach of the city centre, with the IM Marsh campus three miles away in the suburbs for education and community studies. JMU has retained a local commitment, with more than 60 per cent of the students drawn from the Merseyside area, some attracted by the range of diploma courses which still supplement the largely vocational degree programme. A 'learning federation' embracing four further education colleges in St Helens, Southport and Liverpool itself adds to the regional flavour.

A growing research reputation is a source of particular pride, and is reflected in an unusually large number of postgraduates for a new university. JMU was one of only two new universities to have a subject rated internationally outstanding in the latest research assessment exercise. Sports science made the step up from a grade 5 in 1996, while general engineering succeeded in holding onto that score and four more subjects reached the next category. Astronomy has a growing reputation, with a part share in a telescope in the Canary Islands. The International Centre for Digital Content, a partnership with Mersey Television, is developing a range of new courses, including masters programmes in computer games design and e-commerce. A £1.6-million maritime centre features the UK's most advanced 360-degree shiphandling simulator.

Teaching scores improved after a poor start, in which none of the subjects assessed

---

Roscoe Court, 4 Rodney Street,
Liverpool L1 2TZ
T   0151-231 5090
E   recruitment@livjm.ac.uk
W   www.livjm.ac.uk
U   www.l-s-u.com

The Times Rankings
Overall Ranking: 83
(2005 ranking: =85)

Teaching assessment:	=88	(20.6)
Research assessment:	75	(2.6)
Entry standards:	73	(236.1)
Student–staff ratio:	72	(19.0)
Library/IT spend/student:	87	(£396)
Facilities spend/student:	86	(£134)
Good honours:	77	(51.3%)
Graduate prospects:	43	(63.5%)
Expected completion rate:	=82	(77%)

under the original quality system was rated as excellent. The impressive range of courses in hospitality, leisure, sport and tourism achieved a perfect score in 2001, as did physics and the healing and human development courses in the School of Health before them, and the last overall audit by the Quality Assurance Agency found that standards had improved since 1993. An academic review has now rationalised subjects into six faculties.

JMU is one of the most popular of the new universities, judged in terms of applications per place. The demand for places on courses starting in 2005 was up by more than 11 per cent when the official deadline passed. The university's efforts to extend access to higher education are successful: there are more state-educated undergraduates than average for the subjects offered and almost a quarter come from areas where participation in higher education is low. However, the 22 per cent dropout rate is higher than the funding council's benchmark for the university.

Work-based degrees should attract even more non-traditional students. A new programme gives previously unqualified students credit towards their final awards for experience in the workplace and encourages them to build study projects around their job. Degrees can be taken in most subject areas, with at least a fifth of the work taught, usually at JMU.

Facilities for conventional undergraduates have been improving. The conversion of a city-centre hotel was one of a number of residential projects which have allowed the university to guarantee a place for young entrants from outside Merseyside. In addition to the university's own accommodation, a number of private halls, with around 3,500 beds, have been developed in collaboration with JMU.

Accommodation

Number of places and costs refer to 2003–04
University-provided places: 880 plus 18,000 bed-spaces on the books of Liverpool Student Homes.
Percentage catered: 0%
Costs for catered accommodation: n/a
Costs for self-catered accommodation: £47.85–£57.05 a week, based on a 40-week contract.
Policy for first-year students: all first years are guaranteed a place in halls of residence. Students with a Liverpool postcode can apply to the private halls.
Policy for international students: international students are guaranteed a place in halls of residence.
Contact: accommodation@livjm.ac.uk

Students

Undergraduates:	13,500	(4,160)
Postgraduates:	1,170	(1,890)
Mature students:	15.4%	
Overseas students:	9.9%	
Applications per place:	5.2	
From state-sector schools:	95.6%	
From working-class homes:	33%	(2001–02)

Tuition fees 2006	£3,000

See chapter 13 for bursary details.

Teaching Quality Assessments

From 1995 (top score 24):
24 health subjects; hospitality; physics.
23 pharmacy.
22 biological sciences; business and management; economics; land management; media studies; politics.
21 American studies; drama, dance and cinematics; education; mathematics and statistics; nursing.
20 civil engineering.
19 art and design; modern languages; psychology.
18 electrical and electronic engineering; general engineering; sociology; town planning.

University of London

The federal university is Britain's biggest by far, even if some of the most prestigious members have considered going their own way. Indeed its colleges and institutes have already seen their autonomy increased considerably. They are bound together by the London degree, which enjoys a high reputation worldwide. The colleges are responsible both for the university's academic strength and its apparently precarious financial position.

London students have access to some joint residential accommodation, sporting facilities and the University of London Union. But most identify with their college, which is their social and academic base.

The following colleges – some of which have dropped the word 'college' from their title to underline their university status – have separate entries, and each also appears within the main university League Table.

Goldsmiths College
Imperial College of Science, Technology and
    Medicine
King's College London
London School of Economics and Political
    Science
Queen Mary
Royal Holloway
School of Oriental and African Studies
University College London

Many of London's teaching hospitals have now merged with colleges of the university: Imperial College of Science, Technology and Medicine now incorporates St Mary's, Charing Cross and Westminster teaching hospitals.

King's College now incorporates Guys and St Thomas's (the United Medical and Dental Schools of Guys and St Thomas's).

Queen Mary now incorporates St Bartholomew's and the Royal London School of Medicine and Dentistry.

University College now incorporates the Royal Free Hospital Medical School and the Eastman Dental Hospital.

In addition, the School of Slavonic and Eastern European Studies is now part of University College, and Wye College (in Ashford, Kent, and offering degrees in agriculture, rural affairs and environmental studies) is now part of Imperial College.

Senate House, Malet Street,
London WC1E 7HU
T 0207-636 8000
E enquiries@eisa.lon.ac.uk
W www.lon.ac.uk
U www.ulucube.com

Enquiries: to individual colleges, institutes or schools.

Edinburgh
Belfast
Cardiff
LONDON

Colleges not listed separately

Birkbeck College
Malet Street,
London WC1E 7HX
T   0207-631 6000
E   admissions@bbk.ac.uk
W   www.bbk.ac.uk
12,085 undergraduates, mainly part-time.
Apply direct, not through UCAS.

Courtauld Institute of Art
Somerset House,
London WC2R 0RN
T   0207-848 2645
E   ugadmissions@courtauld.ac.uk
W   www.courtauld.ac.uk
125 undergraduates. History of art degree.

Heythrop College
Kensington Square,
London W8 5HQ
T   0207-795 6600
E   enquiries@heythrop.ac.uk
W   www.heythrop.ac.uk.
130 undergraduates. Degrees in theology
and philosophy.

Institute of Education
20 Bedford Way,
London WC1H 0AL
T   0207-612 6000
E   info@ioe.ac.uk
W   www.ioe.ac.uk
Postgraduate education courses.

London Business School
Regent's Park.
London NW1 4SA
T   0207-262 5050
E   help@london.edu
W   www.lbs.ac.uk
Postgraduate MBA and other courses.

*London School of Hygiene and Tropical
Medicine*
Keppel Street,
London WC1E 7HT
T   0207-636 8636
E   registry@lshtm.ac.uk
W   www.lshtm.ac.uk
Postgraduate medical courses.

Royal Academy of Music
Marylebone Road,
London NW1 5HT
T   0207-873 7373
E   registry@ram.ac.uk
W   www.ram.ac.uk
340 undergraduates. Degrees in music.

Royal Veterinary College
Royal College Street,
London NW1 0TU
T   0207-468 5148
E   registry@rvc.ac.uk
W   www.rvc.ac.uk
935 undergraduates. Degrees in veterinary
medicine.

St George's, University of London
Cranmer Terrace,
London SW17 0RE
T   0208-672 9944
W   www.sgul.ac.uk
2,845 undergraduates. Degrees in medicine.

School of Pharmacy
29–39 Brunswick Square,
Lond on WC1N 1AX
T   0207-753 5800
E   registry@ulsop.ac.uk
W   www.ulsop.ac.uk
675 undergraduates. Degrees in pharmacy
and toxicology.

London Metropolitan University

London Met made its debut in our guide two years ago, perilously close to the bottom of *The Times* League Table. It has not appeared since because it has blocked the release of data from the Higher Education Statistics Agency. Last year, senior officials argued that using figures relating to the two universities from which London Met was formed – London Guildhall and North London – would create a misleading impression of the new institution. This objection no longer applies, but still the university chooses to keep its performance secret. Other published statistics do not suggest that its position in this year's table would have been substantially different.

London Met's predecessors both specialised in extending the boundaries of higher education to bring in groups who are under-represented at traditional universities, and the new institution does not shrink from that mission. It has developed 240 new degree courses, which it describes as both intellectual and vocational, and which allow students to study citizenship, ethics or enterprise alongside their main subject. Many prepare students for professional qualifications and give credit for work experience or volunteering.

With 34,000 students and more than 2,000 academic staff, including part-timers, it has become the biggest single institution in the capital. However, until the start of 2005, when a 29 per cent rise in applications was one of the biggest in England, London Met had been struggling to attract full-time UK students through UCAS. The university had its grant for 2005–06 reduced for failing to hit its enrolment targets. Fortunately, many students come through other routes and overseas recruitment has remained healthy. London Met has more undergraduates from other EU countries than any university and is among the biggest recruiters from farther afield.

Economies of scale should improve the university's financial position, but a long-running dispute over academic contracts led to an international boycott by lecturers' unions. The 29 departments at the predecessor universities have been whittled down to 14, with the loss of up to 6 per cent of posts over five years, but the management expects the process to produce a more viable institution.

Sites remain centred on the fringes of the City of London and around north London's Holloway Road. Both universities had been refurbishing and reorganising their premises in the years before the merger. Post-merger, a new graduate school,

---

31 Jewry Street
London EC3N 2EY
T   0207-320 1616
166–220 Holloway Road
London N7 8DB
T   0207-753 3355
E   admissions@
    londonmet.ac.uk
W   www.londonmet.ac.uk
U   www.london
    metsu.org.uk

Edinburgh
Belfast
Cardiff
LONDON

The Times Rankings
London Metropolitan blocked the release of data from the Higher Education Statistics Agency and so we cannot give any ranking information.

designed by Daniel Libeskind, opened in 2004, and a science centre should follow in 2006.

Guildhall had spent £3.5 million bringing order to seven sites in and around the Aldgate area. The business school is one of the largest in Britain, many students coming from City firms to join part-time degrees or professional courses. Retained Guildhall courses include a variety of craft subjects. The silversmithing and jewellery courses are the largest in Britain, while those in furniture restoration and conservation were the first of their kind in Europe.

Courses are also directed at the local community. More than a third of the students are Afro-Caribbean and the proportion of mature students is the highest in England. Unfortunately, so is the projected drop-out rate, which remained close to one in three, despite some improvement, in the latest national survey. One of London Met's first objectives was to improve student retention: student support services, from admission to careers advice, have been remodelled and there is a particular emphasis on academic and pastoral counselling on entry and at other key points of courses.

Quality assessments were patchy at the two predecessor universities. Economics and business studies scored well for teaching quality at Guildhall, while business and management achieved the only perfect score at North London. Research grades were generally low in the last assessments, but London Met has a long-term strategy to bring about improvement. Fewer than 100 Guildhall academics were entered for the latest research assessment exercise, and only German reached the top three grades. American studies was the only subject to make the top three grades at North London, but, in contrast to 1996, none of the 17 entries finished in the bottom two categories.

Residential accommodation is limited, but many of London Met's students live at home. Sports facilities, too, are not extensive but, particularly in north London, the social scene is lively.

Accommodation
Number of places and costs refer to 2004–05
University-provided places: 1,342
Percentage catered: 16%
Costs for catered accommodation: £98.00 a week. (5 evening meals)
Costs for self-catered accommodation: 77.93–£86.94 a week;
Policy for first-year students: all first years accepting a conditional or unconditional offer, live outside the Greater London area and apply before 8 August are guaranteed a place. Priority given to disabled students.
Policy for international students: priority is given to international students.
Contact: accommodation@londonmet.ac.uk

Students

Undergraduates:	16,460	(8,565)
Postgraduates:	2,430	(4,145)
Mature students:	37.7%	
Overseas students:	n/a	
Applications per place:	7.5	
From state-sector schools:	97.0%	
From working-class homes:	43.9%	

Tuition fees 2006   £3,000
See chapter 13 for bursary details.

London School of Economics and Political Science

Always one of the big names of British higher education, the LSE was second only to Harvard University in *The Times Higher Education Supplement's* world rankings for social science in 2004. Now it is planning 20 per cent more places, having seized the chance to tackle a longstanding shortage of teaching space by acquiring former government buildings near the school's Aldwych headquarters.

The LSE took on a new lease of life under Professor Anthony Giddens, the academic face of Tony Blair's Third Way, as big names arrived from a variety of other top universities. Howard Davies, his equally high-profile successor, is building on that progress, having made the move into academic life from the Financial Services Authority. The cosmopolitan feel that derives from the highest proportion of overseas students at any publicly-funded university will continue and many of the new places will be for postgraduates, but there will be some increase in UK undergraduate places.

The LSE has produced 29 heads of state and 13 Nobel prizewinners in economics, literature and peace – including George Bernard Shaw, Bertrand Russell, Friedrich von Hayek and Amartya Sen. The nationals of more than 150 countries take up half of the places. Only the much larger Manchester University had more applications from overseas at undergraduate level at the start of 2005. Its international character not only gives the LSE global prestige but also an unusual degree of financial independence. Less than a fifth of its income comes from the Higher Education Funding Council.

Only Oxford and Cambridge have higher entry standards. A third of British undergraduates are from independent schools – one of the highest ratios in the country and higher than the funding council's benchmark figure, although still significantly less than it was five years ago. Efforts are being made to attract a broader intake with Saturday classes and summer schools. The projected dropout rate of 3 per cent is among the lowest at any university.

Areas of study range more broadly than the name suggests. Law, management and history are among the subjects top-rated for teaching, and there is even a small contingent of scientists. Business, economics, psychology and mathematics all produced good results recently. Only Cambridge outperformed the LSE in the last research assessments, which saw half of

---

Houghton Street,
London WC2A 2AE
T   0207-955 7124
E   UG-admissions@lse.ac.uk
W   www.lse.ac.uk
U   www.lsesu.com

The Times Rankings
Overall Ranking: 4
(2005 ranking: 4)

Teaching assessment:	=34	(22.0)
Research assessment:	=3	(6.4)
Entry standards:	4	(447.1)
Student–staff ratio:	10	(13.0)
Library/IT spend/student:	7	(£1,091)
Facilities spend/student:	73	(£155)
Good honours:	9	(74.5%)
Graduate prospects:	6	(78%)
Expected completion rate:	5	(96.8%)

the school's subjects rated internationally outstanding. The school entered the highest proportion of its academics, at 97 per cent, of any university and just one subject (statistics) slipped below the top two grades.

The LSE does not hide its light under a bushel: it describes itself as 'the world's leading social science institution for teaching and research'. A pan-European survey also showed the school's students to be more active in student associations, more entrepreneurial and more open to opportunities to work abroad than those at other leading universities. The students' union claims to be the only one in Britain to hold weekly general meetings at which every student may attend and vote, while the 120 student societies cover an unusually wide range of interests.

Improvements were being made to the campus long before the opportunity arose to expand. A £30-million Norman Foster-designed redevelopment of the Lionel Robbins Building now houses a much-improved library. The move was a welcome one since the number of books borrowed by LSE students is more than four times the national average, according to a recent survey. Additional buildings have been acquired, routes between buildings are being pedestrianised and a new student services centre has opened.

Partying is not the prime attraction of the LSE for most applicants, who tend to be serious about their subject, but London's top nightspots are on the doorstep for those who can afford them. Despite the high proportion of UK students from independent schools, few can. At least 2,700 residential places for 7,500 full-time students offer a good chance of avoiding central London private sector rents.

Accommodation

Number of places and costs refer to 2005–06
University-provided places: 2,762
Percentage catered: about 46%
Costs for catered accommodation: no longer available at LSE-run halls (students have voted for choice as to whether to take meals).
Costs for self-catered accommodation: £64 (shared room); from £85 (single room) a week.
Policy for first-year students: guarantee an offer of a space to every new first year undergraduate. There are no geographical restrictions placed upon first years.
Policy for international students: same as domestic students.
Contact: accommodation@lse.ac.uk
to apply and submit application forms on-line: www.lse.ac.uk/accommodation

Students

Undergraduates:	3,405	(130)
Postgraduates:	3,585	(1,155)
Mature students:	3.1%	
Overseas students:	47.5%	
Applications per place:	11.8	
From state-sector schools:	66.1%	
From working-class homes:	18.0%	

Tuition fees 2006 £3,000
See chapter 13 for bursary details.

Teaching Quality Assessments

From 1995 (top score 24):
24 business and management.
23 economics; psychology.
22 mathematics; media studies; philosophy; politics.
20 sociology.

London South Bank University

London South Bank ensured that there was no confusion about its location by adding the capital's name to its title in 2003, but there has been no change of direction. Once marketed as 'the university without ivory towers', its mission statement underlines the point with an emphasis on wealth creation and the labour market. Links with the local community are such that 70 per cent of students are from the area, many coming from south London's wide range of ethnic minorities. Of more than 17,000 students, over a third are part-time and half of the undergraduates are on sandwich courses.

Applications soared by more than 30 per cent at the start of 2005, as mature students in particular sought to avoid top-up fees. The proportion of mature entrants is among the highest in Britain, a feat encouraged by initiatives such as the summer school for local people to upgrade their qualifications. The Fast Track to Higher Education programme has been expanded to include numeracy, communication and study skills, as well as the original mathematics. The courses, some of which are tailored to the needs of mature students and some for younger students, start at the end of June and are limited to 15 hours a week so as not to affect students' benefit entitlement.

South Bank has stayed closer than most of the new universities to the technological and vocational brief given to the original polytechnics. Until the recent explosion in demand for health subjects, engineering was second only to business studies in terms of size. Diploma and degree courses run in parallel so that students can move up or down if they are better suited to another level of study. There have been some good teaching assessments, but the university did not quite match the general improvement in scores seen elsewhere in the later stages of subject review. Education, hospitality and town planning produced the best scores, but politics and health subjects also did well.

No subjects reached the top two categories in the last research assessments, but more than four out of ten researchers were in departments on the next rung of the ladder. Computer science, electronic engineering, town planning, social policy and English led the way. The results were considerably better than those in 1996, although a higher proportion of academics entered. Specialist facilities such as the Centre for Explosion and Fire Research show that the vocational theme carries through into research.

The main campus is in Southwark, near the Elephant and Castle, and not far from the South Bank arts complex. The nine-storey Keyworth Centre, which opened in

---

103 Borough Road,
London SE1 0AA
T   0207-815 7815
E   via website
W   www.lsbu.ac.uk
U   www.lsbsu.org

Edinburgh

Belfast

Cardiff

LONDON

The Times Rankings
Overall Ranking: 95
(2005 ranking: 97)

Teaching assessment:	95	(20.0)
Research assessment:	=64	(2.9)
Entry standards:	99	(179.6)
Student–staff ratio:	70	(18.7)
Library/IT spend/student:	=95	(£378)
Facilities spend/student:	97	(£101)
Good honours:	=74	(51.7%)
Graduate prospects:	=49	(62.1%)
Expected completion rate:	78	(78.2%)

2003, has upgraded much of the teaching accommodation and provided a new focal point for the university. Further development of the site is planned, but some projects will have to wait for planning permission. The faculty of the built environment was the latest to be brought onto the site, moving from its own premises three miles away. Some health students are based on the other side of London, in hospitals in Romford and Leytonstone, where there are limited learning resources, supplementing those in Southwark. The university now trains 40 per cent of London's nurses.

The social scene suffers from the fact that the large numbers of mature students are more likely to spend their leisure time with their family or local community than their fellow-students. The capital's attractions are on the doorstep but, with almost half of the students coming from working-class homes, many cannot afford them. The projected dropout rate of one in five represents a big improvement on previous years and is significantly less than the funding councils expected, given the subject mix and entry qualifications.

A new hall of residence means that London South Bank now has 1,400 residential places within ten minutes' walk of the main campus. It is not enough to guarantee places for all first years, but the 2,000 overseas students are all given places if they want them. Sports facilities improved considerably with the extension of the campus sports centre and the launch in 2004 of the Academy of Sport, Physical Activity and Well-being. Representative teams have been quite successful in recent years and sports bursaries of £3,000 are available for elite performers.

Accommodation
Number of places and costs refer to 2005–06
University-provided places: 1,400
Percentage catered: 0%
Costs for catered accommodation: n/a
Costs for self-catered accommodation: £73 (standard); £92 (en suite) a week. This includes utilities, internet connection and basic insurance.
Policy for first-year students: offer of a room not guaranteed; high priority given to first-year UK students who live furthest away.
Policy for international students: offer of a room guaranteed to international and EU first-year students if applications received by 1 August. High priority to final years in 400 returner's rooms.
Contact: accommodation@lsbu.ac.uk

Students

Undergraduates:	8,830	(6,565)
Postgraduates:	1,655	(3,085)
Mature students:	48.7%	
Overseas students:	11.9%	
Applications per place:	5.0	
From state-sector schools:	95.5%	
From working-class homes:	44.0%	

Tuition fees 2006   £3,000
See chapter 13 for bursary details.

Teaching Quality Assessments
From 1995 (top score 24):
23 education.
22 hospitality; Iberian studies; town planning.
21 health subjects; politics.
20 anatomy and physiology; biological sciences; business and management; civil engineering; media studies; nursing; psychology.
19 electrical and electronic engineering; sociology.
18 building; chemical engineering; food science; land and property management.
17 mechanical engineering.

Loughborough University

Best known for its successes on the sports field, Loughborough has enhanced its academic reputation recently, consistently finishing well up *The Times* rankings and rivalling Oxbridge in its teaching ratings, which average no less than 22 points out of 24. Good results are not confined to the technological subjects, which used to be the university's *raison d'être*: information science and human sciences achieved perfect ratings for teaching quality, while economics, sociology, drama and politics were only a whisker behind. The news is not lost on schools and colleges: the number of candidates shot up at the end of the 1990s, when others suffered from the introduction of tuition fees, and the university has maintained its popularity since, with another big rise of more than 12 per cent by the official deadline for places in 2005.

Loughborough merged with the neighbouring colleges of education and art and design, giving a more balanced mix between arts and science, and making the university less male-dominated. The university remains a major centre of engineering with more than 2,800 students in a £20-million integrated engineering complex. Aeronautical, automotive and civil engineering are particularly strong, although art and design, business and sports science now all have more students

than any single branch of the discipline.

The original 216-acre campus has benefited from a construction programme which included a large student union extension and a new business school, as well as the gradual refurbishment of residential accommodation. The 4,989 rooms now all have telephone and internet connections. The size of the campus has been increased by 75 per cent following the purchase of the adjacent Holywell Park site. This will become the focus for research and collaboration with industry, including a £59-million BAE-sponsored Systems Engineering Innovation Centre. The university prides itself on a close relationship with industry, which accounts for its record haul of four Queen's Anniversary Prizes. Arts facilities are improving with the upgrading of the Cope Auditorium to serve the campus and local community.

Most subjects are available either as three-year full-time or four-to-five-year sandwich courses, which includes a year in industry. This has helped to give graduates an outstanding employment record, as well a dropout rate of 6.5 per cent, which is particularly low for the subjects Loughborough offers. The university is a leader in the use of computer-assisted assessment, offering students the chance to

---

Ashby Road, Loughborough,
Leicestershire LE11 3TU
T 01509 222498/9
E prospectus-enquiries@
   lboro.ac.uk
W www.lboro.ac.uk
U www.lufbra.net

The Times Rankings
Overall Ranking: 14
(2005 ranking: 10)

Teaching assessment:	6	(22.8)
Research assessment:	=34	(5.1)
Entry standards:	29	(345.6)
Student–staff ratio:	=81	(20.3)
Library/IT spend/student:	25	(£644)
Facilities spend/student:	14	(£303)
Good honours:	=23	(67.5%)
Graduate prospects:	28	(68%)
Expected completion rate:	=17	(93.4%)

gauge their own progress online.

Only one subject (materials science) has dropped below 22 points since the quality system was changed in 1995, and that by only one point. The built environment, sociology and sports science reached the top rung of the research assessment ladder in 2001, when almost half of the academics entered for assessment were in the top two categories. The university has shown itself prepared to act when subjects are not living up to expectations: primary teacher training and some secondary training specialisms had their last intake in 2000, leaving the university to concentrate on its strengths in physical education, design and science. The Office for Standards in Education now rates Loughborough in its top category in all three areas. Loughborough remains pre-eminent in British university sport, both in terms of facilities and performance. Representative teams have a record second to none and the programme of sports scholarships is the largest in the university system. The heavily-oversubscribed School of Sport and Exercise Science moved into new premises in 2002, and in recent years the campus has acquired a 50-metre swimming pool, national academies for cricket and tennis, a gymnastics centre and a high-performance training centre for athletics. It also opened the UK's only centre for disability sport in 2005.

Social activity is concentrated on the union. The small town of Loughborough, a mile away, is never going to be a clubber's paradise, but both Leicester and Nottingham are within easy reach.

Accommodation

Number of places and costs refer to 2005–06
University-provided places: 4,989
Percentage catered: 58%
Costs for catered accommodation:
£87.47–£128.04 a week.
Costs for self-catered accommodation:
£54.56–£118.47 a week.
Policy for first-year students: guarantee to Loughborough first-choice students.
Policy for international students: guaranteed accommodation for two years of their course.
Contact: SAS@lboro.ac.uk

Students

Undergraduates:	10,165	(185)
Postgraduates:	2,375	(2,360)
Mature students:	4.1%	
Overseas students:	5.3%	
Applications per place:	6.0	
From state-sector schools:	84.5%	
From working-class homes:	23.5%	

Tuition fees 2006   £3,000
See chapter 13 for bursary details.

Teaching Quality Assessments

From 1995 (top score 24):
24 anatomy and physiology; health subjects; information science; psychology.
23 art and design; drama; economics; hospitality; mechanical engineering; physics; politics; sociology; sport and recreation.
22 business and management; chemical engineering; civil engineering; electrical and electronic engineering; mathematics and statistics.
21 materials science.

University of Luton

Luton's teaching ratings have been described by no less an authority than Charles Clarke, then the Education Secretary, as 'bloody brilliant' and recent figures showed that it wins more research contracts per pound of state funding than any other university. But Luton struggles with an unglamorous image. Twice in three years the university was forced to shed academic posts, blaming under-recruitment in particular subjects. The vocational thrust of the university was magnified as it withdrew from a number of academic areas, but applications had merely levelled out since the slump that accompanied the course closures in 2002 until this year's 9 per cent increase.

Never a polytechnic, it had to break all records for expansion to meet the criteria for promotion a year after the other new universities were created. The dash was worth it because tough obstacles were placed in the way of other ambitious colleges subsequently, but the strains showed in the more exalted company the institution was keeping. None of the first dozen departments to be assessed for teaching quality was even claimed to be excellent, and almost all subjects were placed in the bottom two categories in the 1996 research rankings.

Times have changed, however, and Luton is indignant that it is so often the butt of jokes about the expansion of higher education. The first official measure of graduate prospects showed the university to have the lowest unemployment rate of all. Developments costing some £80 million have transformed the main campus, and in the later rounds of teaching assessment Luton outperformed most traditional universities. The last six subjects to be assessed for teaching quality all attracted the equivalent of the old 'Excellent' rating, with health subjects and nursing producing the best score. Research grades improved in the last assessments, although only history and tourism reached the top three categories.

Although there are partner colleges in Bedford, Dunstable and Milton Keynes, most of the university is concentrated in Luton town centre. The borough council is considering making the Park Square campus the centre of a refurbished 'cultural quarter'. The campus, which is in the midst of the shopping area, has acquired an impressive learning resources centre, languages centre and extensive residential accommodation in recent years. Media arts was the most recent beneficiary in a £5-million move that gave the students access to digital facilities. There is an attractive management centre and conference venue

Park Square,
Luton, Bedfordshire LU1 3JU
T   01582 489262
E   admissions@luton.ac.uk
W   www.luton.ac.uk
U   www.ulsu.co.uk

The Times Rankings
Overall Ranking: =91
(2005 ranking: 74)

Teaching assessment:	=51	(21.6)
Research assessment:	94	(1.8)
Entry standards:	95	(194.3)
Student–staff ratio:	=96	(23.8)
Library/IT spend/student:	35	(£593)
Facilities spend/student:	89	(£127)
Good honours:	73	(52.3%)
Graduate prospects:	96	(48.2%)
Expected completion rate:	93	(72.5%)

at Putteridge Bury, a neo-Elizabethan mansion three miles outside Luton, but a graduate business school in Aylesbury was short-lived. Its courses have been transferred to the main campus.

Nursing and midwifery students in the growing Faculty of Health and Social Sciences, are scattered more widely, with Stoke Mandeville Hospital and Wycombe General Hospital the centres in Buckinghamshire, while Bedford, and Luton and Dunstable Hospitals provide the equivalent for Bedfordshire.

The university's commitment to open access is reflected in a high proportion of mature students, many of whom take access courses to bring them up to degree or diploma standard, while about a third of the school-leavers arrive through the clearing system. Luton claims to have the second most diverse intake in Britain, with almost one student in three coming from an ethnic minority and a similar proportion arriving without traditional academic qualifications. The projected dropout rate had improved in the latest official figures, although at almost a quarter, it was still significantly higher than the national average for the subjects on offer.

Courses are strongly job-related. English studies, for example, covers text production, website construction and computer conferencing skills, as well as more traditional English language teaching.

The university also makes the most of its high-tech facilities for assessment. More than 10,000 students in disciplines from accountancy to biology are subject to computer-assisted assessment.

Luton, although not known for its social scene, has its share of pubs, clubs and restaurants. London is only half an hour away by train for those seeking something livelier. Over 1,100 residential places have been added since university status arrived – enough to accommodate all first years. The university's sports facilities are limited, but students have access to top-class provision at the Vauxhall sports centre.

Accommodation

Number of places and costs refer to 2005–06
University-provided places: about 1,118
Percentage catered: 0%
Costs for catered accommodation: n/a
Costs for self-catered accommodation: Band C £60, Band B £67 and Band A £72 (single study bedrooms in flats) a week. Internet provision in all Band A and B rooms. Connection charge £36.31 thereafter usage is free.
Policy for first-year students: all first years are guaranteed a place in hall providing a booking is received by 31 August.
Policy for international students: as for first years. The Accommodation Service is available to International Students for help and advice on choosing suitable accommodation.
Contact: www.thestudentvillage.com

Students

Undergraduates:	6,225	(3,620)
Postgraduates:	1,015	(895)
Mature students:	36.9%	
Overseas students:	27.7%	
Applications per place:	4.0	
From state-sector schools:	98.2%	
From working-class homes:	44.8%	

Tuition fees 2006 £3,000
See chapter 13 for bursary details.

Teaching Quality Assessments

From 1995 (top score 24):
23 health subjects; nursing.
22 anatomy and physiology; art and design; biological sciences; building; media studies; pharmacy; psychology.
21 linguistics.
20 electrical and electronic engineering; modern languages.
18 sociology.

University of Manchester

Always among the giants of British higher education, with 22 Nobel prizewinners to its credit, Manchester became larger and more powerful in 2004 through a merger with neighbouring UMIST. The largest conventional university in Britain has kept its familiar name, but is now headed by a Vice-Chancellor from the other side of the world. Professor Alan Gilbert arrived from the University of Melbourne shortly before the new institution was formed.

Some departments were already administered jointly with UMIST and the two institutions only separated fully in 1993, so the new institution hopes to avoid some of the problems associated with other university mergers. An unprecedented £300-million capital fund is helping to smooth over any difficulties and a raft of new professors are being appointed. The aim is not only to break into higher education's 'golden triangle' of Oxford, Cambridge and London, but to make Manchester one of the top 25 universities in the world by 2015. By then, the aim is to have at least five Nobel laureates on the staff.

Manchester celebrated its 150th anniversary with its best ratings to date, and was already going from strength to strength before the merger. Seven of the last dozen subjects to be assessed achieved maximum points for teaching quality – a record that none of its rivals can match – while the 12 subject areas judged internationally outstanding for research in 2001 trebled the haul five years earlier. The successful departments were spread equally between the arts and sciences, representing a quarter of the academics entered for assessment. Altogether, three quarters of the entrants were in subjects placed in the top two categories.

The university has been climbing *The Times* rankings, as well as reclaiming its place as the university with the largest number of applicants. There has been some slowdown since successive exceptional rises in 2002 and 2003, but the demand for places is still increasing. One of the priorities in the new institution's founding strategy is to broaden the undergraduate intake, with a particular focus on increasing recruitment from the city and its surrounding area. However, in addition to the normal bursary package for British students, Manchester is aiming eventually to have 750 awards for students from educationally-deprived backgrounds in developing countries.

UMIST's legacy is a strong reputation among academics and employers alike in its specialist areas of engineering, science and management. Two thirds of its academics reached one of the top two out of seven

---

Oxford Road, Manchester M13 9PL
T 0161-275 2077
E ug.prospectus@manchester.ac.uk
W www.manchester.ac.uk
U www.umsu.man.ac.uk

The Times Rankings
Overall Ranking: =16
(2005 ranking: 17)
(UMIST: 2004 ranking: 23)

Teaching assessment:	=28	(22.1)
Research assessment:	=10	(5.7)
Entry standards:	17	(372)
Student–staff ratio:	9	(12.7)
Library/IT spend/student:	10	(£838)
Facilities spend/student:	=29	(£249)
Good honours:	20	(68.6%)
Graduate prospects:	30	(67.2%)
Expected completion rate:	22	(92.3%)

categories in the last research assessments. Materials technology and health subjects were both 5* rated. Teaching ratings, too, were good, especially in engineering, and its graduates enjoyed a consistently excellent employment record. Surveys of employers frequently placed UMIST among their favourite recruiting grounds, helping to produce an unrivalled network of industrial sponsorship.

The merger has produced the largest engineering school in the UK, with a £20-million budget and 1,200 students. There already was a federal business school, which is certain to be among the strengths of the new institution, as should the medical school, which was rewarded for impressive teaching ratings with extra places in collaboration with Keele University. A new teaching block caters for the additional 230 places a year.

The city's famed youth culture and the university's position at the heart of a huge student precinct already help to ensure keen competition for places – and hence high entry standards in most subjects. Sports facilities, which were already first rate, have improved still further since the city hosted the Commonwealth Games. Students get discount rates at the aquatics centre opened for the games on campus, for example. The city's reputation for violent crime may be overstated, but the students' union runs late-night minibuses, self-defence classes, and regular safety campaigns. Students tend to be fiercely loyal both to the university and their adopted city.

Accommodation

Number of places and costs refer to 2004–05.
University-provided places: 9,100
Percentage catered: 29%
Costs for catered accommodation: £79–£106 a week, based on 38-week let.
Costs for self-catered accommodation: £47–£78 a week, based on 38-week let.
Policy for first-year students: all unaccompanied students are guaranteed accommodation provided that they have an unconditional place and have submitted an application for accommodation by 31 August. There are no restrictions on local students.
Policy for international students: international students paying the overseas rates of fees are guaranteed accommodation for the duration of their studies.
Contact: Accommodation@man.ac.uk
www.accommodation.man.ac.uk

Students

Undergraduates:	22,480	(2,385)
Postgraduates:	5,935	(4,740)
Mature students:	7.5%	
Overseas students:	13.8%	
Applications per place:	8.3	
From state-sector schools:	80.2%	
From working-class homes:	22.7%	

Tuition fees 2006 £3,000
See chapter 13 for bursary details.

Teaching Quality Assessments

From 1995 (top score 24):
24 business and management; classics and ancient history; dentistry; economics; medicine; pharmacy; philosophy; physics and astronomy; politics; theology.
23 anatomy; archaeology; biological sciences; education; health subjects; nursing.
22 building; chemical engineering; civil engineering; electrical and electronic engineering; leisure management; mathematics and statistics; psychology.
21 drama; German; history of art; linguistics; material science; sociology.
20 aerospace engineering; Iberian languages; Middle Eastern and African studies; town planning;
19 French; Italian; **16** Russian.

Manchester Metropolitan University

With over 31,000 students, including almost 9,000 part-timers, Manchester Metropolitan is neck and neck with its newly-merged neighbour for the title of the largest conventional higher education institution in Britain. But the giant institution boasts quality as well as quantity, as it demonstrated in 2001 with one of the first 5* ratings for research at a new university. Sports science was the area rated internationally outstanding, while seven other subjects were rated in the top three of seven categories.

Although the former polytechnic has not been able to sustain the lead it held briefly over Manchester University in applications, still only a handful of institutions are more popular. There was another 10 per cent increase in the demand for places at the start of 2005. Long-standing commitments to extending access are being continued: even among the full-time undergraduates, a third are over 25 and a higher proportion still are from working-class homes. Nearly 95 per cent of the undergraduates went to state schools and 18 per cent come from areas without a tradition of higher education. Almost 600 courses cover more than 70 subjects, with the menu of programmes including a growing range of two-year foundation degrees.

The university features in *The Times* top 20 for materials technology, librarianship and drama, dance and cinematics. Only mechanical engineering was rated as excellent in the first rounds of assessment, but scores improved subsequently and included near-perfect results for business, drama and philosophy. A dozen subjects achieved at least 22 points out of 24. The university takes teaching seriously: small groups are used whenever possible and staff are encouraged to take a three-year MA in teaching, which has been running since 1992. Many courses also involve work placements.

Education courses have also fared well in the Teacher Training Agency's performance indicators, especially for primary training. The university trains more teachers than any other and has launched a Centre for Urban Education to develop its expertise further. Some 800 trainees and other students taking contemporary arts and sports science are at the former Crewe and Alsager College campuses, 40 miles south of Manchester and now rebranded as MMU Cheshire. The remaining education students are based at Didsbury, five miles out of the centre of Manchester, with those taking community studies. A single Institute of Education covers both centres.

The Crewe and Alsager campuses are six miles apart, but free transport is provided

---

All Saints Building,
Oxford Road, Manchester M15 6BH
T   0161-247 1035/6/7/8
E   prospectus@mmu.ac.uk
W   www.mmu.ac.uk
U   www.mmsu.com

The Times Rankings
Overall Ranking: 75
(2005 ranking: 73)

Teaching assessment:	=62	(21.3)
Research assessment:	=64	(2.9)
Entry standards:	63	(252.7)
Student–staff ratio:	89	(21.4)
Library/IT spend/student:	73	(£458)
Facilities spend/student:	88	(£128)
Good honours:	85	(49.1%)
Graduate prospects:	=84	(54.4%)
Expected completion rate:	=65	(81.6%)

between the two. Although the rural location inevitably makes for a quieter life than in Manchester, Alsager has an arts centre with two theatres, a dance studio and an art gallery, as well as extensive sports facilities, while the Crewe campus has its own nightclub. Eventually, the university intends to develop Crewe as its Cheshire base, adding sports facilities and residential accommodation, as well as more lecture theatres.

There are five sites in Manchester, stretching from leafy Didsbury to the extensive All Saints campus, close to the city centre and Manchester University. The large business school has its own site right in the centre, while health courses – including the recently-incorporated Manchester School of Physiotherapy – are not far away on the Elizabeth Gaskell campus, and clothing, food and hospitality courses are another mile out. Overseas links have expanded rapidly in recent years, offering exchange opportunities in Europe and farther afield, as well as establishing teaching bases abroad.

More than half of the students come from the Manchester area, easing the pressure on accommodation in a city of nearly 70,000 students. Some 85 per cent of hall places are reserved for first years, with priority going to the disabled and those who live furthest from the university. The city's attractions do no harm to recruitment levels, but much depends on where the course is based. Didsbury may offer the best of both worlds, with swift access to the city centre and a peaceful environment, but students at Crewe and Alsager can feel isolated. Some potential applicants are daunted by the sheer size of the university, but individual courses and sites usually provide a social circle.

Accommodation
Number of places and costs refer to 2005–06
University-provided places: 4,500; 8,200 in privately-owned halls.
Percentage catered: 20%; 4% in privately-owned halls
Costs for catered accommodation: £79.50 a week (16 meals).
Costs for self-catered accommodation: £49.25–£65.25 (standard); £68.25–£80.00 (en suite).
Policy for first-year students: all new full-time students who apply for accommodation before the start of the academic year will be offered halls somewhere in Manchester (or at Crewe/Alsager if studying at a Cheshire campus).
Policy for international students: same as above.
Contact: accommodation@mmu.ac.uk

Students

Undergraduates:	20,725	(4,060)
Postgraduates:	2,275	(4,635)
Mature students:	14.3%	
Overseas students:	6.0%	
Applications per place:	5.8	
From state-sector schools:	94.6%	
From working-class homes:	36.3%	

Tuition fees 2006 £3,000
See chapter 13 for bursary details.

Teaching Quality Assessments
From 1995 (top score 24):
23 business and management; drama; philosophy.
22 anatomy and physiology; art and design; biological sciences; health subjects; history of art; hospitality; materials technology; politics; psychology.
21 dentistry;
electrical and electronic engineering; librarianship; modern languages; nursing; sociology.
20 education; mathematics; town planning.
19 food sciences.

University of Middlesex

Middlesex has been changing the character of its intake, reorganising its courses and becoming more international, and now physical changes are on the way. A £100-million building programme will concentrate the university on three sites in north London. The new package should help sustain a revival in recruitment among home students, whose applications had increased substantially at the official deadline for courses beginning in 2004, following a decline in three of the four previous years. There was an even bigger rise by the beginning of 2005, partly fuelled by mature students anxious to escape top-up fees.

Middlesex already had more foreign undergraduates than any UK university, making up a quarter of its intake. A longstanding commitment to Europe sees more than 1,000 students arriving from the Continent and even more come from further afield. There is a network of 11 regional offices, in North and South America, Africa and Asia, producing a student population drawn from 130 countries. Its successes in the overseas market won a Queen's Award for Enterprise in 2003 and the university has now opened its own campus in Dubai.

Now almost 25,000 strong, including part-timers, the university aims to carry on growing. A network of partner colleges at home and abroad participates in exchanges and/or offers Middlesex qualifications. The university has reorganised its schools, having already pulled out of engineering almost entirely, to focus on its strengths in business, computing and the arts.

The highly flexible course system allows students to start many courses in January if they prefer not to wait until autumn, and offers the option of an extra five-week session in July and August to try out new subjects or add to their credits. An experiment bringing forward the start of the academic year to early September has been abandoned, with the result that the first assessments have reverted to after Christmas.

Nine out of ten students take vocational courses, many at postgraduate or sub-degree level. Health and social science is the biggest subject area, but almost a quarter of the undergraduates are on multidisciplinary programmes. More than half are over 21 on entry and half of the full-timers come from London.

Around 97 per cent of the British students are from state schools and over a third of them are from working-class homes, but the dropout rate of more than a quarter is significantly worse than the national average for the university's subjects

---

White Hart Lane,
Tottenham, London N17 8HR
T   0208-362 5898
E   admissions@mdx.ac.uk
W   www.mdx.ac.uk
U   www.musu.mdx.ac.uk

The Times Rankings
Overall Ranking: 79
(2004 ranking: 84)

Teaching assessment:	=72	(21.1)
Research assessment:	=72	(2.7)
Entry standards:	92	(199)
Student–staff ratio:	=57	(17.8)
Library/IT spend/student:	67	(£489)
Facilities spend/student:	60	(£174)
Good honours:	72	(52.4%)
Graduate prospects:	90	(53.6%)
Expected completion rate:	96	(71.7%)

and entry qualifications. Even before the introduction of top-up fees, Middlesex was attempting to attract better-qualified students by offering £1,000-a-year scholarships for UK entrants with 300 UCAS points (the equivalent of three Bs.)

For some time, the university has been reducing the number of campuses dotted around London's North Circular Road. The five remaining locations include a picturesque country estate at Trent Park and a business school campus at Hendon that includes a real tennis court and a new library. The Tottenham site was to have been the new focal point of the university, but ambitious building plans were shelved to the annoyance of some local councillors and MPs.

Nurses and other health students are based in four London teaching hospitals and on a campus at Archway which is shared with the University College and Royal Free Hospital medical schools. There is also a joint degree in veterinary nursing run with the Royal Veterinary College.

Teaching ratings improved considerably after an unspectacular start and Middlesex did well in the first of the new institutional audits in 2003. Philosophy secured the university's best teaching score and also registered one of Middlesex's two grade 5 assessments for research, denoting nationally outstanding work and some of international excellence. History of art was the other top scorer.

The number of residential places is planned to double in the next few years from the current 2,400 beds. Sports facilities have been improving, with a £250,000 refurbishment of facilities on the Enfield campus and the development of an Institute for Sport at Archway.

Accommodation
Number of places and costs refer to 2004–05
University-provided places: 2,075
Percentage catered: 0%
Costs for catered accommodation: n/a
Costs for self-catered accommodation: £68.04–£81.62 a week.
Policy for first-year students: full-year international students have priority, followed by the youngest UK and EU students coming from the furthest distance when Middlesex is their first choice.
Policy for international students: all new full-year international students starting in September are guaranteed a room in halls provided the Accommodation Office receives a completed registration form and £200 caution deposit by 18 August.
Contact: Accomm@mdx.ac.uk

Students

Undergraduates:	13,625	(4,490)
Postgraduates:	2,605	(2,175)
Mature students:	27.0%	
Overseas students:	19.2%	
Applications per place:	6.3	
From state-sector schools:	97.9%	
From working-class homes:	42.3%	

Tuition fees 2006	£3,000

See chapter 13 for bursary details.

Teaching Quality Assessments
From 1995 (top score 24):
23 philosophy.
22 American studies; business; drama, dance and cinematics; education; health subjects; history of art; nursing; politics.
21 art and design; economics; psychology.
20 mathematics.
19 electrical and electronic engineering; modern languages; sociology.

Napier University

Napier was Scotland's first and largest polytechnic, and has been pioneering again with the appointment of the first woman to lead a university north of the border. Professor Joan Stringer moved from neighbouring Queen Margaret University College with the declared aim of making Napier 'one of the leading modern universities in the United Kingdom'. Already an institution of more than 14,000 students, 3,000 of whom are part-timers, it has been developing the facilities to make that possible. Numbers have continued to rise thanks to increased recruitment on the Continent and a better ratio of applications to acceptances, despite a decline in applications seen at most Scottish universities in recent years. However, the 10 per cent drop in applications at the start of 2005 was the biggest at any UK university.

Two new libraries, a purpose-built music centre and refurbishment of the science laboratories underlined Napier's ambitions, with a £5-million computing centre completing the first phase of the university's development plan in 2001. The second is more ambitious, centring on a £30-million centre, opened in 2004, for the biggest business school in Scotland. The university has launched a £50-million fundraising scheme, with the first £10 million intended to meet part of the cost of the business

school. It has given itself a more leisurely period to raise the rest, setting a target date of 2050. A £1-million donation from a Hong Kong businessman got the fund off to a good start, suggesting that success might be achieved somewhat sooner.

Napier has been held up as a model to other universities trying to reduce wastage rates. There is a student mentoring scheme, 'bridging programmes' offering pre-term introductions to staff and information on facilities, and summer top-up courses in a variety of subjects. Nevertheless, the 37 per cent dropout rate projected for students who began courses in 2002 was the highest in Britain and twice the national average for the subjects on offer. Until 2004, Napier had the lowest dropout rate among the new universities in Scotland.

The university is named after John Napier, the inventor of logarithms. The tower where he was born still sits among the concrete blocks of the Merchiston site, in the student district of Edinburgh, where the new computer centre is based. The other main sites are Sighthill, a 1960s development in the west of the city, which is to be used by a number of support departments now that the business school has transferred, and nearby Craiglockhart, a one-time military hospital, where the new school has been built. It features a glass

---

10 Colinton Road,
Edinburgh EH10 5DT

T   0500 353570
E   info@napier.ac.uk
W   www.napier.ac.uk
U   www.napierstudents.com

EDINBURGH

Belfast

London
Cardiff

atrium housing a cyber café and two spherical lecture theatres with a total of 600 seats.

Ambitious plans for a Scottish Centre for Creative Industries Institute to be built at Craighouse, in the south of Edinburgh, have been shelved. But the campus will still bring together the creative subjects for which Napier is popular. A university bus service links the main sites, but there are several teaching outposts where lectures may be scheduled – notably in the Faculty of Health and Life Sciences, the biggest in the university and one of the largest providers of nursing education in Scotland.

Napier failed to register a single Excellent rating before the Scottish system of assessing teaching quality completed its first round of ratings in 1998, despite a string of Highly Satisfactory grades. However, computing and accounting achieved the highest possible scores in repeat assessments under the new quality regime operated in Scotland between 2000 and 2002.

Most of the avowedly vocational courses include a work placement, and the close relationship with industry and commerce helps to produce consistently good graduate employment figures. The modular course system allows movement between courses at all levels and has allowed students the option of starting courses in February, rather than September. Links with a network of partner colleges encourage progression from further to higher education, and off-campus courses that already give access to Napier degrees as far afield as Aberdeen will now be extended to China, where the university will be the first Scottish institution to set up.

The dispersed nature of the university does nothing for the social scene, although Edinburgh is hardly dull. Despite improvements, some students find life too quiet in the evenings and at weekends.

Accommodation

Number of places and costs refer to 2005–06
University-provided places: 929
Percentage catered: 0%
Costs for catered accommodation: n/a
Costs for self-catered accommodation:
£65.00–£69.25 a week.
Policy for first-year students: a guarantee of a place is given to first years if an application is received before the end of August. They must live 30 miles outside of Edinburgh.
Policy for international students: as far as possible, all requests are met if an application is received before the end of August.
Contact: studentaccommodation@napier.ac.uk

Students

Undergraduates:	8,635	(2,110)
Postgraduates:	1,095	(1,495)
Mature students:	34.7%	
Overseas students:	16.1%	
Applications per place:	3.4	
From state-sector schools:	95.9%	
From working-class homes:	30.4%	

Teaching Quality Assessments
1993–95 Rated Excellent:
none.
1993–97 Rated Highly Satisfactory:
building; biological sciences; chemistry; civil engineering; hospitality studies; mass communications; mathematics; statistics.
From 1998 (top score 24):
19 European languages.

See page 245 for recent assessments.

University of Newcastle

Newcastle has been growing in confidence and popularity: applications had been increasing consistently until a dip at the beginning of 2005 and the university was the first to announce that it would charge the maximum £3,000 fee for all of its degrees from 2006. A further 800 places are being added before then, as the university invests £7.5 million in campus facilities. Science and engineering laboratories will be upgraded, disabled access improved and thousands of students provided with internet connections in university flats and halls of residence.

A string of outstanding teaching assessments and the city's burgeoning reputation may have attracted applicants' attention. Originally Durham University's medical school, Newcastle's excellence in that area was confirmed by maximum points for teaching in medicine, anatomy and physiology, pharmacology and pharmacy, reviewed jointly with molecular biosciences, psychology and its department of speech. Dentistry only just missed out on the same score. The medical school's reputation was cemented with its selection as a national centre to disseminate best teaching practice in medicine. A university-wide audit in 2002 confirmed the quality of provision and noted that students found facilities and courses matched the descriptions in the prospectus. Newcastle has been chosen to house two national centres of teaching excellence, in music and healthcare.

The medical school is growing larger in a partnership with Durham, with about a third of trainees spending their first two years at Durham's Stockton campus. Other academic developments include the creation of nine new research institutes, housed in new buildings costing over £30 million. New courses have included Britain's first degree in folk and traditional music, complementing a course in pop and contemporary music, and a four-year business and accounting degree, in conjunction with PricewaterhouseCoopers, which provides a fast-track to professional qualifications.

As well as the normal range of subjects for a traditional university, Newcastle has a number of unusual features, such as a fine art degree which attracts up to 15 applicants per place. It also has a longstanding reputation for agriculture, which recorded good scores for both teaching and research with the benefit of two farms in Northumberland.

Research grades improved in the last assessments, with biological sciences, clinical laboratory sciences, music and psychology all rated internationally

Kensington Terrace,
Newcastle upon Tyne NE1 7RU
T   0191-222 5594
E   admissions-enquiries@ncl.ac.uk
W   www.ncl.ac.uk
U   www.unionsociety.co.uk

Edinburgh

Belfast

NEWCASTLE UPON TYNE

London

Cardiff

The Times Rankings
Overall Ranking: 19
(2004 ranking: 18)

Teaching assessment:	=20	(22.2)
Research assessment:	=30	(5.2)
Entry standards:	19	(366.8)
Student–staff ratio:	45	(16.7)
Library/IT spend/student:	11	(£777)
Facilities spend/student:	19	(£282)
Good honours:	27	(67%)
Graduate prospects:	11	(75%)
Expected completion rate:	20	(93%)

outstanding. Six out of ten academics entered for the exercise were in departments placed in the top two categories.

The campus is spacious and varied, occupying 45 acres close to the main shopping area, civic centre, Northumbria University and Newcastle United's ground. Half of the buildings date from the 1960s onwards. The university also boasts a theatre, an art gallery and three museums, which it hopes to bring together in a 'cultural quarter' for the city.

The university expanded dramatically in the 1990s, and should have more than 17,000 full-time students by 2005–06. It has become popular with independent schools, whose applicants take more than a quarter of the places, but the university has stepped up its contacts with local state schools in order to broaden its intake. The 300 students recruited through the programme have been doing at least as well as those with higher entry grades. Official performance indicators also reveal a healthy 93 per cent completion rate – better than anticipated, given the subject mix.

Few students regret choosing Newcastle for a degree, even if southerners can find the winter temperatures a shock. The city's nightlife is legendary – eighth best in the world, according to one survey – and the university topped a student poll based on computer facilities and student services, as well as the social scene. The cost of living is reasonable and town–gown relations better than in many cities.

Sport is a particular strength, Newcastle claiming to be one of the top ten universities both in terms of performance and facilities. A £5.5-million sports centre is opening on the campus in 2005, supplementing the two existing centres, which have refurbished fitness suites, massage clinics and all the normal indoor services. The main outdoor pitches are two miles from the university. Over £30,000 of sports bursaries are awarded annually to elite athletes.

Accommodation

Number of places and costs refer to 2005–06
University-provided places: 4,406
Percentage catered: 35%
Costs for catered accommodation:
£74.97–£98.98 (en suite) a week.
Costs for self-catered accommodation:
£48.23–£76.85 (en suite) a week.
Policy for first-year students: a student is guaranteed a room in university-managed accommodation if an offer of a place has been firmly accepted and an application has been returned on time. This guarantee does not apply to students who live locally.
Policy for international students: the above guarantee applies to international undergraduates.
Contact: accommodation-enquiries@ncl.ac.uk

Students

Undergraduates:	11,680	(1,170)
Postgraduates:	3,770	(2,290)
Mature students:	8.4%	
Overseas students:	8.4%	
Applications per place:	6.7	
From state-sector schools:	73.8%	
From working-class homes:	20.4%	

Tuition fees 2006	£3,000

See chapter 13 for bursary details.

Teaching Quality Assessments

From 1995 (top score 24):
24 anatomy and physiology; biological sciences; health subjects; medicine; pharmacology and pharmacy; psychology.
23 dentistry; economics; mathematics; politics.
22 agriculture; classics and ancient history; education; linguistics; modern languages.
21 archaeology; chemical engineering; electrical and electronic engineering; town planning.
20 art and design; civil engineering; marine technology.

University of Wales, Newport

Newport recorded the biggest increase in applications anywhere in the UK at the start of 2005, an almost unprecedented 41 per cent to follow the 15 per cent rise in 2004. All subjects experienced increased demand for places, including areas such as computing, which were in decline nationally. Most of the other universities registering big increases benefited from mature students getting in ahead of the introduction of top-up fees in 2006. But, since this policy does not yet apply to Wales, Newport could hope that the rise in popularity was more genuine. A change of name from college to university was thought to be one reason for the boom, but students were also attracted to a range of new courses in creative sound and music, cinema studies and scriptwriting, computer games design and internet technologies.

Full membership of the University of Wales had already encouraged more students to consider Newport and the college had embarked on an ambitious expansion strategy. A futuristic riverside campus that will practically double the number of students, will house the School of Art, Media and Design initially. At the same time, the university will pursue closer links with the University of Wales Institute Cardiff, which was already a partner in a number of subjects.

Art, media and design was awarded a grade 5 rating for research in the last assessments, but other research and teaching ratings have been disappointing. However, both students and employers appear enthusiastic. In the annual student survey, 94 per cent declared themselves satisfied or very satisfied. An equivalent poll of local employers was just as positive.

Just one academic in ten was entered for the latest research assessment exercise, the lowest proportion in the university system. As a result, only one university finished below Newport for average grades per member of staff. Only one subject has been assessed on teaching quality since 1996, but the eight subjects scrutinised before then were all rated Satisfactory, rather than Excellent. Business and management, which was assessed under a different system, was more successful, and Estyn, the Welsh schools inspectorate, commended the teacher-training courses for their excellence.

The university, which was previously Gwent College of Higher Education, now has 9,000 students from 44 different countries. There were merger discussions with Lampeter, University of Wales in 2001, but the two institutions agreed to remain independent.

Virtually all the full-time undergraduates come from state schools and there is a

---

Caerleon Campus,
Newport, South Wales NP18 3YG
T 01633 432432
E admissions@newport.ac.uk
W www.newport.ac.uk
U www.newport
   union.com/

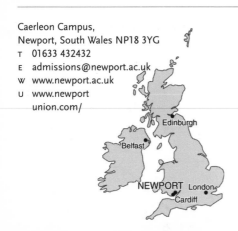

The Times Rankings
Overall Ranking: 93
(2005 ranking: 92)

Teaching assessment:	=92	(20.3)
Research assessment:	=61	(3.0)
Entry standards:	94	(195.5)
Student–staff ratio:	=92	(21.9)
Library/IT spend/student:	89	(£392)
Facilities spend/student:	31	(£239)
Good honours:	=87	(48.1%)
Graduate prospects:	=68	(58.9%)
Expected completion rate:	=82	(77%)

higher proportion from working-class homes than at any other university institution in Wales. However, the dropout rate of 22 per cent is still marginally higher than the benchmark set according to the subject mix. Newport operates a number of access schemes, including one offering students at local schools and colleges guaranteed places if they fulfil certain criteria.

The university is actively involved with a range of local businesses. It was rated the number one university in Wales for enterprise education by the Knowledge Exploitation Fund. Among its innovations is the Corus to Campus project for redundant steelworkers (previously employed by Corus), and it is also a leading player in the Community University of the Valleys. The college also hosts the International Film School Wales.

There are currently two campuses, the smaller of which focuses on engineering and computing, business and professional and social studies. The Caerleon campus is further out, with impressive views, and caters for humanities, science, education and art, media and design. It also contains the student village of 660 self-catered study bedrooms. Free buses link the two existing sites, which are officially among the safest in Britain: the college was the first educational establishment to pass an industry-standard security inspection.

A new sports centre at Caerleon has transformed facilities that previously compared unfavourably with those of other universities. The city of Newport has established a reputation for producing successful rock bands, but students in search of serious cultural or clubbing activity gravitate to nearby Cardiff.

Accommodation
Number of places and costs refer to 2004–05
University-provided places: 661
Percentage catered: 0%
Costs for catered accommodation: n/a
Costs for self-catered accommodation: £49 (standard); £57 (en suite) a week.
Policy for first-year students: accommodation guaranteed until 3 September.
Policy for international students: same as above.
Contact: accommodation@newport.ac.uk

Students		
Undergraduates:	2,535	(4,770)
Postgraduates:	365	(1,310)
Mature students:	36.1%	
Overseas students:	6.5%	
Applications per place:	3.3	
From state-sector schools:	99.3%	
From working-class homes:	42.8%	
Tuition fees 2006	£1,200	

Teaching Quality Assessments
1993–95 Rated Excellent:
none.

University of Northumbria

Always among the leading new universities in *The Times* League Table, Northumbria outperforms the rest of its peer group this year. With 24,000 students, including more than 7,000 part-timers, the former polytechnic begun to benefit as much as it would wish from its high grades and Newcastle's reputation as an exciting student city. It remains predominantly a local institution, with more than half of the students from the North of England. Although the rise in overall applications at the start of 2005 was smaller than in most similar universities, demand has generally been buoyant in recent years. A period of decline ended with a shake-up, in which academic departments were reorganised and the university's name was shortened (from 'Northumbria at Newcastle') as part of a rebranding exercise.

Entry grades for those with A levels are among the highest in the new universities, but more than half of the students are admitted with other qualifications or on the strength of relevant work experience. Free one-day taster courses run between January and July to give local people an idea of what a university course would be like. There is also a network of feeder colleges encouraging applications from adults without traditional academic qualifications.

The latest official figures showed a mixed picture on the university's attempts to widen access: the recruitment of one in five students from areas with little tradition of higher education was better than average for the courses on offer, but the 31 per cent from working-class homes was slightly below Northumbria's benchmark. However, the projected dropout rate remains among the best in the new universities, despite rising over the past two years.

The last big leap in numbers came with the incorporation of a large college of health studies in 1995. Health subjects have now overtaken business studies in terms of student numbers and have been highly successful in teaching assessments: nursing achieved Northumbria's first maximum score and, like modern languages and physics, health subjects managed 23 points out of 24. Education also managed maximum points in 2001 and followed up with a glowing report from the Office for Standards in Education. The university is in the top category for primary training and secondary design and technology. It has also been chosen to run a national centre of excellence in assessment, building on Northumbria's attempts to give students more constructive feedback and teaching them how to assess themselves as future professionals.

Ellison Terrace,
Newcastle upon Tyne NE1 8ST

T   0191-227 4777
E   rg.admissions@unn.ac.uk
W   www.unn.ac.uk
U   www.mynsu.co.uk

Edinburgh

Belfast

NEWCASTLE
UPON TYNE

London

Cardiff

The Times Rankings
Overall Ranking: 49
(2005 ranking: 48)

Teaching assessment:	=28	(22.1)
Research assessment:	=82	(2.3)
Entry standards:	58	(260.6)
Student–staff ratio:	=64	(18.3)
Library/IT spend/student:	28	(£636)
Facilities spend/student:	28	(£259)
Good honours:	=83	(49.2%)
Graduate prospects:	36	(66.1%)
Expected completion rate:	55	(84.1%)

The university also expanded geographically during the 1990s, opening campuses in Carlisle and at Longhirst, 15 miles north of Newcastle. However, the university is now focused on Newcastle itself. The main campus, with its mainly modern buildings, is just the other side of the civic centre from Newcastle University. The majority of subjects are based there, but health, education and community studies are on the Coach Lane campus on the outskirts of the city, where £18 million has been spent upgrading facilities. The campus now incorporates teaching and seminar rooms, a learning resources centre with a fully integrated library, a clinical skills centre and new sports facilities.

Northumbria's best-known feature is its School of Design with its renowned fashion courses, but 20 subjects have achieved the equivalent of the old Excellent grade for teaching. Research ratings improved in 2001 but still three subject areas finished in the last category but one. Only psychology and art and design reached the top three grades. Many degrees are available as sandwich courses, with placements of up to a year in business or industry. Law and business studies have the highest entrance requirements.

All first years from outside the area are offered places in university accommodation or in other housing arranged by the accommodation office. Two large residential developments with en suite rooms are opening in September 2005 and there is a plentiful supply of privately rented flats and houses.

Accommodation

Number of places and costs refer to 2005–06
University-provided places: 3,250
Percentage catered: 12%
Costs for catered accommodation: £85 (full board) a week.
Costs for self-catered accommodation: £41–£68, most commonly £56–£65 a week; £75.00–£77.50 (en suite) a week.
Policy for first-year students: all new students who need accommodation can be offered rooms.
Policy for international students: full-year first years can be guaranteed accommodation if application received in good time.
Contact:
rc.accommodation@northumbria.ac.uk

Students

Undergraduates:	14,375	(5,330)
Postgraduates:	1,735	(2,840)
Mature students:	17.9%	
Overseas students:	11.0%	
Applications per place:	4.7	
From state-sector schools:	89.5%	
From working-class homes:	31.1%	

Tuition fees 2006 £3,000
See chapter 13 for bursary details.

Teaching Quality Assessments

From 1995 (top score 24):
24 education; nursing.
23 health subjects; modern languages; physics.
22 art and design; building;
business and management;
drama, dance and cinematics; economics;
electrical and electronic engineering;
land and property management;
librarianship and information management;
physics; politics; psychology.
21 biological sciences; history of art; hospitality;
mathematics; town planning.
20 sociology.

University of Nottingham

For many years Nottingham has been among the institutions with the stiffest competition for each place, and a striking new campus and extra courses made it even more fashionable. At the start of 2005, it was still the most popular UK destination for overseas students, but overall applications were down by 7 per cent at a time when the national total was up substantially. The university believes that its high entry standards had put off some potential applicants, but extensive media coverage of crime in the city will not have helped.

The university already boasted one of the most attractive campuses in Britain, and has been rising up the pecking order of higher education. In less than 20 years, it has gone from being a solid civic university to a prime alternative to Oxbridge. Constantly among the top 15 universities in *The Times* League Table, it seldom stands still. A £30-million fundraising target was hit a year ahead of schedule and a series of projects have benefited.

The lifting of restrictions on student recruitment allowed the university to make room for 750 more students, but new undergraduates' average A-level grades have not dropped. Once in, they tend to stay the course – only Oxbridge can match the 2.5 per cent dropout rate. But the university is trying to broaden an intake which has more independent school students and fewer from working-class homes than the national average for the subjects offered. There is a well-established summer school for state school teenagers and a bursary scheme for Nottinghamshire students with no history of higher education in their families.

The 30-acre Jubilee campus, which cost £50 million and includes 750 residential places, is barely a mile away from the original parkland site. Futuristic buildings clustered around an artificial lake house the schools of management and finance, computer science and education. An additional building for the fast-growing business school was added in 2004 and a new sports hall is on the way. The medical school is also close to University Park, but the biosciences and the new veterinary school are at Sutton Bonnington, ten miles south of the city.

Nottingham describes itself as 'research-led', with work carried out at the university winning two Nobel Prizes in 2003. Professor Peter Mansfield, who won the prize for medicine for research leading to the development of the MRI scanner, has spent almost all his academic career there. The university received a record £82 million in research contracts in 2003–04, placing it among the top four universities in terms of

---

University Park,
Nottingham NG7 2RD
T   0115-951 5151
E   undergraduate-enquiries@
    nottingham.ac.uk
W   www.nottingham.ac.uk
U   www.students-union
    .nottingham.ac.uk

The Times Rankings
Overall Ranking: 12
(2005 ranking: 14)

Teaching assessment:	=14	(22.4)
Research assessment:	=25	(5.3)
Entry standards:	8	(419.9)
Student–staff ratio:	33	(15.7)
Library/IT spend/student:	17	(£715)
Facilities spend/student:	16	(£298)
Good honours:	7	(76.7%)
Graduate prospects:	22	(69.3%)
Expected completion rate:	4	(97.3%)

private funding. However, the last research assessments were disappointing by the university's high standards, with only five subjects awarded the coveted 5* rating – American studies, German, Iberian languages, music and theology – with 26 more subjects on the next assessment grade.

The university has devoted about £70 million to a research recruitment initiative in advance of the next assessments. It has advertised 20 research chairs and will be investing in the equipment and support posts to accompany them. Recent developments include a £7-million biomedical sciences building on the main campus and a £10-million graduate-entry outpost for the medical school in Derby.

Most teaching assessments have been excellent, with classics, economics and politics joining psychology and manufacturing engineering on perfect scores in 2001. Only one of the last nine assessments produced less than 22 points out of 24, and that by a single point. Nottingham is second only to Cambridge in the number of subjects rated at this level.

Nottingham has long-standing links with the Far East, which provides the majority of its 5,000 overseas students, and has a Chinese physicist, Professor Fujia Yang, as its Chancellor. The university has had a branch in Malaysia since 2000 and launched a new venture in Ningbo, China, in 2004. Purpose-built campuses will open in Ningbo and near Kuala Lumpur in September 2005.

Both main campuses are within three miles of the centre of Nottingham, with a good selection of student-friendly clubs. However, halls of residence and the students' union tend to be the centre of social life for students in both locations. Sports facilities are excellent.

Accommodation

Number of places and costs refer to 2005–06
University-provided places: 6,935
Percentage catered: 58%
Costs for catered accommodation: £84.50 (shared); £138.50 (en suite single) for a 31-week contract.
Costs for self-catered accommodation: £57.85 (standard flat); £94.00 (enhanced en suite) for a 44-week contract.
Policy for first-year students: students who firmly accept a place at Nottingham are guaranteed university-owned, leased, arranged or approved accommodation for one year if they return their preference form by 1 August.
Policy for international students: overseas students are guaranteed a place in university-arranged accommodation for 2 years provided they have firmly accepted a course offer and Accommodation Services receive their application for accommodation by 1 August.
Contact: ugaccommodation@nottingham.ac.uk
www.nottingham.ac.uk/crs

Students

Undergraduates:	17,510	(5,480)
Postgraduates:	4,140	(4,035)
Mature students:	5.4%	
Overseas students:	14.0%	
Applications per place:	8.9	
From state-sector schools:	72.9%	
From working-class homes:	16.9%	

Tuition fees 2006   £3,000
See chapter 13 for bursary details.

Teaching Quality Assessments

From 1995 (top score 24):
24 classics and ancient history; economics; manufacturing engineering; politics; psychology.
23 agriculture; biological sciences; food science; history of art; mathematics; pharmacy; physics; theology.
22 American studies; anatomy and physiology; civil engineering; education; electrical and electronic engineering; German; nursing; philosophy.
21 archaeology; chemical engineering; health subjects; material technology; medicine; sociology.
19 Russian.
17 Iberian languages.
16 French.

Nottingham Trent University

Consistently among the leading new universities in *The Times* League Table, as well as being one of the biggest, Nottingham Trent has demonstrated high quality in an unusually wide range of disciplines. Best known for fashion and other creative arts, which have the largest number of students, it also recorded maximum scores in teaching assessments for physics and biosciences. The law school is one of Britain's largest, offering legal practice courses for both solicitors and barristers, and there is even a commercial farm and equestrian centre on a campus devoted to land-based studies.

The university is particularly proud of the highest entry grades of any new university and a graduate employment record which saw 97 per cent of leavers in work or further study within six months in the last official statistics. It is the only former polytechnic with a projected drop-out rate of less than 10 per cent, although the intake is as diverse as most. Almost a third of the undergraduates come from working-class homes and over nine out of ten attended state schools or colleges.

An ambitious research programme was amply rewarded in the latest assessments, when Nottingham Trent had four subjects judged nationally outstanding, with much of their work considered internationally excellent. The achievements of drama, dance and the performing arts, English, media studies and health subjects was matched by only two other new universities.

An annual opinion survey shows that most of the students are satisfied. These surveys are part of a systematic attempt to involve students in decision-making. Helped by the popularity of Nottingham as a student centre, it grew by a third in five years in the 1990s. It is one of the few new universities to have seen applications increase in each of the last three years, although the 4 per cent rise at the start of 2005 was less than the national average.

There are now more than 26,000 students, including a large contingent of part-timers. The extensive main city site originally housed Nottingham University, but now boasts a mixture of Victorian and modern buildings. Science, education and the arts and media courses are five miles away on the Clifton campus. The last addition to the estate came from a merger with Brackenhurst College, an agricultural college 14 miles from Nottingham, where the university has invested £3 million in modern teaching and laboratory facilities. As well as a farm, the campus also has an equestrian centre with a purpose-built indoor riding area.

Improvements to the original campuses

Burton Street,
Nottingham NG1 4BU
T 0115-941 8418
E marketing@ntu.ac.uk
W www.ntu.ac.uk
U www.su.ntu.ac.uk

The Times Rankings
Overall Ranking: =62
(2005 ranking: 57)

Teaching assessment:	=82	(20.7)
Research assessment:	=67	(2.8)
Entry standards:	55	(268.4)
Student–staff ratio:	=64	(18.3)
Library/IT spend/student:	26	(£641)
Facilities spend/student:	=71	(£157)
Good honours:	=52	(57.3%)
Graduate prospects:	62	(59.8%)
Expected completion rate:	37	(89%)

have seen a new teacher training block and biomedical science building at Clifton and a £2.2 million renovation of the Waverley Building, the Victorian headquarters of art and design. The students' union had already had a £3 million upgrade and there has been a £450,000 refurbishment of the Boots Library. An environmental chamber, offering precise control of temperature, humidity and altitude simulation has helped reinforce sports science as a centre of excellence.

The university was responsible for the largest programme in the first tranche of two-year foundation degrees, covering 14 subject areas. They ranged from garden design to horse management. Pioneering new degrees include Youth Justice, Youth Support and health and social care. Teaching ratings were variable, but showed improvement towards the end of the cycle of assessment, with politics scoring 23 and education and sports science scoring 22 points out of 24 in 2001.

The student body is diverse, with large numbers of mature and overseas students. The university's residential stock has been increasing, with a £10 million development with 446 beds opening on the City campus in 2004. It still is not sufficient to accommodate all first years, but a 300-bed complex is due to open on the Brackenhurst campus in September 2006.

Social life varies between campuses, but all have access to the city's lively cultural and clubbing scene. A late-night bus service links the main campuses and the city's new tram system serves the university.

Accommodation

Number of places and costs refer to 2005–06
University-provided places: 3,400
Percentage catered: 0%
Costs for catered accommodation: n/a
Costs for self-catered accommodation: £67.59–£82.04 for a 40 or 48-week contract.
Policy for first-year students: guarantee of university allocated accommodation for new students (subject to terms and conditions). Students can apply at the conditional firm stage if Nottingham Trent is their first choice of university. Full online service available.
Policy for international students: guaranteed university accommodation if publicised criteria met (see website).
Contact: www.ntu.ac.uk/accommodation

Students

Undergraduates:	15,800	(2,865)
Postgraduates:	1,930	(2,840)
Mature students:	10.7%	
Overseas students:	5.1%	
Applications per place:	5.2	
From state-sector schools:	90.3%	
From working-class homes:	31.2%	

Tuition fees 2006 £3,000
See chapter 13 for bursary details.

Teaching Quality Assessments

From 1995 (top score 24):
24 biological sciences; physics.
23 health subjects; politics.
22 art and design; building; economics; education; psychology; sports science.
21 mathematics and statistics; media studies.
20 civil engineering; electrical and electronic engineering; land management; materials technology.
19 sociology.
17 modern languages.

University of Oxford

After eight years of league table frustration, Oxford finally toppled Cambridge from top place in *The Times* rankings in 2002, and has maintained its grip ever since. The university was also the best-placed British institution, in fifth place, in world rankings published by *The Times Higher Education Supplement* in 2004. With the arrival of a new Chancellor and Vice-Chancellor, Oxford is now braced for organisational changes in order to safeguard its supremacy and compete more effectively on the international stage. That may mean more research students and marginally fewer UK undergraduates, as well as changes in the relationship between the university and its fiercely independent colleges.

Oxford is the oldest and probably the most famous university in the English-speaking world, and it remains almost inseparable from Cambridge in terms of overall quality. Like Cambridge, it attracts world-class academics and takes its share of the brightest students. The pair are head and shoulders above the other non-specialist universities in *The Times* ranking and in the view of most experts.

Yet Oxford briefly slipped to third place in our table, partly because of comparatively low central spending on facilities such as careers and sport. The college structure, which produces an enviable student environment, acted as a handicap. However, a fairer reflection of overall spending, endorsed by the Higher Education Statistics Agency, together with a change in the scoring system to make allowance for the mix of subjects in each university, had a dramatic effect.

There was a 1 per cent rise in applications at the start of 2005 to follow larger increases in the two previous years. But the university is still struggling to broaden its intake and shake of allegations of social elitism. The steady increases in demand for places (which are concentrated in the more job-oriented subjects) are at least partly due to more systematic attempts to get the message through to teenagers that Oxford is open to all who can meet the exacting entrance requirements. Longstanding student visits to comprehensive schools have been supplemented by summer schools, recruitment fairs and colleges' own initiatives, as well as tireless public statements of intent by the university.

For all the university's efforts to shed its 'Brideshead Revisited' stereotype, however, official figures still show 45 per cent of Oxford's students coming from independent schools – the largest proportion at any university. Only 11 per cent come from working-class homes, despite the introduction well before the

---

University Offices,
Wellington Square,
Oxford OX1 2JD
T   01865 270207
E   undergraduate.
    admissions@
    admin.ox.ac.uk
W   www.ox.ac.uk
U   www.ousu.org

The Times Rankings
Overall Ranking: 1
(2005 ranking: 1)

Teaching assessment:	=14	(22.4)
Research assessment:	2	(6.5)
Entry standards:	2	(499.1)
Student–staff ratio:	11	(13.1)
Library/IT spend/student:	1	(£1559)
Facilities spend/student:	=5	(£376)
Good honours:	2	(86.4%)
Graduate prospects:	7	(77.5%)
Expected completion rate:	2	(97.9%)

advent of top-up fees of £2,000 bursaries for all undergraduates who are eligible for full fee remission. New, higher bursaries from 2006 may help broaden the mix further.

Selection is in the hands of the 30 undergraduate colleges, which vary considerably in their approach to this issue and others. Sound advice on academic strengths and social factors is essential for applicants to give themselves the best chance of winning a place and finding a setting in which they can thrive. The choice is particularly important for arts and social science students, whose world-famous individual or small group tuition is based in college. Science and technology, which have benefited from Oxford's phenomenally successful fundraising efforts, are taught mainly in central facilities. Applicants have the option of going straight into the admissions pool without expressing a preference for a particular college.

Recent developments include the new management school, made possible by a £20-million donation from the controversial Syrian businessman Wafic Said, which opened in 2001. An even bigger project has seen the addition of a £60-million chemistry building to house the western world's largest chemistry department, as well as new premises for economics. A £21-million social sciences library followed in 2004.

There was never much doubt about the strength of Oxford's research but, with 25 out of 46 subject areas rated internationally outstanding and 96 per cent of those entered for assessment placed in the top two categories, the latest grades confirmed the university's high standing. The university had the largest number of top-rated researchers and also attracts the biggest amount of research income, at about £200 million. Most teaching assessments have been similarly impressive, with classics and philosophy recording maximum points in 2001.

A major review of the university's activities resulted in some restructuring in August 2000, with the creation of five academic divisions, each headed by a full-time officer. But there will be no change to the eight-week terms and concentration on final examinations, which some students have found too pressurised. Only two in 100 drop out, however, a proportion bettered only by Cambridge.

Accommodation
See Chapter 10 for information about individual colleges.

Students
Undergraduates:	11,455	(4,580)
Postgraduates:	5,040	(1,940)
Mature students:	2.6%	
Overseas students:	10.4%	
Applications per place:	4.1	
From state-sector schools:	55.4%	
From working-class homes:	11.0%	

Tuition fees 2006 £3,000
See chapter 13 for bursary details.

Teaching Quality Assessments
From 1995 (top score 24):
24 art and design; biological sciences; classics and ancient history; philosophy; politics; psychology.
23 economics; general engineering; materials technology; physics; theology.
22 archaeology;East and South Asian studies; mathematics;
Middle Eastern and African studies.
21 anatomy and physiology; linguistics; medicine; modern languages.

Oxford Brookes University

Now firmly established as a leading new university in *The Times* League Table, Oxford Brookes was one of a handful of former polytechnics to have a subject rated internationally outstanding in the latest research assessments. That the 5* rating in history placed the department ahead of its world-renowned neighbour can only have added to the sense of achievement. English and French reached the next grade, although the biggest entry in any new university, representing 41 per cent of the academic staff, meant that overall results were unusually variable.

Applications, always buoyant, increased by another 9 per cent at the start of 2005, following an even bigger rise in 2004. The university's location has always been an advantage in student recruitment, but the quality of provision is the real draw. Its departments feature near the top of *The Times* rankings for several subjects, including a second place for land and property management. Town planning and economics achieved perfect scores for teaching, while art and design, and biological and environmental programmes are among a clutch of subjects where only one point out of 24 was dropped.

The university was chosen to house national centres for the teaching of business and undergraduate research in 2005, having previously won a similar accolade in hospitality, leisure and tourism. Its first two-year foundation degree was in this area and is expected to maintain the university's consistently excellent record for graduate employment. Further foundation degrees have been added in early-years education and for classroom assistants. The Oxford Brookes is also partnering Warwick University in the Government's academy for gifted and talented schoolchildren.

Almost a quarter of the undergraduates come from independent schools – by far the highest proportion among the new universities and twice as many as the benchmark figure calculated from national averages for each subject. The proportion from working-class homes and coming from areas without a tradition of higher education are also well both below funding council expectations, although the university is trying to attract more students from state schools and targeted areas in Oxfordshire.

Brookes made a leap in size in 2000, taking in Westminster College, a merger which added 2,000 students, mainly in teacher training and the humanities, and forming a £2.5-million Institute of Education. The new arrivals joined an institution that is challenging the traditional universities on their own ground, but

---

Headington Campus,
Headington, Oxford OX3 0BP
T   01865 484848
E   query@brookes.ac.uk
W   www.brookes.ac.uk
U   www.thesu.com

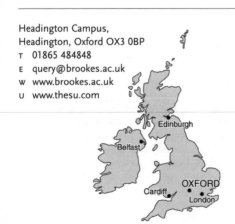

The Times Rankings
Overall Ranking: 53
(2005 ranking: 51)

Teaching assessment:	=40	(21.9)
Research assessment:	=67	(2.8)
Entry standards:	61	(258.8)
Student–staff ratio:	=38	(16.3)
Library/IT spend/student:	=95	(£378)
Facilities spend/student:	=26	(£262)
Good honours:	=55	(57.1%)
Graduate prospects:	27	(68.1%)
Expected completion rate:	=62	(82.6%)

retaining a substantial part-time programme and recruiting large numbers of mature students.

As a polytechnic, Oxford pioneered the modular degree system that has swept British higher education. After more than 20 years' experience, the scheme now offers in excess of 2,000 modules in an undergraduate programme which can pair subjects as diverse as history and physical sciences, or catering management and history of art. Each subject has compulsory modules in the first year and a list of others that are acceptable later in the course. Students are encouraged to take some subjects outside their main area of study, and there is a range of possible exit points. They can qualify for a Certificate in Higher Education after eight modules. The university switched over to semesters of 12 teaching weeks in 2004.

There are four main sites, two of which are only a mile from the city centre and linked to each other by a footbridge. The original Gipsy Lane site was becoming overcrowded when the chance came to acquire the late Robert Maxwell's 15-acre estate at neighbouring Headington Hill. Computing and business are five miles away at Wheatley. The Westminster campus at Botley focuses on teacher education, human development and learning.

A swimming pool and 18-hole golf course have been added to the already impressive sports facilities. Representative teams have a good record, the cricketers now combining with Oxford University to take on county teams. The social scene on campus is not the liveliest and Oxford can be expensive, but there is enough going on to satisfy most students. The university has increased its accommodation stock to more than 4,000 residential places but, while most first years are offered a place, allocation is based on how far from Oxford a student lives. The accommodation office organises house-hunting weekends in September, with free hall places bookable on 01865 483100.

Accommodation

Number of places and costs refer to 2004–05
University-provided places: 3,700
Percentage catered: 23%
Costs for catered accommodation: £3,600–£4,200 a year.
Costs for self-catered accommodation: £2,600–£3,750 a year.
Policy for first-year students: all accommodation is allocated to first-years by distance from Oxford Brookes.
Policy for international students: the policy is the same for all first years.
Contact: accomm@brookes.ac.uk

Students

Undergraduates:	9,695	(2,690)
Postgraduates:	1,975	(4,125)
Mature students:	22.8%	
Overseas students:	17.4%	
Applications per place:	6.5	
From state-sector schools:	76.0%	
From working-class homes:	39.7%	

Tuition fees 2006 £3,000
See chapter 13 for bursary details.

Teaching Quality Assessments

From 1995 (top score 24):
24 business and management; economics; town planning.
23 anatomy and physiology; art and design; biological sciences; building; history of art; land management; psychology; theology.
22 French; hospitality; mathematics; Iberian languages; Italian; politics.
21 education; media studies; sociology.
20 food science; health subjects; nursing.
19 electrical and electronic engineering; German.

University of Paisley

In common with several Scottish universities, Paisley saw the demand for places drop at the start of 2005, but it was already on a high plateau after the biggest surge in popularity at any British university in 2002, and smaller rises in the subsequent years. Students have been flocking to a new range of degrees in subjects such as computer animation, commercial music, computer games technology, sports studies and music technology. The demand for places on the education and media campus in Ayr grew by 50 per cent in a year.

The university is proud of its record in attracting under-represented groups onto courses. Its proportion of students from areas without a tradition of higher education is the highest in Britain, at 36 per cent, and the 42 per cent share of places going to working-class students is exceeded by only a handful of universities. The projected dropout rate has improved considerably but is still well above average for the university's subjects and entry qualifications. Paisley has introduced a range of measures to address the problem, including a new personal tutor system, strengthened counselling support and attendance monitoring. Access measures are continuing, with more than 600 youngsters aged 14 and 15 having attended the 'University Experience' and sampled a week

of student life in what was Scotland's first scheme to target this age group.

Only seven miles from Glasgow, Paisley is Scotland's largest town. The university has more than 10,500 students, including the many part-timers, a high proportion coming from the Glasgow area. Student numbers have grown rapidly in recent years, but staffing levels compare favourably with most new universities. Courses are strongly vocational, with business, multimedia and health subjects by far the most popular choices. There are close links with business and industry, notably with the computer giant IBM and Motorola. All students are offered hands-on computer training, and there is a postgraduate course available in information technology for those who want to move into the industry without a first degree in computing. Paisley was the first UK university approved by Microsoft, Macromedia and Cisco, and has the status of Microsoft Academic Professional Development Centre. A new games development laboratory, supported by Sony, is the latest development in a £300,000 package of investment in multimedia and games facilities.

No subjects were rated Excellent before the teaching quality system changed in 1998, but a majority were graded Highly Satisfactory. Under the new system,

---

Paisley,
Renfrewshire PA1 2BE
T 0800-027 1000
E uni-direct@paisley.ac.uk
W www.paisley.ac.uk
U www.upsa.org.uk

The Times Rankings
Overall Ranking: 76
(2005 ranking: 88)

Teaching assessment:	=66	(21.2)
Research assessment:	96	(1.6)
Entry standards:	72	(236.4)
Student–staff ratio:	=36	(16.2)
Library/IT spend/student:	18	(£695)
Facilities spend/student:	=49	(£194)
Good honours:	=74	(51.7%)
Graduate prospects:	94	(48.9%)
Expected completion rate:	95	(72.2%)

accounting and finance achieved good results in 2002. The university pioneered credit transfer in Scotland, giving credit for non-academic achievement, and its modular course system covers day, evening and weekend classes. Most students either take sandwich degrees or have work placements built into their courses, and earn an average of £10,000 in the process, but the impact on graduate employment has not been as great as in some other universities. Research grades improved in the last assessments, with accountancy achieving the only grade 5 in any new university in Scotland, but still the majority of entrants were placed in the bottom three grades. Applied research and consultancy is concentrated in specialist units on subjects such as alcohol and drug abuse and thin-film technology.

The university has invested over £6 million in student facilities in recent years. The main campus, covering 20 acres in the middle of Paisley, has seen substantial development, including a new library and learning resource centre. The campus in Ayr, acquired through a 1993 merger with a former teacher training college, has seen the establishment of a management centre in an 18th-century mansion. A third campus opened in Dumfries in 1996, in partnership with Glasgow University and a local college. The venture now has over 400 students, and a new teaching centre is increasing the range of courses available for the under-provided southwest of Scotland.

The two main centres could hardly be more different, Paisley industrial and seaside Ayr smaller both as a campus and a town and social life varies accordingly. The university has been investing heavily in improved leisure facilities, with a new students' union already open in Ayr and a £5-million town-centre union building now added in Paisley. Sports provision has also been improving: £1.5 million was spent upgrading Paisley's indoor and outdoor facilities.

Accommodation

Number of places and costs refer to 2004–05
University-provided places: 761 (658 at Paisley; 103 at Ayr campus)
Percentage catered: 0%
Costs for catered accommodation: n/a
Costs for self-catered accommodation: £47–£48 (residences); £39–£48 (flats) a week.
Policy for first-year students: where possible, accommodation is provided for those whose home address lies outside a 25-mile travel zone. Flats are not normally allocated to first years.
Policy for international students: housing is provided for those applicants on the waiting list at the time of allocation. Every effort is made to assist late applicants.
Contact: accommodation@paisley.ac.uk

Students

Undergraduates:	6,025	(3,025)
Postgraduates:	585	(955)
Mature students:	34%	
Overseas students:	5.5%	
Applications per place:	3.8	
From state-sector schools:	98.1%	
From working-class homes:	41.9%	

Teaching Quality Assessments

1993–98 Rated Excellent:
none.
1993–98 Highly Satisfactory:
biological sciences; chemistry; civil engineering; mathematics and statistics; mechanical engineering; psychology; social work; sociology, teacher education.
From 1998 (top score 24):
19 European languages.

See page 245 for recent assessments.

University of Plymouth

One of the first new universities to be awarded a medical school (in collaboration with Exeter University), Plymouth has been carrying out major restructuring. Roland Levinsky, the Vice-Chancellor lured from Imperial College London, set a target of making Plymouth one of Britain's top research universities within 15 years, while still serving the region through teaching. The most controversial element of his plans involved the transfer to Plymouth of courses from the Seale-Hayne agricultural campus, near Newton Abbot, and the arts and humanities programme based in Exeter. The 2,500 places at the two sites will be concentrated on the main North Hill campus from 2005.

The plans were part of an academic reorganisation which divided the university into six faculties and included a three-year programme of capital investment. It has seen the opening of a £30-million headquarters and a second teaching building for the Peninsula Medical School. The library has been extended and upgraded, at a cost of £7 million, with 24-hour study facilities, and the students' union has also been refurbished. The next big project is an arts complex, housing the Faculty of Arts and the Plymouth Arts Centre, and providing the focal point for a 'cultural quarter' around the university.

The Peninsula Medical School admitted its first 130 students in 2002, doubled its applications within a year and has never looked back. At the start of 2005, 12 months after another big increase, applications were up by more than 25 per cent. The university was already responsible for all nursing and midwifery training in the region, and the new medical school sees a variety of health professionals training side by side.

As a polytechnic, its title laid claim to the whole of the southwest of England, but although the university chose to name itself after its Plymouth base, it maintains a strong regional role. It is a partner in the Combined Universities in Cornwall (CUC) initiative, which aims to increase the provision of further and higher education in one of the few counties without its own university. Plymouth has also established a unique relationship with its 18 partner colleges, which spread from Cornwall to Somerset, through a faculty devoted entirely to serving their 5,300 students taking university courses. They have become the University of Plymouth Colleges, sharing £2 million in capital investment.

There are some teaching facilities in Truro and Taunton but only the Exmouth campus will remain open, specialising in education and related subjects. It has acquired a new £2-million teaching centre

---

Plymouth,
Devon PL4 8AA
T   01752 232232
E   admissions@plymouth.ac.uk
W   www.plymouth.ac.uk
U   www.upsuonline.co.uk

Edinburgh
Belfast
London
Cardiff
PLYMOUTH

The Times Rankings
Overall Ranking: 57
(2005 ranking: 53)

Teaching assessment:	=58	(21.4)
Research assessment:	=57	(3.2)
Entry standards:	64	(252.1)
Student–staff ratio:	12	(13.2)
Library/IT spend/student:	61	(£499)
Facilities spend/student:	=35	(£221)
Good honours:	=67	(52.8%)
Graduate prospects:	=79	(56.1%)
Expected completion rate:	=48	(85.3%)

and is scheduled for further investment that will bring the total to £8 million.

The intake reflects Plymouth's position as the working-class hub of the southwest, with nine out of ten students state-educated and almost a third from the poorest social classes. The dropout rate is the best in the new universities. Although the university is still best known for marine studies, its top teaching scores have come in civil engineering, building, psychology, nursing, and hospitality, each of which narrowly missed out on full marks. Plymouth was chosen to house no fewer than four national teaching centres: in health and social care placements, experiential learning in environmental and natural sciences, institutional partnerships and education for sustainable development.

The university also has a longstanding commitment to research. More than a third of the academics were entered for the last research assessment exercise, with computer science, psychology and art history all rated nationally outstanding with significant work of international excellence. But it hit the headlines for introducing a degree in surfing, which it insisted was rigorous as well as vocational. The first graduates all found related employment and the course continues to be oversubscribed. Plymouth has since followed it with a degree in applied marine sports science, in collaboration with the neighbouring College of St Mark and St John.

Plymouth is naturally livelier than Exmouth, offering excellent and recently-upgraded facilities for water sports as well as a thriving nightlife. An £850,000 fitness centre has improved the sports facilities, while a range of sports scholarships and bursaries will help support high-fliers. A £15-million scheme has seen the construction of a 1,300-bed student village and further development has been promised. More rooms are also planned for Exmouth, where the campus has a social scene of its own.

Accommodation

Number of places and costs refer to 2004–05
University-provided places: 1,960
Percentage catered: 0%
Costs for catered accommodation: n/a
Costs for self-catered accommodation:
£45–£80 a week.
Policy for first-year students: all students are guaranteed accommodation for the duration of their course.
Policy for international students: accommodation is guaranteed providing they are confirmed students and their application is received by the specified date in August.
Contact: Plymouth:
accommodation@plymouth.ac.uk
Exmouth: accomexm@plymouth.ac.uk

Students

Undergraduates:	15,960	(6,535)
Postgraduates:	955	(3,570)
Mature students:	21.9%	
Overseas students:	8.6%	
Applications per place:	4.6	
From state-sector schools:	93.3%	
From working-class homes:	32.1%	

| Tuition fees 2006 | £3,000 |

See chapter 13 for bursary details.

Teaching Quality Assessments

From 1995 (top score 24):
23 building; civil engineering; hospitality; nursing; psychology.
22 agriculture; biological sciences; education; land management; politics.
21 art and design;
drama, dance and cinematics; history of art; media studies.
20 health subjects;
mathematics and statistics; sociology.
19 materials technology.
18 electrical and electronic engineering.

University of Portsmouth

Portsmouth only narrowly missed university status before the polytechnics were created, and never gave up the chase. Degree work dates from the beginning of the last century and now four out of five students are at this level or above. Four subjects reached grade 5 of the last research assessments: biomedical and biomolecular studies, cosmology, European studies and Slavonic studies. No new university managed more, and three grade 4s left 45 per cent of the researchers in the top three of the seven categories. Every faculty was involved in research, and the 38 per cent of academics entered for the assessment was among the most in the former polytechnics.

The 15 per cent dropout rate is better than average for the subjects on offer and graduate employment is healthy, especially for a university where a high proportion of the students take arts subjects. Languages are Portsmouth's greatest strength, and one student in five takes a language course of some sort, and the facilities rival those of many traditional universities. About 1,000 Portsmouth students go abroad for part of their course, and at least as many come from the Continent. French achieved a near perfect teaching score and its research was rated internationally outstanding.

The range of subjects has widened in recent years, with the incorporation of the Solent School of Nursing and the Portsmouth School of Art, Design and Further Education. Teaching assessments were variable, but there was a marked improvement in later years of the cycle. Pharmacy recorded a maximum score and education and politics joined radiography and psychology on 23 points out of 24 in 2001. Portsmouth academics have won National Teaching Fellowships in three of the last four years and the university has been chosen to house national teaching centres for the development of foundation degrees and professional development in health subjects.

The main Guildhall campus, dotted around the city centre, is undergoing extensive redevelopment. Earlier developments provided some distinctive buildings, including the aluminium-clad St Michael's Centre and the eco-friendly Portland Building, with its solar panels. The business school has moved into a new £11-million building on the main campus, and an equally expensive library extension is due to be complete by 2006. Facilities for design, including workshops for metalworking, woodworking and ceramics, have been upgraded recently. A £6.5-million student centre opened in 2002, which caters for the multicultural population of the university with alcohol-free areas, an international

---

Winston Churchill Avenue,
Portsmouth PO1 2UP
T   023-9284 8484
E   admissions@port.ac.uk
W   www.port.ac.uk
U   www.upsu.net

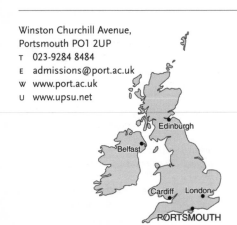

Edinburgh

Belfast

Cardiff   London

PORTSMOUTH

The Times Rankings
Overall Ranking: 77
(2005 ranking: 71)

Teaching assessment:	=66	(21.2)
Research assessment:	=57	(3.2)
Entry standards:	77	(229)
Student–staff ratio:	77	(19.8)
Library/IT spend/student:	78	(£433)
Facilities spend/student:	85	(£136)
Good honours:	93	(46.1%)
Graduate prospects:	=77	(56.5%)
Expected completion rate:	=56	(83.6%)

students' bar and a family area for students with children. Modernised sport, exercise and fitness facilities at St Paul's include resistance and cardiovascular training gyms, dance studios and a sports hall. Facilities for media studies and art and design are being refurbished and extended.

Information technology remains at Milton, with education and English a further mile away at the largely residential Langstone campus. A new department of creative technologies includes a £300,000 virtual reality centre. Only health studies are off Portsea Island, based at Queen Alexandra Hospital, in Cosham. The portfolio of degree courses has expanded considerably in the last two years, in subjects as diverse as criminology, water sports science and money market modelling.

Applications have increased by two thirds over the four years up to the start of 2005, which Portsmouth claims to be the biggest sustained rise at any university. More than a quarter of the undergraduates come from working-class homes, although this is still less than the national average for the subjects and entry qualifications. However, 94 per cent attended state schools or colleges. Efforts are being made to broaden the intake still further with a website for teenagers, which offers discounts as well as stressing the value of higher education. Portsmouth has a larger working-class population and more deprivation than some applicants may realise. But the city also has a vibrant student pub and club scene to supplement a popular students' union. The cost of living is not as high as at many southern universities, and the sea is close at hand. There are not enough hall places to accommodate all first years, and there are restrictions on housing for those who live locally. The students' union runs 'secure a home' days at the beginning of September to help new arrivals with house-hunting.

Accommodation
Number of places and costs refer to 2004–05
University-provided places: about 2,944
Percentage catered: 24.8%
Costs for catered accommodation: £82–£100 for a 36-week let.
Costs for self-catered accommodation: £65–£96 for a 36-week let.
Policy for first-year students: the university aims to offer a hall place to every new full-time student who makes Portsmouth their firm choice by 28 April.
Policy for international students: new international students are guaranteed a room if the application is received by the deadline.
Contact for further information:
Student.housing@port.ac.uk

Students

Undergraduates:	12,320	(2,750)
Postgraduates:	1,620	(2,700)
Mature students:	11.0%	
Overseas students:	20.1%	
Applications per place:	5.0	
From state-sector schools:	94.0%	
From working-class homes:	29.3%	

Tuition fees 2006 £3,000
See chapter 13 for bursary details.

Teaching Quality Assessments
From 1995 (top score 24):
24 pharmacy.
23 education; French;
health subjects (radiography); politics; psychology.
22 biological sciences; mathematics; nursing.
21 economics; German; hospitality.
20 art and design; building;
civil engineering;
electrical and electronic engineering; Italian; land management; physics; sociology.
18 Iberian languages; Russian.

Queen Mary, University of London

More than £100 million has been spent developing London University's East End base into a broadly-based institution of 9,000 students. Professor Adrian Smith, Queen Mary's Principal, believes it has 'punched below its weight' at times, and is trying to put that right with a higher profile and impressive new facilities. Queen Mary was ranked in the top 100 universities in the world by *The Times Higher Education Supplement* and now has the capital's most extensive self-contained campus. A new state-of-the-art learning resource centre with 24-hour access opened in 2003 and a new student village with almost 2,000 en suite rooms followed in 2004. Added to a new £44-million home for Barts and The London, Queen Mary's School of Medicine and Dentistry, the scale of development is unprecedented. More residences and an arts quarter are the next projects planned.

The modern setting is a far cry from the People's Palace, which first used the site to bring education to the Victorian masses, but there is still a community programme as well as conventional teaching and research. In addition to catering for local people, the Open and Distance Learning Unit provides online degrees in computer science for adults without scientific qualifications.

The arts-based Westfield College and scientific Queen Mary came together in 1989, but it took time to mould the new institution and overcome financial difficulties. The sale of Westfield's Hampstead base released the necessary capital to begin to modernise the Mile End Road campus. The new Medical and Dental School is not far away, in Whitechapel. The striking new headquarters, complete with an innovative science centre for schoolchildren, is now fully operational.

Already London University's fourth largest unit, Queen Mary is expected to carry on growing. It is one of London's designated points of expansion in the sciences, although its strength is more obvious on the arts side, which boasts a clutch of high-profile academics. There has been consistent success in attracting overseas students, who make full use of a unit specialising in English as a foreign language. A strategic alliance with City University covers teaching and research initiatives in areas such as engineering, health and history.

Teaching ratings improved after a patchy start. Dentistry produced the only perfect score, with politics and modern languages close behind. The Quality Assurance Agency has given the college a good report in its first institutional audit under the new assessment system. Iberian and Latin American languages, law and linguistics

---

Mile End Road,
London E1 4NS
T   0207-882 5511/5533
E   admissions@qmw.ac.uk
W   www.qmw.ac.uk
U   www.qmsu.org

Edinburgh
Belfast
Cardiff
LONDON

The Times Rankings
Overall Ranking: 44
(2005 ranking: 42)

Teaching assessment:	=46	(21.8)
Research assessment:	=36	(5.0)
Entry standards:	47	(289.8)
Student–staff ratio:	8	(12.5)
Library/IT spend/student:	45	(£561)
Facilities spend/student:	=63	(£165)
Good honours:	45	(59.3%)
Graduate prospects:	21	(69.4%)
Expected completion rate:	30	(90.6%)

were the only subjects rated internationally outstanding for research in the 2001 assessments, but another 13 reached grade 5, leaving almost half of the researchers in the top two categories of seven. The proportion of academics entered for the exercise, at nine out of ten, was among the highest at any university.

The majority of undergraduates take at least one course in departments other than their own, under the modular course system. Most degrees are organised in units to allow maximum flexibility. Interdisciplinary study has always been encouraged: for example, medics can choose selected modules in English and drama. The medical school is to house a national teaching centre for clinical and communications skills. There is a flourishing exchange programme, which includes universities in the United States and Japan, as well as Europe. Each student has an adviser to guide them through the possibilities. Language students can use the University of London Institute, in Paris, while students at Beijing's University of Posts and Telecommunications can take double degrees (awarded by their own institution and Queen Mary) without leaving China.

Queen Mary attracts a socially diverse intake: more than a third of the undergraduates come from the two lowest socio-economic classes, many of them from local ethnic groups. Social life centres on the campus, which features an award-winning student nightclub, but the West End is easily accessible by tube. Students welcome the relatively low prices (for the capital) in East London, which has more to offer than many expect when they apply.

Accommodation
Number of places and costs refer to 2004–05
University-provided places: 2,339
Percentage catered: 9.5%
Costs for catered accommodation:
£106.05 (single) a week; £121.10 (single en suite) a week.
Costs for self-catered accommodation:
£79.03–84.98 (single); £93.45–£107.03 (single en suite) a week.
Policy for first-year students: priority for first years and postgraduates if they apply by 30 June. Offers to those living within a one-hour commute will be deferred until midterm when final numbers are known (most are housed by the start of term 2).
Policy for international students: as above, and will treat as highest priority and extend deadline to accommodate late applicants.
Contact: residences@qmul.ac.uk

Students
Undergraduates:	7,275	(275)
Postgraduates:	1,580	(770)
Mature students:	11.8%	
Overseas students:	16.9%	
Applications per place:	7.4	
From state-sector schools:	84.8%	
From working-class homes:	35.1%	

Tuition fees 2006 £3,000
See chapter 13 for bursary details.

Teaching Quality Assessments
From 1995 (top score 24):
24 dentistry.
23 modern languages; linguistics; politics.
22 biological sciences; health subjects.
21 drama, dance and cinematics; economics; electrical and electronic engineering; mathematics and statistics; medicine; physics and astronomy.
20 materials technology.
19 general engineering.

Queen's University, Belfast

Generally regarded as Northern Ireland's premier university, Queen's has been making big changes to improve its research performance and regain the international standing it enjoyed before the Troubles. Four schools closed, with the early retirement or redeployment of 80 academics and the recruitment of more than 100 others as part of a £25-million investment programme. The strategy worked to some extent – mechanical engineering was again the only subject rated internationally outstanding in the last research assessments, but 15 of the 40 subject areas reached the next grade. An even greater investment programme was announced in 2002, promising £84 million spending on the appointment of new staff and major capital projects to benefit all five faculties.

Queen's enjoyed big increases in applications at the end of the 1990s, as more of the province's students decided to stay at home, and numbers had continued to rise until a downturn at the beginning of 2005, when most UK universities saw healthy increases. However, with 10 per cent more young people going into higher education in Northern Ireland than in England, the university still has some 17,500 undergraduates and postgraduates, with 10,000 more lifelong learners. Queen's was

one of four university colleges for the whole of Ireland in the 19th century, and still draws students from all over the island. The aim now is to revive demand from mainland Britain and add to the 2,400 overseas students.

Teaching assessments have shown the university's all-round strength. Half of the subjects assessed under the original quality system were rated excellent, and none of the 18 areas inspected since 1996–97 yielded less than 21 points out of 24. The last of five subjects to achieve maximum points was economics, but archaeology, business, Celtic studies, education and politics all came close in 2001. Education at St Mary's and Stranmillis colleges (both associated with Queen's) also gained maximum scores.

The university district, which is among the most attractive in Belfast, is one of the city's main cultural and recreational areas. Queen's runs a highly successful arts festival each November, opened a new art gallery in 2001 and has the only full-time university cinema in the UK – one of the best in Ireland. Another £2 million has been invested in arts facilities recently, the lion's share of the cash going into a new studio theatre. Student facilities are being expanded and upgraded to cope with increasing student numbers, with a £50-million student centre bringing services

---

University Road,
Belfast BT7 1NN
T   028-9024 5133
E   admissions@qub.ac.uk
W   www.qub.ac.uk
U   www.qubsu.org

The Times Rankings
Overall Ranking: 31
(2005 ranking: 33)

Teaching assessment:	=40	(21.9)
Research assessment:	=39	(4.9)
Entry standards:	26	(350.4)
Student–staff ratio:	56	(17.7)
Library/IT spend/student:	74	(£457)
Facilities spend/student:	15	(£301)
Good honours:	44	(59.6%)
Graduate prospects:	12	(74.5%)
Expected completion rate:	28	(91%)

together at the heart of the campus and a student village opening, not far away. A new library has also been added recently and more teaching accommodation provided, with better access for the disabled. The university's great hall has had a £2.5-million refurbishment, courtesy of the university's own foundation.

Queen's has been spreading its wings in recent years. It formed a partnership with St Mary's College and Stranmillis College in 1999, with the aim of academic integration, and has established a campus in Armagh City, which now has 400 students. There is a smaller outreach centre in Omagh, Co. Tyrone. Other teaching and research premises are located at the Royal Victoria Hospital, Belfast City Hospital, and the Marine Biology Station in Portaferry on Strangford Lough.

Courses at Queen's are modular and semesters have been introduced. Students are encouraged to take language programmes from a unique 'virtual' language laboratory, which provides online tuition from any computer in the university. IT facilities are good: Queen's was the first institution to meet the national target of providing at least one computer workstation for every five undergraduate students. An unusually large proportion of graduates go on to further study, which does Queen's no harm in the employment league.

The principle of strictly non-denominational teaching is enshrined in a charter which has guaranteed student representation and equal rights for women since 1908. The charter even precluded the teaching of theology – this is done through a network of four associated colleges.

Nightlife has returned to the city centre, but the social scene is still concentrated on the students' union and the surrounding area. Sports facilities, which include a university hut in the Mourne mountains, are of a high standard. A rugby academy opened in 2002 and there are plans to do the same for Gaelic football. Queen's is still not overprovided with residential places, but first years are given priority for accommodation and there is plenty of reasonably-priced private housing to rent.

Accommodation
Number of places and costs refer to 2004–05
University-provided places: 2,000
Percentage catered: 17%
Costs for catered accommodation: £56 (shared room); £67 (single room) a week.
Costs for self-catered accommodation:
£50–£60; £70 (en suite) a week.
Policy for first-year students: priority given to first-year and final-year students.
Policy for international students: international students are given priority.
Contact: s.accommodation@qub.ac.uk

Students
Undergraduates: 12,400 (5,355)
Postgraduates: 1,965 (3,255)
Mature students: 9.8%
Overseas students: 7.1%
Applications per place: 6.0
From state-sector schools: 99.8%
From working-class homes: 36.0%

Tuition fees 2006 £3,000
See chapter 13 for bursary details.

Teaching Quality Assessments
From 1995 (top score 24):
24 dentistry; economics;

electrical and electronic engineering; pharmacy; psychology.
23 archaeology; business; Celtic studies; classics and ancient history; education; physics; politics.
22 anatomy and physiology; civil engineering; mathematics; medicine; nursing; theology.
21 agriculture; biological sciences; chemical engineering; food science; health subjects; Iberian languages; mechanical engineering; town planning.
20 French.
19 German; sociology

University of Reading

Recent assessments in teaching and research have demonstrated an all-round strength that may have surprised those who knew Reading primarily for its highly-regarded agricultural and environmental courses. The university achieved a series of good grades in the arts and social sciences, a perfect score in philosophy following a hat-trick of perfect scores in nursing, physics and psychology. Drama had already achieved this feat.

Several of the successes have come in subjects added when the university took in Bulmershe College a decade ago, although the large education faculty is yet to feature. The college provided a second campus near the original 320-acre parkland site on the outskirts of Reading. The university spent more than £60 million on new buildings in the 1990s, upgrading and extending facilities for meteorology, management, agriculture, archaeology and psychology. More halls of residence have been added recently and a new School of Pharmacy is due to open in 2005.

Reading was the only university established between the two world wars, having been Oxford's extension college for the first part of the last century, but the attractive main campus now has a modern feel. There are also 2,000 acres of university-owned farmland on the Downs, near

Reading, for teaching and research in agricultural and plant sciences. The university's location, a bus ride away from Heathrow Airport, and an international reputation in key areas for developing countries have always ensured a healthy flow of overseas students. Overall applications for full-time degrees were down at the start of 2005, but there had been an increase of more than 8 per cent in the previous year.

Reading was among the universities criticised for missing all three benchmarks for widening access to higher education when official monitoring began. Although the reprimand is now a fading memory and the university has been getting closer to national averages for the subjects on offer, it is still among a handful of universities in that position. Almost 20 per cent of undergraduates come from independent schools and just 7 per cent are from areas without a tradition of higher education. At least the retention rate lived up to expectations, with a little more than 10 per cent of undergraduates who started courses in 2001 expected to leave without a qualification.

All undergraduates take Career Management Skills modules that contribute five credits towards their degree classification. The online system, which has

---

Whiteknights, PO Box 217,
Reading RG6 6AH
T   0118-987 5123
E   information@reading.ac.uk
W   www.reading.ac.uk
U   www.rusu.co.uk/

The Times Rankings
Overall Ranking: 39
(2005 ranking: 30)

Teaching assessment:	=46	(21.8)
Research assessment:	=25	(5.3)
Entry standards:	38	(315.2)
Student–staff ratio:	25	(15.4)
Library/IT spend/student:	36	(£591)
Facilities spend/student:	59	(£175)
Good honours:	36	(64.8%)
Graduate prospects:	=66	(59.4%)
Expected completion rate:	35	(89.2%)

200 web pages of advice, exercises and information, has been bought by 30 other universities and colleges. Sessions are delivered jointly by academics and careers advisors, with input from alumni and leading employers.

Reading has been trying to break down the barriers between the arts and sciences, notably in a joint initiative with the Open University to develop standardised course materials to help under-qualified students cope with physics degrees. Arts and social science students are encouraged to broaden their horizons by taking three subjects from the modular course scheme in the first year of their degree.

Successes in the last research assessment exercise were well spread. Archaeology, English, environmental science, Italian and psychology were all rated internationally outstanding, with 58 per cent of the academics entered for assessment placed in the top two categories of seven. The university is top in *The Times* ranking for environmental science, and second for land management and food science.

The town may not be the most fashionable, but it has plenty of nightlife and an award-winning shopping centre. London is easily accessible by train, but the cost of living is on par with the capital. More than 4,500 residential places include a landscaped student village, while first-rate sports facilities include accessible rowing and sailing boathouses. Representative teams have a good record in inter-university competitions.

Students praise the social scene, although the high proportion from the South East means that many go home at the weekends. The large students' union had a £500,000 refit to improve and extend its popular main venue, and additional refurbishment is planned in 2006. It has been voted among the best in Britain, but students who live in town often avoid the trek back out to the campus.

Accommodation

Number of places and costs refer to 2004–05
University-provided places: about 4,900
Percentage catered: 48%
Costs for catered accommodation: £96–£128 for 30-week year (vacations optional).
Costs for self-catered accommodation: £53–£85 for 30-week year (vacations optional); 39-week options available (£52–£97 a week).
Policy for first-year students: all first-year undergraduates with Reading as first choice are guaranteed a place in halls if they apply by 1 August. Students who apply through Insurance are normally offered places, but Clearing students are not guaranteed accommodation.
Policy for international students: after the normal guarantee period for all students, priority is given to international students.
Contact: accommodation@reading.ac.uk

Students

Undergraduates:	7,885	(2,560)
Postgraduates:	2,315	(2,495)
Mature students:	9.5%	
Overseas students:	9.6%	
Applications per place:	8.4	
From state-sector schools:	80.8%	
From working-class homes:	21.3%	

Tuition fees 2006	£3,000

See chapter 13 for bursary details.

Teaching Quality Assessments

From 1995 (top score 24):
24 dance, drama and cinematics; nursing; philosophy; physics; psychology.
23 archaeology; history of art; typography.
22 classics; food science; land management; mathematics; politics; sociology; town planning.
21 agriculture; American studies; anatomy and physiology; biological sciences; building; business and management; economics; electrical and electronic engineering; French;
20 German; Italian.
19 art and design; education; linguistics.

The Robert Gordon University

So close are links with the North Sea oil and gas industries that Robert Gordon has dubbed itself the Energy University, but nursing and the health sciences are now equally important. A new mission statement has switched the emphasis of the university from vocational to professional education, while the creative industries are also a growth area.

There is full portfolio of courses in business, health, design and engineering. Programmes are flexible, with credit accumulation and transfer making for easy movement in and out of the university for an often mobile local workforce. Work placements, which can last up to a year, are the norm, helping an employment record that has been the best in Scotland for the past three years. In the whole of Britain, only Cambridge saw a higher proportion of leavers go straight into 'graduate-level' employment in 2002.

Efforts to extend access beyond the normal higher education catchment have produced a diverse student population, with more than a third of the undergraduates coming from working-class homes and almost a fifth from areas sending few students to higher education. The projected dropout rate of 16 per cent has been improving but is still marginally higher than the UK average for Robert Gordon's subjects and entry qualifications.

Only two of the subjects assessed in the main rounds of teaching assessment were rated Excellent, but a majority of the rest were considered Highly Satisfactory. Only 120 academic staff were entered for the latest research assessment exercise and none of the subjects featured in the top three of the seven categories. But the university has committed itself to winning international recognition for applied research in the current decade.

There are now about 140 degrees to choose from. There was serious consideration of a merger with Aberdeen University in 2002. Although this was eventually abandoned, there will be continued collaboration between the two institutions. Robert Gordon's finances are now described as 'sound as a pound', and the most secure of any new university in Scotland. Students from the city's two institutions mix easily, and there is healthy academic rivalry in some areas, despite the obvious differences between the universities. Named after an 18th-century philanthropist, Robert Gordon has two sites around the city and an attractive field study centre at Cromarty, in the Highlands. The main Schoolhill site adjoins Aberdeen art gallery, while Garthdee, where 70 per cent of undergraduates are taught, overlooks the

---

Schoolhill,
Aberdeen AB10 1FR
T   01224 262105
E   admissions@rgu.ac.uk
W   www.rgu.ac.uk
U   www.rgunion.co.uk/

The Times Rankings
Overall Ranking: =58
(2005 ranking: 58)

Teaching assessment:	=55	(21.5)
Research assessment:	=91	(1.9)
Entry standards:	45	(294.6)
Student–staff ratio:	=60	(18.1)
Library/IT spend/student:	64	(£496)
Facilities spend/student:	=91	(£122)
Good honours:	51	(58%)
Graduate prospects:	19	(69.9%)
Expected completion rate:	68	(81.4%)

River Dee and has had a £60-million face-lift. Sir Norman Foster designed the business school, while other recent developments made room for art, architecture and the faculty of health and social care (with 3,000 students).

Like most new universities, especially in Scotland, Robert Gordon recruits most of its students locally, 60 per cent of them female. However, overseas recruitment has been growing sharply, with a 30 per cent increase in 2004, and the overall demand for places has been stronger than at most universities north of the border. The Scottish Executive has provided £500,000 in European funding to help more people from disadvantaged communities to take courses. The university already offers four-week intensive access programmes in mathematics, engineering, chemistry and computing during August and September for applicants who narrowly miss the entry requirements to top up their qualifications. If they prefer, prospective students may take access units in these subjects by distance learning, using study packs and with the support of an assigned tutor. The scheme, which runs all year round, is recommended for aspiring students without traditional academic backgrounds.

The university is pinning many of its hopes on new technology. A virtual campus was launched with an online course in e-business for postgraduates, again with European funding, which also enables management undergraduates to receive course materials via an intranet, and other degree and short courses are available.

Aberdeen is a long way to go for English students, but train and air links are excellent, and the city regularly features in the top ten for quality of life. In addition, an £11-million sports and leisure centre opened in 2004, providing a centre for excellence for the region in hockey and several other sports. Although private accommodation can be expensive, low prices in the students' union partially compensate, and there are enough residential places to guarantee accommodation to first years from outside the area.

Accommodation
Number of places and costs refer to 2005–06
University-provided places: 1,216
Percentage catered: 0%
Costs for catered accommodation: n/a
Costs for self-catered accommodation:
£64–£78 a week.
Policy for first-year students: all first years who live outside the Aberdeen city area are eligible to apply for student accommodation.
Policy for international students: international students are guaranteed accommodation for the duration of their studies.
Contact: accommodation@rgu.ac.uk
www.rgu.ac.uk/accommodation

Students

Undergraduates:	6,495	(2,345)
Postgraduates:	960	(2,050)
Mature students:	22.3%	
Overseas students:	11.2%	
Applications per place:	4.1	
From state-sector schools:	95.7%	
From working-class homes:	37.0%	

Teaching Quality Assessments
1994–98 Rated Excellent:
chemistry; nutrition and dietetics.
1994–98 Highly Satisfactory:
architecture; business and management; graphic and textile design; mathematics and statistics; mechanical engineering; pharmacy; physiotherapy; physics; radiography; social work.
From 1998 (top score 24):
19 European languages.

See page 245 for recent assessments.

Roehampton University

Four years after entering a federation with Surrey University, the former Roehampton Institute became a university in its own right in 2004. The two institutions will continue to collaborate on research projects and joint programmes, but undergraduates entering in 2006 will receive Roehampton University degrees.

The new university, with its parkland campus, comprises four distinctive colleges, which still maintain some of the traditional ethos of their religious foundations: the Church of England's Whitelands, the Roman Catholic Digby Stuart, the Methodist Southlands, and the Froebel Institute, following the teachings of the humanist Frederick Froebel. Students do not have to be any of these denominations to study at the university. All four colleges are on or adjacent to Roehampton Lane. Whitelands moved from Putney in 2004 to the 18th-century mansion, Parkstead House, overlooking Richmond Park, which is at the heart of the new 14-acre south campus. Some new building is taking place and refurbishment of the house has provided IT facilities, laboratories and teaching space. A new dance and PE building also opened on the north campus in 2005. The institute had already spent £20 million relocating Southlands, providing a new site for the social sciences.

The colleges all have their own bars and other leisure facilities, although they are open to all members of the university. In line with the colleges' teacher training origins, education remains the largest subject area, accounting for more than a quarter of the students, with others taking combined studies programmes in arts, humanities and languages; business, social sciences and computing; and human and life sciences.

There are over 1,500 subject combinations to choose from, including film studies and biological anthropology, or dance and theology. Among the recent additions were exercise, nutrition and health; journalism and news media; and television studies. Dance was rated internationally outstanding in the latest research assessments, with anthropology and history both in the next-highest category. With 45 per cent of the academics entered for assessment – a higher figure than at any of the former polytechnics – Roehampton outperformed all of its new peer group in terms of average grades per member of staff. The institute had already won a Queen's Anniversary Prize for its research into children's literature. The Quality Assurance Agency has complimented Roehampton on the accessibility of academic staff to students

---

Erasmus House, Roehampton Lane, London SW15 5PU
T 0208-392 3232
E enquiries@roehampton.ac.uk
W www.roehampton.ac.uk
U www.roehamptonstudent.com

The Times Rankings
Overall Ranking: 70
(2005 ranking: 64)

Teaching assessment:	=90	(20.5)
Research assessment:	=57	(3.2)
Entry standards:	=79	(226.6)
Student–staff ratio:	=83	(20.5)
Library/IT spend/student:	48	(£549)
Facilities spend/student:	7	(£356)
Good honours:	80	(50.7%)
Graduate prospects:	=51	(61.9%)
Expected completion rate:	73	(79.4%)

Edinburgh
Belfast
Cardiff
LONDON

and the positive ways in which they responded to student needs. The university is to house a national teaching centre on human rights.

Teaching grades have been less spectacular, but still respectable. Despite the predominance of arts students, biological sciences produced the best score, with psychology and linguistics close behind. A Work and Study Scheme gives local employees credit towards their degree for relevant tasks performed in the workplace. The programme is designed to help employers recruit and retain key staff, as well as helping those who cannot afford to study full time.

Roehampton has been enjoying record intakes at the same time as increasing its entry scores. Nine out of ten undergraduates were educated in state schools and almost a third come from working-class homes – both figures exceeding the national benchmark for the subjects studied. The funding council acknowledges that Roehampton's leafy setting is largely responsible for a low proportion of students from areas without a tradition of higher education. The projected dropout rate had been coming down, but the latest figures suggest that one in five undergraduates will leave without a qualification.

About 80 per cent of first years who want a hall place are offered one, with priority going to those who make Roehampton their first preference. Two new residences opened in 2004, adding almost 450 places to the residential stock. Rents are not cheap for those who miss out on a place or prefer the private sector, but students like the proximity of central London and the lively and attractive suburbs around Roehampton.

Accommodation

Number of places and costs refer to 2005–06
University-provided places: 1,600
Percentage catered: 12.5%
Costs for catered accommodation: £100.50 (standard) a week.
Costs for self-catered accommodation: £83 (standard); £90 (en suite) a week.
Policy for first-year students: students who have nominated Roehampton as their first choice given priority on a 'first come, first served' basis.
Policy for international students: some reserved places for new international students who apply early.
Contact: y.douglas@roehampton.ac.uk
j.marsh@roehampton.ac.uk (Whitelands)
judith.marshall@roehampton.ac.uk (Digby Stuart)
j.rochford@roehampton.ac.uk (Froebel)

Students

Undergraduates:	5,575	(820)
Postgraduates:	1,020	(670)
Mature students:	25.4%	
Overseas students:	7.0%	
Applications per place:	4.0	
From state-sector schools:	92.3%	
From working-class homes:	30.0%	

Tuition fees 2006   £3,000
See chapter 13 for bursary details.

Teaching Quality Assessments

From 1995 (top score 24):
23 biological sciences.
22 linguistics; psychology.
21 drama, dance and cinematics; hospitality.
20 health subjects; sociology.
19 art and design; modern languages.

Royal Holloway, University of London

London University's 'campus in the country' occupies 120 acres of woodland between Windsor Castle and Heathrow. The 600-bed Founder's Building, modelled on a French chateau and opened by Queen Victoria, is one of Britain's most remarkable university buildings. The merger with Bedford College, and the sale of Bedford's valuable site in Regent's Park, enabled Royal Holloway to embark on a major building programme, which has since been extended. The earth sciences, life sciences, mathematics and computing, history and social policy all benefited, and a well-appointed media arts centre and library building have also been added.

The college is in the midst of another ten-year development plan after opening a new sports centre and international building, as well as building up a portfolio of scholarships and bursaries. One offers free places or reduced fees to those who stay on for a postgraduate degree. The conversion of the huge Victorian boilerhouse into a performance space for drama, the launch of a new department of health and social care, and the establishment of formal links with institutions such as New York, Sydney and Yale universities, demonstrate that progress has not just been a matter of bricks and mortar. Closer to home, another link allows

music students to take lessons at the Royal College of Music.

Both partners in the merger which formed the college were originally for women only, their legacy commemorated in the Bedford Centre for the History of Women. The arts and humanities still account for most of the top ratings and a majority of the students are female. French, German, geography and music were considered internationally outstanding in the latest research assessments, when three quarters of the academics entered for assessment were in departments rated in the top two of seven categories. The successes placed Royal Holloway in the top dozen research institutions and have helped cement a place in the top 20 of *The Times* League Table. Several recent high-profile academic appointments should maintain the research record.

Drama, dance and theatre studies led the way in teaching assessments, until psychology and biological sciences registered perfect scores in 2000. Physics had almost beaten them to it, and should benefit from the university's decision to develop science subjects at Royal Holloway. The college already offers a science foundation year at further education colleges in the region, and the balance of disciplines is gradually shifting. All the

---

Royal Holloway
University of London, Egham Hill,
Egham, Surrey TW20 0EX

T   01784 443883
E   undergrad-office@
    rhul.ac.uk
W   www.rhul.ac.uk
U   www.su.rhul.ac.uk

The Times Rankings
Overall Ranking: =16
(2005 ranking: 15)

Teaching assessment:	=46	(21.8)
Research assessment:	=10	(5.7)
Entry standards:	30	(344.7)
Student–staff ratio:	7	(12.3)
Library/IT spend/student:	27	(£638)
Facilities spend/student:	=5	(£376)
Good honours:	35	(65%)
Graduate prospects:	64	(59.6%)
Expected completion rate:	10	(95.4%)

sciences were judged nationally outstanding for research in 2001.

All 21 departments encourage interdisciplinary work, which is facilitated by a modular course structure with examinations at the end of every year. Teaching terms run from the end of September to April, with a five-week examinations term to follow. An Advanced Skills Programme, covering information technology, communication skills and foreign languages, further encourages breadth of study.

Financial problems are now well in the past and Royal Holloway's balance sheet is robust, supported by an increase in research income of nearly 60 per cent in four years. Immediate expansion plans centre on the college's areas of excellence and on distance learning. In 2003, Royal Holloway launched e-degrees in classics, history, business management and an MA in information security to add to its University of London external programme.

The college has an upmarket reputation, with almost a quarter of its undergraduates recruited from independent schools, although the proportion coming from working-class homes has been rising. However, the ethnic mix is above average and the projected dropout rate of less than 5 per cent is among the best in Britain.

Almost 3,000 students are in halls of residence, many of them in the Founder's Building itself. The college's green belt location at Egham, Surrey, an hour's travel from the centre of London by rail, ensures that social life is concentrated on an extended students' union. However, the West End is close for those determined to seek the high life. A high proportion of students come from London and the Home Counties, and the campus can seem empty at weekends.

Accommodation

Number of places and costs refer to 2005–06
University-provided places: 2,569
Percentage catered: 46%
Costs for catered accommodation: £61–£95 a week (the latter includes a £4 weekly charge for data network access). Cost excludes meals but residents are entitled to a 50% discount on most food from the 3 dining halls.
Costs for self-catered accommodation: £51–£94 a week (the latter includes a £4 weekly charge for data network access).
Policy for first-year students: all first years applying through UCAS by the deadline are guaranteed accommodation. Distance is not a criterion.
Policy for international students: international undergraduates are guaranteed accommodation.
Contact: Accommodation-Office@rhul.ac.uk

Students

Undergraduates:	4,215	(640)
Postgraduates:	1,010	(560)
Mature students:	8.7%	
Overseas students:	19.8%	
Applications per place:	5.0	
From state-sector schools:	77.8%	
From working-class homes:	23.5%	

Tuition fees 2006   £3,000
See chapter 13 for bursary details.

Teaching Quality Assessments

From 1995 (top score 24):
24 psychology.
23 classics and ancient history;
drama, dance and cinematics; physics.
22 economics; mathematics.
21 biological sciences;
business and management; French; Italian; sociology.
19 German.

University of St Andrews

As the oldest Scottish university and the third oldest in Britain, St Andrews has long been both well known and fashionable among a mainly middle-class clientele. But its fame became truly global when Prince William chose to study there. There was a 44 per cent surge in applications when the news broke – by far the biggest rise at any university. That kind of increase was unsustainable, but a 20 per cent rise at the beginning of 2005 was again the largest at any university north of the border. A 17 per cent rise 12 months earlier had already left St Andrews more popular than at any time in the last 100 years.

With some 40 per cent of the students coming from south of the border, St Andrews has earned the nickname of Scotland's English university. But almost 20 per cent coming from 75 countries farther afield give a cosmopolitan feel. Fee concessions and exchange schemes have boosted applications, particularly in the United States, which provided a quarter of first-year students on its own in 2003–04.

Peer assessments have shown that there is top quality behind the prestige. St Andrews has the best teaching and research grades in Scotland, although a disputed drop-out rate has cost it the title of the top Scottish university this year. Uniquely, every subject assessed has been rated either Excellent or

Highly Satisfactory for teaching, demonstrating quality across the board. Psychology and English were the only starred research departments, but 15 subjects on the next rung of the ladder put the university into the top ten in terms of the average per member of staff.

St Andrews was one of the universities criticised by its funding council for the narrowness of its intake when performance indicators were introduced. More than a third of the undergraduates come from independent schools, when the UK average for the university's courses and entry scores is only one in five. A dedicated Access Centre has had some success in trying to broaden the intake. The proportion from working-class homes has been rising but, at little more than 15 per cent, is still significantly lower than the university's benchmark. A successful fundraising campaign is building up a bank of £3,000-a-year scholarships for students from poor homes.

The town of St Andrews is steeped in history, as well as being the centre of the golfing world. The university at its heart accounts for about a third of the 18,000 inhabitants. There are close relations between town and gown, both cultural and social. New students ('bejants' and 'bejantines') acquire third and fourth-year

College Gate, North Street,
St Andrews KY16 9AJ
T   01334 462150
E   admissions@
     st-andrews.ac.uk
W   www.st-andrews.ac.uk
U   www.yourunion.net

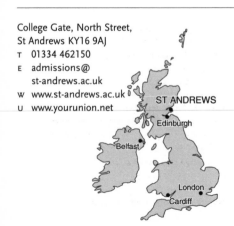

ST ANDREWS

Edinburgh

Belfast

London

Cardiff

The Times Rankings
Overall Ranking: 7
(2005 ranking: 9)

Teaching assessment:	3	(23.1)
Research assessment:	=10	(5.7)
Entry standards:	=9	(414.8)
Student–staff ratio:	3	(10.1)
Library/IT spend/student:	32	(£609)
Facilities spend/student:	46	(£207)
Good honours:	5	(78%)
Graduate prospects:	=24	(68.6%)
Expected completion rate:	44	(86%)

'parents' to ease them into university life, and on Raisin Monday give their academic guardians a bottle of wine in return for a receipt in Latin, which can be written on anything. Another unusual feature is that all humanities students are awarded an MA rather than a BA.

Many of the main buildings date from the 15th and 16th centuries, but sciences are taught at the modern North Haugh site a few streets away. Everything is within walking distance, but bicycles are common. Although small, St Andrews offers a wide range of courses. The university's reputation has always rested primarily on the humanities, which acquired a new £1.3-million research centre recently. It has the largest mediaeval history department in Britain. But a full range of physical sciences is offered, with sophisticated lasers and the largest optical telescope in Britain. A new computer science building opened in 2004.

An academic partnership with Dundee University is being developed in order to expand teaching and research in areas of common interest. A joint degree in electronics and optoelectronics was the first project, followed by shared teaching in medical education and health sciences, and the launch of a course pooling St Andrews' excellence in art history and Dundee's flair for design.

Students do not come to St Andrews for the nightclubs, but there is no shortage of parties in a tight-knit community. More than half of all students live in halls of residence, with another 235 rooms added in 2002 and more since then. Rents rose sharply in 2004, but the students' association accepted that previous subsidies had to be phased out. The sports facilities are excellent.

Accommodation

Number of places and costs refer to 2004–05

University-provided places: 3,284

Percentage catered: 55%

Costs for catered accommodation:
£92.61–£126.28 a week.

Costs for self-catered accommodation:
£45.08–£86.24 a week.

Policy for first-year students: accommodation guaranteed for single entrant undergraduates who apply by 31 May of year of entry.

Policy for international students: as above for first-year students.

Contact: studacc@st-andrews.ac.uk

Students

Undergraduates:	5,940	(465)
Postgraduates:	1,005	(425)
Mature students:	4.3%	
Overseas students:	19.6%	
Applications per place:	6.0	
From state-sector schools:	62.4%	
From working-class homes:	15.5%	

Teaching Quality Assessments
1994–97 Rated Excellent:
biological sciences; chemistry; economics; geography; history;
mathematics and statistics;
physics; psychology.
1994–97 Rated Highly Satisfactory:
business and management; computer studies; English; geology; history of art; medicine; philosophy; theology.
From 1998 (top score 24):
22 European languages.

See page 245 for recent assessments.

University of Salford

In the last five years, Salford has begun to slip below some of the new universities in *The Times* League Table. But consistently good graduate employment rates, carefully-targeted courses and an emphasis on the university's location close to the centre of Manchester appeal to students. Applications were up by more than 10 per cent at the beginning of 2005, returning to a trend that straddled the beginning of the decade.

A merger with University College Salford, with which there were already close links, provided a second opportunity to forge a new type of higher education institution. The main victim of higher education budget cuts in the early 1980s, Salford bounced back as the prototype decentralised, customer-oriented university. The latest model, which was ahead of its time, was the comprehensive post-school institution. Nine years on, however, no further education courses remain.

Instead, Salford stresses its business links and the modern portfolio of courses. Assessment grades have been variable and the projected dropout rate of 20 per cent, although only marginally worse than the national average for the subjects and students' qualifications, is the highest among the old universities. Like most of the institutions with high dropout rates, Salford takes large numbers from under-represented groups: almost four in ten undergraduates come from working-class homes and practically a quarter from areas sending few students to higher education.

Teaching quality grades improved ratings in the latter years of the cycle. The university averaged 21 points out of 24 from 1996 onwards, with perfect scores for politics and biological sciences. Business and health subjects are now big recruiters. The university's growing involvement in health has seen the establishment of a national centre for prosthetics and orthotics, and a high reputation for the treatment of sports injuries. Another innovation was the launch of Europe's first nursing course for deaf students, as part of the Government's 'Making a Difference' strategy. There is also a degree in traditional Chinese medicine, with an acupuncture clinic.

Engineering is the university's traditional strength, attracting many of the 3,000 overseas students, although teaching grades were disappointing. Two thirds of courses offer work placements, half of them abroad and almost all counting towards degree classifications. The tradition of sandwich courses always serves Salford well in terms of graduate employment. A business enterprise support programme helps students set up their own businesses,

---

Salford,
Greater Manchester M5 4WT
T   0161-295 4545
E   course-enquiries@
    salford.ac.uk
W   www.salford.ac.uk
U   www.susu.salford.ac.uk

The Times Rankings
Overall Ranking: 68
(2005 ranking: 69)

Teaching assessment:	=82	(20.7)
Research assessment:	=53	(4.3)
Entry standards:	60	(260.1)
Student–staff ratio:	=60	(18.1)
Library/IT spend/student:	92	(£387)
Facilities spend/student:	=40	(£214)
Good honours:	76	(51.5%)
Graduate prospects:	=49	(62.1%)
Expected completion rate:	74	(79.3%)

providing entrepreneurship training and business skills, as well as a business mentor.

The university has also made headlines with more unusual innovations, such as degrees in business economics with gambling studies, not to mention the appointment of Britain's first Professor of Pop Music. Online degrees have been introduced and Salford has embraced the two-year foundation degree, as well as adding honours courses such as wildlife conservation and physics with aviation.

Salford's extended range of courses meant that fewer than 40 per cent of the academics were entered for the latest research assessment exercise, when the built environment and information management were the only areas considered internationally outstanding. European studies – another longstanding strength – again reached the second rung of the ladder and will benefit from a new £1-million languages centre. The university remains committed to research: it has established 13 interdisciplinary research centres and a graduate school. It also led the way in formally recognising interaction with business and industry as of equal importance to teaching and research.

The modern landscaped campus, a haven of lawns and shrubberies along the River Irwell, is less than two miles from Manchester city centre and has a mainline railway station. The university also has its own TV and radio stations, as part of a partnership with Granada. Salford has spent £68 million on improvements, including £16 million on a new building to bring health courses onto the main campus from nearby Eccles. Another £100 million is scheduled to go into capital projects over the next ten years, starting with more new premises for health-related studies and further development of the Adelphi arts and cultural quarter. Students like the friendly atmosphere and most of the residential places are either on campus or in a student village 15 minutes' walk away. This is important in an area where security is a big issue, one which the university has been addressing in concert with the police and local authority.

Accommodation

Number of places and costs refer to 2005–06
University-provided places: 3,248
Percentage catered: 7%
Costs for catered accommodation:
£84.00–£94.64. A variety of pre-pay SMART cards are available for 10-meal contracts.
Costs for self-catered accommodation:
£49.21–£61.81 (standard); £68.39 (en suite).
Policy for first-year students: all new first years with unconditional offers are guaranteed a place if an application is made by 1 September.
Policy for international students: as above.
Contact: c.saunders@salford.ac.uk
www.salford.ac.uk/crservice/accommod

Students

Undergraduates:	12,695	(2,965)
Postgraduates:	1,470	(2,075)
Mature students:	28.3%	
Overseas students:	10.4%	
Applications per place:	4.8	
From state-sector schools:	96.3%	
From working-class homes:	38.8%	

Tuition fees 2006   £3,000
See chapter 13 for bursary details.

Teaching Quality Assessments

From 1995 (top score 24):
24 biological sciences; politics.
23 physics.
22 anatomy and physiology; health subjects; nursing; social policy; social work; town planning.
21 art and design; drama, dance and cinematics; mathematics.
20 Arabic; economics; modern languages; sociology.
19 civil engineering; hospitality, leisure and tourism.
18 building; land management.

School of Oriental and African Studies, London

As the major national centre for the study of Africa and Asia, SOAS has a global reputation in subjects relating to two thirds of the world's population. Originally only a specialist Oriental college, the school has always worked closely with the Foreign Office, whose staff attend its extensive range of language courses and briefings. The library, with nearly one million volumes, periodicals and audiovisual materials in 400 languages, attracts scholars from around the world.

Students come from over 100 countries, although more than 80 per cent of undergraduates are British. However, the school has a much wider portfolio of courses than its name would suggest, with 400 degree combinations on offer. Degrees are available in familiar subjects such as law, music, history or the social sciences, but with a different emphasis.

Student recruitment is on the rise, especially among independent school candidates, who account for almost a third of the British undergraduates. At the start of 2005, an increase of 33 per cent was one of the largest at any university, and this followed healthy rises in the previous two years. The numbers taking first degrees have risen significantly in past decade, reaching 1,600 in 2002–03, and now the growth area is postgraduate courses, which have helped to tackle a financial deficit. More than 1,500 students (mainly living abroad) are now taking distance learning courses, which won a Queen's Anniversary Prize for innovation in higher education in 1996.

Over 40 per cent of the students are postgraduates, many attracted by a research record which saw history rated internationally outstanding in the last assessments. Seven of the 11 subject areas were placed in the top two categories. Teaching assessments have also been good, a maximum score for history of art leading the way, with East and South Asian studies close behind. The final assessments produced solid results in politics and economics.

Nearly all students take advantage of the unique opportunities for learning one of the wide range of languages on offer: 40 non-European languages are available. There is also an option of spending one, two or three terms of a degree course in one of the school's many partner universities in Africa or Asia. The school has been chosen to house a national teaching centre for languages. Almost two thirds of those graduating recently achieved firsts or upper-

---

Thornhaugh Street,
Russell Square, London WC1H 0XG
T   0207-898 4034
E   study@soas.ac.uk
W   www.soas.ac.uk
U   www.soasunion.org

The Times Rankings
Overall Ranking: 15
(2005 ranking: 19)

Teaching assessment:	=34	(22.0)
Research assessment:	=18	(5.5)
Entry standards:	36	(322.9)
Student–staff ratio:	4	(10.9)
Library/IT spend/student:	3	(£1,230)
Facilities spend/student:	80	(£147)
Good honours:	14	(71.8%)
Graduate prospects:	14	(73.5%)
Expected completion rate:	58	(83.5%)

second class degrees, while the projected dropout rate of 16.5 per cent is only marginally higher than the UK average for the subjects and entry qualifications at SOAS. One in five of the British undergraduates comes from a working-class home.

SOAS is located in Bloomsbury, but in 2001 opened a second campus at Vernon Square, Islington. Less than a mile from the main Russell Square site, and adjacent to the student residences, it provides student-orientated facilities such as an internet café. The centrepiece of the main campus is an airy, modern building with gallery space as well as teaching accommodation, a gift from the Sultan of Brunei. There is no separate students' union building, although the students do have their own bar and catering facilities. The well-equipped and under-used University of London Union is close at hand, with swimming pool, gym and bars. The West End is also on the doorstep.

The 770 residential places, which accommodate first-year students, are within 15 minutes' walk of the school. However, the school has few of its own sports facilities and the outdoor pitches are remote, with no time set aside from lectures. The ethnic and national mix has led to inevitable tensions at times, but SOAS is small enough for most students to know each other, at least by sight, and the normal atmosphere is friendly. Students tend to be highly committed – not surprising since many will return to positions of influence in developing countries.

Accommodation

Number of places and costs refer to 2005–06
University-provided places: 772 (through Shaftesbury Student Housing); 113 (intercollegiate)
Percentage catered: 10%
Costs for catered accommodation: £91.00–£121.10 a week.
Costs for self-catered accommodation: £105.35 a week.
Policy for first-year students: every effort is made to provide first years with accommodation although it cannot be guaranteed.
Policy for international students: no separate policy for international students, although they are a high housing priority.
Contact: student@shaftesburyhousing.org.uk

Students

Undergraduates:	1,970	(25)
Postgraduates:	1,095	(760)
Mature students:	24.8%	
Overseas students:	25.9%	
Applications per place:	4.9	
From state-sector schools:	68.9%	
From working-class homes:	20.5%	

Tuition fees 2006 £3,000
See chapter 13 for bursary details.

Teaching Quality Assessments

From 1995 (top score 24):
24 history of art.
23 East and South Asian Studies.
22 Middle Eastern and African Studies; politics; religious studies.
21 economics.
20 linguistics.

University of Sheffield

Sheffield slipped out of the top 20 in *The Times* League Table after losing the benefit of some of the best grades in the early rounds of teaching assessment, but its stock remains high both in the academic world and among students. Having added 600 extra places in 2002, the university was allocated almost 900 more over three years, accounting for 14 per cent of the extra amount for the whole of England. Two hundred new academic posts have been filled across all seven faculties to cope with the influx.

Only one subject (medicine) scored fewer than 20 points out of 24 for teaching quality, while three quarters of the staff assessed for the last research assessment exercise were placed in the top two categories. Nine starred departments were spread around medicine, science, engineering and social science. The star performers have been electrical and electronic engineering, the biosciences, politics and Russian, each of which achieved maximum scores for both teaching and research. Education was the last subject to record a perfect score for teaching and the university is to house a national teaching centre for the arts and social sciences. The medical school was allocated more places after a reinspection found improvements, and it is now the most popular in Britain in terms of applications per place. Only medicine and dentistry remain outside the modular course system, which operates on semesters.

Research excellence, which takes pride of place in Sheffield's mission statement, has boosted the university's facilities: £100 million for biological and physical sciences, medicine, engineering and social sciences, and £15 million on an aerospace manufacturing research centre in which Boeing is the senior partner, which will form the hub of an advanced manufacturing technology park. The university is the lead institution for systems engineering, smart materials and stem-cell technology in a research network of European, American and Chinese universities. Sheffield has always enjoyed a high ratio of applications to places, despite expanding through much of the 1990s. Although there was a rare dip in the demand for places in 2003, this was reversed in 2004 and had turned into an 8 per cent increase at the start of 2005.

The academic buildings are concentrated in an area about a mile from the city centre on the affluent west side of Sheffield, with most university flats and halls of residence a little further into the suburbs. Recent developments mean that the main university precinct now stretches into an

---

Western Bank,
Sheffield S10 2TN
T 0114-222 8027
E ug.admissions@
   sheffield.ac.uk
W www.sheffield.ac.uk
U www.sheffieldunion.com

The Times Rankings
Overall Ranking: 21
(2005 ranking: 26)

Teaching assessment:	=20	(22.2)
Research assessment:	=18	(5.5)
Entry standards:	12	(398.5)
Student–staff ratio:	=19	(14.7)
Library/IT spend/student:	37	(£583)
Facilities spend/student:	=51	(£190)
Good honours:	13	(72%)
Graduate prospects:	=31	(66.9%)
Expected completion rate:	25	(91.8%)

almost unbroken mile-long 'campus'. The former Jessop Hospital, an imposing building at the heart of the campus, has been purchased by the university for use by academic departments, while another new site adjacent to the engineering departments will house high-tech multidisciplinary facilities. A £16-million learning resources centre, with 1,000 study spaces and 100,000 undergraduate textbooks, will be finished in 2006.

The intake is more diverse than at most leading universities – 83 per cent come from state schools or colleges – and almost one undergraduate in five comes from a working-class home. Yet the dropout rate is among the lowest outside Oxbridge. The students' union's long-established student reception service helps new arrivals settle in, visiting those in private accommodation as well as hall-dwellers. Few have much trouble adjusting to the hectic social scene, which is based on the vibrant union's recently extended facilities but also takes full advantage of the city's burgeoning club life. In addition to its own popular facilities, the union owns two pubs in the western suburbs where most students live. Town–gown relations are much better and the crime rate lower is than in most big cities.

Residential accommodation is plentiful, with most of the 4,900 university-owned places within walking distance of lectures, and private housing reasonably priced. First years from outside Sheffield are guaranteed accommodation. A move to privatise the halls collapsed in 2002 but there are ambitious plans to reorganise and expand provision. The university's excellent sports facilities have been the subject of a £6-million makeover, which includes a 150-station fitness centre and a third Astroturf pitch specifically for soccer and rugby. Top-notch facilities were built by the city for the 1991 World Student Games and a £25-million regional centre for the English Institute of Sport opened in 2003.

Accommodation
Number of places and costs refer to 2005–06
University-provided places: 4,986
Percentage catered: 60%
Costs for catered accommodation: £79.45–£117.18 (en suite) a week.
Costs for self-catered accommodation: £57.61–£79.80 (en suite) a week.
Policy for first-year students: single students accepting by 6 July and confirming a place by 31 August are guaranteed a place (excludes those applying with Sheffield postal codes).
Policy for international students: single first-year international students are covered by the guarantee above.
Contact: studentoffice@sheffield.ac.uk; www.shef.ac.uk/housing

---

Students
Undergraduates:	16,005	(2,645)
Postgraduates:	4,305	(2,550)
Mature students:	6.2%	
Overseas students:	9.6%	
Applications per place:	7.0	
From state-sector schools:	82.6%	
From working-class homes:	19.0%	

Tuition fees 2006	£3,000

See chapter 13 for bursary details.

Teaching Quality Assessments
From 1995 (top score 24):
24 anatomy and physiology; biological sciences; education; electrical and electronic engineering; philosophy; politics; Russian; theology.
23 dentistry; town and country planning.
22 archaeology; East and South Asian studies; librarianship and information management; linguistics; materials technology; physics; psychology.
21 chemical engineering; civil engineering; economics; French; health subjects; Iberian languages; mathematics and statistics; nursing; pharmacy.
20 German; **19** medicine.

Sheffield Hallam University

A series of good teaching scores and a good performance in the last research assessment exercise have cemented Sheffield Hallam's position among the leading new universities in *The Times* League Table. Teaching grades had been improving steadily after a disappointing start in which only one of the first eight subjects was rated as excellent. But physics and later hospitality, sport, leisure and tourism have followed psychology with perfect scores, with education not far behind.

The university has been undergoing a physical transformation designed to alter its image and cater for an even bigger student population. It considered starting afresh in a less central development area, but will now keep its main site in the heart of Sheffield. Eventually, there are to be only two campuses.

Development has been continuing apace, with £140 million earmarked for capital projects over the next decade. They will support key areas for the university, including creative and digital disciplines, health and social care. New buildings for engineering and information technology have already been completed; an atrium provides social space for staff and students; and innovative library developments take pride of place on both campuses. Business and management courses, which account

for easily the biggest share of places, have their own city-centre headquarters. The Collegiate Crescent campus, a former teacher training college, houses education, health and community studies, while art and design are further away in a former art college. This site will close when cultural studies move to the city-centre campus. A £17-million investment will give the school a new building on the site of the students' union, which has taken over the spectacular but ill-fated National Centre for Popular Music. Between them, the faculty and the union will help to raise the profile of the Cultural Industries Quarter, which is on the university's doorstep.

While most of the development has been on the main campus, adjoining the main bus and rail stations, the latest stage has seen the opening of a new social centre on the Collegiate Crescent site. A £14-million headquarters for the Faculty of Health and Wellbeing will follow in 2005, enabling its numbers almost to double, as extra provision is made for nursing, radiotherapy, physiotherapy and social work. The Centre for Sport and Exercise Science, which incorporates a new £6-million research facility, won glowing praise from inspectors, and is one of Europe's largest centres of its kind, with more than 2,000 students.

Sheffield Hallam traces its origins in art

City Campus,
Sheffield S1 1WB
T 0114-225 5555
E undergraduate-admissions@
   shu.ac.uk
W www.shu.ac.uk
U www.hallamunion.com

The Times Rankings
Overall Ranking: 67
(2005 ranking: 68)

Teaching assessment:	=51	(21.6)
Research assessment:	=61	(3.0)
Entry standards:	62	(254.5)
Student–staff ratio:	90	(21.5)
Library/IT spend/student:	82	(£420)
Facilities spend/student:	34	(£222)
Good honours:	92	(46.7%)
Graduate prospects:	=66	(59.4%)
Expected completion rate:	45	(85.8%)

and design back to the 1840s and celebrated the centenary of education and teacher training in 2005. It is now one of the largest of the new universities, with high proportions of part-time and mature students, and more than 1,000 students taught on franchised courses in further education colleges. Business and industry are closely involved in the development of more than 650 courses, with almost half of the students taking sandwich course placements with employers. A new degree for operating department practitioners, for example, provides a novel route to advanced practitioner status. The university is to house two national teaching centres, one for fostering employability and the other to promote individual learning.

Research in art and design, history and materials were all rated nationally outstanding with significant work of international standard in the latest research assessments. The university is creating a 'virtual campus': students are offered e-mail accounts and cheap equipment to access the growing volume of online courses, assignments and discussion groups provided by the university, even when they are at home or on work placements.

Almost 30 per cent of undergraduates come from working-class homes, the majority of them from areas that send few students to higher education. The dropout rate is among the lowest in the new universities and, at 12.5 per cent, significantly better than the national average for the subjects offered and the students' entry qualifications.

Such is Sheffield Hallam's size that it is not possible to guarantee all first years university-owned accommodation, although the large local intake means that many live at home. Sports facilities are supplemented by those provided by the city for the World Student Games. The impressive swimming complex, for example, is on the university's doorstep.

Accommodation
Number of places and costs refer to 2005–06
University-provided places: 3,958
Percentage catered: 10%
Costs for catered accommodation: £84.25 a week for a 39-week contract
Costs for self-catered accommodation: £57.17–£91.00 a week; contract lengths vary between 39 and 44 weeks
Policy for first-year students: all first years offered places either in University-owned, managed, partnership or private sector housing.
Policy for international students: as for first years, except there is a closing date for applications.
Contact: accommodation@shu.ac.uk

Students
Undergraduates:	16,030	(4,160)
Postgraduates:	1,850	(4,440)
Mature students:	16.2%	
Overseas students:	6.0%	
Applications per place:	5.0	
From state-sector schools:	95.2%	
From working-class homes:	29.7%	

Tuition fees 2006	£3,000

See chapter 13 for bursary details.

Teaching Quality Assessments
From 1995 (top score 24):
24 hospitality, leisure, sport and tourism; physics; psychology.
23 education; health subjects; mathematics and statistics.
22 art and design; biological sciences; materials technology; sociology; town planning.
21 building; business; land management; mechanical engineering; nursing.
20 history of art.
19 communication studies; drama
18 civil engineering; electrical and electronic engineering.

University of Southampton

Southampton celebrated its 50th anniversary in 2002, but it has been the last decade which has really made its name as a top university. During that time, student numbers have doubled, and the university has opened two new campuses of its own, as well as acquiring two others in college mergers. The university climbed again in *The Times* League Table last year, and its stock has been rising, as both teaching and research assessments have confirmed the high quality of provision. Its 2001 research grades were among the top ten in Britain, while the last five teaching assessments all produced perfect scores. An increase of more than 11 per cent in applications for 2004, followed by a smaller rise at the start of 2005, show that the message is getting through. Although the proportions of students from working-class homes and areas with little tradition of university education are lower than the national average for the subjects offered, the funding council concluded that this was largely a matter of location.

The university stresses its research strength: the proportion of income derived from research is among the highest in Britain. The 2001 assessments saw the number of subjects rated internationally outstanding shoot up from two to eight, including all branches of engineering.

Physics, computer science, European studies, law and music were the other top-scorers. Economics, education and politics, philosophy and archaeology achieved the five late maximums for teaching.

The medical school, too, enhanced its reputation with a maximum score for teaching quality in a set of assessments that saw more variation than most. It features a common core curriculum for the pre-registration programmes of the 3,000 medical, nursing and other health students from entry to internship. The New Generation curriculum was introduced in 2003, giving each professional group teamworking skills and an understanding of others' roles.

The main Highfield campus, in an attractive location two miles from the city centre, has been the focus of recent development to cater for the expansion in numbers. Nursing, chemistry, electronics and computer science have all benefited, and there is a new commercial services centre and an e-science centre as well as an extended library and a graduate centre for social sciences. A new student services centre is due to open in October 2005, providing learning support and other advisory facilities – all of which will be backed up online for students in other areas of the university.

Highfield,
Southampton SO17 1BJ
T   023-8059 5000
E   prospenq@soton.ac.uk
W   www.soton.ac.uk
U   www.susu.org

Edinburgh

Belfast

Cardiff   London

SOUTHAMPTON

The Times Rankings
Overall Ranking: =26
(2005 ranking: 25)

Teaching assessment:	=46	(21.8)
Research assessment:	=7	(5.8)
Entry standards:	24	(359.2)
Student–staff ratio:	22	(15.1)
Library/IT spend/student:	=19	(£691)
Facilities spend/student:	42	(£212)
Good honours:	19	(68.7%)
Graduate prospects:	42	(63.6%)
Expected completion rate:	15	(94%)

The Waterside Campus, which is in Southampton's revitalised dock area, houses the Oceanography Centre. A £49-million joint project with the Natural Environmental Research Council, it is considered Europe's finest, encompassing teaching, research and knowledge transfer facilities. The Avenue campus, near the main site, is home to the arts departments. Clinical medicine is based at Southampton General Hospital, where a new cancer sciences building opened in 2002.

The incorporation of Winchester School of Art complemented the university's Continental outlook with its own well-established European links. Two new buildings have since doubled the physical size of the school. But the takeover of the former La Sainte Union campus near the city centre to create Southampton New College did not go to plan. The new facility had a regional focus, offering opportunities for students from different backgrounds to the norm for a university where entry requirements are high and a fifth of the successful candidates come from independent schools. Although the drive to widen participation is being maintained, the site is being sold and the courses integrated with existing programmes on the main campus.

The university's social facilities have been expanded and refurbished, with the addition of a new students' union nightclub. Sports facilities have also been upgraded, with the opening in 2004 of an £8.4-million indoor sports complex and swimming pool next to the students' union. Plans are under way, too, for a £4.5-million development of the outdoor facilities. Further residential accommodation will come on stream in 2005.

Accommodation
Number of places and costs refer to 2005–06
University-provided places: 5,000
Percentage catered: 25%
Costs for catered accommodation: £100.24 (standard); £127.82 (en suite single) a week.
Costs for self-catered accommodation: £59.92 (basic); £62.37 (standard); £94.92 (en suite) a week.
Policy for first-year students: all are guaranteed accommodation for their first year except those living within the Southampton city council area; insurance acceptances initially go into lodgings. Students under 18 years are required to live in hall during their first year.
Policy for international students: single overseas fee-paying non-EU students are guaranteed accommodation for the normal duration of their courses.
Contact: accommodation@soton.ac.uk
www.accommodation.soton.ac.uk

Students

Undergraduates:	13,045	(3,305)
Postgraduates:	2,900	(3,075)
Mature students:	12.7%	
Overseas students:	7.3%	
Applications per place:	8.3	
From state-sector schools:	80.9%	
From working-class homes:	18.6%	

Tuition fees 2006 £3,000
See chapter 13 for bursary details.

Teaching Quality Assessments
From 1995 (top score 24):
24 economics; education; electrical and electronic engineering; medicine; philosophy; politics.
23 biological sciences; business and management; general engineering; materials.
22 art and design; nursing; physics.
21 civil engineering; mechanical engineering; psychology; sociology.
20 health subjects; history of art; mathematics.
18 modern languages.

Staffordshire University

Staffordshire claims to offer 'outrageously good courses' and has the ratings to back up its boast. Although there was a 13 per cent increase in applications at the beginning of 2005, British student numbers had been scaled back previously, in line with falling applications, and replaced by overseas recruits. The former polytechnic blamed increased competition from traditional universities, but has found that foreign markets more than compensate for any financial losses. Staffordshire is based on two main sites, the headquarters in Stoke and the other 12 miles away in Stafford. The rural Stafford site features the purpose-built Octagon Centre, in which lecture theatres, offices and walkways surround one of the largest university computing facilities in Europe. A £2.4-million New Technologies Centre, opened in 2003, has helped develop popular courses such as film production technology. Health, engineering and technology are all based at Stafford, while Stoke specialises in the arts, sciences and social sciences. The business school, which acquired a new headquarters in Stoke in 1995, straddles the two campuses in an attempt to foster links with the private sector.

However, a new campus in Lichfield gives a glimpse of the future for Staffordshire. An integrated further and higher education centre, developed in partnership with Tamworth and Lichfield College, is the first purpose-built institution of its kind. The main aim is to act as a resource centre for local businesses. The School of Health has branches in Telford, Shrewsbury and Oswestry, but franchised courses spread the university's net much further afield. There are 5,000 students taking Staffordshire courses outside Britain, almost half of them located around the Pacific Rim.

The university also runs courses for more than 1,000 students at further education colleges in its own region, as well as offering incentives for local people to apply. A priority applications scheme guarantees a place to under-21s from Staffordshire, Shropshire or Cheshire as long as they meet the minimum requirements for their chosen course, while mature students are guaranteed at least an interview if they join one of the range of access courses. Even before the advent of top-up fees, the university was offering £500 awards to disadvantaged students from Shropshire, Cheshire and Staffordshire. The policy has been working – more than a third of the students are from the local area and a new programme, run in conjunction with Keele University, aims to increase the numbers further. A range of courses, including two-year foundation degrees for teaching

---

College Road,
Stoke-on-Trent ST4 2DE
T 01782 294000
E admissions@staffs.ac.uk
W www.staffs.ac.uk
U www.staffsunion.com

The Times Rankings
Overall Ranking: =80
(2005 ranking: =85)

Teaching assessment:	=66	(21.2)
Research assessment:	=84	(2.2)
Entry standards:	83	(223.6)
Student–staff ratio:	59	(17.9)
Library/IT spend/student:	29	(£627)
Facilities spend/student:	53	(£189)
Good honours:	94	(45.5%)
Graduate prospects:	98	(46.9%)
Expected completion rate:	71	(80.3%)

assistants, care managers and e-business specialists, are tailored to the needs of the area and graduates will be encouraged to help develop the local economy. Many courses are available with a January start, a particularly popular arrangement with overseas students who take English language courses before beginning a degree.

Economics registered Staffordshire's first perfect score in 2001, and only one of the last ten assessments yielded less than 20 points out of 24. The university learnt the lesson of the 1996 research assessments, when almost two thirds of the academics were entered, but nearly all were placed in the bottom three categories. In the latest exercise, the proportion of entries was halved and, although no subjects reached the top two grades, media studies and art and design were in the next category.

With 97 per cent of its undergraduates state-educated and more than a third coming from working-class homes, Staffordshire comfortably exceeds all the benchmarks set by the funding council for widening access to higher education. There is good provision for the 700 disabled students. The projected dropout rate of 18.5 per cent is only slightly higher than average for the courses and students' entry qualifications.

Stoke is not the liveliest city of its size, but the campus is close to the railway station, within easy reach of the centre and has a buzzing union. Stafford is much the more attractive setting and offers the best chance of a residential place, but the town is quiet and the campus is a mile and a half outside it. Sports facilities are good, especially in Stafford, where there is a new £1.4-million sports centre and all-weather pitches. Sports scholarships and good coaching have helped attract some outstanding athletes, who have access to a sports performance centre to help with training schedules, psychological support and dietary assessments.

Accommodation
Number of places and costs refer to 2005–06
University-provided places: 1,430 (Stoke); 776 (Stafford)
Percentage catered: n/a
Costs for catered accommodation: n/a
Costs for self-catered accommodation: £52.50–£75.00 a week (includes internet access).
Policy for first-year students: new first years having Staffordshire as their first choice and whose applications are received by 30 June have priority. Exceptions are made for disabled students and those with a serious medical condition.
Policy for international students: full-year students whose applications are received by 8 September have priority.
Contact: Accommodation_stoke@staffs.ac.uk
Accommodation_stafford@staffs.ac.uk

Students

Undergraduates:	9,715	(3,395)
Postgraduates:	640	(1,670)
Mature students:	19.6%	
Overseas students:	6.6%	
Applications per place:	4.8	
From state-sector schools:	96.8%	
From working-class homes:	37.7%	

Tuition fees 2006	£3,000

See chapter 13 for bursary details.

Teaching Quality Assessments
From 1995 (top score 24):
24 economics.
23 philosophy; psychology.
22 art and design; biological sciences; health subjects; hospitality; nursing; physics and astronomy; sport, health and exercise.
21 history of art and design; modern languages.
20 drama; electrical and electronic engineering; media studies.
17 building; materials technology; sociology.

University of Stirling

One of the most beautiful campuses in Britain features low-level, modern buildings in a loch-side setting beneath the Ochil Hills on the former Airthrey Estate, two miles from the centre of Stirling. Even after a 20 per cent expansion over four years, largely due to the incorporation of three nursing colleges at Falkirk, Inverness and Stornoway, in Lewis, the university remains a relatively small institution of 9,000 students. Stirling also has probably the most popular Chancellor: spurning the usual dignitaries, the university chose actress Diana Rigg for the post.

Although highly rated in some research fields, there were no starred departments in the latest research assessments. However, 10 out of the 22 subject areas reached grade 5, denoting national excellence and significant work of international standard. Excellent teaching ratings for economics, sociology, theology, business studies, psychology and English show Stirling's strength in the arts and social sciences. Among the sciences, only environmental science matched this feat, its success reflected in a new School of Biological and Environmental Sciences, with substantially refurbished facilities for both teaching and research. All but one of the subjects assessed for teaching quality were rated at least Highly Satisfactory. Sports studies are particularly popular, as

are film and media studies, which acquired a £40,000 high-tech newsroom in 2004. International exchanges are common, with many students going to American, Asian and European universities each year.

Stirling was the British pioneer of the semester system, which has now become so popular in other universities. The academic year is divided into two 15-week terms, with short mid-semester breaks. Students have the option of starting courses in February, rather than September. Successful completion of six semesters will bring a general degree; eight semesters, honours. The emphasis on breadth is such that there are no barriers to movement between faculties. Undergraduates can switch the whole direction of their studies, in consultation with their academic adviser, as their interests develop. The modular scheme allows students to speed up their progress on a Summer Academic Programme, which squeezes a full semester's teaching into July and August. Full-time students are not allowed to use the programme to reduce the length of their course, but part-timers can use it to make more rapid progress.

The level of competition for places has been unpredictable: there were declines in 2003 and 2004, but the 8 per cent increase in applications at the start of 2005 was one of the largest in Scotland. The intake is

---

Stirling FK9 4LA
T   01786 467044
E   admissions@stir.ac.uk
W   www.stir.ac.uk
U   www.susaonline.org.uk

STIRLING
Edinburgh
Belfast
London
Cardiff

surprisingly diverse, with 92 per cent of undergraduates state-educated and more than a quarter coming from working-class homes. Almost as many come from areas that send few students to higher education, and even before fee differentials encouraged more Scots to stay at home to study, 70 per cent of Stirling's students were from north of the border. Sports facilities are excellent and still improving. The national tennis and swimming centres are both based on the campus, the latter in a new Olympic-sized pool, and there is even a nine-hole golf course. A new golf centre opened in 2004, adding three target greens and a practice area to the existing driving range and indoor facilities. Following the addition of new artificial pitches a few months earlier, it brought Stirling's spending on sport to more than £10 million in five years. Sports bursaries worth between £900 and £2,000, according to performance, are open to overseas students, as well as Britons. The campus also houses the new headquarters of the Scottish Institute of Sport.

The 2,680 campus residential places are enough to accommodate all the first years and most finalists who want them. Chalets offer an unusual alternative to halls of residence. Students appreciate the individual attention a small, campus university can offer, although some find the atmosphere claustrophobic. The original campus buildings have been beginning to show their age and are being refurbished, while applied social science was the latest to acquire new premises in 2003. Stirling is not the top choice of nightclubbers, but the students' union has been named the best in Scotland and there is a lively social programme. The £6.3-million refurbishment of the MacRobert Arts Centre has transformed the cultural programme on campus, while the surrounding scenery offers its own attractions for walkers.

For nurses and midwives, the Highland campus is based in the grounds of Raigmore Hospital in Inverness, with purpose-built teaching accommodation and student flats. The Western Isles campus is located in Stornoway, where the teaching accommodation is an integral part of the recently-built Lewis Hospital.

Accommodation
Number of places and costs refer to 2004–05
University-provided places: 2,840
Percentage catered: 0%
Costs for catered accommodation: n/a
Costs for self-catered accommodation: £55–£71 a week.
Policy for first-year students: all first-years are guaranteed suitable housing arranged by the university.
Policy for international students: guaranteed accommodation as above.
Contact: Accommodation@stir.ac.uk

Students
Undergraduates:	5,950	(1,145)
Postgraduates:	850	(1,025)
Mature students:	14.2%	
Overseas students:	5.0%	
Applications per place:	6.7	
From state-sector schools:	92.2%	
From working-class homes:	26.5%	

Teaching Quality Assessments
1993–98 Rated Excellent:
economics; English; environmental science; psychology; sociology; theology.
1993–98 Rated Highly Satisfactory:
biological sciences; business and management; finance and accounting; French; history; mass communications; mathematics and statistics; philosophy; politics; social work; teacher education.
From 1998 (top score 24):
20 European languages.

See page 245 for recent assessments.

University of Strathclyde

Even as Anderson's Institution in the 18th century, Strathclyde concentrated on 'useful learning'. Some Glaswegians still refer to it as 'the tech'. But if the nickname does less than justice to the current portfolio of courses, the university has never shrunk from its technological and vocational emphasis. Strathclyde aims to offer courses that are both innovatory and relevant to industry and commerce – hence product design and innovation, or international business with modern languages.

Traditional science degrees have continued to prosper, however, with a series of top ratings. All but two of the 26 subjects assessed under Scotland's original system of grading teaching quality were considered Excellent or Highly Satisfactory. The university is in *The Times* top ten for general engineering, health subjects and pharmacy. Its careers service is also rated among the best, having four times won a Government charter mark for customer service. No department reached the top grade of the last research assessments, but ten of the 33 subject areas reached the next rung of the ladder, accounting for 90 per cent of those entered.

Strathclyde's main strength, however, is in the top-rated business school, which is one of the largest in Europe and the only one in Scotland to be accredited by the European Quality Improvement System. Business studies students follow an 'integrative studies' programme, which is designed to place them in a realistic business environment from day one and involves work with a range of major companies. The scheme is now being piloted in other faculties.

The engineering faculty is also the largest in Scotland, and has linked with Glasgow University to provide a joint department of naval architecture and marine engineering.

European focus is evident throughout the university, which has encouraged all departments to adapt their courses to the needs of the single market. Many students combine business or engineering with European studies or languages to give themselves an edge in the job market. Mature students account for a fifth of the places and have a special organisation to look after their interests. With over 20,000 students, including part-timers, Strathclyde is the third-largest university in Scotland, but its numbers are swelled to 60,000 including short courses and distance learning programmes.

Strathclyde actively promotes wider access, almost one student in five coming from an area sending few students to higher education – well above the benchmark for the subjects offered – and more than a

16 Richmond Street,
Glasgow G1 1XQ
T 0141-548 2813
E j.gibson@mis.strath.ac.uk
W www.strath.ac.uk
U www.strathstudents.com

GLASGOW
Edinburgh
Belfast
London
Cardiff

The Times Rankings
Overall Ranking: 32
(2005 ranking: 37)

Teaching assessment:	=7	(22.7)
Research assessment:	=42	(4.7)
Entry standards:	23	(361)
Student–staff ratio:	=52	(17.3)
Library/IT spend/student:	51	(£535)
Facilities spend/student:	=69	(£159)
Good honours:	=28	(66.9%)
Graduate prospects:	=44	(63.4%)
Expected completion rate:	=52	(84.7%)

quarter coming from working-class homes. Its efforts are underpinned by fundraising for a scholarship programme to aid students from poor homes.

The main John Anderson campus is in the centre of Glasgow, behind George Square and near Queen Street station. Apart from the Edwardian headquarters, the buildings are mostly modern. The site of a former maternity hospital in the centre of the campus will eventually provide extra teaching accommodation, but a £73-million refurbishment programme is taking priority. Strathclyde has a second campus on the west side of the city, acquired from a merger with Jordanhill College of Education, Scotland's largest teacher training institution, in 1993. The 67-acre parkland site houses the faculty of education, which is breaking new ground with Scotland's first part-time teacher training degree and also offers courses in speech and language pathology, community arts, social work, sport and outdoor education.

The university is losing its image as a 'nine-to-five' institution, thanks to a student village on the main campus, complete with pub, which has increased the number of residential places. Over 1,400 of these are on campus, all with network access, and another 500 are nearby. The Millennium Student project has delivered full network access from every study bedroom on campus and it is planned to make extensive high-speed dial-up facilities into the University network available for all students in the Glasgow area. The ten-floor union building attracts students from all over Glasgow with its reputation for hard-drinking revelry. For those with more sophisticated tastes, there are several theatres and the city's own variety of cultural venues.

Accommodation
Number of places and costs refer to 2004–05
University-provided places: 1,962
Percentage catered: 7%
Costs for catered accommodation: £72 (single room) a week.
Costs for self-catered accommodation: £51–£76 a week.
Policy for first-year students: accommodation is offered to those students who live 25 miles from the city centre.
Policy for international students: as above.
Contact:
student.accommodation@mis.strath.ac.uk

Students
Undergraduates:	11,530	(2,510)
Postgraduates:	2,875	(6,060)
Mature students:	13.2%	
Overseas students:	5.3%	
Applications per place:	5.6	
From state-sector schools:	92.4%	
From working-class homes:	27.0%	

Teaching Quality Assessments
1993–98 Rated Excellent:
architecture; business and management; chemistry; electrical and electronic engineering; geography; mechanical engineering; pharmacy; physics; politics.

1993–98 Rated Highly Satisfactory:
biological sciences; civil engineering; computer studies; English; history; hospitality studies; law; mathematics and statistics; social work; sociology; teacher education.

From 1998 (top score 24):
22 European languages.
20 chemical engineering.

See page 245 for recent assessments.

University of Sunderland

One of Britain's newest cities also has among the newest university campuses. The Sir Tom Cowie campus at St Peter's, an award-winning 24-acre site by the banks of the Wear, initially housed the business school and the informatics centre. To these is being added a £20-million arts, design and media centre, the first phase of which opened for the 2003–04 academic year. The main campus and a third site in one of Sunderland's suburbs are within walking distance. The university doubled in size in four years, and has taken advantage of urban regeneration programmes to expand its facilities to match. A well-appointed science complex opened on the city-centre site, language laboratories were upgraded and specialist research centres opened for ecology and Japanese studies.

Developments have been planned with an eye to history, for example incorporating a working heritage centre for the glass industry at the heart of the new campus, which is built around a 7th-century abbey described as one of Britain's first universities. The glass and ceramics design degree carries on a Sunderland tradition – the National Glass Centre was one of the features of the new campus – while the courses in automotive design and manufacture serve the region's new industrial base. The large pharmacy department is another strength and the well-equipped School of Computing, Engineering and Technology is one of the largest in the UK with over 3,000 students.

Teaching assessments improved after a poor start. The biosciences recorded the university's only perfect scores, but nursing and anatomy and physiology came close to joining them. The last research assessments were more impressive, registering a big improvement on 1996 and representing the best performance in any new university in terms of average grades per member of staff. Although no subjects reached the top two grades, the 44 per cent of academics entered for assessment was the most in any former polytechnic, and art and design, English and history all managed grade 4. The successes have made the university particularly resentful of the government's plans to concentrate research funding further.

Sunderland is making the most of the opportunity to link up with the multinational companies that have arrived on its doorstep. A new institute for automotive and manufacturing advanced practice has a team of 40 researchers and consultants working with local businesses, while nearby Nissan played an important role in designing a course in automotive product development. The Sony media

---

Langham Tower, Ryhope Road,
Sunderland SR2 7EE
T   0191-515 3000
E   student-helpline@
    sunderland.ac.uk
W www.sunderland.ac.uk
U www.sunderland
    su.co.uk

The Times Rankings
Overall Ranking: =62
(2005 ranking: =76)

Teaching assessment:	=28	(22.1)
Research assessment:	=67	(2.8)
Entry standards:	81	(225.9)
Student–staff ratio:	=48	(17.0)
Library/IT spend/student:	98	(£367)
Facilities spend/student:	54	(£186)
Good honours:	66	(53.2%)
Graduate prospects:	70	(58.4%)
Expected completion rate:	92	(72.6%)

centre is another example, providing students with excellent television and video production facilities.

The university has a determinedly local focus, aiming to double the number of students coming from an area which has little tradition of sending students to higher education. Almost a third now come from 'low participation neighbourhoods' – by far the largest proportion at any English university and more than twice the national average for the subjects on offer. A pioneering access scheme offers places to mature students without A levels, as long as they reach the required levels of literacy, numeracy and other basic skills. The Learning North East initiative, based on Sunderland's successful pilot for the University for Industry, even offers free taster courses to take at home.

More than 40 per cent of the undergraduates have a working-class background, but the downside of Sunderland's access efforts is that the funding council expects more than a quarter to drop out – significantly more than the official benchmark figure for the courses. Provision for disabled students is excellent, with award-winning information produced for those with disabilities, trained support staff in every academic school as well as in the libraries and special modules to help dyslexics. The campus also houses the North East Regional Access Centre, which assesses the learning support requirements of students with disabilities and specific learning difficulties. There is special provision among the 2,200 residential places.

Sunderland itself is fiercely proud of its identity and has the advantage of a coastal location but, despite the city title, with the exception of the impressive new football ground, it has the leisure facilities of a medium-sized town. Those in search of big cultural events or serious nightlife head for Newcastle, which is less than half an hour away by Metro.

Accommodation

Number of places and costs refer to 2003–04

University-provided places: 2,108 (halls); 196 in university managed houses (Head Tenancy scheme).

Percentage catered: n/a

Costs for catered accommodation: n/a

Costs for self-catered accommodation: £37.55–£55.95 (university-managed house); £52.15–£55.25 (hall without internet access); £53.20–£59.50 (in a hall with free internet access); £103.25–£114.70 (family houses and flats) a week.

Policy for first-year students: all first years guaranteed a room in hall.

Policy for international students: no special arrangements.

Contact: residentialservices@sunderland.ac.uk www.sunderland.ac.uk/residential services

---

Students

Undergraduates:	7,570	(6,230)
Postgraduates:	1,560	(755)
Mature students:	17.1%	
Overseas students:	13.7%	
Applications per place:	4.9	
From state-sector schools:	97.1%	
From working-class homes:	44.8%	

Tuition fees 2006	£3,000

See chapter 13 for bursary details.

Teaching Quality Assessments

From 1995 (top score 24):

24 biological sciences.

23 nursing.

22 media studies; pharmacy.

21 art and design; drama, dance and cinematics; education; history of art; sociology.

20 hospitality; psychology; sports science.

18 Iberian languages.

17 French; German.

University of Surrey

Surrey has been one of the unheralded success stories of the university world, remaining true to the technological legacy of its predecessor institution (Battersea Polytechnic Institute) while building a strong research base and a degree of financial independence envied by its peers. Even some of the arts degrees carry a BSc and are highly vocational: four out of five undergraduates in all subjects undertake work experience. Placements of one (or two half) years, often taken abroad, mean that most degrees last four years. The format and the subject balance combine to keep Surrey at the head of the graduate employment league, as well as producing a healthy research income. Indeed, it has taken to describing itself as the 'University for Jobs' to ram the point home. Recent expansion in healthcare, human sciences and performing arts has added to the traditional strengths in science and engineering. The mix has been proving popular with applicants, although the university was one of the few to register a decline in demand for places at the start of 2005.

All students are encouraged to enrol for a course at the European language centre, and a growing number of degrees, including a new range in engineering, have a language component. The cosmopolitan feel is enhanced by one of the largest proportions of overseas students at any university – a feat which won Surrey a Queen's Award for Export Achievement. The 2,700 foreign students come from 140 different countries.

Teaching assessments have been impressive, with economics and education recording near-perfect scores to match those for physics and astronomy, and electrical and electronic engineering, one of Surrey's three top-rated research areas. With health and sociology also starred areas for research, a third of the researchers were in departments considered internationally outstanding – a proportion bettered by only four universities in Britain. Six out of ten reached one of the top two grades. Another indication of the university's research strength lies in the growing proportion of income derived from sources other than Government grants: up from 10 per cent to about 70 per cent in little over a decade. The Surrey Research Park is one of only three science parks still owned, funded and managed by the university that opened it, helping Surrey to amass one of the highest proportions of private funding at any British university.

Both the proportions of undergraduates from working-class homes and from areas without a tradition of higher education are lower than the benchmark figures, which

---

Guildford, Surrey GU2 7XH
T   01483 879305
E   admissions@surrey.ac.uk
W   www.surrey.ac.uk
U   www.ussu.co.uk

take account of the subject mix and entry standards. But the funding council has acknowledged that the explanation lies in the university's location. The projected dropout rate, at less than 9 per cent, exceeded the council's expectations.

The compact campus is a ten-minute walk from the centre of Guildford. Most of the buildings date from the late 1960s, but the new business school and the gleaming European Institute of Health and Medical Sciences offer a striking contrast. Shaped like a giant ship's prow, the steel and glass building houses the large nursing and midwifery departments. A £12-million management building and an Advanced Technology Institute opened in September 2002. The campus includes two lakes, playing fields and enough residential accommodation to enable all first-years and most final-year students to live in. A second campus, adjacent to the Stag Hill headquarters, is now being developed. A postgraduate medical school is intended to be the first stage in the development of a health campus, which will also contain more residential places for students and staff, as well as other academic buildings, leisure and sporting facilities.

As a predominantly middle-class town, Guildford has plenty of cultural and recreational facilities, but riotous nightclubs are not encouraged. The campus, inevitably, is the centre of social life, and has seen recent improvements to leisure facilities. The proximity of London – little more than half an hour away by train – is an attraction to many students, but can leave the campus feeling empty at weekends. It also helps account for the high cost of living, which is not mitigated by the allowances available in the capital.

Accommodation

Number of places and costs refer to 2005–06
University-provided places: 3,373
Percentage catered: 0%
Costs for catered accommodation: n/a
Costs for self-catered accommodation: £49 (shared room); £70 (single with washbasin); £85 (single, en suite) a week.
Policy for first-year students: all first years guaranteed a place, with no restrictions regarding home address, date of application, etc.
Policy for international students: students designated overseas for fees are guaranteed a place for the duration of their course.
Contact: www.surrey.ac.uk/Accommodation

Students

Undergraduates:	6,375	(3,450)
Postgraduates:	2,785	(3,060)
Mature students:	17.2%	
Overseas students:	18.0%	
Applications per place:	5.2	
From state-sector schools:	88.0%	
From working-class homes:	21.5%	

Tuition fees 2006   £3,000
See chapter 13 for bursary details.

Teaching Quality Assessments

From 1995 (top score 24):
23 economics; education; electrical and electronic engineering; physics and astronomy.
22 civil engineering; materials technology; psychology.
21 biological sciences; health subjects; mathematics; sociology.
20 drama, dance and cinematics.
19 art and design; nursing.
18 chemical engineering; modern languages.

University of Sussex

Sussex's all-round academic reputation has seldom been higher. The university appeared in the top 60 in *The Times Higher Education Supplement's* world rankings and was higher still for the arts and social sciences. Sir Harry Kroto won the 1996 Nobel Prize for Chemistry and Professor Anthony Leggett took the 2003 Physics prize for work carried out at Sussex.

Although no subject was considered internationally outstanding in the latest research assessment exercise, more than half were placed in the next category. No subject dropped below grade 4, despite a high proportion of academics entered for assessment. The university now generates more than a third of its income from private sources, largely in research contracts. Philosophy and sociology scored maximum points for teaching quality, with politics and international relations, mathematics and American studies – a long-established strength – the best of the rest.

Applications have seen healthy growth: the 23 per cent increase at the beginning of 2005 was one of the largest at an old university and was the third successive rise. The demand for places in social work practically doubled, environmental science was up by 81 per cent and even physics saw a 35 per cent increase. With the university filling more places with postgraduates in recent years, the result has been increasing competition for degree places. Sussex's success was said to be due partly to targeting schools in London and the South East, as well as to innovations such as weekly campus tours for prospective applicants and drop-in arrangements for mature students. But a revised portfolio of arts subjects seems to have helped; a similar exercise for the sciences will be complete for 2006.

The interdisciplinary approach that has always been Sussex's trademark has been re-examined to adapt this 1960s concept for the 21st century. The 11 schools have been reduced to five and students are being offered a clearer framework so that they are fully aware of the combinations available to them. Student support is being improved through a revamped personal tutor system and a 50 per cent increase in the number of student advisors. Arts and social science students are still in the majority, but the life sciences are not far behind.

Sussex is committed to taking candidates with no family tradition of higher education and has much larger numbers of mature students than most of its peer group of institutions. However, the proportion of working-class students and the share of places going to those from areas with little

Falmer,
Brighton BN1 9RH
T 01273 678416
E UG.Admissions@
   sussex.ac.uk
W www.sussex.ac.uk
U www.ussu.info/

The Times Rankings
Overall Ranking: 37
(2005 ranking: 39)

Teaching assessment:	=62	(21.3)
Research assessment:	=18	(5.5)
Entry standards:	32	(333.3)
Student–staff ratio:	51	(17.2)
Library/IT spend/student:	33	(£601)
Facilities spend/student:	=24	(£263)
Good honours:	17	(69.7%)
Graduate prospects:	53	(61.6%)
Expected completion rate:	=46	(85.6%)

tradition of higher education are both lower than the funding council's benchmark figures. The 14 per cent dropout rate is high, but not significantly worse than the national average for the subjects on offer. And a survey of graduates five years after leaving Sussex showed an enviable employment record.

The university is based in an 18th-century park at Falmer, close to the South Downs and four miles from the centre of Brighton. Sir Basil Spence's original buildings have been supplemented by new developments. The library has been extended and the language centre recenly refurbished. Relations with neighbouring Brighton University are good. The two institutions succeeded in a joint bid for a medical school, which opened in 2003 and has since recorded big increases in applications. The Brighton and Sussex Medical School is split between the Royal Sussex County Hospital and the two universities' Falmer campuses.

Undergraduates can take a year abroad in many subjects, either in Europe or North America. Some courses offer joint qualifications with Continental universities, and those returning from a year abroad are given priority, with first years, for the 3,000 residential places on campus. More accommodation is being built on campus and a new Postgraduate Centre provides dedicated support.

Sussex has always attracted overseas students in large numbers and has seen big increases recently, but a high proportion of the remainder are from the London area, where many return at weekends. As a result, the well-appointed campus can be quiet, although there is no shortage of social events and Brighton has plenty to offer.

Sports facilities are good, and the university has launched a new initiative to attract top performers. Basketball and hockey were the first sports to be highlighted, bringing in coaches from the Brighton Bears, Sussex Magic and Lewes Hockey Club to make use of the two sports halls and a lottery-funded all-weather playing area.

Accommodation
Number of places and costs refer to 2004–05
University-provided places: 3,035
Percentage catered: 0%
Costs for catered accommodation: n/a
Costs for self-catered accommodation: £41–£46 (shared); £57–£67 (standard); £56.50–£78.50 (en suite) a week.
Policy for first-year students: undergraduates applying through UCAS who firmly accept the offer of a place are guaranteed
Policy for international students: certain categories of international students are given priority provided the application is received by 1 August.
Contact: housing@sussex.ac.uk

Students

Undergraduates:	6,565	(2,810)
Postgraduates:	1,720	(1,255)
Mature students:	20.0%	
Overseas students:	13.8%	
Applications per place:	6.5	
From state-sector schools:	85.2%	
From working-class homes:	17.9%	

Tuition fees 2006	£3,000

See chapter 13 for bursary details.

Teaching Quality Assessments
From 1995 (top score 24):
24 philosophy; sociology.
23 American studies; mathematics and statistics; politics.
22 biological sciences; education; French; linguistics; physics.
21 economics; electrical and electronic engineering; media studies; psychology.
20 history of art.
17 modern languages.

Swansea, University of Wales

Swansea is the largest institution within the University of Wales, since the departure of Cardiff. Its attractive coastal location and accessibility to students from outside Wales already made the university a natural alternative to the Welsh capital for thousands of applicants. Numbers have been growing steadily, with rises of 7 per cent in each of the last two years. But a plan to rationalise departments, eventually abandoning five subjects, has caused unrest among academics and students.

A wide variety of new courses have been introduced, as part of a development plan stressing language combinations. There are now more than 500 degree courses in the modular scheme, and undergraduates are encouraged to stray outside their specialist area in their first year. Swansea takes its European interests seriously, with links to more than 90 Continental institutions. The new law school offers options in European and international law, while science students, as well as those on arts courses, can undertake some of their studies abroad.

Swansea has won European funding for some of its projects, including Graduate Opportunities Wales, which steers students towards small firms through industrial placements and vacation jobs. The most important academic development, however, has come with the opening of the Swansea Clinical School, more than 30 years after the first attempt to secure approval for a medical school. The university already had a postgraduate school, but collaboration with University of Wales College of Medicine and Swansea NHS Trust saw the Welsh Assembly back plans for 50 undergraduates to begin training in 2001. From 2004, the 'fast track' programme will allow 70 graduates to qualify as doctors in four years rather than five.

About half of the subjects assessed for teaching quality have received Excellent ratings. Swansea counts physical sciences, management and languages among its strengths, and all branches of engineering are highly rated. Civil engineering was the only top-rated subject in the latest research assessments, but a third of the researchers were placed in one of the top two grades.

For all its concentration on international activities, Swansea has not forgotten its local responsibilities. A Community University of the Valleys offers part-time courses for mature students as part of the effort to regenerate the area. Compacts with schools in the region encourage students in areas of economic disadvantage to aspire to higher education.

The immediate locality is far from depressing, however. The coastal campus two miles from the centre of Swansea offers

---

Singleton Park,
Swansea SA2 8PP
T 01792 295111
E admissions@
   swansea.ac.uk
W www.swan.ac.uk
U www.swansea-union.co.uk

Edinburgh
Belfast
London
SWANSEA Cardiff

The Times Rankings
Overall Ranking: 42
(2005 ranking: 50)

Teaching assessment:	=28	(22.1)
Research assessment:	=48	(4.6)
Entry standards:	53	(275.1)
Student–staff ratio:	=26	(15.5)
Library/IT spend/student:	65	(£495)
Facilities spend/student:	44	(£209)
Good honours:	=55	(57.1%)
Graduate prospects:	37	(65.8%)
Expected completion rate:	36	(89.1%)

ready access to the excellent beaches of the Gower Peninsula, and the university occupies an attractive parkland site overlooking the sea. Apart from Singleton Abbey, the neo-Gothic mansion which houses the administration, most of the buildings are modern. The latest is the £4.3-million Digital Technium Building, which houses the new media and communication studies department. The city has a reasonable range of leisure facilities, but the campus itself is the focus of social life.

Swansea makes a particular effort to cater for disabled students. There are facilities for the blind, deaf and wheelchair-bound, coordinated through a £250,000 assessment and training centre. Other access measures have been reasonably successful: almost 30 per cent of the undergraduates come from working-class homes, while the 18 per cent from areas sending few students to higher education and the 92 per cent share of places going to applicants from state schools and colleges are both significantly higher than the funding council's benchmark for the institution. The projected dropout rate is a respectable 10 per cent.

Sports facilities are good and representative teams (particularly in rugby union) successful. An Olympic-sized swimming pool opened in 2002 and a new athletics track, all-weather pitches and gym are all helping to attract top performers. The 1,800 computers available for student use represent one of the best ratios at any university. Scholarships worth £1,000 a year are offered to students who are outstanding in sport, and both scholarships and bursaries are available for overseas students.

Accommodation

Number of places and costs refer to 2005–06
University-provided places: about 2,750
Percentage catered: 20% (which is part-catered; 7 meals a week).
Costs for catered accommodation: £65 (shared); £91 (en suite). Typical costs: £71.60 (standard single in part-catered) and £84.40 (en suite single in part-catered) for 31-week let.
Costs for self-catered accommodation: £39.50 (shared); £73.50 (en suite). Typical costs: £51.50 (standard single) and £71.50 (en suite single) for 40-week let.
Policy for first-year students: over 98% housed. Students with firm offers are guaranteed places. No distance restrictions except for late Clearing applicants.
Policy for international students: guaranteed for 2 years, but students from outside EU will usually get 3 years if required.
Contact: accommodation@swansea.ac.uk

Students

Undergraduates:	7,465	(3,035)
Postgraduates:	1,275	(1,700)
Mature students:	16.6%	
Overseas students:	8.8%	
Applications per place:	3.9	
From state-sector schools:	91.7%	
From working-class homes:	29.4%	
Tuition fees 2006	£1,200	

Teaching Quality Assessments
1993–98 Rated Excellent:

biological sciences; chemical engineering; civil engineering; classics and ancient history; computer science; electrical and electronic engineering; geography; German; history; Italian; materials engineering; physics; psychology; Spanish.

University of Teesside

Teesside has always described itself as the Opportunity University, stressing its open access and customer-oriented approach. But its latest mission statement adds the rider of 'pursuing excellence' to suggest that there will be no compromise on quality. Teaching ratings improved sharply in the later years of assessment and Teesside was the top new university in this year's *Times* League Table for the proportion of leavers going into graduate-level jobs or further training. Official performance indicators also show the former polytechnic well ahead of the access benchmarks calculated by the funding council. Few English universities draw a larger proportion of undergraduates from areas of low participation in higher education, while more than four students in every ten come from working-class homes. Although the last projected dropout rate was more than one in five, this was no higher than average for the university's courses and entry qualifications.

Although Middlesbrough has never been considered a fashionable student destination, the demand for places had been growing at a time when some new universities were having recruitment problems. Although there was a dip in 2004, the start of 2005 saw an 11 per cent increase in applications. There are now more than 20,000 students, half of them taking part-time courses and nearly 40 per cent over 21 on entry. Teesside is particularly strong in niche markets such as computer games design and animation, sport and exercise, and forensic science.

More than 1,000 students are taking Teesside courses at local further education colleges, which are also involved in the growing range of full-time and part-time two-year foundation degrees. An initial course in chemical technology was the subject of a positive report by the Quality Assurance Agency. In the long term, up to a quarter of the university's students are expected to take their courses off campus, and the university is planning higher education centres attached to further education colleges in Hartlepool and Darlington.

The colleges are also the focus of a Passport scheme which offers help and guidance to students considering going to university. However, the university's best-known access initiative targets a much younger age group. The prize-winning Meteor scheme gives primary schoolchildren a taste of higher education, even offering them the use of a cyber café in the centre of Middlesbrough. University students act as mentors and can earn some useful extra cash and gain experience of working in schools.

Borough Road,
Middlesbrough TS1 3BA
T   01642 218121
E   reg@tees.ac.uk
W   www.tees.ac.uk
U   www.utu.org.uk

Edinburgh
Belfast
MIDDLESBROUGH
London
Cardiff

The Times Rankings
Overall Ranking: =91
(2005 ranking: 96)

Teaching assessment:	=62	(21.3)
Research assessment:	=91	(1.9)
Entry standards:	96	(187.3)
Student–staff ratio:	88	(21.0)
Library/IT spend/student:	100	(£345)
Facilities spend/student:	=91	(£122)
Good honours:	99	(40.3%)
Graduate prospects:	18	(71.1%)
Expected completion rate:	=86	(76.2%)

Only one subject – computer science – was rated Excellent in the original teaching assessments. But nursing, design and health subjects have all achieved the equivalent of the old Excellent rating. The 6,000 health students are now by far the largest group in the university. The last research grades were an improvement on 1996, with history rated as outstanding, but the overall results still left Teesside among the bottom ten universities. It has since announced a £1.5-million research investment plan.

The university is based on one town-centre campus in Middlesbrough, where over £70 million has been spent in recent years. The latest addition is the Olympia Building, which combines indoor sports facilities with teaching and research space for sports science. Before that came an £8-million School of Health, the upgrading of computer science and IT facilities and a state-of-the-art learning resource centre to replace the main library. The redevelopment programme also included an innovation centre, incorporating virtual reality facilities and an array of other high technology, including a cinema and a 20-seater hemispherium giving a 180-degree field of view. Computer provision is generous, with 1,700 PCs available. The new facilities are being used to provide degrees in subjects such as computer games design, animation and virtual reality, as well as one in forensic investigation.

Middlesbrough has more nightlife than sceptics might imagine, and the booming student population has attracted new pubs, cafés and student-orientated shops in and around the Southfield Road area. The cost of living is also among the lowest in the country, with the lively students' union claiming to sell some of the cheapest beer in the country and winning the title of UK students' union of the year in 2004. Outdoor sports facilities include a £1.5-million watersports centre on the River Tees, which is shared with Durham University.

Accommodation

Number of places and costs refer to 2005–06
University-provided places: 737 (managed residences); 550 (managed housing).
Percentage catered: 0%
Costs for catered accommodation: n/a
Costs for self-catered accommodation: £32.90–£56.98 (residences), £33–£37 (in university-managed housing) a week.
Policy for first-year students: all places in university-managed residences are reserved exclusively for first years. Allocations are made on a quota basis: first come, first served.
Policy for international students: international and students designated overseas for fees are guaranteed accommodation provided they apply by the end of May.
Contact: accommodation@tees.ac.uk; direct tel. 01642 342255

Students

Undergraduates:	7,755	(9,850)
Postgraduates:	615	(1,560)
Mature students:	30.2%	
Overseas students:	5.7%	
Applications per place:	4.0	
From state-sector schools:	95.6%	
From working-class homes:	42.6%	

Tuition fees 2006   £3,000
See chapter 13 for bursary details.

Teaching Quality Assessments

From 1995 (top score 24):
23 nursing.
22 art and design; health subjects.
21 electrical and electronic engineering; sport and exercise studies.
20 psychology.
19 building; sociology.
17 chemical engineering; food science.

Thames Valley University

Having survived a tumultuous period in which the university's academic standards were criticised, the high-profile Vice-Chancellor resigned and demand for places collapsed, Thames Valley has embarked on a new future as a much larger institution spanning further and higher education. A merger with Reading College, at the start of 2004, has produced a university of 47,000 students where almost a third of the places are on further education courses and there is even a sixth-form academy. Relaunched as the *New* Thames Valley University in 2005, half of its students are over 30 years old, 60 per cent female and the same proportion part-time.

A new campus in Brentford, West London, is due to open fully in 2006, with 850 residential places as well as extensive teaching accommodation for the largest healthcare faculty in Britain. One of the two campuses in Reading is being completely redeveloped and £9.5 million is being invested in improving the original campus at Ealing. Another £3 million has already been spent on the Slough campus, with more to come.

It is all a far cry from the end of the 1990s, when barely 30 degrees were left. Although the aftermath of that period has left the university rooted to the bottom of *The Times* League Table, the university is virtually unrecognisable from those dark days. The finances are under control, a quality audit has produced a clean bill of health, and even before the merger, there were plans for renewed growth. Applications were up by 29 per cent at the beginning of 2005.

The courses are now concentrated in four faculties – arts, music and design; health and human sciences; professional studies; and technology. Many further education programmes are being extended into degrees or professional qualifications. Among the casualties of the reorganisation, however, were the two top-rated subjects: sociology and linguistics, which also achieved one of the few grade 5 research assessments in the new universities in 1996.

Amid the reconstruction, new honours degrees have been launched in areas such as video production, 3D design, entrepreneurship and web and e-business computing. The portfolio of two-year foundation degrees is growing, with employers such as Compaq, Ealing Studios and the Savoy Hotel Group helping to provide courses. Some are run in conjunction with Stratford-upon-Avon College – one of a number of partner institutions. The university also has 17 outreach centres in and around Reading, at Southall and even Heathrow Airport.

St Mary's Road, Ealing,
London W5 5RF
T   0208-579 5000
E   learning.advice@tvu.ac.uk
W   www.tvu.ac.uk
U   www.tvusu.org.uk

The Times Rankings
Overall Ranking: 100
(2005 ranking: 99)

Teaching assessment:	98	(19.6)
Research assessment:	100	(0.5)
Entry standards:	98	(180.2)
Student–staff ratio:	100	(25.4)
Library/IT spend/student:	=90	(£388)
Facilities spend/student:	100	(£27)
Good honours:	91	(47.3%)
Graduate prospects:	75	(57.3%)
Expected completion rate:	94	(72.4%)

TVU achieved university status only a year after becoming a polytechnic in a merger between two well-established higher education colleges. A policy of open access results in 40 per cent of the undergraduates coming from working-class homes, but also puts the university at a disadvantage in rankings such as ours. Hospitality, leisure and tourism achieved a good score in the final round of teaching assessment, but linguistics and sociology were the only other subjects to manage 22 points out of 24 for teaching quality. TVU also has the worst research record in the university system, having entered fewer than one academic in five for the latest assessments.

Some of the vocational courses have a strong reputation: the school of tourism, hospitality and leisure management, for example, is recognised by the Académie Culinaire de France for its culinary arts programmes. Nursing courses, too, are popular and well regarded. However, the 25 per cent projected dropout rate is among the highest in England.

The town-centre sites in Ealing, Reading and Slough are linked by a free bus service. The business-oriented campus in Slough consists mainly of 1960s buildings, but has been enhanced by an award-winning learning resources centre designed by Sir Richard Rogers. The busier Ealing base was suffering from overcrowding before retrenchment took place. Almost half of the students are from London or Berkshire, despite an unexpectedly large contingent of overseas students.

Residential accommodation is growing from a low base, but students who rely on private housing find the cost of living high. The Slough campus boasts an impressive gym, but otherwise sports facilities are limited.

Accommodation

Number of places and costs refer to 2004–05
University-provided places: 420 (in private rented sector registered with the university accommodation service)
Percentage catered: 30%
Costs for catered accommodation: £75–£100 a week.
Costs for self-catered accommodation: £65–£95a week.
Policy for first-year students: at the start of the academic year priority is given to students who live outside the M25.
Policy for international students: priority is given to international students.
Contact: uas@tvu.ac.uk

Students

Undergraduates:	7,335	(7,355)
Postgraduates:	410	(1,230)
Mature students:	41.3%	
Overseas students:	13.3%	
Applications per place:	5.4	
From state-sector schools:	98.1%	
From working-class homes:	40.1%	

Tuition fees 2006	£2,700

See chapter 13 for bursary details.

Teaching Quality Assessments

From 1995 (top score 24):
22 hospitality, leisure and tourism.
20 health subjects; nursing; psychology.
19 business and management.
18 media studies; modern languages.

University of Ulster

Ulster has notched up a series of recent successes, with rising demand for places and a thriving development programme. The university – the only one in Britain with a charter stipulating that there should be courses below degree level – would like to expand but is constrained by Government policy. UU has had to pull out of its most ambitious project: the proposed 'peaceline campus' linking Belfast's two communities after years of on/off negotiations. But there are plans to improve and expand all four main sites, at a cost of £200 million, during the current decade.

With more Irish students now choosing to stay in the Province to study, there is plenty of scope for expansion, despite the fact that UU already has more than 20,000 students. The main sites in and near Belfast have never been busier, while Magee attracts students from both sides of the border. High technology brings together the university for teaching purposes, but the sites are 80 miles apart at their farthest point and very different in character. Jordanstown, seven miles outside Belfast, has the most students, concentrating on engineering, health and social science. Numbers are being limited to prevent overcrowding and more building is planned. The isolated original university campus, at Coleraine, follows the style of the 1960s, and is the most traditional in outlook, with a focus on science and the humanities. There is a new £11-million Centre for Molecular Biosciences, and further building is in the pipeline. The small Belfast site specialises in art and design, being the former art college, and is earmarked for redevelopment.

Current development is focusing mainly on the Magee campus in Londonderry, although Jordanstown has acquired improved library and computing facilities. Once the poor relation of the university, confined to adult education, Magee is now a thriving centre. Over the next two years, student numbers are expected to grow to about 7,500, including part-timers, with new schools of performing arts, computing and electronics, as well as improved provision for education, nursing and Irish studies. The Institute for Legal and Professional Studies will allow graduates to train as barristers and solicitors. The historic Foyle Arts Centre has become part of the university and a postgraduate medical school is planned

Although often overshadowed by Queen's University, Ulster's community consciousness has worked to its advantage. Almost half the students come from working-class homes – far more than the UK average – and the student profile

---

Cromore Road, Coleraine,
Co. Londonderry BT52 1SA
T   08700-400 700
E   online@ulst.ac.uk
W   www.ulster.ac.uk
U   www.uusu.org

COLERAINE   Edinburgh
Belfast
London
Cardiff

The Times Rankings
Overall Ranking: 55
(2005 ranking: 54)

Teaching assessment:	=72	(21.1)
Research assessment:	56	(3.8)
Entry standards:	59	(260.4)
Student–staff ratio:	=52	(17.3)
Library/IT spend/student:	46	(£558)
Facilities spend/student:	55	(£184)
Good honours:	40	(62.5%)
Graduate prospects:	41	(64.4%)
Expected completion rate:	59	(83.4%)

mirrors the religious balance in the wider population. Mature students are well catered for, with access courses for those who lack the necessary entry qualifications, a nursery and three playgroups in the university.

Teaching ratings were mainly sound, rather than spectacular, although business and management registered maximum points in 2001, while drama and American studies have also produced good scores. Research is not Ulster's principal strength, although grades improved in the latest assessments, with Celtic studies and biomedical sciences rated internationally outstanding.

There has never been a big representation from mainland Britain, but its contingent of overseas students include those from the Republic of Ireland as well as further afield. The Campus One programme provides an alternative mode of study, with a range of courses available online to students all over the world.

As with any split-site university, the student experience varies according to the location. Some courses offer lectures on more than one campus, but for the most part students are based on a single site throughout their university life. With more than half of the students living with their parents or at their own home, the university is not always the focus of social life. The exception is Coleraine, a classic campus university, where there are fewer home-based students, although many gravitate towards the nearby seaside towns of Portrush and Portstewart.

Accommodation

Number of places and costs refer to 2005–06
University-provided places: 2,613
Percentage catered: 0%
Costs for catered accommodation: n/a
Costs for self-catered accommodation:
£40–£80 (en suite) a week.
Policy for first-year students: all first years are guaranteed accommodation if they have accepted a Conditional offer, have Ulster as their first choice and return their application form by 1 July
Policy for international students: same as above, except that a completed accommodation application form must be received by 1 August in the year of entry.
Contact: accommodation@ulster.ac.uk

Students

Undergraduates:	15,010	(4,010)
Postgraduates:	2,175	(3,865)
Mature students:	12.2%	
Overseas students:	9.4%	
Applications per place:	6.3	
From state-sector schools:	100%	
From working-class homes:	46.1%	

Tuition fees 2006 not yet confirmed

Teaching Quality Assessments

From 1995 (top score 24):
24 business and management.
23 hospitality, tourism and sports management; philosophy; psychology.
22 American studies; biological sciences; drama, dance and cinematics; economics; health subjects; mathematics; nursing; politics.
21 building; land management; media studies.
20 electrical and electronic engineering; French.
19 art and design; civil engineering; German.
18 Iberian languages.
17 sociology.

University of the Arts, London

The London Institute resisted the temptation to apply for university status after it was formed in 1986 because the art, design, fashion and media colleges that had come together for administrative purposes were world-famous in their own right. But a change of rules governing university titles and the arrival as rector of Sir Michael Bichard, previously Permanent Secretary at the Department for Education and Skills, prompted a rethink. As a result, the University of the Arts, London was born in 2004, and is already becoming a powerful 'brand' in its own right.

The five component colleges, which continue to use their own names and enjoy considerable autonomy, are Camberwell College of Arts, Central St Martin's College of Art and Design, Chelsea College of Art and Design, the London College of Fashion and the London College of Communication (which changed its name from the London College of Printing in 2004 to reflect a range of courses which now extends to film and other media). Together, they boast a total of more than 24,000 students spread around 18 sites around central London, representing the biggest concentration of art, design and creative arts in Europe.

Teaching and research grades for the Institute – and hence the new university's position in *The Times* League Table – barely do justice to the eminence of the colleges. Although Camberwell and what was then the College of Printing achieved near-perfect scores for teaching quality in art and design, the other colleges' grades in this category and those for business and management, materials technology and media studies were solid rather than spectacular. History of art at Camberwell and Chelsea was a disappointment, while the grade 5 for research in art and design covered relatively few staff. Chelsea and the London College of Fashion have jointly been awarded a national teaching centre for the arts, focusing on practice-based teaching and learning.

However, assessors liked the heavy use of often eminent visiting lecturers, the close links with industry and the broad range of courses, which stretch from further education to postgraduate. A number of two-year foundation degrees have been introduced, including one in interactive games production and another in fashion styling and photography. The mix is going down well with students: applications were up by 13 per cent at the start of 2004 and by twice that figure 12 months later, with recruitment healthy both at home and abroad. The 12 per cent dropout rate is also good for the subjects on offer, but the proportions of undergraduates from

---

65 Davies Street
London W1K 5DA
T   0207-514 6000
E   prospectus@linst.ac.uk
W   www.linst.ac.uk
U   www.lisu.org

The Times Rankings
Overall Ranking: 65
(2005 ranking: 72)

Teaching assessment:	=72	(21.1)
Research assessment:	=42	(4.7)
Entry standards:	68	(248.6)
Student–staff ratio:	87	(20.8)
Library/IT spend/student:	=95	(£378)
Facilities spend/student:	95	(£119)
Good honours:	=67	(52.8%)
Graduate prospects:	95	(48.7%)
Expected completion rate:	41	(86.7%)

working-class homes and areas of low participation in higher education are both lower than average. The university has been running weekend classes and summer schools in an attempt to broaden the intake.

Big changes were already under way before the change of title was agreed: a £70-million development programme has produced prestigious new premises for Chelsea College next door to the Tate Gallery, on Millbank, with extensive workshop facilities, studios and an impressive new library. Another £32 million has been spent on new headquarters for the College of Communication at the Elephant and Castle, south of the Thames. A new £2-million information technology system links all the sites and there are plans to devote a similar sum to a ground-breaking centre for fashion enterprise. There was a series of mergers and property moves during the Institute's 18-year existence, but the basic structure of the new university is expected to remain stable for the foreseeable future.

The colleges vary considerably in character and facilities, although a single students' union serves them all. The university is not overprovided with residential accommodation, although there are nine residences spread around the colleges, 300 more rooms became available in September 2004. Househunting workshops help those who have to rely on what is inevitably an expensive private housing market.

Accommodation

Number of places and costs refer to 2004–05
University-provided places: about 1,500
Percentage catered: 0%
Costs for self-catered accommodation: £79.00–£122.50 a week.
Policy for first-year students: first years whose homes are outside London will be offered a place in managed accommodation.
Policy for international students: as above for first-year students.
Contact: accommodation@linst.ac.uk
www.linst.ac.uk/housing/

The institutions that make up the University of the Arts still operate with a degree of independence; e-mail contact can be made as follows:
Camberwell College of Arts:
enquiries@camb.linst.ac.uk
Central St Martin's:
info@csm.linst.ac.uk
Chelsea College: enquiries@chelsea.linst.ac.uk
London College of Fashion:
enquiries@lcf.linst.ac.uk
London College of Communications:
info@lcp.linst.ac.uk

Students

Undergraduates:	9,175	(590)
Postgraduates:	1,035	(700)
Mature students:	44%	
Overseas students:	34.8%	
Applications per place:	3.9	
From state-sector schools:	98%	
From working-class homes:	22%	

Tuition fees 2006	£3,000

See chapter 13 for bursary details.

Teaching Quality Assessments

23 art and design (Camberwell and London College of Communication).
22 art and design (Central St Martin's and Chelsea); business and management; materials technology.
21 art and design (London College of Fashion).
20 communications and media studies.
19 history of art.

University College London

Such is the breadth and quality of provision at University College (UCL) that it can fairly describe itself not only as a 'university within a university' but also as one of the top multifaculty institutions in England. Its position in *The Times* rankings has regularly confirmed this, and in 2005 it even overtook Oxford and Cambridge for the amount of research support it was allocated by the funding council. The college's excellence is built on a history of pioneering subjects that have become commonplace in higher education: modern languages, geography and fine arts among them. UCL is now emerging from a difficult period, in which it ran up a £12-million deficit and saw the unexpected departure of the Provost and the rejection of a proposed merger with Imperial College London.

Already comfortably the largest of London University's colleges, UCL's incorporation of the School of Slavonic and East European Studies added to the 70 departments. In recent years, several smaller institutes have joined the fold. Medicine started the merger trend, with the Middlesex Hospital Medical School and the Institutes of Laryngology and Otology, of Orthopaedics and of Urology joining forces with UCL in 1987. The institutes of Ophthalmology, Child Health, Neurology and the Eastman Dental Institute have all been added since then. In combination with the Royal Free Hospital, UCL's medical school is a formidable unit, although (apart from the Eastman's near-perfect score) its teaching assessment was a disappointment. A poor rating for learning resources was largely responsible, but new teaching facilities opened in the refurbished Cruciform building during 2000. Medical credentials have been strengthened still further with the announcement that UCL is to be the new home of the National Institute of Medical Research. The various acquisitions mean that the college now has outposts in several parts of central and north London, but the main activity remains centred on the original impressive Bloomsbury site.

Anatomy, archaeology, several branches of engineering, modern languages and pharmacology are among the areas rated internationally outstanding for research. One academic in five was in a top-rated department in the last assessments, with two thirds in the top two categories, but the results did not quite match the high benchmark set in 1996. Economics, health-related subjects, history of art and organismal biosciences have all recorded maximum points for teaching, but most subjects have scored well. A growing number of degrees take four years, and

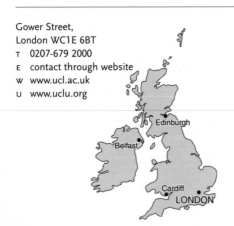

Gower Street,
London WC1E 6BT
T   0207-679 2000
E   contact through website
W   www.ucl.ac.uk
U   www.uclu.org

The Times Rankings
Overall Ranking: 6
(2005 ranking: 6)

Teaching assessment:	=28	(22.1)
Research assessment:	=5	(6.0)
Entry standards:	13	(386.5)
Student–staff ratio:	1	(7.6)
Library/IT spend/student:	6	(£1,131)
Facilities spend/student:	62	(£172)
Good honours:	10	(74.4%)
Graduate prospects:	10	(76%)
Expected completion rate:	16	(93.5%)

most are organised on a modular basis.

Many of UCL's students are from overseas, including more than 1,000 from other EU countries, reflecting the college's high international standing. The proportion is likely to rise further in the coming years. Suitably qualified British applicants are interviewed whenever possible before being offered a place and, once accepted, first-year students in many subjects are given peer tutoring by more experienced colleagues to help them adapt to degree study. The college stresses its commitment to teaching in small groups, especially in the second and subsequent years of degree courses. The approach seems to work: almost three quarters leave with a first or upper second, and the projected dropout rate of only 1 per cent is the best in Britain, a position the college shares with Cambridge University.

UCL is conscious of its traditions as a college founded to expand access to higher education but, while the proportion of places going to independent school students has been dropping, their 38 per cent share is one of the highest in Britain and among the furthest behind the council's benchmark. Less than one undergraduate in five has a working-class background and just 6 per cent come from an area without a tradition of higher education. The college has had some success in broadening its intake through a summer school for state school sixth-formers and increased contact with local schools and further education colleges.

The academic pace can be frantic but, close to the West End and with its own theatre and recreational facilities, there is no shortage of leisure options. Students also have immediate access to London University's underused central students' union facilities. Residential accommodation is plentiful and of a good standard. Indoor sports facilities are close at hand, but the main outdoor pitches, though good enough to attract professional football clubs, are a coach ride away in Hertfordshire.

Accommodation
Number of places and costs refer to 2005–06
University-provided places: 4,156 (including 500 intercollegiate places)
Percentage catered: 30%
Costs for catered accommodation:
£89.32–£116.90 a week.
Costs for self-catered accommodation:
£60.20–£122.94 a week.
Policy for first-year students: accommodation guaranteed for all first- years who have UCL as their first choice and apply before the end of May prior to intake.
Policy for international students: housing guaranteed to all undergraduates who apply by pre-advised deadlines.
Contact: Residences@ucl.ac.uk
www.ucl.ac.uk/admission/accommodation

Students
Undergraduates:	11,480	(340)
Postgraduates:	4,540	(2,540)
Mature students:	8.7%	
Overseas students:	22.3%	
Applications per place:	7.6	
From state-sector schools:	61.4%	
From working-class homes:	17.8%	

Tuition fees 2006   £3,000
See chapter 13 for bursary details.

Teaching Quality Assessments
From 1995 (top score 24):
24 economics; health subjects; history of art.
23 art and design; archaeology; classics and ancient history; German; mathematics and statistics; medicine; physics; philosophy; politics; Scandinavian.
22 anatomy and physiology; biological sciences; Dutch; electrical and electronic engineering; linguistics; psychology.
21 French; medicine.
20 chemical engineering; Italian.
19 civil engineering; Iberian languages.

University of Warwick

The most successful of the first wave of new universities, Warwick was derided by many in its early years for its close links with business and industry. Few are critical today. Tony Blair described the university as 'at the cutting edge of what has to happen in the future' and even brought Bill Clinton there on his last overseas engagement as American President. Both teaching and research are very highly rated, but the university's mission statement still stresses the extension of access to higher education, continuing education and community links.

There is a smaller proportion of independent school students than at most of the leading universities – less than a quarter – but this does not translate into large numbers of working-class undergraduates. The share of places going to students from the lowest social classes and the representation from areas sending few young people to higher education are both lower than the national average for Warwick's subjects and entry qualifications. But the mix helps to produce one of the lowest dropout rates in Britain. Graduates have contributed more than £1 million to a scholarship scheme, which made 105 awards in 2004.

Warwick's teaching assessments were outstanding, with economics and politics bringing the number of maximum scores to seven. The university has been awarded a national teaching centre in theatrical performance, in partnership with the Royal Shakespeare Company, and is collaborating with Oxford Brookes University on another centre to 'reinvent' undergraduate research. Six subjects were rated internationally outstanding for research – business, economics, English, theatre studies and applied mathematics and statistics. Nine out of ten academics entered for assessment were placed in the top two categories, preserving Warwick's place among the top five research universities. The overall standard of the 29 departments brought Warwick a top European award, while the science park, one of the first in Britain, is among the most successful.

While other leading universities were trying to cover the whole range of academic disciplines, Warwick pursued a selective policy. Without the expense of medicine, dentistry or veterinary science to bear, the university invested shrewdly in business, science and engineering. However, the temptation of medicine has proved too much to bear, and the university has gone into partnership with Leicester University to establish a new kind of course for graduates in biological sciences. There are now 330 students in the medical school, which opened in 2000, and numbers are growing.

Coventry CV4 7AL
T 02476 523723
E ugadmissions@
   admin.warwick.ac.uk
W www.warwick.ac.uk
U www.sunion
   .warwick.ac.uk/portal

The Times Rankings
Overall Ranking: 8
(2005 ranking: 5)

Teaching assessment:	=7	(22.7)
Research assessment:	=5	(6.0)
Entry standards:	5	(429.7)
Student–staff ratio:	40	(16.4)
Library/IT spend/student:	12	(£727)
Facilities spend/student:	=35	(£221)
Good honours:	4	(78.6%)
Graduate prospects:	26	(68.5%)
Expected completion rate:	11	(95.3%)

Another deviation from its academic norm has seen the university embracing the Government's two-year foundation degrees. One of the few leading universities to offer the vocational programmes, Warwick is running three courses in education and community enterprise, the latter taught by a local further education college.

Such is the demand for places on conventional degree courses, that many departments stick rigidly to offers averaging more than an A and two Bs at A level. Applications have been buoyant, although there was a 4 per cent dip in 2004 and virtually no movement at the start of 2005, when most universities registered substantial increases. Warwick has been building up its numbers in science and engineering, as other universities have struggled to fill their places. The business school has also been growing rapidly, with a new £15-million extension now complete, while computer science has acquired new, upgraded facilities.

Some £335 million has been spent on the campus, which has often resembled a building site. However, students have welcomed larger union facilities, a number of academic buildings have been improved and the Arts Centre (the second largest in Britain) has been refurbished with a £33-million lottery grant. The 720-acre campus is three miles south of Coventry, where many students choose to live, and three times as far from Warwick. University accommodation is plentiful. The sports facilities are both extensive and conveniently placed on campus, where there is a new sports centre with 25-metre swimming pool and a range of other facilities.

Accommodation
Number of places and costs refer to 2005–06
University-provided places: 5,803 (on campus); 1,650 (head leasing)
Percentage catered: n/a
Costs for catered accommodation: n/a
Costs for self-catered accommodation: £52 (standard); £89 (en suite) a week. A 39-week let is also available.
Policy for first-year students: all first-year undergraduates are guaranteed campus accommodation provided an online application is received before 31 July (with the exception of those coming through Clearing).
Policy for international students: students designated for overseas fees have guaranteed campus accommodation in the first and final years (undergraduates), first year (postgraduates) provided application is received by 31 July.
Contact: accommodation@warwick.ac.uk

Students

Undergraduates:	9,625	(9,165)
Postgraduates:	3,040	(5,520)
Mature students:	5.5%	
Overseas students:	16.6%	
Applications per place:	9.2	
From state-sector schools:	77.8%	
From working-class homes:	17.8%	

Tuition fees 2006	£3,000

See chapter 13 for bursary details.

Teaching Quality Assessments
From 1995 (top score 24):
24 drama and cinematics; economics; education; philosophy; physics; politics; sociology.
23 biological sciences; classics and ancient history; German; media studies.
22 mathematics.
21 French; general engineering; history of art; Italian; psychology.

University of the West of England, Bristol

West of England (UWE) boasts the best teaching quality record in the new universities and has always been regarded among the leaders in its peer group. Perfect scores for education and the joint assessment for biology and biomedical sciences are its best results, but every subject assessed since 1995 was given at least 20 out of 24 points. Business and management, the university's biggest subject area with 3,300 students, and economics also scored well at the end of the cycle of assessments.

This record and a popular location are proving highly attractive to students. The demand for places has been rising steadily, the start of 2005 seeing a rise in applications of more than 16 per cent. However, the university found itself in trouble with the funding council when the monitoring of intakes was introduced for missing its benchmarks for extending access to under-represented groups in higher education. One undergraduate in seven attends a fee-paying school, a proportion exceeded by only one other new university. But more than a quarter of places now go to working-class students and the proportion of students from areas without a history of higher education is no longer significantly out of line with the national average for the subjects offered.

Given the intake, the projected dropout rate of 21 per cent might be lower. But this seems not to put off the thousands who flock to the region's largest university. More than half of the students come from the West Country and there are close links with local business and industry. A network of 15 colleges stretches into Somerset and Wiltshire, offering UWE programmes. Hartpury College, near Gloucester, has become an associate faculty of the university, specialising in agriculture, equine studies and other land-based courses.

A tradition of vocational education regularly helps the university to a healthy graduate employment record. The entrance system credits vocational qualifications and practical experience equally with traditional academic results. Law received a commendation from the Legal Practice Board and the degree in Architecture and Planning won a similar accolade from the Royal Town Planning Institute for bringing together the two disciplines in one joint-honours course giving dual professional qualifications. Industrial links are paying off in a variety of ways, with the university offering a number of employer bursary schemes in addition to its own.

Among the new universities, only Oxford Brookes entered a larger proportion of academics than UWE's 40 per cent in the 2001 Research Assessment Exercise. The

---

Frenchay Campus,
Coldharbour Lane, Bristol BS16 1QY
T   0117-344 3333
E   Admissions@uwe.ac.uk
W   www.uwe.ac.uk
U   www.uwesu.net

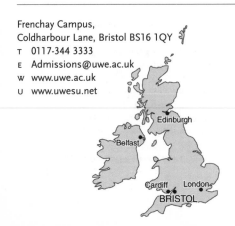

The Times Rankings		
Overall Ranking: 64		
(2005 ranking: 67)		
Teaching assessment:	=40	(21.9)
Research assessment:	=67	(2.8)
Entry standards:	56	(263)
Student–staff ratio:	74	(19.2)
Library/IT spend/student:	=70	(£465)
Facilities spend/student:	=51	(£190)
Good honours:	=57	(56.3%)
Graduate prospects:	=84	(54.4%)
Expected completion rate:	77	(78.7%)

results were an improvement on 1996, with accounting and finance rated nationally outstanding with much work of international standards. However, the scale of the entry also produced more low grades than the university would have wished.

There are four sites in Bristol itself, mainly around the north of the city, with regional centres in Bath, and Swindon concentrating on the growth area of nursing. Only Bower Ashton, which houses art, media and design, is in the south. The main campus at Frenchay, close to Bristol Parkway station but four miles out of the city centre, has by far the largest number of students and includes the Centre for Student Affairs, which brings together the various non-academic services. The St Matthias site (for social sciences and humanities) and Glenside (for midwifery, nursing, physiotherapy and radiography) are more attractive but less lively. Education has moved from the Redland campus, near the city centre, to a £16-million headquarters at Frenchay.

Bristol is a hugely popular student centre: an attractive and lively city, but not cheap. University accommodation has become more plentiful in recent years, with almost 3,700 places available and more on the way. Sports facilities have been a bone of contention for students, but in 2006 there will be a new sports complex as part of a £200-million investment programme, which is one of the largest in UK higher education.

Accommodation

Number of places and costs refer to 2004–05
University-provided places: 3,365
Percentage catered: 0%
Costs for catered accommodation: n/a
Costs for self-catered accommodation: £42.21–£73.00 a week.
Policy for first-year students: applications are processed in the order of receipt. UWE guarantees accommodation for first years accepting an offer at UWE as their firm choice and who return their form by 1 July.
Policy for international students: international students are offered accommodation where possible.
Contact: SAS@uwe.ac.uk

Students

Undergraduates:	15,940 (4,995)
Postgraduates:	1,540 (2,830)
Mature students:	17.8%
Overseas students:	6.5%
Applications per place:	4.5
From state-sector schools:	85.9%
From working-class homes:	26.5%
Tuition fees 2006	£3,000

See chapter 13 for bursary details.

Teaching Quality Assessments

From 1995 (top score 24):
24 biological sciences; education.
23 business and management; economics; sociology and social policy; town and country planning.
22 art and design; land and property management; media studies; nursing; psychology.
21 building; electrical and electronic engineering; health subjects; mathematics; modern languages; politics.
20 agriculture.

University of Westminster

Westminster has just completed a £110 million modernisation of its four sites, which has been going on since the 1990s. Having started with the £33-million transformation of the former Harrow College, in north London, in what was Europe's largest university construction project, the university moved on to an even more costly redevelopment of one of the three central sites, opposite Madame Tussauds. The large business school acquired a 'cloistered environment' in a £9.5-million scheme which creates more space for teaching and research. Now the New Cavendish Street site, near the BT Tower, has been the subject of a £30-million redevelopment. The last stage saw a new teaching, research and administration building named after the Vice-Chancellor, Dr Geoffrey Copland.

The greenfield Harrow campus now boasts a high-tech information resources centre with new facilities for the highly-rated media studies courses. Computing and design are also based on a site designed for 7,500 students. The West End sites provide the perfect catchment area for part-time students, who account for almost half of the 22,000 places. Only the Open University has more. By no means all the students are Londoners, however: one in ten comes from abroad – among the highest proportions among the new universities. Westminster courses are also taught in nine overseas countries, from Oman to the United States, a characteristic which won the university a Queen's Award for Enterprise.

The historic headquarters building, near Broadcasting House, houses social sciences and languages. French and Chinese scored particularly well in teaching assessments, and Westminster claims to offer the largest number of languages – 25 – of any British university. Science and health courses are concentrated on the Cavendish campus. The university's growing interest in health covers degrees from the British College of Naturopathy and Osteopathy and a range of courses in complementary medicine, including a BSc in acupuncture. There are degrees in herbal medicine, homeopathy and nutritional therapy, and a diploma in the traditional Chinese massage technique of Qigong.

A series of good teaching quality scores cemented Westminster's position among the better new universities in *The Times* League Table. Psychology and tourism lead the way with maximum points, with Chinese, media studies, community care and primary health all on the next rung of the ladder. The university weaves work-related skills into its degree programmes.

---

309 Regent Street,
London W1B 2UW
T   0207-911 5000
E   admissions@wmin.ac.uk
W   www.wmin.ac.uk
U   www.uwsu.com

The Times Rankings
Overall Ranking: 69
(2005 ranking: =76)

Teaching assessment:	77	(21.0)
Research assessment:	=67	(2.8)
Entry standards:	71	(240.5)
Student–staff ratio:	21	(15.0)
Library/IT spend/student:	85	(£407)
Facilities spend/student:	=65	(£163)
Good honours:	54	(57.2%)
Graduate prospects:	82	(55.2%)
Expected completion rate:	79	(78.1%)

No new university exceeded Westminster's haul of four subjects on grade 5 in the last assessment exercise, although the decision to enter fewer than 30 per cent of academics limited both the funding rewards and the impact on the university's ranking. Asian studies, law, linguistics and media studies were all rated nationally outstanding with much work of international quality.

More than four out of ten undergraduates are from working-class homes – a much higher proportion than the national average for the subjects offered. The university also exceeds its benchmark for the admission of students from state schools and colleges, although the central London location reduces the share of places going to students from areas without a tradition of higher education. The dropout rate has been improving, but is still almost one in five.

Like those at all the London universities, Westminster's students complain of the high cost of living, particularly for accommodation. The university has added considerably to its residential stock in recent years, but there is no way round the capital's inflated housing market at some stage. The Harrow campus is lively socially, but those based on the other sites tend to be spread around the capital. Sports facilities are also dispersed, with playing fields and a boathouse in Chiswick, west London.

Accommodation
Number of places and costs refer to 2005–06
University-provided places: 1,420
Percentage catered: 0%
Costs for catered accommodation: n/a
Costs for self-catered accommodation:
£65.38–£91.00 (single room) a week.
Policy for first-year students: first years are prioritised. Students from within 25 miles of the university are not prioritised.
Policy for international students: first years whose applications are received by 1 May are normally guaranteed a place.
Contact: www.wmin.ac.uk/accommodation

Students

Students		
Undergraduates:	10,790	(6,735)
Postgraduates:	3,045	(5,210)
Mature students:	25.8%	
Overseas students:	13.9%	
Applications per place:	4.8	
From state-sector schools:	94.9%	
From working-class homes:	44.0%	

Tuition fees 2006 £3,000
See chapter 13 for bursary details.

Teaching Quality Assessments
From 1995 (top score 24):
24 psychology; tourism.
23 Chinese; French; health subjects; media studies; music; politics.
22 building;Middle Eastern and African studies; politics.
21 anatomy and physiology; art and design; biological sciences; electrical and electronic engineering.
20 business and management; civil engineering; German; linguistics; mathematics; town planning.
19 Italian; land management.
18 Iberian languages; Russian; sociology.

University of Wolverhampton

Wolverhampton is the only university in Britain where a majority of undergraduates come from the three poorest socio-economic groups. The last published figure of 51.5 per cent represents twice the proportion at some new universities and almost five times that at Oxford and Cambridge. Almost all the students are from state schools and a quarter come from areas of low participation in higher education. The figures accurately reflect the priority the university gives to extending access to higher education. The downside of the policy is that almost a quarter are projected to drop out, but this has not prevented the university being awarded a national teaching centre focusing on retention, progression and achievement in a diverse student body.

Almost a quarter of the 23,000 students are from ethnic minorities, and more than a third live with their parents. With roots in the 19th-century arts, crafts and technical colleges, Wolverhampton naturally leans towards vocational courses. The university pioneered the high street 'higher education shop' and more recently, a dedicated Student Finance Support Unit and Student Gateway Service, bringing all student support together in one convenient location. Big outreach programmes take courses into the workplace. More than half

of the students come from the region, a quarter from areas without a tradition of higher education. The university has four campuses in the West Midlands and Shropshire, each with their own learning centres, and they are linked by a free bus service. Two are in Wolverhampton, but teacher training is based in Walsall. The original site is in the heart of the city centre, with the Wolves ground nearby. A purpose-built facility in Telford is sited appropriately in an Enterprise Zone, providing a variety of courses for a county with no higher education institution of its own.

Wolverhampton is in the midst of a multimillion-pound infrastructure investment programme known as 'New Horizons', which is due to be completed by 2006–07. The first phase of the project saw the completion of the £26-million development of the City Campus, including the flagship Millennium City Building and extension of the Harrison Learning Centre. The former, now housing some 1,300 students and 200 staff, includes over 10,000 square metres of new teaching space, incorporating a 300-seat lecture theatre, dedicated science labs, social learning space, cyber café, exhibition hall and refectory.

Since then, a Lottery-funded specialist Judo, Sports Science and Medicine Centre has opened on the university's Walsall

---

Wulfruna Street,
Wolverhampton WV1 1SB
T   01902 321000
E   admissions@wlv.ac.uk
W   www.wlv.ac.uk
U   www.wolvesunion.org

Edinburgh
Belfast
WOLVERHAMPTON
Cardiff
London

The Times Rankings
Overall Ranking: 84
(2005 ranking: 89)

Teaching assessment:	=80	(20.8)
Research assessment:	=89	(2.0)
Entry standards:	91	(200.2)
Student–staff ratio:	=67	(18.6)
Library/IT spend/student:	=76	(£451)
Facilities spend/student:	13	(£305)
Good honours:	71	(52.5%)
Graduate prospects:	=88	(54%)
Expected completion rate:	=90	(73.3%)

campus, where 350 residential places are under construction. An IT tower is planned for the City Campus and a new technology centre for the Telford site. The Compton campus has become the centre for postgraduate business courses and home of the Leadership Centre for school managers throughout the region.

Teaching assessments improved after a poor start, with philosophy achieving a perfect score and business and education only one point behind. Inspectors were once critical of quality control on the many courses franchised to further education colleges, but procedures have since been tightened up. Wolverhampton claims a number of firsts for its academic programmes, pioneering interactive multimedia communication degrees, as well as offering the only one in British sign language and one of the first in virtual reality design and manufacturing. It was the first university to be registered under the British Standard for the quality of its all-round provision. The university was also the first to open a dedicated student employment bureau with an online student and graduate jobs vacancy service that has since been adopted by a number of other institutions.

Research ratings are among the lowest in the university system, however, with less than one academic in five entered for assessment and no subjects in the top two of the seven categories. History and Spanish achieved the best results in the last assessments.

Social facilities vary considerably between sites, although they are close enough for students to come together for big events. Wolverhampton claims the fastest growing nightlife in the UK, although the basis of comparison is unclear, but there is no doubt that the cost of living is reasonable. The art gallery was refurbished in 2000 and the cultural attractions of Birmingham are now only a metro tramride away.

Accommodation
Number of places and costs refer to 2005–06
University-provided places: 2,123
Percentage catered: 0%
Costs for catered accommodation: n/a
Costs for self-catered accommodation:
£50–£70 a week.
Policy for first-year students: no restrictions. First come, first served, but more than 90% get a place in hall. Accommodation will normally be allocated to students who live beyond a 25-mile radius of the university.
Policy for international students: same as above, but most get a place.
Contact: residences@wlv.ac.uk

Students
Undergraduates:	12,835	(6,295)
Postgraduates:	945	(2,925)
Mature students:	25.4%	
Overseas students:	14.6%	
Applications per place:	4.3	
From state-sector schools:	98.7%	
From working-class homes:	51.5%	

Tuition fees 2006   £3,000
See chapter 13 for bursary details.

Teaching Quality Assessments
From 1995 (top score 24):
24 philosophy.
23 biological sciences;
business and management; education; politics.
22 economics; health subjects; Russian.
21 American studies; art and design; linguistics; nursing; psychology; theology.
20 building; general engineering;
Iberian languages; mathematics and statistics; sociology.
19 drama, dance and cinematics; French; media studies.
17 German.

University of York

York is another university to have demonstrated in successive *Times* rankings and academic assessments that comparative youth is no bar to excellence. No university has a better record for teaching quality in our table. Almost half of the subjects assessed since 1995 – archaeology, economics, education, electrical and electronic engineering, biosciences, philosophy, physics, politics and psychology – have achieved perfect scores, and none has slipped below 21 points out of 24. The university is increasingly recognised as a permanent fixture in the top rank of British higher education.

Like Warwick, a contemporary that has been running neck and neck in our ranking, York has chosen its subjects carefully. There are still only 10,000 students, with no veterinary science, dentistry or law. This will change if the university is able to develop the nearby 'Heslington East' site, which will make room for 50 per cent more students and a new range of subjects. These may include business, finance and law, and a new department of theatre, film and television.

The existing subjects are offered in a variety of unusual combinations, many including a language component. Among the more recent additions have been nursing and midwifery, which grew out of the incorporation in 1996 of the former North Yorkshire College of Health Studies. Since 2003, there has also been a medical degree, which saw applications grow by 50 per cent in the first year and another 20 per cent at the start of 2005. A joint initiative with Hull, the school will have a strong focus on learning in community settings.

There are nine applications to each place in most subjects, the total rising gradually in each of the last few years, so entrance requirements are high. Although nearly eight out of ten undergraduates are state educated, less than 18 per cent come from working-class homes. However, the 5 per cent dropout rate is among the lowest in Britain. The proportion of local students may rise with the establishment of the Higher York programme, linking the university with the city's further and higher education colleges.

Unlike most universities, York concentrated on science and technology in expanding its entry during the 1990s, balancing an initial bias towards the arts and social sciences. The university won a Queen's Anniversary Prize for its work in computer science, which is rated internationally outstanding for research as well as excellent for teaching. Psychology and English were the other starred research departments in the last assessments, which

---

Heslington,
York YO10 5DD
T   01904 433533
E   admissions@york.ac.uk
W   www.york.ac.uk
U   www.yusu.org

The Times Rankings
Overall Ranking: 9
(2005 ranking: 7)

Teaching assessment:	2	(23.2)
Research assessment:	=7	(5.8)
Entry standards:	=9	(414.8)
Student–staff ratio:	=15	(14.0)
Library/IT spend/student:	31	(£610)
Facilities spend/student:	57	(£181)
Good honours:	22	(68.3%)
Graduate prospects:	35	(66.3%)
Expected completion rate:	13	(94.7%)

placed 84 per cent of the academics in the top two of seven categories.

Since 1990, York has been reviewing its courses every three years. External audits have also been complimentary, with surveys showing most students satisfied with their tuition. Every student has a supervisor responsible for their academic and personal welfare. Existing courses include language and computer literacy training, and the programme will expand this year to include courses on personal effectiveness, financial management, active citizenship and introduction to accounting. The business community is involved at every level. Undergraduates can also take the 'York Award', comprising a range of courses, work placements and voluntary activities which aim to prepare students for the world of work. Over 400 students work as volunteer teaching assistants in local schools.

The university is set in 200 acres of parkland, a mile outside the picturesque city centre. Students join one of seven colleges, which mix academic and social roles. Most departments have their headquarters in one of the colleges, but the student community is a deliberate mixture of disciplines, years and sexes. Nursing apart, only archaeology and medieval studies are located off campus, sharing a medieval building in the centre of the city.

Social life on campus is lively, despite the absence of a student union building, with colleges the main focus. There are two newspapers, television and radio stations, as well as several magazines, to keep students abreast of campus issues. Sports facilities are good, and have been improved further with the opening of a new sports pavilion. Playing fields are on campus and the River Ouse fosters a strong rowing tradition. Cultural events abound in the city, which is also famous for a high concentration of pubs. The club scene has improved, but students still head for Leeds for the top names.

Accommodation

Number of places and costs refer to 2005–06
University-provided places: 3,895
Percentage catered: 0%
Costs for catered accommodation: n/a
Costs for self-catered accommodation:
£58.45–£74.06 (single room) a week.
Policy for first-year students: first-year single undergraduates are provided with university accommodation if an application is received by 8 September (UK residents) or 15 September (resident outside UK).
Policy for international students: overseas students (non-EU) are provided with university accommodation for the full duration of the course provided application is made each year by the appropriate deadline date.
Contact: accommodation@york.ac.uk
www.york.ac.uk/admin/accom

Students

Undergraduates:	6,555	(1,400)
Postgraduates:	2,230	(1,055)
Mature students:	4.7%	
Overseas students:	8.7%	
Applications per place:	9.0	
From state-sector schools:	79.3%	
From working-class homes:	17.7%	

Tuition fees 2006	£3,000

See chapter 13 for bursary details.

Teaching Quality Assessments

From 1995 (top score 24):
24 archaeology; biological sciences; economics; education; electrical and electronic engineering; philosophy; physics; politics; psychology.
23 sociology.
22 business; linguistics; mathematics and statistics; modern languages.
21 history of art; nursing.

12

University Cities

One glance at their glossy prospectuses shows that universities today are well aware that students look almost as carefully at their future surroundings as at their chosen courses. Those set in rolling countryside, or a lively city, flaunt their advantages. The lecture room and library are only part of the story, and students are not going to achieve peak performance if they are tied for three or four years to a place they do not like. These pages offer a brief guide to the main student centres. All have at least two universities.

Fashions change quickly among students, and a popular city can soon lose its attractions. London, for example, used to be a magnet for students, but some of the capital's universities have struggled to fill their places recently because of the high cost of living. Manchester, by contrast, with its student community of nearly 70,000, has become a popular draw while Newcastle is also challenging for the position of the students' favourite city.

Cost of living variations between cities tend to be the result of differences in the cost of services, including accommodation, transport and entertainment, rather than differences in the price of goods in shops which tend to be similar across the UK. The weekly magazine *The Grocer* (www.thegrocer.co.uk/) produces 'The Grocer 33', a weekly shopping basket survey that provides price information throughout eight regions across the country. It tracks price variations on 33 staple foods across the major supermarket chains within the regions. And it shows that, in the supermarkets at least, food prices are not subject to significant regional variation.

See pages 174–5 for some information on the level of crime in the major university cities.

The following pages profile:

Aberdeen	**Glasgow**
Belfast	**Leeds**
Birmingham	**Leicester**
Brighton	**Liverpool**
Bristol	**London**
Cambridge	**Manchester**
Cardiff	**Newcastle**
Coventry	**Nottingham**
Dundee	**Oxford**
Edinburgh	**Sheffield**

Aberdeen

Known as the Granite City, Aberdeen is Scotland's third largest city and home to Scotland's third oldest university, yet it is still compact enough to get around on foot. The city is close to the Grampian Mountains and beautiful beaches, as well as being a bustling social and commercial centre. The expansion of oil-related industries in the 1980s pushed up living costs, but the low local rate of unemployment means that part-time jobs are a real possibility for students. Social life tends to be focused on the students' unions, especially the older university's facilities, to which all students have access.

Getting Around

Local bus services are plentiful and student passes are available. However, short distances mean that walking or cycling are reliable alternatives. Aberdeen is 490 miles from London. Direct rail services link Aberdeen and London, including a sleeper service. The journey takes around 8 hours. Aberdeen is served by its own airport (Dyce).

Attractions for Students

Sport: Sports enthusiasts are well catered-for with swimming pools, the largest bowling alley in Scotland, 11 golf courses and a Premier League football team. The hinterland offers opportunities for skiing, sailing, windsurfing, hill climbing, canoeing and most other outdoor activities.

Culture and nightlife: There are three cinemas showing all the usual latest releases. His Majesty's Theatre plays host to drama, ballet, opera and musicals whilst the Aberdeen Arts Centre, the Music Hall and the Exhibition and Conference Centre are the venues for other major musical events. The Lemon Tree and the Beach Ballroom cater for the student market. There is an enviable selection of eating places, pubs and clubs. The City Art Gallery has an excellent collection of fine and applied art, and the Arts Centre has a small gallery for contemporary arts and crafts. The Maritime Museum, the Marischal College Museum, the Zoology Museum and the Grampian Transport Museum and Satrosphere, the science discovery centre, are all worth a visit

Shopping: The most recently completed indoor shopping centre is The Academy, which offers a range of bars, cafés and specialist shopping.

Population: 212,000
Student population: 17,000

Proximity to the city centre:
University of Aberdeen: King's College about 1 mile north of the city, Foresterhill a 20 minute walk
The Robert Gordon University: 5 sites around the city, with its base in the city centre

For more information:
Aberdeen and Grampian Visitor Information Centre
23 Union Street
Aberdeen AB11 5BP
T 01224 288828
E info@agtb.org
W www.aberdeencity.gov.uk
   www.aberdeen-grampian.com

Belfast

Belfast is the largest city in Northern Ireland, and is both the cultural and political capital. Recently, the peace process has stimulated applications from the mainland. Queen's campus is within Belfast's Golden Mile of pubs, clubs, café bars, restaurants and entertainment venues. Student life tends to concentrate here, for the Golden Mile provides part-time job opportunities as well as recreation.

Getting Around

There is a fast, reliable and reasonably priced integrated bus and rail network run by Trans-link. Travel cards are available. Within the city cycling is possible but the weather puts many off. Ferry services operate out of Belfast and Larne. Flights to London take about 1 hour. There are low-cost flights from Belfast International Airport to many major centres. The cross-border train service travels from Belfast to Dublin and back 8 times daily.

Attractions for Students

Sport: Belfast Giants ice hockey team is based in the new Odyssey arena. Ulster rugby is played at Ravenhill Stadium. There are 11 golf courses and centres within the city boundary. The Millennium National Cycling Network incorporating a newly completed 20-mile route in the greater Belfast area serves cycling enthusiasts. Ten-pin bowling is offered at two venues and the Dundonald International Ice Bowl is one of Northern Ireland's principal leisure and entertainment facilities with an Olympic-size ice rink. There are five leisure centres within Belfast with swimming pools. The Belfast City Marathon in May is a major sporting event.

Culture and nightlife: Belfast has over 400 bars and restaurants and many theatres, galleries and cinemas. Major concerts are staged at the Waterfront Hall and the Odyssey. There are plenty of clubs and live music is part of the scene, ranging from impromptu folk music sessions in the pubs to big-name concerts at the Queen's Union. Odyssey is the £100 million Landmark Millennium Project which features Ireland's largest all-seater indoor venue, the Arena; W5, Ireland's only interactive discovery centre; the Pavilion, a development of restaurants, bars, shops and the Sheridan Imax. A free monthly, listings guide *What About* details entertainment in the city.

Shopping: The high street names and designer labels are amply represented. Lisburn Road is the location for designer names and Donegall Pass is the antiques sector. Northern Irish crafts are also on offer in abundance.

Population: 297,300
Student population: 33,000

Proximity to the city centre:
Queen's University: main campus half-mile south
University of Ulster: only about 850 of the student population are based in Belfast, but many of those who study at Jordanstown (7 miles) live in the city

For more information:
Belfast Welcome Centre
47 Donegall Place
Belfast BT1 5AD
T 028-9024 6609
E info@belfastvisitor.com
W www.gotobelfast.com
   www.belfast.net
   www.belfastcity.gov.uk

Birmingham

Massive investment and bold cultural initiatives have transformed the cityscape and underpinned Birmingham's renaissance as a major European city. Much still remains to be done but the brutalism of 1960s town planning is giving way to new skyscraper hotels, pedestrianised squares and rejuvenated historic areas. Among the most recent developments are The Water's Edge at Brindleyplace, the Mailbox and Millennium Point, the region's landmark project. The reopened Bullring complex is now home to five retail markets. With a further £5 billion investment planned, Birmingham aims to continue its transformation as a vibrant, dynamic city.

Getting Around

Birmingham is at the centre of the UK motorway system, and is connected to 500 destinations via the national coach network. Rail links are excellent and London is a 90-minute journey. Birmingham International Airport, just 8 miles from the city centre, is a major hub with destinations throughout the UK, Europe, North America and Asia. Buses, trains and trams provide a comprehensive network of local transport. Cycling is possible, but heavy traffic and busy roads are best avoided.

Attractions for Students

Sport: The National Indoor Arena hosts many national sporting events. There are two Premiership football teams, and Test and County cricket is played at Edgbaston. Bowling alleys, golf, rock climbing, go-cart racing, ice-skating, squash, tennis and swimming are on offer.

Culture and nightlife: There is a full range of clubs, bars, music venues and restaurants, including over 50 different restaurants within the famous 'Balti Triangle'. Birmingham Royal Ballet is based at the Hippodrome, whilst Symphony Hall is the home of the City of Birmingham Symphony Orchestra. There are numerous theatres and galleries including Star City, a new leisure complex housing a 30-screen cinema. The Waterhall Gallery of Modern Art is Birmingham's newest venue for contemporary art, with the stylish Ikon Gallery displaying the best of international and British art. Birmingham Museum and Art Gallery is famous for its collection of Pre-Raphaelite works. The National Exhibition Centre stages major exhibitions and pop concerts.

Shopping: Usual high street stores and many designer shops can been found in the city centre. Students may prefer browsing in the Victorian arcades. The markets are good. More exclusive boutique shopping can be found on The Mailbox where there is also a Harvey Nicholls.

Population: 977,000
Student population: 42,000

Proximity to the city centre:
Aston University: campus a 10-minute walk
Birmingham University: campus 3 miles southwest at Edgbaston
University of Central England in Birmingham: 9 sites; the main site is at Perry Barr, 3 miles north

For more information:
Marketing Birmingham
Millennium Point
Level L2, Curzon Street
Birmingham B4 7XG
F   0121-202 5116
E   info@marketingbirmingham.com
W   www.birmingham.org.uk
www.birmingham.gov.uk
www.itchybirmingham.co.uk
http://icbirmingham.ic24.com

Brighton

Located 50 miles south of the capital, the overwhelming majority of Brighton's students come from the London area, contributing to its reputation as 'London by the Sea'. The similarity to the capital manifests itself not only in Brighton's variety and vitality, helped by large numbers of international students, but also in high prices and frenetic pace. Relaxed places, such as the North Laine, do exist, if you know where to look for them. The variety of nightlife in the city means that Brighton's students' unions are less well used than those at other universities, but they do benefit from easy accessibility compared with those in the city centre.

Getting Around

Brighton is compact and easy to get around on foot. Bus services are plentiful and there is a flat rate fare in the central area. There is a network of cycle lanes. Car parking is at a premium but there is a park-and-ride system. Trains to London take 50 minutes. London Gatwick Airport is 25 miles away with international links.

Attractions for Students

Sport: The Brighton Bears basketball team is based at the Brighton Centre; Brighton and Hove Albion plays football at Withdean Stadium and Sussex County Cricket Club has its ground in the area. The marina contains a leisure complex with a health club and bowling alley. The city has two golf courses, three swimming pools, 24 cricket pitches, more than 60 tennis courts and around 70 football pitches.

Culture and nightlife: The city has 19 cinema screens, and five major theatres. The Brighton Centre plays host to the large pop and rock tours, whilst the Dome is home to the Brighton Philharmonic Orchestra. There are 10 museums. The Royal Pavilion epitomises Regency Brighton. The Victorian Brighton Pier is packed with traditional seaside amusements. The new-look Beachfront area buzzes with bars, cafés, clubs, basketball and volleyball, artists' and fishing quarters. England's largest arts extravaganza, the Brighton Festival, is in May and the London to Brighton Veteran Car Run takes place in November. Arguably the clubbing capital of the south coast, Brighton attracts big name DJs from all over the country.

Shopping: North Laine with its Saturday fleamarket is popular with students, while The Lanes provides trendy and expensive shops. Churchill Square has all the High Street favourites under one roof. The Marina contains a factory outlet-shopping village.

Population: 248,000
Student population: 31,000

Proximity to the city centre:
University of Brighton: 1 site in Eastbourne and 3 in and around Brighton
University of Sussex: about 4 miles north-east in Falmer

For more information:
Brighton Visitor Information Centre
10 Bartholomew Square,
Brighton BN1 1JS
T 0906-711 2255 (calls cost 50p a minute)
E brighton-tourism@brighton-hove.gov.uk
W www.visitbrighton.com
    www.brighton-hove.gov.uk
    www.thisisbrightonandhove.co.uk
    www.itchybrighton.co.uk

Bristol

Bristol, the largest city in south-west England, has benefited from National Lottery funding and other grants to finance major regeneration projects. This has created a new civic cultural heart, buzzing with activity in the waterfront bars, restaurants, museums and art galleries. The thriving local economy means high prices and generally expensive accommodation. Bristol is on the whole welcoming to students although pubs in the town tend to be more segregated. Bristol is perennially popular as a student destination.

Getting Around

Travel by car is not easy; parking is difficult and expensive. Walking and cycling are preferable and the cycle tracks are good. There is an extensive and reasonably priced bus network. Travel cards are available. The Studentlink bus service operates during the week. London is 1 hour 30 minutes away by train. National Express operates coach links to many UK destinations. Bristol International Airport now serves many European destinations. Bristol's waterfront attractions are served by various ferry services with guided tours from spring to autumn.

Attractions for Students

Sport: Bristol has two football clubs – City and Rovers – and Gloucestershire County Cricket Club. Tennis, swimming, ice-skating, golf, rowing and sailing are all available. Bristol Climbing Centre offers indoor climbing while the Avon Gorge is a popular venue for outdoor climbing.

Culture and nightlife: The city is well provided with cinemas, both multiscreens and independents, plus an IMAX. The Bristol Old Vic theatre company is based at the Theatre Royal, whilst the Hippodrome is the venue for musicals, ballet and opera. The Colston Hall is host to a variety of comedy, rock, pop and orchestral concerts and exhibitions. The Arnolfini and the Harbourside Watershed Media Centre also offer a lively programme of exhibitions, films and theatre. The Harbourside includes three interactive and hands-on attractions. The British Empire and Commonwealth Museum opened in 2002. Bristol has an excellent range of pubs and clubs from the traditional to stylish late-night bars. A vibrant scene can be found at the Harbourside, Corn Street and Whiteladies Road.

Shopping: Broadmead, the Galleries and The Mall at Cribbs Causeway have all the high street names. Park Street is useful for music and second-hand clothing. Clifton Village has many specialist shops, but can be expensive. St Nicholas Markets, established in 1743, has stalls selling a range of food, second-hand books, old clothes, CDs and a range of unusual goods.

Population: 381,000
Student population: 34,000

Proximity to the city centre:
University of Bristol: campus in Cotham area, close to the city centre
University of the West of England at Bristol: 5 campuses; the main purpose-built Frenchay Campus lies about 4 miles north

For more information:
Bristol Tourist Information Centre
The Annexe, Wildscreen Walk
Harbourside, Bristol BS1 5DB
T   0906-7112 1914 (calls cost 50p a minute)
E   ticharbourside@bristol-city.gov.uk
W www.bristol-city.gov.uk
    www.visitbristol.co.uk
    www.venue.co.uk
    www.itchybristol.co.uk

Cambridge

Cambridge is a town-sized city easy to navigate on foot or bike and students and tourists throng its streets. The city has also become the centre of the hi-tech 'Silicon Fen' industries. Despite the bustle, the atmosphere in a small city of such beauty can feel cloistered or even stifling, especially to those from larger and livelier places. The gulf between new and old universities is nowhere wider than in Cambridge. Nonetheless, the two universities' students do mix, and those at Anglia enjoy access to a wide range of social events, which is fortunate because the university rather than the town is the main host. Town–gown relations are generally good.

Getting Around

Walking and cycling are the most popular modes of transport as much of the city is flat and easily accessible. Buses are fairly reliable, but expensive. However, travel cards are available. Cars are not recommended in the centre. London is 60 miles away, and trains take 50–70 minutes. London Stansted International Airport is 30 minutes away by train.

Attractions for Students

Sport: For sports enthusiasts there are two football teams based in the city – Cambridge United and Cambridge City – and the usual range of football, cricket, climbing and swimming is available, although many sports facilities are based within the university.

Culture and nightlife: The Cambridge Corn Exchange is the largest arts and entertainment venue and hosts a full range of events. The Junction is popular for bands, dance and experimental theatre whilst the ADC Theatre is owned by a student society and managed by the university. The Arts Picture House shows foreign and cult classics and hosts the two-week Cambridge Film Festival in July. Cambridge has a good array of pubs but few clubs. The Strawberry Fair is held each June, and the Cambridge Folk Festival in July. The Fitzwilliam Museum offers free admission to its exhibitions of paintings and ceramics. Kettles Yard Gallery is very popular with those who enjoy modern art and sculpture. An excellent way to see the sights of Cambridge is to hire a punt, rowing boat or canoe and travel along The Backs at a leisurely pace or to go upriver to Grantchester. There are also daily walking tours of the City and University from the Tourist Information Centre.

Shopping: Shopping is located in the market place, the Grafton Centre and Lion Yard City Centre shopping arcade.

Population: 109,000
Student population: 30,000

Proximity to the city centre:
Cambridge University: ancient buildings form the city centre
APU: campus 10 minute walk; its other campus is 40 miles away in Chelmsford

For more information:
Visit Cambridge Tourist Information Centre
The Old Library
Wheeler Street
Cambridge CB2 3QB
T   0906-586 2526
W www.visitcambridge.org
    www.cambridge.gov.uk
    www.itchycambridge.co.uk

Cardiff

There is much to be proud of in this prosperous and attractive city. It is bounded by an historic waterfront area on one side and beautiful countryside on the other, with good public transport systems. Cardiff has all the cultural and commercial facilities one would expect in the home of the National Assembly for Wales, whilst the cost of living is lower than in most capital cities. Recent huge regeneration projects have resulted in the Cardiff Bay waterfront development (including The Pierhead) and the Millennium Stadium. This facelift has really put Cardiff on the map as a forward-looking, modern European city.

Getting Around

Within the city, public transport is efficient and reasonable. Most students use the bus service but cycling and walking are popular. The UWIC bus service links all the sites and the city. London is 154 miles away, and trains take under 2 hours. There are direct flights from Cardiff International Airport to a number of European destinations.

Attractions for Students

Sport: Famous for rugby, the Millennium Stadium, the largest covered stadium in Europe, is the also venue for international football fixtures. Other sports catered for in the city include squash, ice-skating, golf, swimming and football.

Culture and nightlife: A range of cinemas and theatres includes the Chapter Arts Centre with two cinemas, three theatres, a visual arts centre plus café and bars. Cardiff has a vibrant nightlife with bars and pubs for all tastes. The city also hosts an annual Mardi Gras in September, now one of the biggest festivals of its kind in the UK. The magnificent Millennium Centre, a multi-purpose cultural and entertainment venue, and the new home for the Welsh National Opera was completed in 2004. The Atlantic Wharf entertainment complex offers a 12-screen cinema, bowling alley, nightclub, bars and restaurant. Admission to the National Museum and Gallery, which houses the largest collection of impressionist painting in Europe outside of Paris, is free. St David's Hall is the national concert hall of Wales, and the BBC National Orchestra of Wales is based in Cardiff. Two comedy venues, the Jongleurs and the Glee Club are also in the city.

Shopping: The Edwardian arcades of the Capitol Centre offer a variety of unusual shops and cafés. The main shopping areas are Queen Street and the St David's Centre with the full range of high street and designer names.

Population: 305,000
Student population: 25,000

Proximity to the city centre:
Cardiff University: buildings all round the city centre
University of Wales, College of Medicine: based at the University Hospital of Wales, 2 miles from the city centre
Cardiff, University of Wales Institute: 4 main teaching campuses situated around the city centre

For more information:
Cardiff Visitor Centre
St. David's House, 16 Wood Street
Cardiff CF10 1ES
T   029-2022 7281
E   visitor@thecardiffinitiative.co.uk
W   www.cardiff.gov.uk
    www.visitcardiff.info
    www.itchycardiff.co.uk

Coventry

A prosperous medieval town, modern Coventry's success was based on motor manufacture and engineering. It enjoys good communications and low prices, and its image is currently undergoing a major makeover. The Phoenix Initiative is a multimillion-pound scheme to revitalise one area of the city with a series of public squares and gardens alongside cafés, bars and shops. Town–gown relations are generally relaxed, and entertainment is more plentiful than the city's image suggests. Students from the two universities rarely cross paths. Warwick's tend to stay on campus and prefer Kenilworth and Leamington Spa for off-campus accommodation. Coventry's make the most of the city centre, which complements their own sports centre and students' union.

Getting around

There is a good bus service with special student rates between the city and Warwick University. The area is good for cycling and walking. London is 86 miles away, and trains take 75 minutes; Birmingham is less than 30 minutes away. Birmingham International Airport is 20 minutes by train. Coventry airport also provides passenger flights to many European destinations.

Attractions for students

Sport: Coventry City Football Club will be playing at the new Coventry Arena next season. This huge complex will also have a large concert facility, conference space and banqueting hall. Coventry Rugby Club has also moved to its new ground at the Butts Arena. Coventry Sports Centre includes a 50-metre Olympic-standard pool. Speedway is available in the city and there is an ice rink.

Culture and nightlife: Cinema lovers are well catered-for between the Odeon cineplex, the Film Theatre, and the Showcase Cinema. The Belgrade Theatre offers musicals, pantomime and traditional theatre whilst the Warwick Arts Centre plays host to popular music, dance, classical concerts and opera. It is also home to the Mead Gallery, exhibiting paintings, art, sculpture, craft and photography. The Museum of British Road Transport holds the largest collection of British cars in the world. The Toy Museum and the Herbert Art Gallery and Museum are also worth a visit. The Cathedral quarter links old and new Coventry and has been revived with a range of pubs, cafés and restaurants. Spon Street houses reconstructed medieval buildings and the Heritage Museum.

Shopping: Coventry has a traditional indoor market. The West Orchards Shopping Centre houses all the usual high street names, whilst out-of-town shopping is provided at the Central Six Retail Park.

Population: 301,000
Student population: 26,000

Proximity to the city centre:
Coventry University: purpose-built campus in the city centre
University of Warwick: modern campus about 3 miles from the city centre

For more information:
Coventry Tourist Information Centre
4 Priory Row, Coventry CV1 5EX
T   024-7622 7264/6
E   tic@coventry.gov.uk
W   www.coventry.gov.uk
    www.visitcoventry.co.uk

Dundee

Called the 'City of Discovery', Dundee has been cleaned up and relaunched in recent years and enjoys a cost of living estimated at 12 per cent lower than the UK average. Jute and jam may have disappeared, but the city is still home to DC Thomson, publishers of *The Beano* and *The Dandy*. It certainly benefits from its location on the Firth of Tay, with the Highlands within easy reach for outdoor pursuits.

Getting around

There is a decent local public transport network. The students' association at the University of Dundee runs a free nightbus for students within the city boundary. The city is on the main East Coast route with direct services to Newcastle, York and London, 430 miles away, taking around 6 hours 30 minutes. Trains to Edinburgh and Glasgow each take about an hour. Dundee Airport has daily flights to London City Airport and a new service to Manchester. Major airports are at Aberdeen, Edinburgh and Glasgow.

Attractions for Students

Sport: Dundee is home to two Premier League football clubs. Golfers are spoiled for choice. A running and cycling track is available at the Caird Park. Keen skiers and snowboarders have easy access to Scotland's slopes and Dundee is ideally placed for river fishing and canoeing enthusiasts. The Olympia Leisure Centre hosts a range of activities, including a climbing wall and leisure pool, while Dundee Ice Arena features an Olympic-size ice rink and is a venue for curling and ice hockey.

Culture and nightlife: The Dundee Contemporary Arts Centre is a popular venue for exhibitions, film and theatre. The Repertory Theatre, the Caird Hall, Marryat Hall complex and the Whitehall Theatre offer venues for concerts and dance. The Odeon Multiplex and UGC Cinemas boast 15 screens between them. Discovery Point is home to Scott of the Antarctic's vessel, *Discovery*, as well as the 19th-century frigate, *Unicorn*. The Verdant Works is a living museum depicting a working jute mill. The McManus Galleries host an exhibition of history, art and natural history, whilst the Barrack Street Museum's natural history exhibition includes a 40-foot whale skeleton. The Mills Observatory is the only full-time public observatory in the UK. 'Sensation' brings science to life with interactive exhibits.

Shopping: Shopping is centred on the Wellgate and the recently revamped Overgate Centres. Cheap and cheerful furniture is often found at the Dens Road Market. City Quay factory outlets provide designer labels at cheap prices.

Population: 146,000
Student population: 12,000

Proximity to the city centre:
University of Dundee: main campus in city centre
University of Abertay: campus in city centre

For more information:
Angus and Dundee Tourist Board
Castle Street
Dundee DD1 3AA
T   01382 527527
E   enquiries@angusanddundee.co.uk
W   www.angusanddundee.co.uk
www.dundeecity.gov.uk

Edinburgh

An elegant and cultured capital city, historic Edinburgh, visually spectacular, vibrant and cosmopolitan, is one of the most sought-after cities by students. Now the home of the Scottish Parliament, Edinburgh is enjoying a prosperous time. The compact city centre has an enviable range of pubs, bars and nightclubs, many with extended hours of opening. Students make up a good proportion of the population, and are generally welcomed. Areas such as Marchmont and the New Town are popular, but the city is expensive for accommodation. Shopping and entertainment costs are comparable with other major UK cities.

Getting Around

Edinburgh's seven hills make cycling hard work, but the city centre is easy to walk around. The local bus service is comprehensive. Bus lanes and cycle paths exist. Travel cards are available, though more expensive than in some cities. The National Express coach network links to many destinations. London is 373 miles away, and trains take 4 hours 30 minutes. Trains to Glasgow are frequent and the journey takes about 50 minutes. Edinburgh International Airport is 6 miles west, and the number of budget flights is expanding.

Attractions for Students

Sport: Murrayfield Stadium is home to Scottish Rugby Union and the city supports two football clubs – Hibs and Hearts – as well as an American football squad, ice hockey and basketball. There are three major golf courses, an Olympic-size swimming pool, a sports stadium and the largest artificial ski slope in Europe.

Culture and nightlife: Edinburgh offers six commercial cinemas and three independents. Theatres are plentiful. The world famous Edinburgh Festival takes place every August. The city is home to a wealth of art galleries, including the Queen's Gallery at Holyroodhouse, and museums as well as the Castle and botanical gardens. The recently developed dockland area of Leith is alive with bars, restaurants and clubs.

Shopping: Princes Street is the main shopping area in the city with most national chains as well as Edinburgh institutions, such as Jenners. George Street, Rose Street, the Grassmarket, the Royal Mile and the Stockbridge area of the city have more unusual shops. Ocean Terminal, a new shopping and leisure complex is situated on the waterfront at Leith.

Population: 450,000
Student Population: 37,000

Proximity to the city centre:
University of Edinburgh: in the centre, with science and engineering 2 miles south
Heriot-Watt University: campus 7 miles west of the city centre
Napier University: 2 miles south of the city centre

For more information:
Edinburgh and Scotland Information Centre
3 Princes Street
Edinburgh EH2 2QP
T   0845-225 5121
E   info@visitscotland.com
W www.edinburghguide.com
    www.edinburgh.org
    www.visitscotland.com
    www.itchyedinburgh.co.uk

Glasgow

Glasgow is Scotland's largest city, and one of Britain's liveliest. Glasgow has campaigned vigorously and successfully to change its 'mean city' image. Home of Charles Rennie Mackintosh and the Glasgow School of Art, it is Scotland's cultural capital. Scotland's opera, ballet and national orchestra are based in the city, which also boasts a profusion of art galleries, museums and theatres. Students find the locals generally very friendly. The three universities are within easy reach of one another and many students live in the attractive West End, though the area's desirability has led to an increase in prices over recent years.

Getting Around

There is a good cheap local bus service and a reliable underground. Few cycle because of the hills and heavy traffic. London is 392 miles away, and trains take 5 hours. Glasgow International Airport, 7 miles to the west of the city, receives national and international flights including transatlantic flights as well as budget flights. Coaches depart from Buchanan Street Bus Station to all major UK cities.

Attractions for Students

Sport: Two famous football clubs – Rangers and Celtic – are based in the city and the range of participative sports includes football, rugby, sailing and skiing on the city's two dry ski slopes. The Trossachs and Loch Lomond National Park is within easy reach, and rail and ferry links make the nearby islands such as Arran and Bute accessible.

Culture and nightlife: Glasgow boasts a variety of theatres and performing and visual arts venues. Glaswegians are famously fond of their pubs, and the city's club scene rivals those of London and Manchester. Live music is very popular and numerous venues range from the SECC to the Barrowlands. The city is home to a great variety of classical music concerts, and has many cinemas, including four multiscreens and two independents. The Glasgow Science Centre features a Science Mall and an IMAX cinema. Glasgow's medieval roots can be explored in the Cathedral and Provand's Lordship. Glasgow has 35 museums and art galleries, including the famous Burrell Collection, many without an entry fee.

Shopping: A plethora of designer shops in the Buchanan Galleries, Princes Square and the Merchant City cater for the label-conscious Glaswegian. The Barras street market offers variety for the cash-strapped student.

Population: 580,000
Student population: 45,000

Proximity to the city centre:
University of Glasgow: 3 miles from the centre in the West End
Glasgow Caledonian University: situated in the city centre
Strathclyde University: main campus in the city centre

For more information:
Greater Glasgow and Clyde Valley Tourist Board
11 George Square
Glasgow G2 1DY
T   0141-204 4480
E   enquiries@seeglasgow.com
W www.seeglasgow.com
    www.glasgow.gov.uk
    www.itchyglasgow.co.uk

Leeds

Leeds is a sophisticated commercial centre with more law and accountancy firms than anywhere outside London. The city itself is friendly and lively, and the cost of living is generally low. The two universities live and work together in the city centre, and there is much interchange between their students' unions. Students who live out also tend to live in the same area, making a compact student enclave. Property rental prices are low, helped by the surplus accommodation in the city.

Getting Around

A new Supertram network is under development. Buses provide a cheap and efficient method of transport and a very reasonably priced student Metrocard is available. Cycling is possible, but unpopular because of the hills and heavy traffic. London is 190 miles away, and trains take 3 hours. Leeds–Bradford International Airport is 8 miles north.

Attractions for Students

Sport: Leeds United plays at Elland Road and two international sporting venues – Yorkshire County Cricket Club and Leeds Rugby League Club – are both located in Headingley. There are 160 tennis courts in the city's parks as well as pitches for rugby, football, cricket and hockey. The city has an Olympic-sized swimming pool and a skateboard park. The Yorkshire Dales, North Yorks Moors and the Vale of York are within easy reach of Leeds.

Culture and nightlife: Music lovers are well provided for with chamber music, jazz, classical and rock at live venues across the city. The gas-lit Hyde Park Picture House offers a unique cinema experience. The City Art Gallery houses the new Henry Moore Centre for the Study of Sculpture. The Abbey House Museum and the Royal Armouries are just two of Leeds' museums. There is a dazzling array of clubs. The recently developed Waterfront is now a dining quarter and restaurants, cafés and bars also surround the Millennium Square.

Shopping: Excellent shopping facilities exist in the Corn Exchange, Granary Wharf and the Victoria Quarter with Harvey Nicholls. Many designer shops and major retail outlets thrive in the heart of the city centre.

Population: 715,000
Student population: 38,000

Proximity to the city centre:
University of Leeds: compact redbrick campus a mile away
Leeds Metropolitan University: high-rise campus near the city centre; Beckett Park campus 3 miles away

For more information:
Gateway Yorkshire Leeds Tourist Office
PO Box 244
The Arcade,
City Station
Leeds LS1 1PL
T   0113-242 5242
W www.leeds.gov.uk
     www.bbc.co.uk/leeds
     www.leedsguide.co.uk
     www.itchyleeds.co.uk

Leicester

Leicester is a compact and friendly place, rich in green spaces. Students find the city ideally sized and its central location means that it attracts students from all over the UK. Student social life tends to be spread evenly all over the city centre. A strong ethnic diversity has contributed to a cosmopolitan and cultured atmosphere and the strength of the local economy recently has resulted in much new development. Life in the city is inexpensive, and the fresh food market, the largest outdoor market in Europe, helps stretch tight student budgets. Accommodation is still not too hard to find and the rents are among the lowest in the country.

Getting Around

There is a good cheap bus service and travel cards are available. Leicester has miles of cycleways. London is 93 miles away, and trains take 1 hour 15 minutes. The nearest airports are Nottingham East Midlands (less than half an hour away) and Birmingham. Road links are good and Leicester is well served by the coach network.

Attractions for Students

Sport: Leicester has a selection of sports and leisure centres, including swimming, tennis, rugby, golf and squash. Leicester City Football Club, Leicestershire County Cricket Club and the Leicester Tigers Rugby Club are based here. Nearby Rutland Water is popular for a range of watersports.

Culture and nightlife: Leicester is bursting with bars, clubs, pubs and restaurants. The city attracts big name bands, DJs and classical music performances. Jazz can be found at the Y Theatre and new bands play at pubs such as the Charlotte. The Haymarket Theatre, the Phoenix Arts Complex and De Montfort Hall, which hosts major concerts, are the big venues. Leicester enjoys a number of annual festivals reflecting the city's cultural diversity, such as the Caribbean Carnival and the Diwali Festival of Light. The annual Comedy Festival is held in the city each February. The New Walk Museum, the Jewry Wall Museum, the Abbey Pumping Station and the National Space Centre are the main visitor attractions.

Shopping: The Shires and Haymarket shopping centres have all the usual high-street names. The arcades of St Martins Square, Silver Street and the Leicester Lanes offer more individuality in shopping. Belgrave Road, also known as the Golden Mile, offers jewellery shops and saris.

Population: 280,000
Student population: 30,000

Proximity to the city centre:
De Montfort University: one campus in the city centre, another nearby at Scraptoft
University of Leicester: campus about 1 mile away

For more information:
Leicester Tourist Information Centre
7–9 Every Street
Town Hall Square
Leicester LE1 6AG
T 0906-294 1113 (calls cost 25p a minute)
E info@goleicestershire.com
W www.goleicestershire.com

Liverpool

Liverpool has always been a vibrant city and a centre of cultural wealth and diversity. The announcement that it is to be European Capital of Culture 2008 is already having a huge impact on the city and it is currently enjoying a period of investment and development with the help of funding from central Government and the EU. The Albert Dock development is evidence of great progress. Liverpool is a friendly and economical base for students, with excellent opportunities for part-time work and one of the lowest costs of living in the UK. Students tend to live and socialise around the central Smithdown Road area because of the cheap rents, but the Kensington area is also popular.

Getting Around

Merseyrail (the Metro) supplements an efficient bus service. JMU operates a free shuttle bus between its sites. Cycling is possible but not popular. London is 197 miles away, and trains take 3 hours. National Express coaches operate to many destinations. Flights from Liverpool Airport are expanding, and there are flights to many European cities. Manchester International Airport is less than an hour away for other destinations.

Attractions for Students

Sport: Home to both Liverpool and Everton Football Clubs, it also offers Rugby Union, golf, cricket, gymnastics and basketball. Rugby League teams such as St Helens, Widnes and Wigan play nearby. Watersports enthusiasts are catered for close to the Albert Docks and climbing is available at the Awesome Walls centre. Aintree Race Course, home of the Grand National, has a visitor centre.

Culture and nightlife: Liverpool has a reputation as a lively city and there are about 130 clubs and hundreds of bars and pubs. The city has many cinemas and numerous theatres including the Liverpool Empire and the Everyman. The Philharmonic Hall is the venue for classical concerts. National Museums Liverpool represents the eight museums and galleries in and around the city. Tate Liverpool is famous for its modern art exhibitions and the Maritime Museum gives an account of Liverpool's seafaring history. The Waterfront and the redeveloped Albert Dock with its shops, cafés and bars are popular as are the new Fact Centre art house cinema and multimedia gallery in the developing Ropeworks.

Shopping: As well as the usual high-street stores, Cavern Walks caters for those who like designer gear. St John's Centre and Bold Street are popular with bargain hunters.

Population: 439,000
Student population: 32,000

Proximity to the city centre:
University of Liverpool: modern campus in the city centre
Liverpool John Moores University: two main sites on opposite sides of the city centre

For more information:
Liverpool Tourist Information Centre
Queen's Square Centre
Queen Square
Liverpool L1 1RG
T   0845-601 1125
E   info@visitliverpool.com
W www.visitliverpool.com
www.itchyliverpool.co.uk
www.liverpool.gov.uk

London

London is by far the largest city in the UK and it has universities located both in the centre of the city – University College London and the University of Westminster – and well away from the centre – Kingston, Greenwich and Brunel. Check carefully the location of any London university that you are considering.

Whether you are interested in parks or pubs, theatres or cinemas, shopping or sightseeing, museums or art galleries, dancing non-stop throughout the weekend or eating every cuisine under the sun, London can meet your requirements. The city will also present you with a fairly hefty bill for most of the above, and for travel between them. That said, the diligent hunter will find bargains, but the temptation to spend is everywhere.

Whatever bargains can be found, accommodation will be a major expense for every student. Even if rents away from the smart areas of the city centre are slightly less astronomical, travel to and from college can easily eat away any savings made although efforts by ULU (the University of London's Students' Union) mean most students can get money off bus and underground fares. The capital city's hectic pace can overwhelm as easily as it excites, and loneliness can be a problem in a city where you might be living miles away from your college. Nevertheless, London is justly renowned as one of the most exciting cities in the world and, for those who can strike a balance between making the most of life and avoiding spending their way to bankruptcy, it is the ideal place to be a student.

Getting Around

London is well served by an extensive bus, railway and underground network with special price deals available for students. In many areas the roads are very busy, making cycling a hazardous occupation. The main airports serving London are Heathrow, Gatwick, Stansted and Luton.

Attractions for Students

London is such a large city with so many attractions that a description of particular activities is not given. There are many guidebooks to London.

Population: 7.2 million
Student population: 306,000

Twelve separate universities. The University of London is a loose affiliation of almost 50 colleges and other institutions.

For more information:
w www.london.gov.uk
www.bbc.co.uk/london
www.londontown.com
www.timeout.com/london
www.londonnet.co.uk
www.londoneye.com
www.londontheatre.co.uk
www.tate.org.uk/modern
www.tfl.gov.uk
www.itchylondon.co.uk
http://uk.visitlondon.com

Manchester

Manchester is a thriving, prosperous northern hub and considers itself the commercial and cultural capital of the North of England. The city is also probably the most fashionable student location in Britain. The success of the 2002 Commonwealth Games and the worldwide fascination with Manchester United Football Club enhance its reputation for glitz and glamour.

Getting Around

The city is well served by bus, train and tram, and the lack of hills means that cycling is a viable alternative. Road and rail links are good. Manchester is 184 miles from London, and trains take 2 hours 30 minutes. National Express coaches travel to many destinations. Manchester International Airport is 10 miles south of the city and has a full range of international flights.

Attractions for Students

Sport: Both Manchester United and Manchester City football clubs are based here, as well as the Lancashire County Cricket Club. There are extensive sporting facilities, including the National Cycling Centre and Manchester Aquatics Centre. It also has the country's largest martial arts club, and is home to the English Wrestling Association and the British Mountaineering Council.

Culture and nightlife: Manchester boasts over 400 pubs, clubs and café bars in the city centre, and many bands have originated on the Manchester scene. It also boasts one of the largest Chinatowns in Britain, a 'Curry Mile' in Rusholme, and a 'Gay Village' in the city centre. There are numerous cinemas including the Cornerhouse with its three screens, café and gallery. Manchester is home to the Royal Exchange Theatre Company, BBC Philharmonic Orchestra and the Hallé Orchestra, housed in the new Bridgewater Hall. The Lowry Centre, consisting of an arts centre and theatres, and the Imperial War Museum North are both on the waterside at Salford Quays.

Shopping: The compact city centre contains an extensive shopping area, a magnet for the region. As well as all the high-street stores, there are trendy designer shops and boutiques.

Population: 410,000
Student population: 68,000

Proximity to the city centre:
University of Manchester: city-centre campus
Manchester Metropolitan University: city-centre campus plus sites in south Manchester, Crewe and Alsager
University of Salford: campus in Salford, 1 mile from the city centre

For more information:
Manchester Visitor Centre
Town Hall Extension
Lloyd Street, Manchester M60 2LA
T 0161-234 3157
E manchester.visitor.centre@
   notes.manchester.gov.uk
W www.manchester.gov.uk
   www.visitmanchester.com
   www.manchesteronline.co.uk
   www.itchymanchester.co.uk

Newcastle

Newcastle is known as a very friendly, lively city. Students enjoy living in Newcastle with its vibrant nightlife, excellent shopping facilities and one of the lowest costs of living in the north. Bars and pubs in the city centre are cheap and welcoming to students at weekends and on special student nights. The addition of CCTV has made it a safer place after dark, as has the redevelopment of the Quayside area.

Getting Around

Newcastle's Metro connects the city centre with Gateshead, Sunderland, the coast, Newcastle Airport and the railway station. There is also good bus network. London is 274 miles away, and trains take 3 hours. Newcastle Airport is 6 miles north of the city. There is a daily ferry from the International Ferry Terminal at North Shields (7 miles) to Amsterdam, and other services to Bergen and Gothenburg.

Attractions for Students

Sport: Newcastle United Football Club is based at St James's Park. Rugby, basketball and ice-hockey are all played, and the Great North Run is hosted by Newcastle every year. Athletics are at Gateshead's International Stadium across the river. Newcastle is fully equipped with swimming pools, gyms and cycle paths.

Culture and nightlife: A commercial cinema with nine screens is at the Gate, with the independent Tyneside Cinema showing cult and art films. The Metro Radio Arena plays host to major music tours in addition to basketball and ice hockey. The City Hall, Journal Tyne Theatre and Foundation complement a range of smaller venues. Four theatres and five art galleries provide a range of cultural activities. The Discovery Museum is the largest museum complex in the region; Life Science Centre, a virtual reality journey through life. The Gateshead Millennium Bridge now links the Quayside area, with its many pubs, clubs, restaurants and hotels, to Gateshead Quays and BALTIC, the Centre for Contemporary Art, for pedestrians and cyclists. Above the Quays, Norman Forster's SAGE regional music centre opened to great acclaim last year. The Hoppings, a traditional fair, arrives on the Town Moor for ten days annually at the end of June. Many sites on Hadrian's Wall in Northumbria are within easy reach.

Shopping: Shoppers can spend their money in Eldon Square or Monument Mall, or can visit the area around the City Library where designer label shops are located. The famous Metro Centre, a vast covered shopping centre, is across the river in Gateshead.

Population: 260,000
Student population: 31,000

Proximity to the city centre:
University of Newcastle: campus in the city centre
University of Northumbria: two sites in the city centre, another three miles outside; one in Longhirst (15 miles) and one in Carlisle (55 miles)

For more information:
Tourist Information Centre
132 Grainger Street,
Newcastle NE1 5AF
T   0191-277 8000
E   tourist.info@newcastle.gov.uk
     bookonline@gateshead.gov.uk
W www.newcastle.gov.uk
     www.visitnewcastle.co.uk
     www.visitnewcastlegateshead.com

Nottingham

Nottingham is probably still most famous for the legendary Robin Hood, whose redistribution of income policy would be welcome to most of the city's students. The locals are generally friendly to students, and many choose to settle here after graduation. The distance between the two universities means that their students tend not to fraternise and live out in different areas. Lenton is favoured by students at the older university and Forest Fields by those at Nottingham Trent. Accommodation takes some finding, but it is not over-priced.

Getting Around

Buses are reasonable, and a new tram network opened in spring 2004. Cycle lanes and relatively flat terrain make cycling popular. Nottingham is easily accessible by road, rail and air. London is 122 miles away, and trains take 1 hour 45 minutes. The nearest airport is Nottingham East Midlands.

Attractions for Students

Sport: The National Ice Centre has two Olympic-sized rinks, whilst the National Watersport Centre at Holme Pierrepoint offers white-water rafting in addition to rowing, canoeing and water skiing. Test and county cricket are played at Trent Bridge. Nottingham is equipped with ample leisure centres and swimming pools. The nearby Peak District National Park offers excellent walking and climbing.

Culture and nightlife: Nottingham has a thriving nightlife, from venues such as Rock City, the Rescue Rooms and the Marcus Garvey Centre catering for most musical tastes, to a good selection of clubs. Certain venues may be expensive, but there are plenty of student nights. Theatre is provided at the Theatre Royal and the Nottingham Playhouse and concerts at the Concert Hall. There is no shortage of cinemas, including the Savoy with its double seats and the recently opened UGC at the Cornerhouse. The Broadway Arts Cinema caters for more esoteric tastes. Nottingham offers a host of pubs – including the 'oldest pub in the world', The Trip to Jerusalem, dating back to 1189. The redeveloped canalside area has three bars and a comedy club. The Galleries of Justice is an award-winning museum of the history of crime, punishment and British justice throughout the ages. The annual Goose Fair is a three-day event held in October on the Forest Recreation Ground. Many of the 400 caves lying under the city are open for tours.

Shopping: The small and compact city centre offers the full range of high-street brands and designer names.

Population: 267,000
Student population: 39,000

Proximity to the city centre:
University of Nottingham: campus about 4 miles from the city centre
Nottingham Trent University: one city-centre campus; two other sites about 4 miles from the city centre

For more information:
City Information Centre
1–4 Smithy Row
Nottingham NG1 2BY
T 0115-915 5330
E enquiries@experiencenottinghamshire.com
W www.experiencenottinghamshire.com
   www.leftlion.co.uk
   www.nottinghamcity.gov.uk
   www.bbc.co.uk/nottingham
   www.itchynottingham.co.uk

Oxford

The city is beautiful, ancient and expensive. Medium-sized, it has a cosmopolitan and youthful atmosphere. A thriving nightlife and dynamic music scene have added to the buzz of the place. Its historical architecture is world-famous and attracts many tourists each year. High costs are probably one reason why student social life tends to be concentrated in college bars and in the Brookes' Students' Union. Contact between the two universities is minimal, though probably greatest in the cosmopolitan Cowley Road area where many students look for non-collegiate, and often overpriced, accommodation.

Getting Around

Most students use bikes, and cycle lanes and cycle parking are abundant. Local buses are inexpensive and services are good. Cars are actively discouraged in the city centre. London is 59 miles away, and trains take 1 hour. Coaches run to London 24 hours a day. There are special coach links to Heathrow (half hourly) and Gatwick (hourly) airports.

Attractions for Students

Sport: The city has a range of swimming pools and leisure centres, an ice rink and an athletics track. Many of the Oxford colleges have their own sports facilities, Oxford Brookes has a pool at Westminster College as well as its own sports provisions. The river provides opportunities for rowing. Rugby, football, basketball and ice hockey are all played.

Culture and nightlife: A number of famous bands has come out of Oxford in recent years, and there are now several venues for live music with gig nights for up and coming bands. Bars, clubs and restaurants are proliferating and a varied club scene with special student nights is attracting students to the city centre. Oxford has two cinemas, plus the Phoenix and the Ultimate Picture Palace. The Oxford Playhouse is the main theatre. The New Theatre is a venue for concerts. The Museum of the History of Science, the Ashmolean, the University Museum of Natural History and the adjacent Pitt Rivers are examples of the many museums. The Oxford Art Weeks takes place in May and June each year. There are walking tours of Oxford and the colleges, which provide an interesting and informed view of the city. The tours leave Oxford Information Centre daily at 11am and 2pm.

Shopping: Cornmarket and Queen Streets are popular shopping areas, as are the Westgate and Clarendon Centres and the traditional Covered Market. Book lovers are spoilt for choice.

Population: 142,000
Student population: 28,000

Proximity to the city centre:
Oxford University: the colleges are an integral part of the city, with most of the undergraduate colleges being in or near to the city centre
Oxford Brookes University: two campuses in Headington, 2 miles from the centre; one site at Wheatley, 6 miles east; and one in Botley, 3 miles west

For more information:
Oxford Information Centre
15–16 Broad Street
Oxford OX1 3AS
T 01865 726871
E tic@oxford.gov.uk
W www.visitoxford.org
   www.oxford.gov.uk
   www.dailyinfo.co.uk
   www.itchyoxford.co.uk

Sheffield

The rejuvenation of the city has put Sheffield back on the map, with the multimillion-pound remodelling of the city centre a major contributory factor. Known for its friendliness, it has long been a popular city with students, a high proportion of whom choose to stay - or return - and settle here. Students live throughout the city, rather than in isolated enclaves, demonstrating just how easy it is to get around. Rents and the cost of living are generally reasonable.

Getting Around

The Supertram serves both universities, the city centre and a number of the main venues and buses are reliable but not cheap. Cycling is only for the fit or the determined as Sheffield is built on hills. London is just over160 miles away with frequent train services taking about 2 hours 30 minutes. The nearest airports are Manchester, Nottingham East Midlands and the new Robin Hood Airport at Doncaster. Coaches serve many UK destinations.

Attractions for Students

Sport: Sheffield has two climbing centres; a ski village for skiing and snowboarding; an Olympic-size swimming pool and the world's deepest diving pool. Ice hockey (Sheffield Steelers) and basketball (Sheffield Sharks) are both based at the Arena. There are two football teams, Sheffield Wednesday and Sheffield United, and Rugby League. The National Ice Centre opened in 2003. One third of Sheffield is within the Peak District National Park, a Mecca for hill walking and rock climbing enthusiasts.

Culture and nightlife: Sheffield has more than 30 cinema screens, including those at the acclaimed independent Showroom Cinema. Two main theatres, the Crucible and Lyceum, along with the smaller Studio theatre provide the largest theatre complex outside London's South Bank. The Hallam FM Arena and Sheffield City Hall are just two of the venues hosting major concerts whilst the Leadmill, Boardwalk and Octagon Centre put on regular gigs. Sheffield has a reputation for a vibrant music scene and legendary clubs. The Millennium Galleries house major exhibitions from the V & A and the Tate. Magna, the science adventure centre, celebrates the natural elements of earth, air, fire and water. Kelham Island Museum provides an insight into Sheffield's steel and cutlery industries.

Shopping: All the high-street brands (and more) can be found in the city centre with the Devonshire Quarter being a particular favourite for independent designers. Ecclesall Road offers a range of boutiques whilst the Meadowhall complex is one of the largest shopping malls in Europe.

Population: 513,000
Student population: 48,000

Proximity to the city centre:
University of Sheffield: campus about half a mile west of the city centre
Sheffield Hallam University: campuses in the city centre and approx. 1 mile south-west of city centre.

For more information:
Sheffield Tourism
Blades Enterprise Centre
Sheffield S2 4SW
T 0114-221 1900
E visitor@sheffield.gov.uk
W www.sheffieldtourism.co.uk
   www.itchysheffield.co.uk

13

Bursaries and Scholarships in England and Northern Ireland from 2006

The UK Parliament has passed a law allowing English universities to charge students variable tuition fees for each year of their studies. These so-called 'top-up fees' will start for students entering these universities in 2006 and the maximum fee allowed will be £3,000. Apart from an annual adjustment to allow for inflation, this fee is fixed by law until 2010 and can only be changed by Parliament itself. But the Labour Government was, and is, committed to 50 per cent of young people experiencing higher education and wants to ensure individuals are not deterred from coming to universities because of lack of funds. Coupled, therefore, with the introduction of variable tuition fees is an extensive system of support for students from low-income families, including new bursaries and scholarships all designed to encourage wider access to higher education. In developing these, the universities seem not to have made any clear cut distinction between the words 'bursary' and 'scholarship' but rather to use these interchangeably.

The Office for Fair Access

All of these new arrangements are being overseen by a new body, the Office for Fair Access (OFFA) which has been in existence for less than a year. It required universities to submit Access Agreements by March 2005 outlining what fees they intend to levy and how they still plan to widen access. A significant feature of these rather complex documents is a description of the new bursaries and scholarships available from 2006. These are really important to readers of this *Guide*; OFFA suggests that some 400,000 students are likely to benefit. The Access Agreements contain much other helpful information for would-be university applicants and copies of all of them can be found at www.offa.org.uk. You are strongly encouraged to read those of particular interest to you. We must also emphasise that these bursaries and scholarships are targeted at specific groups and hence the list is by no means comprehensive. The grid below together with the notes that follow summarise a particular Government initiative aimed principally – but not exclusively – at students from low-income families, but universities have always offered a small number of bursaries and scholarships to undergraduates. If you are interested in the full range on offer, you will need to consult the websites of the individual universities. Some have even produced booklets with listings and there are invariably references to university awards in the prospectuses. Even this is not the whole story because there is nothing to stop a university enhancing the offers made in its Access Agreement with OFFA. What it cannot do is lower the offer. So the message has to be 'watch this space' and urge you to look at the relevant websites when you come to apply to universities.

Tuition Fees and Bursaries

Whilst the universities are being allowed to charge fees anywhere between £1,200 and £3,000 a year, the vast majority have opted for the maximum of £3,000. Only three universities will be charging less (Ulster has yet to announce its plans), but others may decide to do so later in the light of experience. The three are:

Greenwich	£2,500
Leeds Metropolitan	£2,000
Thames Valley	£2,700

These three are not required to provide bursaries for students from low-income families but all the other universities must, and the **minimum** bursary will be £300 a year. However, as the grid shows, many universities are offering a standard bursary well above this minimum, together with an array of other bursaries and scholarships. These are in addition to the means-tested Higher Education Maintenance Grant (HEMG), the upper limit of which is £2,700, plus any student loan from the Student Loans Company to which you might be entitled (see chapter 7 for information on these). The HEMG and any bursary or scholarship is yours to keep – it does not have to be repaid. Loans are loans and, with few exceptions, will have to be repaid some day. However, for those from the Student Loans Company you don't have to start repaying whilst still a student.

When it comes to application procedures, a number of universities are quite specific and indicate both timing and availability of online applications, including a timetable for notification of decisions. Some universities have gone out of their way to keep it simple and will not require an application at all; entitlement will be calculated by direct reference to your LEA financial assessment without your having to do anything else. Others are very vague and some make no mention of this at all. On payments, some expect to make these through the Student Loans Company whilst others plan to administer their schemes in-house. There is some indication in some of the Access Agreements about whether the bursary will be made in advance of the academic year or as staged payments during the year. Generally, the information suggests that if your personal circumstances change part-way through the course, for example, through unsatisfactory academic progress or a change in residual family income, then your entitlement will be reviewed. If this all sounds rather vague, we are assured that all the missing detail will be revealed by the early part of next year.

All of this argues for a great deal of help and advice and most universities plan to provide web-based or hard copy information nearer the time, even help lines in some cases. In addition, most universities plan to deploy support staff to assist the implementation of these new arrangements and some institutions will even provide direct, over-the-counter help to students like you. Yet again, we cannot emphasise enough the value of consulting individual university web sites for up-to-date information. If all else fails, phone the university; this is particularly the case where you come across inconsistencies or difficulties in understanding or interpreting the bursaries and scholarships information. We have lived in universities most of our lives but have still found all of this something of a quagmire, so don't be afraid to ask!

The Bursaries and Scholarships Grid

The grid summarises the types of bursaries(B) and scholarships(S) available. It is followed by a listing of further details for each university. An explanation of the headings follows:

- **In receipt of full HEMG** are bursaries for students from the lowest income families and these will have a HEMG (Higher Education Maintenance Grant) of £2,700 and a mandatory non-repayable bursary of at least £300. But, as the grid shows, this bursary will often be considerably higher than this minimum.
- **In receipt of partial HEMG** are students from low-income families who, whilst not receiving the full £2,700 HEMG, will still receive a lower HEMG and, in addition, at many universities also the bursary shown.
- **Living in region** is defined by the university itself. For most, this will be the city or county where the university is located but it could be wider than that, particularly for universities in rural areas.

- **Living in specified postcodes** will usually be for students who live in deprived parts of towns and cities where there is little tradition of entry to universities. But the university may also have other good reasons for targeting these districts.
- **Progression from outreach** will be for students who have already been involved in the outreach activities of the university. Most higher education institutions have developed strong links, sometimes called Compacts or Partnerships, with schools and colleges with which they have special arrangements for encouraging their students to apply to universities.
- **Ethnic minorities** are students from black and other ethnic communities where these are under-represented in the university student population.
- **Disabled** because, again, these students are often under-represented in universities.
- **Sport** is seen as an increasingly important factor in widening access to universities. Some, most notably Loughborough, have fine reputations and have long since offered scholarships but here is a new selection to consider.
- **Shortage subjects** are those which the universities find difficult to fill yet ones which are crucial to the UK economy. They tend to be modern languages, the physical sciences and engineering.
- **Academic achievement** is usually defined by the universities in terms of high entry qualifications (A level grades or points, UCAS tariff scores, etc). But note that many of the scholarships for academic achievement are only open to certain individuals (eg first generation, ethnic minorities, low-income).

The notes for particular universities refer to the money set aside for bursaries by the universities from the £3,000 tuition fees they receive. This is generally stated in the form: **X per cent of the additional tuition fee income will be earmarked for bursaries**. Clearly, the higher the proportion ploughed back for redistribution the more likely you are to benefit.

Another regular comment refers to the fact that **eligibility for bursaries will be assessed using UUK/SLC model bursary scheme**. This is a scheme developed by the heads of the universities (UUK) and administered by the Student Loans Company (SLC) on behalf of the university rather than by the university itself. At the time of publication, no further information was available from the Student Loans Company website (www.slc.co.uk) on how this will operate but the plan is to make it transparent and avoid duplication. The scheme is expected to be a simple add-on to the existing system for the administration of grants and loans.

Reduced tuition fees and bursaries will normally apply for any part of the university course spent on placement elsewhere. This might be as part of a sandwich degree, for a year abroad within a modern language degree, or whilst undertaking professional training. Where this is the case, it is detailed in the footnotes. Foundation year studies also often attract lower fees and/or bursaries. Some Access Agreements specifically mention that the university has a Hardship Fund or runs a Job Shop to help you find local employment. You should not assume that this is unique; most universities have these now but have chosen not to highlight these to OFFA.

Points to Ponder

- **Is the bursary automatic or conditional?** If it is conditional, when will I know? For those bursaries dependent on family income, you will have a good idea of eligibility when you apply and will know for definite when you get your LEA assessment. For others, you won't know until you get your exam results, well after you have made all the crucial decisions.

And if you are doing unusual entry qualifications (especially any not in the UCAS tariff), you may not know until you or your parents have had a debate with the University Admissions Office!

- **Is the bursary application procedure complex**? Or does it all follow from LEA assessments, postcodes or exam results without your having to do anything?
- **How many applicants will benefit from the large headline sums?** Check both the value of the bursary and the number on offer. Be realistic – but not pessimistic – about your chances.
- **Do you qualify?** If your parents are high-income earners, then you are likely only to be eligible for scholarships linked to your academic achievement and desire to study 'shortage' subjects. So if your Dad or Mum is a successful barrister, forget it unless you are going to get straight AAAs at A level and plan to do Physics!
- **Look out for special (unadvertised) offers** when you go to interviews and open days or in Clearing, particularly in this first year when everyone (including the universities!) is working in the dark.
- **Some universities offer fee remission rather than a bursary.** This is really a choice between reduced debt in the future versus cash in hand now.

The table on the following four pages summaries the position at each English university. It is then followed by more detailed information on each institution. The chapter concludes with details for Queen's, Belfast. The University of Ulster had not released its details when this book went to press.

University	In receipt of full HEMG (£)	In receipt of partial HEMG (£)	Living in region	Living in specified postcodes	Progressing from outreach	Ethnic minorities	Disabled	Sport	Shortage subjects	Academic achievement
Anglia	800 min	500 max	•B	•B	•B	•B	•B			
Aston	750 min	750 max								
Bath	1,500 min	300–1200								
Birmingham	1,100	800							•S	•S 1,200
Bolton	300	Sliding scale to min 50			•S 700					
Bournemouth	1,000	Sliding scale based on level of HEMG						•S		•S
Bradford	300	300			•S 300					
Brighton	1,000 max	500 min		•B			•B			•B
Bristol	1,100	700	•B	•S	•S				•S	•S
Brunel	300	200			•S	•S				•S
Cambridge	3,000	700–2,300					•B			
Central England	300	300								
Central Lancashire	1,000	1,000	•B		•B				•S	
City	800	800		•S					•S	
Coventry	500	500			•S 1,000			•S		•S 2,000
De Montfort	300	500	•S					•S 1,000		•S 1,000
Derby	800	200–600								
Durham	3000	600–1,500								
East Anglia	540	108–432								
East London	300							•S 1,000		•S 1,000

	In receipt of full HEMG (£)	In receipt of partial HEMG (£)	Living in region	Living in specified postcodes	Progressing from outreach	Ethnic minorities	Disabled	Sport	Shortage subjects	Academic achievement
Essex	300	More than 300, so that the bursary plus the HEMG total 3,000								
Exeter	2,000	50–1,500	•B		•B					
Gloucestershire	300–910									
Goldsmiths College	1,000	300								•S
Greenwich*	500	500								•S 500
Hertfordshire	1,350	Up to 1,350							•S	•S
Huddersfield	1,000	500–750								
Hull	1,000	500–1000		•B						
Imperial College	300	200–500								•S 4,000
Keele	300	Up to 5,000	•B	•B	•B	•B			•S Maths	•B
Kent	1,000	500–750	•B	•B	•B			•S		•S
King's College London	1,350	Up to 1,350								
Kingston	300–1,000	300–1,000			•B					
Lancaster	300–2,000	500–700							•B	•B
Leeds	1,300	300–1,300		•S	•S					
Leeds Metropolitan*	n/a	n/a								
Leicester	1,300–1,500	50–950								
Lincoln	600	Sliding scale based on level of HEMG	•B 100–300		•B 100–300					•B 500

Institution								
Liverpool	1,300	1,000		•B			•S	•B
Liverpool John Moores	1,000	400			•S		•S	•100 S
London School of Economics	2,500	Up to 1,700						
London Metropolitan	1,000	Up to 975			•S			•S
London South Bank	300							
Loughborough	1,300	200–1,100					•S	•S
Luton	1,750	300–1,000						
Manchester	1,000	Up to 1,000		•S	•S		•S	•S
Manchester Metropolitan	1,000	Sliding scale % of HEMG received						
Middlesex	300							•S
Newcastle	1,300	1,000						
Northumbria	300		•B	•S	•S	•S		
Nottingham	1,000	1,000	•B	•B				
Nottingham Trent	1,000	250	•B	•B			•S	
Oxford	3,000	1,500–2,600						
Oxford Brookes	1,200	200–1,200		•S				
Plymouth	300		•B	•B	•B		•S 500	
Portsmouth	500	Up to 500						
Queen Mary	1,000	800						•S
Reading	1,300	325–1,300	•B	•B				
Roehampton	300						•S 1,000	
Royal Holloway	500							•S
Salford	300	Sliding scale						
SOAS	700	400	•B 400					

University	In receipt of full HEMG (£)	In receipt of partial HEMG (£)	Living in region	Living in specified postcodes	Progressing from outreach	Ethnic minorities	Disabled	Sport	Shortage subjects	Academic achievement
Sheffield	650	400			•B				•B	•B
Sheffield Hallam	700	700			•B					•B
Southampton	1,000	Up to 1,000	•B		•B					•S
Staffordshire	1,000	500–1,000								
Sunderland	500	500								•S
Surrey	1,000	Up to 1,000		•S					•S	•S
Sussex	1,000			•S		•S				•S
Teesside	1,300	500			•S					•S
Thames Valley*	1,000	1,000								
University of the Arts London	300	50% of HEMG value	•B	•B						
University College London	1,350–2,500	300–2,416								
Warwick	1300–3000	300–3000								
West of England	1,250	750		•S					•S	
Westminster	300	Up to 300								
Wolverhampton	300	More than 300, so that the bursary plus the HEMG total 3,000								•S
York	1,400	600–1,000								

*Greenwich will charge a tuition fee of £2,500 rather than the full £3,000
*Leeds Metropolitan will charge a tuition fee of £2,000 rather than the full £3,000
*Thames Valley will charge a tuition fee of £2,700 rather than the full £3,000

Bursaries and Scholarships by University

The pages that follow contain a summary of the bursary and scholarship schemes that English universities (and Queen's, Belfast) will be offering in 2006, based on the Access Agreements submitted to OFFA.

For each university, the information is presented as follows

Aston

In receipt of full HEMG	£750 min
In receipt of partial HEMG	£750 max

- Scholarship scheme to be announced
- Tuition fee for placement year is £600
- 12.5% of tuition fee to be earmarked for means-tested bursaries
- Eligibility for bursaries to be assessed using UUK/SLC model bursary scheme

The headings in the first column are the same as those in the table on pages 477–80. An explanation of each heading is given on pages 474–5.

The second column indicates the value of any bursary linked to those receiving a full Higher Education Maintenance Grant (HEMG) or a partial HEMG. There is also information on whether a bursary (B) or scholarship (S) is available for a particular purpose.

The third column gives specific details relating to the university. This can cover such issues as the proportion of tuition fee income that will be earmarked for bursaries (see page 475), the use of the UUK/SLC model bursary scheme (see page 475), as well as details of particular scholarship and bursary schemes, and arrangements for foundation and placement years.

Anglia

In receipt of full HEMG	£800 min	
In receipt of partial HEMG	£500 max	
Living in region	Bursary	
Living in specified postcodes	Bursary	
Progressing from outreach	Bursary	
Ethnic minorities	Bursary	
Disabled	Bursary	

- Anglia also plans to target people living in areas remote from higher education institutions
- Eligibility for bursaries to be assessed using UUK/SLC model bursary scheme

Aston

In receipt of full HEMG	£750 min
In receipt of partial HEMG	£750 max

- Scholarship scheme to be announced
- Tuition fee for placement year is £600
- 12.5% of tuition fee to be earmarked for means-tested bursaries
- Eligibility for bursaries to be assessed using UUK/SLC model bursary scheme

Bath

In receipt of full HEMG	£1,500 min
In receipt of partial HEMG	£300-£1200

- Tuition fee for placement year is £600. Financial assistance in the form of bursaries will be available for eligible students on their placement year
- 21% of the additional fee income will be used to assist students from low income families
- Eligibility for bursaries of students from Wales, Scotland and Northern Ireland to be decided
- Eligibility for bursaries to be assessed using UUK/SLC model bursary scheme

Birmingham

In receipt of full HEMG	£1,100
In receipt of partial HEMG	£800
Shortage subjects	Scholarship
Academic achievement	Scholarship
	£1,200

- Scholarship scheme will be means-tested and open only to those students receiving a bursary and having at least 28 A-level points
- Part-time employment, paid volunteering and placement opportunities will be created by the university as supplementary income sources.
- Eligibility for bursaries may be assessed using UUK/SLC model bursary scheme
- Payment will be made in instalments

Bolton

In receipt of full HEMG	£300	• No tuition fee will be charged for year-out placement students
In receipt of partial HEMG	Sliding scale to min £50	• 33% of the additional fee income will be earmarked for bursaries and outreach
Progressing from outreach	Scholarship £700	• Payment will be made in instalments

Bournemouth

In receipt of full HEMG	£1,000	• Bursary available for eligible students completing written application form prior to enrolment
In receipt of partial HEMG	Sliding scale based on level of HEMG	• Tuition fee will be all-inclusive, with no extra charges for equipment, field trips etc
Sport	Scholarship	• Incentive schemes such as discounts for up-front fee payments will be introduced
Academic achievement	Scholarship	• Scholarship scheme to reward academic and vocational merit and success in sport, music and citizenship. No values available to date
		• Placement year tuition fee will be £500
		• 27% of additional tuition fee income will be earmarked for bursaries

Bradford

In receipt of full HEMG	£300	• Targeted scholarships for all students of Bradford University Academy holding full or partial HEMG
Progressing from outreach	Scholarship £300	• Individual custom support packages for students to be offered by a Learning Support Fund
		• Placement year tuition fee will be £600
		• 30% of additional tuition fee income (£955,000 in 2006–07) will be earmarked for bursaries

Brighton

In receipt of full HEMG	£1,000 max	• 100 Governors' bursaries available to students showing the most academic potential of which 50 will be earmarked for students of low-income families and/or living in low-participation neighbourhoods
In receipt of partial HEMG	£500 min	
Living in specified postcodes	Bursary 50 at £1,000	
Disabled	Bursary	• 10 disabled athletes bursaries worth £1,000 available in 2006–07; 5 a year thereafter (see next page)
Academic achievement	Bursary	

Brighton CONT.

- Placement year tuition fee will be £650
- 25% of additional fee income (£1.34 million in 2006–07) will be earmarked for bursaries

Bristol

In receipt of full HEMG	£1,100
In receipt of partial HEMG	£700
Living in region	Bursary
Shortage subjects	Scholarship
Academic achievement	Scholarship

- Bursaries take the form of a package comprising a cash component, support with course-related costs and a free sports pass
- 100 scholarships will be available for bursary holders and for non-bursary holders with high academic potential in specified shortage subject areas. Scholarships take the form of a fee remission up to a value of £2,500
- Pre-existing bursaries and scholarships will continue to be offered in 2006–07
- 17% of additional fee income (£987,000 in 2006–07) will be earmarked for bursaries

Brunel

In receipt of full HEMG	£300
In receipt of partial HEMG	£200
Living in specified postcodes	Scholarship
Progressing from outreach	Scholarship
Ethnic minorities	Scholarship
Academic achievement	Scholarship

- 150 scholarships worth up to £3,000 each for students from under-represented groups with a minimum of 280 tariff points
- 50 scholarships worth up to £2,000 available for late applicants in specific subjects, for first in family, and those who do better than expected in A levels
- Up to 25 scholarships worth up to £3,000 for high performing students from partnership schools in low participation boroughs
- Placement year tuition fee will be £600–£1,200
- Payment will be made in instalments

Cambridge

In receipt of full HEMG	£3,000
In receipt of partial HEMG	£700–£2,300
Disabled	Bursary

- Mature students who are Cambridge residents and are recipients of the full HEMG will be eligible for an enhanced bursary of £5,000. Also bursaries for disabled students and students with dependent children

Cambridge CONT.

- Students from Scotland, Wales and Northern Ireland may be eligible for bursaries, subject to assessment
- 30% of additional fee income (£7 million in 2010–11) will be earmarked for bursaries

Central England

In receipt of full HEMG	£300
In receipt of partial HEMG	£300

- 11% of additional fee income to be earmarked for bursaries
- Eligibility for bursaries to be assessed using UUK/SLC model bursary scheme

Central Lancashire

In receipt of full HEMG	£1,000
In receipt of partial HEMG	£1,000
Living in region	Bursary
Progressing from outreach	Bursary
Shortage subjects	Scholarship

- Harris Bursary Fund is for local students. Excellence Scholarships for about 100 high-entry students in subject areas to be specified. Partner Company Scholarships to be developed
- Placement year tuition fee will be £1,500 and a 50% bursary will be available
- Bursaries do not apply to other EU students
- Payment will be made in instalments

City

In receipt of full HEMG	£800
In receipt of partial HEMG	£800
Living in specified postcodes	Scholarship
Shortage subjects	Scholarship

- Placement year tuition fee will be £1,000. Fees for part-time students will be on a sliding scale. Fees for Foundation year will be £1,500
- Scholarships for able students from low-income backgrounds in subject areas Law (£800), Business (£750) and Engineering (£1,000)
- 15% of additional fee income will be earmarked for bursaries; 2% for scholarships
- Eligibility for bursaries to be assessed using UUK/SLC model bursary scheme

Coventry

In receipt of full HEMG	£500
In receipt of partial HEMG	£500

- £750 bursary for those with residual income up to £10,000 higher than the qualifying amount for HEMG eligibility (see next page)

Coventry CONT.

Progressing from outreach	Scholarship £1,000 More than 300 points	
Sport	Scholarship	
Academic achievement	Scholarship £2,000 More than 320 points	

- Students will be eligible for a bursary plus a scholarship
- Scholarships also for new courses and for performance in music, enterprise and artistic endeavour (£2,000)
- Foundation year fee £2,000
- 75% of estimated additional fee income to be earmarked for bursaries and scholarships by 2010–11

De Montfort

In receipt of full HEMG	£300
In receipt of partial HEMG	£500
Living in region	Scholarship
Sport	Scholarship £1,000
Academic achievement	Scholarship £1,000

- Access scholarships for those in local schools and colleges who are first generation university entrants. Details to be finalised
- 23% of additional fee income to be earmarked for bursaries and scholarships
- Eligibility for bursaries to be assessed using UUK/SLC model bursary scheme
- Bursary for students receiving partial HEMG may be higher than the bursary for students receiving full HEMG to assist the many students not qualifying for full HEMG but still perceived as being in great need of financial assistance
- Payment will be made in instalments

Derby

In receipt of full HEMG	£800
In receipt of partial HEMG	£200–£600

- Additional support to be announced
- Placement year tuition fee will be £1,500 but no bursary will be available for that year
- 28% of additional fee income to be earmarked for bursaries
- Payment will be made in instalments

Durham

In receipt of full HEMG	£3,000
In receipt of partial HEMG	£600–£1,500

- Durham Grant Scheme and Student Opportunities Fund available to UK domiciled, home, full-time undergraduates. Means tested by LEA/SLC. 725 grants available in 2006–07 rising to 2,569 in 2010–11
- Placement year tuition fee will be £1,500. Fees for Foundation year will be £1,200
- 22% of additional fee income to be earmarked for bursaries/grant scheme

East Anglia

In receipt of full HEMG	£540	• 16% of additional fee income to be earmarked for bursaries
In receipt of partial HEMG	£108–£432	• Eligibility for bursaries to be assessed using UUK/SLC model bursary scheme

East London

In receipt of full HEMG	£300	• Bursary also available to all EU students
Sport	Scholarship £1,000	• 200 Achievement Scholarships per year for academic, sporting and performance arts achievement
Academic achievement	Scholarship £1,000	• 50 Refugee Scholarships to cover the difference between home and overseas fees
		• In kind benefits include books, equipment, fees for field trips (package valued at £750 over three years)

Essex

In receipt of full HEMG	£300	• For students in receipt of partial HEMG it is intended to bridge the gap between the HEMG and the tuition fee with a bursary
In receipt of partial HEMG	More than £300, so that the bursary plus the HEMG total £3,000	• Foundation year tuition fee will be £1,200 • 25% of additional fee income to be earmarked for bursaries

Exeter

In receipt of full HEMG	£2,000	• Local Access to Exeter scheme designed to attract first generation applicants and those facing major obstacles (eg difficult family circumstances, adverse peer pressure, etc). Also Exeter Foundation Bursary scheme.
In receipt of partial HEMG	£50–£1,500	
Living in region	Bursary	
Progressing from outreach	Bursary	• Placement year tuition fee will be £1,500 • 22% of additional fee income to be earmarked for bursaries, rising to 24% in 2010–11. • Eligibility for bursaries to be assessed using LEA means-testing process

Gloucestershire

In receipt of full HEMG	£300–£910	• £200 start-up payment for all full-time students on entry to first year of course under consideration • Placement year tuition fee will be £1,000 • 10% annual rebate of fees for successful completion of each year of study issued as

Gloucestershire CONT.

- cash at the beginning of the next academic year
- 15% of additional fee income to be earmarked for bursaries
- Payment will be made in instalments

Goldsmiths College

In receipt of full HEMG	£1,000
In receipt of partial HEMG	£300
Academic achievement	Scholarship

- Part-time tuition fee will be £1,500
- 16% of additional fee income will be earmarked for bursaries

Greenwich

In receipt of full HEMG	£500
In receipt of partial HEMG	£500
Academic achievement	Scholarship
	£500
	More than 300 points

- Greenwich will charge a tuition fee of £2,500 rather than the full £3,000
- Bursary of £500 available to mature, full-time students receiving HEMG

Hertfordshire

In receipt of full HEMG	£1,350
In receipt of partial HEMG	Up to £1,350
Shortage subjects	Scholarship
Academic achievement	Scholarship

- Bursary is to be calculated on the basis of 50% of the student's HEMG
- Scholarship scheme to be announced
- Payment will be made in instalments

Huddersfield

In receipt of full HEMG	£1,000
In receipt of partial HEMG	£500–£750

- Bursaries open to all EU students
- No fee to be charged for placement year. Foundation year tuition fee will be £1,200
- 27% of additional fee income to be earmarked for bursaries

Hull

In receipt of full HEMG	£1,000
In receipt of partial HEMG	£500–£1,000
Living in specified postcodes	Bursary

- Foundation year and placement year tuition fee will be £1,500

Imperial College

In receipt of full HEMG	£300
In receipt of partial HEMG	£200–£500
Academic achievement	Scholarship £4,000

- Home students only eligible for awards
- Scholarships of £4,000 each year for up to four years for excellent academic performance

Imperial College CONT.

(3 As at A-level or equivalent) to students receiving HEMG
- Additionally, Student Opportunities Fund disbursed according to financial or educational disadvantage
- 29% of additional fee income to be earmarked for bursaries
- Eligibility for bursaries to be assessed using UUK/SLC model bursary scheme

Keele

In receipt of full HEMG	£300
In receipt of partial HEMG	Up to £5,000
Living in region	Bursary
Living in specified postcodes	Bursary
Progressing from outreach	Bursary
Ethnic minorities	Bursary
Shortage subjects	Scholarship Maths
Academic achievement	Bursary

- Target groups for non-mandatory bursaries: rural, black and ethnic minorities (15 awards), post-code (20 awards) and first generation students
- Limited number of non-mandatory bursaries with carefully-defined criteria (135 available)
- Additionally, medical education bursaries, work-based bursaries, study abroad (15 available) bursaries, widening participation mentoring (6 available) bursaries and 25 contingency bursaries
- 20% of additional fee income to be earmarked for bursaries
- Partial HEMG bursary higher than full HEMG to assist the many students not qualifying for full HEMG but still perceived as being in great need of financial assistance
- In kind benefit is a reduction in accommodation costs worth £500

Kent

In receipt of full HEMG	£1,000
In receipt of partial HEMG	£500–£750
Progressing from outreach	Bursary
Sport	Scholarship
Academic achievement	Scholarship

- Foundation year tuition fee will be £1,200
- 40 bursaries for students from regional schools (worth £1,000); scholarships for academic attainment, excellence in sport and outstanding contribution to the university community
- A condition of holding a bursary is attendance at a student support programme, eg financial counselling
- Eligibility for bursaries to be assessed using UUK/SLC model bursary scheme
- Payment will be made in instalments

King's College London

In receipt of full HEMG	£1,350
In receipt of partial HEMG	Up to £1,350

- Bursary is to be calculated on the basis of 50% of the student's HEMG
- King's scholarships to be announced
- 25% of additional fee income to be earmarked for bursaries
- Eligibility for bursaries to be assessed using LEA means-testing process

Kingston

In receipt of full HEMG	£300–£1,000
In receipt of partial HEMG	£300–£1,000
Progressing from outreach	Bursary

- University Compact Scheme provides £300 for 150 (rising to 500) new entrants
- Variable Fees Fund, a discretionary hardship fund, is available to students not receiving HEMG
- 25% of additional fee income to be earmarked for bursaries
- Eligibility for bursaries to be assessed using UUK/SLC model bursary scheme

Lancaster

In receipt of full HEMG	£300–£2,000
In receipt of partial HEMG	£500–£700
Shortage subjects	Bursary
Academic achievement	Bursary

- Bursaries will be available to UK students
- Subject awards worth £1,000 to UK and EU students of science, modern languages and engineering
- Academic excellence awards worth £1,000 for students of all subjects
- Student employment scheme to be developed
- Eligibility for bursaries to be assessed using UUK/SLC model bursary scheme

Leeds

In receipt of full HEMG	£1,300
In receipt of partial HEMG	£300–£1,300
Living in specified postcodes	Scholarship
Progressing from outreach	Scholarship

- Targeted scholarship scheme (58 available by 2010) to attract first generation students, students from low socio-economic groups and from schools with no tradition of progression to HE. This scheme is available to students receiving full HEMG and is in addition to bursary. Worth £3,000
- Foundation year tuition fee will be £1,200; placement year and year abroad tuition fees £800
- £8.7 million of additional fee income to be earmarked for bursaries by 2010–11

Leeds Metropolitan

In receipt of full HEMG	n/a	• Leeds Met will charge a tuition fee of £2,000 rather than the full £3,000
In receipt of partial HEMG	n/a	• Leeds Met Bursary Scheme will continue to offer discretionary hardship awards of about £2,000 over 3 years to 15–20 students each year

Leicester

In receipt of full HEMG	£1,300–£1,500
In receipt of partial HEMG	£50–£950

- Bursaries will be available to UK students only
- Eligibility for bursaries to be assessed using UUK/SLC model bursary scheme
- In kind benefits include loan of laptop computers, free local bus pass for term 1, allowance for food from university catering, print card and bookshop allowance (package valued at £1,200)

Lincoln

In receipt of full HEMG	£600
In receipt of partial HEMG	Sliding scale based on level of HEMG
Living in region	Bursary £100–£300
Progressing from outreach	Bursary £100–£300
Academic achievement	Bursary £500

- 18% of additional fee income to be earmarked for bursaries
- Eligibility for bursaries to be assessed using UUK/SLC model bursary scheme

Liverpool

In receipt of full HEMG	£1,300
In receipt of partial HEMG	£1,000
Living in region	Bursary
Living in specified postcodes	Bursary
Shortage subjects	Scholarship
Academic achievement	Bursary

- Bursaries will be available to UK students only, subject to means-testing
- Targeted attainment scholarships in chemistry, physics, engineering, computer science, earth and ocean sciences
- Placement year tuition fee will be £600; foundation year fee will be £1,200. These students are eligible for bursaries
- Eligibility for bursaries to be assessed using UUK/SLC model bursary scheme

Liverpool John Moores

In receipt of full HEMG	£1,000	• only; scholarships open to UK and EC
In receipt of partial HEMG	£400	students
Progressing from outreach	Scholarship	• Scholarships worth £1,000 except for 6
Sport	Scholarship	awards of £10,000 to outstanding,
Academic achievement	Scholarship	academically-gifted applicants
	100 awards	• Placement year tuition fee will be £1,500

London Metropolitan

In receipt of full HEMG	£1,000	• Discretionary hardship fund available
In receipt of partial HEMG	Up to £975	• Scholarships for academic achievement to be announced
Academic achievement	Scholarship	

London School of Economics

In receipt of full HEMG	£2,500	• Students from low-income families and disabled students have access to hardship funds and accommodation awards
In receipt of partial HEMG	Up to £1,700	• A Job Shop provides part-time employment opportunities for students
		• 25% of additional fee income to be earmarked for bursaries

London South Bank

In receipt of full HEMG	£300	• 20%–30% of additional fee income to be earmarked for bursaries
		• Some payments to be in kind

Loughborough

In receipt of full HEMG	£1,300	• The value of the bursaries is doubled for mature students
In receipt of partial HEMG	£200–£1,100	• Merit-based entry scholarships to science and perhaps engineering to be announced
Shortage subjects	Scholarship	• Placement year tuition fee will be £600
Academic achievement	Scholarship	• £3.2 million of additional fee income to be earmarked for bursaries by 2010–11
		• Eligibility for bursaries may be assessed using m UUK/SLC model bursary scheme

Luton

In receipt of full HEMG	£1,750	• 40% of additional fee income to be earmarked for bursaries
In receipt of partial HEMG	£300–£1,000	• Eligibility for bursaries will be assessed using UUK/SLC model bursary scheme

Manchester

In receipt of full HEMG	£1,000	• Eligibility for scholarships subject to
In receipt of partial HEMG	Up to £1,000	means-testing (worth £5,000). Targeted access scholarships designed to attract
Living in region	Scholarship	students from under-represented groups
Living in specified postcodes	Scholarship	in Greater Manchester and first
Shortage subjects	Scholarship	generation students (worth £2,000)
Academic achievement	Scholarship	• Subject-specific scholarships worth £1,000 for excellence in exam results

- Eligibility for scholarships subject to means-testing (worth £5,000). Targeted access scholarships designed to attract students from under-represented groups in Greater Manchester and first generation students (worth £2,000)
- Subject-specific scholarships worth £1,000 for excellence in exam results
- Faculty and school-based scholarships to be defined

Manchester Metropolitan

In receipt of full HEMG	£1,000
In receipt of partial HEMG	Sliding scale based on level of HEMG

- 33% of additional fee income to be earmarked for bursaries and access work
- Eligibility for bursaries will be assessed using UUK/SLC model bursary scheme

Middlesex

In receipt of full HEMG	£300
Academic achievement	Scholarship

- Academic scholarships worth £1,000 to students entering with greater than 300 tariff points at A2 or equivalent
- 12% of additional fee income to be earmarked for bursaries and access

Newcastle

In receipt of full HEMG	£1,300
In receipt of partial HEMG	£1,000

- Scholarship scheme, open to all based on achievement, to be announced
- Payment to be made in instalments

Northumbria

In receipt of full HEMG	£300
Living in region	Bursary
Living in specified postcodes	Scholarship
Ethnic minorities	Scholarship
Disabled	Scholarship

- Regional bursaries worth £300 and scholarships for target groups worth £250, £500 and £1,000 to be offered
- Placement year tuition fee will be £750
- 33% of additional fee income to be earmarked for bursaries
- Eligibility for bursaries will be assessed using UUK/SLC model bursary scheme

Nottingham

In receipt of full HEMG	£1,000
In receipt of partial HEMG	£1,000
Progressing from outreach	Bursary

- Additional bursaries worth £250–£1,000 for students with residual income of £32,000–£42,500, ie just above threshold for partial HEMG (see next page)

Nottingham CONT.

- Further bursaries for target groups
- £2.5 million of additional fee income to be earmarked for bursaries

Nottingham Trent

In receipt of full HEMG	£1,000
In receipt of partial HEMG	£250
Living in specified postcodes	Bursary
Academic achievement	Scholarship

- Discretionary Hardship Fund available
- Scholarship scheme will offer 25 competitive scholarships of £2,000
- Eligibility for bursaries will be assessed using UUK/SLC model bursary scheme

Oxford

In receipt of full HEMG	£3,000
In receipt of partial HEMG	£1,500–£2,600

- Additional one-off award of £400–£1,000 in first year for students from low-income families
- Existing bursary schemes, scholarship schemes and hardship funds to run in parallel
- 30% of additional fee income to be earmarked for bursaries

Oxford Brookes

In receipt of full HEMG	£1,200
In receipt of partial HEMG	£200–£1,200
Progressing from outreach	Scholarship

- Scholarship scheme to be announced
- Hardship fund available

Plymouth

In receipt of full HEMG	£300
Living in region	Bursary
Progressing from outreach	Bursary
Academic achievement	Scholarship
	£500

- Discretionary Hardship Fund available
- One-off awards of £500 to target groups: first generation students and those from low income families
- £1,500 relocation award to mature students
- Additional support for disabled students
- Eligibility for bursaries will be assessed using UUK/SLC model bursary scheme

Portsmouth

In receipt of full HEMG	£500
In receipt of partial HEMG	Up to £500

- Bursary scheme not available to EU students
- Placement year tuition fee will be £600
- 21% of additional fee income to be earmarked for bursaries
- Eligibility for bursaries will be assessed using UUK/SLC model bursary scheme

Queen Mary

In receipt of full HEMG	£1,000
In receipt of partial HEMG	£800
Academic achievement	Scholarship

- £4,000 for students receiving full HEMG and achieving 3A grades at A level
- Eligibility for bursaries will be assessed using UUK/SLC model bursary scheme

Reading

In receipt of full HEMG	£1,300
In receipt of partial HEMG	£325–£1,300
Progressing from outreach	Bursary

- Students from Scotland and Wales eligible for bursaries
- Pre-application, pre-entry bursaries to target groups.
- Outreach schools to nominate candidates for Vice-Chancellor's Bursary scheme. Up to 2 bursaries may be held by each student
- Hardship Funds available
- More than 25% of additional fee income to be earmarked for bursaries
- Eligibility for bursaries will be assessed using UUK/SLC model bursary scheme

Roehampton

In receipt of full HEMG	£300
Academic achievement	Scholarship
	£1,000

- 13% of additional fee income to be earmarked for bursaries
- Eligibility for bursaries will be assessed using UUK/SLC model bursary scheme

Royal Holloway

In receipt of full HEMG	£500
In receipt of partial HEMG	£500
Academic achievement	Scholarship

- Scholarships of £500 for all in receipt of HEMG and with more than 320 UCAS tariff points. Competitive Thomas Holloway Scholarships of £3,500 for 'outstanding' students receiving HEMG. Competitive Bedford Scholarships of £1,000 for 'outstanding' students
- 19% of additional fee income to be earmarked for bursaries

Salford

In receipt of full HEMG	£300
In receipt of partial HEMG	Sliding scale

- Additional bursaries available for UK and EC students receiving full HEMG to cover course-related costs worth about £500 in kind; pro-rated for partial HEMG
- Bursaries available to students on international placements consisting of fee remission and £500 per semester abroad (see next page)

Salford CONT.

- Eligibility for bursaries will be assessed using UUK/SLC model bursary scheme

SOAS

In receipt of full HEMG	£700
In receipt of partial HEMG	£400
Progressing from outreach	Bursary Worth £400

- 18% of additional fee income to be earmarked for bursaries

Sheffield

In receipt of full HEMG	£650
In receipt of partial HEMG	£400
Progressing from outreach	Bursary
Shortage subjects	Bursary
Academic achievement	Bursary

- Additional bursaries for students receiving full or partial HEMG with outstanding entry grades; amounts vary according to number of A grade A levels achieved and according to subject to be studied. Worth £750–£1,550
- Regional outreach bursaries linked to Compact Scheme worth £100–£750
- 14% additional fee income to be earmarked for bursaries

Sheffield Hallam

In receipt of full HEMG	£700
In receipt of partial HEMG	£700
Progressing from outreach	Bursary

- Partnership Bursaries of £300 for students progressing from partner schools and colleges
- Discretionary bursaries worth up to £1,000
- Eligibility for bursaries will be assessed using UUK/SLC model bursary scheme

Southampton

In receipt of full HEMG	£1,000
In receipt of partial HEMG	Up to £1,000
Living in region	Bursary
Progressing from outreach	Bursary
Academic achievement	Scholarship

- Hampshire and Isle of Wight Bursaries available by competition to 150 first generation students from low-income families in the region, especially those in partner schools and colleges. Worth £1,000
- Medicine bursaries worth £1,000
- Academic scholarships worth £1,000–£2,000; details to be finalised
- 22% of additional fee income to be earmarked for bursaries
- Eligibility for bursaries will be assessed using UUK/SLC model bursary scheme

Staffordshire

In receipt of full HEMG	£1,000
In receipt of partial HEMG	£500–£1,000

Sunderland

In receipt of full HEMG	£500
In receipt of partial HEMG	£500
Academic achievement	Scholarship

- Progression Scholarships to all students progressing from year one to year two and year two to year three, etc, of a course, worth £500

Surrey

In receipt of full HEMG	£1,000
In receipt of partial HEMG	Up to £1,000
Living in specified postcodes	Scholarship
Shortage subjects	Scholarship
Academic achievement	Scholarship

- Scholarships for students with outstanding A levels (3 grade As) worth £1,000. A-level requirement may be relaxed for students from low participation areas and/or studying shortage subjects
- Scholarships for academic progression based on excellent performance (first class) on university course. Worth £1,000 each year
- Extended programme award of £1,500 for final year of, eg, MEng courses
- Value of bursaries doubled for students also in receipt of scholarship
- Placement year tuition fee will be £450; foundation year fee £1,200

Sussex

In receipt of full HEMG	£1,000
Living in specified postcodes	Scholarship
Ethnic minorities	Scholarship

- £200 Chancellor's Scholarships available to first generation students from low-income families or experiencing educational or social disadvantage. Also open to students who make a significant contribution to the community. Worth £1,000 (80% earmarked for applicants under 21 years of age)
- 20% of additional fee income to be earmarked for bursaries
- Eligibility for bursaries will be assessed using UUK/SLC model bursary scheme

Teesside

In receipt of full HEMG	£1,300
In receipt of partial HEMG	£500
Progressing from outreach	Scholarship
Academic achievement	Scholarship

- 250 scholarships worth up to £1,000 to be allocated on the basis of academic performance and outreach
- Students whose residual family income is in the upper income threshold for HEMG will receive bursary in year 1 only
- 31% of additional fee income to be earmarked for bursaries

Thames Valley

In receipt of full HEMG	£1,000
In receipt of partial HEMG	£1,000

- Thames Valley will charge a tuition fee of £2,700 rather than the full £3,000
- All students not receiving HEMG will receive a bursary of £500

University of the Arts, London

In receipt of full HEMG	£300
Living in region	Bursary
Living in specified postcodes	Bursary

- Bursaries will be available to UK students only
- Bursary of £1,000 is available on application by first-generation students receiving full or partial HEMG living in specified postcodes
- 12.5% of additional fee income to be earmarked for bursaries

University College London

In receipt of full HEMG	£1,350–£2,500
In receipt of partial HEMG	50% of HEMG value

- All students in receipt of HEMG to receive a bursary calculated at 50% of its value but enhanced to £1,500–£2,500 for those from families with lowest residual income
- For students on longer undergraduate courses eg with a year abroad or MEng and MSci degrees the bursary will be doubled or valued at 100% HEMG, whichever is the higher, for the final year
- Hardship Fund available

Warwick

In receipt of full HEMG	£1,300–£3,000
In receipt of partial HEMG	£300–£2,416

- 170 means-tested Philanthropic Scholarships available on application
- Work/study scheme devised to provide participating students with 5 hours paid work a week

Warwick CONT.

- 26% of additional fee income to be earmarked for bursaries
- Bursary for students receiving partial HEMG may be higher than the bursary for students receiving full HEMG to assist the many students not qualifying for full HEMG but still perceived as being in great need of financial assistance

West of England

In receipt of full HEMG	£1.250
In receipt of partial HEMG	£750
Living in specified postcodes	Scholarship
Shortage subjects	Scholarship

- Scholarships for target groups worth £1,000 over 3 years. Details to be finalised
- 44% of additional fee income to be earmarked for bursaries
- Eligibility for bursaries will be assessed using UUK/SLC model bursary scheme

Westminster

In receipt of full HEMG	£300
In receipt of partial HEMG	Up to £300
Academic achievement	Scholarship

- Bursaries are open to non-UK EU students
- Scholarship fund will support academic excellence in under-represented groups and students progressing from foundation level
- There will be no tuition fee for any placement year
- 15% of additional fee income to be earmarked for bursaries
- Eligibility for bursaries will be assessed using UUK/SLC model bursary scheme

Wolverhampton

In receipt of full HEMG	£300
In receipt of partial HEMG	More than £300, so that the bursary plus the HEMG total £3,000

- Regional fee discount scheme to be introduced giving a £1,000 discount on first year fees only to Aimhigher applicants from the region
- For students in receipt of partial HEMG it is intended to bridge the gap between the HEMG and the tuition fee with a bursary
- Eligibility for bursaries will be assessed using UUK/SLC model bursary scheme

York

In receipt of full HEMG	£1,400
In receipt of partial HEMG	£600–£1,000

- Bursaries available to students from England, Scotland and Northern Ireland. The position regarding Wales is not yet known. EU students are not eligible
- Bursaries for the Hull-York Medical School are under consideration
- 19% of additional fee income to be earmarked for bursaries

Northern Ireland

Queen's Belfast

In receipt of full HEMG	£1,100
In receipt of partial HEMG	£100–£600

- Part of the bursary (£100) paid in kind for sports facilities and buying books
- 20% of additional fee income earmarked to be for bursaries
- Access agreement approved by DEL in consultation with OFFA

University of Ulster

Details still to be confirmed.

Colleges of Higher Education

This listing gives contact details for higher education institutions not mentioned elsewhere within the book. All the institutions of the University of London which do not have their own entry are listed under the main entry for the University of London. All the institutions listed below offer degree course, some providing a wide range of courses while others are specialist colleges with a limited range of courses and a small intake. Those marked with a * are members of SCOP (the Standing Conference of Principals; www.scop.ac.uk).

The Arts Institute at Bournemouth*
Wallisdown, Poole, Dorset BH12 5HH
T   01202 533011
E   courseoffice@aib.ac.uk
W   www.aib.ac.uk

Bath Spa University College*
Newton Park campus,
Newton St Loe, Bath BA2 9BN
T   01225 875875
E   enquiries@bathspa.ac.uk
W   www.bathspa.ac.uk

Bell College
Almada Street, Hamilton ML3 0JB
T   01698 283160
E   inform@bell.ac.uk
W   www.bell.ac.uk

Birmingham College of Food, Tourism and Creative Studies*
Summer Row, Birmingham B3 1JB
T   0121-604 1000
E   marketing@bcftcs.ac.uk
W   www.bcftcs.ac.uk

Bishop Grosseteste College, Lincoln*
Newport, Lincoln LN1 3DY
T   01522 527347
E   registry@bgc.ac.uk
W   www.bgc.ac.uk

Buckinghamshire Chilterns University College*
Queen Alexandra Road, High Wycombe,
Buckinghamshire HP11 2JZ
T   01494 522141
E   marketing@bcuc.ac.uk
W   www.bcuc.ac.uk

Canterbury Christ Church University College*
North Holmes Road, Canterbury CT1 1QU
T   01227 767700
E   admissions@cant.ac.uk
W   www.cant.ac.uk

Central School of Speech and Drama*
Embassy Theatre, 64 Eton Avenue,
London NW3 3HY
T   0207-722 8183
E   enquiries@cssd.ac.uk
W   www.cssd.ac.uk

Conservatoire for Drama and Dance
c/o London Contemporary Dance School
The Place, 17 Duke's Road,
London WC1H 9AB
T   0207-387 0145
W   www.theplace.org.uk
and **Royal Academy of Dramatic Arts**
62-64 Gower Street, London WC1E 6ED
T   0207-636 7076
W   www.rada.org.uk

Cumbria Institute of the Arts*
Brampton Road, Carlisle,
Cumbria CA3 9AY
T   01228 400300
E   info@cumbria.ac.uk
W   www.cumbria.ac.uk

Dartington College of Arts*
Totnes, Devon TQ9 6EJ
T   01803 862224
E   registry@dartington.ac.uk
W   www.dartington.ac.uk

Edge Hill College*
St Helens Road, Ormskirk, Lancs L39 4QP
T   01695 575171
E   enquiries@edgehill.ac.uk
W   www.edgehill.ac.uk

Edinburgh College of Art
Lauriston Place, Edinburgh EH3 9DF
T   0131-221 6000
E   registration@eca.ac.uk
W   www.eca.ac.uk

Glasgow School of Art
167 Renfrew Street, Glasgow G3 6RQ
T   0141-353 4500
E   registry@gsa.ac.uk
W   www.gsa.ac.uk

Harper Adams University College*
Edgmond, Newport, Shropshire TF10 8NB
T   01952 820280
E   admissions@harper-adams.ac.uk
W   www.harper-adams.ac.uk

Kent Institute of Art and Design*
Oakwood Park, Maidstone, Kent ME16 8AG
T   01622 757286
New Dover Road,
Canterbury, Kent CT1 3AN
T   01227 769371
Fort Pitt, Rochester, Kent ME1 1DZ
T   01634 830022
E   info@kiad.ac.uk
W   www.kiad.ac.uk

Liverpool Hope University College*
Hope Park, Liverpool L16 9JD
T   0151-291 3000
E   admission@hope.ac.uk
W   www.hope.ac.uk

Newman College of Higher Education*
Genners Lane, Bartley Green,
Birmingham B32 3NT
T   0121-476 1181
E   registry@newman.ac.uk
W   www.newman.ac.uk

North East Wales Institute
Plas Coch Campus, Mold Road,
Wrexham, N. Wales LL11 2AW
T   01978 290666
E   admissions@newi.ac.uk
W   www.newi.ac.uk

Northern School of Contemporary Dance
98 Chapeltown Road, Leeds LS7 4BH
T   0113-219 3000
E   admissions@nscd.ac.uk
W   www.nscd.ac.uk

Norwich School of Art and Design*
St George Street, Norwich NR3 1BB
T   01603 610561
E   info@nsad.ac.uk
W   www.nsad.ac.uk

Queen Margaret University College
Clerwood Terrace, Edinburgh EH12 8TS
T   0131-317 3247
E   admissions@qmuc.ac.uk
W   www.qmuc.ac.uk

Ravensbourne College of Design and Communication*
Walden Road, Chislehurst, Kent BR7 5SN

T   0208-289 4900
E   info@rave.ac.uk
W   www.rave.ac.uk

Rose Bruford College*
Lamorbey Park Campus, Burnt Oak Lane,
Sidcup, Kent DA15 9DF
T   0208-308 2600
E   enquiries@bruford.ac.uk
W   www.bruford.ac.uk

Royal Agricultural College*
Stroud Road, Cirencester,
Gloucestershire GL7 6JS
T   01285 652531
E   admissions@rac.ac.uk
W   www.royagcol.ac.uk

Royal College of Art
Kensington Gore, London SW7 2EU
T   0207-590 4444
E   admissions@rca.ac.uk
W   www.rca.ac.uk

Royal College of Music
Prince Consort Road, London SW7 2BS
T   0207-589 3643
E   info@rcm.ac.uk
W   www.rcm.ac.uk

Royal College of Nursing*
FREEPOST, 23Lon20336,
London W1E 0DW
T   0207-647 3700
E   distance.learning@rcn.org.uk
W   www.rcn.org.uk

Royal Northern College of Music
124 Oxford Road, Manchester M13 9RD
T   0161-907 5200
E   info@rncm.ac.uk
W   www.rncm.ac.uk

Royal Scottish Academy of Music and Drama
100 Renfrew Street, Glasgow G2 3DB
T   0141-332 8901
E   registry@rsamd.ac.uk
W   www.rsamd.ac.uk

Royal Welsh College of Music and Drama
Castle Grounds, Cathays Park,
Cardiff CF10 3ER
T   029-2034 2854
    music.admissions@rwcmd.ac.uk
E   drama.admissions@rwcmd.ac.uk
W   www.rwcmd.ac.uk

The College of St Mark and St John*
Derriford Road, Plymouth, Devon PL6 8BH
T 01752 636890
E admissions@marjon.ac.uk
W www.marjon.ac.uk

St Martin's College*
Bowerham Road, Lancaster LA1 3JD
T 01524 384384
E admissions@ucsm.ac.uk
W www.ucsm.ac.uk

St Mary's College*
Waldegrave Road, Twickenham,
Middlesex TW1 4SX
T 0208-240 4000
E enquiry@smuc.ac.uk
W www.smuc.ac.uk

St Mary's University College
191 Falls Road, Belfast BT12 6FE
T 028-9032 7678
E admis@stmarys-belfast.ac.uk
W stmarys-belfast.ac.uk

Southampton Institute*
East Park Terrace, Southampton SO14 0YN
T 023-8031 9000
E enquiries@solent.ac.uk
W www.solent.ac.uk

Stranmillis University College
Stranmillis Road, Belfast BT9 5DY
T 028-9038 1271
E registry@stran.ac.uk
W www.stran.ac.uk

Surrey Institute of Art and Design*
Falkner Road, Farnham, Surrey GU9 7DS
T 01252 722441
E registry@surrart.ac.uk
W www.surrart.ac.uk

Swansea Institute of Higher Education
Mount Pleasant, Swansea SA1 6ED
T 01792 481085
E enquiry@sihe.ac.uk
W www.sihe.ac.uk

Trinity and All Saints College*
Brownberrie Lane, Horsforth,
Leeds LS18 5HD
T 0113-283 7100
E admissions@tasc.ac.uk
W www.tasc.ac.uk

Trinity College Carmarthen
College Road, Carmarthen, Wales SA31 3EP

T 01267 676767
E registry@trinity-cnm.ac.uk
W www.trinity-cm.ac.uk

Trinity College of Music
King Charles Court, Old Royal Naval Court,
Greenwich, London SE10 9JF
T 0208-305 4444
E info@tcm.ac.uk
W www.tcm.ac.uk

University College, Chester*
Parkgate Road, Chester CH1 4BJ
T 01244 375444
E enquiries@chester.ac.uk
W www.chester.ac.uk

University College Chichester*
Bishop Otter Campus, College Lane,
Chichester, West Sussex PO19 4PE
T 01243 816000
E admissions@ucc.ac.uk
W www.ucc.ac.uk

University College Falmouth*
Woodlane Campus, Falmouth,
Cornwall TR11 4RH
T 01326 211077
E admissions@falmouth.ac.uk
W www.falmouth.ac.uk

University College Northampton*
Park Campus, Boughton Green Road,
Northampton NN2 7AL
T 01604 735500
E marketing@northampton.ac.uk
W www.northampton.ac.uk

University College Winchester*
Hampshire SO22 4NR
T 01962 841515
E admissions@winchester.ac.uk
W www.winchester.ac.uk

University College Worcester*
Henwick Grove, Worcester WR2 6AJ
T 01905 855111
E admissions@worc.ac.uk
W www.worc.ac.uk

University of the Highlands and Islands
UHI Millennium Institute, Caledonia House,
63 Academy Street, Inverness IV1 1LU
T 01463 279000
E eo@uhi.ac.uk
W www.uhi.ac.uk

Wimbledon School of Art*
Merton Hall Road, London SW19 3QA
T   0208-408 5000
E   info@wimbledon.ac.uk
W www.wimbledon.ac.uk

Writtle College*
Chelmsford, Essex CM1 3RR
T   01245 424200
E   info@writtle.ac.uk
W www.writtle.ac.uk

York St John College*
Lord Mayor's Walk,
York YO31 7EX
T   01904 716598
E   admissions@yorksj.ac.uk
W www.yorksj.ac.uk

Internet Resources

Abbreviations
EEA European Economic Area
ELB Education and Library Board (Northern Ireland)
EU European Union
FTE Full-Time Equivalent
HE Higher Education
LEA Local Education Authority
SLC Student Loans Company
TQA Teaching Quality Assessment
(later called Subject Reviews)

General
DEL Department for Employment and Learning (Northern Ireland)
www.delni.gov.uk
DfES Department for Education and Skills
www.dfes.gov.uk
HEFCE Higher Education Funding Council for England
www.hefce.ac.uk
HEFCW Higher Education Funding Council for Wales (part of Education and Learning Wales)
www.elwa.ac.uk
HESA Higher Education Statistics Agency
www.hesa.ac.uk
Mayfield University Consultants
www.mayfield-uc.org.uk
NUS National Union of Students
www.nusonline.co.uk
OFSTED Office for Standards in Education
www.ofsted.gov.uk
QAA Quality Assurance Agency for Higher Education
www.qaa.ac.uk

RAE Research Assessment Exercise
www.hero.ac.uk/rae
SCOP Standing Conference of Principals
www.scop.ac.uk
SHEFC Scottish Higher Education Funding Council
www.shefc.ac.uk
UniversitiesUK (formerly The Committee of Vice-Chancellors and Principals)
www.universitiesuk.ac.uk

Applying to University
Aimhigher
www.aimhigher.ac.uk
BBC
www.bbc.co.uk/schools/aimhigher
www.bbc.co.uk/radio1/onelife/education
www.bbc.co.uk/ouch/lifefiles/student
BUSA (British Universities Sports Associations)
www.busa.org.uk
Course Discover Database
www.coursediscoveronline.co.uk
Foundation Degrees
www.foundationdegree.org.uk
HERO Higher Education and Research Opportunities in the United Kingdom
www.hero.ac.uk
NISS National Information Services and Systems
www.hero.ac.uk/niss
SKILL National Bureau for Students with Disabilities
www.skill.org.uk
UCAS Universities and Colleges Admissions Service for the UK
www.ucas.com

UCS University and College Sport
www.ucsport.net
UKCourseFinder.com
www.ukcoursefinder.co.uk
UKSport
www.uksport.gov.uk
Uni4me
www.uni4me.co.uk
University Open Days
www.opendays.com
University Options
www.universityoptions.co.uk
University of Wolverhampton UK Sensitive Maps
Universities and HE Colleges
www.scit.wlv.ac.uk/ukinfo/uk.map.html
Unofficial Guides
www.unofficial-guides.com
Woody's Web-Watch
www.woodyswebwatch.com

Paying Your Way
CDL Career Development Loans
www.lifelonglearning.co.uk/cdl/index.htm
DfES Higher Education Student Support
www.dfes.gov.uk/studentsupport
Department of Health
Financial Support for Healthcare Students
www.dh.gov.uk
EGAS Educational Grants Advisory Service
www.egas-online.org.uk
The Inland Revenue
www.inlandrevenue.gov.uk/students
Moneyfacts
www.moneyfacts.co.uk
NAMSS National Association for Managers in Student Services (Student Finance and Benefits)
www.support4learning.org.uk/money
Need 2 Know
www.need2know.co.uk
SAAS Student Awards Agency for Scotland
www.saas.gov.uk
Scholarship Search
www.studentmoney.org
SLC Student Loans Company
www.slc.co.uk
Student Finance Direct
www.studentsupportdirect.co.uk
www.studentfinancedirect.co.uk

Student Finance Wales
www.studentfinancewales.co.uk
UNIAID
www.uniaid.org.uk

Gap Year
CSV Community Service Volunteers
www.csv.org.uk
FCO Foreign and Commonwealth Office
Know Before You Go Campaign
www.fco.gov.uk/travel
GAP Activity Projects
www.gap.org.uk
Gap Year Company Ltd
www.gapyear.com
Millennium Volunteers
www.mvonline.gov.uk
Project Trust
www.projecttrust.org.uk
Raleigh International
www.raleigh.org.uk
Timebank (volunteering)
www.timebank.org.uk
Volunteering
www.volunteering.org.uk
Worldwide Volunteering
http://wwv.org.uk
Year in Industry
www.yini.org.uk
Year Out Group
www.yearoutgroup.org
Young Volunteer Challenge
www.dfes.gov.uk/volunteering

Coming From Overseas
The British Council
www.britishcouncil.org
English UK
www.englishuk.com
DfES Department for Education and Skills
www.dfes.gov.uk/studentsupport/eustudents
www.dfes.gov.uk/international-students
Education UK (British Council course search)
www.educationuk.org
Education UK (Scholarships Database)
www.educationuk.org/scholarships
Embassy World
www.embassyworld.com

FCO Foreign and Commonwealth Office
Visa Information
www.i-uk.com
www.ukvisas.gov.uk
Sources of Funding for International Students (British Council)
www.britishcouncil.org/learning-funding-your-studies.htm
UKCOSA The Council for International Education
www.ukcosa.org.uk
UK NARIC National Academic Recognition Information Centre for the UK
www.naric.org.uk

Studying Abroad
ACU Association of Commonwealth Universities
www.acu.ac.uk
ERASMUS/ SOCRATES EU Activites
http://europa.eu.int/comm/education/programmes/socrates/erasmus/erasmus_en.html
The European Choice
www.eurochoice.org.uk
Fulbright Commission
www.fulbright.co.uk
LEONARDO DA VINCI EU Vocational Training Action Programme
http://europa.eu.int/comm/education/programmes/leonardo/leonardo_en.html
see also
European Training in the UK
www.leonardo.org.uk
UK Socrates–Erasmus Council
www.kent.ac.uk/ERASMUS/erasmus/index.html
Worldwise
www.brookes.ac.uk/worldwise

Work Experience and Graduate Employment
Activate
www.activate.co.uk/
AGCAS The Association of Graduate Careers Advisory Services
www.agcas.org.uk
BUNAC
www.bunac.co.uk
CSU Prospects Graduate Careers
www.prospects.ac.uk

Graduate Careers in Ireland
www.gradireland.com
STEP Shell Technology and Enterprise Programme
www.step.org.uk
Student Employment Offices
www.nases.org.uk
SummerJobs.com
www.summerjobs.com
TTA Teacher Training Agency
www.useyourheadteach.gov.uk
Vacation Work Publications
www.vacationwork.co.uk
Worktrain
www.worktrain.gov.uk
Work Experience
www.work-experience.org.uk

Where to Live
BBC
www.bbc.co.uk/radio1/onelife/housing
Student Accommodation
www.thestudentvillage.com
Council Tax
www.ukonline.gov.uk
Housing Benefit/ Council Tax Benefit
www.dwp.gov.uk/lifeevent/benefits/housing_benefit.asp
www.dwp.gov.uk/lifeevent/benefits/council_tax_benefit.asp
Letlink
www.letlink.co.uk
CAB Citizens Advice Bureau
www.citizensadvice.org.uk
www.adviceguide.org.uk
Public Transport Information
www.pti.org.uk
Safety
www.good2bsecure.gov.uk
www.crimereduction.gov.uk
studentcrime1.htm
www.menduk.org
www.suzylamplugh.org
UNITE
www.unite-student.co.uk

Index